The **Rough Guide** to

Laos

written and researched by

Jeff Cranmer and Steven Martin

D0970776

ROUGH
GUIDES

NEW YORK • LONDON • DELHI

www.roughguides.com

Contents

Festivals colour section
following p.112

The hill tribes colour
section following p.208

◀◀ Landscape at Vang Viang ◀ Buddhas at Haw Pha Kaew, Vientiane

Introduction to
Laos

Just over a decade ago, Laos was largely unknown to Western travellers. Other than for a brief period during the 1960s, when the country became a player in the Vietnam War, it has remained a backwater – a situation that only intensified after the 1975 revolution and the ensuing years of xenophobic communist government. However, in the 1990s Laos reluctantly reopened its doors to the outside world, after its major source of aid dried up with the collapse of the Soviet Union. The major towns and cities now offer visitors good-value accommodation and a surprisingly diverse array of cuisines, and while conditions in the countryside remain primitive and challenging, travellers willing to brave them are rewarded with sights of a landscape and people not much changed from those that greeted French explorers over one hundred years ago.

Laos's lifeline is the Mekong River, which runs the length of the landlocked country, at times bisecting it and at others serving as a boundary with Thailand. The rugged Annamite Mountains also run much of the country's length and historically have acted as a buffer against Vietnam, with which Laos shares its eastern border. Despite intensive logging, there are still tracts of dense forest inhabited by myriad animal species, including tigers and other majestic cats, all but vanished from neighbouring countries, and new mammals are still being discovered, such as the deer-like soala or spindlehorn. There is even a pod of rare freshwater dolphins inhabiting an isolated stretch of the Mekong.

For such a small country, Laos is surprisingly diverse in terms of its people. Colourfully dressed hill tribes populate the higher elevations, while in the lowland river valleys, coconut palms sway over the Buddhist monasteries of the ethnic Lao. The country also retains some of the French influence

it absorbed during colonial days: the familiar smell of freshly baked bread and coffee mingles with exotic local aromas in morning markets.

Laos has relatively few proper tourist sights, but even so, you haven't really seen the country unless you've spent some time aboard some ancient jalopy or slow boat, taking in the rugged natural beauty and witnessing the country's rich ethnic mosaic at leisure. If you want to see something of the northern mountains as well as the islands of the far south, and have enough time to absorb a little of the serene Lao way of life, you really need to be in Laos for two to three weeks. With up to two weeks at your disposal, you can either do a whirlwind trip up the Mekong River Valley or, perhaps better, focus on one region and enjoy it at an easy pace. Internal flights, while unreliable, can speed up an itinerary substantially and are cheap enough not to break your budget.

Fact file

- The Lao People's Democratic Republic, whose capital is **Vientiane**, is Southeast Asia's only landlocked country. Modern Laos covers more than 236,000 square kilometres, yet has a **population** of just 6.2 million.

- A constitutional monarchy until 1976, Laos is today a one-party dictatorship and one of the world's last official **communist** states. It is also one of the world's poorest countries, heavily reliant on aid. Despite economic reforms undertaken in the early Nineties, fledgling entrepreneurs and foreign investment have been hindered by official corruption.

- **Lowland Lao** (Lao Loum) comprise approximately seventy percent of the population, **upland Lao** (Lao Theung) and **highland Lao** (Lao Soung) roughly twenty and ten percent respectively; within these broad definitions, there are many smaller divisions. **Chinese** and **Vietnamese** are a small but economically significant portion of the population. The national **language** is Lao, a tonal language closely related to Thai, although the written scripts differ. English is the most popular European language.

- Laos is a predominately **Buddhist** country and follows the Theravadan school of Buddhism, in common with neighbouring Thailand, Burma and Cambodia. Up to forty percent of the population, particularly in the highlands, follow **animist** beliefs.

Where to go

Set on a broad curve of the Mekong, **Vientiane** is perhaps Southeast Asia's most modest capital city. Yet, although lacking the buzz of Ho Chi Minh City or Bangkok, Laos's capital has been transformed in the past decade and a half from a desolate city of boarded-up shopfronts into a quaint backwater, with a string of cosmopolitan restaurants and cafés to complement charming rows of pale yellow French-Indochinese shophouses. Robbed of its more splendid temples in battles with Siam long ago, Vientiane is more a place for adjusting to the pace of Lao life, and indulging in herbal saunas and sunset drinks on the banks of the Mekong, than one for breakneck tours of monuments and museums. Few tourists passing through the capital miss a chance for a half-day journey out to **Xiang Khouan**, its river-side meadow filled with mammoth religious statues, one of Laos's most arresting and bizarre sights.

With Vientiane seen off, most tourists venture north, the overwhelming majority to Louang Phabang. Doing the journey by bus rather than dashing up by air gives you a chance to take in **Vang Viang**, a town set in a landscape of glimmering green paddies and sawtoothed karst hills, a popular spot for caving, kayaking, rock climbing and long walks in the countryside. From here the road to Louang Phabang rollercoasters through some of Laos's most stunning scenery along the mountainous old Royal Road. The more intrepid can indulge in a road-and-river expedition through Laos's northwestern frontier, stopping off in the remote outpost of **Xainyabouli**, home to a large portion of the country's diminishing elephant population.

Despite the ravages of time, the gilded temples and weathered French-Indochinese shophouses of tiny, cultured **Louang Phabang** still possess a spellbinding majesty that make this Laos's most enticing destination. You won't want to leave without having taken a few day-trips out of the city, whether it's messing about on the Mekong en route to the sacred **Pak Ou Caves**, two riverside grottoes brimming with thousands

▲ Schoolkids, Vang Viang

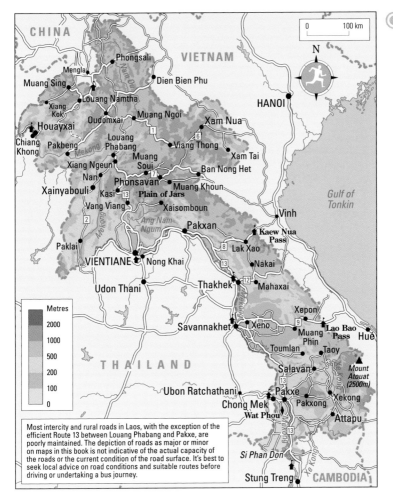

Most intercity and rural roads in Laos, with the exception of the efficient Route 13 between Louang Phabang and Pakxe, are poorly maintained. The depiction of roads as major or minor on maps in this book is not indicative of the actual capacity of the roads or the current condition of the road surface. It's best to seek local advice on road conditions and suitable routes before driving or undertaking a bus journey.

of Buddha images, or meandering through hillside ethnic minority villages on the way to **Kouang Si waterfall**.

To the north of Louang Phabang, the wild highlands of the **far north**, part of which falls within the notorious, opium-rich Golden Triangle, aren't the easiest to get around, but this often spectacular region is home to a patchwork of upland tribal groups. **Louang Namtha** and the easy-going village of **Muang Sing** are both centres for treks to nearby hill-tribe villages, while the former also offers kayaking opportunities. A corkscrew ride from Muang Sing through **Akha** country to the Burmese border lands you in the village of **Xiang Kok**, perched on the Mekong. Downriver

▼ Monks receiving alms, Louang Phabang

from here is **Houayxai**, an entry point popular with travellers arriving from northern Thailand in search of a slow boat for the picturesque journey south to Louang Phabang. Even more scenic is the trip from Louang Phabang up the **Nam Ou River**, an emerald waterway lined with sandy beaches and craggy limestone hills; on its banks, the breathtaking village of **Muang Ngoi** has justifiably become a popular travellers' haunt. Those looking for more of a challenge can continue upriver to Laos's chilly northernmost province, **Phongsali**, or hop onto a pick-up chugging off into the country's isolated **northeast**.

Lost in the misty mountains of the far northeast, **Houa Phan** province was the nerve centre of communist Laos during the Second Indochina War, and remains well removed from the Mekong Valley centres of lowland Lao life. If you make it as far as the provincial capital of **Xam Nua**, you'll find it hard to resist the temptation to visit **Viang Xai**, where the communist Pathet Lao directed their resistance from deep within a vast cave complex, and where the last Lao king was exiled until his untimely demise. South along

> **Si Phan Don is home to a handful of Irrawaddy dolphins**

Route 6 from Houa Phan is **Xiang Khouang** province, the heartland of Laos's **Hmong** population. **Phonsavan**, a dusty ramshackle town, is a good base from which to visit the region, in particular the premier attraction, the mystical **Plain of Jars**.

To the **south**, the tail of Laos is squeezed between the formidable Annamite Mountains to the east and the Mekong River as it barrels towards

Riding the rivers

Although the rivers of Laos have for years served as the country's highways, it is only recently that their potential for kayaking, rafting and canoeing has started to be realized. Most of the action is currently limited to areas where there are white-water travel companies on the ground, the best developed centres being Vang Viang (see p.118), Louang Phabang (see p.166) and Louang Namtha (see p.210). Most such operators offer a choice of day-trips or multi-day adventures, the cost of which usually pays for equipment, an experienced guide and meals and lodging.

Cambodia. **Thakhek** is somewhat overshadowed by the other two major Mekong towns here, but distinguishes itself with its crumbling colonial facades and proximity to the jagged sea of limestone hills that shelter the **Tham Lot Kong Lo**, an underground river that can be navigated by canoe. Genial **Savannakhet** is the south's most famous town, almost as culturally Vietnamese as it is Lao, a pleasant urban retreat with an architectural charm second only to Louang Phabang. Downriver, the market town of **Pakxe** lacks Savannakhet's appeal, but good transport links make it a convenient base for trips to the remoter parts of the **far south**. Visitors rarely venture across the fertile Bolaven Plateau, where most of Laos's **coffee** is grown, to Laos's wild east, preferring to strike south towards diminutive **Champasak**, with its red-dirt streets and princely villas. The ruins of **Wat Phou**, the greatest of the Khmer temples outside Cambodia, perch on a forested hilltop nearby. Anchoring the tail of Laos, the countless river islands of **Si Phan Don** lie scattered across the Mekong, swollen

▼ Sticky rice

to 14km from bank to bank, all the way to the Cambodian border. One of the most significant wetlands in the country, Si Phan Don is home to a handful of **Irrawaddy dolphins**, and harbours scores of long-established fishing communities as well as centuries-old lowland Lao traditions.

▼ Customers and traders at the morning market, Muang Sing

When to go

November to January are the most pleasant months to travel in lowland Laos, when daytime temperatures are agreeably warm and evenings are slightly chilly. However, at higher elevations temperatures are significantly cooler, sometimes dropping to freezing point. In February, temperatures begin to climb, reaching a peak in April, when the lowlands are baking hot and humid. During this time, the highlands are, for the most part, equally hot if a bit less humid than the lowlands, though there are places, such as Pakxong on the Bolaven Plateau, that have a temperate climate year round. The **rainy season** (generally May to September) affects the condition of Laos's network of unpaved roads, some of which become impassable after the rains begin. On the other hand, rivers which may be too low to navigate during the dry season become important transport routes after the rains have caused water levels to rise.

Average daily maximum temperatures and monthly rainfall

	Jan	Feb	Mar	Apr	May	Jun	Jul	Aug	Sep	Oct	Nov	Dec
Vientiane												
°C	28	30	33	34	32	32	31	31	31	31	29	28
mm	5	15	38	99	267	302	267	292	302	109	15	3
Louang Phabang												
°C	28	32	34	36	35	34	32	32	33	32	29	27
mm	15	18	31	109	163	155	231	300	165	79	31	13

21

things not to miss

It's not possible to see everything that Laos has to offer in one trip – and we don't suggest you try. What follows is a selective and subjective taste of the country's highlights: stunning temples, colourful festivals and great activities. They're arranged in five colour-coded categories to help you find the very best things to see, do, eat and experience. All highlights have a page reference to take you straight into the guide, where you can find out more.

01 A slow boat down the Mekong Page **225** • The lifeline of a landlocked nation, the Mekong figures in every visit to Laos, supplying the fish for dinner, a stunning array of sunsets and a route to travel along.

02 Wat Xiang Thong Page **150** • Spared wars, fires and overzealous restorations, the jewel of temple-rich Louang Phabang is as elegant as it is historic.

04 Haw Pha Kaew Page **94** • Once the king's personal shrine, the Temple of the Emerald Buddha now houses the best collection of Lao art in the country.

03 Kouang Si Falls Page **169** • A dip in the cool blue pools below Louang Phabang province's most picturesque waterfall is a refreshing respite from the tropical heat.

06 Lao food Page **46** • Lao cuisine offers a surprising range of delights, from spicy salads to ubiquitous grilled chicken – and there's excellent Beerlao lager with which to wash them down.

05 Textiles Page **57** • Weavers plying their craft still work the looms under their homes in the countryside, where each ethnic group is known for having its own style of textiles.

07 **Louang Phabang**
Page **133** • At the confluence of the Mekong and the Nam Khan, Laos's most enchanting city boasts atmospheric temples and a variety of excursions.

09 **Royal Palace, Louang Phabang** Page **147** • The home of the country's last king provides a glimpse into Laos's fading royal past.

08 **Trekking** Page **205** • Rugged mountain forests set the scene for hikers seeking to explore the remote hill villages of the north.

10 **Wat Phou**
Page **280** • The most evocative Khmer ruin outside of Cambodia, this rambling mountainside complex dates from the sixth to twelfth centuries.

11 **Markets** Page **47** • With fresh greens, food stalls and bootlegged DVDs of the latest Hollywood thriller all on offer, the country's markets make for a rich hunting ground for intrepid shoppers.

12 **Boat races** See *Festivals* **colour section** • Rooted in ancient planting rituals, boat races are held near the end of the rainy season throughout the country.

13 **Plain of Jars** Page **194** • Ancient funerary urns, the remnants of a lost civilization, lie scattered across the heart of the northeast.

14 **Wat Sisaket** Page **93** • Buddha images nestle in temple walls at Vientiane's oldest temple, the only religious site spared the torch of invading Siamese in the 1820s.

15 **Vang Viang** Page **114** • A spectacular landscape dotted with sawtoothed karsts, Vang Viang offers a chance to romp in the outdoors, with kayaking, rock climbing and caving all on hand.

16 **That Chomsi** Page **153** •
Offering some excellent panoramas, this golden spire crowns Louang Phabang's sacred hill.

17 **The Nam Ou** Page **232** •
Whether you're travelling by speedboat or on a lazy cruise, a journey along this tropical waterway in the mountainous north is an experience not to be missed.

18 Buddha Caves Page **168** • Hundreds of Buddhas gaze serenely across the Mekong from their riverside perch.

19 Colonial shophouses Page **256** • French-Indochinese shophouses add character to city streets in Mekong River towns, such as Savannakhet.

20 Si Phan Don Page **287** • This picturesque collection of Mekong islands, close to the Cambodian border, is dotted with rustic fishing villages and offers the chance to view river rapids and – if you're lucky – rare dolphins.

21 Herbal healing Page **66** • Rejuvenate yourself with a visit to a traditional Lao sauna, where the herbal remedies in the steam bath and the tea are jealously guarded secrets.

Basics

Basics

Getting there

The quickest and easiest way to get to Laos is to fly. Vientiane is the main gateway into Laos, but in the absence of direct flights from Europe, North America or Australasia, most visitors fly to Bangkok, and from there take an hour-long flight to Vientiane or Louang Phabang with Thai Airways, Bangkok Airways or Lao Airlines.

The **high season** for flights to Southeast Asia is from the beginning of July through to the end of August and also includes most of December, during which period fares can be twenty percent higher than at other times of year. Flights get booked solid at this time and should be reserved several weeks in advance. Note also that flying at weekends adds to the fare. Fares on to Vientiane from Bangkok rarely fluctuate, hovering around $200/£120 return; you may as well book this leg from home if possible, as you'll save very little buying tickets in Bangkok. Slightly discounted **youth or student fares** are available to under-25s on some airlines, but tickets need to be booked as far in advance as possible, as seat availability at these prices is limited.

Generally, **specialist flight agents** (including online travel companies) are your best bet for tickets, as these firms can usually undercut airline prices. If you're travelling on a discounted ticket, however, bear in mind that penalties for changing your plans can be stiff, and that only a percentage refund may be available if you need to cancel your journey.

If Laos is only one stop on a longer journey, you might want to consider buying a **Round-the-World (RTW) ticket**. Some travel agents can sell you an "off-the-shelf" RTW ticket that will have you touching down in about half a dozen cities; others will have to assemble one for you, which can be tailored to your needs but is apt to be more expensive. Also worth considering if you live in Australia, New Zealand or the West Coast of North America are **Circle Pacific** tickets, which feature Bangkok as a standard option.

Package tours to Laos, some of which take in the country as part of a wider Indochina trawl, are inevitably more expensive and less spontaneous than if you travelled independently, but are worth investigating if you have limited time or a specialist interest. It's also sometimes possible to use a package as a starting point to your holiday, allowing you to get the feel of the place with minimal hassle – just check before booking that you can stay on independently and fly back at a later date. Note that the handful of tour companies based in Laos (see p.43) offer a wider range of tours than agencies based abroad, and charge lower prices, too.

Online booking agents

Ebookers ⓦ www.ebookers.com (UK), ⓦ www.ebookers.ie (Ireland).
Expedia ⓦ www.expedia.com (US), ⓦ www.expedia.ca (Canada), ⓦ www.expedia.co.uk (UK).
Flightcentre ⓦ www.flightcentre.com (US, Canada, UK, Australia, New Zealand and South Africa).
Lastminute.com ⓦ www.lastminute.com (multiple locations).
Opodo ⓦ www.opodo.co.uk (UK).
Travelocity ⓦ www.travelocity.co.uk (UK), ⓦ www.travelocity.com (US), ⓦ www.travelocity.ca (Canada), ⓦ www.zuji.com.au (Australia), ⓦ www.zuji.co.nz (New Zealand).

Flights from the US and Canada

There are direct flights to Bangkok from Vancouver, Seattle, San Francisco and Los Angeles on the West Coast, from Detroit in the Midwest and from New York and Newark on the East Coast. Flying time from the West Coast to Bangkok is sixteen to eighteen hours, twenty hours from the New York area and Detroit.

Fares to Bangkok vary widely. Count on being able to get a better deal via Asia than on flights via Europe, especially if you're departing from the West Coast. Note also that flying on weekends can add as much as $200 to a round-trip fare. Low-season round-trip fares are $750–1000 from the West Coast, $900–1200 from the East Coast (add $300–400 in high season). From Canada, expect to pay around Can$2000 from Vancouver in low season (Can$300–400 more in high season).

Airlines

Air Canada ☏ 1-888/247-2262, ⊚ www .aircanada.ca. Daily flights from most major Canadian cities to Japan or Hong Kong, with onward connections to Bangkok through partner airlines.
Air France US ☏ 1-800/237-2747, Canada ☏ 1-800/667-2747, ⊚ www.airfrance.fr. Daily flights to Bangkok via Paris from several US and Canadian cities.
Asiana Airlines ☏ 1-800/227-4262, ⊚ www .flyasiana.com. To Seoul from several US cities, with onward flights to Bangkok operated by itself or partner airlines.
British Airways ☏ 1-800/AIRWAYS, ⊚ www .ba.com. Daily nonstop services from many North American cities to London, with connections to Bangkok.
Cathay Pacific US ☏ 1-800/233-2742, Canada ☏ 1-800/268-6868, ⊚ www.cathaypacific.com. To Bangkok from New York, Vancouver and Los Angeles via Hong Kong.
China Airlines ☏ 1-800/227-5118, ⊚ www .china-airlines.com. Flights to Bangkok from Taipei, with connections from Los Angeles, San Francisco and New York.
EVA Airways ☏ 1-800/695-1188, ⊚ www.evaair .com. To Bangkok via Taipei from New York, Seattle and Vancouver, among other cities.
Japan Airlines ☏ 1-800/525-3663, www .japanair.com. To Bangkok via Japan from San Francisco, Los Angeles, Chicago, Detroit, Seattle and New York.
Korean Airlines ☏ 1-800/438-5000, ⊚ www .koreanair.com. To Bangkok via Seoul from New York, Los Angeles and Vancouver.
Northwest/KLM ☏ 1-800/447-4747, ⊚ www .klm.com. To Bangkok via Japan from most major US cities, and via Amsterdam.
Swiss US ☏ 1-800/221-4750, Canada ☏ 1-800/ 267-9477, ⊚ www.swiss.com. Daily flights to

Bangkok via Zürich from several North American cities.
Thai Airways International US ☏ 1-800/426-5204, Canada ☏ 1-800/668-8103, ⊚ www.thaiair .com. From Los Angeles to Bangkok (nonstop, though you may have to pay a premium for this), with an onward connection to Vientiane.
United Airlines ☏ 1-800/538-2929, ⊚ www.ual .com. Daily flights to Bangkok via Japan from most major US cities.

Discount travel agents

Air Brokers International ☏ 1-800/883-3273, ⊚ www.airbrokers.com. Specialist in RTW and Circle Pacific tickets.
Airtreks ☏ 1-877/AIRTREKS, ⊚ www.airtreks.com. RTW and Circle Pacific tickets.
Educational Travel Center ☏ 1-800/747-5551 or 608/256-5551, ⊚ www.edtrav.com. Student/youth discount agent.
Flightcentre US ☏ 1-866/967-5351, ⊚ www .flightcentre.us, Canada ☏ 1-877/967-5302, ⊚ www.flightcentre.ca. Rock-bottom fares worldwide.
STA Travel ☏ 1-800/781-4040, ⊚ www.sta-travel .com. Worldwide specialists in independent travel; also student IDs, travel insurance, etc.
Travel Cuts Canada ☏ 1-866/246-9762, US ☏ 1-800/592-2887, ⊚ www.travelcuts.com. Canadian student-travel organization.

Specialist tour operators

Adventures Abroad ☏ 1-800/665-3998, ⊚ www .adventures-abroad.com. Small-group tour specialists with several regional tours which include Laos on their itinerary, plus one trip out of Bangkok that concentrates exclusively on Laos.
Adventure Center ☏ 1-800/227-8747, ⊚ www .adventurecenter.com. Plenty of trips to Laos, sometimes in combination with neighbouring countries, each lasting at least twelve days.
Asian Pacific Adventures ☏ 1-800/825-1680, ⊚ www.asianpacificadventures.com. Cultural travel specialists with a couple of Indochina offerings.
Asian Transpacific Journeys ☏ 1-800/642-2742, ⊚ www.asiatranspacific.com. A luxury small-group Indochina tour that will set you back at least $7400 – not including long-haul flights.
Bestway Tours ☏ 1-800/663-0844, ⊚ www .bestway.com. Cultural tour specialist with a two-week excursion to Laos and Myanmar (Burma), plus an eighteen-day Indochina package, though Laos coverage in both trips is limited to Louang Phabang and Vientiane.

Fly less – stay longer! Travel and climate change

Climate change is a serious threat to the ecosystems that humans rely upon, and air travel is the fastest-growing contributor to the problem. Rough Guides regard travel, overall, as a global benefit, and feel strongly that the advantages to developing economies are important, as is the opportunity of greater contact and awareness among peoples. But we all have a responsibility to limit our personal impact on global warming, and that means giving thought to how often we fly, and what we can do to redress the harm that our trips create.

Flying and climate change

Pretty much every form of motorized travel generates CO_2 (the main cause of human-induced climate change) but planes are far and away the worst offenders, not just because of the sheer distances they allow us to travel, but because they release a selection of greenhouse gases high into the atmosphere. The statistics are frightening: two people taking a return flight between Europe and the US will contribute as much to climate change as an average household's gas and electricity over a whole year.

Fuel-cell and other less harmful types of plane may emerge eventually. But until then, there are really just two options for concerned travellers: to reduce the amount we travel by air (take fewer trips – stay for longer!), and to make the trips we do take "climate neutral" via a carbon offset scheme.

Carbon offset schemes

Offset schemes run by climatecare.org, carbonneutral.com and others allow you to make up for some or all of the greenhouse gases that you are responsible for releasing. To do this, they provide "carbon calculators" for working out the global-warming contribution of a specific flight (or even your entire existence), and then let you contribute an appropriate amount of money to fund offsetting measures. These include rainforest and other indigenous reforestation, and initiatives to reduce future energy demand – often run in conjunction with sustainable development schemes.

Rough Guides, together with Lonely Planet and other concerned partners in the travel industry, are supporting a carbon offset scheme run by climatecare.org. Please take the time to view our website and see how you can help to make your trip climate neutral.

www.roughguides.com/climatechange

Cox and Kings ☎1-800/999-1758, ⓦwww .coxandkingsusa.com. Luxury tour operator with a week-long Laos itinerary covering Vientiane, Louang Phabang, Pakse and Don Khong.
Far Horizons ☎1-800/552-4575, ⓦwww .farhorizons.com. Specialists in archeological and cultural trips. Their twenty-day "Discover Angkor Wat and Laos" tour, which devotes a week to Laos, costs around $8300 (including flights).
Geographic Expeditions ☎1-800/777-8183, ⓦwww.geoex.com. A couple of Southeast Asian circuits that include Laos.
Journeys International ☎1-800/255-8735, ⓦwww.journeys-intl.com. Specialists in small-group nature and culture explorations, with a couple of six-day Laos offerings, including a tour taking in Louang Phabang and Vientiane.

Mountain Travel-Sobek ☎1-888/687-6235, ⓦwww.mtsobek.com. Adventure-travel outfit covering Laos as part of their "Treasures of Indochine" package, a sixteen-day journey visiting historic sites in Laos and ethnic minority villages in northern Vietnam.
Pacific Holidays ☎1-800/355-8025, ⓦwww .pacificholidaysinc.com. A couple of Indochina packages, taking in Vientiane and Louang Phabang.

From the UK and Ireland

There are nonstop flights from **London to Bangkok** with British Airways, EVA Airways, Qantas and Thai International; journey time is around twelve hours. Thai Airways offers onward connections to Vientiane. Many scheduled airlines operate indirect flights from London, as well as from UK regional airports and the Republic of Ireland; these usually take up to four hours longer depending on the stopovers en route, but can work out significantly cheaper than flying nonstop.

During the **high season**, a discounted London–Bangkok flight is likely to cost around £550. Prices drop considerably at other times of the year, when you should be able to find a fare for under £450. If you're flying Thai Airways, you may be able to get a London–Vientiane return ticket for as little as £500.

Airlines

Austrian Airlines UK ☎0870/124 2625, ⓦwww .aua.com. From London Heathrow to Bangkok, via Vienna.
British Airways ☎0870/850 9850, Republic of Ireland ☎1890/626 747, ⓦwww.britishairways .com. Heathrow–Bangkok nonstop, daily.
Emirates UK ☎0870/243 2222, ⓦwww.emirates .com. From London Heathrow, London Gatwick and Manchester to Bangkok via Dubai.
Eva Airways ☎020/7380 8300, ⓦwww.evaair .com. Nonstop London Heathrow to Bangkok.

Gulf Air UK ☎0870/777 1717, ⓦwww.gulfairco .com. London Heathrow to Bangkok via Bahrain.
KLM UK ☎0870/507 4074, ⓦwww.klm.com. Amsterdam to Bangkok, with connections from UK and Irish airports.
Qantas ☎0845/774 7767, ⓦwww.qantas.co.uk. Daily nonstop flights from Heathrow to Bangkok.
Royal Jordanian UK ☎020/7878 6333, ⓦwww .rja.com.jo. From Heathrow to Bangkok via Amman.
Thai Airways ☎0870/606 0911, ⓦwww.thaiair .com. Daily nonstop to Bangkok from Heathrow, with an onward connection to Vientiane.

Discount flight agents

Lee Travel Republic of Ireland ☎021/427 7111, ⓦwww.leetravel.ie. Flights worldwide.
North South Travel UK ☎ & ☎01245/608 291, ⓦwww.northsouthtravel.co.uk. Discounted fares worldwide; profits are used to support projects in the developing world.
STA Travel UK ☎0870/160 0599, ⓦwww .statravel.co.uk. Worldwide specialists in low-cost flights and tours for students and under-26s, though other customers welcome.
Trailfinders UK ☎0845/058 5858, ⓦwww .trailfinders.com; Republic of Ireland ☎01/677 7888, ⓦwww.trailfinders.ie. Efficient agent geared up to independent travellers.
Travel Bag UK ☎0800/082 5000, ⓦwww .travelbag.co.uk. Discount long-haul flights.
USIT Northern Ireland ☎028/9032 7111, ⓦwww .usitnow.com, Republic of Ireland ☎01/602 1904, ⓦwww.usit.ie. Student and youth travel.

Specialist tour operators

Exodus ☎0870/240 5550, ⓦwww.exodus.co.uk. Various Indochina packages from this specialist in cultural and adventure tourism, including one marrying Laos and Cambodia.
Explore Worldwide UK ☎0870/333 4001, Ireland (c/o Maxwell's Travel) ☎01/677 9479, ⓦwww .exploreworldwide.com. A variety of Laos offerings, including the eighteen-day "Spirit of Laos" tour, which includes Northern Laos, the Plain of Jars, and the Bolaven Plateau.
Guerba Expeditions UK ☎01373/826611, ⓦwww.guerba.co.uk. Guerba run a fifteen-day Bangkok–Hanoi overland tour that takes you down the Mekong to Louang Phabang, then to Vientiane and Pak Lao, and across Route 9 to Hanoi.
Magic of the Orient ☎0117/311 6051, ⓦwww .magic-of-the-orient.com. Upmarket tour company offering several Laos packages, including a four-day "Laos Classic" tour concentrating on Louang Phabang.

Peregrine ☏01635/872 300, ⓦwww
.peregrineadventures.com. Established adventure-
tour operator, covering Laos and Cambodia in one
package.

Regent Holidays ☏0870/499 0911, ⓦwww
.regent-holidays.co.uk. Their "Undiscovered Laos"
offering is an eleven-day affair featuring encounters
with hill tribes, rounded off with a stay in Louang
Phabang.

Steppes East ☏01285/651010, ⓦwww
.steppeseast.co.uk. Tailor-made, exclusive holidays
in Indochina.

Symbiosis ☏0845/123 2844, ⓦwww
.symbiosis-travel.com. An environmentally aware
and exclusive outfit. Organized tours include one
centred around the Louang Phabang Boat Race
Festival and specialized kayaking tours.

Transindus ☏020/8579 3739, ⓦwww.transindus
.co.uk. A small number of Laos offerings, including
river cruises in a boat-hotel, plus a pricey Indochina
tour lasting nearly three weeks.

World Expeditions ☏0800/074 4135, ⓦwww
.worldexpeditions.co.uk. A cycling package in the
Louang Phabang area and northern Thailand is one of
the more unusual of their several Laos excursions.

From Australia and New Zealand

Bangkok is the best choice of gateway
city to Laos, as Thai Airways fly here from
both Australia and New Zealand and have
connections to Vientiane. Return **fares** to
Bangkok vary between A$1000/NZ$1300
and A$1500/NZ$1800 depending on the
season. Several airlines have a set fare from
major eastern Australian cities to Bangkok;
fares from Perth and Darwin are around
A$100–200 cheaper. From Christchurch and
Wellington you'll pay NZ$150–300 more than
from Auckland.

Airlines

Air New Zealand Australia ☏13 24 76, New
Zealand ☏0800/737 000, ⓦwww.airnewzealand
.com. Flights to Singapore with onward connections to
Bangkok through partner airlines.

British Airways Australia ☏1300/767 177, New
Zealand ☏09/966 9777, ⓦwww.britishairways
.com. Sydney to Bangkok daily.

Garuda Australia ☏02/9334 9970, New Zealand
☏09/366 1862, ⓦwww.garuda-indonesia.com.
Daily service from Auckland, Adelaide, Brisbane,
Cairns, Melbourne and Sydney to Bangkok via
Denpasar or Jakarta.

Malaysia Airlines Australia ☏13 26 27, New
Zealand ☏0800/777 747, ⓦwww.mas.com.my.
Daily service from Sydney, Melbourne and Auckland to
Bangkok via Kuala Lumpur.

Qantas Australia ☏13 13 13, New Zealand
☏0800/800 767, ⓦwww.qantas.com. Daily flights
from major Australian and New Zealand cities to
Bangkok.

Singapore Airlines Australia ☏13 10 11, New
Zealand ☏09/303 2129, ⓦwww.singaporeair
.com. Daily service to Bangkok from Sydney, Adelaide,
Melbourne and Auckland via Singapore.

Thai Airways Australia ☏1300/651 960; New
Zealand ☏09/377 3886, ⓦwww.thaiair.com. To
Vientiane from Sydney, Brisbane, Melbourne and
Auckland via Bangkok (an overnight connection may
be required).

Discount flight agents

Destinations Unlimited New Zealand ☏09/414
1680, ⓦwww.travel-nz.com. Good deals on airfares
and holidays.

STA Travel Australia ☏1300/733 035, ⓦwww
.statravel.com.au, New Zealand ☏0508/782 872,
ⓦwww.statravel.co.nz. Worldwide specialists in
"learning travel", with low-cost flights for students and
under-26s; other customers also welcome. Over 200
branches overseas.

Trailfinders Australia ☏1300/780 212. ⓦwww
.trailfinders.com.au. Australian branch of large UK-
based independent travel specialists.

Specialist tour operators

Abercrombie & Kent Australia ☏1300/851 800,
New Zealand ☏0800/441 638, ⓦwww
.abercrombiekent.com.au. Luxury tour operator with
a couple of Indochina offerings.

Adventure World Australia ☏02/8913 0755,
ⓦwww.adventureworld.com.au; New Zealand
☏09/524 5118, ⓦwww.adventureworld.co.nz.
Agents for Orbitours' customized packages for
independent travellers, including trekking and hill-tribe
visits.

Intrepid Travel ☏1300/360 667, ⓦwww
.intrepidtravel.com.au. A long list of Laos trips, most
combining the country with visits to its neighbours.

Peregrine Adventures ☏03/9663 8611, ⓦwww
.peregrine.net.au. Small-group adventure and cultural
tours, with a Laos/Cambodia joint offering.

San Michele Travel Australia ☏1800/222 244,
ⓦwww.asiatravel.com.au. Short Laos trips that can
be plugged into tours of Indochina.

Travel Indochina ☏1300/138 755, ⓦwww
.travelindochina.com.au. Goes beyond the obvious
sights and can arrange cross-border visas for

Thailand, Laos, Vietnam, China and Cambodia. Among several Laos offerings is a two-week "Inside Laos" trip that takes you from Pakbeng to Don Khong.
World Expeditions Australia ℡ 1300/720 000, ⓦ www.worldexpeditions.com.au; New Zealand ℡ 0800/350 354, ⓦ www.worldexpeditions.co.nz. Most unusual among their handful of Laos tours is a trip combining southern Laos, including the Bolaven Plateau and Si Phan Don, with the Isaan region of northeast Thailand.

Getting there from neighbouring countries

As regards air travel, both Vientiane and Louang Phabang are most easily reached from Bangkok. Laos in general is accessible overland via a number of border crossings with its neighbouring countries. Visas to Laos are obtainable from embassies and consulates in neighbouring countries (see pp.26–27 for further details).

From Thailand

The most convenient way to get to Laos from Thailand is by **flying** from **Bangkok** or **Chiang Mai** to Vientiane or Louang Phabang. All journeys take about an hour.

If cost is a concern, you can fly from Bangkok to the northeastern Thai city of Udon Thani for roughly half the price of a Bangkok–Vientiane flight; from Udon Thani, Thai Airways provides a van ($3) for the forty-minute drive to the Friendship Bridge (see below).

Crossing **overland** allows you ample time to visit Thailand's mountainous north or explore the northeast, an area heavily populated by ethnic Lao. As of the time of writing, there are five routes across the Thai border into Laos: Chiang Khong–Houayxai (see p.226); Nong Khai–Vientiane (via the Friendship Bridge, see p.83); Nakhon Phanom–Thakhek (see p.249); Mukdahan–Savannakhet (see p.254); and Chong Mek–Pakxe (see p.274). All these border crossings now have **visa-on-arrival** services; $30 and a passport photo will buy you two weeks of Lao time. If you intend to stay for longer, it's best to apply for a business visa at the Lao Embassy in Bangkok or at the consulate in Khon Kaen (see p.27). In theory, a sixth crossing, namely Beung Khan–Pakxan, is also open to foreigners, but there have been reports of travellers being turned back there; if you're keen on trying this route, it's best to seek local advice on the latest situation.

It is no longer possible to cross from Nong Khai to Thadua by ferry: tourists must use the Friendship Bridge, a few kilometres west of Nong Khai town.

From Vietnam

Vietnam Airlines flies from **Hanoi** and **Ho Chi Minh City** (Saigon) to Vientiane (1hr), the latter route also being served by Lao Airlines. It's also possible to travel **overland** into Laos at four border points. Route 8 across the **Kaew Nua Pass** (the Cau Treo/Nam Phao crossing), which links Vinh with Vientiane, is paved and served by daily direct buses connecting Vientiane to a number of cities on the coast of Vietnam, including Hanoi and Ho Chi Minh City. Route 9 across the **Lao Bao Pass** (the Lao Bao/Daen Sawan crossing) links the Vietnamese city of Dong Ha with the Mekong River town of Savannakhet, and is also served by direct buses. The latest crossings to open are in the north and are, so far, little used by Western visitors. The busiest of these is on Route 7 at **Namkan**, just east of Nong Het, connecting Vietnam's Nghe An province with Xiang Khouang province. Further north still, just beyond Viang Xai, is the **Na Meo** crossing from Vietnam's Thanh Hoa province.

Bear in mind that **Vietnamese officials** are notorious sticklers for paperwork. Vietnamese embassy officials have been known to incorrectly stamp exit/entry points in visitors' passports – and making changes means paying a surcharge.

From Cambodia

Lao Airlines operates direct **flights** from both **Phnom Penh** and **Siem Reap** to Vientiane (3hr). The Mekong **border crossing** between Cambodia and Laos has not been officially opened at the time of writing, but a steady stream of Western travellers has been going through in both directions without incident (you'll need a Lao visa in advance). Boats can sometimes be hired at Stung Treng for the journey north to Ban Hang Khon on Don Khon. Both Lao and Cambodian border officials will exact a toll from passing tourists ($5–10).

From China

From China's southwestern **Yunnan** province, it's possible to travel by road or air into Laos. Lao Airlines operates **flights** from Kunming to Vientiane (2 weekly; 1hr 15min). Travelling **by road**, you'll pass through the virgin rainforests of Xishuangbanna, a region whose history and peoples have close ties with Laos. There are direct buses from Jinghong to Oudomxai and Louang Namtha; from Mengla, it takes ninety minutes by minibus to reach Mo Han, 6km from the border, beyond which lies the Lao town of Boten. The **river route** from China to Laos down the Mekong is currently only open to cargo boats, but there is talk of allowing foreign tourists to use this route in the near future.

From Burma

Western tourists are not officially permitted to cross between **Burma** (Myanmar) and Laos at Muangmom or Xiang Kok, the two official border points between the two countries, although a few foreigners have reportedly slipped through.

Airlines

Bangkok Airways Bangkok ☎ 02 265 5555, Ⓦ www.bangkokair.com. Bangkok to Louang Phabang.

Lao Airlines Bangkok ☎ 02 236 9822, Chiang Mai ☎ 053 404033, Hanoi ☎ 04/942 5362, Ho Chi Minh City ☎ 08/822 6990, Kunming ☎ 0871/3163000, Phnom Penh ☎ 023/216563, Siem Reap ☎ 063/963283, Ⓦ www.laoairlines.com. Daily flights to Vientiane from Bangkok, plus less frequent flights from Chiang Mai, Hanoi, Kunming, Phnom Penh and Siem Reap. Also flights to Louang Phabang from Bangkok, Chiang Mai, Hanoi and Siem Reap; plus to Pakxe from Phnom Penh and Siem Reap.

Thai Airways Bangkok ☎ 02 545 3690, Ⓦ www .thaiair.com. Bangkok–Vientiane.

Vietnam Airlines Hanoi ☎ 04/825 0888, Ⓦ www .vietnamairlines.com. Hanoi and Ho Chi Minh City to Vientiane.

Red tape and visas

Visas are required for all non-Thai visitors to Laos, but you don't need to obtain a visa in advance; fifteen-day visas can be bought on entry to the country. To apply for an advance visa, which is good for longer than fifteen days, you will have to go through a Lao embassy or a tour agency. Note that all visitors to Laos must have a passport that is valid for at least six months from the time of entry into Laos.

Visas on arrival take just a few minutes to process, cost $30 and are available to passengers flying into Wattay Airport in Vientiane, Louang Phabang Airport or crossing into Laos from any of Thailand's border crossings that are open to foreign tourists. Only US dollars are accepted as payment and a passport-size photograph is required. If you forget the photo, the border officials will usually overlook this for another $5. Note that when entering or exiting Laos via the Friendship Bridge, there is an entry/exit fee of less than $1 that can be paid in kip or Thai baht.

Many visitors opt to apply for a Lao visa **in advance** while staying in Bangkok or Hanoi in order to stay longer than the two weeks given as visas on arrival. In any case, you'll find it much easier to apply for your visa in, say, Bangkok (same-day service) than in the West (where visas can take up to a month to process). Wherever you get your visa, it's worth bearing in mind that

Lao visa regulations and prices are subject to frequent change.

In **Bangkok**, you can obtain visas directly from the **embassy** (see opposite for the address). Fifteen-day visas cost approximately 750 baht ($21). Thirty-day visas cost 1000 baht ($23) for nationals of Britain, Australia and New Zealand, 1200 baht ($27) for Americans and 1400 baht ($32) for Canadians. Two passport-size photographs are required and processing is done on the same day provided you apply before noon. It's also possible to get more than one visa at a time, that is, two thirty-day visas, for double the price. Note that the Lao embassy in Bangkok only accepts Thai baht for transactions. If you don't fancy the trip out to the embassy, which is on the outskirts of the city, and you're willing to pay a bit extra, you can go through one of the many **travel agents** concentrated on and around Khao San Road. Prices charged by agents start at 750 baht for a fifteen-day visa, up to twice

Lao visas

Visa on arrival: Fifteen days, extendable for two extra weeks. Available at Wattay International Airport (Vientiane), Luang Phabang International Airport, and all Thai-Lao border crossings open to foreigners.

Tourist visa (VT): Fifteen days, extendable.

Visitor visa (B3): One-month stay. Extendable for two extra weeks.

Transit visa (VTR): Maximum five days for a stay. Offered at the Lao embassy in Hanoi and the consulate in Kunming, China, for travellers flying to Bangkok who wish to make a short stopover in Vientiane. For this reason, the visa may only be valid for one province. Transit visas are also available in Da Nang, Vietnam, for travellers wanting to take Route 9 to Thailand. Costs $25–30, depending on your nationality, and takes three working days to process.

Business visa (B2): One-month stay. Multiple extensions. Requires a Lao sponsor.

Multiple entry visa: Only issued by the Ministry of Foreign Affairs, Consular Department.

as much for a thirty-day visa depending on nationality; visa applications take about three working days to turn around. If you decide to go through a Bangkok travel agency, make sure you actually get the class of visa you have paid for (see the box opposite). A Lao consulate in **Khon Kaen** in Thailand's northeast can also issue visas, though the fees being charged and the time taken to process the visa here are somewhat erratic.

The Lao embassy in **Hanoi**, and consulates in **Ho Chi Minh City** and **Da Nang**, can also issue visas but it's important to note that the types of visas issued and the prices charged vary from place to place, and the regulations and conditions change frequently. Lao visas issued in Vietnam are also significantly more expensive than those issued in Thailand. If you are going to cross overland into Laos from Vietnam be sure to **specify the crossing** you intend to use – Lao Bao or Cau Treo – when applying for the visa. Immigration officials on the Vietnam side have been known to refuse exit to travellers whose visa does not specify where they intend to cross, although this could be just another incidence of fishing for bribes.

At the time of writing, one-month visitor visas issued in Hanoi cost $50–70 depending on the nationality of the applicant and require three working days. The one-day express service costs an extra $20. In Ho Chi Minh City, you can get a thirty-day visitor visa ($50; same-day service), but in Da Nang, you can only get a fifteen-day tourist visa ($50; 2 working days) or a five-day transit visa ($30; 2 working days), which will allow you to take Route 9 over to Mukdahan in Thailand.

Extending visas

Visa extensions are fairly easy to obtain, but the rules are far from uniform and the price of an extension varies from place to place or day to day. Officially, only the immigration office on Hatsady Road in Vientiane can issue extensions, costing $2 per day; the maximum length of an extension is fifteen days but this is up to the official on duty. It is sometimes possible to get a visa extended in other towns, and it's certainly worth asking about this if you are in some remote provincial capital and nearing the end of your visa.

Should you accidentally **overstay** your visa, both airport and border immigration offices generally charge $10 per day for overstays.

Lao embassies and consulates

Australia 1 Dalman Crescent, O'Malley, Canberra ☎02/6286 4595, ℻6290 1910.
Cambodia 15–17 Keomani Rd, Phnom Penh ☎23/26441.
China 11 E 4th St, Sanlitun, Chaoyang, Beijing ☎010/65321224; Camelia Hotel, Suite 3226, 154 E Dong Feng Rd, Kunming ☎0871/3176624.
France 74 Avenue Raymond Poincaré, Paris ☎01/45 53 02 98, ℻47 27 57 89.
Germany Bismarckallee 2A, 14193 Berlin ☎49/30 89 06 06 47, ℻30 89 06 06 48.
Hong Kong Room 1002 Arion Commercial Centre, 2–12 Queen's Road West, Hong Kong ☎2544 1186.
India Panchsheel Park, New Delhi ☎011/642 7447, ℻011/642 8588.
Indonesia 33 Jalan Kintamani Raya, Kuningan Timur, Jakarta ☎021/520 2673, ℻522 9601.
Japan 3-3-22, Nishi-Azabu, Minato-ku ☎03/54112291, ℻54112293.
Malaysia 25 Jalan Damai, Kuala Lumpur ☎03/2148 7059, ℻2145 0080.
Myanmar (Burma), Diplomatic Headquarters, Taw Win Road, Yangon (Rangoon) ☎01/22482.
New Zealand Contact embassy in Canberra.
Philippines 34 Lapu-Lapu St, Magallanes, Makati, Metro-Manila ☎02/833-5759.
Singapore 101 Thomson Road #05–03A, United Sq ☎6250 6044, ℻6250 6014.
Thailand 502/13 Ramkhamhaeng Soi 39, Bangkapi, Bangkok ☎02 539 6668; 19/1–3 Phothisan Rd, Khon Kaen ☎043 223 698.
USA 222 S St NW, Washington DC ☎202/332-6416, ℻332-4923, ⊛www.laoembassy.com.
Vietnam 40 Quang Trung, Hanoi ☎04/845 3836; 181 Hai Ba Trung, Ho Chi Minh City ☎08/829 7667; 12 Tran Quy-Cap, Da Nang ☎051/21208.

Customs

Lao **customs regulations** limit visitors to 500 cigarettes and one litre of distilled alcohol per person upon entry, but in practice bags are rarely opened unless a suspiciously large amount of luggage is being brought in. A **customs declaration form** must be filled out along with the arrival form, but typically nobody bothers to check that the information is correct. There is no limit on the amount of **foreign currency** you can bring into Laos.

Information

The Lao National Tourism Administration (LNTA or NTAL for short; ⓦwww .tourismlaos.gov.la) operates offices in a few places, including Vientiane and Louang Phabang. They will usually have a few brochures and perhaps a map of Vientiane, but their local information is generally good. Privately owned travel companies, such as Sodetour and Diethelm, can often provide reliable information in provincial capitals (see p.43 for more on tour companies). Queries directed at Lao embassies abroad often elicit no response.

For visitors, tour agencies, guesthouse owners and fellow travellers are much better sources of information, particularly as conditions in Laos change with astonishing rapidity. No one will better be able to describe the condition of the road between Xiang Kok and Muang Sing than someone who has just traversed it.

Online resources

Below is a selection of useful **websites** for all-round information on Laos. The mother of all Lao **links pages** is found at ⓦwww .vientianetimes.com.

Recommended websites

ⓦ**www.laopdr.com** A good jumping-off point, this is an excellent general info site with lots of links.

ⓦ**www.mekongexpress.com** Huge general info site.

ⓦ**www.global.lao.net/laoVL.html** A good source of facts and information with useful links and a virtual library.

ⓦ**www.laoembassy.com** The website of the Lao Embassy to the United States posts visa regulations and an updated list of border crossings.

ⓦ**www.ecotourismlaos.com** A slick website by the Lao National Tourism Administration.

ⓦ**www.visit-laos.com** A good all-round travel site on Laos.

ⓦ**www.laos-travel.itgo.com** Another promising general site for tourist information.

ⓦ**www.savannanet.com** A good travel page with articles and links.

ⓦ**www.theboatlanding.laopdr.com** An excellent site on travel in Northern Laos. Features information on independent trekking and eco-tourism, has great links and is visually one of the best Lao websites.

Governmental travel advice

Australian Department of Foreign Affairs ⓦwww.dfat.gov.au.

British Foreign and Commonwealth Office ⓦwww.fco.gov.uk/travel.

Canadian Foreign Affairs Department ⓦwww .dfait-maeci.gc.ca.

US State Department Travel Advisories ⓦwww.travel.state.gov.

Costs, money and banks

Laos is one of the world's poorest nations, and consequently one of the cheapest Asian countries to travel in. Accommodation and transport are very inexpensive, though restaurant prices tend to be slightly higher than in neighbouring Thailand. For this reason, it's not uncommon to spend as much or more on meals than on accommodation.

By eating at noodle stalls and cheap restaurants, using public transport and opting for basic accommodation, you can travel in Laos on a **daily budget** of less than $20. Staying in upmarket hotels and resorts, eating in top-notch restaurants and hiring a car with a driver will push your budget up to something like $30–50 a day, a very reasonable sum, though note that many Lao towns lack upmarket accommodation and eating options.

Official **price tiering** does exist in Laos, with foreigners paying more than locals for some services. The dual system applies for airfares, speedboat tickets and entry fees to museums and famous sites. Frequently, you'll come across bus, sawngthaew and boat drivers who feel entitled to levy their own foreigner surcharge. Indeed, cases of foreign visitors being overcharged for goods and services have now become fairly common, as anywhere else in the world. But be cautious about causing a scene until you've established the cost of things, and remember prices vary throughout Laos as you enter more remote areas. The best way to avoid being overcharged is simply to know the correct price before you buy or ride.

While restaurants and some shops have fixed prices, in general merchandise almost never has price tags, and the lack of a fixed pricing scheme can take some getting used to. Buying anything other than food in a market should always be negotiated, as should the cost of chartering transport (as opposed to fares on passenger vehicles, which are not negotiable). Hotel and guesthouse operators are usually open to bargaining, particularly during off-peak months.

Bargaining is very much a part of life in Laos, and an art form, requiring a delicate balance of humour, patience and tact. It's important to remain realistic, as vendors will lose interest if you've quoted a price that's way out of line, and to keep a sense of perspective: cut-throat haggling over 1000K only reflects poorly on both buyer and seller. As the Lao in general – with the exception of drivers of vehicles for hire and souvenir sellers in Vientiane and Louang Phabang – are less out to rip off tourists than their counterparts in Thailand and Vietnam, they start off the haggling by quoting a fairly realistic price and expect to come down only a little.

Incidentally, Laos relies heavily on products imported from Vietnam, China and Thailand. If you are arriving from Thailand, it pays to buy everyday items (such as toiletries) in Thailand, or you'll find yourself paying double for the same items in Laos.

Entrance fees

Museums, monuments and anything else popular with tourists charge a small **entrance fee**, usually around $1. A growing number of monasteries and holy sites in Vientiane and Louang Phabang charge for admission, though only a fraction of the money collected reverts back to the monastery.

Currency

Due to the instability of the national currency, the **kip**, American dollars and Thai baht are also widely used; in fact, Thai currency makes up an estimated thirty percent of all cash circulating in the Lao capital. At the time of writing, the official **exchange rate** was 10,500 kip to the US dollar, 260 kip to the Thai baht.

Lao currency is available in 20,000K, 10,000K, 5000K, 2000K, 1000K and 500K notes; there are no coins in circulation. For the last edition of this book, the largest denomination banknote was 5000K, a fact which should give an idea as to the stability (or lack thereof) of the kip.

Although a law passed in 1990 technically forbids the use of foreign currencies to pay for goods and services in local markets, many hotels, restaurants and tour operators routinely quote their prices in dollars or baht, and it is perfectly acceptable to pay in either of these currencies, regardless of what the price is quoted in. One exception, however, is the government-owned Lao Airlines, which only accepts payment in American dollars cash. This is not too surprising when you consider that a round-trip ticket from Vientiane to Phongsali costs over a million kip.

Carrying large sums of money in kip can be cumbersome. Indeed, most travellers tend to retain the bulk of their cash in dollars or baht, changing money when they need to. Bear in mind that you cannot convert your kip back into dollars or baht when leaving the country – and that you won't be able to burn up your kip at the duty-free shops, as they only accept dollars and baht.

Banks and exchange

Banking **hours** are generally Monday to Friday 8.30am to 4pm, although some banks in the provinces keep different hours. Exchange kiosks keep longer hours but are rare – with a couple operating in downtown Vientiane and others found in provincial post offices, airports and at some border checkpoints. **Exchange rates** tend to be better in Vientiane, decreasing slightly in major urban centres, and slipping again in the satellites of provincial centres. Before travelling into smaller towns, **change enough money** to see you through until the next major town. It's also a good idea to stay atop of the daily fluctuations of the market, so that you don't get an inferior rate.

For a period, the re-emergence of the **black market** in foreign currencies provided some Lao with a means of supplementing their incomes by moonlighting as freelance currency traders. Such traders used to hang around outside the markets in Vientiane and Louang Phabang, but are now rare. In most towns your best bet for a rate more favourable than the bank is to enquire at a gold shop or your guesthouse.

Traveller's cheques, cash and cards

The most convenient way to travel in Laos is to arm yourself with an ample supply of American dollars and Thai baht in cash. **Traveller's cheques** are available for a small commission from most banks and travel agents at home (keep the purchase agreement and a record of cheque serial numbers separate from the cheques), but although they are the safest

Kip and dollars

Given the **volatility of the kip**, prices for accommodation, river travel and car hire in the Guide have been given in their more stable dollar equivalents. Indeed, many hotels and guesthouses have opted to fix their rates to the dollar, or simply to quote the price in dollars outright, and some restaurants do the same. Throughout the Guide, prices quoted in kip for transport, museum entrance fees, etc were correct at the time of research and have been retained to give a relative idea of costs, though in practice many of these prices will be higher. The kip stood at a comparatively stable 10,500 to the dollar at the time of writing. **Current rates** as well as a commodities basket reflecting the current prices of various goods and services in kip are published on Ⓦ www.vientianetimes.com, and daily rates are posted at all foreign exchange counters in Laos.

way to carry your money, you'll have trouble cashing them outside Vientiane and major cities such as Louang Phabang, Savannakhet and Pakxe. Sometimes, provincial banks will make an exception, usually when someone needs dollars to buy an airline ticket, and then usually only when presented with a letter from Lao Airlines.

Major **credit cards** – American Express, Visa and Mastercard – are slowly catching on in Vientiane and are accepted at many hotels, upmarket restaurants and shops catering to tourists. **Cash advances** on Visa

cards, and less frequently Mastercard, are possible in major urban centres – you can count on this service in Louang Phabang, Vientiane, Savannakhet and Pakxe – but you will most likely be required to withdraw a minimum of $100 in kip, incurring a commission of 2.5 to 3 percent. Cash advances in dollars are possible at a rate of 3.5 percent at BCEL in Vientiane. The American Express representative is Diethelm Travel, based in Vientiane. At the time of writing, it's not possible to withdraw cash from **ATMs** in Laos – there aren't any.

Insurance

Most people find it essential to take out a good travel insurance policy to cover against theft, loss and illness or injury. Before paying for a new policy, however, it's worth checking whether you are already covered. Credit and charge cards often have certain levels of medical or other insurance included, and travel insurance may also be included if you use a major credit or charge card to pay for your trip. Similarly, some all-risks home insurance policies may cover your possessions when overseas, and many private medical schemes include cover when abroad.

A typical travel insurance policy usually provides cover for the loss of baggage, tickets and – up to a certain limit – cash or cheques, as well as cancellation or curtailment of your journey. Most of them exclude

so-called **dangerous sports** unless an extra premium is paid: in Laos this can mean white-water rafting, rock-climbing and trekking. Many policies can be chopped and changed to exclude coverage you don't

Rough Guides travel insurance

Rough Guides has teamed up with Columbus Direct to offer you travel insurance that can be tailored to suit your needs.

Readers can choose from many different travel insurance products, including a low-cost backpacker option for long stays; a short break option for city getaways; a typical holiday package option; and many others. There are also annual multi-trip policies for those who travel regularly, with variable levels of cover available. Different sports and activities (trekking, skiing, etc) can be covered if required on most policies.

Rough Guides travel insurance is available to the residents of 36 different countries with different language options to choose from via our website – ⓦ www .roughguidesinsurance.com – where you can also purchase the insurance.

Alternatively, UK residents should call ☎0800 083 9507; US citizens should call ☎1-800 749-4922; Australians should call ☎1 300 669 999. All other nationalities should call ☎+44 870 890 2843.

need – for example, sickness and accident benefits can often be excluded or included at will. If you do take medical coverage, ascertain whether benefits will be paid as treatment proceeds or only after return home, and whether there is a 24-hour medical emergency number. When securing baggage cover, make sure that the per-article limit – typically under £500 – will cover your most valuable possession. If you need to make a **claim**, you should keep receipts for medicines and medical treatment, and in the event you have anything stolen, you must obtain an official statement from the police.

Health

Health care in Laos is so poor as to be virtually nonexistent; the average life expectancy is just over 55. Malaria and other mosquito-borne diseases are rife, and you'll need to take a number of precautions to avoid contracting these, especially if you plan on spending long periods of time in rural regions. The nearest medical care of any competence is in neighbouring Thailand; if you find yourself afflicted by anything more serious than travellers' diarrhoea, it's best to head for the closest Thai border crossing and check into a hospital.

Plan on consulting a doctor at least two months before your travel date to discuss which diseases you should receive immunization against. Some antimalarials must be taken several days before arrival in a malarial area in order to be effective. Travelling with small children requires special precautions, and a doctor will be able to advise on what over-the-counter drugs to bring. If you are going to be on the road for some time, a **dental check-up** is also advisable, as Laos is no place to have a toothache.

Vaccinations

While there are no mandatory **vaccinations** for Laos (except yellow fever if you are coming from an infected area), a few are recommended. Hepatitis A, typhus, tetanus and polio are the most important ones, but you should also consider hepatitis B, rabies and Japanese encephalitis. All shots should be recorded on an **International Certificate of Vaccination** and carried with your passport when travelling abroad.

Hepatitis A is contracted via contaminated food and water and can be prevented by the Havrix vaccine which provides protection for up to ten years. Two injections two to four weeks apart are necessary, followed by a booster a year later. The older one-shot vaccine only provides protection for three months. **Hepatitis B** is spread via sexual contact, transfusions of tainted blood and dirty needles. Vaccination is recommended for travellers who plan on staying for long periods of time (six months or more). Note that the vaccine can take up to six months before it is fully effective.

Rabies can be prevented by a vaccine that consists of two injections over a two-month period with a third a year later and boosters every two to five years. If you haven't had shots and are bitten by a potentially rabid animal, you will need to get the jabs immediately.

Japanese encephalitis, a mosquito-borne disease, is quite rare, but doctors may recommend a vaccination against it. The course of injections consists of two shots at two-week intervals plus a booster.

Medical resources for travellers

Besides the resources here, you might want to check the *Rough Guide to Travel Health* by Dr Nick Jones.

Websites

ⓦ **www.csih.org**. The website of the Canadian Society for International Health contains an extensive list of travel health centres in Canada.

ⓦ **www.cdc.gov/travel** The US government's official site for travel health.

ⓦ **www.istm.org** The website of the International Society for Travel Medicine, with a full list of clinics specializing in international travel health.

ⓦ **www.tripprep.com** Travel Health Online provides an online-only comprehensive database of necessary vaccinations for most countries, as well as destination and medical service provider information.

ⓦ **www.fitfortravel.scot.nhs.uk** UK Scottish NHS website carrying information about travel-related diseases and how to avoid them.

Travel medicine

USA and Canada

MEDJET Assistance ☎ 1-800/863-3538, ⓦ www .medjetassistance.com. Annual membership programme for travellers which, in the event of illness or injury, will fly members home or to the hospital of their choice in a medically equipped jet.

Travel Medicine ☎ 1-800/872-8633, ⓦ www .travmed.com. Sells first-aid kits, mosquito netting, water filters, reference books and other health-related travel products; the website includes a list of US travel clinics.

UK and Ireland

Hospital for Tropical Diseases Travel Clinic 2nd floor, Mortimer Market Centre, off Capper St, London WC1E 6AU ☎ 020/7388 9600, ⓦ www .thehtd.org (Mon–Fri 9am–5pm by appointment only). A consultation costs £15, which is waived if you have your injections or buy your malaria pills here. A recorded Health Line (☎ 020/7950 7799; for Laos info key 57 at the voice prompt) gives hints on hygiene and illness prevention as well as listing appropriate immunizations.

Liverpool School of Tropical Medicine Pembroke Place, Liverpool L3 5QA ☎ 0151/708 9393, ⓦ www.liv.ac.uk/lstm/about/TravelClinic. htm. Walk-in clinic available; contact them for current times.

MASTA (Medical Advisory Service for Travellers Abroad) ☎ 0870/606 2782, ⓦ www .masta.org. Travel clinics around the UK.

Nomad Travel ⓦ www.nomadtravel.co.uk. Vaccinations, anti-malarials and medical kits at their stores in London (Victoria, Russell Square and Turnpike Lane), Bristol and Southampton. Also a travel

health info line (☎ 0906/863 3414; 60p/min).

Trailfinders Immunization clinic (no appointment necessary) at 194 Kensington High St, London (Mon–Fri 9am–5pm except Thurs to 6pm, Sat 10am–5.15pm; ☎ 020/7938 3999).

Travel Health Centre Department of International Health and Tropical Medicine, Royal College of Surgeons in Ireland, Mercers Medical Centre, Stephen's St Lower, Dublin ☎ 01/402 2337. Expert pre-trip advice and inoculations.

Travel Medicine Services PO Box 254, 16 College St, Belfast 1 ☎ 028/9031 5220. Offers medical advice before and after trips.

Tropical Medical Bureau Grafton Buildings, 34 Grafton St, Dublin 2 ☎ 01850/487 674, ⓦ www .tmb.ie. Travel clinics in Dublin and elsewhere across the Republic of Ireland.

Australia and New Zealand

Travel Doctor Australia ☎ 1800/245499, ⓦ www .tmvc.com.au; New Zealand ☎ 09/373 3531, ⓦ www.traveldoctor.co.nz. Clinics in major Australian and New Zealand cities; travel health factsheets available online.

General precautions

The average traveller to Laos has little to worry about as long as they use common sense and exercise a few precautions. The changes in climate and diet experienced during travel collaborate to lower your resistance, so you need to take special care to maintain a healthy intake of food and water and to try to minimize the effects of heat and humidity on the body. Excessive alcohol consumption should be avoided, as the dehydrating effects of alcohol are amplified by the heat and humidity.

Bacteria thrive in the tropics and the best way to combat them is to keep up standards of **personal hygiene**. Frequent bathing is essential; hands should be washed before eating, especially given that much of the Lao cuisine is traditionally eaten with the hands. Cuts or scratches, no matter how minor, can become infected very easily and should be thoroughly cleaned, disinfected and bandaged to keep dirt out.

Most health problems experienced by travellers are a direct result of something they've eaten. Avoid eating uncooked vegetables and fruits that cannot be peeled. Dishes containing raw meat or fish are considered a delicacy in Laos but people who eat them

What about the water?

The simple rule while travelling in Laos is not to drink **river** or **tap water**. Contaminated water is a major cause of sickness due to the presence of pathogenic organisms: bacteria, viruses and cysts. These microorganisms cause **diseases** such as diarrhoea, gastroenteritis, typhoid, cholera, dysentery, polio, hepatitis A, giardia and bilharzia, and can be present even when water looks clean.

Safe **bottled water** is available almost anywhere, though when buying, check that the seal is unbroken as bottles are occasionally refilled from the tap. Chinese **tea** made from boiled water is generally safe, but travellers should shun **ice** that doesn't look factory-made.

risk ingesting worms and other parasites. According to NGO doctors posted in Laos, the most common fatal disease among the rural Lao is **diarrhoea**; the majority of the victims are infants who actually die from the resulting dehydration. Cooked food that has been sitting out for an undetermined period should be treated with suspicion. While the communal nature of Lao dining makes it difficult to do so, you should avoid sharing glasses and utensils.

Stomach trouble and viruses

Most travellers experience some form of **stomach trouble** during their visit to Laos, simply because their digestive system is unaccustomed to the local germs and needs time to adapt. To deal with travellers' diarrhoea, it is usually enough to drink lots of liquids and eat lightly, avoiding spicy or greasy foods in favour of bland noodle soups, until your system has had time to recover. The use of Lomotil or Imodium should be avoided, as they just prevent your body clearing the cause of the diarrhoea, unless long-distance road travel makes it absolutely necessary. Diarrhoea accompanied by severe stomach cramps, nausea or vomiting is an indication of **food poisoning**. As with common diarrhoea, it usually ends after a couple of days. In either case, be sure to increase your liquid intake to make up for lost fluids. It's a good idea to bring **oral rehydration salts** with you from home. Otherwise, you could try a Thai-made athletes' rehydration beverage called "Sponsor", which is available at restaurants and drink stands in many parts of Laos, and which, when mixed with bottled water,

is good for replacing lost salts. If symptoms persist or become worse after a couple of days you should consider seeking medical advice in Thailand.

The presence of blood or mucus in the faeces is an indication of dysentery. There are two types of dysentery and they differ in their symptoms and treatment. **Bacillary dysentery** has an acute onset, with severe abdominal pain accompanied by the presence of blood in the diarrhoea. Fever and vomiting may also be symptoms. Bacillary dysentery requires immediate medical attention and antibiotics are usually prescribed. **Amoebic dysentery** is the more serious of the two and the onset is gradual with bloody faeces accompanied by abdominal pain. The symptoms may eventually disappear but the amoebas will still be in the body and will continue to feed on internal organs, causing serious health problems in time. The treatment of amoebic dysentery by a physician should not be delayed. In the case of contracting either type of dysentery, medical advice in Thailand should be sought.

Hepatitis A, a viral infection contracted by consuming contaminated food or water, is quite common in Laos. The infection causes the liver to become inflamed and resulting symptoms include nausea, abdominal pains, dark-brown urine and light-brown faeces that may be followed by jaundice (yellowing of the skin and whites of eyes). Vaccination is the best precaution; if you do come down with hepatitis A, get plenty of rest and eat light meals of non-fatty foods.

Another scatological horror is **giardia**, symptoms of which include a bloated stomach, evil-smelling burps and farts, and diarrhoea or floating stools. As with dysentery, treatment by a physician in Thailand should be sought immediately.

Occasional outbreaks of **cholera** occur in Laos. The initial symptoms are a sudden onset of watery but painless diarrhoea. Later nausea, vomiting and muscle cramps set in. Cholera can be fatal if adequate fluid intake is not maintained. Copious amounts of liquids, including oral rehydration solution, should be consumed and medical treatment in Thailand should be sought immediately.

Like cholera, **typhoid** is also spread in small, localized epidemics. The disease is sometimes difficult to diagnose, as symptoms can vary widely. Generally, they include headaches, fever and constipation, followed by diarrhoea.

Mosquito-borne illnesses

Malaria, caused by the plasmodium parasite, is rife in much of Laos. The **symptoms** include chills, a high fever and then sweats, during which the fever falls; the cycle repeats every couple of days. Of course these symptoms aren't so different to those of flu, making diagnosis difficult without a blood test; if you think you've contracted malaria, you should immediately check into a Thai hospital.

While urban Vientiane is said to be malaria-free, visitors to other parts of Laos should take all possible precautions to avoid contracting this sometimes fatal disease. Night-feeding mosquitoes are the carriers, so you'll need to take extra care in the evening, particularly at dawn and dusk. High-strength mosquito **repellent** that contains the chemical compound DEET is a necessity, although bear in mind that prolonged use of DEET may be harmful. A natural alternative is citronella oil, found in some repellents. Wearing trousers, long-sleeved shirts and socks gives mosquitoes less skin to target.

If you plan on travelling in remote areas, bring a **mosquito net**; nets treated with repellent are available for $20 from the Australian Embassy Clinic in Vientiane (see p.105). Most accommodation can provide mosquito nets, but some of these have holes, a problem easily remedied with a few rubber bands: gather up the offending section of net and twist a rubber band around it. Many newer hotels have replaced nets with screened-in windows, which is fine if the room door remains shut at all times, but unfortunately doors are usually left wide open when maids are tidying up the rooms between guests, and invariably mosquitoes fly in by the dozen. If you can't get hold of a mosquito net, you can resort to another defence against mosquitoes, namely **coils** – lit with a match – which can usually be found in most markets or general stores in Laos.

In addition to these precautions, it's advisable to take **antimalarial tablets** for added insurance against the disease. Though **doxycycline** and **mefloquine** are the most commonly prescribed antimalarials for Laos, the plasmodium parasites are showing resistance to the latter drug. While none of the antimalarials guarantees that you will not contract malaria, the risks will be greatly reduced. Note that some antimalarials can have unpleasant side effects. Mefloquine in particular can sometimes cause dizziness, extreme fatigue, nausea and nightmares. Pregnant or lactating women are not advised to take mefloquine.

Day-feeding mosquitoes are the carriers of **dengue fever**. The disease is common in urban as well as rural areas, and outbreaks occur annually during the rainy season. The symptoms are similar to malaria and include fever, chills, aching joints and a red rash that spreads from the torso to the limbs and face. Dengue can be fatal in small children. There is no preventative vaccination or prophylactic. As with malaria, travellers should use insect repellent, keeping skin covered with loose-fitting clothing and wearing socks. There is no specific treatment for dengue other than rest, lots of liquids and paracetamol for pain and fever. Aspirin should be avoided as it can aggravate the proneness to internal bleeding which dengue sometimes produces.

Sun-related maladies

The Lao deal with the hottest hours of the day by getting horizontal in the shade, and for good reason. The Lao **hot season**, roughly March to May, can be brutal, especially in the lowlands. Visitors from temperate climes may not immediately appreciate the dangers that the tropical sun presents. To prevent **sunburn**, fair-skinned people should wear sun block and consider purchasing a wide-brimmed straw hat. Most people find UV protective sunglasses are essential to cut the sun's glare, which can be especially harsh during river journeys. The threat of **dehydration** increases with physical exertion. Even if you don't feel thirsty, do drink plenty of water. Not having to urinate or passing dark-coloured urine are sure signs that your system is not getting enough liquids.

Heat exhaustion, signified by headaches, dizziness and nausea, is treated by resting in a cool place and increasing your liquid intake until the symptoms disappear. **Heatstroke** can be life-threatening if not treated immediately and is indicated by high body temperature, flushed skin and a lack of perspiration. Reducing the body's temperature by immersion in tepid water is an initial treatment but is no substitute for prompt medical attention. Heat and high humidity sometimes cause **prickly heat**, an itchy rash that is easily avoided by wearing loose-fitting cotton clothing. A Thai-made remedy, "St Luke's Prickly Heat Powder", available in Vientiane and towns along the Mekong, provides relief and prevents the rash from recurring.

Critters that bite and sting

In Laos the **bugs** are thick, especially during the rainy season when they swarm round light bulbs and pummel bare skin until you feel like the trampoline at a flea circus. Fortunately, most flying insects pose no threat and are simply looking for a place to land and rest up.

Visitors who spend the night in hill-tribe villages where hygiene is poor risk being infected by **scabies**. These microscopic creatures are just as loathsome as their name suggests, causing severe itching by burrowing under the skin and laying eggs. Scabies is most commonly contracted by sleeping on dirty bedclothes or being in prolonged physical contact with someone who is infected. More common are **head lice**, especially among children in rural areas. Like scabies, it takes physical contact, such as sleeping next to an infected person, to contract head lice, though it may also be possible to contract head lice by wearing a hat belonging to someone who is infected.

The **leeches** most commonly encountered in Laos are about the size and shape of an inchworm, and climb foliage to wait for a suitable "host" to pass by. Travellers are most likely to pick them up while trekking through wooded areas. Take extra care when relieving yourself during breaks on long-distance bus rides. The habit of pushing deep into a bush for privacy gives leeches just enough time to grab hold of your shoes or trousers. Later they will crawl their way beneath clothing and attach themselves to joint areas (ankles, knees, elbows) where veins are near the surface of the skin. An anaesthetic and anticoagulant in the leeches' saliva allows the little vampires to gorge themselves on blood without the host feeling any pain. Usually the victim is not even aware they have been bitten until the bloated leech drops off and blood continues to flow from the small wound. Tucking your trouser-legs into your socks is an easy way to foil leeches. Wounds left by sucking leeches should be washed and bandaged as soon as possible to avoid infection.

Laos has several varieties of **poisonous snakes**, including the king cobra, but the Lao habit of killing every snake they come across, whether venomous or not, keeps areas of human habitation largely snake-free. Travelling in rural areas greatly increases the risk of snakebite, but visitors can lessen the chances of being bitten by not wearing sandals or flip-flops outside urban areas. While hiking between hill-tribe villages especially, take the precaution of wearing boots, socks and long trousers. If you are bitten, the number-one rule is not to panic; remain still to prevent the venom from being quickly absorbed into the bloodstream. Snakebites should be washed and disinfected and immediate medical attention sought – a challenge in most parts of Laos, making avoidance of the problem vital. Huge, black **scorpions** the size of large prawns lurk under the shade of fallen leaves and sting reflexively when stepped on, another solid reason to restrict flip-flop-wearing to urban areas. While the sting is very painful, it is not fatal and pain and swelling usually disappear after a few hours.

A traveller's first-aid kit

Among items you might want to carry with you – especially if you're planning to go trekking – are:

- ❏ Antiseptic cream
- ❏ Antifungal cream
- ❏ Insect repellent
- ❏ Plasters/band aids
- ❏ Water sterilization tablets or water purifier
- ❏ Gauze and sealed bandages
- ❏ Imodium or Lomotil for emergency diarrhoea treatment
- ❏ Paracetamol/aspirin
- ❏ Multivitamin and mineral tablets
- ❏ Rehydration salts
- ❏ Hypodermic needles and sterilized skin wipes (more for the security of knowing you have them, than any fear that a local hospital would fail to observe basic sanitary precautions)

Animals that are infected with **rabies** can transmit the disease by biting or even by licking an open wound. Dogs are the most common carriers but the disease can also be contracted from the bites of gibbons, bats and other mammals. Travellers should stay clear of all wild animals and resist the urge to pet unfamiliar dogs or cats. If bitten by a suspect animal, wash and disinfect the wound with alcohol or iodine. Seek medical help immediately as the disease is fatal if left untreated.

Sexually transmitted diseases

Prostitution is on the rise in Laos, and with it the inevitable scourge of **sexually** transmitted diseases (STDs). Gonorrhoea and syphilis are common but are easily treated with antibiotics. Symptoms of the former include pain or a pus-like discharge when urinating. An open sore on or around the genitals is a symptom of syphilis. In women symptoms are internal and may not be noticed. The number of cases of **AIDS** is also rising in Laos, mostly the result of Lao prostitutes contracting HIV in Thailand.

Condoms are the best prevention for all STDs. Bringing condoms from home is a good idea; most condoms sold in Laos are imported from Thailand, where surveys have found that over ten percent of Thai-made condoms are defective.

Getting around

Getting around on Laos's transport system is an adventure in itself, what with its barely seaworthy boats, aged jalopies with hard seats and hot, crowded buses. Don't be fooled by maps and distance charts – seemingly short rides can take hours, as tired vehicles slow to a crawl in their uphill battle against muddy, mountainous roads. Take heart though, in knowing that many visitors have their best encounters with the people of Laos amid the adversity of a bad bus ride.

Laos's road system has improved over the last few years. Roads have been upgraded, and getting around is easier than ever, though often still challenging. Keep in mind, however, that a newly graded and paved road this year may get no maintenance, and after just two or even one rainy season the road will revert to being nothing but a potholed track. Some roads are only built to last a season, being washed away each year by the monsoon.

The country's main thoroughfare is **Route 13**, which stretches from Louang Phabang to the Cambodian border, passing through Vientiane, Savannakhet and Pakxe. Route 13 sees a steady flow of bus traffic, and it's usually possible to flag down a vehicle during daylight hours provided it's not already full. Off Route 13, you'll encounter a wide range of road conditions – from freshly paved to bone-rattlingly potholed. Note also that some roads remain off-limits because of security problems (see p.64). With the improved road conditions, **buses** have largely supplanted **river travel**, the traditional means of getting around.

You only need to travel for a week or two in Laos before you realize that **timetables** are irrelevant: planes, buses and boats leave on a whim and estimated times of arrival are pointless. Wherever you go in Laos, the driver does not seem to be in any hurry to arrive.

For an idea of frequency and duration of bus services between towns, check the **travel details** at the end of each chapter. Given the poor condition of many roads and buses, as well as the many unscheduled stops en route, all travel times in these sections should be taken as rough estimates.

Inter-town transport

Visitors hoping to see anything of the country can expect hours of arduous, bone-crunching travel on Laos's motley fleet of lumbering jitter-boxes. Buses link only larger towns and on many routes can be few and far between, a fact which makes a number of attractions, such as ruins and waterfalls, difficult to reach. Even when there is transport, you may find that the limited bus timetable will allow you to get to a particular site, but not make a same-day return trip – something of a problem given the dearth of accommodation in far-flung spots. In the rainy season, unpaved roads dissolve into rivers of mud, slowing buses to a crawl or swallowing them whole. Even vehicles in reasonably good condition make painfully slow progress, as drivers combat **mountainous roads** and make frequent (and at times long) stops to pick up passengers, load goods and even haggle for bargains at roadside stalls.

Buses

Ordinary buses provide cheap transport between major towns and link provincial hubs with their surrounding districts. Cramped, overloaded and designed for the smaller Lao frame, these buses are profound tests of endurance and patience. Seats have either torn cushions or are nothing more than a hard plank. Luggage – ranging from roosters, with the runs, to sloshing buckets of fish and the inevitable fifty-kilo sacks of rice – is piled in every conceivable space, filling up the aisle and soaring skywards from the roof. **Breakdowns** are commonplace and often require a lengthy roadside wait as the driver repairs the bus on a lonely stretch of road. Typical fares are of the order of 75,000K for Vientiane to Louang Phabang, 100,000K for Vientiane to Pakxe, though expect fares to rise rapidly if fuel prices increase.

Operating out of Vientiane, a fleet of blue, **government-owned buses** caters mostly to the capital's outlying districts, although it does provide a service to towns as far north as Vang Viang and as far south as Pakxe. While newer than most vehicles in Laos, these Japanese- and Korean-built buses are not air-conditioned and have cramped seats, a situation that worsens as rural passengers pile in. Buses plying **remote routes** tend to be in worse shape: aged jalopies cast off from Thailand or left behind by the Russians, which reach new lows in terms of discomfort and are even more prone to breakdowns. These vehicles range in style from buses in the classic sense of the word to souped-up tourist vans. Converted Russian flat-bed trucks, once the mainstay of travel in Laos, still operate in remote areas.

Only in larger towns such as Vientiane, Savannakhet and Louang Phabang is it necessary to **buy a ticket** at the station before boarding the bus. On most routes it's common practice to buy them on board, although some buses do not issue tickets at all. Lao bus operators are generally honest, but you may find a few drivers who charge foreigners a somewhat higher rate, not usually more than double the standard fare.

At the other end of the spectrum, a handful of companies offer an air-conditioned **express bus service**, such as the daily $10 coach service from Vientiane to Louang Phabang. Such services leave Vientiane from their own private "stations", and reservations, which can be made through the companies' respective Vientiane offices, are recommended. Additionally, several van and minibus services have started up, offering services to Vang Viang and even as far afield as Savannakhet. The situation changes rapidly at this end of the market, so check with travel agents in Vientiane for the latest information on routes and bookings.

Timetables only exist in regional hubs like Vientiane, Louang Phabang and Savannakhet; elsewhere it's best to go to the bus station the night before you plan to travel to find out the schedule for the next day. Where there is no information, it's best to get to the bus station **early** (often between 6 and 7am), as that is when the majority of Lao passengers prefer to travel, especially on long-distance runs. Very few buses leave after midday. Buses often won't depart if empty; many drivers will sit in the bus station long after their stated departure time, revving their engines in an attempt to lure enough passengers to make the trip worthwhile.

Sawngthaews

In rural areas, away from the Mekong Valley, the bus network is often replaced by **sawngthaews** – converted pick-up trucks – into which drivers stuff as many passengers as they possibly can. Passengers are crammed onto two facing benches in the back ("sawngthaew" means "two rows"); latecomers are left to dangle off the back, with their feet on a running board, an experience that, on a bumpy road, is akin to inland windsurfing.

Sawngthaews also ply routes between larger towns and their satellite villages, a service for which they charge roughly the same amount as buses. They usually depart from the regular bus station, but will only leave when a driver feels he has enough passengers to make the trip worth his while. Some drivers try to sweat extra kip out of passengers by delaying departure. Your fellow passengers may agree to this, but most often they grudgingly wait. In some situations, you can save yourself a lot of trouble and waiting by getting a few fellow travellers together and flat-out **hiring the driver** to take you where you want to go. In any case the fares are ridiculously low so this is quite affordable. To catch a sawngthaew in between stops, simply flag it down from the side of the road and tell the driver where you're headed so he knows when to let you off. The fare is usually paid when you get off or at the end of the ride. If the driver is working without a fare collector, he will tend to stop on the outskirts of his final destination to collect fares. For more on sawngthaews, see p.207.

City and town transport

With even the capital too small to support a local bus system, transport within Lao towns and cities is left to squadrons of motorized **samlaw** (literally, "three wheels") vehicles, more commonly known as jumbos and tuk-tuks. Painted in primary reds, blues and yellows, the two types of *samlaw* look alike and both function as shared taxis, with facing benches in the rear to accommodate four or five passengers. **Jumbos** are the original Lao vehicle, a homemade three-wheeler consisting of a two-wheeled carriage soldered to the front half of a motorcycle, a process best summed up by the name for the vehicle used in the southern town of Savannakhet – Skylab (pronounced "sakai-laeb"), after the doomed space station that fell to earth, piece by piece, in the late 1980s. **Tuk-tuks**, offspring of the three-wheeled taxis known for striking terror in Bangkok pedestrians, are really just bigger, sturdier jumbos, the unlikely product of some Thai factory, which take their name from their incessantly sputtering engines. Lao tend to refer to these vehicles interchangeably.

Although most northern towns are more than manageable on foot, the Mekong towns tend to sprawl, so you'll find tuk-tuks particularly useful for getting into town from a bus station. To catch a tuk-tuk, flag it down as it passes in the street by waving your hand, palm face down and parallel to the ground. Tell the driver where you're going, bargain the price and pay at the end of the ride.

There are also **tuk-tuks** which operate within towns and cities, collecting people from markets or stations and then doing a run into the centre or vice versa. In this case the payment is per person according to the distance travelled and your bargaining skills. Rates vary from town to town and are prone to fluctuate in step with rising petrol prices, but figure on paying around 5000K per kilometre. In some towns, tuk-tuks run set routes to the surrounding villages and leave from a stand, usually near the market, once full. Chartering tuk-tuks is also a good way to get to sites within 10 to 15km of a city.

Boats

With the country possessing roughly 4600km of navigable **waterways**, including stretches of the Mekong, Nam Ou, Nam Ngum, Xe Kong and seven other arteries, it's no surprise to learn that rivers are the ancient highways of mountainous Laos. Road improvements in recent years, however, have led to the decline of river travel between many towns, with buses and sawngthaews replacing the armada of boats that once plied regular routes.

The main **Mekong routes** that remain link Houayxai to Louang Phabang, and Pakxe with Si Phan Don. Since the upgrading of Route 13, boats only rarely ply the stretch of river between Louang Phabang and Pakxe. Aside from the larger, so-called "slow boats" on the Mekong routes, smaller passenger boats still regularly cruise up the wide Nam

---

Addresses and street names

Lao addresses can be terribly confusing, firstly because property is usually numbered twice – when numbered at all – to show which lot it stands in, and then to signify where it is on that lot. To add to the confusion, some cities have several conflicting address systems – Vientiane, for example, has three, although no one seems to use any of them. To avoid confusion, numbers are often omitted from addresses given in the Guide, and locations are described using landmarks instead.

Only five cities in Laos actually have **street names** – and that's just the start of the problem. Signs are few and far between and many roads have several entirely different names, sometimes changing name from block to block. If you ask for directions, locals most likely won't know the name of a street with the exception of the three or four largest avenues in Vientiane. Use street names to find a hotel on a map in the Guide, but when asking directions or telling a tuk-tuk driver where to go you'll have better luck mentioning a landmark, monastery or prominent hotel. Fortunately, Lao cities, even Vientiane, are relatively small, making it more of a challenge to get lost than it is to figure out where you're going.

Ou River (Muang Khoua–Hat Sa), the Nam Tha (Louang Namtha to Pak Tha), and a few others, provided water levels are high enough.

Slow boats and passenger boats

The diesel-chugging cargo boats that lumber up and down the **Mekong routes** are known as **"slow boats"** (*heua sa*). Originally hammered together from ill-fitting pieces of wood, and powered by a jury-rigged engine that needs to be coaxed along by an on-board mechanic, these boats once offered one of Asia's last great travel adventures, but you'll need to speak Lao to arrange a trip. Much easier is to take advantage of the **passenger boats** with seating for a couple of dozen people, which have been introduced on the river journey most popular with Western visitors, namely Houayxai to Louang Phabang.

On smaller rivers, river travel is by long, narrow boats powered by a small outboard engine. Confusingly, these are also known as "slow boats", although, unlike the big Mekong cargo boats, they only hold eight people and never attempt the Mekong. They never have a fixed schedule and only leave if and when there are enough passengers.

Due to the casual nature of river travel in Laos, the best way to deal with uncertain departures is to simply **show up early** in the morning and head down to the landing and ask around. Be prepared for contradictory answers to questions regarding price, departure and arrival time, and even destination. Given variations in currents and water levels and the possibility of breakdowns and lengthy stops to load passengers and cargo, no one really knows how long a trip will take. On occasion, boats don't make their final destination during the daytime. If you're counting on finding a guesthouse and a fruit shake at the end of the journey, such unannounced stopovers can take you out of your comfort zone, as passengers are forced to sleep in the nearest village or aboard the boat. It's also a good idea to bring extra water and food just in case.

The **northern Mekong** services (Houayxai–Pak Beng–Louang Phabang) are somewhat better managed, with **tickets** sold from a wooden booth or office near the landing (buy tickets on the day of departure) and ports overseen by a local government official, who will generally shepherd you in the right direction. Fares are generally posted, but foreigners pay significantly more than locals. Always arrive early in the morning to get a seat.

Southern Mekong services (Pakxe–Champasak–Don Khong) are more haphazard. Unlike in the north, you won't need to buy a ticket, the downside of which is that you won't know what the exact fare is. The crew may try to overcharge you a few thousand kip, but usually never so much as to provoke indignation. The recent completion of Route 13 means that traffic along this route will surely decline in coming years, although the presence of far-flung villages on the right bank and on various islands means that a boat service should continue to Si Phan Don for the foreseeable future.

Travel by slow boat can be dangerous and reports of boats **sinking** are not uncommon. The Mekong has some particularly tricky stretches, with narrow channels threading through rapids and past churning whirlpools. The river can be particularly rough late in the rainy season, when the Mekong swells and uprooted trees and other debris are swept into the river.

Speedboats

On both the Mekong and its tributaries, **speedboats** (*heua wai*) are a costlier but faster alternative to slow boats. Connecting towns along the Nam Ou and the Mekong from Vientiane to the Chinese border, these five-metre-long terrors are usually powered by a 1200cc Toyota car engine and can accommodate up to eight passengers.

Donning a crash helmet and being catapulted up the Mekong River at 50km an hour may not sound like most people's idea of a holiday in Laos, but if you're up for it, speedboats can shave hours or days off a river journey and give you a thrilling spin at the same time. It's by no means safe, of course, although captains swear by their navigational skills. The boats skim the surface of churning whirlpools and slalom through rapids sharp enough to turn the wooden hull into toothpicks. In one particularly nasty accident in 1998, two boats collided head-on, killing all on board.

Speedboats have their own **landings** in Vientiane, Thadua, Paklai, Louang Phabang, Pakbeng and Houayxai, and depart when full. Seating is incredibly **cramped**, so you may want to consider paying for the price of two seats. **Crash helmets** are handed out before journeys – to spare your hearing from the overpowering screech of the engine. Although the roar of the engine is less annoying on board than it is from the banks, consider bringing along **ear plugs**. Some drivers also provide life jackets.

Tickets cost as much as two to three times what you might pay to take a slow boat: the journey from Louang Phabang to Pakbeng, for example, is around $12. Speedboats can also be **chartered** for around $50 per hour – Louang Phabang to Phongsali, for example, costs around $200, Louang Phabang to Houayxai $100.

Cross-river ferries

Clunky metal car **ferries** and **pirogues** – dug-out wooden skiffs propelled by poles, paddles or tiny engines – are both useful means of fording rivers in the absence of a bridge. Both leave when they have a sufficient number of passengers and usually charge 1000K, unless you're taking a vehicle across, in which case you can expect to pay 2000–5000K. If you don't want to wait, pirogues are always open for hire. In the outback, fishermen can usually be persuaded to ferry you across to the opposite bank for a small sum of money.

Planes

The government-owned **Lao Airlines** (ⓦwww .laoairlines.com), the country's only domestic carrier, had a dubious safety record in its previous incarnation as Lao Aviation. Along with the name change came a supposed increase in maintenance of aircraft on flights between Vientiane and Louang Phabang, and Vientiane and Phonsavan. At any rate, domestic routes were cut by almost half as the airline downsized in the last couple of years.

As with other forms of transport in Laos, you'll need to remain flexible. Reliability increases on key routes: Vientiane–Louang Phabang, Vientiane–Pakxe and Vientiane–Phonsavan. Given the popularity of such routes in the peak season it's even wise to **book ahead**. On other routes, you may find it better to reconfirm the departure of your flight by stopping by the Lao Airlines office.

Sample one-way **fares** are Vientiane to Phonsavan $53; Vientiane to Xam Nua $75; Louang Phabang to Vientiane $60; Vientiane to Louang Namtha $84. Note that Lao Airlines only accepts US dollars cash.

Vehicle and bike rental

Renting a **private vehicle** is expensive, but is sometimes the only way you'll be able to get to certain spots, given the limitations of Laos's transport network. Self-drive is an option, and cars can be rented from a couple of agencies in Vientiane only. However, it's usually easier and cheaper to hire a **car and driver**. Tour agencies will rent out air-conditioned vans and 4WD pick-up trucks as well as provide drivers. Prices are inflated by the rates paid by UN organizations, and can be as high as $80–100 per day, sometimes more if you're hiring a car to head upcountry from Vientiane. When settling on a price, it's important to clarify who is responsible for what: check who pays for the driver's food and lodging, fuel and repairs, and be sure to ask what happens in case of a major breakdown or accident.

Motorbikes

One of the best ways to explore the countryside is to rent a **motorbike**. Unfortunately, this is only an option in Vientiane, Vang Viang, Louang Phabang, Thakhek and Pakxe, and even then you'll only be able to find smaller bikes, usually 100cc step-throughs such as the Honda Dream. Rental prices for the day are generally $6–10, depending on the age and condition of the bike. More powerful 125cc **dirt bikes** suitable for cross-country driving are available only in Vientiane and cost $20 a day.

A licence is not needed, but you'll be asked to leave your passport as a deposit and may be required to return the bike by dark. Insurance is not available, so it's a good idea to make sure your travel insurance covers you for any potential accidents.

Before zooming off, be sure to **check the bike** thoroughly for any scratches and damaged parts and take it for a test run to make sure the vehicle is running properly. As far as **equipment** goes, a helmet is good protection, although few rental places will have one to offer you; it's not against the law to ride without a helmet. **Sunglasses** are essential in order to fend off the glare of the tropical sun and keep dust and bugs out of your eyes. Proper shoes, long trousers and a long-sleeved shirt are all worthwhile additions to your biking outfit and will provide a thin layer of protection if you take a spill.

Bicycles

Bicycles are available in most major tourist centres; guesthouses, souvenir shops and a few tourist-oriented restaurants may keep a small stable of Thai- or Chinese-made bikes (though rarely mountain bikes) to rent out for $1–2 per day.

Hitching

Hitching in Laos does not exist in the Western sense, although there is a tradition of people flagging down passing trucks and catching rides in exchange for a small payment. Given the rather limited amount of traffic on Laos's highways, you won't want to count on hitching your way around the country, although you may find yourself flagging down a truck if you miss the last bus or if the one you're already on breaks down. As with hitching anywhere in the world, think twice before hitching solo, especially if you're a woman.

Organized tours

Although less spontaneous and considerably more expensive than independent travel, **organized tours** are worth looking into if you have limited time or prefer to have someone smooth over the many logistical difficulties of travelling in Laos. Although the government encourages travellers to visit Laos through an authorized tour company, the tours aren't bogged down in political rhetoric and guides tend to be easy-going and informative.

About a dozen **tour companies** have sprung up in Vientiane, all offering similar tours in roughly the same price range, although it never hurts to shop around and bargain. A typical multi-day package might include a private cruise down the Mekong River on a slow boat operated by the tour company, with guided day-tours around Louang Phabang and other towns. While some tours include accommodation, meals and entry fees, others don't, so check what you're getting before paying.

Organized **adventure tours** are rapidly gaining popularity in Laos. These can be single- or multi-day programmes and usually involve hill-tribe trekking or river kayaking, or a combination of both. Rafting tours are also available and organized rock-climbing is just starting to take off. The main centres for adventure tours are Vientiane, Vang Viang, Louang Phabang, Louang Namtha and Muang Sing.

All Laos's tour companies are authorized by the Lao National Tourism Administration, which ensures that you won't be dealing with a fly-by-night organization.

Guides are generally flexible about adjusting the itinerary, but if you want more **freedom**, an alternative is to set up your own custom-made tour by gathering a group of people and renting your own vehicle plus driver.

Local tour operators

Diethelm Travel Laos Nam Phou Place, PO Box 2657, Vientiane ☏ 021/215920, ⓕ 217151. In Bangkok ☏ 02 255 9150, ⓦ www.diethelmtravel .com.
Green Discovery 54 Setthathilat Rd, Vientiane ☏ 021/251564, ⓦ www.greendiscoverylaos.com. Branches in Louang Namhtha, Louang Phabang and Vang Viang.
Inter-Lao Tourisme Louang Phabang Rd, PO Box 2912, Vientiane ☏ 021/214232 or 214832, ⓦ www .interlao.laopdr.com.
Lane Xang Travel Pangkham Rd, PO Box 4452, Vientiane ☏ 021/213198 or 212469, ⓕ 215804.
Lao National Tourism Administration ⓦ www .ecotourismlaos.com.
Sodetour 16 Fa Ngum Rd, PO Box 70, Vientiane ☏ 021/216314, ⓕ 216313.

Accommodation

The influx of foreign visitors has meant a rapid increase in hotels and improved standards in tourist centres, although out in the boondocks change comes more slowly and comfort can be harder to come by. Expect to find higher standards of accommodation, as well as the greatest variety, in larger towns. Provincial towns, with the exception of popular stopovers on backpacker routes, tend to lag far behind, with small towns on well-travelled highways offering at best one or two rather rustic guesthouses.

Outside Louang Phabang, Vang Viang and the capital, finding a place to stay is a far simpler process than in most Southeast Asian countries – often because there are only one or two places in town and they're often a short walk from one another. Few towns have touts or taxi drivers trying to influence your decision.

Once you've found a spot, ask to see a number of rooms before reaching a decision, as standards and room types can vary widely within the same establishment. You'll need to look at the bed arrangement for starters (a double can be two single beds or one large bed, among other permutations), but also check the water pressure, whether or not the drains work, as well as the air conditioning if you've opted for this facility. Also make sure that there's a mosquito net if the windows are lacking screens, and a functioning lock on the door.

In cities that lack a constant supply of electricity, you should weigh the added cost of an air-conditioned room against the number of hours you'll have power. Some hotels may give you the option of not switching on the air-con and billing you for a fan room. En-suite

showers and flush toilets are the norm only in mid-range and top-end hotels.

When you **check in** at a hotel or guesthouse, you're asked to fill in a brief **registration form** and to pay for your first night in advance, although some places don't mind billing you at the end of your stay. Establishments that do not already quote their prices in dollars or baht keep a close eye on the volatile exchange rate and change their prices frequently, keeping the room rate at roughly the same dollar value. **Payment** can generally be made in Lao kip, US dollars or Thai baht; count on being able to use credit cards only at higher-end establishments in Louang Phabang and Vientiane. Hotels and guesthouses generally have exchange rates close to the official rate.

Prices for the most basic double room start at around $3–5 in the provinces and $6–8 in Vientiane and Louang Phabang. At these prices rooms can be pretty shabby, although there are a few diamonds in the rough. Moving up the scale to $25 lands you a cosy room in a restored French villa.

Most places are open to **negotiation**, especially in the low season, so it's a good

Accommodation price codes

Accommodation throughout the Guide has been categorized according to the following price codes, reflecting the minimum you can expect to pay for a **double room**:

❶ Less than $3	❹ $10–15	❼ $40–60
❷ $3–6	❺ $15–25	❽ $60 and above
❸ $6–10	❻ $25–40	

In cases where an establishment charges per bed the price is given in the text rather than indicated by a price code.

idea to try and bargain; your case will be helped if you are staying for several days. You should also establish whether both parties are talking about a per-person or per-room rate before you begin haggling.

Not all accommodation places have **phones**, which is why some listings in this Guide don't have numbers alongside. Online booking services include Ⓦwww.laos-hotels .com and Ⓦwww.laos-hotel-link.com.

Budget accommodation

The distinction between a **guesthouse** and a **budget hotel** is rather blurry in Laos. Either can denote anything ranging from a bamboo-and-thatch hut to a multistorey concrete monstrosity. There's very little that's standard from place to place – even rooms within one establishment can vary widely – although in tourist centres the cheapest bet is generally a fan room with shared washing facilities, at best kitted out with a ceiling fan and mosquito net. As you tack on extra dollars, you'll gain the luxury of a private bathroom with a hot-water shower and an air conditioner. In small towns in remote areas you'll find that the facilities are rustic at best – squat toilets and a large jar of water with a plastic scoop with which to shower. The further off the beaten track you go the greater the chances are that you'll be pumping your own water from a well or bathing in a stream.

There are no youth hostels as yet in Laos, though some government-owned flop houses operate as dorms, charging by the bed, and sometimes **dormitory accommodation** is an option at guesthouses.

Mid-range accommodation

Mid-range hotels have been opening up in medium-sized towns all over Laos over the last few years, greatly improving the accommodation situation. Most of these hotels are compact, of up to five storeys, and offer spacious rooms with tiled floors and en-suite bathrooms with Western-style toilets for between $5 and $10. The mattresses are usually hard – but at least the sheets and quilts are consistently clean. The bathroom fittings in such hotels are usually brand new but a few don't have water heaters. Because the standard of construction is poor and there is no concept of maintaining buildings, such hotels tend to age quickly.

Upmarket hotels

Once you've crossed the $25 threshold, you enter a whole new level of comfort. In the former French towns on the Mekong this level of expense translates into an atmospheric room in a restored colonial villa or accommodation in a recently built establishment where rooms boast some of the trappings of a high-end hotel, such as cable television, fridge, air conditioning and a hot-water shower.

Colonial-era hotels often have a limited number of rooms, so **book ahead** if you want to take advantage of them – well in advance if you plan to visit during the peak months (Dec & Jan). Many of these places are firmly ensconced on the tour-group circuit, so push for a discount if you're travelling independently.

Thanks to foreign investors, a few **top-end hotels** have opened their doors in Vientiane and Louang Phabang, charging upwards of $60 a night. The best hotels in the capital, such as the *Settha Palace Hotel* and the *Novotel Belvedere*, have international-class facilities, including business centres and gyms. At the moment, there's a glut of high-end hotel accommodation in the capital, so don't hesitate to ask for discounts, especially for longer-term stays.

Staying in villages

Should you find yourself stuck in a small town for the night, a victim of the tired machinery of Laos's infrastructure or the yawning distances between villages, villagers are usually kind enough to find space for you in the absence of a local guesthouse. Don't expect much in the way of luxuries: you'll most likely find yourself bathing at the local well or in the river and going to the bathroom under the stars. Many small towns don't have so much as a noodle shop, so you'll also need to prepare yourself for some very authentic cooking. Before leaving, you should offer to remunerate your host with a sum of cash equivalent to what you would have paid in a budget guesthouse.

If there's a local **police station**, you should make yourself known to them, otherwise ask for permission to stay from the **village headman**; the government doesn't encourage foreigners to spend the night at a villager's house.

Eating and drinking

Fiery and fragrant, with a touch of sour, Lao food owes its distinctive taste to fermented fish sauces, lemon grass, coriander leaves, chillies and lime juice. Eaten with the hands along with the staple sticky rice, much of Lao cuisine is roasted over an open fire and served with fresh herbs and vegetables. Pork, chicken, duck and water buffalo all end up in the kitchen, but freshwater fish is the main source of protein in the Lao diet. Many in rural Laos, especially in the more remote mountainous regions, prefer animals of a wilder sort – mouse deer, wild pigs, rats, birds or whatever else can be caught – much to the dismay of tourists and wildlife conservationists.

Closely related to Thai cuisine, Lao food is, in fact, more widely consumed than you might think: in addition to the more than two million ethnic Lao in Laos, Lao cuisine is the daily sustenance for roughly a third of the Thai population, while more than a few Lao dishes are commonplace on the menus of Thai restaurants in the West. Although Lao cuisine isn't strongly influenced by that of its other neighbours, Chinese and Vietnamese immigrants have made their mark on the culinary landscape by opening restaurants and noodle stalls throughout the country, while the French introduced bread, pâté and pastries.

Vientiane and **Louang Phabang** are the country's culinary centres, boasting excellent Lao food and international cuisine at fabulous value. Outside the Mekong corridor, however, Laos can be a culinary wasteland where you'll be lucky to find anything more than a simple bowl of noodles.

Hygiene is an important consideration when eating anywhere in Laos. Away from

settlements in the Mekong River valley, the kitchen is often just a shack without proper lighting or even running water, and the cooking is done over an open fire. Furthermore, in many rural towns there is limited electricity to run refrigeration. As a rule, sticking to tourist-class restaurants is the safest bet, but is no guarantee of not getting an upset stomach. The Lao have poor knowledge of food preparation, storage and hygiene and, although the food is much safer than in Nepal or India, you can pretty much expect to get the trots at some point.

While it's important to be careful where and what you eat, in some of the smallest towns you may have no choice but to catch as catch can. It's also a good idea to go easy on your stomach by avoiding chillies and excessive amounts of fresh fruit during your first few days and by always drinking bottled or boiled water. As a general rule, noodle stalls and restaurants that do a brisk business are safe bets, though this is not much of a guide in smaller towns and villages, as so few people eat out. In some remote places, you may need to wait while the stall-holder goes to the market to buy the ingredients for your meal.

For a **food and drink glossary**, see pp.375–377.

Where to eat

Generally speaking, there are four types of outlet from which to choose when getting your food. **Hawkers** peddle fruit from handcarts and sell roasted bugs on sticks to bus passengers; a step up from these are **markets**, usually starting late in the afternoon, where inexpensive, pre-cooked takeaways can be purchased. Also inexpensive are **street stalls**, often to be found in and around the market or on a town's main road, offering simple dishes such as spring rolls, baguettes and noodles. **Restaurants** in Laos come in all shapes and sizes, ranging from unpretentious noodle shops or open-air places to fancy French establishments serving quality wine by candlelight.

Markets, street stalls and noodle shops

Morning markets (*talat sâo*), found in most towns throughout Laos, remain open all day despite their name and provide a focal point for noodle shops, coffee vendors, fruit stands and sellers of crusty loaves of French bread. In Louang Phabang and Vientiane, vendors hawking pre-made dishes gather towards late afternoon in **evening markets** known as *talat láeng*. Takeaways include grilled chicken (*pîng kai*), spicy papaya salad (*tam màk hung*) and in some instances a variety of dishes, displayed in trays and ranging from minced pork salad (*làp mu*) to stir-fried vegetables (*khùa phák*).

While many market vendors offer only takeout food, **noodle shops** (*hân khãi fõe*) and a few other food stalls feature a makeshift kitchen surrounded by a handful of tables and stools, inhabiting a permanent patch of pavement or even an open-air shophouse. Most stalls specialize in one general food type, or, in some cases, only one dish; for example a stall with a mortar and pestle, unripe papayas and plastic bags full of pork rinds will only offer spicy papaya salad and variants on that theme. Similarly, a noodle shop will generally only prepare noodles with or without broth – they won't have meat or fish dishes that are usually eaten with rice.

A step up from street stalls and noodle shops are *hân kin deum*, literally "**eat-drink shops**", where you'll find a somewhat greater variety of dishes and be able to quench your thirst with beer and whisky.

In the smallest of towns you're only likely to find a noodle shop, but many noodle-shop proprietors will be happy to make you a proper meal with rice providing you give them enough advance warning.

Restaurants

Proper **restaurants** (*hân ahãn*) aren't far ahead of eat-drink shops and noodle shops in terms of comfort; most are open-air establishments of dubious hygiene tucked beneath a thatch or corrugated tin roof. Ethnic **Vietnamese** and **Chinese** dominate the restaurant scene in Laos; indeed it can be downright difficult to find a Lao restaurant in some towns, as many Lao simply don't eat out, preferring the less expensive option of eating at home. A Lao-food restaurant is identifiable by the *típ khào* (lidded wicker basket for sticky rice) on the tables next to diners. Many of these basic eating places won't have any **menus** – in Lao or English – so it's a good idea to have a few stock dishes on the tip of your tongue when ordering.

Increasingly, restaurants catering more to foreigners have been cropping up in tourist centres. Such establishments, which have an English menu, offer a hotchpotch of dishes ranging from fried noodles and fried rice to the occasional sandwich, in addition to a variety of Lao, Chinese and Thai dishes intended to be eaten with steamed rice.

For more relaxed dining, **Vientiane** has a range of more expensive restaurants specializing in gourmet Lao cuisine as well as some of the best and best-value international food in Southeast Asia. The most popular non-Lao cuisine on offer is **French**, although good Italian, Japanese and Indian are all well represented. The cost of a meal in one of these restaurants is hardly prohibitive – it's unlikely to set you back more than $15 per person, and many offer even less expensive set menus.

Although restaurants stay open later in the capital, as a rule the Lao **eat early**: outside the major cities and tourist centres, street stalls and noodle shops rarely stay open beyond 8pm and may close even earlier. Many restaurant listings in the Guide do not include telephone numbers, as you won't need to make **reservations** while eating your way through Laos, even at Vientiane's poshest establishments.

When it comes to **paying**, the normal sign language will be readily understood in most restaurants, or simply say "*khāw sék dae*" ("the bill, please"). You'll only be able to use major **credit cards** at upscale establishments in Vientiane and high-end hotel restaurants in Louang Phabang. **Tipping** in restaurants isn't a Lao custom, although upmarket Vientiane restaurants expect a gratuity of around ten percent.

What to eat

So that a variety of tastes can be enjoyed during the course of a meal, Lao **meals** are eaten communally, with each dish being served at once, rather than in courses. The dishes – typically, a fish or meat dish and soup, with a plate of fresh vegetables such as string beans, lettuce, basil and mint served on the side – are placed in the centre of the table, and each person helps him- or herself to only a little at a time. When ordering a meal, if there are two of you it's common to order two or three dishes, plus your own individual servings of rice, while three diners would order three or four different dishes.

The staple of Lao meals is **rice**, with **noodles** a common alternative for breakfast or as a snack. Most meals are enjoyed with **sticky rice** (*khào niaw*), which is served in a lidded wicker basket and eaten with the hands. Although it can be tricky at first, it's fairly easy to pick up the proper technique if you watch the Lao around you. Grab a small chunk of rice from the basket, press it into a firm wad with your fingers and then dip the rice ball into one of the dishes. Replace the lid of the *típ khào* when you are finished eating or you will be offered more rice.

Plain steamed **white rice** (*khào jâo*) is eaten with a fork and spoon, with the former held in the left hand and the latter in the right (reverse for southpaws) – the spoon and not the fork is used to deliver the food to your mouth. If you're eating a meal with steamed white rice, it's polite to only put a small helping of each dish onto your rice at a time. Chopsticks (*mâi thu*) are reserved for

noodles, the only exceptions being Chinese-style rice served in bowls (usually encountered at Chinese restaurants where you'll only be given chopsticks) and spicy papaya salad as eaten by the people of Louang Phabang. Attempting to eat sticky rice with chopsticks will only serve to baffle the Lao.

If you are **dining with a Lao family** as a guest, wait until you are invited to eat by your host before taking your first mouthful. While dipping a wad of sticky rice into the main dish, try not to let grains of rice fall into it, and dip with your right hand only. Resist the temptation to continue eating after the others at the table have finished. Custom dictates that a little food should be left on your plate at the end of the meal.

Flavours

In addition to chillies, coriander, lemon grass and lime juice, common flavouring ingredients used in Lao food include ginger, coconut milk, galingale, shallots and tamarind pulp. Another vital addition to certain Lao dishes is *khào khùa*, raw rice roasted in a wok until thoroughly browned and then pounded into powder; it's used to add both a nutty flavour and an agreeably gritty texture to food.

The definitive accent, however, comes from the fermented fish mixtures that are used to salt Lao food. An ingredient in nearly every recipe, *nâm pa*, or **fish sauce**, is made by steeping large quantities of fish in salt in earthen containers for several months and then straining the resulting liquid, which is golden brown. Good fish sauce, it has been said, should attain the warm, salty smell of the air along a beach on a sunny day. Most Lao use *nâm pa* imported from Thailand.

While *nâm pa* is found in cooking across Southeast Asia, a related concoction, **pa dàek**, is specific to Laos and northeastern Thailand. Unlike the bottled and imported *nâm pa*, thicker *pa dàek* retains a homemade feel, resembling fish sauce but with chunks of fermented fish as well as rice husks, and possessing a scent that the uninitiated usually find foul. Although cherished by the Lao, *pa dàek*, along with the liquid strained from it, carries with it the risk of liver flukes. (*Pa dàek* found in Vientiane and Louang Phabang, however, is considered much safer than that found in rural areas, particularly in the far south.)

Use of **monosodium glutamate** (MSG) is also quite common. The seasoning, which resembles salt in appearance, sometimes appears on tables in noodle shops with various other seasonings. If you'd prefer to avoid MSG, try saying *baw sai phõng sú lot* when ordering your food and hope for the best.

Standard dishes

If Laos were to nominate a national dish, a strong contender would be *làp*, a "**salad**" of minced meat or fish mixed with garlic, chillies, shallots, eggplant, galingale, fried rice and fish sauce. *Làp* is eaten either raw (*díp*) – a culinary experience you may want to avoid – or *súk* (cooked) and served with a side dish of lettuce, which is good for cooling off your mouth after swallowing a chilli. The notion of a "meat salad" is a common concept in Lao food, although in Louang Phabang you'll find Lao salads closer to the Western salad, with many falling into the broad category of *yam*, or "mixture", such as *yam sìn ngúa*, a spicy beef salad.

Another quintessentially Lao dish is *tam màk hung*, a spicy **papaya salad** made with shredded green papaya, garlic, chillies, lime juice, *pa dàek* and, sometimes, dried shrimp and crab juice. One of the most common street-vendor foods, *tam màk hung*, is known as *tam sòm* in Vientiane. Stalls producing this treat are identifiable by the vendor pounding away with a mortar and pestle. Each vendor will have their own particular recipe, but it's also completely acceptable to pick out which ingredients – and how many chilli peppers – you'd like when you order. One of several variants on *tam màk hung* is *tam kûay tani*, which replaces shredded papaya with green banana and eggplant.

Usually not far away from any *tam màk hung* vendor, you'll find someone selling *pîng kai*, basted **grilled chicken**. Hawkers wander onto buses to sell *pîng kai* on a stick, and a few restaurants in Vientiane specialize in the dish, serving up plump, whole chickens along with sticky rice and draught Beer Lao. Fish, *pîng pa* is another grilled favourite, with whole fish skewered and thrown on the barbecue.

Soup is a common component of Lao meals and is served along with the other main courses during a meal. Fish soups, *kaeng pa* (or *tôm yám paw* when lemon grass and mushrooms are included), frequently appear on menus, as does *kaeng jèut*, a clear, mild soup with vegetables and pork, which can also be ordered with bean curd (*kaeng jèut tâo hû*).

A speciality of southern Laos and Louang Phabang, well worth ordering if you can find it, is **mók pa** or fish steamed in banana leaves. Other variations, including *mók kheuang nai kai* (chicken giblets grilled in banana leaves) and *mók pa fa lai* (the same recipe made with freshwater stingray), are also worth sampling, though they appear less frequently on restaurant menus.

Restaurants catering to travellers can whip up a variety of **stir-fried dishes**, which tend to be a mix of Thai, Lao and Chinese food, and are usually eaten with steamed rice. **Fried rice** is a reliable standby throughout the country, as are quasi-Chinese dishes such as pork with basil over rice, *mũ phát bai holapha*, chicken with ginger, *khùa khing kai*, and mixed vegetables, *khùa phák*.

Vegetarian fare

Although very few people in Laos are vegetarian, it's fairly easy to persuade cooks to put together a vegetable-only rice or vegetable dish. In many places that may be your only option unless you eat fish. If you don't eat fish, keep in mind that most Lao cooking calls for fish sauce so, when ordering for a veggies-only dish, you may want to add "*baw sai nâm pa*" ("without fish sauce"). You could survive a meal or two on biscuits or instant noodles. Sadly for vegans and others with strict vegetarian diets, eating vegetarian at all but a handful of real vegetarian restaurants means ordering from the vegetables-only page of the menu.

Noodles

When the Lao aren't filling up on glutinous rice, they're busy eating *fõe*, the ubiquitous **noodle soup** that takes its name from the Vietnamese soup *pho*. Although primarily eaten in the morning for breakfast, *fõe* can be enjoyed at any time of day, and, outside of large towns, visitors to Laos often have to fall back on *fõe* for a lot of meals, owing to the lack of any eating places other than noodle shops.

The basic bowl of *fõe* consists of a light broth to which is added thin rice noodles and slices of meat (usually beef, water buffalo or grilled chicken). It's served with a plate of fresh raw vegetables, usually including lettuce, mint and coriander leaves and bean sprouts. Flavouring the broth is pretty much up to you: containers of chilli, sugar, vinegar and fish sauce (and sometimes lime wedges and MSG) are on the tables of every noodle shop, allowing you to find the perfect balance of spicy, sweet, sour and salty. Also on offer at many noodle shops is *mi*, a yellow wheat noodle served in broth with slices of meat and a few vegetables. It's also common to eat *fõe* and *mi* softened in broth but served without it (*hàeng*), and at times fried (*khùa*).

Many other types of noodle soup are dished up at street stalls. *Khào biak sèn* is another soup popular in the morning, consisting of soft, round rice noodles, slices of chicken and fresh ginger and served in a chicken broth, though it's hard to find outside bigger towns. More widely available, and a favourite at family gatherings during festivals, is *khào pûn*, a dish of round, white, translucent flour noodles, onto which is scooped one of any number of sweet, spicy coconut-milk based sauces. These noodles also find their way into several Vietnamese dishes, such as barbecued pork meatballs (*nâm néuang*) and spring rolls (*yáw*), in which they are served cold with several condiments and a sauce. There's also a Lao incarnation of *khào soi*, the spicy noodle curry eaten throughout northern Thailand and the Shan States of Myanmar; the version common in Laos (in Louang Phabang and certain northwestern towns) consists of rice noodles served in almost clear broth and topped with a spicy meat curry.

Fruits and desserts

The best way to round off a meal or fill your stomach on a long bus ride is with **fresh fruit** (*màk mâi*), as the country offers a wide variety, from the more commonly known bananas, papayas, mangoes, pineapples, watermelons and green apples imported from China (you might want to rinse in drinking water to remove possible pesticide residues) to more exotic options: crisp green guavas; burgundy lychees, with tart, sweet white fruit hidden in a coat of thin leather; wild-haired, red rambutans, milder and cheaper than lychees; dark purple mangosteen, tough-skinned treasures with a velvety smooth inside divided into succulent sweet segments; airy, bell-shaped green rose apples; pomelos, gigantic citruses whose thick rinds yield a grapefruit without the tartness; fuzzy, brown sapodillas, oval in shape and almost honey-sweet; large, spiky durian, notoriously stinky yet divinely creamy; oblong jackfruit, with sweet, yellow flesh possessing the texture of soft leather; and rare Xiang Khouang avocados, three times the size of those in France, with a subtle perfumed flavour. Restaurants occasionally serve fruit to end a meal, and, in Vientiane, handcart-pushing hawkers patrol the streets with ready-peeled segments. Elsewhere, track down your fruit directly from stands at the market.

Desserts don't really figure on many restaurant menus, although some Vientiane restaurants will usually have a few featuring **coconut milk** or cream, notably banana in coconut milk (*nâm wān màk kûay*). Markets often have a food stall specializing in inexpensive coconut-milk desserts, generally called *nâm wān*. Look for a stall displaying a dozen bowls, containing everything from water chestnuts to corn to fluorescent green and pink jellies, from which one or two items are selected and then added to a sweet mixture of crushed ice, slabs of young coconut meat and coconut milk. Also popular are light Chinese **doughnuts**, fried in a skillet full of oil and known as *khào nõm khu* or *pá thawng ko*, and another fried delight, crispy bananas (*kûay khaek*).

Sticky rice, of course, also turns up in a few desserts. As **mangoes** begin to ripen in March, look for *khào niaw màk muang*, sliced mango splashed with coconut cream served over sticky rice; those who don't mind the smell of durian can try the durian variant on this dessert. *Khào lăm*, another treat, this one popular during the cool season, is cooked in sections of bamboo, which is gradually peeled back to reveal a tube of sticky rice and beans joined in coconut cream.

What to drink

The Lao don't drink **water** straight from the tap, and nor should you. Plastic bottles of drinking water (*nâm deum*) are sold countrywide for around 2000K, even in smaller towns. Noodle shops and inexpensive restaurants generally serve free pitchers of weak tea or boiled water (*nâm tóm*), which is fine to drink, although perhaps not as foolproof as bottled water. In some cases you'll find that budget hotels provide complimentary bottles of water, which can be refilled with boiled water. If the seal of the water bottle has been broken you might not want to take your chances with it.

Given the extraordinarily hot weather in Laos, it can be difficult to resist the temptation to cool off by filling your drink with **ice**. Most ice in Laos is produced in large blocks under hygienic conditions, but it can become less pure in transit or storage, so be wary, or simply avoid it altogether.

Soft drinks and juices

Brand-name **soft drinks**, such as 7-Up, Pepsi and Fanta, are widely available for around 2000K per bottle (cans are somewhat more expensive). Bottles are returnable so, if you're on the go, you'll have to drink the bottle at the shop. Most vendors will pour the drink into a plastic packet (which is then tied with a string or rubber band and inserted with a straw) for takeaways.

Also refreshing are the **fruit shakes** churned out by many restaurants and drink shops in larger towns. These *màk mâi pan* consist of your choice of fruit blended with ice, liquid sugar and sometimes a hint of salt and sweetened condensed milk. Look for a blender stationed next to bowls of fruit. Even

more readily available are freshly squeezed **fruit juices**, such as lemon (*nâm màk nao*), plus coconut water (*nâm màk phao*) enjoyed directly from the fruit after it has been dehusked and cut open. Also popular is the exceptionally sweet sugar-cane juice, *nâm oi*.

Hot drinks

Laos's best **coffee** is grown on the Bolaven Plateau, outside Pakxong in southern Laos, where it was introduced by the French in the early twentieth century. Twenty thousand tons of coffee are produced in Laos annually, most of which is robusta, although some arabica is grown as well. Quality, although much improved in recent years, can still vary widely. Some establishments that are accustomed to foreigners may serve instant coffee (*kafeh net*, after the Lao word for Nescafé, the most common brand); if you prefer locally grown coffee ask for *kafeh Láo* or *kafeh thông*, literally "bag coffee", after the traditional technique of preparing the coffee. A few bakeries and restaurants catering to foreigners in Vientiane may serve imported coffee, while in more remote areas you may only be able to find instant coffee.

The Lao drink *kafeh hâwn*, very strong coffee made by pouring hot water through a sock-like bag filled with the ground coffee, and then served in a short glass filled with a generous dollop of sweetened condensed milk and a spoonful of sugar. Traditionally, hot coffee is served with a complimentary glass of weak Chinese tea or hot water, to be drunk in between sips of the very sweet coffee. If you prefer your coffee black, and without sugar, order *kafeh dam baw sai nâm tan*. More appropriate for Laos's hot weather is *kafeh yén*, in which the same concoction is mixed and poured into a mug of crushed ice or a plastic bag.

Black and Chinese-style **tea** are both served in Laos. Weak Chinese tea is often found, lukewarm, on tables in restaurants and can be enjoyed free of charge. Stronger Chinese tea (*sá jin*) you'll need to order. If you request *sá hâwn*, you usually get a brew based on local or imported black tea, mixed with sweetened condensed milk and sugar; it's available at most coffee vendors.

Alcoholic drinks

Many foreign **beers**, including Heineken, Singapore's Tiger and ABC Stout, Vietnamese 333 and Singha from Thailand, are available in Laos, although **Beer Lao** (Bia Lao in Lao), with a 98 percent market share, is far and away the most popular and the cheapest at just 9000K per 660ml bottle (330ml cans are also sold). Containing five percent alcohol, the beer owes its light, distinctive taste to the French investors who founded the company in 1971, although the company was later state-owned, with Czechoslovakian brewmasters training the Lao staff, until it was privatized in the mid-1990s. Nearly all that goes into making Beer Lao is imported, from hops to bottle caps, although locally grown rice is used in place of twenty percent of the malt.

In Vientiane and Louang Phabang, **draught** Beer Lao, known as *bia sót* and sometimes appearing on English signs as "Fresh Beer", is available at bargain prices by the litre. Often served warm from the keg, the beer is poured over ice, though some establishments serve it chilled. There are dozens of *bia sót* outlets in the capital, most of which are casual outdoor beer gardens with thatch roofs. You can usually get snacks here too, known as "**drinking food**" or *káp kâem* – typical dishes include spicy papaya salad, fresh spring rolls, omelette, fried peanuts (*thua jeun*), shrimp-flavoured chips (*khào kiap kûng*) and grilled chicken.

In Vientiane, you can find a selection of **Western spirits** and an excellent (for Southeast Asia) selection of **French wines**, sometimes for as little as $2 for a drinkable bottle of table wine. Elsewhere you'll have trouble finding anything other than bottles of spirits

Lào-láo and other rice spirits

Drunk with gusto by the Lao is **lào-láo**, a clear rice alcohol with the fire of a blinding Mississippi moonshine. Although the government distils its own brand, Sticky Rice, which is sold nationally, most people indulge in local brews, the taste varying from region to region and even town to town. *Lào-láo* is usually sold in whatever bottle the distiller had around at the time (look twice before you buy that bottle of Fanta) and sells at drink shops and general stores for around 10,000K per 750ml. You can indulge in some of the best *lào-láo* in Si Phan Don and Phongsali.

Drinking *lào-láo* often takes on the air of a sacred **ritual**, albeit a rather boisterous one. After (or sometimes during) a meal, the host will bring out a bottle of *lào-láo* to share with the guests. The host begins the proceedings by pouring a shot of *lào-láo* and tossing it onto the ground to appease the house spirit. He then pours himself a measure, raising the glass for all to see before throwing back the drink and emptying the remaining droplets onto the floor, in order to empty the glass for the next drinker. The host then pours a shot for each guest in turn. After the host has completed one circuit, the bottle and the glass are passed along to a guest, who serves him- or herself first, then the rest of the party, one by one. Guests are expected to drink at least one shot in order not to offend the house spirit and the host, although in such situations there's often pressure, however playful, to drink much more. One polite escape route is to take a sip of the shot and then dump out the rest on the floor during the "glass emptying" move.

Another rice alcohol, *lào hái*, also inspires a festive, communal drinking experience. Drunk from a large earthenware jar with thin bamboo straws, *lào hái* is fermented by households or villages in the countryside and is weaker than *lào-láo*, closer to a wine in taste than a backwoods whisky. Drinking *lào hái*, however, can be a bit risky as unboiled water is sometimes added to the jar during the fermentation process.

Several brand-name **rice whiskies**, with a lower alcohol content than *lào-láo*, are available for around $1 at local general stores. Chevreuil d'Or, Mae Khong and Sing Thong all taste similar to Thailand's Mekong whisky and are more enjoyable over ice with Pepsi or soda water than neat.

produced by the Lao Winery Company ($1–2), but if you look hard enough you'll usually be able to hunt down a bottle of Johnnie Walker Black or Red Label. In the case of foreign brands, check that the cap is properly sealed and the bottle doesn't look used, as fakes sometimes find their way into Laos from Vietnam and Thailand.

Communications

Laos's communications network has improved dramatically in recent years, but many glitches remain, and outside Vientiane and other Mekong towns standards are low.

The Lao **postal system** is less than reliable, though when it does work, mail takes seven to fourteen days in or out of Laos, depending on where you are. Overseas postal rates are reasonable: a postcard costs around $0.30 and a standard letter runs for under $1. An Express Mail Service operates to most Western countries and certain destinations within Laos; the service cuts down on delivery time and automatically registers your letter. Alternatively, several **international couriers**, including DHL and FedEx, have offices in Vientiane.

Post offices throughout the country are recognizable by their mustard-yellow colour scheme, and open at least five days a week, normally from 8am until noon and from 1pm to 4pm. When sending **parcels**, leave the package open for inspection.

Poste restante services are available in Vientiane and Louang Phabang. Post offices in both towns charge a small fee for letters (postcards received this way are free) and keep mail behind the counter for two or three months. Bring your passport on the off chance that you're asked to show identification when picking up your mail. Mail should be addressed: name, GPO, city, Lao PDR. To avoid misfiling, your surname should be underlined or capitalized; when checking your mail, it doesn't hurt to check under your first name as well. If you're moving to Laos, you may want to rent a **post office box** to receive mail, as there are no household deliveries.

Phones

Laos has entered the age of satellite telecommunications, but the network is still shaky at best. International connections are made via satellite to Hong Kong, Japan and Australia, with provincial outposts hooked up to the main telephone exchange in Vientiane. But

---

Dialling codes

To **call Laos** from abroad, dial your international access code, then ☏856 + area code minus first 0 + number. To **call abroad from Laos**, dial 00, then the relevant country code and the number. Useful country codes include:

Australia ☏61
Canada ☏1
Ireland ☏353
New Zealand ☏64
South Africa ☏27
UK ☏44
USA ☏27

although IDD is widely available in Vientiane, the telephone service in many provincial outposts is still in comparatively poor shape. These days, however, a small number of Internet cafés, particularly in Vientiane and Louang Phabang, offer **Internet-routed calls** which cost a fraction of what a regular international call would cost.

The best place to make conventional international calls is the **Telecom Office** – you'll find these offices, normally open from 8am until 9pm, in Vientiane and most provincial capitals; otherwise, international calls can be placed at the post office. Calls abroad are charged by the minute. Calls to the UK and North America cost approximately $3 per minute, whereas calling New Zealand is somewhat cheaper at roughly $1.50, while Australia calls cost less than $1 a minute. It's also quite cheap to call Thailand, although calls to Vietnam and Cambodia will cost you the same as it would to ring Wellington. Calling overseas from a hotel invariably results in surcharges. **Local calls** can be made at hotels and guesthouses for a small fee.

There's no facility for collect or reverse-charge international calls, but you can almost always ask the operator for the minimum call abroad and get the phone number of the post office you're calling from, so that you can be **called back** at the post office. For this you'll pay a small service charge on top of the cost of the initial call.

Public phones are wired for both domestic and international calls and are usually stationed outside post offices in provincial capitals; larger towns have several booths, although many seem to be out of service much of the time. Phone cards (*bat tholasap*) for these phones, which are available at shops, post and telephone offices, come in several denominations, costing between $2.50 and $6. Because of high charges for overseas calls and the low amount of time units available, it's difficult to make an overseas call that lasts for more than a few minutes before you're cut off.

Regional codes are given throughout the Guide: the "0" must be dialled before all long-distance calls. Some hotels have consecutively numbered phone lines – thus ☎021/221200–5 means that the last digit can be any number between 0 and 5.

International and domestic **fax** services are available at upmarket hotels in Vientiane and Louang Phabang and at most provincial post offices.

Cell phones

If you have a GSM **mobile phone** (most phones except some used in the US are GSM), you can use it in Laos, though you may need to ask your phone provider to activate **roaming**. It's worth asking what the call charges are, not just to make calls but also to receive them in Laos. If your phone isn't locked to one network, it can be cheaper to make Lao calls with a SIM card from a major local service provider, such as Lao Telecom (Ⓦwww.laotel.com) or Tangolao (Ⓦwww.tangolao.com). Note that cell-phone coverage is limited to major cities and towns.

Internet access

There are **cybercafés** and **computer shops** with Net access in the major cities, as well as some of the smaller towns. Charges range from 100K to 200K per minute, or 10,000K per hour. If you're moving to Laos, a local ISP to contact is GlobeNet (☎021/218841), which shares an office with KPL News Service on the first floor of the *Lao Hotel Plaza*.

The media

Tightly controlled by the communist party since the Pathet Lao came to power in 1975, Laos's minuscule media struggles to compete with flashy Thai TV game shows and the multitude of channels offered by satellite dishes. With only one-tenth the population of neighbouring Thailand, it's very hard for Laos to compete with Thailand.

Newspapers and magazines

Laos has only one **English-language newspaper**, the *Vientiane Times*, established in 1994. Despite being somewhat thin, self-censored and nearly impossible to find outside the capital, it is nonetheless a good window on Laos. Published by the Ministry of Information and Culture, the *Vientiane Times* focuses primarily on business and trade issues, although interesting cultural pieces do slip in from time to time, and the occasional column showcasing people's opinion on a selected social topic is a worthwhile read. You'll also find ads for restaurant specials and a brief listings section on the back page.

There are two **Lao-language dailies** and five weeklies. Of the two dailies, *Wieng Mai* and *Pasason*, the latter is more widely read. Both get their international news from KPL, the government news agency, and, for the most part, have their own reporters who file domestic news. Neither is known for independent-minded reportage. In fact it's fair to say you'll find much more news about Laos online (a list of recommended websites appears below) than you can in the country.

Foreign publications are extremely difficult to find outside Vientiane, and even in the capital there are scant copies. *Newsweek*, *Economist* and *Time* are sold at major hotels, and the *Bangkok Post* is sold in minimarkets in Vientiane.

Online news about Laos

ⓦ **www.vientianetimes.com** The website of the *Vientiane Times* is the best place to start. It contains most of the stories from Laos's only English-language newspaper and related news from other publications around the world.

ⓦ **www.laosguide.com** A good source of news and articles.

ⓦ **www.laosnews.net** Has articles and extensive links.

ⓦ **www.muonglao.com** An excellent online magazine with many good articles on Laos.

ⓦ **www.bangkokpost.net** The website of Thailand's leading English-language daily.

ⓦ **www.asiaobserver.com** The *Asian Observer*'s selection of articles on Laos is particularly extensive.

Television

Lao television's two **government-run channels** broadcast a mix of news, cultural shows and Chinese soaps for several hours a day, with no English programming. Reception is poor, however, in rural areas, and in general Lao TV struggles to compete with flashy Thai TV game shows and the multitude of channels offered by satellite dishes. One of the oddest sights in Laos is that of rickety bamboo and thatch huts and houses all over the country with huge, modern satellite dishes attached to the roofs.

Many mid-range and top-end hotels provide **satellite TV** – though often these show only a handful of channels – as do a few coffee shops and bakeries in Louang Phabang and Vientiane.

Radio

Lao radio thrives, helped along by the fact that newspapers rarely find their way outside Vientiane and that the country's two national TV stations are not available to many people in the countryside. The main radio station, **Lao National Radio**, can be picked up in the vicinity of Vientiane or on shortwave in roughly seventy percent of the country. LNR gets its international news from a number of sources, including CNN, BBC, Xinhua and KPL, and broadcasts news in English twice a day. Tuning into LNR will also give you a chance to hear traditional **Lao music**, which you otherwise may only get to hear at festivals.

With a **shortwave radio**, you can pick up Voice of America (🖫www.voa.gov), BBC World Service (🖫www.bbc.co.uk/worldservice) and a variety of other international stations in most parts of Laos. Schedules and frequencies are available on broadcasters' websites.

Opening hours and public holidays

The official working hours of all government offices were adjusted back in 1998: the two-hour lunch break was shortened to one, and government workers were given Saturday off. Old habits die hard though, and many civil servants have found it difficult to give up the two-hour siesta that was a relic of French rule. This means that while official hours for government offices are Monday to Friday from 8am until noon and 1pm to 5pm, very little gets done between 11am and 2pm.

Opening hours for private businesses vary, but almost all close on Sunday. During the heat of the day many shop owners will partly close their doors and snooze to escape the heat. If you need to buy something it is perfectly acceptable to wake them up. Daily **markets** are always best in the morning, the earlier the better, and by mid-afternoon most have all but shut down. Details of banking and post offices hours are given on p.30 and p.53 respectively.

The posted hours on **museums** are not scrupulously followed, and on slow days (almost every day) the curators and staff are often tempted to pack up and head home. Unless a festival is taking place (see the Festivals colour section for background on traditional celebrations), **monasteries** should only be visited during daylight hours as monks are very early risers and are usually in bed not long after sunset.

Public holidays

Two decades ago when they were created, most of the **holidays** listed below were celebrated in Vientiane with rallies and speeches. Today, little if anything happens officially, but

a holiday is a holiday: government offices and banks are closed. Very infrequently, the Lao government holds **national elections**, which temporarily paralyze the country. Even border crossings are shut down for a few hours.

Although the Vietnamese and Chinese **lunar new year** isn't a public holiday, it is celebrated privately by the Vietnamese and Chinese communities of Vientiane, Thakhek, Savannakhet and Pakxe, with parties and visits to Mahayana Buddhist pagodas. Most businesses in these towns are closed for at least three days during the lunar new year, which coincides with the new moon in late January or early to mid-February.

January 1 New Year's Day
January 6 Pathet Lao Day
January 20 Army Day
March 8 Women's Day
March 22 Lao People's Party Day
April 15–17 Lao New Year
May 1 International Labour Day
June 1 Children's Day
August 13 Lao Issara
August 23 Liberation Day
October 12 Freedom from France Day
December 2 National Day

Shopping

One of the pleasures of shopping in a non-industrial country like Laos is the availability of hand-crafted goods. Because items made by hand can only be produced in limited quantities, they are usually sold or bartered in the village in which they were made, and seldom get very far afield. Hand-made baskets, bolts of cloth and household utensils are best acquired at the village level, as everything is cheaper at the source, though it's not all that easy for non-Lao-speaking visitors to turn up and make known what they're after. Provincial markets are the obvious alternative; prices here are usually just a bit more than what you would pay were you to buy directly from village artisans. Of course, if village-made objects make it all the way to the boutiques of Vientiane, their "value" will have multiplied many times over.

As with the rest of Southeast Asia, merchandise often has no price tag and the buyer is expected to make a spirited attempt at **haggling** the quoted price down. Even if an item is sporting a price tag, it's still perfectly acceptable to ask for a discount. Bargaining takes patience and tact, and knowing what an item is really worth is half the battle. The first price quoted will usually be inflated. If you feel the price is way out of line, it is better to just smile and walk away than to squawk in disbelief and argue that the price is unfair – no matter how loud or valid your protestations, nobody will believe that you cannot afford to buy.

On the whole, **Louang Phabang** is better for shopping than Vientiane, as much of what is for sale in Louang Phabang is produced locally, meaning you get a better selection of goods and at better prices.

Textiles

A surprisingly large number of the ethnic groups that make up the population of Laos produce cloth of their own design, which is turned into men's and women's sarongs, shoulder bags, and headscarfs and shawls. Traditionally, most textiles stayed within the village where they were woven, but the increasing popularity of Lao textiles with visitors has led urban textile merchants to employ buyers to comb isolated villages for **old textiles** that might be resold at a profit. The result is that many merchants

have only a vague idea of where their old textiles are from or which group made them. This doesn't seem to deter foreign buyers, however, and sales are brisk, which has given rise to the practice of boiling new textiles to artificially age them. Some of these so-called antique textiles sell for hundreds of dollars.

To some shopkeepers "old" can mean ten years or so and most will have little idea what the age of a certain piece is, but if you persist in asking, they will often claim an item has been around for a couple of centuries. As textiles are difficult to date, it's best to take such claims with a pinch of salt. All in all, though, it is rare for the local merchants to go to great lengths to deceive customers.

These days, though, the vast majority of the textiles for sale are **new textiles** specifically made for the tourist market. These may have the same patterns and motifs as the traditional sarongs and so forth, but are cut and sewn into items such as pillowcases. If you're after antique textiles you have to ask; unless you are an expert or have money to burn, it is a good idea to stick to new textiles, which can be had for as little as $5 and are just as pleasing to the eye as the older pieces.

Lao weavers have a long tradition of combining **cotton** and **silk**: a typical piece may have a cotton base with silk details woven into it. Modern pieces of inferior quality substitute synthetic fibres for silk, and some vendors have been known to try to pass off hundred-percent synthetic cloth as silk. Lastly, the synthetic dyes used by most weavers are not colourfast, something to bear in mind when laundering newly purchased textiles.

Silver

Although Thai antique dealers have made off with quite a bit of old Lao **silver** (and marketed it in Thailand as old Thai silver) there is still a fair amount of the stuff floating around. Items to look out for are paraphernalia for **betel chewing**: egg-sized round or oval boxes for storing white lime, cone-shaped containers for holding betel leaves and miniature mortars used to pound areca nuts. Larger silver boxes or bowls with human or animal figures hammered into them were once used in religious ceremonies. C-shaped **bracelets** and anklets are found in a variety of styles. Bracelets and anklets of traditional Lao style, as opposed to hill-tribe design, have a stylized lotus bud on each end.

Hill-tribe silver jewellery (traditionally made by melting down and hammering silver French piastres) is usually bold and heavy – the better to show off one's wealth. With few exceptions, the hill-tribe jewellery being peddled in Laos is the handiwork of the Hmong tribe. In **Louang Phabang**, the old silversmith families that once supplied the monarchy with ceremonial objects are again practising their trade, and their silver creations represent some of the best-value souvenirs to be found in Laos.

Antiques

Thai merchants regularly scour Laos for **antiques** so there are probably more authentic Lao antiques for sale in the malls of Bangkok and Chiang Mai than anywhere in Laos. Conversely, many of the "antiques" for sale in Laos are actually reproductions made in Thailand or Cambodia. This is particularly true in the case of metal Buddhist or Hindu figurines.

As with so many antique shops in Asia, Lao shop proprietors will tell you whatever you want to hear about the age and rarity of that patinaed bauble you're dying to own. Therefore, the best advice to visitors interested in purchasing Lao "antiques" is not to pay more than what you think the item's visual worth is: the days when Laos sold valuable heirlooms for a fraction of their international price are long gone. If looking at it only gives you ten dollars' worth of pleasure, don't pay twenty for it.

Wooden **Buddha images** are often genuine antiques, but were most likely pilfered from some temple or shrine. Refraining from buying them will help discourage this practice. Prospective buyers should also be aware that there is an **official ban** on the export of Buddha images from Laos. Although this is aimed primarily at curbing the theft of large Lao bronze Buddhas from rural monasteries, small images are also included in the ban. That said, it is highly unlikely that Lao officials will confiscate new Buddhas from foreign visitors. If the ban doesn't put you off buying a Buddha image, note how the Lao, when acquiring a Buddha image, pay particular attention to the expression on the Buddha's face. Does the Buddha look serene? If so, the image is considered auspicious.

Antique brass weights, sometimes referred to as "**opium weights**", come in a variety of sizes and shapes. Those cast in zoomorphic figures (stylized birds, elephants, lions, etc) are an established collectable and command high prices, sometimes selling for hundreds of dollars. Weights of simpler design, such as those shaped like miniature stupas, are much more affordable and can be bought for just a few dollars in provincial towns.

Opium pipes come in sundry forms as well. Although very few are genuine antiques, the workmanship is generally quite good as they are produced by pipemakers who once supplied Vientiane's now-defunct opium dens. A typical pipe may have a bamboo body, a ceramic bowl and silver or brass ornamentation, and should sell for about $50. During the past few years Laos has been flooded with reproduction opium pipes from Vietnam. These are more colourful and ornate than the Laos-made pipes, but aren't worth spending more than $10 or so to buy. Discerning what is what can be kind of tricky, and don't expect the merchants who sell antiques of any sort to answer your questions with any truthfulness.

Banknotes, coins and stamps

While antiques are risky business, old **stamps**, **coins** and **banknotes** are excellent value. The iconography and symbolism these display speak volumes about the country's history and culture, giving an immediate sense of the values of the government that issued them. And being so easy to transport and weighing almost nothing, they make ideal souvenirs.

Banknotes

On sale in antique shops, pre-revolution **banknotes** are the most easily acquired mementos of the old monarchy. Specimens from the French era were also legal tender in what is now Vietnam and Cambodia and motifs reflect the three main cultures that were encompassed by French Indochina. The denominations were also written out in Lao, Khmer, Vietnamese and Chinese, as well as French.

Banknotes issued soon after independence from France bear colourful portraits of King Sisavang Vong and, despite countless stacks being ceremonially burned by zealous communists after the revolution, small caches are still commonly found in antique shops.

Immediately after the revolution, from 1976 to 1979, the Lao government issued the so-called "**liberation kip**" with illustrations of revolutionary combat themes. Most interesting are the ten-kip note with armed villagers setting booby traps; the two-hundred kip note with porters and elephants traversing the Ho Chi Minh Trail; and the five-hundred kip note, with anti-aircraft guns shooting down American planes over the Plain of Jars.

The series of banknotes currently in circulation was issued to replace the liberation kip in the late 1970s, but inflation has forced the government to stop printing small-denomination banknotes and, as soon as they went out of circulation, stacks of them began appearing in souvenir shops. The tiny, post-revolution one-kip note, barely larger than a business card, was the first to make the transformation from currency to curio. The five-, ten- and twenty-kip notes soon followed. The twenty-kip note is probably the most interesting of this series, having an illustration on the reverse of a tank pointing its big gun across the Mekong towards Thailand.

Coins

Gold and silver shops often have a hoard of old silver **coins**, including French piastres and, to a lesser extent, British-Indian rupees. These are still used as currency by some tribal peoples, such as the Akha and Hmong, who wear the coins as jewellery or ornamentation on clothing and pawn them when necessary. Use caution when buying though, as craftsmen in Thailand make fakes that invariably find their way into Lao antique shops. It's not so difficult to discern these fake coins as nobody bothers to artificially age them – if the century-old coin looks new then it almost certainly is.

Both the Kingdom of Laos and the Lao People's Democratic Republic issued coins made of a lightweight aluminium alloy that are easily differentiated by their iconography. Coins of the royal government have a hole in the middle and a three-headed elephant. The hammer and sickle embossed coins issued by the PDR lost their value to inflation so quickly that few made it into circulation and they are now quite rare. Both types of coinage are sometimes found in antique shops.

Stamps

Learned philatelists know that Lao **stamps** from the 1950s and early 1960s are some of the most exquisitely designed and coloured stamps ever issued. Of these, the works of French artist **Marc Leguay** stand out. Leguay's scenes of rural Lao life and depictions of characters from Lao mythology, printed in Paris, are mini-masterpieces. Most antique shops in Vientiane have a selection of old stamps and at least one shop specializes in philately.

Lao stamps from the early 1970s depicting American astronauts and their achievements in space were replaced in the late 1970s by stamps commemorating the celestial exploits of Soviet cosmonauts. Since the revolution, Lao stamps have been made in Cuba and

Shipping

It is not advisable to ship anything of value home from Laos. If you're planning to travel onwards to **Thailand**, it would be a good idea to wait and ship it from there.

are not gummed, hence the little glue pots to be found in every Lao post office.

Royalist regalia

With the memories of the war that divided Laos fading, paraphernalia associated with the defunct kingdom is less likely to offend officials of the present regime. Brass buttons, badges and medals decorated with the Hindu iconography of the Lao monarchy are sometimes found in gold or silver jewellery and antique shops. Royal Lao Army hat devices depicting Shiva's trident superimposed on Vishnu's discus and brass buttons decorated with Airavata, the three-headed elephant, are typical finds.

Souvenir hunters should keep in mind that attaching medals or badges of the Kingdom of Laos to your clothes and wearing them in public would be considered, in the words of one Louang Phabang antiques merchant, "poor form".

Woodcarving, rattan, wicker and bamboo

Until tourism created a demand for souvenirs, nearly all examples of Lao **woodcarving** were religious in nature – for example, the small, antique, wooden Buddha images which are finding their way into curio shops (see p.58). For those who have bought a stunning, hand-woven textile but are unsure of how to display it, there are ornately **carved hangers** made expressly for this purpose. Workmanship varies, however, so inspect carefully to ensure that there are no splinters or jagged edges which may damage the textile. Keep in mind also that large woodcarvings sometimes crack when transported to less humid climes.

That **baskets** are an important part of traditional Lao culture is reflected in the language: Lao has dozens upon dozens of words for them, and they're used in all spheres of everyday life. Many different forms of basket are used as **backpacks**; those made by the Gie-Trieng tribe in Xekong province are probably the most expertly woven. Baskets are also used for serving food, such as sticky rice. These mini-baskets come with a long loop of string so they can be slung over the shoulder when hiking, as sticky rice is the perfect snack on long treks, road or boat trips. **Mats** made of woven grass or reeds can be found in sizes for one or two people. The one-person mats are dirt-cheap, easily carried when rolled up and make a lot more sense than foam rubber mattresses. Woven mats are especially handy when taking a slow boat down the Mekong, as the passenger holds are often not the cleanest of places. Ordinary sticky rice baskets and mats can be found at any provincial market and should cost no more than a couple of dollars.

While most **rattan and bamboo furniture** in Laos is much cheaper than at home, the cost of shipping it back tends to equal things out. Recently a couple of companies have begun producing stylish, high-quality rattan and bamboo furniture that is comparatively pricey. Either way, rattan and bamboo are the favourite food of a tiny but voracious beetle that commonly infests furniture of this type made in this part of the world. In the end, buying and shipping furniture is probably not worth the trouble.

Culture and etiquette

While history may have given them ample reason to distrust outsiders, the Lao are a genuinely friendly folk and interacting with them is one of the greatest joys of travelling through Laos. Always remember, though, that Laos is a Buddhist country and that foreigners need to moderate their dress and behaviour appropriately.

Because of the sheer diversity of **ethnic groups** in Laos, it is difficult to generalize when speaking of "Lao" attitudes and behaviour. The dominant group, the so-called "Lao Loum", or **lowland Lao**, who make up the majority in the valleys of the Mekong and its tributaries, are Theravada Buddhists and this has a strong effect on their attitudes and behaviour. In this article the focus is on do's and don'ts within that culture; customs among the **hill-tribe peoples** are often quite different from those of the lowlanders (see the "Trekking Etiquette" box on p.215 for more).

Travellers who have spent some time in Thailand will note that the Lao and Thai share many cultural traits, so that lessons learned in Thailand can be applied to Laos as well.

Dress and appearance

Appearance is very important in Lao society. **Conservative dress** is always recommended, and visitors should keep in mind that the Lao dislike foreigners who come to their country and dress in what they deem a disrespectful manner. This includes men appearing shirtless in public, and women walking around braless. Be aware also that dreadlocks, tattoos and body-piercing are viewed with disfavour by lowland Lao, although hill-tribe people are usually more accepting. Dressing too casually (or too outrageously) can also be counterproductive in dealings with Lao authorities, such as when applying for visa extensions at immigration.

When in urban areas or visiting Buddhist monasteries or holy sites, visitors should refrain from outfits that would be more suited to the beach. Women especially should avoid wearing anything that reveals too much skin or could be conceived of as provocative – this includes shorts and sleeveless shirts. Sandals or flip-flops can be worn for all but the most formal occasions; in fact, they are much more practical than shoes, since footwear must be **removed** upon entering private homes, certain Buddhist monastery buildings or any living space. The habit of leaving your footwear outside the threshold is not just a matter of wanting to keep interiors clean, it is a long-standing tradition that will cause offence if flouted.

Manners

Lao **social taboos** are sometimes linked to Buddhist beliefs. **Feet** are considered low and unclean and care should be taken not to touch or even point at things with your feet. Be careful not to step over any part of people who are sitting or lying on the floor (or the deck of a boat), as this is also considered rude. If you do accidentally kick or brush someone with your feet, apologize immediately and smile as you do so. That way, even if the words aren't understood, your intent will be. Conversely, people's **heads** are considered sacred and shouldn't be touched. Playful hair tousling is not a sign of adoration among the Lao.

Besides dressing conservatively, there are other conventions that must be followed when visiting **Buddhist monasteries**. Before entering monastery buildings such as the *sim* or *wihan*, or if you are invited into monks' living quarters, footwear must be removed. Women should never touch Buddhist monks or novices, or hand objects directly to them. When giving something to a monk, the object should be placed on a nearby table or passed to a layman who will then hand it to the monk. This is an example of the many precepts that Buddhist monks must adhere to and which apply even when a monk interacts with his mother. All Buddha images are objects of veneration, and some are also considered to be great works of art, so it should go without saying that touching Buddha images disrespectfully (such as giving them a thump to ascertain what they are made of) is inappropriate. When sitting on the floor of a monastery building that has a Buddha image, never point your feet in the direction of the image. If possible, observe the Lao and imitate the way they sit: in a modified kneeling position with legs pointed away from the image. The same position should be taken when sitting on the floor (or the deck of a boat) near a monk.

The lowland Lao traditionally **greet** each other with a *nop* – bringing their hands together at the chin in a prayer-like gesture. After the revolution the *nop* was discouraged, but it now seems to be making a comeback. This graceful gesture is more difficult to execute properly than it may at first appear, however, as the status of the persons giving and returning the *nop* determines how they execute it. Most Lao reserve the *nop* greeting for each other, preferring to shake hands with Westerners, and the only time a Westerner is likely to receive a *nop* is from the staff of upmarket hotels or fancy restaurants. In any case, if you do receive a *nop* as a gesture of greeting or thank you, it is best to reply with a smile and nod of the head.

As for the **Lao temperament**, most visitors will find it by turns charming, baffling and maddening. With foreign visitors the Lao are almost unfailingly gracious and hospitable, especially in the remoter parts of the country where foreigners are a rarity. The patient and unflappable Lao, however, have found that foreigners can be quick to anger and will vent their spleen in situations where it is clear that losing tempers will get them nowhere. The Lao are likely to find amusement in such situations, smiling or chortling at the foreigner's vein-popping fury. If the foreigner still fails to see the futility of displaying rage, the Lao are likely to flee the scene,

giving the hothead some time to cool. No matter what happens, **showing anger** is a useless endeavour in Laos.

The Lao also feel that many foreign visitors seem to be a bit aloof. They have obviously spent a lot of time and money to get so far from home, but once they get to Laos they walk around briskly, looking at the locals, but rarely bothering to smile or greet those they have come so far to see. The Lao are unsure of what to make of this, for in Laos it is customary for strangers to smile at each other to show that they mean well. Foreign visitors who are not grin-stingy will find that a smile and a nod will break the ice of initial reservation some locals may have upon seeing a foreigner, and will invariably bring a smile in response.

The Lao realize that their country is poor and know that foreign visitors might be put off by their rustic lifestyles, particularly in the countryside. Partly to make up for these perceived shortcomings, the Lao are very hospitable and enjoy **offering food or drinks** to visitors. This will certainly be the case if visitors are invited into a Lao home. Sadly, some foreigners are not interested in partaking of the humble offerings, declining sometimes to even have a taste. The humiliated host may continue to urge the guests to partake, but will hide any signs of feeling insulted if they flat-out refuse his hospitality. In the future the spurned host will think twice before issuing another such invitation.

Sexual attitudes

As with showing anger, **displaying affection** in public is just not done in Laos. The Lao attitude, which might seem "old-fashioned" to Westerners, is to keep a lid on such passions while in public. What to Westerners are innocent displays of affection, a little hug here, a little kiss there, will be perceived by the Lao as ill-concealed lust. This is not to say that the Lao are prudes. They can be quite forward and frank when discussing sexual matters, but any display of affection in public is considered tasteless.

Particularly disturbing to the Lao are incidents, increasingly common in touristed areas, in which foreign couples are caught having sex in a public or semi-public place.

No matter what the foreigners' intentions were, in Lao eyes such behaviour is insulting. The Lao won't see such an act as being the result of two lovers caught up in the moment: dogs copulate outdoors, people do not. Another growing problem is Western tourists coming to Laos and bringing male or female prostitutes from Thailand with them as travelling companions.

Interestingly, while public displays of affection between the sexes are discouraged, Lao friends of the same sex, especially inebriated men, fairly drape themselves around each other. This type of behaviour should not be taken to be homosexual, however. Travellers who have spent some time in Thailand and noted the high number of gays who seem to

be out and about there, will notice that the Lao are more conservative in comparison. Unlike Thailand, the **gay scene** in Laos Is very underground. and while foreign gay couples travelling through Laos will never be hassled or threatened, any behaviour that draws attention to one's gayness is likely to instigate mirth among the Lao.

Sexual relations between an unmarried Lao national and a Westerner are officially illegal in Laos. This is partly due to government fears that a Thai-style sex industry could take root in Laos. In Vientiane especially, a law prohibiting Lao nationals from sharing hotel rooms with foreigners is sometimes enforced. Outside the capital the law seems to be much more lax.

Crime and personal safety

Laos is a relatively safe country for travellers, although certain areas remain off-limits because of banditry and unexploded ordnance left over from decades of warfare. As a visitor, however, you're an obvious target for thieves (who may include your fellow travellers), so keep your wits about you wherever you go.

Carry your passport, traveller's cheques and other valuables in a concealed **money belt** and don't leave anything important lying about in your room, particularly when staying in rural bungalows. A few hotels have safes which you may want to use, although you should keep in mind that you never know who has access to the safe. A **padlock** and chain, or a cable lock, is useful for doors and windows at inexpensive guesthouses and budget hotels and for securing your pack on buses, where you're often separated from your belongings. It's also a good idea to keep a reserve of cash, photocopies of the relevant pages of your passport, insurance details and traveller's cheque receipts separate from the rest of your valuables.

As tranquil as Laos can seem, petty theft and serious crimes do happen throughout the country – even on seemingly deserted country roads. On the whole, petty crime is

more common in **Vientiane** than anywhere else in the country, and although even here incidents are limited, it's best to be on the safe side. Be on your guard in darker streets outside the city centre, and along the river. Motorbike-borne thieves ply the city streets and have been known to snatch bags out of the front basket of other motorbikes that they pass.

If you do have anything stolen, you'll need to get the **police** to write up a report in order to claim on your insurance: bring along a Lao speaker to simplify matters if you can. While police generally keep their distance from foreigners, they may try to exact "fines" from visitors for alleged misdemeanours. With a lot of patience, you should be able to resolve most problems and, if you keep your cool, you may find that you can bargain down such "fines". It helps to have your passport with you at all times – if you don't, police

Drugs

In recent years Laos has seen a steady rise of "drug tourism". **Ganja** (marijuana) is widely available in Laos, although it's illegal to smoke it. Tourists who buy and use ganja risk substantial "fines" if caught by police, who do not need a warrant to search you or your room. As in Thailand, there have been many instances of locals selling foreigners marijuana and then telling the police. In Muang Sing police have even been known to go around the guesthouses in the evening smelling for hemp.

In northern towns, tourists are sometimes approached by **opium** addicts who, in return for cash, offer to take the visitors to a hut or some other private place, where opium pipes will be prepared and smoked. For some it's hard not to have a go – many Westerners feel the romanticism of doing this all but extinct drug is just as appealing as the promise of intoxication. The opium prepared for tourists is often not opium at all, but **morphine**-laden opium ash that has been mixed with painkillers. The resulting "high" is, for many, several hours of nausea and vomiting. While real **opium** is not as addictive as its derivative, heroin, withdrawal symptoms are similarly painful. Visitors caught smoking opium (or even opium ash) are usually fined, and sometimes have to endure a spell in jail, before they're deported.

have greater incentive to ask for money and may even try to bring you to the station. In some instances police may puzzle over your passport for what seems like an awfully long time. Again, such situations are best handled with an ample dose of patience. If your papers are in order, you shouldn't have anything to worry about.

Banditry

With far more serious consequences than petty theft, **banditry** is a possible threat in Laos, although you can greatly reduce the risks by sticking to the main highways. In the past, buses, motorcyclists and private vehicles on certain highways have been held up, their passengers robbed and, in some instances, killed. Because information in Laos is tightly controlled, no one knows exactly if rumoured bandit attacks have actually occurred or if other incidents have happened and gone unreported. Therefore it's always good to ask at a Western embassy in Vientiane for any **travel advisories** before heading out into remote regions.

Security has improved greatly along **Route 13** between Kasi and Louang Phabang since the mid-1990s, when this section of the highway was considered completely unsafe. The insurgent/bandit group generally thought to be responsible for the attacks in this area, the **Chao Fa**, is still active in parts of Xiang Khouang province (see p.189). While bus drivers working this route maintain that the area is now free of such incidents and have stopped carrying guns, as recently as 2004 two European tourists were killed, along with six Lao, when a shadowy group attacked a bus on Route 13 just north of Vang Viang. Since punitive attacks on nearby Hmong villages by the Lao army in 2004 and 2005, the road is said to have been quiet. However, the Lao penchant for tightly controlling the news means that there is a chance that there have been unreported incidents. During 2003 there were also attacks against buses on **Route 7** between Phou Khoun and Phonsavan. Before travelling either Routes 13 or 7 it is a good idea to be aware of the potential risks, and perhaps contact your embassy for advice – keeping in mind of course that embassies tend to be overly cautious. Locally based expats in both Vientiane and Louang Phabang will often have the best idea of whether or not the routes are safe to travel.

Unexploded ordnance

The **Second Indochina War** left Laos with the dubious distinction of being the most heavily bombed country per capita in the history of warfare. The areas of the country most affected by aerial bombing are along the border of Vietnam – especially in southern Laos where the border runs parallel to the former Ho Chi Minh Trail; also heavily targeted was Xiang Khouang province in the northeast. Other provinces, far from the border with Vietnam, were the site of land battles in which both sides lobbed artillery and mortar shells at each other. A fair quantity of this ordnance did not explode.

These dangerous relics of the war, known as **UXO** (unexploded ordnance), have been the focus of disposal teams since the 1980s. According to the Lao government, most areas that tourists are likely to visit have been swept clean of UXO. That said, it always pays to be cautious when in rural areas or when trekking. UXO unearthed during road construction can be pushed onto the shoulder, where it becomes overgrown with weeds and forgotten. Disposal experts say that fast-growing bamboo has been known to unearth UXO, lifting it aloft as the stalk grows and then letting it fall onto a trail that was previously clean. Consequently, it's best to stay on trails and beware any odd-looking metallic objects that you may come across. Picking something up for closer inspection (or giving it a kick to turn it over) can be suicidal. When taking a toilet break during long-distance bus journeys, it's not a good idea to penetrate too deeply into the bush looking for privacy.

In some southern towns locals use old bombs, bomb cases, mortar shells etc for a variety of functions, from demarcating plots of land to decorating. These will have been checked by UXO disposal experts, and should pose no threat. Still, it pays to have a healthy respect for all UXO. After all, these are weapons that were designed to kill or maim.

Alternative therapies

During their period of colonization, the French regarded traditional Lao therapies as quaint and amusing, and this attitude was passed on to the Lao elite who studied in France. In an essay about traditional Lao medicine written in the 1950s by a former Minister of Health, the traditional Lao doctor is repeatedly referred to as "the quack". But renewed interest, partially fuelled by a similar rekindling of enthusiasm in neighbouring China, has seen a resurgence of confidence in traditional techniques.

Recently, a government-sponsored traditional medicine **hospital** opened on the outskirts of Vientiane. Known as the *hong maw pin pua duay ya pheun meuang* in Lao, the founding of this institution is a sign that the Lao are once again taking their traditional healing techniques seriously. Tourism has likewise been partially responsible for renewed interest in traditional massage and herbal sauna, though these alternative therapies are limited to larger towns and cities. Besides the obvious physical benefits the Lao massage and sauna afford the recipient, administering massage and sauna to others is believed to bring spiritual merit to those who perform the labour, making Lao massage and sauna a "win-win" proposition for all involved.

Lao massage

Lao massage owes more to **Chinese** than to Thai schools, utilizing medicated balms and salves which are rubbed into the skin. Muscles are kneaded and joints are flexed while a warm compress of steeped herbs is applied to the area being treated. Besides massage, Lao doctors may utilize other "exotic" treatments that have been borrowed from neighbouring countries. One decidedly Chinese therapy that is sometimes employed in Laos is **acupuncture** (*fang khem*), in which long, thin needles are inserted into special points that correspond to specific organs or parts of the body. Another imported practice is the application of **suction cups** (*kaew dut*), a remedy

Traditional remedies

In the not-too-distant past Westerners believed that malaria was caused by noxious vapours (indeed *malaria* is Latin for "bad air"). In a similar vein the Lao believed that many illnesses were the result of an offended spirit out to get revenge, or possibly caused by the spell of a hired black magician. To this day many uneducated Lao (the vast majority of the population) still adhere to these beliefs and will seek out **traditional remedies**, often in addition to Western medicines, to cure stricken family members.

Before an illness can be treated it must be **diagnosed**, and the Lao employ an egg as a tool to this end. The egg is rolled along the affected part of the body and then broken, and its yolk examined to determine the source of the illness. If it is determined that the illness was caused by an offended spirit, a spirit-doctor will visit the patient, make the appropriate offerings and then call out the names of spirits until the culprit is found. After a discussion with the family of the patient to ascertain what action offended the spirit in the first place, an animal, usually a chicken, is sacrificed and the placated spirit will loosen its grip on the patient. If it is determined that the patient has been stricken by a foreign object (usually a chicken bone or piece of water buffalo skin) that has been projected into the body by a black magician, a doctor will exorcise the object from the victim using deft fingers to pull the object directly from the skin. In some cases incantations and smoke are used to make the victim vomit and expel the foreign object.

popular in neighbouring Cambodia. Small glass jars are briefly heated with a flame and applied to bare skin; air within the cup contracts as it cools, drawing blood under the skin into the mouth of the cup. Theoretically, toxins within the bloodstream are in this way brought to the surface of the skin.

Lao herbal saunas

Before getting a massage, many Lao opt for some time in the **herbal sauna**. Sometimes found in the grounds of monasteries, the setup usually consists of a rustic wooden shack divided into separate rooms for men and women; beneath the shack a drum of water sits on a wood fire. Medicinal herbs boiling in the drum release their juices into the water and the resulting steam is carried up into the rooms. The temperature inside is normally quite high and bathers should spend only a few minutes at a time in the sauna, taking frequent breaks to cool off by lounging outside and sipping herbal tea to replace water that the body so profusely sweats out. The **recipes** of both the saunas and teas are jealously guarded but are known to contain such herbal additives as carambola, tamarind, eucalyptus and citrus leaves.

The basi

Visitors to Laos will notice that many lowland Lao wear one or more bracelets of white thread around their wrists. This is a sign that the wearer has recently taken part in a **basi**, the quintessential Lao ceremony of **animist** bent, which is performed throughout the year. Also known as *sukhuan*, the ceremony is supposed to reunite the body's multiple souls, which are thought to succumb to wanderlust and depart from the body every now and again. *Basi* ceremonies are held during Lao New Year as well as being a part of weddings, births and farewell parties. While not believed to be medicinal per se, the *basi* is sometimes performed in addition to other therapies to remedy an affliction.

Before the ceremony can be performed, an auspicious time must be gleaned from an astrologer, and a *phakhuan* – made from rolled banana leaves and resembling a miniature Christmas tree – must be prepared. The *phakhuan* is decorated with marigolds and other flowers, and draped with white threads. This arrangement sits in a silver bowl filled with husked rice, which is placed in the centre of a mat laid out on the floor. Participants sit in a circle around the *phakhuan* and offerings of food and liquor are placed near it. These are used to entice the absent souls to return. An animist **priest**, known as a *maw phawn* or "wish-doctor", presides over the ceremony, inviting the souls to return with a mixture of Pali and Lao chants. The white threads that are draped over the *phakhuan* are then removed and tied around the wrists of the participants while blessings are invoked. During the *basi* ceremony performed at Lao New Year, each thread tied around the wrist may be accompanied by a shot of rice liquor, and this sometimes leads to an impromptu *lam wong*, or "circle dance", performed by euphoric participants.

Sports and outdoor adventure

Laos is one of the better outdoor-adventure destinations in Southeast Asia: there are trekking opportunities, cave systems to be explored and white-water rivers to be rafted. With the emergence of a number of specialized travel companies offering inexpensive, organized, adventure tours in previously remote reaches, it's now easier than ever to experience the wild side of Laos.

Laos is wild country. Over seventy percent of it comprises high terrain, with chains of **mountains** reaching heights of over 2800m running its entire length. Covering many of these ranges are expanses of virgin **rainforest**. And from these highlands run steep, narrow valleys through which **rivers** rush down from the mountain heights to join the "Mother of Waters", the mighty Mekong River, which flows the entire length of the country.

Trekking

The easiest and most popular adventure sport in Laos is **trekking**, in the northern provinces. Although trekking in Laos has yet to reach the stage of being an industry as in Nepal or Thailand, there are still rich opportunities for both hiking and multi-day treks.

The **far north** has mountain scenery, forest areas and colourful ethnic hill tribes living in traditional villages. Although there was an initial mad rush in the late Nineties to "see Laos before it's spoiled", the truth is that there has never been a better time to come to Laos to experience the tribal cultures of the north. There are excellent **tourist facilities** available in many northern towns, and **Guide Service Offices** are gradually being opened throughout the north, to support tourists who want to take part in guided treks that are both environmentally friendly and have a low impact on the local peoples.

For visitors interested in hill tribes and **organized trekking**, the best towns to head for are Louang Namtha, Muang Sing, Louang Phabang and Vang Viang, all of which have developed programmes for travellers wanting to make a series of day-trips based out of town or take part in multi-day treks involving camping and village stays. If you want to take a more independent, "do-it-yourself" approach, other towns highly suitable for **independent trekking** opportunities using self-hired local guides include Muang Long, Xiang Kok, Houayxai, Vieng Phoukha, Muang Khoua and Nong Khiaw, all of which have guesthouses and are close to tribal areas.

NBCAs and eco-tours

A handful of Lao companies organize **eco-tours** to wilderness areas featuring rare and exotic flora and fauna. Here, nature lovers and birdwatchers will find some of the rarest species on the planet and vast forest canopies. Although Laos does not have any national parks in the Western sense,

Traditional sports and pastimes

While the Lao can often be seen glued to the television whenever Thailand broadcasts a sporting event, relatively few people play the usual team sports simply because equipment is prohibitively expensive. The honourable exception is **kataw**. Played with a grapefruit-sized woven wicker ball, *kataw* is thought to have originated in the Malay Archipelago, but is also quite popular in Thailand. *Kataw* is something like a no-hands version of volleyball and is played both with and without a net. The acrobatics involved are simply astounding. Games are played just about anywhere, but are commonly seen in schoolyards or in monastery grounds.

As with the rest of Southeast Asia, **cockfighting** is a celebrated diversion in Laos. This should come as no surprise, as the blood sport originated in this region. **Betting** is, of course, the whole point. Cockfights take place on Sundays and the local cockpit can usually be found by wandering around and listening for the exuberant cheers of the spectators. Unlike in some Southeast Asian countries, knives are not attached to the rooster's legs in Laos, which means that cockfights last much longer and the birds don't usually die in the ring.

Another sport that relies on a wager to sharpen excitement is **rhinoceros beetle fighting**. Although it is difficult to say just how far back the tradition of beetle fighting goes, it is known to be popular among ethnic Tai peoples from the Shan States to northern Vietnam. The walnut-sized beetles hiss alarmingly when angered and it doesn't require much goading to get them to do battle. Pincer-like horns are used by the beetles to seize and lift an opponent, and the fight is considered finished when one of the two beetles breaks and runs. The fighting season is during the rains when the insects breed. They are sometimes peddled in markets tethered to pieces of sugar-cane.

since 1993 the government has established twenty **National Biodiversity Conservation Areas (NBCAs)**, many still with villagers and hill tribes living within their boundaries. Unfortunately, though NBCA status means government recognition of their biodiversity, this status has not conferred any real protection (see p.355).

The NBCAs are scattered around the country, often in remote border areas without roads. While many of the parks are inaccessible short of mounting a professional expedition, several have been developed for eco-tourism and have **visitor centres** and **guided walks**. The best developed NBCAs for tourists are Phou Khao Khouay (see p.111), Louang Namtha (see p.214) and Phou Hin Poun (see p.252), all of which can be reached by road.

Water sports

While most river-journey enthusiasts are satisfied with a slow boat down the Mekong between Houayxai and Louang Phabang, many opportunities exist for exploring Laos's faster waterways. Several companies offer **white-water rafting** trips out of Louang Phabang on a number of northern rivers, including the Nam Ou, the Nam Xuang and the Nam Ming.

Even more popular are **river-kayaking** adventures ranging from easy day-trips for beginners to multi-day adventures down rivers with grade 5 rapids. Professional guided kayaking tours are currently operated on a regular basis on eight northern rivers as well as the Ang Nam Ngum Reservoir near the capital. The best bases for kayaking tours are Vientiane, Vang Viang, Louang Phabang and Louang Namtha. Another fantastic region for kayaking is the Khammouane Limestone NBCA (see p.252). Among other scenic wonders, this NBCA features a seven-kilometre-long natural river-tunnel through the heart of a mountain, and is becoming popular for organized tours out of Vientiane.

Caves and rock-climbing

With its great forests of limestone karst scenery receding into the distance like an image in a Chinese scroll painting, Laos is a great destination for cave exploring, spelunking and rock-climbing. Prime areas for limestone karst scenery in Laos include Vang Viang, Kasi, Thakhet and Viang Xai. For most tourists, **cave exploring** is limited to climbing up to and wandering around in caves that are fairly touristy and have clearly defined pathways. Serious spelunkers can find vast cave and tunnel systems to explore in the Khammouane Limestone NBCA and the Hin Nam No NBCA, but should seek local permission before launching any major expeditions as many caves have yet to have archeological surveys done. With so many awesome unclimbed and unnamed peaks, **rock-climbing** is one sport that seems to have a huge future in Laos. At present the sport is still in its infancy with the country's first bolted cliff face, featuring sixteen routes graded 5b to 8c, recently opened in Vang Viang, but new routes should follow soon.

Mountain biking

With some of the best untamed scenery in Southeast Asia, many unpaved roads, and little traffic, Laos is becoming a very hot destination for cross-country **mountain-bike touring**. A lot of independent travellers do self-organized mountain-bike touring in northern Laos, bringing their bikes with them from home. **Route 13** from Louang Phabang to Vientiane seems to be the most popular route, but be warned that despite the beautiful scenery, the route is also extremely mountainous, crossing several large ranges before reaching the Vientiane Plain. There are much better routes in **Houa Phan** and **Xiang Khouang** provinces where you'll find fantastic landscapes, plenty of remote villages and paved roads with very few vehicles on them.

It's a good idea to plan carefully. What appear to be very short distances on the map can often take many hours, even in a vehicle. One good thing about bicycle touring in Laos is that should things get too difficult, you can always flag down a passing *sawngthaew* and throw the bike on the roof. Another alternative is to join an **organized cycling tour**, of which there are many.

The environment and ethical tourism

While tourism has been a boon for the economy, it has potentially disruptive effects environmentally, socially, culturally and economically. The worst example in Laos was the rapid rise of "drug tourism", with many young Westerners coming to the country purely to buy cheap ganja and experiment with opium. Laos is also now established on the backpacker circuit and is experiencing all of the positive and negative effects which this can bring on its fragile culture.

Local issues have been covered throughout this book. If you are concerned about the impact of tourism or environmental matters, get in touch with the organizations listed below.

Contacts

EarthWise Journeys ⓦ www.teleport .com/~earthwyz. American organization promoting environmentally responsible travel.

Partners in Responsible Tourism ⓦ www .pirt.org. An organization of individuals and travel companies promoting responsible tourism to minimize harm to the environment and local cultures. Their website features a "Traveler's Code for Traveling Responsibly".

Tourism Concern ⓦ www.tourismconcern.org .uk. Campaigns for the rights of local people to be consulted in tourism developments affecting their lives, and produces a quarterly magazine of news and articles.

Travelling with children

Travelling through Laos with children can be both challenging and fun. The presence of children helps break the ice with strangers, but it's worth giving some thought as to whether your children – and you – can handle the attention. You'll also need to take precautions in light of Laos's poor sanitation, animals and demanding roads.

Bear in mind that Laos lacks adequate **health-care** facilities, worrisome given that children, especially the very young, are more vulnerable to illness. If children do become sick, keep up their fluid intake so as to avoid dehydration. Remember too that diarrhoea can be dangerous for children: rehydration solutions are vital if your child comes down with it. Rabies is a common problem in Laos, so explain to your children the dangers of playing with animals and consider a rabies shot.

In tourist areas it should be no problem finding food that kids will **eat**, although some children may turn up their noses at Lao food. Before leaving for your trip, it might be an idea to take the kids out for a few sample meals at Thai, Lao or Vietnamese restaurants, to help their taste buds adjust.

You'll also want to plan a more comfortable itinerary than you might if travelling on your own. Laos's bumpy, windy **roads** and the long distances between tourist centres can be tough on younger children, so take shorter bus journeys and consider renting a van. At more expensive hotels, children under 12 can usually stay free of charge in their parents' rooms, while many guesthouses and budget hotels have rooms with double beds or can add an extra cot for a small extra cost.

If you're travelling with babies, you'll have difficulty finding **nappies** (diapers) throughout Laos. For short journeys, you could bring a supply of nappies from home; for longer trips, consider switching over to washables.

For more **advice** on travelling with children in developing countries, consult *Travel with Children* by Maureen Wheeler (Lonely Planet) or the "tips and advice" section of Ⓦwww.nomadtravel.co.uk. For specific advice about children's health issues, contact your doctor, or consult one of the travellers' medical services listed on p.41.

Travellers with disabilities

Laos makes zero provisions for the disabled, so you'll need to be self-reliant. The important thing is to check beforehand with tour companies, hotels and airlines that they can accommodate you specifically. The list below details organizations that can advise you as to which tour operators and airlines are the most reliable.

Public transport will present the biggest challenge: it's difficult to board and cramped inside. In Vientiane and Louang Phabang, wheelchair users may find the uneven sidewalks, which lack ramps, difficult to negotiate. Elsewhere there are no pavements and most of the roads are dirt. Hotels and guesthouses do not have rooms adapted for the needs of the disabled and very few hotels have lifts: the best bet is a ground-floor room.

The best way to alleviate transport difficulties is to take internal flights and hire a private minibus with a driver. You should also consider hiring a local tour guide to accompany you on sightseeing trips – a Lao speaker can facilitate access to temples and museums. Flying an international carrier whose planes are suited to your needs is also helpful. Keep in mind that airline companies can cope better if they are expecting you, with a wheelchair provided at airports and staff primed to help.

When preparing for your trip, it's a good idea to pack spares of any clothing or equipment that might be hard to find. If you use a wheelchair, you should have it serviced before you go and carry a repair kit. If you do not use a wheelchair all the time but your walking capabilities are limited, remember that you are likely to need to cover greater distances while travelling (often over rougher terrain and in hotter temperatures) than you are used to.

Insurance and medication

It's advisable to read your travel **insurance** small print carefully to make sure that people with a pre-existing medical condition are not excluded. A **medical certificate** of your fitness to travel, provided by your doctor, is also extremely useful; some airlines or insurance companies may insist on it. If there's an association representing people with your disability, contact them early in the planning process as they will be able to advise on travel insurance as well as other travel-related issues.

Make sure that you have extra **supplies of medication** – carried with you if you fly – and a prescription including the generic name in case of emergency. As medical facilities in Laos are generally poor, it is unlikely you will be able to find your medication at short notice; indeed you may not be able to find what you need at all. It's a good idea to carry a doctor's letter about your medication prescription with you at all times – particularly when passing through customs

at Lao border checkpoints and any Southeast Asian airports that you might be passing through en route to Laos.

Contacts for travellers with disabilities

The following organizations can provide general advice on arranging your trip (and in a couple of cases may actually be able to book a trip for you), though little by way of specific advice on the country itself.

US and Canada

Access-Able ⓦ www.access-able.com. Online resource for travellers with disabilities.
Directions Unlimited 123 Green Lane, Bedford Hills, NY 10507 ☎ 1-800/533-5343 or 914/241-1700. Tour operator specializing in custom tours for people with disabilities.
Mobility International 451 Broadway, Eugene, OR 97401, voice and TDD ☎ 541/343-1284, ⓦ www.miusa.org. Information and referral services, access guides, tours and exchange programmes.
Society for the Advancement of Travelers with Handicaps (SATH) 347 5th Ave, New York, NY 10016 ☎ 212/447-7284, ⓦ www.sath.org. Non-profit educational organization that has actively represented travellers with disabilities since 1976.

UK and Ireland

Holiday Care Service 2nd floor, Imperial Building, Victoria Rd, Horley, Surrey RH6 7PZ ☎ 0845/124 9971, ⓦ www.holidaycare.org.uk. Provides general travel advice.
Irish Wheelchair Association Blackheath Drive, Clontarf, Dublin 3 ☎ 01/818 6400, ⓦ www.iwa.ie. Useful information provided about travelling abroad with a wheelchair.

Australia and New Zealand

ACROD (Australian Council for Rehabilitation of the Disabled) PO Box 60, Curtin ACT 2605 ☎ 02/6282 4333, ⓦ www.acrod.org.au. Provides lists of travel agencies and tour operators for people with disabilities.
Disabled Persons Assembly 4/173–175 Victoria St, Wellington, New Zealand ☎ 04/801 9100, ⓦ www.dpa.org.nz. Resource centre with lists of travel agencies and tour operators for people with disabilities.

Directory

Bookshops With only 65 percent of the population literate and surveys showing that only four percent of the people are readers, it should come as no surprise that books keep a relatively low profile in Laos. English-language books are expensive in Laos, but the selection is better now than in the past, though still not vast. You'll find a small selection of imported paperbacks and magazines at book stores in Vientiane and Louang Phabang. The best place to buy books on all subjects Lao is Bangkok.

Contraceptives Bring condoms from home rather than relying on those found in Laos.

Better-quality condoms and birth control are available at pharmacies in Thailand.

Departure tax When leaving Laos by air or via the Friendship Bridge, you'll have to pay a departure tax equivalent to US$10, payable in US dollars, Thai baht or kip. Tax is not yet collected at other border points, although officials may attempt to find other ways to "tax" you – levying small fees for arriving or departing during lunch hour, late in the day or on the weekend seem to be the most popular techniques.

Electricity Supplied at 220 volts AC. Two-pin sockets taking plugs with flat prongs

Useful things to bring

An **internal-frame backpack** is probably the easiest way to lug your things around, with a lightweight daypack for day-trips. A few small padlocks help to keep the curious out of your belongings during those long journeys when your pack is on the roof of the bus.

It's important to bring **clothes** that are comfortable for Laos's hot and humid weather; lightweight cotton garments that are loose-fitting are best. Long-sleeved shirts and pants help to ward off sun and bugs; shorts and a swimsuit are also good to bring. Be sure to also include one sweater if you plan to travel in the north, where it's cold from October to February. Sport sandals, with good traction, are a good choice for footwear, given the long rainy season and the many rivers and streams you're bound to encounter. If you're bringing trainers (sneakers), you might also consider bringing flip-flops, which are great for slipping out of during temple tours as well as shared showers at guesthouses. A sarong doubles as a towel and is useful for maintaining your modesty while changing or bathing in rivers. If you plan on doing your own laundry, bring along a length of cord for drying clothes.

For **protection from the sun**, bring sunscreen, sunglasses and a brimmed hat; an umbrella (available locally) acts as a parasol and is a must during the rainy season.

Toiletries are easy to come by in towns, but bring anything out of the ordinary. While you can count on basic medications being available at pharmacies, it's advisable to bring a medical kit (see p.37). **Insect repellent** is a must, and a **mosquito net** is a good idea. If you wear glasses or contact lenses, make sure you bring a spare pair (contact lens users should also bring enough contact lens solution for their trip).

Carry your valuables in a **money belt** or neck purse. **Earplugs** come in handy if you plan on travelling by speedboat. **Photos** of home help to break the ice and are a helpful tool in learning a few words of basic Lao. A few other **essentials** include a torch (flashlight), Swiss army knife, a small towel, a sewing kit, a universal sink plug, eye protection for dusty bus trips, sealable zip-lock plastic bags for keeping things separate in your pack and protecting important documents from getting wet, and a travel alarm clock for those early bus departures. Also bring along photocopies of your passport and a few extra passport-size photos.

are the norm. Many smaller towns, including several provincial capitals, have power for only a few hours in the evening or none at all. Blackouts are not uncommon, so bring a torch. Electrical wiring in budget guesthouses is sometimes an accident waiting to happen. It's advisable to exercise caution when fiddling with light switches and plugging in appliances.

Laundry Most guesthouses and hotels offer a same-day laundry service, and in larger towns a few shops offer laundry service which can be cheaper than what you'll be charged at your accommodation. In either situation, the charge is usually per item. Your clothes will take a beating, so it's best not to entrust prized articles to these services. If you want to wash clothes yourself, you can buy small packets of detergent in many general stores and markets around the country. Hang out your underwear discreetly – women should take particular care, as women's undergarments are believed to have the power to render Buddhist tattoos and amulets powerless.

Measurements Laos follows the metric system.

Photography Louang Phabang and the capital are the best places to stock up on film; elsewhere you never know how long the film has been sitting on the shelf in the heat. Lithium batteries can be difficult to find outside of these cities. Developing film is expensive in Laos and the quality isn't top-notch as shops tend to use their chemicals over and over. You'll have better luck developing film in Thailand; otherwise you might want to wait until you get home – it's always easier to carry film canisters than a bunch of photos anyway. If you use a digital camera, bring as many memory cards as you think you might need, as at the time of writing they were virtually impossible to buy in Laos. If you are running out of space on your memory cards, you may be able to find a cybercafé which can burn your pictures to CD.

Showers Bathing takes a bit of finesse in Laos. Traditional Lao showers, sometimes found in accommodation in rural areas, consist of a large, ceramic jar or a cement tub resembling an oversized bathtub without a drain. Standing next to the tub, you use the plastic scoop provided to sluice water over your body. While it may look tempting on a hot day, don't get into these tubs or try to use them for doing your laundry, as the water has to be used by others. In some towns villagers opt for an even more traditional technique – the river. Men usually bathe in their underwear, women in sarongs.

Tampons Hard to find outside Vientiane's minimarkets, which have a very limited selection. Bring supplies.

Time zone Ignoring daylight saving time abroad, Laos is 7 hours ahead of London, 15 hours ahead of Vancouver, 12 hours ahead of New York, 3 hours behind Sydney and 5 hours behind Auckland.

Toilets Squat toilets are the norm throughout Laos, although almost all hotels and guesthouses have Western-style porcelain thrones. Public toilets are not common in Laos – you'll only find them at airports and some bus stations; at the latter a small fee is usually collected. Carry toilet paper with you – you can buy it in most places. Most squat toilets require manual flushing – you'll find a bucket of water with a scoop floating on the surface for this purpose. In some small, rural villages people tend to take to the woods because of a lack of plumbing. On long road trips this is also a perfectly acceptable way to relieve yourself, and many Lao women usually bring along a sarong (if they're not already wearing one) to lend them a shred of privacy for such occasions. Keep in mind that many parts of Laos have UXO (see p.64), so it's not wise to wade too far into the bush when the bus stops for a bathroom break.

Work Without a prearranged job and work permit, don't count on finding work in Laos. Teaching English is probably the easiest job to land (a TEFL – Teaching English as a Foreign Language – qualification is useful but not essential) although it's hard to make enough money to live on.

Guide

Guide

1

Vientiane and the northwest

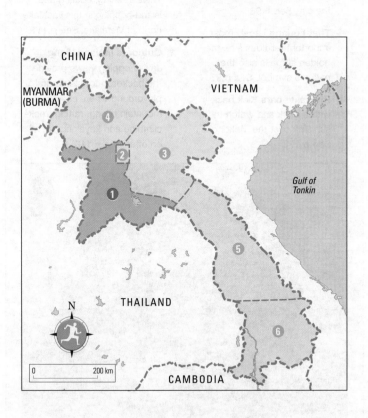

CHAPTER 1 # Highlights

✱ **Lao National Museum** Lao history meets Marx in Vientiane's funky relic of the class struggle. See p.92

✱ **Wat Sisaket** Vientiane's oldest wat, the only temple spared by the invading Siamese in their 1828 sack of the city. See p.93

✱ **That Louang** Laos's most important religious site, the golden stupa is also the national symbol. See p.97

✱ **Riverside bars** Kick back with a drink and watch the sun sink over the Mekong. See p.103

✱ **Phou Khao Khouay NBCA** Laos's most accessible wilderness park, home to elephants and tigers, and just two hours from the capital. See p.111

✱ **Ang Nam Ngum Reservoir** There's fishing, boating and island-hopping in this vast lake north of Vientiane. See p.111

✱ **Outdoors in Vang Viang** Jaw-dropping views provide the backdrop to this natural playground where caving, mountain biking, rafting, rock-climbing and kayaking are all on offer. See p.118

△ Buddha images at Wat Sisaket

Vientiane and the northwest

Hugging a bend of the Mekong River on the Vientiane Plain, **Vientiane** looks more like a rambling collection of numerous villages, dotted with a few grandiose monuments, than a capital city. However, in the mere decade and a half since Laos reopened its doors to foreign visitors, the city has changed with dizzying rapidity. At the beginning of the Nineties, Vientiane wallowed in an economic stupor brought about by a fifteen-year near-ban on free enterprise and a heavy reliance on Soviet aid. But with the collapse of the Soviet Union in 1991, economic restrictions were relaxed; soon afterwards, Vientiane's collection of billboards proclaiming the glories of socialism were outnumbered by advertisements for Pepsi, and the hammer and sickle that had been erected atop the abandoned French cultural centre was removed. Shophouses that had long been padlocked and disused were opened up and transformed into minimarts and video rental shops. Despite these changes, Vientiane is still quaint and easy-going compared to Southeast Asia's other capital cities, and the people have managed to retain their hospitality and sense of humour.

Two days is sufficient to see Vientiane's sights, and if the small-town atmosphere of Vientiane gets too claustrophobic, you'll find several worthwhile excursions in the vicinity of the city. The most popular of the **day-trips** is to Xiang Khouan or the "**Buddha Park**", a Hindu-Buddhist fantasy in ferro-concrete surrounded by raintrees on the banks of the Mekong. North of Vientiane, the **Ang Nam Ngum Reservoir** attracts locals and foreign visitors alike for relaxing weekend retreats, offering hiking and camping and boat trips to many small islands. Off the beaten track and a bit more of an effort to reach is the resort of **Lao Pako**, on the banks of the Nam Ngum River, which offers a rural Lao experience within relatively easy distance of the capital.

Slightly further afield but still within day-tripping range of Vientiane is the laid-back resort town of **Vang Viang**. Set amid spectacular scenery on Route 13, Vang Viang is a popular halfway stop between the capital and Laos's other major tourist city, Louang Phabang, and a major recreational centre in its own right, with hiking, river tubing and cave exploring among the activities on offer. An alternative route to Louang Phabang involves road and river travel through the remote left-bank province of **Xainyabouli**.

VIENTIANE & THE NORTHWEST

N

Vientiane and around

High on the list of any visitor to **VIENTIANE** should be the Buddhist monastery known as **Wat Sisaket**, which offers a couple of hours' diversion, as does **Wat Simuang**, Vientiane's most popular temple and monastery. Another top attraction is **That Louang**, Laos's most important religious building, best viewed at sundown for the effects of the sunset on its golden surface. Aside from temples and stupas, the **museum of Lao art**, housed in the former royal temple of **Haw Pha Kaew**, and the socialist-era **Lao National Museum** are also worth a visit.

As with other urban centres in the region, the majority of Vientiane's merchant class are ethnic Chinese and Vietnamese, whose forefathers emigrated to Laos during the French era. Foreign expatriate workers comprise a significant percentage of the capital's population, a fact which adds a **cosmopolitan** touch to the place and has given rise to a surprisingly wide choice of places to eat.

Some history

Vientiane's history has been a rather turbulent one, as its meagre collection of structures from the past suggests. An old settlement, possibly dating back to the eighth century, Vientiane had been occupied and subsequently abandoned by the Mon and then the Khmer long before the Lao king Sett-hathilat moved his **capital** here from Louang Phabang in 1560. Vientiane is actually pronounced "Wiang Jan" (the modern Romanized spelling is a French transliteration), *wiang* being Lao for a "settlement with a stock-ade", while *jan* means "sandalwood". The wooden ramparts of the "City of Sandalwood" were evidently of little use for repelling invaders, for Vientiane was overrun or occupied several times by the Burmese, Chinese and, most spectacularly, by the **Siamese**. During one punitive raid in 1828, the Siamese levelled the entire city. Lao residents who were unable to escape into the jungle were taken prisoner and resettled in areas where they could be controlled and taxed by the victors. (To this day, there are pockets of ethnic Lao in the Thai provinces surrounding Bangkok, descendants of Lao who survived the force-marched exile into Siam.) For the next four decades, Vientiane was almost completely abandoned. When **French explorers** arrived in 1867, they found the city all but reclaimed by the jungle.

Within a few decades, the French controlled most of what is now Laos, Cambodia and Vietnam. When Vientiane was chosen by the French to be the capital of an administrative division of French Indochina, they rebuilt the city and laid out its system of roads. It is from this period, roughly 1899 to 1945, that the city's crumbling collection of French colonial mansions dates. However, the French presence in Laos was never very strong, and this is reflected in the modest number of old French buildings to be found here compared to the other former French Indochinese capital cities of Saigon, Hanoi and Phnom Penh.

The end of the First Indochina War between France and Vietnam in 1954 saw a flood of **Vietnamese refugees** enter Vientiane from Ho Chi Minh's newly independent Democratic Republic of Vietnam. As North Vietnamese troops began to infiltrate into South Vietnam while simultaneously occupying large areas of northeastern Laos, the United States started pouring massive amounts of unregulated aid into Vientiane, causing widespread corruption among government and military officials. In August 1960, a disgruntled army captain who resented the vast difference in lifestyles between his high-living superiors and his hard-bitten troops staged a successful **coup d'état**. This was soon followed by the Battle of Vientiane in December of that year, in which two Lao factions, one supplied by the US and the other by the USSR, managed to level whole blocks of the city with mortars and artillery.

As the **war in Vietnam** steadily escalated with growing US involvement, Laos was pulled deeper into the conflict, but while the thunder of bombs shook the countryside, the residents of the capital were relatively unaffected. For most of the war, Vientiane was like an island of calm surrounded by violent seas. A steady influx of refugees, shell-shocked villagers from the outer provinces, arrived in the city seeking sanctuary. The population of the capital swelled and rows of squatters' shanties appeared along the tree-lined avenues, contrasting sharply with the Mercedes-Benz automobiles of wartime profiteers.

When author Paul Theroux passed through Vientiane just before the end of the war he found a morally bankrupt kingdom with "baffling pretensions to Frenchness". After the fall of Saigon in 1975, the **Lao communists** suddenly gained power and, with coaching from the Vietnamese, set out to create the Lao People's Democratic Republic. The princes and prostitutes with whom Theroux made acquaintance during his visit either fled or were imprisoned. Undesirables were rounded up and held captive on two small islands in the nearby Ang Nam Ngum Reservoir, one for men and the other for women.

But, perhaps owing to the Lao temperament, revolutionary fervour never reached the extremes seen in China or Cambodia. Still, a large percentage of the population of Vientiane found it necessary to escape across the Mekong and were replaced by immigrants from the former "liberated zone" in north-eastern Laos, further changing Vientiane's ethnic make-up.

The 1980s were a time of quiet stagnation. Soviet aid helped ease the transition to **socialism**, but the majority of Lao with any education were in some form of exile, either "attending seminar" in a re-education camp located in some remote province or squatting in a Thai refugee camp while awaiting resettlement in a third country. Grand plans for progress were announced by the communist government and then promptly forgotten. Not until the collapse of the Soviet Union in 1991 and the suspension of Soviet aid was the government forced to rethink its opinions of capitalism. A number of **economic reforms** were implemented, leading to an explosion of new ventures and businesses.

In the mid-Nineties, the first bridge to span the Mekong River between Laos and Thailand was constructed outside the city. Dubbed the "**Friend-ship Bridge**", it declares the direction from which much of Vientiane's foreign investment now comes; in fact, the look and feel of Vientiane these days is not unlike that of some backward provincial capital in Thailand rushing to modernize. With Laos stretching out a conciliatory hand to its neighbour and former enemy, Thailand, Thai entrepreneurs were soon arriving in Vientiane to scout around for economic potential. Some of the city's precious few French colonial mansions have been restored and are being used as places of business, but scores of venerable old shade trees were cut down in order to widen roads to accommodate an ever-multiplying number of cars and motorbikes. Taking their cue from Thai television, Vientiane's exuberant youth emulate fads and fashions of Japan and the West, filtered through the catholic (some would say none-too-discerning) tastes of Bangkok. Official fears of being infected by Thailand's social ills occasionally see the police setting up road blocks to snare motorcycle-racing teenagers, or closing night-clubs at midnight, all in the name of preserving Lao culture. However, the Lao inability to sustain enthusiasm for anything *baw muan* ("no fun") ensures that crackdowns are short-lived.

Recent years have also seen a trickle of former refugees, sporting new nation-alities, returning to Vientiane to visit long-missed relatives and sniff around for business opportunities. However, any accompanying political reforms that might have been expected have not been forthcoming, and the government still does not tolerate dissent in any form.

Arrival

Whichever way you arrive, there's no need to panic if you don't have Lao kip for your trip into town, as taxi drivers will happily accept Thai baht or Ameri-can dollars. A useful reference point is a humble fountain in the middle of a square known as **Nam Phou** (actually Lao for "fountain"), which marks the heart of **downtown Vientiane**, though grandiose monuments elsewhere may suggest otherwise. Situated in a quarter built by the French, Nam Phou lies at the heart of a cosmopolitan, commercial district populated by Vietnamese, Chinese and a smattering of Indians, as well as Lao. Here, you'll find the city's greatest concentration of accommodation, restaurants and shops catering to visitors.

By air

Wattay International Airport, Vientiane's main airport as well as the terminus for most internal flights, is located on Louang Phabang Avenue, roughly 6km west of downtown Vientiane. Airport facilities include **visas on arrival**, duty-free, exchange services and an upstairs restaurant. The easiest way to get to the city centre is by taxi ($3) – numerous tuk-tuk and car-taxi drivers will greet you as you emerge from the terminal. A cheaper option is to take a shared taxi in the form of a tuk-tuk or jumbo ($1). If money is really tight, just walk a few hundred metres from the terminal out to Louang Phabang Avenue, and hail a sawngthaew coming from the north (5000K), which will drop you off at the main bus station next to the Morning Market in the city centre. The prices above represent what locals pay for these journeys; expect to have to haggle if you want to be charged the correct fare.

Via the Friendship Bridge

Completed in 1994, the **Thai–Lao Friendship Bridge** is the primary land crossing into Laos. The 1240-metre bridge spans the Mekong River at a point 5km west of Nong Khai in Thailand, and 20km east of Vientiane. **Minibuses** (10 baht) shuttle passengers across the bridge, leaving every fifteen to twenty minutes between 8am and 7.30pm. The minibuses stop at Thai immigration control at the base of the bridge, where passengers must clear Thai customs before reboarding and continuing on to Lao immigration on the opposite side of the river. **Motorcycles** may cross the bridge, but you should have the registration papers with you. At the Lao immigration booth, you can get a **visa on arrival**. Nearby facilities include duty-free, an exchange booth and a post office.

Tuk-tuks ($3 to charter) and car-taxis ($5) for the thirty-minute run into Vientiane can be found just beyond Lao immigration. If you have to get into town on the cheap, wait till you have enough people to fill a tuk-tuk and share the expense. The #14 bus to downtown Vientiane runs past the bridge but doesn't always stop, particularly if potential passengers are carrying big packs or a lot of luggage.

By bus

Most buses from the south arrive at Vientiane's compact **main bus station**, next to the Morning Market (Talat Sao) on Khou Viang Road, about 1500m from Nam Phou fountain. From here it's only a short tuk-tuk ride to all the central hotels and guesthouses. Most **buses from the north**, however, arrive at the **Khoua Louang bus stand**, near the Evening Market, about 2km northwest of the city centre. From here, a shared tuk-tuk into the centre costs around 500K. Somewhat typically, other buses from the north may (or may not) stop at the sawngthaew station on Route 13 at the northern edge of town. Either way, the routine is the same, with tuk-tuks providing a cheap shuttle service to your destination.

By boat

Speedboats and slow boats from the north arrive at **Tha Hua Kao Liaw pier**, located on the Mekong River 10km west of the centre of Vientiane. The only way to get to the city centre from here is by tuk-tuk (50,000K). No regular boat traffic arrives in Vientiane from points south.

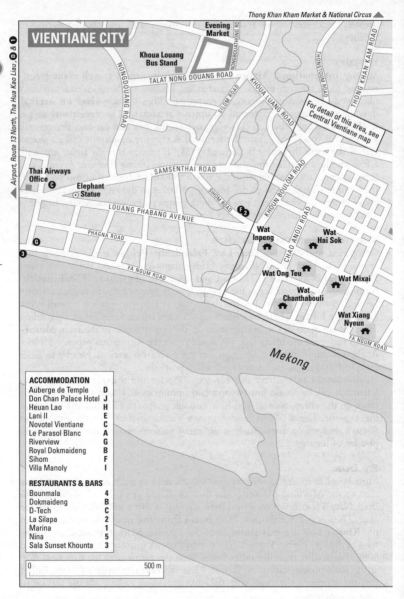

VIENTIANE CITY

ACCOMMODATION
Auberge de Temple	**D**
Don Chan Palace Hotel	**J**
Heuan Lao	**H**
Lani II	**E**
Novotel Vientiane	**C**
Le Parasol Blanc	**A**
Riverview	**G**
Royal Dokmaideng	**B**
Sihom	**F**
Villa Manoly	**I**

RESTAURANTS & BARS
Bounmala	**4**
Dokmaideng	**B**
D-Tech	**C**
La Silapa	**2**
Marina	**1**
Nina	**5**
Sala Sunset Khounta	**3**

0   500 m

Information and city transport

The **Lao National Tourism Administration** (LNTA) operates out of an imposing building on Lane Xang Avenue (Mon–Fri 8am–5pm; ☎021/212248 or 212251), near the Morning Market. Apart from a few free pamphlets, however, the office and staff aren't of much assistance to tourists; you'll get

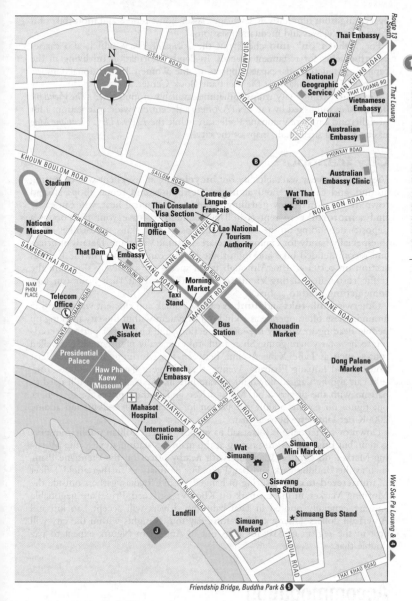

Route 13 South

Thai Louang

Wat Sok Pa Louang & **○**

Friendship Bridge, Buddha Park & **⑤** ▼

better information from talking to other travellers. For maps and reading material on Laos it's better to stock up in Thailand if possible, but in Vientiane itself the best bets are Monument Books and the Vientiane Book Center (see p.99). Phimphone minimarkets and some of the more popular coffee shops, such as the *Scandinavian Bakery* and *Le Croissant D'Or* (both are marked on the Central Vientiane map, pp.90–91), maintain noticeboards, displaying information on everything from film festivals, language classes, house rentals and motorbikes for sale to yoga classes and meditation sessions.

For **"what's on" info** check out the *Vientiane Times*, which also carries advertisements for restaurant specials. In-depth information on living in the capital, geared towards expats, appears in the Women International Group's *Vientiane Guide*, available at the Vientiane Book Center.

There are two free city **maps** sometimes available around town. *The Vientiane Tourist Map*, published by the LNTA, offers a decent citywide orientation, a list of sights and a map of Vientiane Prefecture, while the *LAO-ITEC Vientiane Map* has large- and small-scale maps of the city.

City transport

Vientiane is a very walkable city, but **bicycles** are an excellent way of getting around, and can be rented at many guesthouses and rental shops around town. If you don't fancy pedalling about in the tropical heat, you can easily find a **motorbike** to rent (you'll be required to leave your passport as a deposit), depending on the bike and your bargaining skills; motorbikes come in especially handy for exploring the areas around Vientiane. Details of prices and recommended bike and motorbike outlets can be found in the Listings section on p.105 & 106. Although travel speeds are relatively slow and the traffic rustic, negotiating Vientiane's cluttered roads at rush hour can take some getting used to at first.

Otherwise, **tuk-tuks** and **jumbos** can be a quick and efficient way of getting around. These often operate as a kind of bus system within the city (picking up people heading in vaguely the same direction), and charge per person according to how far you're going. Shared tuk-tuks generally ply frequently travelled routes, such as Lane Xang Avenue between the Morning Market and That Louang, and Louang Phabang Avenue; they charge a flat fee of 2000K. Tuk-tuks can also be flagged down for private hire like taxis, though you'll need to bargain with the drivers a bit. Many drivers inflate their prices for foreigners, but figure on paying 5000K per person for distances of 1–2km, and adding 2000K per kilometre beyond that.

Downtown Vientiane is too small to support a metropolitan public transport system, but **bus routes** originating at the main bus station, next to the Morning Market, do connect Vientiane with nearby places on the Vientiane Plain, such as the Buddha Park and Ban Pako. For destinations further afield, a fleet of **unmetered taxis**, consisting of banged-up old Toyotas, gathers outside the Morning Market, in the car park on Khou Viang Road. Prices are negotiable and are generally quoted in Thai baht, but drivers will accept Lao kip and American dollars. Hiring a driver for a day tour of sights within the city will cost in the region of $10; for trips out to Ang Nam Ngum, expect to pay double that.

Accommodation

Vientiane offers a wide range of tourist **accommodation**, from cheap backpacker dives to four-star hotels like the *Novotel Belvedere*. The majority of the city's seventy hotels and guesthouses are located in the centre around Nam Phou, within the general area formed by Khoun Boulom Road and Lane Xang Avenue. However, other establishments, especially larger hotels, have opened up beyond this area, particularly along Lane Xang Avenue in the vicinity of

Patouxai, as well as on Louang Phabang Avenue, a quick tuk-tuk ride into the centre.

Budget hotels in the central area are generally housed in renovated older buildings. As many of them have a wide range of room types, from cheaper fan singles to expansive triples with air-conditioning and en-suite bathrooms, it's worth asking to see more than one room and always worth haggling, as the price is never really fixed. Prices run from just under $2 for a dorm bed to between $5 and $10 for a single with fan. Note that rooms at any of the handful of budget standouts, such as the *MIC* or *Saybaidee*, tend to fill up very quickly, even in low season. It's not uncommon to see late arrivals desperately pounding the pavement around the central district looking for a reasonably priced budget room, as what's left by that time tends to be towards the top end of the budget range without meriting the price. This being the case, it helps to check in by noon, just after people begin checking out for that day. Guesthouses and budget hotels rarely take advance bookings unless they know you already.

There are much better deals to be found in the **mid-range** establishments. For $15–20 you can buy yourself considerably more comfort, whether it's the luxuries of a standard hotel or the cosiness and hospitality of an upmarket guesthouse with a garden, tucked away in a quiet side street. If you're willing and able to spend the extra money, you can actually get something quite luxurious for $25.

Moving further up the scale, a handful of **expensive hotels** has appeared on the scene, and with the existing upmarket hotels struggling to fill their rooms, many managers are amenable to discounts, especially in low season. Before settling on a price at mid-range and high-end hotels, check whether service charge and tax are included in the quoted price.

Wherever you stay, your case will be helped if you are booking in for a few days and paying in dollars or baht. For **long-stay accommodation** – basically, anything over a few days – you should always push for a discount. Some hotels and guesthouses even have set weekly and monthly rates, designed to accommodate expatriates working in Vientiane on short-term projects, and even those that don't will be open to negotiating a long-term room rate.

Hotels listed under "Central Vientiane" below appear on the map on pp.90–91; for hotels listed under "Outside the centre", see the Vientiane City map on pp.84–85.

Central Vientiane

Anou Hotel Corner of Heng Boun and Chao Anou roads ☎021/213630, ⨎213635, ⊛www .anouhotel.com. Forty unremarkable but perfectly decent rooms in a quiet, convenient location. The lobby is spacious and cool, and all the usual facilities are available. ⑤

Chaleunxay Hotel Khou Viang Rd, west of the Morning Market ☎021/223407, ⨎223529. The location of this large business-oriented hotel on a big busy street leaves much to be desired, but it's a good deal for Vientiane. The fact that it's mostly Thai businessmen staying here rather than falang tourists makes it a better deal than a lot of tourist hostels in the centre.

Day Inn Hotel 059/3 Pangkham Rd, behind the *Lao Hotel Plaza* ☎021/223847, ⨎222984, ⓔdayinn@laotel.com. Located just a few steps away from the bustle of Samsenthai Rd, the *Day Inn* offers light, airy rooms fitted out with rattan furniture, potted plants and a huge TV. Well run, it combines all the mod cons with a real Fifties ambience. One of the few hotels in the city with a bit of style and attitude, and excellent value. ⑥

Douang Deuane 6 Nokeo Koummane Rd ☎021/222301, ⨎222300. The rooms are fairly standard for the price, but the smart, efficient staff and the location near the Mekong help make this a worthy option, though the windowless first-floor rooms are best avoided. Motorbike and bicycle rental, as well as airport pick-up. ⑤

Haysoke I 083/1–2 Heng Boun St ☎021/219711, ⨎219755, ⊛haysok.laopdr.com. Chinese-run place with no-nonsense, good-value, fairly priced rooms. ④

Hua Guo 359 Samsenthai Rd, opposite the *PVO* and Boualian Travel. Singles and doubles with a/c, phone, hot water and satellite TV, for hostel prices. **❸**

Lane Xang Fa Ngum Rd ☎021/214102, ℻214108. Once Laos's premier hotel, this place has a retro Fifties feel, with a kidney-shaped pool, and spacious grounds lush with tropical foliage and a tiki torch or two. The rooms are large and have bathrooms decked out with heavy porcelain and chrome fixtures of another era. Facilities include tennis courts, snooker parlour and a putting green. The only drawback is noise on weekends, when the hotel is a popular venue for wedding receptions. Otherwise, tremendously good value. **❺**

Lani I Setthathilat Rd, opposite Wat Ong Teu ☎021/216103, ℗www.lanigh.laotel.com. Supremely pleasant accommodation in a centrally located house, decorated with antiques and handicrafts, with the added attraction of a terrace dining area. All twelve rooms have a/c, hot water and phone, but the rooms in back are small, gloomy and overpriced. It's worth the extra kip to upgrade to the priciest rooms for the light and space. Reservations recommended. **❻**

Lao Plaza Hotel 63 Samsenthai Rd ☎021/218800, ℻218808, ℗www.laoplazahotel .com. Located in the heart of town, this huge Thai-built hotel is, not surprisingly, popular with Thai package tourists and conventioneers, but it is starting to look a tad worn. All 142 rooms have a/c, hot water, IDD phone, satellite television and refrigerator. Tucked away in the imposing complex are a wide range of facilities: boutique shops, a health club, a swimming pool, a hair salon, a nightclub and an array of restaurants. The hotel has been known to offer substantial discounts. **❻**

Mali Namphou Guesthouse Phangkham Rd, just north of Nam Phou ☎021/215093. The land behind what was once a tailor's tiny shophouse has been converted into two floors of rooms situated around a grassy courtyard. Rooms are smallish but clean. Discounts are sometimes given – just make sure any offer is put down in writing when you check in. **❹**

MIC (Ministry of Information and Culture) Manthatoulat Rd ☎021/212362. This fifteen-room guesthouse is the budget travellers' perennial favourite. The stairwells are a bit nasty, but the rooms, all with attached bathrooms, are reasonably clean. While it doesn't have dorms, backpackers travelling solo tend to link up to split the cost of the three-bed rooms. If it's full you can always try to get in at *Saybaidee* and the *Mixok*, which are both very close by. **❷**

Mixay 039 Nokeo Koummane Rd ☎021/217023. Perhaps the cheapest place in town, with spartan rooms ranging from fan singles to triples with either attached bathrooms or shared facilities. There's hot water and a reception room with TV. Two rooms have balconies overlooking the street. Fills up very quickly. **❶**

Mixok 188 Setthathilat Rd, next door to ITIC Computer ☎021/251606. Backpacker hostel similar to the *Mixay*, with singles, doubles, triples, and dorms with shared facilities. Rock-bottom prices and a terrific location on the city's prettiest street. **❶**

Orchid Guesthouse 33 Fa Ngum Rd ☎021/252825, ℻021/216588. Given the location right on the main restaurant strip and facing the Mekong, the prices here are extremely reasonable. One of the few places in its price bracket with a river view. **❹**

Praseuth 312 Samsenthai Rd ☎021/217932. Old and run-down, this backpacker establishment offers very basic rooms with shared facilities. The a/c rooms cost only $1 more than those with a fan. A last-resort option. **❸**

Santisouk 77/79 Nokeo Koummane Rd ☎021/215303. Situated above the *Santisouk Restaurant*, with nine a/c rooms and an upstairs balcony. It's run-down and certainly no great shakes, but is well known on the backpacker circuit. **❷**

Saybaidee Setthathilat Rd. One of the top backpacker options and in the same class as *Mixok* and *Mixay*. Very low prices and a great location mean it fills up very quickly. **❷**

Settha Palace Hotel 6 Pangkham Rd ☎021/217581, ℻217583, ℗www .setthapalace.com. Until recently, Vientiane was the only Southeast Asian capital without a historic colonial-era hotel. This palatial 1932 building is filled with French period furniture, but the hotel's 29 rooms have all the mod cons, including mini-bar and safe. Beautiful colonial architecture, period furnishings and landscaped gardens. The published rate is around $200 for a double, though discounts may be available. **❽**

Sihom Sihom Rd, along the dirt alley to the west of *La Silapa* restaurant ☎021/214562. Eleven tastefully decorated rooms fitted out with rattan double beds, a/c, refrigerator and satellite TV. The a/c rooms are only $1 more than those with a fan. Particularly recommended for couples travelling on a budget. **❷**

Syri Saigon Rd ☎021/212682, ℻217252. A large house on a quiet lane in the Chao Anou residential district, with spacious double and triple a/c rooms and a nice balcony. Motorbikes and bikes for rent. **❹**

Tai-Pan 2–12 François Nginn Rd, near the Mekong ☎021/216906–9. Still Vientiane's best-value small business hotel. Rooms, and the array of suites, come with all mod cons. There's also a business centre with Internet access, sauna and fitness room. ❹

Thawee 64 Du Puits Rd ☎021/217903, ☏251609. Comfortable, well-decorated rooms for less than a lot of the older, run-down places charge. Fan rooms are half the a/c room price. When there's a lull in business they drop their "high season" price by thirty percent, making it about the best deal in town. Because it's good value it's often full, so be sure to book in advance. ❹

Vannasinh 51 Phnom Penh Rd, near Chao Anou Rd ☎021/218707, ☏222020. Very well-known backpacker place with fan doubles and more spacious a/c doubles, all en suite. Some of the cheaper fan rooms are cramped, despite the high ceilings. Relative to the competition, such as the *Vayakorn*, it's no longer as good a deal as it once was. ❹

🏃 **Vayakorn Guesthouse** Nokeo Koummane Rd, just opposite Carol Cassidy Lao Textiles ☎021/214911. One of the best new guesthouses to open up in a long time, *Vayakorn* goes above and beyond for cleanliness and efficiency. All rooms have satellite TV and en-suite bathroom, and are decorated with more attention to detail than is usual for rooms in this bracket. Good value. ❸

Outside the centre

Auberge de Temple Sikhotabong Rd ☎021/214844, ☏214844. Down a quiet lane off Louang Phabang Ave, this French-owned guesthouse has eight attractively decorated rooms, some with baths. It's west of the city centre, but close to a slew of casual sunset restaurants and bars. ❹

Don Chan Palace Hotel Fa Ngum Rd ☎021/244288, ☏244111, ⊛www .donchanpalacelaopdr.com. On reclaimed land on a sandbar in the middle of the Mekong, this massive new eleven-storey hotel is perhaps the beginning of the end of Vientiane's reign as Southeast Asia's most low-rise capital, and is the tallest building in Laos at the time of writing. The rooms have the best views in town, but it remains to be seen how long it takes before the gloss of the facade starts to fade. ❼

Heuan Lao Off Samsenthai Rd, near Wat Simuang ☎021/216258, ☏216258. This friendly upmarket guesthouse is located on a quiet lane opposite a park and offers singles, doubles and triples, all en suite. ❹

Lani II Off Sailom Rd, near Lane Xang Ave ☎021/213022, ☏215639. Tucked away on a quiet lane off Sailom Rd, the Lani II has all the mellow atmosphere of the *Lani I* (see opposite) for slightly less money. The veranda, complete with wicker furniture, makes a great spot for a lazy breakfast. Accommodation consists of seven tastefully decorated a/c singles and doubles, the more expensive sporting en-suite bathrooms with hot water. Although not so well located as its sister establishment, it's only a short walk from the town centre. ❺

Le Parasol Blanc Sibounheuang Rd ☎021/215090 or 216091, ☏222290. Quiet hotel set in a leafy compound just north of Patouxai and popular with French tourists. A swimming pool and a good restaurant serving French, Lao and Thai food, with an outdoor dining area, make this a fine place to relax. Some of the rooms are a bit too dark, but all is forgiven after morning coffee under the vines in the garden. ❻

Novotel Belvedere Vientiane Samsenthai Rd ☎021/213570–1, ☏213572–3, ⊛www.novotel .com. Although quite pokey for a *Novotel*, it's still the best of the modern hotels in Vientiane, with a wide array of facilities, including a pool, 24hr business centre with Internet access, airport reservation desk, French restaurant and tennis courts. If that's not enough, try the beer garden, bar, sauna, snooker hall, bookstore or disco – to name a few of the other amenities – and be sure to try out the excellent Sunday brunch as well. All the two hundred-plus rooms come with WiFi, minibar, a/c and satellite TV. If you really want to splash out, there's a range of suites costing up to $650. ❾

Riverview Corner of Fa Ngum and Sithan Nua roads ☎021/216231, ☏216232. Located a few kilometres west of the town centre in the middle of the strip of riverside bars, this Thai-owned hotel is in much better shape than the run-down exterior suggests. Spacious and quiet, the rooms have a/c, hot water and phones. An extra $10 secures a room with a view of the Mekong. ❺

Royal Dokmaideng Lane Xang Ave, near Patouxai ☎021/214455, ☏214454, ⊛www .dokmaidenghotel.laopdr.com. Commonly known as the "Royal Hotel", this five-storey three-star hotel is a good option, particularly for business travellers. There's a business centre with Net access and a herbal sauna and nightclub for winding down. ❻

Villa Manoly Ban Simuang, next to Honour International School and around the corner from Wat Simuang ☎ & ☏021/218907, ✉manoly20@ hotmail.com. Indeed a villa and an attractive place too, with a pleasant upstairs terrace and spacious grounds. The singles and doubles all have high ceilings and en-suite hot showers. Just a short walk from the river, it also has its own swimming pool. ❺

The City

Three main streets run parallel to the river to form the backbone of the city centre, cutting across narrower streets to form an easily deciphered grid. Tree-lined **Setthathilat Road**, just south of Nam Phou, is unarguably the city's most scenic thoroughfare, particularly the west end, with its four monasteries. Further north

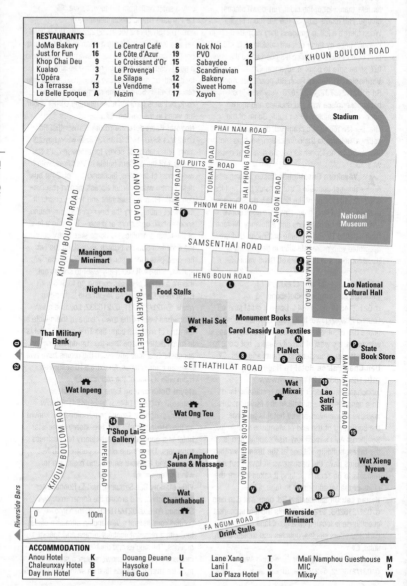

RESTAURANTS

JoMa Bakery	11	Le Central Café	8	Nok Noi	18
Just for Fun	16	Le Côte d'Azur	19	PVO	2
Khop Chai Deu	9	Le Croissant d'Or	15	Sabaydee	10
Kualao	3	Le Provençal	5	Scandinavian	
L'Opéra	7	Le Silapa	12	Bakery	6
La Terrasse	13	Le Vendôme	14	Sweet Home	4
Le Belle Epoque	A	Nazim	17	Xayoh	1

ACCOMMODATION

Anou Hotel	K	Douang Deuane	U	Lane Xang	T	Mali Namphou Guesthouse	M
Chaleunxay Hotel	B	Haysoke I	L	Lani I	O	MIC	P
Day Inn Hotel	E	Hua Guo	I	Lao Plaza Hotel	H	Mixay	W

runs **Samsenthai Road**, Vientiane's principal commercial district and site of the massive *Lao Plaza Hotel*, as well as the **Lao National Museum**, an anachronistic hangover from the days of banner-hoisting socialism. **Fa Ngum Road**, fronting the river, has recently lost some of its behemoth rain trees to the renovation work that was intended to spruce up the riverfront area. A row of refreshment stands on the bank of the river are favoured vantage points for viewing sunsets.

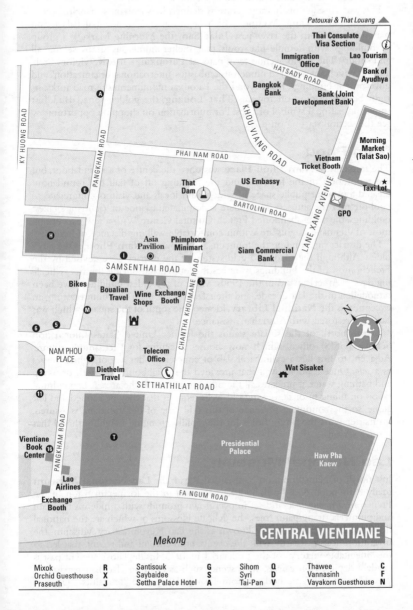

CENTRAL VIENTIANE

Mixok	R	Santisouk	G	Sihom	Q	Thawee	C
Orchid Guesthouse	X	Saybaidee	S	Syri	D	Vannasinh	F
Praseuth	J	Settha Palace Hotel	A	Tai-Pan	V	Vayakorn Guesthouse	N

Fa Ngum Road follows the river as it bends southeast and skirts behind the Presidential Palace. The palace is off-limits to visitors, but the **Haw Pha Kaew**, which occupies the western corner of the palace compound, has been converted into a museum, housing the largest collection of Lao art and antiquities in the country. Roughly opposite the Haw Pha Kaew, across Setthathilat Road, stands **Wat Sisaket**, a picturesque Buddhist monastery containing what is thought to be the oldest structure in Vientiane.

The eastern edge of the city centre is defined by Vientiane's principal thoroughfare, **Lane Xang Avenue**, which begins at the Presidential Palace and marches away from the river past **Talat Sao** (the Morning Market), a group of buildings with temple-like roofs that shelter numerous shops selling all and sundry. The broad avenue terminates at **Patouxai**, a massive victory arch, around which are scattered numerous embassies, international organizations and government buildings. Just beyond the Patouxai monument, the road forks, its right branch leading off towards **That Louang**, the golden-spired Buddhist stupa and national symbol of Laos. For information on shopping opportunities, see the section starting on p.98.

Nam Phou

The fountain of **Nam Phou Place** was once the centre of a roundabout, but the renovation of the fountain and the blocking off of half the roundabout created a pleasant public space in which both locals and visitors congregate to cool off after the sun sets. The square is dominated by one of Vientiane's tallest buildings, the semi-abandoned French Cultural Centre. With a few exceptions, most of Vientiane's sights are within comfortable walking distance of here.

The district surrounding the fountain, also known as **Nam Phou**, is the city's oldest. Although the roads and grid system of the district were devised by the French, most of the buildings were hastily constructed during the free-wheeling days of American aid in the 1950s. Many of the oldest buildings have been remodelled in the last decade, and their facades are plain and uninteresting; an exception is the **National Library**, located due south of the square, which was carefully restored with Australian assistance.

To the north of the square stands the former United States Information Service (USIS) office, which now houses a centre for Vietnamese culture. Adjacent to this lies a cylindrical slab of concrete under a roof, which serves as a *sala*. Once a public well that provided the neighbourhood with drinking and bathing water, it predates all the other structures in the area. A Lao cultural taboo on filling in or destroying old wells requires that they be capped and left alone, so the continued presence of this odd relic of old Vientiane is assured, no matter what the future holds for the rapidly changing neighbourhood that it once served.

Lao National Museum

Just north of Nam Phou, on Samsenthai Road, the **Lao National Museum** (daily 8am–noon & 1–4pm; 5000K) is housed in the former mansion of the French *résident supérieur* and set in overgrown grounds with a hideous fountain and plumeria (frangipani) trees, the delicate blossoms of which are the national flower of Laos. Until recently known as the Lao Revolutionary Museum, the institution deals primarily with the events, both ancient and recent, that led to the "inevitable victory" of the proletariat in 1975. Inside, Laos's ancient past is crudely depicted on canvas, with scenes such as crimson-clad Lao patriots of yore liberating the motherland from Thai and Burmese "feudalists". Upstairs there are more crude oils: "French colonialists" are depicted as hair-faced ogres bullwhipping tightly trussed Lao villagers or tossing Lao tots down a well. Black-and-white **photographs** take over to tell the story of the struggle against "the Japanese fascists" and "American imperialists". Most of the best artefacts on display, including a wonderfully detailed **Khmer sculpture of Ganesh** and a bronze frog-drum, possibly used in ancient rain-making rituals, didn't fit neatly into the official socialist story line, and were, until recently, very neglected.

Setthathilat Road

Running parallel to and one block south of Samsenthai Road is **Setthathilat Road**, with its shady trees and monasteries. Not all of the monasteries are particularly deserving of attention, however. If time is limited, the four at the street's western end – wats Ong Teu, Mixai, Inpeng and Hai Sok – can be skipped in favour of **Wat Sisaket** and **Wat Simuang** at the eastern end.

Wat Sisaket

East of Nam Phou, on Setthathilat Road, **Wat Sisaket** (daily 8am–noon & 1–4pm; 2000K) is the oldest wat in Vientiane. Constructed by King Anouvong (Chao Anou) in 1818, the monastery was the site of a ceremony in which Lao lords and nobles swore an oath of loyalty to the king. During the 1828 sack

---

The Lao wat

The **wat**, or Buddhist **monastery**, is the centrepiece of most villages populated by ethnic Lao. A contingent of monks and novices lives in each wat, providing the laypeople with an outlet for **merit-making** (see p.340). The wat also serves as a hub for social gatherings and, during annual festivals and Buddhist holy days, a venue for entertainment.

Sometimes referred to as a "temple" in English, a wat is actually composed of a number of religious and secular structures, some of which could also be described as a temple. The **sim** is usually the grandest structure in the monastery grounds, as it houses the monastery's principal Buddha images, as well as being the place where monks are ordained. The *that*, or **stupa**, is generally a pyramid or bell-shaped structure which contains holy relics, usually a cache of small Buddhas. Occasionally, a *that* will be the reputed repository of a splinter of bone belonging to the historic Buddha himself, while miniature stupas, or *that kaduk*, contain the ashes of deceased adherents. The *haw tai* is a solid structure, usually raised high off the ground, for storing palm-leaf manuscripts, and *kuti* are monks' quarters. Because the latter two buildings are not considered as important as other religious structures in the monastery grounds, they are not as frequently restored, and are thus most likely to exude that "timeless Asia" charm. Minor buildings sometimes found at a wat include a bell tower and a **sala**, or open-air pavilion. Many monasteries also have a venerable specimen of a bodhi (*Ficus religiosa*), a wonderfully shady tree of spade-shaped leaves that is said to have sheltered the Buddha while he meditated his way to enlightenment.

Because the wat and resident monks depend on adherents for support, the extravagance of a monastery's **decoration** is directly related to the amount of cash flow in the host village or town. In poor villages, the wat may consist of just a *sim*, which will be a large but simple hut-like structure, raised on stilts without any ornamentation. The only clue to the outsider that this is a monastery will be the freshly laundered monks' robes hanging out to dry alongside a piece of junk metal or war scrap, such as an old artillery-shell casing, which when struck serves as a bell to wake the monks or call them to assemble.

of Vientiane by the Siamese, this was the only monastery not put to the torch and, once the smoke had cleared, the Siamese brought the surviving Lao nobility here and made them swear another oath of loyalty, this time to their new overlords. Later, in 1893, the whole ceremony was repeated again at this very same wat before new masters – the French.

Surrounded by a tile-roofed cloister, the *sim* contains some charming **murals** similar in style to those found at Bangkok's Wat Phra Kaew. The murals, together with the niches in the upper walls containing small Buddha images, and the ornate ceiling, are best taken in while kneeling on the floor (taking care not to point your feet towards the altar – see p.61 for more on etiquette). The Buddha images on the altar are not particularly notable, but a splendidly ornate *hao thian*, or candle holder, of carved wood situated before the altar is an example of nineteenth-century Lao woodcarving at its best.

Outside, the interior walls of the **cloister** echo those of the *sim*, with countless niches from which peer diminutive Buddhas in twos and threes. Lining the galleries are larger images that survived the destruction of 1828 and, in a locker at the western wall, a heap of Buddhas that did not. The shaded galleries are a cool and pleasant place to linger and soak up the atmosphere. Breaching the wall that runs along Lane Xang Avenue, the structure with the multi-tiered roof is the monastery's former **library** (closed to the public), where its palm-leaf manuscripts were once kept.

Haw Pha Kaew

Opposite Wat Sisaket stands the **Presidential Palace**, a rather unimpressive French Beaux Arts-style structure, built to house the French colonial governor, and nowadays used mainly for government ceremonies. Just west of the palace, the **Haw Pha Kaew** (daily 8am–noon & 1–4pm; 2000K) was once the king's personal Buddhist temple, but now functions as a **museum of art and antiquities**. Said to date from the mid-sixteenth century, the structure was destroyed by marauding Siamese during the sack of Vientiane in 1828 and was later earmarked for restoration by the French. The temple is named for the **Emerald Buddha**, or Pha Kaew, which, along with the Pha Bang (see box, p.148), the most sacred Buddha image in Laos, was pilfered by the Siamese in 1779 and carried off to their capital. The Pha Bang was eventually returned to Laos and is enshrined in its namesake city of Louang Phabang, but the Pha Kaew remains in Bangkok to this day, much to the resentment of Lao Buddhists.

The museum houses the finest collection of Lao art in the country. **Bronze Buddhas**, many looted of the inlay that once decorated their eyes, line the terrace surrounding the building. Inside are some exquisite works, one of the most striking being a Buddha in the "Beckoning Rain" pose (standing with arms to the sides and fingers pointing to the ground) and sporting a jewel-encrusted navel. Also of note are a pair of eighteenth-century terracotta *apsara*, or celestial dancers, and a highly detailed "naga throne" from Xiang Khouang that once served as a pedestal for a Buddha image. Next to the throne stands an elaborate candle holder of ornately carved wood and almost identical to one still in use at Wat Sisaket. An arched metal rod attached to the wood is where the lighted candles were placed.

Outsized bronze **statues** of a kowtowing Lao boy and girl on the lawn outside the museum were once part of a tableau that included the statue of explorer Auguste Pavie. The Frenchman's statue is now located inside the French embassy compound across the street. Sheltered under an adjacent pavilion is a sample stone urn from the Plain of Jars, but this small, broken jar is a rather poor specimen and not really typical of those at the site.

Wat Simuang

Roughly 500m east of Haw Pha Kaew, down Setthathilat Road, sits **Wat Simuang**. While Vientiane has its share of Buddhist monasteries, this wat stands out in terms of the number of worshippers it receives. Numerous pavement stalls stationed outside the walls give some indication of its popularity and sell all the ingredients for a proper tray of offerings (flowers, fruit, incense and candles). The monastery itself was built on an ancient Khmer site, the ruins of which are piled behind the *sim* and consist of laterite bricks with traces of stucco ornamentation. The *sim* of Wat Simuang houses the city's *lak meaung*, a sacred stone pillar. It is believed that the guardian spirit of Vientiane inhabits the pillar, which was consecrated with a human sacrifice at the time of the city's founding. Covered with gold leaf and wrapped in sacred cloth, the pillar is the centrepiece of an altar crowded with Buddha images. That great multitudes of worshippers come here is evident from a glance at the ceiling, coal-black with a thick coating of soot, which is constantly rising from sputtering candles and smouldering joss sticks.

By quietly taking a seat on the floor you can observe the **rituals** of devotees seeking answers or favours. Two baby-sized, crude images resting on their own pillows are the main focus of the worshippers' attention. After a question is posed or a favour requested, the devotee attempts to lift one of the images while kneeling towards the altar. Being able to lift the image three times over one's head is considered an auspicious sign. Worshippers whose wishes are granted must return and appease the guardian spirit with an offering; marigolds, coconuts and bananas are particularly popular tokens of gratitude. The **monastery grounds** surrounding the *sim* contain a dozen or so brightly painted sculptures of animals, Buddhist-Hindu deities and mythological figures from Lao legends, making this a favourite playground for local kids.

On a small wedge of land outside the south wall of the monastery towers a monolithic **statue of King Sisavang Vong**, who reigned from 1904 to 1959. The statue survived the revolution, having been executed by a Soviet sculptor and presented to the Lao government in 1972 after a visit to the Soviet Union

△ Wat Simuang

by King Sisavang Vatthana. Ironically, within a few short years of the statue being erected in 1974, the royalist government collapsed, and the newly installed communist government banished King Sisavang Vatthana and his family to a cave near the Vietnamese border, where they all perished. A plaque that was once attached to the pedestal has long been missing and, if asked, many locals will only be able to say that the massive statue depicts "an old king".

Patouxai

It has been said that, along with coffee and baguettes, the Lao inherited a taste for pompous town planning from the French. **Lane Xang Avenue**, leading off north from Setthathilat Road, was to be Vientiane's Champs Elysées and **Patouxai**, 1km from the Presidential Palace, its Arc de Triomphe. While it would be impossible to mistake seedy Lane Xang Avenue for Paris's most famous thoroughfare, if you were to stand at a fair distance and squint, you might be able to convince yourself that Patouxai resembles its Parisian inspiration. Popularly known as *anusawali* (Lao for "monument"), this massive reinforced concrete monument (daily 8am–5pm; 1000K), situated in a roundabout at the end of Lane Xang Avenue, was built in the late 1950s to commemorate casualties of war on the side of the Royal Lao Government. The structure, said to have been completed with concrete donated by the US government for the construction of an airport, has been jokingly referred to as "the vertical runway". If the story is true, then Patouxai is also the most notable structure left to show for the millions of dollars of aid that were pumped into Laos during the early years of American involvement in Indochina. After the revolution, the arch was given its current name and partially redecorated – some Hindu iconography symbolic of the defunct Lao monarchy was chipped away – so the communists could feel more comfortable with this behemoth reminder of the detested royalists in their midst.

Patouxai is best visited in the early morning before the structure has had time to absorb much heat from the sun's rays. A handful of vendors selling souvenirs

△ Patouxai

and refreshments are sheltered by a ceiling adorned with **reliefs** of the Hindu deities – Rahu devouring the sun, Vishnu, Brahma, and Indra on Airavata, the three-headed elephant. Decorating the walls just below the ceiling are characters from the *Ramayana*. Up close, it looks somewhat crude and unfinished, but the **view** of Vientiane from the top is worth the climb.

That Louang

One and a half kilometres east of Patouxai stands the Buddhist stupa, **That Louang** (daily except Mon & public holidays 8am–noon & 1–4pm; 3000K), Laos's most important religious building and its national symbol. The present building dates from the 1930s and is a reconstruction; the original That Louang is thought to have been built by King Setthathilat in the mid-sixteenth century, and it is his statue that is perched jauntily on a pedestal in front of the stupa.

Archeological evidence suggests that, like most central and southern Lao Buddhist structures of significance, That Louang was built on top of an ancient Khmer site. What the original Buddhist stupa looked like is a mystery, but a Dutch trader, Gerritt van Wuysthoff, who visited Vientiane in 1641, left an awestruck account of the gold-covered "pyramid" he saw there. Between then and the early nineteenth century, the stupa was embellished and restored periodically, but this ceased after the 1828 Siamese raid which left the capital deserted. When French explorers Francis Garnier and Louis Delaporte stumbled upon That Louang in 1867, it was overgrown by jungle, but still largely intact. A few years later, Chinese-led bandits plundered the stupa looking for gold, and left it a pile of rubble. A photo on display in the National Museum, taken in the late 1800s to commemorate the visit of a group of Frenchmen, gives some indication of the extent of the devastation.

A French attempt at **restoration** was made in 1900, after which the stupa was disparagingly referred to as the "Morin Spike", a snipe at the architect, whose idea of a Buddhist stupa resembled a railroad spike turned on its head. Dissatisfaction with the design eventually led to another attempt in the 1930s. Using sketches done by Delaporte as a model, a re-restoration in brick and stucco was carried out over four years, and what you see today are the results of this effort.

The tapering **golden spire** of the main stupa is 45m tall and rests on a plinth of stylized lotus petals, which crowns a mound reminiscent of the first-century-BC Buddhist stupa at Sanchi, India. The main stupa is surrounded on all sides by a total of thirty short, spiky stupas, which can be reached via any of four gates in the crenellated walls that support the monument. The whole is in turn surrounded by a cloistered wall, vaguely Chinese in style. Within the **cloisters** is a collection of very worn Buddha images, some of which may have been enshrined in the original Khmer temple that once occupied the site. Until just a few years ago, only the stupas' spires were "gilded", but with the passing years, more and more gold paint has been applied, so that now even the inner walls and their crenellations are gold. The effect is best seen just before sunset or during the evenings leading up to the **That Louang Festival** (see Festivals colour section), when the stupa is festooned with strings of lights, and moths the size of sparrows circle and cling to its glowing surface.

Wat Sok Pa Louang

The majority of Vientiane's most famous temples are found close to the Mekong – there are twenty temples between the riverbank and the length of Setthathilat Road from Wat Simuong to Wat Tainiai, an area that roughly corresponds to the old city. That said, there are over a dozen other temples scattered across the city in an east–west arc to the north that seldom see any tourists, and which make a great excuse for a bicycle ride through Vientiane's quiet outer neighbourhoods. Once outside of the tourist centre, you'll find a completely different Vientiane that most tourists don't even realize exists, where children play games in the dirt lanes, neighbours casually chat under the palm and banana trees, and saffron-robed monks with shade umbrellas return to their temples after errands.

One example of a worthwhile outlying temple is **Wat Sok Pa Louang**, mainly of interest to enthusiasts of **herbal sauna** and **traditional massage**. Originally outside the city limits and surrounded by forest, the wat now lies approximately 3km southeast of central Vientiane in a suburb that spreads out from the highway south to the village of Thadua. The easiest way to get here is by tuk-tuk (10,000K). Wood-fired saunas are started early in the morning and tended all day, enveloping bathers in clouds of healing steam; impurities are sweated out and the vapours of medicinal herbs soak in. Traditional Lao massage is available as well and is said to interact with the effects of the sauna. Visitors should dress modestly and bring a sarong to wear into the sauna. A soak in the sauna is $1, and $2 pays for forty minutes of massage.

Shopping

Fifteen years ago, immediately after Laos opened its doors to visitors, bargain-hunting in Vientiane was an experience. Capitalism had been stifled for over a decade, and in the Morning Market and the handful of shops around town, antique textiles and silver could be had for a song, while staples such as rice and cooking oil were unbelievably expensive. The situation has since stabilized and Vientiane's merchants now know the correct value of antiques and handi-crafts. In fact, the city's proximity to Thailand tends to keep the price of **Lao handicrafts** higher than they might otherwise be, with Thai buyers regularly snapping up Lao handicrafts for resale in the stores of Bangkok. You're better off shopping in Louang Phabang, where silverwork and textiles are produced and prices are generally cheaper.

Vientiane's **Morning Market** (Talat Sao) is the best place to begin a shopping tour of the capital. While many of the goods on offer will be of little inter-est to foreigners – Chinese electronics and cheap consumer goods proliferate – there are bargains to be had when it comes to homespun cotton clothing and handicrafts. Most of the other textile, souvenir and antique shops are found on **Samsenthai** and **Setthathilat roads** and along the lanes running between them. As with anywhere else, avoid shops in the lobbies of top-end hotels unless you don't mind paying huge mark-ups. See the Shopping section of Basics (pp.57–60) for further details on what to look out for in the items mentioned below.

Vientiane's other markets are either "wet" markets selling produce, "dry" markets selling manufactured goods, or, more commonly, a mixture of both. Other significant markets close to the centre include Talat Khouadin, Talat Dong Palane, Talat Nongduang and Talat Thong Khan Kham.

Antiques and reproductions

Antique shops can be found in the Morning Market and elsewhere in the centre of Vientiane. As ever, virtually all metal images or figurines of Buddhist or Hindu deities are reproductions from Thailand and Cambodia, though vendors won't admit this. **Opium weights**, usually seen in antique stores but also found in upscale textile shops, are priced at levels way out of line when compared to the rest of Laos, with merchants asking two to five times more for weights than their counterparts in Louang Phabang and the other provinces. Reproduction **opium pipes** can be found in the antique shops on Samsenthai Road. The cheapest are gaudy things made in Vietnam from tusk-shaped bone, but if you look patiently you may come across bamboo and brass or silver pipes made locally by a couple of craftsmen who are the sole remaining pipemakers in Southeast Asia. Local pipes may go for as much as $100, but newly made Vietnamese pipes can be bought for as little as $10.

Books
The recently opened Monument Books (℡021/243708) on Nokeo Koummane Road, opposite Carol Cassidy Lao Textiles, has Vientiane's largest selection of **English-language books**. The Vientiane Book Center on Pangkham Road (℡021/212031), south of the Nam Phou, is an old standby. The government-run State Bookstore, on the corner of Manthatoulat and Setthathilat roads, carries just a small selection of English-language books and a few comical, dusty titles from the communist era, including such useful tomes as Lao language guides to the customs and culture of the Soviet Republic of Tajikistan.

Rattan, wicker and bamboo
Check the antique stores of the Morning Market and the downtown area for old or rare **baskets** made by the tribal peoples of Laos, which can sell for as much as $200. Sticky rice baskets and mats costing $1–3 can be found in several shops that line Thong Khan Kam Road beyond the Thong Khan Kham Market. Pai Exclusive, Thong Tum Road (℡021/214804), near the defunct National Circus (*hong kanyasin*), produces chic if pricey designs, and can arrange shipping. They also have a shop in the lobby of the *Lao Plaza Hotel*.

Stamps, coins and banknotes
Most antique and curio shops have a small stash of **stamps, coins** and **banknotes** from present and previous regimes – the shops on Samsenthai and Setthathilat roads are your best bet. A no-name antique shop near Vinothèque La Cave always has a small selection of stamps, including some designed by the incomparable Marc Leguay (see p.59).

Textiles
Once a tremendous bargain in Vientiane, antique Lao weavings are now more expensive in Vientiane than in Thailand. If you're determined to buy **old textiles** in Vientiane, the Morning Market is your best bet. **New textiles**, however, are another matter. Lao silk and cotton textiles can be purchased in bolts of plain coloured cloth or as ready-made clothing for $2–5 per item. If you're looking to make a smart purchase without shelling out too much cash, Lao shoulder bags, or *nyam*, are a cheap and functional choice. Hand-woven *pha biang*, a long, scarf-like textile, can be found in a wide variety of colours and patterns, and chequered *pha khao ma*, the knee-length men's sarong, are also good buys. The Morning Market has the best selection; the merchants here are used to foreign tourists and enjoy a spirited haggle.

Aside from the markets, Vientiane boasts an increasing number of upmarket **shops** and **boutiques** carrying, and sometimes specializing in, Lao textiles. They often have the best range and most attractively displayed products and, unsurprisingly, the highest prices. Most of these new boutiques and galleries are located **south of Samsenthai Road** between Khoun Boulom and

Manthatoulat roads and can be taken in during a single, short walking tour. Perhaps the most impressive of these boutiques is Carol Cassidy Lao Textiles (☎021/212123), housed in a French-era mansion on Nokeo Koummane Road, which produces hand-woven wall hangings tinted with natural dyes under the supervision of an American designer. Other top-drawer places include Satri Lao Silk, 79/4 Setthathilat Road (☎021/219295); Lao Gallery, Nokeo Koummane Road (☎021/212943), and T'Shop Lai Gallery, Inpeng Road (☎021/223178, ℱ223178). Not so fancy, but certainly one of the earliest pioneers of traditional textiles, is the Lao Women's Union shop called The Art of Silk, on Manthatoulat Road. This unpretentious shop has good deals on lengths of plain silk and cotton cloth from all over the country, including hard-to-find ethnic textiles from Laos's remote southern provinces.

Woodcarving

Unlike Chiang Mai in Thailand, Vientiane is not a centre of **woodcarving** and the merchandise on offer tends to be crudely carved and garishly lacquered. An exception is the handicrafts of the T'Shop Lai Gallery on Inpeng Road next to *Le Vendôme* restaurant, which specializes in unique mosaics and other handicrafts made from coconut shell. Prices are fixed, though, and certainly not cheap.

Eating

The **culinary scene** in Vientiane has improved remarkably since the early 1990s, when ordering a plate of fried rice usually meant precisely that – fried rice, no meat, no vegetables. The huge rise in tourism and the establishment of a permanent foreign community have given rise to restaurants catering to virtually every taste, from sausage and sauerkraut to Korean BBQ. Vientiane also has a large concentration of French and Italian restaurants, the best of which compare favourably to those in Bangkok. Although the prices such restaurants charge are prohibitive for Lao, foreign visitors will be pleasantly surprised by the comparatively low cost of eating out. If you plan to head out in the provinces for a while, take the opportunity to indulge in the capital's Western culinary offerings before hitting the trail.

If, on the other hand, it's cheap food you're after, one area to focus on is the zone around Heng Boun and Khoun Boulom roads. Here you'll find a good night market (see below), *mi pét* (duck noodle) restaurants, fruit stands and French bread vendors all nearby, and the ice cream and pastry shops of Chao Anou Road, between Setthathilat and Heng Boun roads.

Food stalls and markets

For cheap, home-style cooking, seek out the outdoor **food stalls** found near any of the city's markets. Riverside food stalls can be found along the Mekong on Fa Ngum Road approximately opposite Wat Chanthabouli, with most offering Lao staples like *tam màk hung* (spicy papaya salad), *pîng kai* (grilled chicken) and refreshing fruit shakes from morning until nearly midnight. These stalls also provide an excellent spot to enjoy sunset over the Mekong.

A **night market** offering similar fare, and with tables on the street, sets up on Khoun Boulom Road and along Heng Boun Road in the early evening and stays open till about 10pm. This area is a popular night-time spot for cheap Chinese, Lao and Vietnamese food with several *föe* (noodle soup) stalls. A more extensive night market for good Lao food is at **Dong Palane Market** on Dong Palane Road near Wat Ban Fai – you'll find all the Lao standards on offer. For daytime food, try the **Morning Market stalls** on Lane Xang Avenue near the Lao National Tourism Administration office: here you'll find good Lao-style *khào pûn* (noodles with sauce), *tam màk hung* and excellent shakes. But if it's *khào biak sèn* (rice noodles in chicken broth) you're after, hop into a tuk-tuk in the afternoon and head straight for Wat Phaxai on That Khao Road, where you'll find noodle shops dishing up bowls of this soup that are second to none.

Crusty **baguettes** (*khào jî*) are a speciality of Vientiane, and vendors selling these French-inspired loaves, plain or filled with Lao-style pâté, can be found around downtown.

Bakeries and cafés

The legacy of the French is most deliciously apparent in the range of **cafés** and **bakeries** that crop up all over town. The **coffee** served at these places varies, with some offering Lao coffee and some using imported beans. While places like the *Scandinavian Bakery* may charge over three times what you would pay for coffee at one of the long-running Lao bakeries opposite the defunct cinema on Chao Anou Road, the quality of both coffee and baked goods at the former is worth the expense to most.

Cafés and bakeries tend to open early and close by 7pm. At a good café on Setthathilat Road you'll pay $2 for a **breakfast** special such as coffee and a couple of croissants. **Brunch buffets** are on offer at the big international-style hotels like *Novotel* and *Lao Hotel Plaza* for roughly $8 – quite expensive for Laos.

All the places below appear on the Central Vientiane map, pp.90–91.

Le Croissant d'Or 78/6 Nokeo Koummane Rd. The place to come for outstanding chocolate croissants and chocolate eclairs filled with cream mousse.

JoMa Bakery Setthathilat Rd, just west of Nam Phou. Reputedly a front for Catholic missionaries from Canada (JoMa is said to be a contraction of "Joseph and Mary"), this does good breakfasts and delicious sandwiches.

Scandinavian Bakery Nam Phou. Vientiane's most popular bakery, with outdoor seating, offers sandwiches and a wide selection of pastries

and cookies. Despite having expanded, it's often completely overrun and has a big following among Westerners. The breakfasts are a tad expensive, but if you get a table out front and the sun isn't too hot, it's a great place to laze away the morning reading and sipping.

Sweet Home Chao Anou Rd. A café with banquettes and signs featuring a dead ringer for cartoon legend Mighty Mouse on the walls, and serving pastries, cheap breakfasts and fine fruit shakes. The pastries lack the flair of those at the foreign-run bakeries, but the price is right.

Restaurants

Most of Vientiane's **restaurants** open for lunch and then again for dinner; no-frills eateries are usually open throughout the day, closing around 9pm. In most Western restaurants you'll pay on average $3 for each course, and even in more upmarket restaurants you'll rarely spend more than $15 unless you get into the wine.

The restaurants reviewed below are subdivided for convenience into "Asian" and "Western" places, but Laos isn't a place for culinary purism, and thus many supposedly Asian places do offer Western snacks and light meals, while even the fancier, supposedly Western, restaurants often have a Lao noodle dish or two lurking in the menu.

Most of the restaurants reviewed are scattered all over the riverside section of central Vientiane. In as much as Vientiane has a main restaurant centre,

Nam Phou is it. All the restaurants below are on the "Central Vientiane" map apart from the *Bounmala* and *Le Silapa*, which appear on the "Vientiane City" map.

Asian

Bounmala Khou Viang Rd, near Wat Phaxai. Classic, inexpensive Lao beer and roast-chicken joint under a tin roof. Also worth sampling is the roast beef, served with *khào pun*, star fruit and lettuce.

Just for Fun Pangkham Rd. Time your meal at this tiny, vegetarian-friendly restaurant to avoid the lunchtime crowds, as the tasty over-rice dishes are very good value. Also does some of the best cakes and pies in town and a great selection of herbal teas. Closed Sun.

Kualao 111 Samsenthai Rd ☏021/215777. Somewhat overpriced, but offers a unique deal, namely traditional Lao music and dance performances in a beautifully restored old house. The food itself is largely Lao (though many dishes are actually Thai) and priced at around $5 a dish; set menus are available for $10 and $15 per person. Tends to cater mostly to large tour groups.

Nazim Fa Ngum Rd. Inexpensive Indian restaurant facing the river, with indoor and outdoor seating. Strong on vegetarian dishes and immensely popular with backpackers. It's so packed most evenings that the whole pavement is taken over by its tables.

Nok Noi At the corner of Fa Ngum and Nokeo Koummane Rd. The best of five popular travellers' cafés facing the river, with the cleanest kitchen and very cheap Lao, Thai and Western dishes. The three friendly girls here do everything from sandwiches to stir-fries, with most dishes costing under $1.

PVO Samsenthai Rd. Inexpensive and full-flavour food, which you select from a picture menu, wins this shopfront eatery a high recommendation. Among the offerings are fantastic submarine sandwiches, spring rolls, *nâm neuang* and *baw bun*, served on the spot or to take out. Great value.

Sabaydee Setthathilat Rd, diagonally across from the PlaNet Internet centre. One of the few places to enjoy East Asian food (Lao, Thai and Chinese) in the centre of town. Meals are served on an outdoor patio well shielded from the traffic.

Western

L'Opéra Nam Phou. Considered *the* place in Vientiane for wining and dining, with excellent Italian food, impeccable service, a selection of Italian coffees and wines, and opera pumping through the sound system. In a word, classy; a favourite with the diplomatic and business sets.

La Terrasse Nokeo Koummane Rd, near Wat Mixai. Fills its tables nightly by offering outstanding steaks, pizzas, Mexican food and salads at prices lower than most of the other Western joints. Seating in a covered courtyard or chic bar/dining area. Highly recommended. Closed Sun.

Le Belle Epoque 6 Pangkham Rd, in the *Settha Palace Hotel*. The classiest act in town, serving French food in an elegant dining room. There is nowhere else in Vientiane even remotely like this. Even if you don't dine here, you can have a drink at the bar and soak up the colonial atmosphere.

Le Central Café Setthathilat Rd, opposite Wat Ong Teu. Reasonable prices with a menu offering pizzas, rotisserie chicken, pasta, salads and sandwiches. The quality bar has Beer Lao on tap and you can also sit outside in the narrow outdoor garden.

Le Côte d'Azur Fa Ngum Rd, near Nokeo Koummane Rd. This bright, airy place is one of Vientiane's better restaurants and has a good location facing the river. It has terrific service and a great menu, featuring Provençal-style seafood and pasta, plus a large selection of excellent pizzas. Closed Sun lunchtime.

Le Provençal Nam Phou. Lost customers when its chef left and opened *Le Côte D'Azur*, but the menu remains the same and the pizza is still first-rate. Closed Sun.

Le Silapa 17/1 Sihom Rd, west of the Thai Military Bank ☏021/219689. French-managed restaurant serving French food (by a French chef) in a beautifully restored colonial shophouse. The à la carte menu is very reasonable at around $5 each for mains and starters. The lunchtime $5 set menu is also extremely good value. Daily except Sun 11.30am–2pm & 6–10pm.

Le Vendôme Inpeng Rd, near Wat Inpeng. Cosy restaurant in an old house with seating inside or on a pleasant bamboo-curtained terrace. The food runs the gamut from French and Thai fare to good pizzas and very tasty calzone. Closed Sat & Sun lunchtime.

Xayoh Corner of Samsenthai and Neokeo Koummane facing the wedding-cake style Lao National Cultural Hall. One of Vientiane's most reliable restaurants, serving pizzas and salads as well as very cold beer. There's also a branch in Vang Viang.

Minimarkets and wine shops

For many travellers, especially Europeans, one of the great pleasures of returning to Vientiane after a long journey upcountry is the availability of cheeses,
wine and other imported goods to accompany those crusty baguettes which
are a speciality of the capital. There are several **minimarkets** where you
can stock up. Maningom Supermarket (corner of Khoun Boulom and Heng
Boun), Riverside Minimarket (Fa Ngum Road, near the *Orchid Guesthouse*)
and Phimphone Minimarket (with two outlets on Samsenthai Road near
Chantha Khoumane Road) all have a selection of cheeses, wine, imported
beer and chocolate, as well as imported body-care products you won't
be able to find elsewhere in Laos. Les Boutiques Scoubidou at the eastern
end of Samsenthai Road, near Wat Simuang, boasts the best selection of
speciality **gourmet products** in town, with French wines, olives, anchovies,
pâté, cured meats and sausages. The best selections of **wine** in Laos can be
found at Vinothèque La Cave and Le Wine Cellar, both on Samsenthai Road,
opposite the *Asia Pavilion Hotel*.

Drinking, nightlife and entertainment

Vientiane's location along an east–west stretch of the Mekong makes for spectacular sunsets, with the fiery orb lighting up the water before slowly descending into Thailand. Taking advantage of this backdrop, makeshift **stalls** selling
bottles of Beer Lao and fruit shakes set up along the sidewalk on Fa Ngum
Road opposite Wat Chanthabouli from afternoon till early evening. If you're
looking for something even closer to the water and away from the bustle of
the city centre, continue west along Fa Ngum Road, where for the next 2km
you'll find a long row of over twenty **beer gardens** with wooden terraces
overhanging the riverbank. These laid-back, open-air venues offering cheap
pitchers of golden "Fresh Beer" (*bia sót*) under a thatch roof define the quintessential Vientiane pub experience. The largest and fanciest of these are all in the
vicinity of the *Riverview Hotel*.

Believe it or not, Vientiane's once notorious **nightlife** helped earn it the name
of Wonderland. To hear Paul Theroux tell it in *The Great Railway Bazaar*, opium
was easier to find than beer. However, the brothels and strip joints vanished
when the old regime fell in the mid-1970s, and these days nightspots pop up
here and there only to be simultaneously shut down during fits of socialist
puritanism that grip the capital semi-annually.

Many of the **nightclubs** are Japanese-style, with costumed pop singers, dim
lighting, hostesses and deep couches. These places are fairly innocuous – the
absurdly overdressed hostesses will only sit with you, for a fee. The city's larger
hotels often have nightspots like this (the one in the *Novotel* is a decent choice),
but if you do visit one, keep in mind that the hotel venues are favourites of the
spoiled offspring of the Party elite, who seem to get their jollies by picking
fights on the dance floor. As you might expect, many of these clubs also feature
karaoke lounges.

Of more interest to Western visitors, a number of **dance clubs** playing
Thai pop and international dance mixes, and catering to well-heeled teenagers, have cropped up along Louang Phabang Avenue, just beyond the *Novotel*.
Smaller clubs are sometimes able to bend the rules more and go until the wee
hours depending on the political climate. There's usually no cover charge,
but if there is it will include a bottle of Beer Lao. Vientiane's **live music**

scene is largely derivative, with popular taste being overwhelmed by a flood of Made-in-Thailand pop churned out by the massive music industry across the river.

Bars and clubs

Broadway *Lao Plaza Hotel*, Samsenthai Rd. The dance club in the *Plaza's* basement has been eclipsed by the club at the *Novotel*, but this means that there's less chance of seeing a fight on the dance floor. There are deep plush sofas to sink into and black lights to make your gin and tonic glow a pale shade of blue.

Dokmaideng Club *Royal Dokmaideng Hotel*, Lane Xang Ave. A very similar scene to the *Lao Plaza Hotel* and popular with the 20-something expat crowd and children of the new elite. An interesting place to just sit with a cocktail and people-watch.

D-Tech Club *Novotel*, Louang Phabang Ave. The in-spot of the moment.

Khop Chai Deu Nam Phou. Recently expanded and located in a big French-period house, this is the most popular hangout for foreign tourists. Downstairs, in the outdoor patio bar, you can get cheap pitchers of draught beer; up the big spiral staircase you'll find another very pleasant bar on the roof. You can eat inside – the mixed menu has reasonable Lao and Indian dishes, though the falang food is a bit hit and miss. The most fun place in town.

Lao Plaza Beer Garden *Lao Plaza Hotel*, Samsenthai Rd. Nowhere near as popular as the *Khop Chai Deu*, but still a fine place to sit outside overlooking Samsenthai Rd and have a cold, $1-a-pint draught beer in the evening. Nightly 6–10pm.

Marina Louang Phabang Ave, 3km west of the centre. The longest-running of two big discos on the edge of town for Lao teenagers to shake their groove thang, and very much in the Thai disco style. Has a good dance floor, separate bar and plenty of couches for breaks between dancing.

Nina Thadua Rd, 3km east of centre. When you tire of *Marina*, make the 6km trek through town to *Nina*, the other big disco that has managed to survive the crackdowns that periodically wipe the slate clean downtown. Expect a local crowd and Thai hits played at deafening volume.

Sala Sunset Khounta Fa Ngum Rd. The longest-running of the riverside bars, and long known to old hands as "The End of the World", harkening back to a time when this bar was as far as a foreigner could travel from downtown Vientiane without official permission. Nowadays the bar is most commonly called "The Sunset Bar", which is not inappropriate given that this was the original spot for sundowners in Vientiane. There is some quite good finger food on the menu as well.

Cultural entertainment

Four hundred and fifty years after superseding Louang Phabang as the centre of political power, Vientiane still lacks the natural **cultural life** of the old royal capital, but a few venues offer a taste of Laos's heritage, even if just for the entertainment of foreigners. The **Lao National Theatre** on Manthatoulat Road near Wat Xieng Nyeun has performances featuring lowland Lao music, dance and even a mock wedding ceremony. Also colourful are lowland renditions of the music and dance of the hill-tribe peoples. While the costumes and numbers aren't always strictly traditional, the enthusiasm of the performers compensates. Shows are nightly at 8.30pm, except the third Sunday of every month, and cost $7 for adults and $4 for children under 12. The *Kualao* (see p.102) also stages traditional dancing and music – the daily dance show starts at 7pm and lasts two hours.

With Lao singers selling out to demand for Thai music and the capital's cinemas shut since the advent of video, Vientiane's grassroots cultural life really only reawakens during **festivals**. The best time to get a taste of Lao music is in November during the **That Louang Festival** (see Festivals colour section), when the nation's best singers and musicians are featured in a string of performances during the two weeks leading up to the festival.

Listings

Airlines Lao Airlines, Pangkham Rd ☎021/212051, or at the airport ☎021/512000; Thai Airways, Louang Phabang Ave ☎021/222527; Vietnam Airlines, Samsenthai Rd, mezzanine floor of the *Lao Plaza Hotel* ☎021/21756. For Bangkok Airways, see p.165.

American Express Their representative agent in Laos is Diethelm Travel, on the corner of Setthathilat Rd and Nam Phou (☎021/213833).

Banks and exchange Banks, hotels, guesthouses and shopkeepers all over downtown Vientiane will happily exchange foreign currency. Thai and Lao banks, many of which are located along Lane Xang Ave, can cash traveller's cheques, but a more convenient option for tourists is bank exchange booths, which can be found on Samsenthai Rd as well as on Fa Ngum Rd by the *Lane Xang Hotel*. There are also exchange booths at the Friendship Bridge and the airport. Banque pour le Commerce Extérieur Lao (BCEL), Pangkham Rd, has the best exchange rates and the widest range of services, including changing traveller's cheques into US dollars and dollar cash advances on Visa; for Mastercard head to Siam Commercial Bank, Lane Xang Ave.

Bicycle rental Bicycles are available at rental shops and some guesthouses for $1 per day. There are three bike and motorbike rental outlets in a row on Samsenthai Rd, including PVO (☎021/214444) and Boualian Lao Travel (☎021/213061, ☎219649).

Car rental Asia Vehicle Rental, Lane Xang Ave (☎021/217493, ☎217493); Khounta Rental, Luang Phabang Rd (☎020/513127); PVO (☎021/214444) and Boualian Lao Travel (☎021/213061, ☎219649), both on Samsenthai Rd. Many guesthouses and hotels can make car-rental arrangements that may be cheaper than agencies.

Courier services DHL Worldwide Express ☎021/214868 or 216830; United Parcel Service ☎021/414392.

Embassies and consulates Australia, Nehru Rd ☎021/413610 or 413805; Canada, c/o embassy in Bangkok ☎+66 2/636 0540; Cambodia, near That Khao, Thadua Rd ☎021/314952 or 315251; China, near Wat Nak Noi, Wat Nak Noi Rd ☎021/315100 or 315103; France, Setthathilat Rd ☎021/215253 or 215257–9; Germany, Sok Pa Louang Rd ☎021/312110–3; India, near Wat Phaxai, That Louang Rd ☎021/413802; Indonesia, Phon Kheng Rd, Ban Phon Sa-at ☎021/413909 or 413910; Ireland, c/o embassy in Kuala Lumpur

☎+60 3/2161 2963; Malaysia, near Wat Phaxai, That Louang Rd ☎021/414205 or 414206; Myanmar (Burma), Sok Pa Louang Rd ☎021/314910; New Zealand, c/o embassy in Bangkok ☎+66 2 254 2530; Philippines, near Wat Nak, Salakoktane Rd ☎021/315179; Singapore, Ban Naxay, Unit 12 Nong Bon Rd ☎021/416 860; Sweden, near Wat Nak, Sok Pa Louang Rd ☎021/315018; Thailand (visa section), across from the Lao National Tourism Administration building, Lane Xang Ave ☎021/214582; UK ☎021/413606, but most enquiries should go to the embassy in Bangkok ☎+66 2/305 8333; United States, near That Dam, Bartholonie Rd ☎021/213966 or 212581; Vietnam, near Wat Phaxai, That Louang Rd ☎021/413400–4.

Emergencies Dial ☎190 in case of fire, ☎195 for an ambulance, or ☎191 for police.

Health clubs *Tai-Pan Hotel*, François Nginn Rd ($4 per day).

Hospitals and clinics Australian Clinic, Nehru Rd ☎021/413603 (by appointment only, with vaccinations Thurs); International Clinic, Mahosot Hospital Compound, Fa Ngum Rd ☎021/214022 (open 24hr); Mahosot Hospital, Mahosot Rd ☎021/214018; Swedish Clinic, near Wat Nak, Sok Pa Louang Rd ☎021/315015.

Immigration department Hatsady Rd, not far from the tourist office ☎021/212520 (Mon & Wed–Sat 8–11.30am & 2–4.30pm).

Internet access PlaNet CyberCentre, on the corner of Manthatoulat and Setthathilat roads (Mon–Sat 8.30am–10pm & Sun 9am–8pm), is the biggest player in town, but there are well over a dozen small Internet centres scattered around the city, all charging 100K a minute and closing at about 10pm.

Language courses Centre de Langue Française, Lane Xang Ave ☎021/215764; Lao-American Language Center, Phon Kheng Rd, Ban Phon Sa-at ☎021/414321, ☎413760. Short-term courses and private tutorials are available.

Laundry Most hotels and guesthouses will wash clothes for you; a faster and cheaper alternative is one of the laundries on Heng Boun Rd, near the *Anou Hotel*.

Massage and herbal sauna Ajan Amphone, tucked away behind Wat Chanthabouli on Fa Ngum Rd, offers massage at $3/hr, and a sauna for $1 (Mon–Fri 2–5pm, Sat & Sun 10am–7pm); Hôpital de Médicine Traditionnelle, near Wat Si Amphon, does massage for $1 per hour and sauna for $0.50, and offers acupuncture; Mixay Massage, near Wat

Moving on from Vientiane

Lao Airlines operates several domestic **flights** out of Vientiane, for details of which, see "Travel details", p.129. International flights from Vientiane include Lao Airlines' services to Bangkok and Chiang Mai, Hanoi, Phnom Penh and Siem Reap.

Buses

The situation regarding bus-stop locations and departure times can only be described as chaotic. **Buses** heading to all points **south** leave from the Talat Sao bus station, adjacent to the Morning Market. If you want to spend a bit more and get an express a/c bus to southern destinations (book a day ahead with the operator, Laody; ☏021/740112) such as Thakek, Savannakhet and Pakxe, head to the Simuang bus stand, near Wat Simuang. It's also possible to charter a twelve-seater a/c minibus to points south from Boualian Travel Company (☏021/213061). Buses to the **north** and northeast leave from the northern bus station (Khiw Lot Khoua Louang in Lao) near the Evening Market (sometimes called Nongduang Market or Talat Laeng) on Talat Nongduang Road, 2km northwest of the city centre. Note that you generally have to go first to Louang Phabang and find buses onward from Louang Phabang's northern bus station.

To the Friendship Bridge: Bus #14 departs every 45 minutes from the main bus station; a much, much faster alternative is to take a taxi from the lot at the southeast corner of the Morning Market ($5) or charter a tuk-tuk ($3).

To Nong Khai and Udon Thani: Direct buses to Nong Khai and Udon Thani in Thailand are mostly used by Lao and Vientiane-based expats to make shopping runs to Udon, but they are also a convenient way to get over the Friendship Bridge without having to change vehicles. Four buses leave daily for both destinations from behind Talat Sao. From Nong Khai, overnight buses and trains to **Bangkok** leave between 5pm and 7pm. If you intend to catch the train, get a taxi to the Friendship Bridge; once on the Thai side, take a tuk-tuk to the train station (40 baht).

To Louang Phabang: Buses north and northeast to Louang Phabang, Phonsavan and Xam Nua leave from the northern bus station. There is also an a/c tourist coach

---

Mixai on Nokeo Koummane Rd, offers massage only, for $5/hr. Also worth considering is Wat Sok Pa Louang (see p.98).

Meditation An hour of sitting and walking meditation is led by Ajan Paan on Saturday afternoons at 4pm at Wat Sok Pa Louang (see p.98).

Motorbike rental Rental motorbikes in Vientiane are mostly little 100cc step-throughs like the Honda Dream. Most of the bikes are older second-hand models imported from Thailand. The asking price is usually $8–10 depending on how new the bike looks, but it's possible to bargain this down to $6 a day, especially if you want it for a few days. The *Douang Deuane Hotel*, Nokeo Koummane Rd (☏021/222301–3), PVO, Samsenthai Rd (☏021/214444), and Boualian Lao Travel Company, 346 Samsenthai Rd (☏021/213061, ☏021/219649), all have small fleets of Honda Dreams, but PVO is the only place in town with eight proper Yamaha 225cc enduro dirt bikes. These run to $20 a day, about double the price of rental in Thailand.

Newspapers The *Vientiane Times* is sold at the big hotels and most minimarkets; the *Bangkok Post* is sometimes available at the Phimphone minimarket on Samsenthai Rd.

Pharmacies The best pharmacies are on Mahosot Rd, north of the main bus station.

Post office The GPO is located on the corner of Khou Viang Rd and Lane Xang Ave (Mon–Fri 8am–5pm, Sat 8am–4pm, Sun 8am–noon), opposite the Morning Market. The poste restante counter will hold mail for up to three months with a minimal charge. There's also a philatelic counter.

Skating There is a line-skating ring on Thadua Rd heading east out of town.

Swimming *Lane Xang Hotel*, Fa Ngum Rd ($2 per day); *Lao Plaza Hotel*, Samsenthai Rd ($5); *Novotel*, Louang Phabang Ave ($5); *Royal Dokmaideng Hotel*, Lane Xang Ave ($2.50); Sok Pa Louang swimming pool, Sok Pa Louang Rd ($0.50).

Telephone services The Telecom office, on the corner of Setthathilat and Chantha Khoumane roads (daily 7am–10pm), handles international calls

($10) between Vientiane and Louang Phabang which departs up to three times daily, depending on the season, and can be booked through most guesthouses.

To Vang Viang: Several government buses depart from the Talat Sao bus station daily; alternatively, sawngthaews leave twice an hour. The location of the sawngthaews stand tends to change every few months, but it usually in the vicinity of the Talat Sao bus station.

To Vietnam: Buses for Hanoi leave from the Vietnam bus booth at the southwest corner of the Morning Market on Mondays, Wednesdays, Fridays and Saturdays at 8pm, and should arrive in Hanoi 24 hours later. Two companies provide this service. The fare is $25, which is supposed to get you a "good" bus; the size of the bus used depends on the number of advance bookings. There are also buses to Vinh, Hue and Da Nang.

Sawngthaews

The main staging area for **sawngthaews** and unmetered **taxis** is the big lot at the southeast corner of the Morning Market just opposite the bus station. Here you'll find both shared sawngthaews for towns around the Vientiane Plain, and vehicles for hire. North of town, about 8km up Route 13, there is a second bus lot for sawngthaews heading north towards Vang Viang, with departures every thirty minutes until late afternoon.

Boats

There are now only very infrequent boat services to the **northwest** and **north**; most people take the bus nowadays. When they do run, speedboats and slow boats leave from Tha Hua Kao Liaw pier, on the Mekong River 10km west of the centre of Vientiane; tuk-tuks there from the centre cost 50,000K. You will have to make a trip out here to inquire if any boats will be departing soon. By slow boat it takes three days to get to Louang Phabang. More common are speedboats to Paklai, 217km upriver from Vientiane, which cost $20 per person (or you could charter one for $100).

and faxes; you can place calls through the operators inside or use their card phones just out front. IDD calls can be made from most hotels.
Travel/tour agencies Beside the companies listed in Basics on p.43, you can also contact Boualian Lao Travel Company, 346 Samsenthai Rd (℡021/213061); or Lao Travel Service, Lane Xang Ave (℡021/216603–4).

Visa services Boualian Lao Travel Company (see opposite) can arrange visas for Vietnam, Cambodia, Thailand and China, as well as Lao visa extensions ($2 per day). The proprietor, Mrs. Boualian Dangmani, a Vietnamese–Lao, is sharp as a tack; she speaks fluent English, French, Vietnamese, Thai and Lao. For visa extensions, see "Immigration department", p.105.

Excursions from Vientiane

If you need a break from Vientiane or have time to kill while your visa is being processed, it's easy enough to get out of the city in under an hour, and shuttle around the expansive Vientiane Plain by public transport or on a private tour. The most popular destination for a half-day jaunt is the other-worldly **Buddha Park**, southeast of town, while those who have never seen a "Buddha's footprint" might consider travelling further east to **Wat Phabat Phonsan**. North of the capital, the huge **Ang Nam Ngum Reservoir** is a pleasant retreat for boating, fishing and swimming, with scores of islands to explore, as well as a casino. At the southern edge of the reservoir is the vast **Phou Khao**

Khouay NBCA, which can be visited on an adventure tour from the capital. Downstream on the Nam Ngum River, **Ban Pako** is an eco-tourism lodge that makes a fine day-trip, though most visitors end up staying on to relax for a few days, visiting country villages and exploring nature trails. Of the two state-sanctioned tourist destinations on the edge of the city, the **National Ethnic Cultural Park** and the **Kaysone Memorial Museum**, the latter is the more worthwhile, making an interesting diversion into the personality cults surrounding communist leaders.

Buddha Park and National Ethnic Cultural Park

Situated some 25km southeast of downtown Vientiane on the Mekong River, Xiang Khouan or the "**Buddha Park**" (daily 8am–5pm; 5000K) is surely Laos's quirkiest attraction – a tacky tourist trap to some travellers, one of the most interesting sights in Vientiane to others. This collection of massive ferro-concrete sculptures, dotted around a wide riverside meadow, was created under the direction of Louang Pou Bounleua Soulilat, a self-styled holy man who claimed to have been the disciple of a cave-dwelling Hindu hermit in Vietnam. Upon returning to Laos, Bounleua began the sculpture garden in the late 1950s as a means of spreading his philosophy of life and his ideas about the cosmos. After the revolution, Bounleua was forced to flee across the Mekong to Nong Khai, Thailand, where he established an even more elaborate version of his philosophy in concrete. Ironically, the Lao National Tourism Authority chose Bounleua's sculptures as the symbol of their "Visit Laos Year" campaign, and posters depicting the exiled guru's works can be seen in government offices throughout the country.

Besides the brontosaurian reclining Buddha that dominates the park, there are statues of every conceivable deity in the Hindu-Buddhist pantheon and even a handful of personalities from the old regime. Near the park's entrance is a strange edifice that resembles a giant pumpkin with a dead tree sprouting from its crown. Entering the structure through the gaping maw of devouring time, you can explore representations of the "three planes of existence": hell, earth and heaven. The crude and cobwebby figures that populate these rooms are reminiscent of a child's nightmare and, although the interior is rigged with electric lights, they aren't always turned on, so bring a torch (flashlight) if you want to see anything. A spiral stairway leads to the roof of the building, which affords a view of the park.

Bus #14 from Vientiane's main bus station (every 40min) stops outside the Buddha Park. Alternatively, get a shared tuk-tuk from the stand near the Morning Market to Thadua, and then charter a tuk-tuk for the remaining 3km to the park. Easiest is to charter a tuk-tuk for the round trip (around $5, including a 2hr wait).

National Ethnic Cultural Park

En route to the Buddha Park you'll pass the **National Ethnic Cultural Park** (daily 8am–6pm; 3000K), some 18km from the capital. This is Laos's answer to the tour-the-country-in-one-hour theme park, which almost every Southeast Asian country finds it necessary to construct. Concrete replicas of the traditional dwellings of Laos's ethnic minorities double as snack stands, and there are cement models of dinosaurs. If you're heading for the Buddha Park with a rental car or motorcycle, a swing through here isn't much trouble.

The Kaysone Memorial Museum

The Kaysone Memorial Museum (Tues–Sun 8–11.30am & 2–4.30pm; 2000K) is the most visible attempt of the Lao government to build a personality cult around the shadowy man who, according to Party legend, led the Thirty Year Struggle (see p.258). It lies on the edge of Vientiane, in the former American compound known during the Second Indochina War as **Six Klicks City** – after its location, 6km from the centre. An oasis during the years that the US embassy was the seat of power in Vientiane, Six Klicks City was a slice of suburban Americana with nicely paved roads lined with ranch-style homes and swimming pools out back. One month after Saigon and Phnom Penh fell in April 1975, and with Pathet Lao troops surrounding the barbed-wire-enclosed compound, American residents inside received a phone call telling them not to leave. Three days later, the first busload of Americans headed to Wattay Airport, beginning the end of an era. In December 1975, 264 delegates gathered in the compound's gymnasium and proclaimed the formation of the Lao People's Democratic Republic. Having just emerged from their wartime hide-out in the caves of Viang Xai, the Lao communist party members promptly moved into the American fortress, which was to become Kaysone's headquarters until his death in 1992.

The Memorial Museum is strikingly modest compared to the mausoleum of Kaysone's Vietnamese counterpart, Ho Chi Minh. Opened in 1994, the museum originally consisted only of the tiny ranch house where Kaysone lived, though a more conventional museum was opened next door a year later. The guide will show you Kaysone's exercise bike and the spot where he used to meditate, as well as cabinets containing Buddha images and bottles of Johnnie Walker scotch – so much for communist austerity, though the guide duly notes that they were gifts of the people. Also on display are gifts to Kaysone from the leaders of Indonesia, Thailand, Vietnam and China, as well as the books – many of which, ardent Lao nationalists might note, are in Vietnamese – of his well-stocked library. Next door, the later part of the museum is heavy on the sort of revolutionary photographs common to other Lao museums, but also features objects from various stages of Kaysone's life: his desk from his Savannakhet school, the winnowing tray on which he was placed during the first days of his life, and his mother's bed, along with a model of Kaysone's Viang Xai cave, his binoculars, revolver and other items from his time with the resistance movement.

Getting to the museum is easiest by rental motorbike or tuk-tuk. Southbound sawngthaews, departing from the main bus station, pass the road leading to the compound, 6km from the city along Route 13 South; the turn-off is on the left just before the Children's Home. The road leads 300m to the gate of an army outpost, at which point you turn left and continue along the road, which curves right, for 1km. The museum entrance is on the right.

Ban Pako (Lao Pako) Resort

A quick trip you can make out of the capital is to **BAN PAKO**, 50km northeast of Vientiane, which has a rustic resort on a bend in the Nam Ngum River, reached by road and a short river journey. Once there you could easily spend a couple of days soaking up the laid-back atmosphere at this woodsy getaway, affording ample opportunity for swimming, bird-watching and day hikes to nearby villages. You can also follow self-guided nature trails, along one of which is a herbal steam bath, modelled on the wood-fired saunas at Wat Sok Pa Louang (see p.98), and near a refreshingly cool spring.

To get to the resort, you first catch the blue government **bus** bound for Pakxap from the main bus station (at 6.30am, 11am or 3pm), getting off at Somsamai (alternatively, chartering a tuk-tuk costs about $5), where there's a sign reading "Boat to LAO PAKO". From here boatmen will ferry you down the tranquil Nam Ngum River (25min; 15,000K) to the resort (☎021/451970, ⑩www.banpako.com; ⑤, dorms $10). **Accommodation** ranges from an eight-bed dorm in a Lao-style longhouse with a huge veranda, to more private detached bungalows, also with en-suite facilities and verandas. Rooms are limited, so it's best to call ahead for reservations. An **open-air restaurant** overlooking the river serves up Lao staples plus a few decent Western dishes.

Wat Phabat Phonsan

The somewhat isolated monastery of **WAT PHABAT PHONSAN**, 80km east of Vientiane, is best known for its **"Buddha's footprint"**, probably one of the most elaborate of the handful of examples in Laos. As with most so-called footprints of the Buddha, the one at this monastery was originally a larger-than-life recess in stone that vaguely resembled a human footprint. In ancient times, the sandstone bluff upon which the monastery now sits was submerged by the nearby river and, over time, the swirling currents carved deep bowls into its surface. When the water receded, one of these indentations looked enough like a footprint for it to become enshrined as one of those left behind by the historic Buddha during his wanderings through Laos. Never mind that there is no record of Gautama Buddha ever having got this far east, his footprints have been found all over Laos wherever there is a population of Buddhists.

The footprint was embellished with stucco (and later concrete) and the 108 auspicious marks said to be found on the Buddha's foot were carved into the wet stucco. Red paint and gold leaf were then applied to the surface and offerings were made. Nowadays, most pilgrims toss banknotes into the footprint for luck and a wire-mesh cage has been built around it to keep thieves from pocketing the offerings. Still, say resident monks, naughty kids have been known to put blobs of chewing gum on the end of sticks and poke away until their pockets bulge with banknotes.

Next to the building containing the Buddha's footprint is another, housing a concrete **reclining Buddha**. The nearby stupa is said to date from the early twentieth century and is decorated with whimsical motifs reminiscent of Savannakhet's That In Hang (see p.260). Because this monastery is considered to be of high holiness, donations have rolled in from lay Buddhists wishing to dilute some of their sins. These donations have been used to make "improvements" to the wat, including monks' quarters to replace the charmingly rustic colonial-era teakwood buildings. Even the river-carved bowls in the sandstone bluff are being filled in with concrete so that the monks don't stumble when traversing the compound at night.

The best time to come here is during the annual **temple fair** (*bun*) held during the full moon in July when thousands of pilgrims flock to the monastery to make offerings, play games of chance and dance to electric *lam wong* music until late into the night.

Any **public transport** bound for Savannakhet, Thakhek or Pakxan will pass by Wat Phabat Phonsan, which is roughly halfway between Vientiane and Pakxan, about an hour and a half's drive from each. There is no accommodation in the vicinity of Wat Phabat Phonsan, so it's best visited as a day-trip or en route to or from the south.

Phou Khao Khouay NBCA

Located 90km northeast of the city, this huge NBCA straddles three different administrative districts and forms the southern edge of the Ang Nam Ngum Reservoir. Within easy striking distance of the capital, **PHOU KHAO KHOUAY** basically is to Vientiane what Khao Yai National Park is to Bangkok. The NBCA features several large ranges and includes two peaks of over 1600m, one of which, Phou Xang, at 1666m, towers over the southern end of the Nam Ngum Lake. There are also several large **waterfalls**, including Tad Xay, Tad Leuk and Tad Phou Khao Khouay, which can be reached by road, and a smaller dam and reservoir, Nam Luek Reservoir, which can also be reached by motor vehicle from the east. Fauna includes **Asian elephants**, **tigers** and **gibbons**.

There is a **visitor centre** at Tad Leuk and **accommodation** at the *T&M Guesthouse* (❶) in the town of **Thabok**, where the road into the NBCA meets Route 13. Enquire with Vientiane **tour agencies** about organized packages to Phou Khao Khouay.

Ang Nam Ngum Reservoir

Ninety kilometres north of Vientiane, the vast **Ang Nam Ngum Reservoir** sits above the northern edge of the Vientiane Plain, where the rice-growing flatlands surrounding the capital meet the mountainous terrain of the north. Created when the Nam Ngum River was dammed in 1971, the deep green waters of the reservoir are dotted with scores of forest-clad islands stretching to a dramatic horizon lined with mountains, their peaks lost in mist. Foreign travellers, usually in a rush to head upcountry, tend to bypass Ang Nam Ngum as they make for nearby Vang Viang, but those who do stop off discover a pretty 250-square kilometre expanse of water with islands, secluded beaches and swimming spots. There are a number of convenient options for visiting Ang Nam Ngum, either as a day-trip from Vientiane or Vang Viang or en route between the two; short package trips are also available.

Built with foreign expertise and funding, the reservoir is the driving force behind Laos's production of **hydroelectricity** – the country's largest export earner until the late 1980s – and provides power for Vientiane and surrounding villages on the Vientiane Plain. Most of the power, however, flows across the Mekong into Thailand, which has an agreement to purchase Laos's surplus electricity. The reservoir is also slowly being developed for tourism and now boasts a two-star hotel on the southern shoreline, the **DanSaVanh Nam Ngum Resort**, complete with casino, golf courses and a marina.

At the time the dam was built, the Royalist government had only just plugged Vientiane into the hydroelectric dam before they were forced to cede power to the communist Pathet Lao. In an all too typical example of poor environmental planning, the builders of the dam had flooded a vast area of valuable forest 50m underwater. The rotting vegetation sucked oxygen out of the water and blocked up the turbines, a problem that was later turned into profit by underwater logging ventures, whose frogmen drop to the reservoir floor to cut submerged trees with underwater saws. Meanwhile, the new communist government found a novel use for the reservoir. After 1975, prostitutes, thieves and teenagers "infected with foreign ideas" were rounded up from the streets of Vientiane, a Lao Sodom in the eyes of the Pathet Lao, and were confined on islands in the middle of the lake for "re-education".

These days, day-tripping Lao head for Ang Nam Ngum with relaxation in mind, descending on the scenic reservoir in droves on weekends and hiring out wooden boats for picnic cruises. Aside from tourism and timber, the main occupation here is **fishing**, with much of the catch sold in the markets of Vientiane. Around sunset you'll even see a few of the fishermen heading out to fish for the night, armed with spear guns and crude oxygen machines – so large they nearly overwhelm their slim pirogues – which allow the fishermen to stay underwater for long stretches of time.

Reaching the reservoir

Getting to Ang Nam Ngum by public transport is easy enough. **From Vientiane**, four blue government buses depart from the main bus station daily for the town of **Thalat** (there are also more frequent sawngthaews here, leaving from the stand in front of the bus station). From Thalat, you can get a shared tuk-tuk for the short run to the reservoir or the regular tuk-tuk shuttle service to **Na Nam**, near the dam on the western shore of the reservoir, and the most logical base for independent travellers to explore the lake by chartering a taxi for $20 return, in which case you might consider making a scenic detour en route along the quieter **Route 10** via Ban Keun. Southbound sawngthaews **from Vang Viang** pass right by the town of **Tha Hua** at the northern end of the reservoir, or you can switch vehicles at the Phonhong junction and cut in to Thalat and Na Nam. If you want to use the lake as an alternative route from Vientiane north to Vang Viang, charter a boat from Na Nam for the five-hour trip to Tha Hua and then continue by road to Vang Viang.

Several travel companies offer very affordable one- to three-day **package tours** to the reservoir out of Vang Viang, which combine hiking, boating and camping.

Accommodation

Accommodation ranging from grass huts to casino suites is available at a few locations around the reservoir. Near the dam itself, a few kilometres away from the reservoir, there's *EDL Bungalows* (⑤), built to house Japanese engineers who worked on the dam, and featuring air-conditioning and hot water. To reach it, take a shared tuk-tuk from Thalat bound for Na Nam; the bungalows are about halfway along the route, near the dam, on the left. If you fancy your luck at the gaming tables, you could splash out at the *DanSaVanh Nam Ngum Resort* (see opposite). Don Dok Khoun Kham offers the most accessible **island-based accommodation** (see opposite), although the views from the run-down guesthouse and restaurant here are of the dam and the less than picturesque port of Na Nam. Further out, better views can be had on Don Mittaphab, but its only hotel (①) is even more run-down than the one on Don Dok Khoun Kham, and has no electricity. Basic food only is available, so it's best to bring extra provisions. A ride out here from Na Nam takes about half an hour. Another paradisiacal island with extemely basic accommodation is Don Santiphap, a tiny little islet with a simple guesthouse fit for Robinson Crusoe.

Na Nam

Although relatively few people live in **NA NAM**, a port of rickety shacks suspended above the water, it does have a clutch of tourist restaurants, basic accommodation, and a fleet of wooden tourist boats – some seating up to forty passengers – for **lake cruises**. Freelance boatmen down at the waterfront restaurants generally ask for $4 per hour but are willing to negotiate day rates in the vicinity of $12. Na Nam guesthouses can also arrange boat tours. Obviously, the more people you have, the more affordable it becomes. Beyond simply touring the reservoir, possibilities for boat trips include Don Dok Khoun Kham, where there's a rustic restaurant; the secluded beach at Don Keng Phou Viang – the hour-long trip to which passes the scenic Pha Tao or "star cliff" island – or

Festivals

All major Lao festivals, whether Buddhist or animist in nature, are multi-faceted affairs with parades, games, music and dancing, not to mention the copious consumption of lào-láo, a liquor made from sticky rice. Besides the nationwide festivals listed here, there are numerous local festivals (called bun wat), centred around a monastery; ask at your accommodation for details. If you happen to be in a town or village that is gearing up for a festival, consider altering your plans so that you can attend – unless you're a teetotaller, in which case you're advised to clear out immediately. In rural areas especially, a festival can transform an entire village into a wild, week-long party.

Major festivals

Because the Lao calendar is dictated by both solar and lunar rhythms, the dates of festivals change from year to year, and even just a few days prior to a parade or boat race, there is sometimes confusion over just when it will take place. For the Lao this is not really a problem, as the days leading up to and immediately following large lunar festivals are filled with merrymaking as well.

Makkha Busa (full moon in February)

This Buddhist holy day, observed by merit-making, commemorates a legendary sermon given by the Buddha after 1250 of his disciples spontaneously congregated around the enlightened one.

Lao New Year (April 15–17)

Called *pi mai lao*, the beginning of the Lao New Year is fervently celebrated all over Laos, most stunningly in Louang Phabang. There, the town's namesake Buddha image is ritually bathed by

townsfolk; a procession led by Phu Nyoe and Nya Nyoe (the guardian spirits of Louang Phabang), and the Seven Daughters of Brahma, is held; sand stupas are erected in monastery grounds; and Buddhists make a pilgrimage to nearby caves to bathe the Buddha images stored there.

In villages and small towns, the lunar new year is marked with *basi* ceremonies (see p.66) and merrymaking. If you're in the right place at the right time, you may be ambushed by young people carrying pails of water and armed with squirt guns. After being forced to down a few shots of *lào-láo*,

▲ New Year high jinks

you will be given a thorough drenching followed by a liberal dusting with talcum powder and frenzied smearing with blood-red lipstick.

▲ Monks making fireworks

Bun Bang Fai (May)

Also known as the rocket festival, this rain-making ritual predates Buddhism in Laos, and is a madcap combination of fireworks and firewater. Crude rockets are fashioned from stout bamboo poles stuffed with gunpowder and, after being blessed, are propped up on wooden launch platforms that resemble rickety ladders to heaven. As villagers dance and cheer, the rockets are shot skywards. The thundering noise and clouds of smoke reassuringly simulate rainy season conditions, which is in turn supposed to inspire the spirits to produce the real thing. Celebrations in the south can be wonderfully bawdy: men brandishing foot-long, wooden phalluses give the local maidens something to giggle about. The rocket festival is also very popular with the ethnic Lao in northeastern Thailand, where it has evolved into more of a sporting event, with participants wagering on what heights the rockets will attain.

Wisakha Busa (full moon in May)

Commemorating the historic Buddha's birth, enlightenment and passing into nirvana, this is celebrated in much the same way as Makkha Busa.

Lai Heua Fai (full moon in October)

A festival of lights, this event is most magically celebrated in Louang Phabang. In the days leading up to the festival the different neighbourhoods, or *ban*, that make up the city build large floats and festoon them with lights. On the appointed evening, the floats are paraded along Xiang Thong Road to Wat Xiang Thong, where they are judged for aesthetic merit, and are then carried down to the Mekong and set atop boats for a second procession on the river. All evening, along the Mekong River road, vendors offer saucer-sized floats made from banana stalks and leaves and containing flowers, incense and a candle. After selecting one, celebrants take the little offerings down to the river and launch them on the current.

▲ Illuminated float, Lai Heua Fai

Lai Heua Fai is celebrated concurrently with Awk Phansa, the end of the three-month "rains retreat", a time when laypeople donate new robes and other offerings to Buddhist monasteries.

Suang heua (October to December)

What at first glance may seem to be a mere sporting event is actually rooted in ancient beliefs that predate Buddhism in Laos. To this day, many lowland Lao believe that the Mekong and other local waterways are the abode of *naga*, serpent-like creatures that leave the river during the rainy season and inhabit the flooded paddy fields (see box on p.146). The boat races, held near the end of the rainy season, seek to lure the *naga* out of the fields and back into the rivers, so that ploughing may begin.

▲ Boat race on the Mekong

During the days of the monarchy, the quasi-religious ceremonies involved in building and launching the boats were as important as the races themselves. Sadly, though, these rituals have been suppressed since the revolution. Still, the Lao thoroughly enjoy themselves at the races, finding in them yet another reason to imbibe large quantities of *lào-láo*.

That Louang Festival (full moon in November)

In the days leading up to this, the great That Louang stupa in Vientiane comes to resemble the centrepiece of a fairground, as vendors hawking everything imaginable set up booths in the open spaces around it. The week-long festival kicks off with a mass **alms-giving** to hundreds of monks and a **procession** from Wat Simuang to That Louang. Over the next few days a series of bands and performances occupy a stage near the stupa, and *tikhi*, a game resembling field hockey in which the ball traditionally symbolizes the skull of a demon, is played. On the last evening, the whole city shows up to process with offerings around That Louang.

Bun Pha Wet (December or January)

Commemorating the Jataka tale of the Buddha's second-to-last incarnation as Pha Wet, or Prince Vessantara, this celebration takes place at the local monastery, where a contingent of monks recite the tale as a long chant. In larger towns, entertainment in the form of a live band and dancing takes place.

▼ Procession to That Louang, Vientiane

even down to the *DanSaVanh Nam Ngum Resort*. Some of the islands are quite large; Don 516, for instance, supports a community of five hundred families and is connected to Na Nam twice daily by a passenger ferry (almost 3hr).

Eating figures highly in the weekend plans of Lao tourists, and several restaurants have set up shop in and around Na Nam to cater to this demand. *Nam Ngum*, in the port overlooking the water, delivers with freshly caught reservoir fish cooked in a variety of ways, and has an exceptional view of the lake. Just down the hill, *Boathouse*, a ramshackle barge with pleasant views, does good, moderately priced food. When there's an order, fish kept under the boat are netted and pulled right into the middle of the restaurant.

Don Dok Khoun Kham

Just a ten-minute boat ride from Na Nam, small, densely forested **Don Dok Khoun Kham**, the most accessible of the islands, boasts a pleasant restaurant and a rapidly decaying two-storey **guesthouse** (❷) that will be a sure hit with horror-film fans. The eight rooms, of varying shapes and sizes, are all a little the worse for wear. During the week, few guests stay here and the house can at times be without water or electricity, although this is usually only the case if you've arrived after sunset and the caretaker is off spear-fishing for the night. If you don't mind roughing it a bit, the island makes for a pleasant, quiet stay. You might want to bring added provisions and a deck of cards, although the guesthouse is well stocked with necessities such as rice, water and Beer Lao, and fresh fish is always on the restaurant menu. Guests are shuttled by pirogue between the guesthouse and the restaurant across a small cove. The islanders will ferry you back to the mainland for significantly less than what the boatmen in Na Nam charge to pick you up.

DanSaVanh Nam Ngum Resort

A joint venture between the Lao military and a private Malaysian company, the *DanSaVanh Nam Ngum Resort* is located on the southwestern shore of the lake (℡021/217594-6, ⓦwww.dansavanh.com; ❻). Besides a swimming pool, eighteen-hole golf course, spa and Thai–Chinese restaurant, it also has post-communist Laos's first **casino**, mainly aimed at gamblers from Thailand – and the Thai baht is the currency of the tables (kip aren't even accepted). The 24-hour gaming centre includes tables for blackjack, baccarat and tai-sai (the Chinese three-dice game), roulette and Australian slot machines. This self-styled "mega eco-tourism resort" also offers (and this is where the "eco-resort" tag really starts to stretch thin) speedboat rides, mountain-biking, disco and, of course, karaoke. After all that activity, the hotel website suggests that the "cheerful massage girls can pamper your tired body".

While you can get to the **resort** by chartered boat from Na Nam, it's more practical to come directly from Vientiane by road. There are free casino shuttle-buses from both the Friendship Bridge and major hotels in the capital.

The northwest

Although Vientiane and Louang Phabang are both on the banks of the Mekong River, the land between them is extremely mountainous, while the opposite left bank of the Mekong, composed of huge ranges separating Laos and Thailand, forms its own remote province of **Xainyabouli**. As almost everyone's itinerary in Laos includes the journey between Vientiane and Louang Phabang, you're highly likely to cross this stunning terrain at some point, and there are three main options to choose from for travel between the two cities.

The first and simplest option is to follow **Route 13** north from Vientiane through the karst mountains of Vang Viang and up the **old Royal Road** through the mountains north of **Kasi**. Route 13 was first completed by the French in 1943, and although it was improved in the 1960s with American aid, there was very little maintenance on the road until the mid-1990s, when it was properly sealed. Until that time, this rough track of a road took at best a full 24 hours to traverse, and often as long as three days. The highway was finally completed in 1996 after years of toil by Vietnamese road workers, twenty of whom were killed by guerrillas in the process. The breathtaking mountain scenery from Kasi to Louang Phabang makes this one of the most **scenic routes** in all Southeast Asia.

If you don't fancy making the ten-hour bus journey from Vientiane to Louang Phabang in one go, **Vang Viang** makes an ideal stopover and is well worth an extended visit in its own right, with beautiful caves and **ethnic minority villages** nearby, and a host of outdoor activities to keep you occupied, floating down the Nam Xong on huge tractor inner tubes being among the most popular. The **Phou Phanang NBCA** runs close to Route 13 for 75km, but although two tracks lead into the reserve off of Route 13, the NBCA is still fairly inaccessible to tourists. However, if you're prepared to rent a four-wheel-drive vehicle or dirt bike from Vientiane, you could try a dirt track running the entire western boundary of the reserve and linking several villages.

The second route, a detour through **Xainyabouli**, the sparsely populated region of rugged valleys and wild elephants on the western side of the Mekong, is more complicated, and takes you along a path well off the banana-pancake backpacker circuit. Unless you have your own four-wheel-drive vehicle, the Xainyabouli route necessitates travelling at least part of the way by boat along the Mekong – the lack of decent roads west of the capital makes Xainyabouli much more remote than it appears on maps. The third route is to travel the whole way by **boat** (see p.107), an attractive option but requiring at least three days of travel time by slow boat, although speedboats can make the trip in a day.

Vang Viang

VANG VIANG reclines on the east bank of the Nam Xong River, snugly settled between a spectacular spread of sawtoothed limestone karsts to the west and rolling hills to the east. You could easily spend up to a week here cycling, cave exploring, tubing, rafting and hiking, or simply relaxing and enjoying the lazy country atmosphere, good food and idyllic landscape. The town was already a popular backpacker destination way back in the Seventies, when the trip took a full day from the capital. Today, Vang Viang has quickly responded to the new wave of budget travellers and offers a huge range of backpacker-oriented guesthouses and other amenities, including Internet cafés, video bars, massage, laundry services and pizzerias.

Depending on when you get here, the town can in the space of a few days become totally packed out or almost empty, as the tourist crowds ebb and flow. When Vang Viang is crowded, it can feel *very* crowded, and the centre of town can seem like an inland version of Thailand's Hat Rin on Ko Pha Ngan. Still, a pleasant walk in the cool of the morning to a nearby cave, or a lazy float down the river, will dispel any notions that Vang Viang has become irredeemably spoiled.

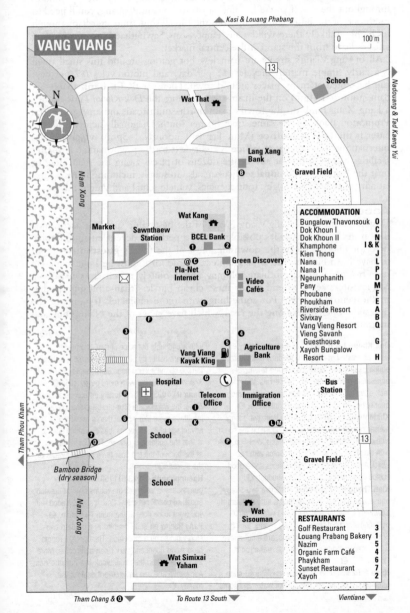

VANG VIANG

0   100 m

▲ Kasi & Louang Phabang

▶ Naduoang & Tad Kaeng Yui

N

Nam Xong

Wat That

School

Lang Xang Bank

Gravel Field

Market

Sawnthaew Station

Wat Kang

BCEL Bank

Green Discovery

Pla-Net Internet

Video Cafés

Vang Viang Kayak King

Agriculture Bank

Hospital

Telecom Office

Immigration Office

Bus Station

School

School

Bamboo Bridge (dry season)

Nam Xong

Gravel Field

13

Wat Sisouman

Wat Simixai Yaham

▲ Tham Phou Kham

▼ Tham Chang & ⊙   ▼ To Route 13 South   ▼ Vientiane

ACCOMMODATION	
Bungalow Thavonsouk	O
Dok Khoun I	C
Dok Khoun II	N
Khamphone	I & K
Kien Thong	J
Nana	L
Nana II	P
Ngeunphanith	D
Pany	M
Phoubane	F
Phoukham	E
Riverside Resort	A
Sivixay	B
Vang Vieng Resort	Q
Vieng Savanh Guesthouse	G
Xayoh Bungalow Resort	H

RESTAURANTS	
Golf Restaurant	3
Louang Prabang Bakery	1
Nazim	5
Organic Farm Café	4
Phaykham	6
Sunset Restaurant	7
Xayoh	2

Practicalities

Sawngthaews and buses to and from Vientiane and Louang Phabang arrive at the **bus station**, on Route 13 just to the east of town, and within walking distance of most accommodation. **Buses** and **sawngthaews** going north and south along Route 13 stop at the bus station. If you're heading to Vientiane, sawngthaews are much more convenient, leaving every twenty minutes throughout the day. If you're heading north to Louang Phabang, you'll need to catch one of the buses coming up from the capital sometime after 9am, though it's highly unlikely there will be any empty seats. Sawngthaews to surrounding villages leave from the stand at the central market.

All of Vang Viang's streets are nameless, but getting around this small town is a fairly simple matter. Bicycles ($1 per day) and motorcycles ($7 per day) can be rented at many places around town. There's a BCEL **bank** (Mon–Sat 8am–noon & 1–4pm) on the main street opposite the *Dok Khoun I* guesthouse, a Lang Xang Bank on the town's main north–south road, and an Agricultural Promotion Bank on the same street further south. Diagonally across from the latter is the **telecom office** (Mon–Fri 8am–noon & 1–5pm), which handles international calls; the **post office** is right next to the town market. **Internet** facilities can be found at any of the dozens of places along the main drag or near the market. All the usual services are also in supply, including herbal sauna, laundry, massage, photo labs, tour agencies, vehicle rental and video movies.

Accommodation

Despite its small size, Vang Viang is one of the best-value spots for accommodation in the country – it's possible to find a perfectly decent en-suite double here for under $5. On the downside, most of the town's **guesthouses** seem to have been built by the same architect, whose forte must be huge, concrete monstrosities with Corinthian columns and absolutely no charm whatsoever. Most visitors seem to end up in these cheap but less-than-atmospheric digs in the centre of town. For something with more character, try one of the bungalow operations along the river, which have views of the Nam Xong and mountains beyond.

Dok Khoun I & II Clean, tiled rooms, many en suite and with hot water, in modern multistorey buildings at three locations around town. Very popular, and so big there's no worries about a lack of vacancies. Reasonably good value and quality but no personality or atmosphere. ❸

Khamphone ☏023/511062. Two large two-storey houses opposite one another. The house on the south side of the road has eighteen spacious, well-lit rooms with tile floors and en-suite bathrooms with hot water. A cut above other similar places and a good choice if you're not on too strict a budget. ❹

Kien Thong ☏023/511069. Attractive two-storey house with a spiral staircase and a little restaurant downstairs. Has 21 doubles, most with en-suite bathrooms and hot water. The a/c rooms, which are double the price of fan rooms, are a cut above with queen-sized bed and a fridge in the room. Good value. ❸

Nana ☏023/511036. Fourteen spacious en-suite doubles in a big house, all with hot water and some with a/c (double the price of fan). The upstairs rooms are better by far and there's also a pleasant terrace on the second floor. Same quality as the *Dok Khoun* next door but with more personality. ❸

Nana II ☏023/511070. Totally different from the *Nana*, the *Nana II* is a four-storey, L-shaped building that's more like a hotel than a guesthouse. The advantage of its 25 rooms, besides being cheap, is that the building is newish. The corner rooms at the back of the top floor have the best views of the karsts. ❸

Ngeunphanith ☏023/511150. A two-storey guesthouse in which all the rooms are not created equal, so check out a few first. It's well placed – if you want to be right at the main T-junction. ❶

Pany Roomy en-suite doubles in a modern two-storey house on a quiet lane. The upstairs rooms have wood floors and very clean bathrooms. More atmosphere than the usual block-like guesthouses. Above average and an excellent deal for the money. ❷

Phoubane South of the market, just in from the river road ☎023/511037. One of the best deals in town, in a pleasant, leafy compound, with decent rooms, some en suite. There's also a Lao herbal sauna that non-residents can use. ❶

Phoukham Directly behind the *Dok Khoun I*. An ugly building with gaudy pillars and rooms that are better value than in similar places, though not great in themselves. Several of the upstairs rooms have good views of the karsts. ❶

Riverside Resort On the northern edge of town ☎023/511035. A great location and sturdy wooden bungalows with small verandas make this a relaxing spot. The original cheap huts are being slowly converted into bungalows, but there are still a few left, and they share a spotless bathroom. ❸

Sivixay ☎023/511030. These two modern buildings, set in a large compound, aren't much to look at from the outside, but contain seventeen very decent, tiled en-suite doubles with fan and hot water, at below-average prices. ❶

Thavonsouk Resort ☎023/511096, ⓦwww .thavonsouk.com. At the bamboo bridge. Superbly located deluxe en-suite bungalows with a total of 35 units spread along the banks of the Nam Xong. Prices depend on the size and quality of bungalow, some of which have private balconies facing the karsts. ❺

Vang Vieng Resort A 15min walk south along the river from the market ☎023/511050. Standard en-suite bungalows with decent facilities and hot shower. Good if you want to get as far away from the hustle and bustle of town as possible. ❻

Vieng Savanh Guesthouse East of the hospital ☎023/511112. A large, white block of concrete, inside which the acoustics amplify every door slam. Still, if you can tolerate a little noise, this place is fairly good value overall. ❶

Xayoh Bungalows On the river road. The bungalows have en-suite bathrooms and are comfortable and spacious, but lackadaisical service sometimes makes this Xayoh-run place feel like a ship with no one at the helm. Happily, things are still new and in working order, so there is little reason to have to look for the staff anyway, and there's a popular restaurant. ❻

Eating and drinking

Vang Viang has no lack of newly arrived dreamers from abroad who are willing to sink their cash into a new restaurant or watering hole, despite a purge of foreign-owned businesses in 2001 (a *Time* magazine article about drug use among backpackers was used as a pretext), which allowed these firms to be overtaken by locals. Thanks to these wide-eyed foreign entrepreneurs, and lax regulations and the low start-up costs associated with the town, foreign-run eating and drinking establishments aren't unusual in Vang Viang – in fact, they're proportionally more common here than in Vientiane or Louang Phabang – and it's possible to get anything from vindaloos to fish tacos in Vang Viang. Budget travellers tend to gravitate to the main north–south road where there's a whole strip of cheap restaurants offering a choice of Western-style seating or mats or cushions at low tables, and often showing DVD movies. Aside from restaurants in town, there are a few decent places overlooking the river.

Golf Restaurant Despite the name, there's no connection with the game. The food is better-than-average traveller fare. Try the tuna melt on whole rye bread. Regular runs to Udon keep the menu fresh and interesting.

Louang Prabang Bakery Near BECL Bank. This only has a couple of tables, but is the place to come for brekky. Lao coffee is served blond and very sweet in short glasses: stir up the sweetened condensed milk with one of those little aluminium spoons made from recycled jet-fuel canisters.

Nazim ☎023/511214. Serving vegetarian and non-vegetarian Indian food, and absolutely packed most evenings, though there have been many next-day reports of the food being a little too authentically Indian.

Organic Farm Café Popular with vegetarians, this restaurant, which is an outlet for a local experimental organic farm, is definitely worth seeking out. The harvest curry with fresh veggies in a creamy curry broth is particularly good.

Phaykham This old favourite serves basic Lao grub and sandwiches.

Sunset Restaurant At *Bungalow Thavonsouk* by the bamboo bridge ☎023/511096. A decent place for a sundowner, boasting a million-dollar view across the Nam Xong, and quite good Western and Lao food.

Xayoh A good place for a drink or meal, and boasting a view that is sure to induce a contented sigh. The thin, crispy pizzas are recommended. You can eat either inside or on the outdoor patio. There's also an attached Internet centre.

Around Vang Viang

The **countryside** surrounding Vang Viang is full of enough day-trip options to easily fill up a week. Scores of **caves** in limestone karst outcrops, tranquil lowland Lao and minority villages, and **Kaeng Yui Waterfall**, all make worthy destinations for a rewarding day's hike (if walking isn't your thing, you can hire bicycles or motorbikes from various outlets around town), while the Nam Xong River makes for a fun afternoon of **tubing**, **kayaking** or **rafting** – tubes can be rented at a number of shops on the main street leading to the market. Aside from a number of organized tours around Vang Viang itself, there are also one- to three-day excursions to Ang Nam Ngum Reservoir (see p.111) which can be booked through most guesthouses.

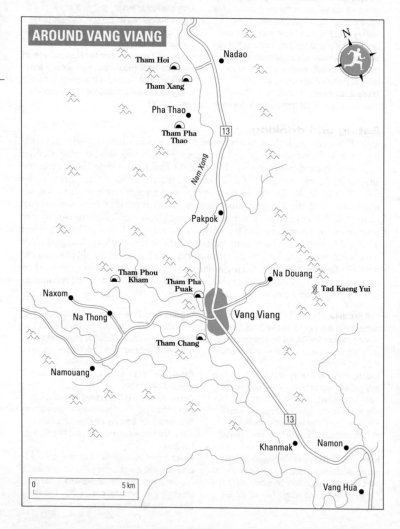

Dress for success in Vang Viang

The **varied terrain** surrounding Vang Viang can turn treacherous in a hurry, particularly during the rainy season. **Exercise caution** while wandering through caves and scrambling about on the steep slopes of the karst formations, as serious injuries incurred by foolhardy travellers while tramping about in the area are common. Slippery trails demand that proper shoes be worn – Teva-style sandals with good traction are the best for conquering Vang Viang's alternately rocky and muddy trails. Bermuda-type shorts are also a good sartorial choice as you may end up knee-deep in water at some point if you intend to enjoy the countryside to the fullest. A re-sealable plastic bag for valuables such as money and your passport is an excellent idea. Do not leave your valuables with local youths, who may offer to "look after them for you" while you explore a cave.

Finally, while it may be tempting to wander around in your swimming gear (and it's not uncommon to see travellers sunbathing half-naked on the banks of the Nam Xong), always remember that in Laos gratuitous displays of flesh are considered a form of rudeness and disrespect.

Organized day tours, many of which combine both caving and tubing with lunch in between, are a fast and convenient way for the uninitiated to get into the Vang Viang groove: once you've done the tour you can go back for more on your own. It's not hard to find a guided tour – just look for signs posted in restaurants and guesthouses. If you do opt to join a tour, be sure to check how many people will be in the group. Some agents have few qualms about stuffing twenty people into a single sawngthaew, which not only spoils a good walk but can seriously hasten the onset of claustrophobia if tramping about several hundred metres underground.

If you decide to visit the caves on your own, it's worth getting hold of one of the hand-drawn **maps** of the Vang Viang area which show all the **caves** and **trails**; they're available from several of the restaurants and guesthouses in town. Otherwise just ask around; everyone in Vang Viang has their favourite cave, swimming hole or countryside getaway. The local people are more than happy to point you in the right direction, and other travellers will also enthusiastically recommend the best places. If you're looking to explore areas north or south of town, there's enough local transport in the form of buses and sawngthaews plying Route 13 to get you up and down the highway cheaply. Or, if you prefer something quick and easy, just hire a tuk-tuk (the stand is at the market), which will gladly wait for you for the right price.

Most of Vang Viang's attractions lie on the **west bank** of the Nam Xong. There still isn't a permanent bridge so you have to cross either via the rickety bamboo bridge (foreigners are sometimes charged 1000K to cross outbound) by the *Nam Song Hotel* or, during the rainy season when the bridge is dismantled, by pirogue. On the other side, Chinese-made tractors trundle along the bumpy paths to nearby villages, acting as makeshift shared taxis that aren't entirely comfortable but are at least faster than walking. These wait at the river's edge; elsewhere you can simply flag them down as you would a bus or tuk-tuk.

There are three **kayaking** and **rafting** companies operating in Vang Viang. For more strenuous outdoor activities, Green Discovery (☎023/511230, ⓦwww
.greendiscoverylaos.com) has a number of options, including day-trip packages as well as overnight hiking and kayaking excursions. The same company is also behind Laos's first fully operational **rock-climbing** site, featuring fifty different bolted routes (graded from 5b to 8c on the French grading system) in the Vang Vieng area. A day's climbing costs $45 with equipment, a guide and lunch.

△ Bemboo bridge, Vang Viang area

Chang Cave

Vang Viang's best-known cave, **Tham Chang**, has been developed for tourism to such an extent that the proprietors of *Vang Vieng Resort*, whose land you have to cross to get to the cave, levy a fee to enter the resort and again at the cave's entrance (10,000K). In the nineteenth century, the cave earned its nom de guerre when it was used for defence during an invasion of Chinese Haw from the north ("chang" means steadfast). Chinese bandits would have an easy run of the place these days, with steep stairs leading up the side of the cliff to the cave mouth. Inside, gaudy coloured lights illuminate cement pathways leading through the cavern, past rock formations that bear an uncanny resemblance to monkeys, frogs, a white elephant and the three-headed elephant, symbol of Lao royalty. Follow the path to the left and you'll wind up at a second cave mouth which affords a bird's-eye view of the valley below. At the base of the cave, cross a stream to find a third cave mouth out of which flows a spring leading into the Nam Xong. It's possible to swim up the stream about 50m into this cave, which also has a Buddha image inside. The grassy lawn around the base of the cave is a pleasant spot to catch some rays.

Pha Puak Cave

A little more than 1km north of Ban Houay Nye lies **Tham Pha Puak**, a cave tucked into a karst encircled by Pha Daeng, or the Red Cliffs. Pha Daeng is considered particularly sacred and some locals even maintain that planes flying over the cliff do so at their peril, no doubt a legend with roots in the Second Indochina War, when Vang Viang was used as an airbase, known to pilots as Lima Site 6. Although in and of itself nothing special, the cave makes a good short walk out of Vang Viang. To get there, cross the river then follow the signs on the path through the rice fields north of Ban Houay Nye.

Tubing the Nam Xong

One of Vang Viang's most popular activities, a lazy afternoon floating down the **Nam Xong** on huge tractor inner tubes, runs a close second to caving on many travellers' itineraries, and some people make several trips. It's a good way to relax, take in the view and just be mellow, with enough rapids and tiny islands to keep things interesting. You can also stop at beaches along the way for a rest or a walk, and some enterprising villagers even sell cold soft drinks from the river bank. **Tubes** are available from a number of shops in town for $3, and this includes a tuk-tuk ride upriver to the launching point.

The main launching point is near the village of **Pakpok**, roughly 4km north of Vang Viang, which makes for a two- to three-hour trip. If you're in for something longer, jump in at the bend in the river at the Kilometre 10 marker (see p.122), which will have you in the water for at least five hours. But before you grab your tube and race for the river, take note that a few people have drowned tubing down the river, which is swift in spots; it's quite easy to become temporarily separated from your tube. If you can't swim or are a weak swimmer, wear a life jacket while tubing – the shops supplying the inner tubes should provide them (and don't go tubing if you happen to be drunk or stoned). You'll also need a good sunblock and a hat if you don't want to come out looking like a lobster; the tropical sun is powerful, even on overcast days. Exercise common sense and ask about river conditions before you float off down the river, and, unless you want to end up entering the Mekong 70km east of Vientiane, be sure to position yourself towards the east bank when you see Vang Viang town to your left, so you can get out at the *Nam Song Hotel*.

Phou Kham Cave

Six kilometres west of Vang Viang, **Tham Phou Kham** makes a rewarding half-day trip that takes in some fine scenery and affords the chance to visit a cave and enjoy a good swim along the way. Cross the river by pirogue at the launch near the *Nam Song Hotel* and follow the road through a pretty valley, ringed by imposing karsts, to **Na Thong**, 4km west. Hop the fence at the bend in the road just past the village school house and walk through the rice fields towards the cliff face, 1km in the distance. When you see the bizarrely arched bamboo bridge, cross it and you'll reach the path leading to the cave. It's a short steep climb to the entrance and the path is extremely slippery in the rainy season, but there's plenty of bamboo to grab on to on the way up. In the main cavern reclines a bronze Buddha, while there are tunnels branching off the main gallery that you can explore if you have a torch. Outside the cave, the Hollywood-swimming-pool-blue stream is a great spot for a swim, and you can buy cool drinks and fruit nearby. If you've come by bike, it's best to leave it at the *tam màk hung* stall across from the village school.

Kaeng Yui Waterfall

While it may seem counterintuitive to turn your back on Vang Viang's majestic karsts, a day spent out east at **Tad Kaeng Yui**, with its twin thirty-metre-high waterfalls, is well worth the trip. Off the beaten track, Tad Kaeng Yui nestles in the forest among the hills protecting Vang Viang's eastern flank. Besides offering a refreshingly cool picnic spot, with small pools of water directly under the falls to lounge in, it rewards the journey with the sense of being smack in the middle of the tropics, miles from anywhere.

To find the falls, first cross Route 13 just north of the old airstrip, and follow this road, flagged by the secondary school on the corner, 3km east to the village of **Na Douang**. As the path to the waterfall, another 3km from the village, can be completely obscured by bamboo (the falls are rarely visited, even by locals), your safest bet is to pay a villager from Na Douang to show you the way. From Na Douang, head southeast towards the hills by cutting through the village rice fields; beyond the fields lies a path leading uphill, through scrub forest, across a number of small streams, and then into the woods. Once you've reached the woods, push on for another 300m; the path turns left and the falls become audible.

Plans to exploit the waterfall's tourism potential by building a road out to the falls, which will undoubtedly spoil the spot's secluded beauty, are a sign that times have changed. For now, getting there remains a muddy affair much of the year – even travelling as far as Na Douang. If you plan to do the trip by bicycle, a sit-up-and-beg model risks turning the trip into a Sisyphean feat, but it might be a good splash on a mountain bike.

Pha Thao Cave

A descent into **Tham Pha Thao** is the most satisfying caving trip you can make from Vang Viang. Stretching for more than 2km, the tunnel-like cave is pitch-black and filled with huge and presumably ancient stalactites and stalagmites. It also contains a **swimming hole**, formed in an underground river that winds through the cave. The cave is best visited near the end of the rainy season, when the water level is perfect for a swim in the subterranean pool 800m into the cave. In the height of the dry season, it's possible to go beyond this point and explore the full length of the cave – not an option during the rains when the water level is too high.

The cave is located in the cliff face behind **Pha Thao**, a smallish village populated by former Hmong refugees. The Hmong living here fled the northern mountains of Laos during the post-revolutionary turmoil of the late 1970s and early 1980s and wound up in a Thai refugee camp where they lived until being repatriated in the mid-1990s. Essentially, they are some of the Hmong who were denied visas to the United States and other Western nations and were forced to go "home". The village lies 13km north of Vang Viang; to reach it, turn left after the bridge just beyond the Kilometre 10 marker on Route 13 – a road sign points the way to the "Nam Xong-Pha Thao Irrigation Project" – and head for the river. Here, you'll have to ford the river or hail a pirogue to take you across for a few thousand kip. This spot also makes a good launching point for **tubing**. Once you've made it across the river, make your way to the village, which lies at the base of the cliff. Here, you'll find a few simple restaurants serving drinks and Hmong food, and the villagers will be happy to point you in the direction of the cave mouth which, obscured by boulders and trees, isn't terribly apparent. If you explore the cave during the rainy season, you'll be up to your chest in water at times – so travel light and don't bring along anything that you don't want to get wet. A waterproof torch and camera are a good idea. Tour groups often pull through this cave during the morning, so you may want to go in the afternoon.

Tham Xang and Tham Hoi

Situated in a karst outcrop that seems to rise from a bed of vibrant-green rice paddies, **Tham Xang** is easily visible from Route 13 about 13km north of Vang Viang. To get there turn left on the dirt road in the village of **Sinsomxai**, just beyond the Kilometre 13 marker, and follow the dirt road to the river. Climb the fence and walk along the paddies downriver, climb a second fence and walk past a sugar-cane field and down along the riverbank until you spot a bamboo bridge worthy of an Indiana Jones B-movie. Cross the river here to reach Tham Xang; if you're not feeling acrobatic you can hail a pirogue. Although it's more of an opening than a cave, Tham Xang is roomy enough to house a large Buddha image and is a popular attraction at Lao New Year.

If you've made it to Tham Xang, it's well worth continuing to **Tham Hoi**, a nearby cave as wide as a subway tunnel that reportedly stretches 2–4km into a nearby cliff, although patriotic locals profess it to be 20km deep. In mid-April, New Year revellers take advantage of a makeshift lighting scheme to visit the cave and a few feel the urge to express their inner Michelangelo; suffice to say, the cave isn't unspoilt, yet it's still a treat to visit. To get there from Tham Xang, head north, cross a small footbridge and then zigzag through the rice paddies in a northwesterly direction towards the cliff, 500m from Tham Hoi; a Buddha image stands guard just inside the cave mouth. A caretaker with a torch, who will lead the way for a small tip, claims that if the water level in the cave is right – usually late in the year – it's possible to make it far enough inside to reach a decent swimming hole.

The Royal Road: Kasi to Louang Phabang

KASI is the northernmost town before Route 13 begins its wild 170-kilometre stretch of highway along steep ridges and around hairpin bends, with headlong views of rugged valleys and remote mountains as far as the eye can see. The road runs right through the centre of town forming the main street, but the town itself lies in the attractive **Nam Lik river valley** surrounded by rice paddies and low hills, with the occasional karst adding an exotic touch to a pretty landscape. Within easy day-tripping distance of Kasi are numerous vast cave systems rumoured to dwarf anything found at Vang Viang, 60km to the south, but so far plans to develop the Kasi area into a tourist region have come to nought. If the rumours of Olympic-pool-sized cave lakes and caverns large enough to house cathedrals are only half true, then Kasi's crack at being the next Vang Viang may some day become a reality.

Buses plying the road between Vientiane and Louang Phabang usually make a lunch stop here, so there's half a dozen decent **places to eat** up and down the street. There are also three guesthouses, including the comfortable *Vanphisith Guesthouse* (**①**) near the centre of the strip. If you're staying here, you might want to go down to the sawmill by the river to watch the **elephants** that are still occasionally used to haul logs.

Vieng Kham

Perched on a narrow mountain ridge 39km north of Kasi and just 5km before Phou Khoun, the village of **Vieng Kham** offers good views to the west of one of Laos's most magnificent **peaks** – a gigantic, lone 2097-metre crag that rises like a giant tooth out of the flatlands below. If you're travelling south, Vieng Kham affords the first view of this breathtaking peak and its more distant companion, which stands at an equally impressive 2089m. Just beyond the second peak, out of view, is the Mekong River, and beyond that the distant mountains of Xainyabouli. Whether you're travelling north or south on Route 13, it's well worth getting a window seat on the west-facing side of the bus in order to photograph this spectacular peak. South of Vieng Kham there's a long, slow winding decent towards Kasi that provides good photo opportunities of this unforgettable mountain.

Phou Khoun and Route 7 to Phonsavan

A former French outpost, the mountain village of **PHOU KHOUN**, 44km north of Kasi, is the junction of Route 13 and Route 7. The village has sweeping views of the deep valleys below, and is the main market for people living in isolated villages around the area. Given the mountain location, be warned that the weather can get quite chilly here.

From Phou Khoun, **Route 7** branches off from Route 13 and travels due east across the Xiang Khouang Plateau to **Phonsavan** (see p.191) on the Plain of Jars. At the time of writing, the surfacing of Route 7 was behind schedule, and there was still a fifty-kilometre stretch of loose dirt road to cross, making the trip to Phonsavan a dusty ten- to twelve-hour run. This last stretch should be paved very soon, however, reducing the travelling time by several hours and opening up a whole new route to Phonsavan and Xam Nua. Once the work is complete, you can also expect to see more guesthouses in Phou Khoun as well as private sawngthaews doing the Phonsavan run. In the meantime, catching the daily bus to Phonsavan remains an ordeal. By the time the bus reaches Phou Khoun from Vientiane it is packed, so chances are you'll be standing all the way unless another passenger is prepared to sell you their seat. Should you get stuck at the junction, there's a single guesthouse, the *Chiher* (**①**), a two-storey shophouse with a green roof, which has no running water and very basic rooms.

Phou Khoun to Xiang Ngeun

Tiny picturesque villages cling to the mountain ridges every 20km or so for the rest of the journey north, none yet offering accommodation and only a few providing a table at which to eat a bowl of *fõe*. If you're travelling by rented or chartered vehicle, you could try the proper noodle shop at **Pha Keng Noi**, a small village perched on a narrow ridge 15km north of Phou Khoun. **Kiou Ka Cham**, 45km north of Phou Khoun, is an even larger town, populated by **Hmong**, and located high up in the mountains. It has several restaurants, tiny pharmacies and general stores selling basic goods and petrol out of old oil drums, the walls plastered with Vietnamese pin-ups and family snapshots of relatives living abroad – Hmong women dressed to the nines in extravagant traditional garb standing beside their sons and husbands in cheap suits in their suburban American homes. To the north the highway continues to wind through the green-blue mountains, passing ethnic-minority villages and swidden fields cutting bare the hillsides, until it reaches **Xiang Ngeun**, a large settlement 24km south of Louang Phabang. Xiang Ngeun is another important junction: from here **Route 2** heads southwest 110km to the provincial capital of Xainyabouli, on the western side of the Mekong River.

The Xainyabouli circuit

While the vast majority of visitors use Route 13 between Louang Phabang and the capital, it is possible to swing through Laos's northwestern frontier provided you're willing to allow three to four days for the journey. You can make the entire journey by slow boat, but if you opt for the road-and-river journey, **Paklai** and **Xainyabouli** are the best places to make stopovers. As there are still only rugged tracks between Vientiane and the south of Xainyabouli province, river travel is the best way to do that section of the trip. Route 2, running the length of **XAINYABOULI PROVINCE** between Louang Phabang and Kenthao, is especially beautiful, particularly in the rice-growing season (June–Nov), with the electric-green paddies set against a sea of bluish mountains – some as high as 2000m – receding in waves towards Thailand.

Something of a Lao Wild West, this remote, densely forested and mountainous province is home to elephants, tigers and the Sumatran rhino. Recognizing it as the perfect place to disappear, CIA operatives active in the Second Indochina War saw Xainyabouli as the escape route for **Vang Pao** and his band of Hmong irregulars (see p.330) should their "secret war" go wrong. They figured the Hmong would be at home in this province peopled by numerous hill tribes, among them Mien, Khamu and Akha, who migrate freely across the western border with Thailand. The untamed nature of the province is perhaps best illustrated by the traditional lifestyle of the **Mabri**, a tribe of nomadic hunter-gatherers numbering only a few hundred people, who are known to the Lao as *kha tawng leuang* or "slaves of yellow banana leaves" – the name is derived from the tribal custom of moving on as soon as the leaves of their huts turn yellow.

Some of the villages are so remote that they hardly feel part of Laos, finding it far more convenient to trade with Thai towns across the border, or to simply exist in relatively isolated self-sufficiency. Seizing upon the Lao government's seeming neglect of its far-flung villages, the Thais claimed three Lao villages near the border as their own in a land grab during the 1980s – an incident that sparked two skirmishes between the historic rivals during the course of four years and highlighted the vagueness of the border.

These days the line separating Laos from its larger neighbour has been sketched somewhat more permanently on the map, and it's back to business as usual for traders on either side, with the bustling border town of **Kenthao** functioning as a gateway for goods flowing across the Nam Huang River. A fair number of smuggled cars, sparkling new and without plates, also pass through here and continue on to Vientiane, where they change hands for a fraction of their tax-heavy cost. Amphetamine production is another thorny cross-border issue, with Thai police accusing clandestine factories on the Lao side of producing *ya ba*, or methamphetamine, which ends up on the streets of the Thai capital Bangkok.

A 150-kilometre-long section of the border with Thailand consists of the massive **Nam Phoun NBCA**, Laos's westernmost bio-conservation area. The chain of mountains forming the park's spine includes peaks as high as 1790m. Two significant streams, the Pouy and the Phoun, flow down from heights above and cross the width of Xainyabouli province before flowing into the Mekong. Although the town of Nakong on Route 2 sits right on the edge of the park, the NBCA has yet to be developed for trekking.

As you might expect, getting to Xainyabouli's remotest corners isn't easy. Secluded caves and waterfalls are out there, but none lies on the tourist route. The region will probably be one of the last places to benefit from the country's rapid improvements in tourist infrastructure, which is inspiration enough to try this route.

The Mekong River: Vientiane to Paklai

Speedboats take about four hours to complete the 217-kilometre journey between Vientiane and the Mekong river-port town of **Paklai**. The boats depart from Tha Hua Kao Liaw pier 10km west of Vientiane (see p.107) – be sure to get to the pier early in the morning, as it's first come first served for space on the speedboat ($20). If there are no other passengers, it's possible to charter a speedboat for $100. **Slow boats** are only for cargo these days, and are very infrequent.

Upstream from Vientiane, the Mekong forms the Lao–Thai border. Golden stupas dot the banks of Laos's richer cousin, a marked contrast to the shaggy bamboo- and forest-clad hills on the right, many bearing the scars of logging. Further upriver, the Mekong swings north and the Lao tricolour flies from both banks for the first time since Champasak.

Paklai

PAKLAI, a port town 210km south of Louang Phabang, is the best stopover between Xainyabouli and Vientiane. Although not as developed as the border town of Kenthao, 60km to the south, Paklai is bigger, its wooden houses spreading for several kilometres along the riverbank. The town's economic mainstay is timber and timber products, a trade lucrative enough to draw Chinese businessmen from Singapore, Malaysia and China in their land cruisers and banged-up pick-ups to this remote town. Speedboats dock at the **boat landing** on the far southern end of town, 3km from the town square, where you'll find a few restaurants and guesthouses. Some captains will take you to Paklai's main port, which lies in the centre of town near the square; failing that, there's usually a tuk-tuk (1000K) at the top of the hill overlooking the pier.

You need look no further than the town square to see that Paklai's not up to much. A scruffy patch of grass with a puny white stupa, crudely crafted from stucco, and topped with a red communist star, provides a backdrop for schoolchildren to play tag but little else. Here you'll find the town's main **restaurant**, which serves, among a variety of rice dishes, generous helpings of fried rice with a tasty sauce on the side. Further up the street is a small noodle shop, also nameless, popular for its *foe*. The restaurant can also handle a few rice dishes and makes decent Lao coffee. Across the street stands the *Khemekong* (❶), a wooden **guesthouse** with thirteen rooms, usually reserved for government employees. A better option is the friendly *Ban Na* (❶), a short walk upriver on the right, which has clean rooms and a seating area with a nice view of the river. If you're desperate, a third, government-owned guesthouse, the *Pak Lay* (❶), lies at the end of this road on the left. Nearly 1km away from the main ferry landing, next to a sawmill, this is a bit run-down and there are no restaurants nearby; the manager does her best, however, and her pet monkey provides entertainment gratis.

Moving on, sawngthaews leave from the market in the morning for the 100-kilometre journey to Xainyabouli town (25,000K), departing when full. Speedboats sometimes make the trip up and down the Mekong, but you may have to charter one if they don't have enough passengers.

Xainyabouli

XAINYABOULI (pronounced "sai NYAboolee"), a dusty, independent-minded town, sits on the Nam Houng River, with the massive grey and white Pha Xang limestone cliffs – so named because they bear a passing resemblance to a herd of elephants in motion – providing a distant backdrop. At the centre of the town, there's a massive thirty-room hotel, an aborted government building begun by a former governor whose political largesse mocks the decidedly rustic atmosphere of Laos's most remote provincial capital. To add to the incongruity, Xainyabouli is also a training town for budding traffic cops, who are occasionally seen in groups of five or six waving their arms and blowing their whistles at

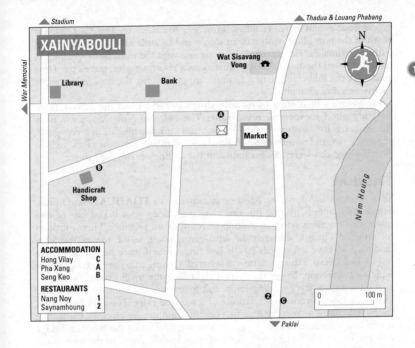

the town's empty roundabout. Unlike the traffic, the town's expat international aid and development community has grown significantly, as Xainyabouli province is one of the country's least developed areas.

The bustling **market** is the focus of the town's energies, and manages to maintain a buzz throughout the day. People from the local **hill tribes** often come down to buy and sell, spreading out their weird and wonderful range of produce (roots and forest creatures among other things) on swaths of cloth in neat rows around the fringe of the market proper, while members of the Mien tribe run the more established stalls. Few of the ethnic minorities in the market wear traditional clothes, however, preferring to dress in the style of the lowland Lao. The textiles available in this section of the market are mostly from Vientiane, so you won't find many treasures here. But east of the market, near the *Seng Keo*, there's a small **handicraft shop** selling eye-joltingly colourful Tai Leu textiles, of a style rarely found outside the province, as well as textiles from nearby Tai Dam villages.

Practicalities

Xainyabouli has two **bus stations**, the one at the southern end of town for pick-ups shuttling the one-hundred-kilometre all-weather road between Xainyabouli and Paklai, and the other at the northern end of town for vehicles making the forty-minute run to the Thadua ferry landing on the Mekong. Tuk-tuks make the trip into town from the bus stations, stopping at the central market (1200K). From the northern bus station there are direct sawngthaews to Louang Phabang, though sometimes the trip requires separate sawngthaews for each side of the river.

The *Seng Keo* (**1**), a two-storey house with a stone facade set in a grassy compound one block east of the post office, is the best **guesthouse**, with decent doubles and shared facilities. If the *Seng Keo* is full, try *Pha Xang* (●), just north of the post office, with sixteen rooms and an attractive courtyard flowing with bougainvillea. The town's disco, complete with the usual hostess scene, sits directly behind the hotel. Finally, situated on a riverfront plot, there's the *Hong Vilay* (●); the lobby and shared facilities are grubby but the double and triple rooms are clean enough.

Along with a smattering of **noodle shops** in and around the market, there are a few good, inexpensive **restaurants**. The well-run *Nang Noy*, across from the market, is the most established – it may not look like much, but serves good, expensive rice and noodle dishes. A few hundred metres away, the clean, well-lit *Saynamhoung* also serves decent food and has an English-language menu.

Thadua

Slow boats up and down the Mekong usually stop in **THADUA**, 35km north-east of Xainyabouli, making this tiny river port, along with Paklai, one of two towns that travellers wind up visiting in Xainyabouli province. There's little to recommend Thadua, although the aqua-green house at the top of the ferry landing does have a few beds (●). If you find yourself stuck here, a short hike out to **Tad Chao**, a thirty-metre-tall waterfall flowing into the Mekong, makes a pleasant diversion. To get there, turn right after the small market, which sits at the top of the ferry landing ramp, and follow the road until it ends (about 1km) at a small stream on the far side of a wooded ridge. The path leading off to the left climbs a short distance to a pair of unimpressive grottoes, containing a *rishi* and a Buddha image. To get to the waterfall, cross the wooden bridge and you'll eventually come to a flight of stairs leading down to the base of the fall. Tad Chao is not Laos's most spectacular fall, but the fact that this popular Sunday picnic spot perches at the side of the Mekong River certainly adds to its appeal.

From Thadua, **speedboats** make the trip to Louang Phabang regularly, taking about two hours, but unless there are other passengers you'll have to charter the whole boat. Slow boats for Louang Phabang take nearly four times as long. Pirogues skirt across the river regularly, although if you've come by your own transport you're at the mercy of the Thadua ferry, which can take up to an hour. Large sawngthaews bound for Louang Phabang queue up along the ferry landing ramp on the opposite bank, a gathering of petrol stations and thatch huts known as **Pakkhon**.

Muang Nan and the road to Louang Phabang

At first glance, **MUANG NAN**, around 20km northeast of Thadua on the road to Louang Phabang, seems little more than a dusty truck-stop whose only saving grace is its location in a slim, pretty valley full of rice fields. But walk off the highway and you'll find a town of traditional homes and old temples hugging the palm-lined banks of the babbling Nan River. The spirited villagers dam up the tiny river annually near the end of the monsoon and hold boat races with long, slender pirogues. While it's difficult to imagine the narrow river offering much sport to a flock of ducks, let alone a fleet of boats, enough city folk from Louang Phabang make the trip down to Nan for the event, held to celebrate Awk Phansa (see Festivals colour section), to make it a lively affair.

A government **guesthouse** stands on a small hill along the highway and has clean doubles and triples with shared facilities ($2 per person). The **restaurant** across from the guesthouse serves *fŏe* with an excellent homemade sauce of tamarind, peanuts and garlic, known as *jaew sakki*, on the side. If you order in advance, they can also prepare vegetable and chicken dishes with a country flair.

Sawngthaews in either direction usually pause briefly on their hourly run through the town. From here, it takes two to three hours to Louang Phabang by sawngthaew, but the gentle rollercoaster of a dirt road is scenic, negotiating uneven hills pocked with remote caves and swinging through narrow valleys of terraced rice fields cut in irregular rectangles, farmed by the hill tribes whose dusty bamboo-and-thatch huts hug the road. A kilometre north out of town, the highway cuts past Muang Nan's school on the right, with the makeshift huts of boarding students from far-flung ethnic minority villages clustered around the wooden school and football pitch along the road. Predominantly Mien, the children have been forced by the government to live in these temporary huts. It is hoped the children, growing up far from their highland villages, will acquire a taste for town life, as well as unlearn anything their tribal parents may have taught them. Thus the Lao government hopes to assimilate a potentially subversive minority.

Travel details

Buses

Pakkhon to: Louang Phabang (5 daily; 3hr); Muang Nan (5 daily; 2hr 30min).

Paklai to: Kenthao (1–2 daily; 1–2hr); Xainyabouli (1–3 daily; 3–4hr).

Vang Viang to: Louang Phabang (5 daily; 6hr); Vientiane (8 daily; 3hr).

Vientiane to: Friendship Bridge (every 45min; 45min); Kasi (8 daily; 5hr); Lak Xao (3 daily; 8hr); Lao Pako (3 daily; 1hr); Louang Phabang (5 daily; 10–12hr); Oudomxai (1 daily; 19hr); Pakxan (12 daily; 2hr); Pakxe (3 daily; 14hr); Phonsavan (2 daily; 18hr); Savannakhet (8 daily; 8 hr); Thakhek (10 daily; 6hr); Thalat (hourly; 2hr); Vang Viang (8 daily; 3hr 30min); Xam Nua (daily; 30hr).

Xainyabouli to: Paklai (1–3 daily; 3–4hr); Thadua (4 daily; 40min).

Boats

Thadua to: Louang Phabang (variable; 7–9hr).

Vientiane to: Louang Phabang via Paklai (infrequent; 3–4 days).

Domestic flights

Vientiane to: Houayxai (3 weekly; 1hr 20min); Louang Namtha (3 weekly; 1hr 10min); Louang Phabang (up to 4 daily; 40min); Oudomxai (4 weekly; 50min); Pakxe (1 daily; 1hr 20min); Phonsali (2 weekly; 1hr 30min); Phonsavan (4 weekly; 40min); Xainyabouli (3 weekly; 45min); Xam Nua (3 weekly; 1hr 10min).

Xainyabouli to: Vientiane (3 weekly; 45min).

Louang Phabang

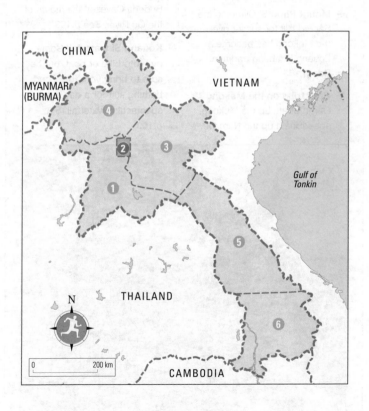

CHAPTER 2

Highlights

✳ **The Royal Palace Museum**
Tour the French-built palace, once home to the last of the Lao kings. See p.147

✳ **Wat Xiang Thong** Laos's most historic wat is one of the jewels of Southeast Asian architecture. See p.150

✳ **Mount Phou Si** Climbing the Sacred Hill for sunset over the Mekong has become a Louang Phabang tradition. See p.153

✳ **Boat trips on the Mekong** Cargo boats up the Mekong, speedboats up the Nam Ou, or a ferry across the river – you'll find a boat trip for every budget down at the landing. See p.165

✳ **Pak Ou Buddha Caves** Cruise up the Mekong to see Louang Phabang's most popular pilgrimage site, the old Buddha Caves at the mouth of the Ou River. See p.168

✳ **Kouang Si waterfall** Come by motorbike or boat, but be sure to bring your towel and bathing suit for a day at this spectacular waterfall. See p.169

△ Wat Xiang Thong

2

Louang Phabang

Nestling in a slim valley shaped by lofty, green mountains and cut by the swift Mekong and Khan rivers, **LOUANG PHABANG** (also known as Louang Prabang) exudes remote tranquillity and casual grandeur. A tiny mountain kingdom for more than a thousand years and designated a World Heritage site in 1995, Louang Phabang is endowed with a legacy of ancient red-roofed temples and French-Indochinese architecture, not to mention some of the country's most refined cuisine, its richest culture and its most sacred Buddha image, the Pha Bang. For those familiar with Southeast Asia, the very name Louang Phabang conjures up the classic image of Laos – streets of ochre colonial houses and swaying palms, lines of saffron-robed monks gliding through the morning mist, the sonorous thump of the temple drums hours before dawn, and, of course, longtail boats racing down the Mekong before the river slips out of view through a seam in the mountains.

It is this heritage of Theravada Buddhist temples, French-Indochinese shop-houses and **royal mystique** that lends Louang Phabang a pull unmatched by any other city in Laos. This is not only where the first proto-Lao nation took root, it's also the birthplace of countless Lao rituals and the origin of a line of rulers, including the rulers of Vientiane, Champasak and Lane Xang. Louang Phabang people are tremendously proud of their pivotal role in Lao history. Indeed, they're somewhat known for their cultured ways in the rest of the country; in Lao soap operas, the doctor or the intellectual invariably speaks with a Louang Phabang accent.

Inevitably, the city has lost some of its sleepy charm and dreamy serenity as a result of the recent influx of tourists, but it's still relatively unspoilt. Louang Phabang's strict building code, drawn up by UNESCO, keeps it from becoming another modern architectural nightmare without turning it into a museum. Still, it is a constant battle to keep commercialism at bay. The massive tour buses that squeeze through Louang Phabang's streets, for example, do so in contravention of arrangements agreed with UNESCO. It can only be hoped that compliance will improve in future, or Louang Phabang could go the way of other tourist-oriented cities in the region.

Most travellers spend only a few days here on a whistle-stop tour of Laos, though the city really demands longer. If time is limited, top priority should go to the **old city**, dubbed by the UNESCO World Heritage team as a "historic preservation zone". In a day, you can easily tour the sights from newly renovated **Dala Market** along the peninsula to Louang Phabang's most impressive temple, **Wat Xiang Thong**, taking in the **Royal Palace Museum** along the way and still managing to climb up to the golden cone of **Phou Si** for a dazzling sunset perch. If you're here for a second day, enjoy some of the

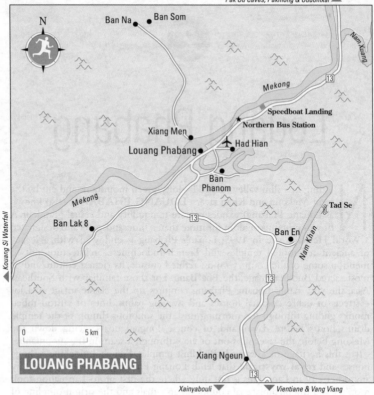

▲ Pak Ou Caves, Pakmong & Oudomxai

Ban Na ● Ban Som

Mekong

13

Nam Xiang

N

Speedboat Landing
★ Northern Bus Station

Xiang Men ●

Louang Phabang ●

✈ Had Hian

Ban
Phanom

Tad Se

Mekong

Ban Lak 8 ●

Ban En ●

Nam Khan

13

Kouang Si Waterfall

0   5 km

13

Xiang Ngeun ●

LOUANG PHABANG

13

Xainyabouli ▼   ▼ Vientiane & Vang Viang

sights around Louang Phabang by taking a boat up the Mekong River and contemplating the hundreds of Buddhas within the holy **Pak Ou Caves**, or travelling south through the surrounding hills to one of the area's two major **waterfalls**, Kouang Si and Tad Se. But whatever you do, be sure to soak up Louang Phabang's languid atmosphere by wandering the streets at dawn, when the town's legion of monks receives alms and life attains all the buzz of a country village, or at dusk, when the air fills with otherworldly chants wafting from the temples.

Louang Phabang's air of serenity is disturbed only at **festival** time. The most famous festivals last for days and inspire a carnival atmosphere that makes it easy to forget that these complex rituals held the very structure of the kingdom in place for centuries. **Lao New Year** in April is perhaps the town's biggest festival, but near the end of the monsoon, two holidays – the boat races and the Festival of Lights – also bring Louang Phabang to a festive standstill. A visit coinciding with one of these festivals would certainly enhance your stay, though the most popular time to visit remains the cooler months of December and January, when the weather is clear and dry.

Some history

Knowledge of Louang Phabang's early history is sketchy, at best. The earliest Lao settlers made their way down the Nam Ou Valley sometime after the tenth

The myth of the birth of the Lao

In the early days, when humankind grew unruly and refused to honour the gods, the **chief of the gods** flooded the earth. Three lords managed to survive the flood, floating up to heaven on a raft. They paid homage to the chief of the gods, and once the floods had subsided the lords returned to earth in the vicinity of Dien Bien Phu with a water buffalo, which helped them sow the rice fields in the plain. When the buffalo died, a large vine bearing three gourds grew from its nostrils, and from the gourds came shouts and cries. One of the lords pierced the gourds with a hot poker and a mass of people struggled out of the blackened holes. These were the **Lao Theung**, the Lao of the hillsides. Seeing their plight, a second lord cut more holes with a chisel and from these larger openings emerged the **Lao**. The lords taught the Lao how to grow rice and build homes, but when the population grew too big, the chief of the gods sent his son, **Khoun Borom**, to earth.

Descending to earth on an elephant with crossed tusks, Khoun Borom brought with him teachers and courtiers, teaching the Lao how to make tools and schooling them in the arts of dance and music. After a prosperous reign of 25 years, Khoun Borom sent his seven sons to rule over the Tai–Lao world. The eldest went to **Louang Phabang** and the others to Xiang Khouang, Chiang Mai, Xishuangbanna (in southwestern China), Ayuthaya and to regions of lower Myanmar and northern Vietnam.

century, absorbing the territory on which the city lies. At the time, the area was known as Muang Sawa, a settlement thought to have been peopled by the Austroasiatic ancestors of the Lao Theung. According to folklore, this migration of the Lao to Louang Phabang was led by Khoun Lo, son of Khoun Borom, the legendary first ancestor of the lowland Lao. Khoun Lo, it is said, descended the Nam Ou River, claimed the area for his people and called the settlement **Xiang Dong Xiang Thong**. By the end of the thirteenth century, Xiang Dong Xiang Thong had emerged as one of the chief centres of Lao life in the Upper Mekong region, a principality significant enough to be a vassal state of the great Siamese kingdom of Sukhothai.

However, it wasn't until the legendary Lao warrior **Fa Ngum** swept down the Nam Ou with a Khmer army in 1353 and captured Xiang Dong Xiang Thong that the town emerged as the heart of a thriving, independent kingdom in its own right. Fa Ngum, whose exploits are shrouded in myth, looms large in Lao histories, many of which trace Laos's fragile claims of nationhood to the warrior's rise to power in Louang Phabang. Claiming the throne of his grandfather, Fa Ngum founded the kingdom of **Lane Xang Hom Khao** – the Land of a Million Elephants and the White Parasol – and established the line of kings that was to rule Laos for six centuries.

With Fa Ngum came monks, artisans and learned men from the Khmer court and, according to histories written a century and a half later, a legal code and Theravada Buddhism. Yet Fa Ngum was still very much the fourteenth-century warrior. After his ministers grew weary of his military campaigns and his rather uncivilized habit of taking his subject's wives and daughters as concubines, he was exiled and replaced on the throne by his son, Oun Heuan, in 1373. Oun Heuan is remembered as **Samsenthai**, [King of] Three Hundred Thousand Tai, a name signifying the number of Lao men that the king of Xiang Dong Xiang Thong could call upon for labour and military service. He's also remembered for his long peaceful reign, during which the city flourished.

Five columns of Vietnamese troops swept through the city in 1478, only to be chased out a few years later by the humiliated Lao king's younger brother. The

The exile of Fa Ngum

Most histories of Laos trace the origins of the country back to warrior-king **Fa Ngum**, a man whose accomplishments on the throne, the battlefield and in the bedroom are the subject of wild exaggeration and a wealth of legends, perhaps befitting a man touted as the founder of his country and whose exploits were only first recorded more than a century after his death. One of the best-known legends records his **exile** from Louang Phabang and his spectacular **return**.

In the year of the Naga, Fa Ngum was born into the royal house of Xiang Dong Xiang Thong with a set of 33 teeth. Worried that this miraculous abnormality was an **omen** spelling doom for the kingdom, the superstitious royal advisers talked the king into floating the infant prince down the Mekong. A Lao Moses with a crocodile smile, Fa Ngum drifted downstream for a year, his raft heavy with an entourage of advisers, wet nurses and servants – 33 in all – until he reached the Khone Falls. Here, a Buddhist monk found Fa Ngum and took the child to the Khmer court, where he was educated in the manner of a Khmer prince and given a Khmer princess as a bride.

In the many versions of the myth of Fa Ngum's exile there is one detail on which the tales never vary: not long after his expulsion, Fa Ngum returned to Xiang Dong Xiang Thong and fulfilled the omen foretold by his birth. Backed by an army of Khmer soldiers, Fa Ngum forced the king from the throne and established the Kingdom of a Million Elephants and the White Parasol.

sacking of the city proved a catalyst for the ushering in of the city's **golden age**: striking temples, including the *sim* of Wat Xiang Thong, were built, epic poems composed, sacred texts copied and the administration of the kingdom fine-tuned over the next century. Lane Xang was, for the moment, a major power on the Indochinese peninsula. In 1512, King Visoun brought the **Pha Bang**, a sacred Buddha image, to Xiang Dong Xiang Thong, a distinguishing event for the identity of the Lao people and the city itself, and a sign that Theravada Buddhism was flourishing. Visoun's pious son **Phothisalat** helped the faith along by issuing a decree banning worship of spirits, which resulted in animist shrines being torched and their altars thrown into the river. However, King Phothisalat spent much of his time in Vientiane, a more central location for a kingdom whose population had been shifting south along the Mekong. His son, **King Setthathilat**, wary of encroaching Burmese, officially moved the capital to Vientiane in 1563, leaving the Pha Bang behind and renaming the city after the revered image. The Pha Bang may have been known for its protective properties, but they were no match for the might of the Burmese, and Louang Phabang was engulfed by the chaos of successive **Burmese invasions** that swept through the Tai world.

From then on, the city had a roller-coaster ride. With the disintegration of Lane Xang at the turn of the eighteenth century, **Kingkitsalat** became the first king of an independent Louang Phabang. The kingdom was never able to attain Lane Xang's glory but Louang Phabang did manage a semblance of independence by paying tribute to Hué, Bangkok and Beijing, and receiving vassalage from Houa Phan and Xiang Khouang.

When **French explorers** Doudart de Lagrée and Francis Garnier arrived in 1867, they found a busy market and port town of wooden homes situated in parallel rows along streets positioned at right angles, a town that Garnier called "the most eminent Laotian centre in Indochina". With Louang Phabang firmly in Siam's orbit, the explorers' suggestion that the kingdom would be better off French was scoffed at by King Oun Kham, but the explorers were proved right two decades later when the Siamese left the town virtually undefended and the city was set ablaze by a group of marauding **Haw** led by Deo Van Tri. A White Tai chieftain from Sipsong Chao Tai, Tri was out to avenge himself on the Siamese who had captured his brothers during a mission to subdue unrest on Louang Phabang's frontier. During the siege, French vice-consul Auguste Pavie plucked the ageing Lao king from his burning palace and brought him downriver to safety. From that moment, the king offered tribute to France.

Almost everything was lost during the sacking of the city, but the event provided Pavie with the ammunition he needed to "conquer the hearts" of the Lao and usher in Louang Phabang's **French period**. The town was quickly rebuilt, with the French counting ten thousand people and more than a thousand homes a year after the town's destruction. When the novelty of living in wooden Lao houses on piles finally wore off, the French hired Vietnamese workers to build the homes that lend the city its classic French–Indochinese character, a trend quickly followed by Lao nobility. The city remained remote however: even in 1930 it took longer to travel by river from Saigon to Louang Phabang than it did to travel from Saigon to France. Louang Phabang's rituals – intertwined with the pomp and ceremony of the kingdom's royal family, by this point the only active royal line left in Laos – continued under the French.

During the two **Indochina wars**, Louang Phabang fared better than most towns in Laos, although the city did play a pivotal role in events leading up to France's ultimate defeat in Indochina. In early 1953, invading Viet Minh forces nearly reached Louang Phabang, causing the French to hastily reinforce their garrison and the town's Chinese community to board up their shops. Much to the consternation of the French, the town's ethnic Lao majority remained calm, as a blind monk had prophesied that the invaders would not take the city. The king refused to leave his palace, while Crown Prince Sisavang Vatthana cruised confidently around town in his blue Chrysler as preparations for defence of the town gave way to celebrations long before the Viet Minh ran out of supplies and retreated. The French, on the other hand, were somewhat less relaxed about the near-attack upon Laos's royal city. In order to maintain their campaign against the Viet Minh on Vietnamese soil while still protecting northern Laos, the French massed troops in **Dien Bien Phu**, where they suffered their ultimate setback in their attempt to restore their grip on Indochina (see p.326).

While Louang Phabang itself remained intact during the fighting that consumed Laos over the next two decades, the Second Indochina War ultimately took its toll on Louang Phabang's ceremonial life, which lost its regal heart when the **Pathet Lao** ended the royal line by forcing King Sisavang Vatthana to abdicate in 1975. Two years later, Louang Phabang and Laos lost the king himself, as the new **communist government**, fearful that he might become a rallying point for a rebellion, allegedly exiled him to a Houa Phan cave, a journey from which he and his family never returned.

Arrival, information and city transport

Most people arrive in Louang Phabang at the **airport**, just over 2km northeast of the city. It's possible to get a fifteen-day **visa on arrival** here (see p.26). There are also **exchange** facilities and an **immigration checkpoint**, where you'll need to get your passport stamped. Tuk-tuks (12,000K per six-person vehicle) and touts from hotels and guesthouses are both on hand to ferry you into the centre.

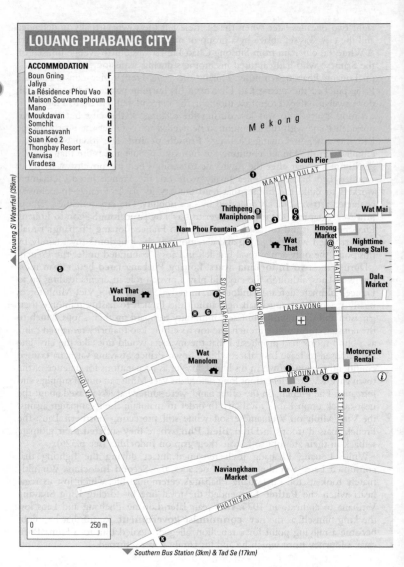

LOUANG PHABANG CITY

ACCOMMODATION

Boun Gning	F
Jaliya	I
La Résidence Phou Vao	K
Maison Souvannaphoum	D
Mano	J
Moukdavan	G
Somchit	H
Souansavanh	E
Suan Keo 2	C
Thongbay Resort	L
Vanvisa	B
Viradesa	A

Mekong

South Pier

MANTHATOULAT

Wat Mai

Thithpeng
Maniphone

Nam Phou Fountain

Hmong
Market

Nighttime
Hmong Stalls

PHALANXAI

Wat That

Dala
Market

Wat That
Louang

LATSAVONG

SOUVANNAPHOUMA

BOUNKHONG

Wat
Manolom

Motorcycle
Rental

VISOUNALAT

Lao Airlines

SETTHATHILAT

Naviangkham
Market

PHOTHISAN

◀ Kouang Si Waterfall (35km)

0   250 m

▼ Southern Bus Station (3km) & Tad Se (17km)

Buses from Vientiane, Vang Viang and other points south along Route 13 stop at the **Southern Bus Station**, 3km south of the centre. Nearby is the **Pakkhon depot** used by buses from Xainyabouli. Buses and sawngthaews from the north arrive at the **Northern Bus Station**, 6km north of town. It's possible to find **shared tuk-tuks** at all three bus stations, which act as shuttles to similar destinations in town (2000K). Hiring your own will cost around 10,000K, depending on your haggling skills.

Slow boats dock at the ferry landing directly behind the Palace Museum. From here it's a short walk to old-city guesthouses on the peninsula and Ban

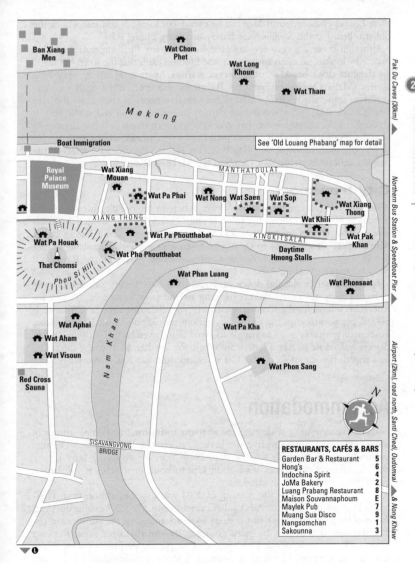

Ban Xiang Men

Wat Chom Phet

Wat Long Khoun

Wat Tham

Mekong

Boat Immigration

See 'Old Louang Phabang' map for detail

Royal Palace Museum

Wat Xiang Mouan

MANTHATOULAT

Wat Pa Phai   Wat Nong   Wat Saen   Wat Sop

Wat Xiang Thong

XIANG THONG

Wat Khili

Wat Pa Phoutthabat

KINGKITSALAT

Wat Pak Khan

Wat Pa Houak

Wat Pha Phoutthabat

Daytime Hmong Stalls

That Chomsi

Phou Si Hill

Wat Phan Luang

Wat Phonsaat

Wat Aphai

Nam Khan

Wat Pa Kha

Wat Aham

Wat Visoun

Wat Phon Sang

Red Cross Sauna

N

SISAVANGVONG BRIDGE

RESTAURANTS, CAFÉS & BARS	
Garden Bar & Restaurant	5
Hong's	6
Indochina Spirit	4
JoMa Bakery	2
Luang Prabang Restaurant	8
Maison Souvannaphoum	E
Maylek Pub	7
Muang Sua Disco	9
Nangsomchan	1
Sakounna	3

Wat That, a good area for accommodation near the river, although tuk-tuks are usually close at hand should you want one. If you've arrived by speedboat, you'll land at the **speedboat pier** 7km northeast of town and will need to hire a tuk-tuk into the centre (20,000K).

Information

The Lao National Tourism Administration runs the **Tourism Information Centre** at 3 Visounalat Road (Mon–Fri 8am–5pm; ☏071/212487), next to the Red Cross. It's much more helpful than branches elsewhere in Laos, and their *Louang Phabang Tourist Map* can be useful. For local ads and info, check the bulletin board at the *Scandinavian Bakery* on Xiang Thong Road.

Although there are very few street signs in Louang Phabang, you'll quickly realize by looking at maps and guesthouse business cards that the town has made an absolute dog's breakfast of its **street names**. Apart from having very long names (Maha Ouphalathphetsalath Road, for example), often with multiple spellings, some roads change names four or five times as they cross the city. For clarity's sake, we've sometimes chosen one street name and stuck with it throughout the chapter – not that street names mean much to locals anyway. As elsewhere in Laos, local inhabitants prefer to use landmarks, such as monasteries, to identify parts of town: thus Ban Wat That ("Wat That district") refers to the neighbourhood between Wat That and the Mekong River.

City transport

Although you can comfortably walk everywhere in the old city, **bicycles** are a great way of getting around the town at large. Heavy Chinese models are available at most budget guesthouses and at tourist shops on Xiang Thong Road. **Motorbikes** – a great way to see out-of-town attractions – are available to rent for $8 a day at guesthouses, rental shops, and along Xiang Thong Road, but must be returned before dark.

Tuk-tuks can be flagged down easily on most busy streets, and in the early morning there are always drivers hanging around guesthouse areas waiting for foreigners bound for the stations or airport. Typically, a ride anywhere in town is 5000K per person; trips out to the bus stations should cost about $1 per person. Foreigners generally need to haggle to avoid being overcharged, although a few drivers will refuse to take a tourist anywhere for less than $1. If you're interested in a trip to the waterfalls or Pak Ou caves, tuk-tuks can easily be arranged.

Accommodation

Louang Phabang has a wide range of **accommodation**, from simple rooms in inexpensive guesthouses to five-star luxury resorts. The high season is December and January (festivals, such as Lao New Year, are also very busy times), but regardless of the season, it's a good idea to book in advance if you have a particular establishment in mind.

An unforeseen result of the tsunami of 2004 was a shift of visitors from Thailand's beaches to Southeast Asia's inland destinations, such as Louang Phabang. Accommodation managers and owners took advantage of the situation in the time-honoured fashion – by price gouging. Rooms that once went for $5 a night were suddenly worth $10–15, and subsequently proprietors were reluctant to reduce prices. The result is that rock-bottom accommodation in Louang Phabang is now virtually nonexistent, and even in low season (May–Oct), most guesthouses and hotels are much less amenable than before to negotiating over rates.

For most people, a location within the **old city**, occupying a finger of land created by the confluence of the Mekong and the Nam Khan, is the first choice. Here you'll find not only most of the city's best attractions but also many shops and restaurants. However, while there's no shortage of charming mid-range colonial guesthouses here, inexpensive places to stay are few. One possible compromise if you want to be close to the old city is the **Ban Wat That** neighbourhood, just south of Setthathilat Road, between Wat That and the Mekong

River. Similar in atmosphere to the old city, the area has four parallel lanes holding a dozen of the cheaper guesthouses. However, the area's overblown reputation as a backpacker centre means that many of these guesthouses aren't good value. A better choice for budget travellers, though a bit further from the old city, is the area between the Nam Phou Fountain on **Phalanxai Road** and **Visounalat Road** to the southeast. Scattered in this grid of streets are over a dozen guesthouses and inns, many of which are a slightly better value than their Ban Wat That rivals. The fourth centre for tourist accommodation is **Phou Vao Road**, which runs from the Kaysone Monument up to Naviengkham Road and forms the southern limit of the new city. Controls on building in the old city have resulted in many new hotels springing up here – along the length of this wide boulevard, you'll find over a dozen decent hotels and guesthouses as well as many restaurants, though the distance from the old city is a drawback.

All the places reviewed below appear on the map on pp.138–139, except for the places in the old city, which are on the map on p.144–145. If you're staying in a guesthouse or small hotel, be sure to enquire what time doors are locked at night.

The old city

Apsara Kingkitsalat Rd ☏ 071/254670, ℱ 254252, ⓦ www.theapsara.com. A pair of nicely done-up two-storey shophouses in a superior setting facing the Nam Khan, with views of river life and the mountains beyond. Upstairs are high-ceilinged rooms, with en-suite baths. Downstairs rooms are less atmospheric, but not by much. There's also an excellent restaurant. ❹

Auberge Le Calao Inn Manthatoulat Rd ☏ 071/212100, ℱ 212085, ⓦ www .calaoinn.laopdr.com. An intimate guesthouse in a beautifully restored Sino-Portuguese mansion dating from 1904, near Wat Xiang Thong. Each of the six tastefully decorated rooms has an arched balcony with a Mekong view that takes in the temples on the opposite bank and beautiful sunsets. It's an excellent alternative to the over-hyped *Villa Santi* (see p.142), but you'll need to reserve well in advance. The patio restaurant outside overlooking the street is a nice place for a drink. ❼

Bounthieng Manthatoulat Rd ☏ 071/252488. If you can't afford the *Auberge Le Calao*, consider this very comfortable colonial-era guesthouse, which likewise faces the Mekong. The more expensive upstairs rooms have hot water en-suite bathrooms and balconies looking right out over the river. Good value. ❸

Heritage Near Wat Pa Phai ☏ 071/252537. Once one of the best deals in town, this two-storey colonial house has badly deteriorated. Still, the location just off Xiang Thong Rd is unequivocally superb. Doubles and singles are the same price and all the rooms have en-suite facilities. ❸

Les 3 Nagas Xiang Thong Rd ☏ 071/253888, ⓦ www.3nagas.com.

Styling itself a boutique hotel, and actually lives up to the claim. Rooms are tastefully decorated, comfortable and have Internet connectivity for laptops, and the service is impeccable. ❼

Mekong Manthatoulat Rd, near the slow-boat pier ☏ 071/212752. This well-located guesthouse in a large 1960s building is run by a friendly family. Inside, behind the shophouses, you'll find seven rooms ranging from doubles with shared bathrooms to the massive upstairs front room, with its two big double beds, balcony and huge en-suite bathroom. ❸

Pa Phai Opposite Wat Pa Phai ☏ 071/212752. A quirky little guesthouse with a pleasant tree-shaded patio, set up above a quiet street. There are ten decent rooms, with clean shared facilities. Run by the former Royal Lao Airforce pilot who also owns the *Mekong*. A rare find indeed in the heart of the old city, so book ahead if possible. ❷

Pathoumphone Kingkitsalat Rd ☏ 071/212946. Run by a friendly couple, and spread out across three rustic old houses. The main draw is the great views of the Nam Khan and surrounding mountains from the balconies. It's also ideally placed if you're in town for the boat races. Some rooms are en suite. ❸

Phounsab Sisavang Vong Rd ☏ 071/212595. In a prime location on the old city's restaurant and souvenir strip, this two-storey hotel has high-ceilinged rooms, some of which are en suite. The ground-floor restaurant is a good place for watching the flow of people along Sisavang Vong Rd. ❸

Saynamkhan Kingkitsalat Rd ☏ 071/212976, ℱ 213009, ⓦ www.saynamkhanhotel.laopdr.com. The interior of this marvellous re-styled 1939 shophouse lacks the elegance of the exterior – the original building was more Bauhaus than

French-Indochinese – but the location on the Nam Khan is great nonetheless, and there's a pleasant, if narrow, terrace for sunrise coffees. The rooms come with a/c, TV and private bathroom; a larger corner room has a bathtub. One of the best choices in its price bracket. ⑤

Sayo Facing Wat Xiang Mouan ☎071/252614, Ⓔsayo@laotel.com. This grand old colonial mansion overlooking the Xiang Mouan temple has absolutely enormous rooms with wooden floors and ceilings. Aside from the nicely furnished rooms and modern bathrooms, the building has tons of character and the views over the temple are superb. A great choice and terrific value. ⑤

Senesouk Xiang Thong Rd, opposite Wat Sene ☎071/212074, Ⓕ071/212074. Location doesn't get much better than this – right on a quiet stretch of Xiang Thong between the most interesting wats and the restaurant strip. The building itself, a two-storey, colonial-style house, features pleasantly decorated rooms with a/c and TV. ⑤

Tum Tum Cheng Xiang Thong Rd, next to Wat Xiang Thong ☎071/253224, Ⓕ071/253262. Friendly and well run, this place is one of only a handful situated this far down the peninsula. Rooms all have en-suite bathrooms and a/c, and are decorated with some attention to detail. A good place to be if you want to have some space between you and the crowds on lower Sisavang Vong Road. ⑤

Villa Santi Xiang Thong Rd ☎ & Ⓕ071/212267, Ⓦwww.villasantihotel.com. More than a century old, and once home to King Sisavang Vong's wife. Subsequently converted into a hotel, it was the best place to stay in Louang Phabang for many years, but while resting on its laurels it has been overtaken, and the experience no longer justifies the tariffs. The fourteen-room annexe, around the corner, was built in the late 1990s, but is already looking quite worn. ⑦

Villa Xieng Mouane Facing Wat Xiang Mouan ☎071/252152. Stately rooms with wooden floors in an attractive white colonial-style villa with light-blue trim. The guesthouse takes its name from the nearby monastery, named for its old temple drum which produces a particularly sonorous thump (*xieng mouane* means "jolly sound"). There's a new annexe with very modern rooms in the same colonial style in the back of the building for less money. Family rooms and the grassy lawn between the two buildings make this a great spot if you're travelling with kids. ⑤

Ban Wat That

Suan Keo 2 Koksak Rd. The best of the four budget guesthouses in this lane, with eight rooms

in a two-storey colonial-style house, with blue shutters, tiled floors and a spacious terrace. ③

Vanvisa Kokkiang Rd ☎071/212925. Owned by a university professor of French, this yellow Sixties villa on a quiet street in the former silversmithing district is the most charming of the Wat That guesthouses. There are just eight rooms, three of which use shared facilities. The leafy front courtyard and ground-floor living room filled with antiques and textiles add to the character of the place. ③

Viradesa Vatthat Rd ☎071/252026. This true backpacker's spot has a wide range of cheap rooms, including dorms, in a wooden house with a small front yard facing the lane. The restaurant here is good, and is a focal point for everyone staying in the neighbourhood. Dorms $5, ②

Between Phalanxai and Visounalat roads

Boun Gning Souvannaphouma Rd ☎071/212274. A well-run backpacker's place, though note that the en-suite bathrooms look as though they were built as an afterthought – not for those who are shy about making or hearing toilet noises. The building itself is a rustic two-storey wooden affair, on a quiet street. ②

Jaliya Visounalat Rd ☎071/252154. Across from Lao Airlines are a dozen en-suite rooms tucked away behind a shophouse travel agency. They're all very clean and comfortable, and face onto a private garden. Cheaper but less attractive rooms are available in the older part of the building. The Lao lady owner organizes anything and everything you might need. ②

Maison Souvannaphoum Phalanxai Rd ☎071/212200, Ⓦwww.coloursofsangana.com. Recently renovated by a Singaporean company, the two dozen handsomely appointed rooms, all with private balcony, are housed in regal white buildings set among spacious gardens. The hotel was once the residence of former neutralist prime minister Prince Souvannaphouma. You can stay in the room he was born in – now the master suite with a deluxe bathtub. ⑧

Mano Visounalat Rd ☎071/253112. If you don't mind the busy road, this little hotel is good value, offering comfortable rooms in a modern colonial-style building. ④

Moukdavan Latsavong Rd ☎071/252402. Newish, Lao-style two-storey house with a nice balcony and a red-tile roof, not dissimilar to the *Somchit*. With en-suite bathrooms, it's much better value than a lot of the so-called backpacker places in Ban Wat That. ②

Somchit Latsavong Rd ☎071/212522. Wooden house with perfectly decent rooms plus a slim, communal balcony. The bathrooms are a bit run-down, but the wooden floors are nice. Better value than most Wat That places. **②**

Souansavan Bounkhong Rd ☏071/213020. The *Souansavan* is the perfect place to try if your first selection is full or you've just arrived and don't feel like tramping around. Set in a huge compound on a quiet street, the hotel consists of three separate buildings, all in the same attractive style, with 27 rooms. **③**

Out of the centre

La Residence Phou Vao On Kite Hill at the eastern end of Phou Vao Rd ☏071/212194, ☏071/212534, ⊛www.pansea.com/laos.html. Louang Phabang's first and only truly five-star hotel. All the rooms mix Asian-style wood floors, hardwood furniture and wooden blinds with modern comforts like king-size beds, mini-bar, IDD phones, TV and a/c. The eighteen superior rooms feature double private balconies and garden-style bathrooms big enough to get lost in. The place also has one of the classiest restaurants in town, over-looking an outdoor swimming pool. **③**

Thongbay On the banks of the Nam Khan river, about 2km from the old city ☏071/219686 or 253234, ⊛www.thongbay-guesthouses.com. Run by two cheerful sisters, this collection of eight deluxe Lao-style bungalows features wood floors, native furnishings and huge bathrooms; the four choicest units all look out over the river. You could spend hours lounging on the balcony watching the villagers tend their vegetable gardens on the oppo-site bank, with Mount Phou Si in the background. A phenomenal deal, but don't expect such good prices once the word gets out. **⑤**

The City

The majority of Louang Phabang's architecture of merit – temple monasteries, Asian shophouses and French-influenced mansions – is found in the **old city**, along the main thoroughfare of **Sisavang Vong/Xiang Thong Road**. Sett-hathilat Road divides the old city from the commercial parts of Louang Phabang which, though newer, still contain plenty of colonial-era mansions scattered about, as well as a number of other important monasteries (most are open daily 8am–5pm or sometimes until 7pm), including **Wat Aham** and **Wat Visoun**. The most interesting areas outside the old city for tourists are the **riverbanks**, **Ban Wat That**, the old silversmithing district south of the GPO between Wat That and the Mekong, and **Visounalat Road**, which is a shopping and accom-modation thoroughfare. The boulevard of Phou Vao Road, which has many new hotels and restaurants but little character, forms the southern limit of town, while to the north and west, the opposite banks of the Mekong and Nam Khan have nothing in the way of tourist facilities but are extremely charming.

While other urban centres in the country are heavily populated by ethnic Vietnamese and Chinese, Louang Phabang is the only city in Laos where ethnic Lao are in the majority. The **Lao character** is particularly stamped on the backstreets and cobblestoned lanes, which have a distinctly village-like feel, in marked contrast to the shophouses and commercial scenes that you find on the streets of other Lao cities. One of the joys of a stay in Louang Phabang is simply strolling these lanes and absorbing the unhurried rhythms of traditional Lao culture.

For shopping opportunities throughout Louang Phabang, see the section starting on p.158.

The old city

The **old city** is concentrated on a long finger of land, approximately 1km long by 300m wide. The thicker southern end of the peninsula is dominated by a steep, forested hill, **Phou Si**, crowned by a Buddhist stupa that can be seen for miles around. As the city grew it expanded outwards from the peninsula to the south and east, and continues to do so to this day.

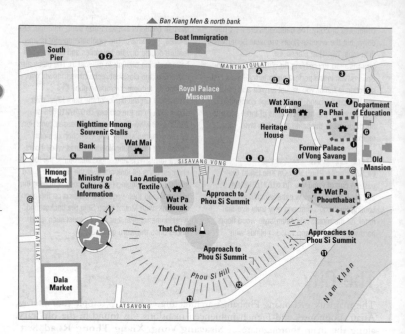

Just four parallel streets run the length of the peninsula, but there are enough cross streets, lanes and dead ends to keep things interesting. Amazingly, each area seems to exude its own distinct personality. Although it is possible to knock off all the attractions in the old city in a couple of days, it's far more enjoyable to explore it a little at a time, and really soak up the atmosphere; the many temples and monasteries are certainly too charming be rushed through.

The main thoroughfare in the old city, lined by the bulk of Louang Phabang's tourist restaurants and shops, has two names, **Sisavang Vong** and **Xiang Thong**, after Laos's penultimate king and Louang Phabang's royal temple, respectively. Aside from the main attractions of the **Royal Palace Museum**, **Mount Phou Si** and **Wat Xiang Thong**, there are a dozen historic wats, or temples, within the old city area, as well as hundreds of French colonial shophouses and mansions. In the early morning (around 7am) you can watch the ritual of long lines of monks collecting alms along Sisavang Vong/Xiang Thong Road.

Wat Mai

Just south of the Royal Palace on Xiang Thong Road, Wat Mai Suwannaphumaham, or **Wat Mai** for short ($1), has what must surely be Louang Phabang's most photographed *sim* after that of Wat Xiang Thong. The monastery dates from the late eighteenth or early nineteenth century (depending on whom you believe), but it is the *sim*'s relatively modern facade with its gilt stucco reliefs that forms the main focus of attention. Depicting the second-to-last incarnation of the Buddha set amid traditional Lao scenes, the facade was created in the 1960s and restored in the 1990s. Like most examples of modern Lao temple ornamentation, it looks interesting from a distance, but disappointing up close.

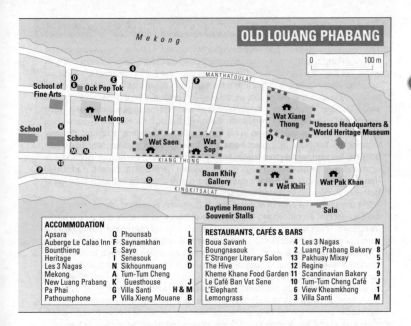

OLD LOUANG PHABANG

Mekong

0   100 m

MANTHATOULAT

School of Fine Arts

Ock Pop Tok

Wat Nong

School

School

Wat Saen

Wat Sop

XIANG THONG

Wat Xiang Thong

Unesco Headquarters & World Heritage Museum

Baan Khily Gallery

KINGKITSALAT

Wat Khili

Wat Pak Khan

Daytime Hmong Souvenir Stalls

Sala

It was at Wat Mai that **Auguste Pavie** and his party resided while trying to establish a foothold in Louang Phabang in the late nineteenth century. Siamese officials, who controlled the Lao court at the time, had billeted the Frenchmen in an isolated hut, hoping this would make them give up and leave, but the abbot of Wat Mai befriended Pavie and invited him to stay at the wat. Soon Pavie and King Oun Kham were communicating via the abbot while the Siamese stood by and watched helplessly. Decades later, France celebrated Pavie's contribution to the colonization of Laos by erecting a statue of him where the post office now stands. After the revolution, the statue disappeared, and in the mid-Nineties Pavie's home town in France attempted to find it, but without success. During **Lao New Year** festivities, Wat Mai is a hive of activity, as it is here that the Pha Bang (see p.148) is put on display so that the faithful may ritually bathe the image.

Wat Pa Phai to Wat Sop

In the area immediately north of the palace are three temples of note, **Wat Choum Khong**, **Wat Xiang Mouane** and **Wat Pa Phai**, the Bamboo Forest Monastery. The principal attraction at Wat Pa Phai is the facade of the *sim*, painted and lavishly embellished with stylized naga and peacocks. The stucco and mirror work closely resemble that commonly seen on Buddhist structures in Chiang Mai. Directly across from Wat Pa Phai sits a curious old **mansion** which is a fine example of a type of architecture that could be termed "French-Indochinese": the design of the house itself is unmistakably European, but the ornamentation is obviously Asian. The finely carved hardwood doors were almost certainly crafted by Chinese or Vietnamese, and hint at the origin of the curious "Buddha" on the facade posing in a very non-traditional *mudra*.

Naga and ngeuak: water serpents of Lao legend

The ubiquitous **naga** of Lao mythology is sometimes mistaken by visitors for the dragon of China, with which it shares a major characteristic: both are associated with water. For the most part, though, the similarity ends there. The origins of the naga are debated. Snake cults are thought to have existed in Southeast Asia long before the arrival of Buddhism in the region, particularly in Cambodia, so it is possible that this snake-like icon is indigenous. Another possibility is that the naga is a cultural migrant from Hindu India. In Hindu mythology, the naga, Sanskrit for serpent, is sometimes associated with the god Vishnu in his incarnation as Narayana, a cosmic dreamer reclining on the body of a giant naga and floating on an endless sea. Buddhism adopted the icon, and a story relates how, while meditating, the historic Buddha was sheltered by a seven-headed naga during a violent rainstorm. In Laos, it is probable that the present-day form of the naga, called *nak* or *phayanak* in Lao, is a fusion of both indigenous and imported beliefs.

The naga is both a symbol of water and its life-giving properties, and a protector of the Lao people. An old legend is still related of how a naga residing in a hole below Vientiane's That Dam stupa was known to rise up at critical moments and unleash itself upon foreign invaders. While the naga is mainly a benign figure, a similar water serpent, the **ngeuak**, is especially feared by Lao fishermen. Believed to devour the flesh of drowning victims, *ngeuak* are said to infest the waters around Si Phan Don. As for the existence of naga in modern-day Laos, the Lao point to "proof" that can be seen in a photograph displayed in some homes, eateries and places of business. The photo shows a line of American soldiers displaying a freshly caught deep-sea fish that is several metres long; some copies of the photograph have the Lao words *nang phayanak* (Lady Naga) printed below. Where and when the photo was taken is a mystery, but many Lao believe that the photo depicts a naga captured in the Mekong by American soldiers during the Second Indochina War.

The whitewashed mansion up the street on the corner of Xiang Thong Road is the former **palace of Crown Prince Vong Savang**. Its proximity to the street makes you wonder at the extraordinary blend of official pomp and casual familiarity that must have existed between the ordinary inhabitants of Louang Phabang and its rulers. To the north stand French-built primary and secondary schools, and every afternoon in the school yard you'll see *kataw* being played. The massive tamarind trees that shade the road in front of the schools once lined the route all the way up to Wat Xiang Thong.

On the next corner is the **Villa Santi**, formerly the Villa de la Princesse and once the residence of Princess Manilai, widow of Crown Prince Vong Savang. Still owned by her family, this charming little palace-turned-hotel caused controversy when it opened in the early Nineties. Government pressure was successful in bringing about a name change, but the hotel continues to thrive on the mystique of erstwhile royalty.

On the next block north, **Wat Saen**, is the first of a row of monasteries that monopolize the west side of the street for nearly two blocks. Of interest at Wat Saen is an ornate boat shed housing the monastery's two **longboats**, used in the annual boat race festival. Held at the end of the rainy season, the boat races are believed to lure Louang Phabang's fifteen guardian naga back into the rivers after high waters and flooded rice paddies have allowed them to escape (see box above). Fittingly, the boathouse is decorated with the carved wooden images of these mythical serpentine creatures.

In 1888, the French counted nearly fifty monasteries in Louang Phabang and its environs. Today, there are just over thirty. Close inspection of the grounds of **Wat Sop**, just beyond Wat Saen, yields some clues as to the reason for the disappearance of many wats. The large Buddha image out in the open and the section of unmatched wall in front of it are evidence that this half of the grounds was once the site of a separate monastery. Sometime in the past the *sim* that once sheltered the Buddha was destroyed, and the monastery was absorbed by Wat Sop.

Beyond Wat Sop are four other temples of note, two on each side of the street: Wat Si Boun Heuang, Wat Khili (see p.152), Wat Pak Kham at the furthest tip of the peninsula, and the greatest of Louang Phabang's temples, Wat Xiang Thong (see p.150).

The Royal Palace Museum

Occupying a fittingly central location in the old city, between Phou Si Hill and the Mekong River, the former **Royal Palace** (daily 8.30–11.30am & 1.30–3.30pm; $2) is now a museum preserving the trappings and paraphernalia of Laos's recently extinguished monarchy. The palace, at the end of a long drive lined with stately palms, was constructed in 1904 by the French and replaced an older, smaller palace of teak and rosewood. The new palace was supposed to be crowned by a European-style steeple, but King Sisavang Vong insisted on modifications, and the graceful stupa-like spire that you see today was substituted, resulting in a tasteful fusion of European and Lao design. Another striking feature is the pediment over the main entrance adorned with a gilt rendition of the symbol of the Lao monarchy: Airavata, the three-headed elephant, being sheltered by the sacred white parasol. This is surrounded by the intertwining bodies of the fifteen guardian naga (see opposite) of Louang Phabang.

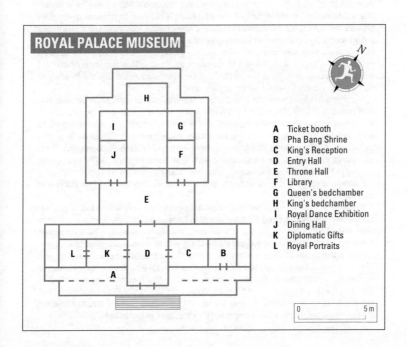

ROYAL PALACE MUSEUM

A Ticket booth
B Pha Bang Shrine
C King's Reception
D Entry Hall
E Throne Hall
F Library
G Queen's bedchamber
H King's bedchamber
I Royal Dance Exhibition
J Dining Hall
K Diplomatic Gifts
L Royal Portraits

0   5 m

At the far end of the gallery to the right of the main entrance is a small, barred room that once served as the king's personal shrine room. It is here that the **Pha Bang**, the most sacred Buddha image in Laos (see box below), is being kept until the completion of the Haw Pha Bang – the temple in the eastern corner of the palace compound. Flanking the Pha Bang are numerous other Buddha images, including ancient Khmer stone images and several pairs of mounted elephant tusks. One pair, deeply incised with rows of Buddhas, was noted by Francis Garnier on the altar of Wat Visoun in the 1860s. Displayed nearby in richly carved wooden frames are silk panels embroidered with gold and silver thread that depict yet more images of the Buddha.

On entering the palace, visitors are directed through the entry hall to the **king's reception room**, full of huge Gauguinesque canvases portraying what appears to be "a day in the life of old Louang Phabang", with scenes of the city as it appeared in the early twentieth century. The paintings, executed by Alex de Fautereau in 1930, are meant to be viewed at different hours of the day when the light from outside is supposed to illuminate the panels depicting the corresponding time of day. In practice the lack of sunlight entering this room renders the effect less than stunning.

More impressive is the **Throne Hall**, located just beyond the entry hall. Its high walls spangled with mosaics of multicoloured mirrors set in a crimson background, the throne hall dazzles even in the dim light. These mosaics, along with others at Wat Xiang Thong, were created in the mid-Fifties to

The Pha Bang

Much more than an ancient image of the Buddha, the **Pha Bang** is the palladium of Laos. The pursuit and enshrining of palladial images has a long history in Southeast Asia, full of intrigue and Byzantine plotting. Like Thailand's "Phra Kaew" and Myanmar's "Mahamuni" Buddha images, the Pha Bang is believed to possess miraculous powers that safeguard the country in which it is enshrined. Formerly, palladial images were thought to legitimize the sovereignty of a king who had one in his possession. Only a pious king with sufficient religious merit could hope to hold on to such an image, and losing it was thought to be proof that a kingdom and its ruler did not deserve to possess it. Thus the histories of certain palladia read like the itinerary of some much coveted sacred sword or holy grail.

According to Lao legend, the Pha Bang image was cast of gold, silver, copper, iron and precious stones. Overseen by the god Indra, who donated gold for its creation, the image was crafted in the heavens above the Himalayas and then delivered to the capital of Sri Lanka. From there the image made its way to Cambodia and then to the city of Xiang Dong Xiang Thong, later renamed Louang Phabang (the Great Pha Bang) in honour of the image. In the early eighteenth century, the Pha Bang was moved to **Vientiane**, now the capital. Twice the Siamese invaded Vientiane, capturing the image, and twice they returned it to the Lao, believing that the Pha Bang was bad luck for Siam.

Since 1867, the Pha Bang has been kept in Louang Phabang, where to this day it is considered the most sacred Buddha image in Laos and centrepiece of the Lao New Year festival. At least, that's the official story. Persistent **rumours** have circulated since the revolution that the authentic Pha Bang was removed from its ornate pedestal and given to the Soviets in return for assistance to the Pathet Lao during the war. The image on display is said to be a copy, while the real Pha Bang is locked away in some vault in Moscow, its powers no longer serving as a talisman for Laos. Whether the story has any truth to it (and it seems highly doubtful), a significant number of Lao believe it, which is perhaps, as one expert on Lao culture pointed out, "a comment on the illegitimacy of the Lao government" in the eyes of the people.

commemorate the 2500th anniversary of the historic Buddha's passing into Nirvana. On display in this room are rare articles of royal regalia: swords with hilts and scabbards of hammered silver and gold, an elaborately decorated fly-whisk and even the king's own howdah (elephant saddle). Also on show is a cache of small crystal, silver and bronze Buddha images taken from the inner chamber of the "Watermelon Stupa" at Wat Visoun. Somehow these treasures escaped the plundering gangs of "Black Flag" Chinese who, led by a White Tai warlord, sacked Louang Phabang in 1887. The stupa was destroyed, rebuilt in 1898, but collapsed in 1914. It was then that the Buddhas were discovered inside.

Leaving the Throne Hall via the door on the right, you come to the **royal library**, which is almost exclusively made up of official archives of the Ming and Ching dynasties, a gift from China during the Cultural Revolution. Succeeding rooms are the **queen's bedchamber**, with a very retro collection of Sixties furniture, and another room filled with glass cabinets containing Royal Lao Government awards, seals and decorations. In a third room is a display of theatrical masks, headdresses and musical instruments used by the **royal dance troupe** in their performances of the Lao version of the ever-popular classical Indian legend, the Ramayana.

King Sisavang Vong's bedchamber, located at the very back of the palace, is surprisingly modest. The only thing that looks especially regal is the massive hardwood bed, the headboard of which sports the king's initials and a carved Buddha sheltered by a seven-headed naga. The footboard bears a rendition of the royal emblem of Laos, this time with a two-tiered parasol. The curious arrangement of tall lamps at each of the bed's four corners makes you wonder if reading in bed was a royal pastime. Above the bed is a frame for suspending a mosquito net.

Exiting through the throne hall and into the entry hall, you'll find a final set of displays located in the rooms to your right. The near room houses **diplomatic gifts** presented to the people of Laos by a handful of nations, as well as the rather tatty-looking flag of the Kingdom of Laos that was given a symbolic ride up into space and back on one of the Apollo missions. Not long afterwards, the Kingdom of Laos ceased to exist. In the far room hang larger-than-life **portraits** of King Sisavang Vattana, his wife Queen Kham Phoui and their son Prince Vong Savang. These are the only officially displayed portraits of the last members of the 600-year-old dynasty anywhere in Laos. Had they not been painted by a Soviet artist they almost certainly would not have survived the years following the revolution. The same goes for the bronze sculpture of King Sisavang Vong in the museum grounds near the front gate. This statue may look familiar if you have already passed through Vientiane, where a larger version stands in the park adjacent to Wat Simuang.

The artefacts on public view are but a small portion of the royal relics in storage here, many of which have been packed away and forgotten about since the revolution. The price of admission also includes a peek into the garage housing the late king's motorpool; here, among other dust-covered classics, you'll see an ivory-coloured 1960 Ford Edsel convertible with royal red upholstery.

Ban Jek

The neighbourhood just north of the former Royal Palace is still known to locals as "**Ban Jek**" or Chinatown, as the rows of shophouses along Sisavang Vong Road were once mostly owned by ethnic Chinese shopkeepers. Here you'll find some fine examples of Louang Phabang **shophouse architecture**, a hybrid of French and Lao features superimposed on the basic South China style that was once the standard throughout urban Southeast Asia. Downstairs was a shop or other place of business, while upstairs the residents lived under a roof of fired-clay shingles supported by brick and stucco walls. This combination kept interior temperatures cool during the hot season and warm during the chilly early morning hours of Louang Phabang's "winter". Shuttered windows, introduced by the French, were coupled with transoms of filigreed wood above doors and windows. This allows air to circulate even when doors and windows are bolted shut.

Many of the shops here are now rented out to entrepreneurs from Vientiane, but even with their inevitable conversion to souvenir and tourist outlets, the streets which they line retain much of the charm they exuded before the outbreak of World Heritage fever.

Wat Xiang Thong

The most historic and enchanting Buddhist monastery in the entire country, **Wat Xiang Thong**, the Golden City Monastery ($1), should not be missed. Near the northernmost tip of the peninsula, the main temple or *sim* was built in 1560 by King Setthathilat (who then promptly moved the capital of the Kingdom of a Million Elephants downriver to Vientiane). It is this wonderfully graceful building that dominates the monastery. Unlike nearly every other temple in Louang Phabang, this *sim* was not razed by Chinese marauders in the nineteenth century or overenthusiastically restored in the twentieth. Indeed, an old photograph taken under Auguste Pavie's direction shows the temple to have changed little in the last century.

You'll need to stand at a distance to get a view of the **roof**, the temple's most outstanding feature. Elegant lines curve and overlap, sweeping nearly to the ground, and evoke a bird with outstretched wings or, as the locals say, a mother hen sheltering her brood. The **walls** of the *sim* are decorated inside and out with stencilled gold motifs on a black or maroon background. As you enter the dimly lit temple and your eyes adjust to the lack of light, the gold-leaf patterns seem to float on the blackened walls.

Besides stylized floral designs, the motifs depict a variety of tales, including the Lao version of the Ramayana, scenes from the Jataka and stories about the lives of the Buddha, as well as graphic scenes of punishments doled out in the many levels of Buddhist hell. Such depictions were meant to give a basic education in religion to illiterate laypeople. In one of these punishment scenes, on the wall to the right of the main entrance, an adulterous couple is being forced to flee a pack of rabid dogs by climbing a tree studded with wicked thorns. In the branches above perches a flock of crows, awaiting the chance to peck out the sinners' eyes. Other unfortunate souls are being cooked in a copper cauldron of boiling oil (for committing murder) or are suspended by a hook through their tongues (guilty of telling lies).

In the rafters above and to the right of the main entrance runs a long wooden **aqueduct** or trough in the shape of a mythical serpent. During Lao New Year, lustral water is poured into a receptacle in the serpent's tail and spouts from its mouth, bathing a Buddha image housed in a wooden pagoda-like structure situated near the altar. A drain in the floor of the pagoda channels the water through pipes under the floor of the *sim* and the water then pours from the mouth of a mirror-spangled elephant's head located on the exterior wall. The water is considered to be highly sacred and the faithful use it to anoint themselves or to ritually bathe household Buddhas. Covering the exterior of the back wall of the *sim* is a **mosaic**, said to depict a legendary flame tree that stood on the site when the city was founded. This particular composition is especially

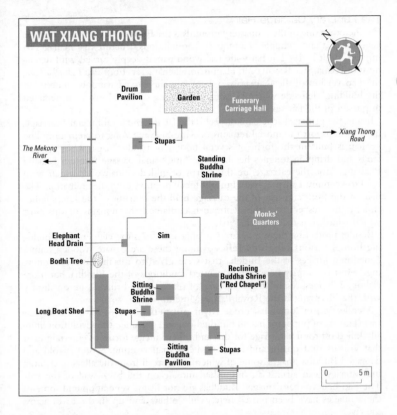

WAT XIANG THONG

Drum Pavilion

Garden

Funerary Carriage Hall

Xiang Thong Road

The Mekong River

Stupas

Standing Buddha Shrine

Monks' Quarters

Elephant Head Drain

Sim

Bodhi Tree

Reclining Buddha Shrine ("Red Chapel")

Sitting Buddha Shrine

Long Boat Shed

Stupas

Sitting Buddha Pavilion

Stupas

0   5 m

beautiful during the Festival of Lights, when the *sim* is decked out with *khom fai dao*, star-shaped lanterns constructed of bamboo and mulberry paper. The flickering candlelight illuminates the tree and animals in the mosaic, making them twinkle magically.

To the left of the *sim*, as you face it, stands a small brick-and-stucco **shrine** containing a standing Buddha image. The purple and gold mirrored mosaics on the pediments of the structure are especially intricate and probably the country's finest example of this kind of ornamentation, which is thought to have originated in Thailand and spread to Myanmar as well.

Directly behind the shrine is a larger structure known to French art historians as "La Chapelle Rouge", the **Red Chapel**. The red- and gold-coloured reliefs covering this building look modern and uninspiring, but the **reclining Buddha** image enshrined within is one of Laos's greatest sculptures in bronze. Thought to date from the sixteenth century, it was taken to Europe in 1931 and put on display at the Colonial Exposition in Paris, alongside treasures from Angkor and other sites in France's Indochinese colonies. Adorning the walls of this shrine are countless clay votive tablets stamped with Buddhas. A donation box at the altar is provided for visitors interested in contributing to the upkeep of the monastery. Supposedly only a fraction of the admission fee collected at the gate goes to the monastery, however; the remainder is said to go to the government.

On the other side of the monastery grounds is the **Funerary Carriage Hall** or *haw latsalot*, a rare example of a modern Lao religious structure that manages to impress. Built in 1962, it has wide teakwood panels deeply carved with depictions of Rama, Sita, Ravana and Hanuman, all characters from *Pha Lak Pha Lam*, the Lao version of the Ramayana. Check out the carved window shutters on the building's left side where Hanuman, the King of the Monkeys, is depicted in pursuit of the fair sex.

Inside, the principal article on display is the *latsalot*, the royal funerary carriage, used to transport the mortal remains of King Sisavang Vong to cremation. The vehicle is built in the form of several bodies of parallel naga, whose jagged fangs and dripping tongues heralded the king's final passage through Louang Phabang. Atop the carriage are three urns of gilded sandalwood, which were used to keep royal corpses in an upright foetal position until the cremation. The urns at the front and rear of the carriage held the remains of the king's father and mother respectively; the centre urn contained the remains of the king, which were cremated in April 1961.

Besides protecting these funerary paraphernalia from the elements, the building houses various **religious relics**. Among these are ornate wooden frames containing images of the Buddha that were given to the monastery as offerings. Most on display here feature painted renditions of the Buddha, but more elaborate images, resembling a tapestry of silver or gold thread, are on display with the Pha Bang at the Royal Palace Museum.

A collection of somewhat crude **royal puppets** occupies a wood and glass case. The art of puppetry has all but died out in Laos since the revolution literally killed off royal patronage for this and other vintage forms of entertainment that visitors find quaint and locals find less than riveting. Scores of old and damaged Buddha images, some of which were taken from the altars of defunct monasteries, lean against an unfinished mosaic on the back wall of the hall. The Lao believe that damaged Buddhas are not fit for veneration and some of these images have been retired here, while others end up in the caves across the river.

The leafy **garden** beside the hall contains some grand bougainvillea, coconut trees and two grey-green fan palms. It was from this species of palm that traditional **palm-leaf manuscripts** were made. Using a stylus to scratch characters onto the palm leaves, monks wrote down Pali-language chants and recorded historical events that affected the kingdom. Before access to paper and cheap printing made palm-leaf manuscripts obsolete, two or three of these trees could be found growing at every wat.

Wat Khili

On the opposite side of Xiang Thong Road, **Wat Khili** is a rare example of a Xiang Khouang-style temple. Louang Phabang once boasted at least three temples in this low, squat design, which originated on the windy plains of the province and former kingdom after which the style is named. Legend has it that the Chinese "Black Flag" rebels who sacked and looted Louang Phabang in 1887 took special care to destroy Xiang Khouang-style temples because their shape resembled Chinese coffins. It's also said that the Buddha at Wat Khili broke into a cold sweat in 1958, a dark omen signalling the coming war. The province of Xiang Khouang was heavily bombed during the Second Indochina War, leaving no trace of Xiang Khouang-style architecture there and making the *sim* at Wat Khili possibly the last surviving example. The monastery is said to have been founded for the commemoration of the marriage of a Phuan prince from Xiang Khouang to a Louang Phabang princess in the early nineteenth century.

Phou Si

Phou Si (Sacred Hill; daily 8am–7pm; $1) is the geographical as well as spiritual centre of the city. Believed to have once harboured a powerful *naga* who dwelt in its bowels, the hill is also seen as a miniature Mount Meru, the Mount Olympus of Hindu-Buddhist cosmology. Though there is nothing to see on the hill itself, save for an ancient-looking *sim* at its foot, and it's not particularly picturesque up close in any case, Phou Si is striking from a distance. Indeed, the golden spires of **That Chomsi** at its summit are the first glimpse of the city that visitors get if they are arriving by boat. Likewise, the peak affords a stunning panorama of the city it crowns, and the shimmering rivers beyond, jungle-clad mountains and moody skies are mesmerizing. Viewing the **setting sun** from the summit of Phou Si has become a kind of tourist ritual, so don't expect to enjoy the moment alone. A quieter spot from which to watch the sunset is Santi Chedi on a hill due east of Phou Si, which affords a marvellous view back towards Phou Si, without the crowds.

There are **three approaches** to the summit. The first and most straightforward is via the stairway directly opposite the main gate of the Royal Palace Museum. The second approach, on the other side of the hill, is up a zigzag stairway flanked by whitewashed naga, and can be used for descending to Phou Si Road. The third and most rambling approach is via Wat Pha Phoutthabat near Phou Si's northern foot (across from the *Saynamkhan Guesthouse*).

The entrance fee must be paid before ascending, and, if you're using the first approach, this is when you should ask to be let into the adjacent *sim*, which is normally padlocked shut. Known as **Wat Pa Houak**, this fine little temple is exquisitely situated, nestled amid dense foliage and overlooking Xiang Thong Road. Its charmingly weathered facade features a rendition of Indra seated on Airavata. The **interior murals**, which French art historian Henri Parmentier once described as "ridiculous", are actually the city's most fascinating, and appear to depict Louang Phabang as a celestial city. Besides Lao characters in classical costumes, there are Chinese, Persians and Europeans in the city, but it is not clear whether they have come as visitors or invaders. After soaking up the murals it's a steep climb through a tunnel of shady plumeria trees to the peak.

Wat Pha Phoutthabat

Entering via **Wat Pha Phoutthabat** affords the most atmosphere. There are actually three monasteries in this compound, one of which is a school for novice monks. The most interesting structure in the compound is the *sim* of **Wat Pa Khe**, a tall, imposing building with an unusual inward-leaning facade. Most noteworthy here is a pair of carved shutters on the window to the left of the main entrance, said to depict seventeenth-century Dutch traders, and a similar if poorly preserved pair of shutters thought to depict Venetians. Why Dutch and Italians are part of the ornamentation on a Buddhist temple in Louang Phabang has been the subject of much conjecture. Perhaps it commemorates the visits of a travelling merchant of the Dutch East India Company who arrived in Vientiane in 1641, and an Italian missionary who arrived soon after, though the penned accounts of neither of these men ever mention reaching Louang Phabang. Perhaps more likely is the theory that these carvings were executed in the mid-nineteenth century and were meant to serve the same function as the images of demons commonly found carved on temple doors and windows: to keep evil spirits at bay.

△ Detail of carvings at Wat Pa Khe

Behind and to the left of the *sim* is a stairway leading to the "**Buddha's footprint**" after which Wat Pha Phoutthabat was named. The balustrade flanking this shady stairway is decorated with four pairs of curious sandstone carvings. The carvings resemble *somasutra*, found in ancient Khmer temple architecture, which were used to channel lustral water over a phallic stone sacred to the Hindu god Shiva. However, these carvings look distinctly Chinese, and fittings on the rear ends seem to indicate that the carvings were a decorative feature of a large structure before being incorporated into the balustrades of this stairway.

The shrine housing the Buddha's footprint is usually locked. However, if you were to find somebody with a key you would see a larger-than-life stylized footprint complete with the 108 auspicious marks said to be found on the historic Buddha's foot (for more on "Buddha's footprints", see the account of Wat Phabat Phonsan, p.110). On festival days, this shrine is open and pilgrims make offerings by tossing banknotes into the footprint. Adjacent to the shrine is a concrete pavilion where Cambodia's Prince Sihanouk held informal press conferences during the cremation ceremony of King Sisavang Vong.

Continuing up the path, you come to a small concrete grotto with an image of Pha Kajai, the Mahayanist deity most Westerners associate with the Buddha. The path meanders up past stone monks' quarters and the remains of an old anti-aircraft gun, a glowing photo opportunity if you happen to pass by when the resident novice monks are having a spin on the thing. Just beyond the gun is the summit, crowned by the stupa That Chomsi, which looks dented and dull up close.

Outside the old city

The old city may have the highest concentration of monasteries and old build-ings, but there is plenty of interest on and beyond Setthathilat Road including over twenty temples, several markets, and a choice of scenic walks. The most historically important of the temples are **Wat That**, **Wat Visoun** and **Wat Aham**, although a trip to the opposite banks of the Mekong and Nam Khan

Along the banks of the Mekong and the Nam Khan

Surrounded by **rivers** on three sides, Louang Phabang not surprisingly feels almost waterborne, and the ship-like contour of the peninsula enhances this impression. Numerous stairways, flanked with whimsical guardian images, link palaces, monasteries and homes with nearby rivers, and are a statement of the importance of the **Mekong** and the **Nam Khan** in the lives of Louang Phabang's population. The banks along the Mekong side are the more lively, but the Nam Khan side is more evocative of old Louang Phabang, and on either side the show is a never-ending affair.

When the French arrived in Louang Phabang they noted a "floating suburb" anchored in the shallows on the Mekong's banks. Francis Garnier described how arriving boats and rafts would slowly poke among the houseboats looking for a place to land and discharge their passengers and cargo. With paved roads conveying much of the traffic into Louang Phabang, life along the river is less of a circus now, but sights and sounds of riparian commerce linger. Spend enough time **strolling the river road** and you will surely witness the tragicomic spectacle of a shipment of pigs, squealing like the crack of doom, being manhandled off boats and up steep embankments. On the Nam Khan side, groups of residents tend tidy riverside gardens and make their way down to the river to bathe during dusk's waning light. It is scenes like these, all but vanished and forgotten in more developed countries, that make Louang Phabang such a fascinating place.

On the banks of both rivers can be found huge umbrella-shaped **somsa trees**, easily distinguished by the furry growth of parasitic vegetation that covers the trees' trunks and branches. In the old days, people would plant a somsa tree near their house for its generous shade-producing canopy and also in the hope that a guardian spirit would take up residence in the tree and protect the house.

rivers will reward you with many other venerable riverside temples, as well as a relaxed rural ambience and good views back over the old city.

Dala Market and the Hmong Market

Louang Phabang's main market, **Dala Market** (Talat Dala), is on Setthathilat Road, not far from the main post office. The market has been undergoing renovations for a couple of years, and the high fence around the site gives little clue as to what the end result will be. Near Dala Market, a small "**Hmong Market**" (so called because the majority of the good-natured grannies who gather here to sell hats and bags are from nearby Hmong villages) occupies a lot on the corner of Setthathilat and Sisavang Vong roads, diagonally opposite from the main post office. Dominating the market, a gigantic billboard extolling socialism and featuring ecstatic factory workers, soldiers and peasants and a giant portrait of Kaysone peels and flakes away in big strips as the women in its shadow count their cash. For more on both markets, and other markets in the city, see the box on p.159.

Wat That

Wat That ($1), officially known as Wat Pha Mahathat, is situated on a low hill to the west of Phou Si Hill and is reached via a stairway flanked by some impressive and undulating seven-headed naga spewing from the mouths of snaggle-toothed *makara*. At the top of the stairs is the most photographed **window** in all of Louang Phabang, a blend of Lao, Chinese and Khmer design framed in ornately carved teak. Other elements of the wat suggest influence from northern Thailand, namely the gold-topped *that* after which the monastery was named. The graceful **stupa** is very similar to examples found in Chiang

Mai, Thailand. This monastery is also the resting place of Prince Phetsarath and his younger brother Prince Souvanna Phouma; their ashes are interred in a family stupa here.

Wat Visoun and Wat Aham

Wat Visoun and **Wat Aham** (each $1) share a parcel of land on the opposite side of Phou Si from the Royal Palace Museum. The *sim* of the former, as seen in a wood-block print executed by French artist Louis Delaporte in 1873, was once a lavishly decorated example of the all-but-extinct Xiang Khouang style. The original *sim* was razed during the sack of Louang Phabang in 1887 by Chinese bandits, and the bulbous, finial-topped stupa, known as *that makmo* – the **watermelon stupa** – was destroyed as well. The looters made off with treasures stored within, but fortunately didn't take everything. What they left behind is now on display in the throne room of the Royal Palace Museum. Wat Visoun's reconstructed *sim* is an unremarkable mix of Louang Phabang and Vientiane styles, but the watermelon stupa is still quite unique.

Neighbouring Wat Aham features a delightfully diminutive *sim* and a couple of mould-blackened *that*, one with a picturesque slant. This wat is associated with **Phu Nyoe** and **Nya Nyoe**, the shaggy, red-faced spirits that are believed to be the founders and protectors of Louang Phabang (see box below). Effigies of the two deities head the parade during the Lao New Year festivities in April, and they are believed to inhabit the two venerable banyan trees whose shade-giving canopies make this a pleasant place to linger.

Across the Mekong: Xiang Men and around

Surprisingly few tourists bother to cross the Mekong and explore the sleepy village of **XIANG MEN**, but it makes a good half-day trip and gives you a chance to view Louang Phabang from across the river. A passenger ferry operates between Louang Phabang and Xiang Men, leaving from the landing west of the Royal Palace Museum. Alternatively, you could strike a deal with one of the many boats to be found along the riverbank. The short journey should cost around 5000K per person, more if you have the boatman wait for you. You

The founding of Louang Phabang

Louang Phabang's guardian spirits, **Phu Nyoe** and **Nya Nyoe**, emerge annually to participate in the New Year's festival, sharing a place in Lao legend with Khoun Lo, Fa Ngum and assorted betel merchants and hermits, all of whom hold claim to the title of **city founder**, as recounted in the following version of the establishment of Louang Phabang. Hacking their way through thick jungle, Phu Nyoe and Nya Nyoe arrived at a hill that resembled a mound of rice, a sign that the settlement was meant for great things. Down the hill, which came to be known as Phou Si, flowed a stream which they followed until they arrived at the confluence of the Mekong and the Khan rivers, where they found a flame tree, hundreds of metres tall and bursting with brilliant red flowers. After vanquishing the evil spirits inhabiting the land with their axes, the ancestors placed a flat rock beneath the great tree, pronouncing it the spot for the palace of the town's future king. They then threw large stones along the banks of the two rivers to mark the boundaries of the town. When they finished, they called forth fifteen *nagas* from the rivers and commanded these water spirits to guard the new city, for which they would receive tribute from the king. From that point forward, the spirits would emerge from the trunks of their banyan trees once a year to participate in the ritual purification of the kingdom.

could ask him to let you off at Wat Xiang Men, almost directly across from the Royal Palace, or cut across the river to Wat Tham, opposite Wat Xiang Thong in the old city, and then walk back to Wat Xiang Men.

Originally built in 1592, **Wat Xiang Men** ($1) has been extensively rebuilt in modern times, but retains its beautiful carved doors. The forest behind the wat conceals a royal cemetery for those members of royalty who, for religious reasons, could not be cremated. An easy climb to the top of the hill north of Wat Xiang Men brings you to the *sim* and stupas of **Wat Chom Phet**. At dusk the views of the sunset from here are spectacular, further enhanced by the sounds of the city carrying across the water. Walking down the hill to the north brings you to **Wat Long Khoun**, once used by Louang Phabang's kings as a pre-coronation retreat involving ritual baths, meditation and reflection. The wat was restored in 1995 by the École Française d'Extrême Orient. Of note are the two Chinese door guardians painted either side of the main entrance to the *sim*, and the murals within.

The next and final sight to the north is Wat Tham Xiang Maen or **Wat Tham**, which is actually a **cave** repository for old and damaged Buddha images. As with Tham Ting upriver (see p.168), this cave is a focus of activity during Lao New Year, when the residents of Louang Phabang come here to gain merit by ritually bathing the Buddhas.

Across the Nam Khan

Although a long walk along the Mekong foreshore and even around the point and back down Kingkitsalat Road is considered *de rigueur* on any walking tour of the old city, very few tourists make the short hop across the river to the **opposite shore of the Nam Khan**. Here, facing the old city and running for several kilometres alongside the Nam Khan and the Mekong to the village of Ban Don, is a string of old **wats** and **monasteries**, quiet neighbourhoods that see relatively few foreign faces, and boast a few crumbling old French mansions ready to tumble into the Mekong. To reach the far shore, simply cross the Sisavangvong Bridge, and turn left at the first big intersection. This puts you on Maha Ouphalathphetsalath Road, which follows the banks of the Nam Khan all the way to the Mekong and then continues along the Mekong shore through several small villages all the way up to **Ban Don**, where the speedboat landing is located. Along the way you can visit many charming temples such as Wat Phan Luang, Wat Pa Kha or Wat Phonsaat, and take in superb views back across the Nam Khan towards the old city.

Santi Chedi

About 3km east of town stands Louang Phabang's largest religious monument. Constructed in 1988 and christened **Santi Chedi**, or "Peace Stupa", this modern, concrete pagoda is best known for its mural-splashed interior (open Mon–Fri 8–10am & 2–4pm), though its carved windows are great works of art in themselves. However, the main reason to come up here is for the impressive **views** of Phou Si and the Nam Khan River, which needless to say are especially attractive at sunset, as is Santi Chedi itself when its golden surface catches the glow of the setting sun – most impressive from a distance. On the way to Santi Chedi, the road passes the old **French cemetery**, where only a few broken tombstones remain. After the revolution the new government used the cemetery as a rubbish dump. Finally, after normalization, the French Government exhumed the bodies and took them back to France.

Shopping

As the royal capital of Laos, Louang Phabang was traditionally a centre for skilled **artisans** from around the former kingdom. Weavers, gold- and silver-smiths, painters, sculptors of bronze, wood and ivory all held a place of importance in old Louang Phabang, and the most gifted artisans were awarded royal patronage. After the revolution these arts were seen as decadent and officially suppressed, while the artisans associated with the former royalty were shunned. Unable to practise their trade, many drifted to more acceptable occupations or fled the country. These days, with the boom in tourism, the traditional arts have been experiencing a revival, and there is a wide array of different crafts on sale – as well as the usual selection of tourist junk. **Silver** and **textiles**, in particular, can be good buys in Louang Phabang, but only if you buy from the right people and haggle.

One of the best places to see everything in one place is the **Pathana Boupha Antique House** (daily 8.30am–7pm; ☎071/212262), southeast of Phou Si Hill and across the street from Wat Aham. This beautiful colonial mansion operates as a private museum and showroom and has a large collection of antique handicrafts and textiles for sale. The women of the Boupha family are fascinating to talk to and can show you the family photo albums spanning several generations. Another showroom for Lao handicrafts is the Blue House (☎071/252383, ⊜bluehouse@lao.tel.com) on Xiang Thong Road, next to *Le Café Ban Vat Sene*. Also housed in a lovely old colonial building, the Blue House acts as a kind of display room and gallery for handicraft artists.

There are over twenty other **handicraft shops** and **boutiques** located on Sisavang Vong/Xiang Thong Road and plenty of good boutiques in the side streets to check out. Shops selling textiles often hang out their wares in colourful displays to lure the curious. Handicraft and antique shops are also to be

△ The Hmong Market

Louang Phabang markets

Dala Market, the city's popular dry market, was undergoing a major renovation at the time of writing. Its location on Setthathilat Road, on the edge of the historic district, gives reassuring credence to the rumours that some of the market's original colonial-era elements will be preserved in the new design, though it is also being said that Louang Phabang's current mayor is not a huge fan of historical architecture. In any case, by the time you read this, the renovation should be nearly completed. The old Dala Market was mainly given over to the usual stacks of toiletries and clothing, but careful inspection of the hardware stalls revealed items such as wild chicken calls, bags of saltpetre and sulphur for making gunpowder, lead shot, and other accoutrements of the rural hunter. Vials of mercury, utilized by gold-panners to separate gold dust from river silt, were also on sale. Stalls acting as pawn shops usually displayed a selection of royalist regalia – brass buttons, badges and medals decorated with the Hindu iconography of the old kingdom.

In the evenings you can browse for souvenirs at the stalls of the nearby **Hmong Market**, on the corner of Sisavang Vong and Setthathilat Roads. The quality of cloth here is not what you'll find in the old city boutiques, but there are many good items and with a bit of bargaining you can get a great deal. More such stalls line Sisavang Vong Road between this corner and the Royal Palace Museum, which is closed to vehicular traffic in the evenings from sunset to 9pm. During the day there are a few Hmong souvenir stalls along Kingkitsalat Road where it runs along the Nam Khan. Other interesting city **markets** include Naviangkham Market and Vieng Mai Market.

found in the old city. See the Shopping section of Basics (pp.57–60) for further details on what to look out for in the items listed below.

Antiques, antiquities and fakes

Instant antiques produced in Thailand, and to a much lesser extent Cambodia, are finding their way back up to Louang Phabang. Buddhist or Hindu figurines cast in any kind of metal are mostly Thai or Cambodian reproductions: some years back, a Ganesh figurine of the kind that sells in Bangkok for four to six dollars was seen for sale at Ban Phanom for an asking price of $800. **Opium weights**, also mostly reproductions, are well represented in the silver shops of Louang Phabang.

Basketry

Baskets made in the nearby hill-tribe villages are widely available in Louang Phabang. Vintage baskets are hard to come by, but some of the tribal villages around the city have met the demand for their basketry by smoking newly woven baskets over an open fire to give them a rich patina. Tribal baskets can be found in the souvenir shops along Sisavang Vong Road.

Mulberry paper products

Observant visitors to Louang Phabang may notice the bustling trade in what first appears to be bundles of white garlic. The "garlic" is in fact *Broussonetia papyrifera*, the raw material for **mulberry paper**, known in Lao as *jia sa*. This paper is used throughout Tai cultures, and in Laos is utilized in the construction of *khom fai*, mulberry-paper lanterns that decorate houses and monasteries during the *lai heua fai* festival (see Festivals colour section). Notebooks and photo albums made from mulberry paper have found a ready market in the handicraft shops of Louang Phabang. **Baan Khily Gallery** on Xiang Thong Road (opposite Wat Sop) offers a good selection of originally designed paper lanterns, including easily transported collapsible models. This German-run operation also produces tasteful stencil work on mulberry paper, featuring traditional Lao–Buddhist motifs inspired by the walls of Louang Phabang's many gaily decorated *sims*.

Royalist regalia

It stands to reason that Louang Phabang, being the former royal capital, should be awash with dusty relics evoking the **monarchy**, and indeed its curio shops have more than anywhere else in Laos, though not as many as you might imagine. Considered a royalist hotbed by suspicious communist officials after the revolution, Louang Phabang and its inhabitants were especially targeted for "re-education". During the early years of the LPDR, royal items were buried, thrown into rivers or melted down by people anxious to forget their own ties to the previous regime. What remained eventually appeared in antique stores, and souvenir-hungry tourists have rid Louang Phabang of these mementos with more thoroughness than the threat of re-education ever did.

Silver

Although Thai antique dealers have made off with quite a bit of old Lao silver (and marketed it in Thailand as old Thai silver), there is still a fair amount of the stuff floating around. Items to look out for include paraphernalia for betel chewing, boxes or bowls and jewellery. With a few exceptions, the **hill-tribe jewellery** peddled in Louang Phabang is the handiwork of the Hmong. All of these articles are sold in the shops along Sisavang Vong/Xiang Thong Road.

New silver of superior quality can and should be bought directly from Louang Phabang's expert **silversmiths**. The best known of these is Thithpeng Maniphone, whose workshop is located just down the small lane opposite Wat That. As for the quality of the merchandise, suffice to say that when Thailand's Princess Sirindhorn visited Louang Phabang she made a point of patronizing Thithpeng's shop. Other silversmiths are located near the Royal Palace and opposite Wat Aham. New silver for sale at souvenir shops and in the market is less expensive than that of the silversmiths, but the difference in workmanship is quite evident.

Textiles

Traditional **textiles** are practically Louang Phabang's signature product, and both antique and new textiles can be bought here. The city has many **boutiques** specializing in high-quality Lao textiles; the outlets themselves are often every bit as upscale as the best boutiques in Bangkok or Chiang Mai, from which they draw their inspiration.

Ock Pop Tok Textiles Gallery and Workshop at 73/5 Ban Wat Nong (☏071/253219, ⊛www.ockpoptok.com), next to *L'Elephant*, is typical of the kind of chic shops popping up around this end of town. It is foreign-managed, has knowledgeable sales staff, and is run as a kind of cooperative with the villagers who produce the weavings for sale here. Another good boutique is Satri Lao on Siphouthabath Street (☏020/252708). On the same strip are two other boutiques also selling Lao textiles.

One of the longest-running places in town is **Lao Antique Textiles Collection** on Sisavang Vong (☏071/212775), which has an excellent selection of textiles. The owner, Mr Keomontri, is very knowledgeable about what he sells and can tell you just which of Laos's many ethnic groups produced a certain piece. There's also a selection of weaving accoutrements, such as hand-carved shuttles and loom pulleys, on offer.

Cheaper, lower-quality wares and utilitarian articles such as *nyam* – shoulder bags – and the all-purpose *pha khao ma*, a chequered, wrap-around sarong that Lao men also use as a turban or scarf, can be found at shops all over town. Eye-catching examples of **Hmong embroidery** are sold at the Hmong Market and along Sisavang Vong Road in the evenings (see p.159).

Woodcarving

Lao **woodcarving** is traditionally religious in nature, but the increase in tourism has created a demand for souvenirs, and so woodcarvers are now whittling a wide range of objects. These include wooden hangers for displaying textiles, carved with motifs such as the watermelon stupa and the three-headed elephant. Small, antique wooden **Buddha images** turn up occasionally in antique stores, but visitors should resist the temptation to purchase, as they are likely to have been pilfered from the caves at Pak Ou. New Buddhas are the better alternative, and examples carved in a variety of hardwoods can be found alongside the textiles and old silver in the shops on Sisavang Vong Road.

Eating

Louang Phabang is a city that prides itself on its food. Some dishes are unique to the royal city, and others are simply done better here than elsewhere – all of which conspires to make this the town in which to dig into **Lao food** with a sense of mission, despite the wide availability of international cuisine. At the top of your list should be *aw lam*, a bittersweet soup, heavy on aubergines and mushrooms. Another local speciality, *jaew bong*, a condiment of red chillies, shallots, garlic and dried buffalo skin, makes a nice addition to the pâté sandwiches on sale around town, although it's most commonly eaten with dried beef.

You're less likely to use your *jaew bong* as a dipping sauce for *nang nyam*, a local treat consisting of small squares of water buffalo skin left to rot, then dried and fried to burn off the hair before being folded over and tied with a slim strip of bamboo. If the sound of that is enough to turn you into a committed veggie, you'll delight in *phak nam*, a type of **watercress** particular to the area and widely used in salads. The most common style of salad appears on menus alternatively as "watercress salad" or "Louang Phabang salad" and is in fact quite similar to a Western salad – a light alternative to the meat salads more commonly served in Lao restaurants. Another green delight is *khai paen*, a highly nutritious **river moss** that's usually fried in oil and eaten as patties sprinkled with sesame seeds. Mekong River *khai paen* is chewy, while the moss from the Nam Khan is considered a bit harder in texture.

For other local favourites timing is everything. In July, fried freshwater **prawns**, known as *jeun kung*, with a delicate taste, hit the markets. As the rains ebb, *màk deuy* – one Lao–English dictionary translates this mysterious plant's name as "Job's tears" – in olive-green bouquets, takes the town by storm, appearing in piles on street corners and in the hands of virtually every Lao woman. It's the slightly oily nut at the top of the stem that they're after, a tasty diamond that's a cross between a pea and a peanut. With the arrival of the cooler weather of November, *màk deuy* is supplanted by buttery-tasting papayas. The locals' serious approach to food begins with the way they grow their fruit: Louang Phabang inhabitants claim to shun chemical fertilizers, preferring fruit small in size but large in flavour.

Locals even add a twist to the Lao staple, *tam màk hung*, **papaya salad**: the distinctive Louang Phabang flavour of this dish comes from the addition of crab juice. It's okay to reach for your chopsticks while munching on this one, as the civilized folk of Louang Phabang shun the fingers-and-sticky rice technique favoured elsewhere in the country.

With so much ado about food, it's only right that Louang Phabang should have its own tipple, and indeed, *lào khào kam*, a dark-red fizzy **wine**, is a welcome respite from *lào-láo*.

Cafés

All the cafés reviewed below appear on the "Old Louang Phabang" map except for the *JoMa Bakery*, which is on the "Louang Phabang City" map.

Le Cafe Ban Vat Sene Xiang Thong Rd, next to the Blue House Gallery. Recently opened by the owners of *L'Elephant*, this atmospheric little coffee shop is housed in a colonial shophouse with a beautiful interior and features truly decadent desserts.

E'Stranger Literary Salon South side of Phou Si. This two-storey house is a laid-back place for secondhand books, coffee and world music.

JoMa Bakery Xiang Thong Rd. Does great baked goods and excellent set breakfasts. The cinnamon buns and banana breads are top-notch.

Luang Prabang Bakery Sisavang Vong Rd. With two branches nearly next door to each other, and serving very tasty "tea-bread" sandwiches and good fruit shakes.

Regine Adjacent to Wat Pa Phai. A recently opened café that does its busiest trade in the morning hours, luring customers in with French crepes and many other excellent breakfast options.

Scandinavian Bakery Xiang Thong Rd. A Louang Phabang institution, very popular (and sometimes crowded), but a handy spot to catch up on the Bangkok newspapers, read the bulletin boards and get a satellite TV news fix.

Restaurants

Thanks to the huge growth in tourism, Louang Phabang boasts more **restaurants** than anywhere else in the country outside of the capital. But the city is no centre for street food – there's nothing even remotely like the kind of food-stall scene you find in Thailand, although basic noodle shops, street stalls and *khào ji pateh* vendors can be found scattered around town. The vast majority of Louang Phabang residents only eat at home.

Many of the city's flash tourist eating places are located along a five-hundred-metre strip of **Sasavang Vong Road**. Here you'll find almost twenty tourist restaurants, most of which serve Western and Lao dishes and almost all of which tend to be pricey by Lao standards. That said, with the exception of upmarket restaurants in fancy hotels like the *Villa Santi* or the *Maison Souvannaphoum* (see p.142), a two-course meal in Louang Phabang usually only costs $5–10; seldom will you spend more than $15 unless you are drinking imported wine. Cheaper and often tastier meals can be found at the delightful **riverside restaurants** along the western end of Manthatoulat Road. The riverside places are the perfect spot to be at sunset and after dark for alfresco dining. All of the restaurants along the waterfront offer indoor seating but also set up tables and chairs outside along the riverbank. Don't come here if you're looking for Western food; the house specials are all Lao, Thai and Chinese. In the morning, try the little places up towards the northern end, like the *Boua Savanh*, with a view of the Mekong and serving a full American breakfast for a dollar.

Generally, the further you get from Sisavang Vong Road, the cheaper things get. Restaurants open daily for lunch and stop serving food by 9pm.

The old city

L'Elephant Straight towards the Mekong from the *Villa Santi* ☏071/252482, ⓦwww .elephant-restau.com. A cross between southern California and Casablanca, this is one of Louang Phabang's more chic restaurants. With the cane chairs and potted plants, it's the kind of place where you almost expect to see Humphrey Bogart stroll in. A three-course meal with coffee runs to about $20 here, but the quality is superb. There are also some creative vegetarian dishes to be had here.

Les 3 Nagas Xiang Thong Rd ☏071/253888. The restaurant of this excellent boutique hotel is one of the better choices in town: the food is Lao with a French accent, and there is a decent wine list. Try the buffalo *laap*, a minced and fried meat and mint dish that is usually done with pork, but prepared here with water buffalo, which has a wonderfully gamey flavour. Prices are moderate; look to pay $10–20 per person without drinks.

Pakhuay Mixay Near Wat Xiang Mouan. The main draw here is the tranquil, garden atmosphere in a quiet residential corner of the old city, near to but worlds away from the bustle and hype of the main drag. The place is sometimes packed out with package tourists, but many expats and well-heeled locals are also drawn by the excellent Lao cuisine.

Villa Santi Xiang Thong Rd ☏071/212267. Although the hotel service has slipped of late, the restaurant is still one of the classiest places in town to sample Lao cuisine, featuring recipes by the daughter of the legendary Phia Sing, the last chef to cook for the Lao royal family. If you're looking for a romantic meal by candlelight, on a balcony overlooking the relaxed evening scene of Xiang Thong Rd, it's hard to beat. A drink at the garden bar of this former royal residence is also something of a Louang Phabang tradition. Give the house drink, "Return of the Dragon", a try; it's a mixture of local *lào khào kam* and banana liqueur.

Tum-Tum Cheng Café Sisaleumsak Rd, uphill from Wat Xiang Thong. This restaurant/cooking school, located downstairs in a cool old colonial building, offers Lao food as well as giving lessons on how to prepare it.

Riverside establishments

Boungnasouk Souvanbaniang Rd ☏071/212726. Excellent views of the Mekong and lovely lamps make this a good place to spend sunset. The fruit shakes are particularly delicious. The menu is mostly Lao-Thai and very inexpensive, with vegetable and meat dishes at $1 and $2 respectively.

Kheme Khan Food Garden Kingkitsalat Rd. High on the bank of the Nam Khan River behind Phou Si, this is a great venue for traditional Lao food with lovely views of the river. There's a big wooden deck over the river with wooden tables and chairs, so come early enough to enjoy the view. The bird's-eye view of river life also gets a little help from a tidy selection of Western-style cocktails. The *keng kai màk nao*, a soup served with chicken, and the *sai-ua Louang Phabang*, Lao-style sausages, are standouts on this solid menu of traditional Lao food. An added touch is the substitution of purplish balls of *khào kam* for standard sticky rice.

View Kheamkhong Souvanbaniang Rd ☏071/212726. A lovely outdoor restaurant right on the banks of the Mekong River, with candle-lit tables and big white umbrellas. The menu is quite extensive and the food inexpensive and delicious. Probably the best of the riverside options.

The new city

Garden Bar & Restaurant *Le Parasol Blanc Hotel*, off Phou Vao Rd ☏071/252124. For a bit of a splurge, the Lao restaurant of *Le Parasol Blanc* is really something to behold. Surrounded by the Lao-inspired buildings and a lush tropical garden, this Lao-Thai restaurant is set in a traditional open *sala* with a huge hardwood deck opening on to a lovely lotus pond. There's traditional live music some nights. Pricey but worth the experience.

Indochina Spirit Xiang Thong Rd, just north of the Nam Phou Fountain ☏071/252372. The best Lao-Thai restaurant in Louang Phabang, if not Laos, this absolutely charming old house with hardwood floors and Thai and Lao antiques is a gem. Eat inside at a table, or Lao-style on cushions and mats, or alfresco on the lovely brick patio with live, traditional music.

Luang Prabang Restaurant Visounalat Rd, just north of the circle ☏071/252981. A very popular travellers' café (one of three using this moniker), catering to people staying in the Visounalat Rd area. Best of the seven places north of the circle and packed most evenings.

Nangsomchan Souvanbaniang Rd, straight down from the Nam Phou fountain. The southernmost riverside restaurant and the cheapest too. Wooden chairs and tables with big shade umbrellas set the scene along the bank of the Mekong; you should find plenty to tempt your taste buds on the eight-page menu.

Sakounna Xiang Thong Rd. This cream French-colonial building with green shutters and doors makes a good alternative to the tourist restaurants on the opposite side of the palace further north. The menu is pretty standard tourist fare, but the price is right and it draws the Ban Wat That dinner crowd in the evenings.

Drinking, nightlife and entertainment

In the evening, you might be content to sip a cool drink at one of the town's riverfront restaurants, but if you're looking for something with more of a local spin, head over to the popular *Muang Sua* disco (nightly 9–11.30pm; $1) on Phou Vao Road. A fun **dance club** attached to the hotel of the same name, it has a laid-back dance floor where both Lao and foreign clientele are welcome. Just behind Phou Si hill on Latsavong is the coolest bar in town, *The Hive*, a low-key venue with DJ-driven sounds that stays open later than most, usually until 1am; most other venues close by midnight. Most of the more stylish places to stay have equally stylish places to enjoy a drink, including *Les 3 Nagas* (see p.163) and the long-running *Maison Souvannaphoum* (see p.142), which has been spruced up since being taken over by a group of Singaporeans. *Lemongrass*, next to Wat Xiang Mouan, is a wine bar with minimalist decor and trendy music that could be mistaken for ambient noise.

Louang Phabang is the cultural heart of Laos, and during the high season (November through February) a building on the grounds of the Royal Palace Museum serves as the home of the Royal Ballet Theatre, which gives performances three nights a week (Mon, Wed & Fri 6pm; $5). The shows include excerpts from the Lao version of the Ramayana, a mock Lao wedding ceremony, as well as some Lao interpretations of the dances of their tribal neighbours. The glittering costumes are stunning, and the traditional Lao music will be playing in your head long into the night.

Listings

Banks and exchange There are several exchange places along Xiang Thong Rd, including the main branch of Lane Xang Bank, opposite the Hmong Market, which changes traveller's cheques and can do cash advances on Visa. Lane Xang Bank also maintains an exchange bureau on Latsavong Rd (cash and traveller's cheques only; daily 8.30am–4pm). The official exchange rates in Louang Phabang are better than anywhere further upcountry.

Bicycle rental Numerous shops on Xiang Thong Rd rent out bicycles ($2–3 for the day) although mountain bikes are harder to find. Most budget guesthouses also rent out bikes.

Boat charters Boatmen tend to congregate at the Boat Immigration Office behind the palace or at the nearby "South Pier", just to the south. If you need a boatman who can act as a guide,

contact Mr Thongdi at Bouchane Rice Shop, Manthatoulat Rd (☏071/212910), next to the *Auberge Calao*, who speaks excellent English and has two boats.

Hospitals and clinics The main hospital is located on Setthathilat Rd; an International Clinic (☏071/252049) is around the corner on the hospital's western side. In case of a serious illness, flying to Bangkok for treatment is the best option.

Internet access Pla-Net CyberCentre has two branches, one on Sisavang Vong Rd and another on Setthathilat Rd just up from the post office (both daily 8am–9pm; 200K/min). Several other Internet places can be found along Sisavang Vong Rd.

Laundry Most hotels and guesthouses will wash clothes for you.

Lao Airlines (Visounalat Road; ☏071/212172) operates **flights** to Vientiane, Pakxe and Phonsavan, as well as internationally to Bangkok, Chiang Mai, Hanoi and Siem Reap. For Bangkok, Bangkok Airways is also an option (57/6 Sisavang Vong Rd; ☏071/253334).

Buses and sawngthaews

Buses to Vientiane and Vang Viang and **points south** along Route 13 use the Southern Bus Station, best reached by tuk-tuk. There are several buses a day to Vientiane, with the final departure at 5pm. Tickets are sold at the bus station. There are also air-con **tourist coaches to Vientiane** ($10), which can be booked through most guesthouses. Southwest-bound **buses to Xainyabouli and Muang Nan** pull out of the Pakkhon depot, near the Southern Bus Station, and depart until mid-afternoon. Buses and sawngthaews to all **points north** use the Northern Bus Station. Almost all northbound buses depart in the morning; there's no need to buy your ticket in advance.

Boats

Slow boats leave from the Navigation Office landing behind the former Royal Palace in the old city. Departures down to Vientiane or up to Houayxai, as well as up the Nam Ou River, are all posted on a chalk board here, but arrive at the pier early as there are no real fixed departure times. A quick visit to the Navigation Office the day before you plan to depart is prudent. Boats to Xainyabouli may leave from the "South Pier" landing a little downriver, at the foot of Setthathilat Road, so make your enquiries beforehand. **Charter boats** to the Buddha Caves, Kouang Si and other nearby destinations are easily found along the riverfront south of the Navigation Office – you'll be approached by boatmen offering a variety of tour options. While they are not recommended due to safety issues, eight-seater **speedboats** leave from a separate landing in the suburb of Ban Don, 7km north of the centre on the banks of the Mekong. They travel to points north and south along the Mekong River, as well as destinations along the Nam Ou River.

Massage and herbal sauna The Red Cross on Visounalat Rd (☏071/252856 or 212303; daily 5–9pm) has traditional Lao massage at $3 per hour (reserve ahead) and an excellent sauna for $1 (bring a sarong or pay 5000K to rent one). Proceeds go to help poor villagers. There are a number of places on Sisavang Vong Rd offering "traditional massage", but note that the massage is Thai.

Minimarkets Small minimarts selling everything from Kodak film to American chocolate bars can be found all along Sisavang Vong Rd, especially in the Ban Jek area.

Motorbike rental Motorbikes are rented out for around $10 per day plus deposit of your passport. Pinekham Service, on the corner of Setthathilat and Visounalat roads, is the biggest outlet in town. Many guesthouses also have motorbikes available.

Pharmacies The best pharmacies are opposite Dala Market.

Photographic services Lithium batteries are available at VDO on Xiang Thong Rd.

Post office The GPO is on the corner of Sisavang Vong and Setthathilat roads (Mon–Fri 8am–noon & 1–5pm, Sat 8am–noon).

Telephone services It is usually possible to make Internet long-distance calls at the Internet cafés along Sisavang Vong Rd. Prices are a fraction of what they would be if you were to use a long-distance telephone line. The telecom office (daily 8am–9pm), located behind the GPO, handles international calls and faxes. International direct dial phones are located outside the GPO and phone cards are available at many convenience stores. IDD calls can be made from most hotels.

Tour agencies Diethelm, Xiang Thong Rd ☏071/212277; Lane Xang, Visounalat Rd ☏071/212793; Lao Travel Service, Xiang Thong Rd ☏071/212725; Sodetour, Manthatoulat Rd ☏071/212092; Wildside/Green Discovery, 37 Sisavang Vong Rd ☏071/212093, ⊛www .greendiscoverylaos.com.

Around Louang Phabang

Once you've exhausted Louang Phabang's many monasteries and temples, you'll still find many more attractions in the surrounding countryside, all within easy reach of the city. An excursion to the village of **Ban Phanom** rewards with textiles shopping, together with a look at a traditional lowland Lao village, and can be combined with a pilgrimage to the tomb of French explorer Henri Mouhout and a stop at the Santi Chedi viewpoint (see p.157). The popular **Pak Ou caves** trip gets you out on the water, a wonderful day-trip, especially if you haven't had a chance to travel the Mekong by boat. There are also two picturesque **waterfalls** nearby, Tad Se and Kouang Si, both of which are good spots for a picnic and splashing around in turquoise waters. All the trips described here can be done in half a day. While it's possible to get to these sites by local public transport, it's much faster and easier to get there on your own by hiring a tuk-tuk with a few fellow travellers or renting a motorbike.

The swift rivers, pretty rural areas and impressive mountains around Louang Phabang also offer many opportunities for **adventure sports**, including white-water rafting, mountain-bike touring, kayaking, and trekking tours. Enquires for adventure tours can be made through your guesthouse or one of the tour agents listed on p.165. Green Discovery, for example, offers a number of possibilities around Louang Phabang, including rock-climbing, caving, trekking and kayaking on the Nam Xuang and Nam Khan rivers.

Ban Phanom

A few hundred metres beyond the golden stupa of Santi Chedi, **BAN PHANOM** attracts its share of the tourist dollar through its pedigree as a former royal weaving village. The palace resettled a Thai Leu community from the northern town of Louang Namtha to provide weavers and dancers for King Sisavang Vong's court. Young girls from Ban Phanom were chosen to be classical dancers and would begin the intensive training regime as young as 7 years old – a necessity if they were to learn how to bend their limbs and fingers at the alien angles demanded by Lao classical dancing. The only traces of this tradition left in Ban Phanom lie in the tales woven by older village women who long ago danced for the king. Elsewhere, classical dancing is only a little easier to find, showcased for tourists at restaurants such as the *Kualao* in Vientiane or at upmarket hotels like Louang Phabang's *Maison Souvannaphoum*.

Just off the main road, the Ban Phanom **textile market** has textiles of comparable quality to those in town, at slightly lower prices. The market sells cotton and silk sarongs, as well as a selection of trousers and shirts in sizes large enough to fit Westerners, plus a sampling of colourful shoulder bags. If you take the time to wander Ban Phanom's quaint, red-dirt streets you'll find a few independent textile shops as well as women hard at work weaving in the relatively cool space beneath their raised, traditional wooden homes.

Ban Phanom is easily reached by **bicycle** or **motorbike** by following Patoupakmao Road and turning left at the first major intersection beyond the *Wiang Mai* restaurant. After 500m, turn right onto a dirt road leading uphill; Ban Phanom is about 300m further on. Shared tuk-tuks for Ban Phanom (10,000K) leave Louang Phabang several times throughout the day from a stand near Dala Market.

Henri Mouhot's tomb

Four kilometres up the Nam Khan from Ban Phanom is the final resting place of **Henri Mouhot**, the Anglophile French naturalist and explorer best known as the "discoverer" of Angkor Wat (see box below). A simple memorial, made from stone donated by the Lao king Tiantha and erected by Doudart de Lagrée of the Mekong Commission in 1867, marks the spot, which is easily located by looking for the sign posted on the road above it. As you leave Ban Phanom, follow the right fork 3.7km until you reach a steep dirt path leading down to the bank of the river, a spot favoured by picnicking Lao from Louang Phabang on weekends. The whitewashed memorial lies 200m upriver from the path and about 20m from the river's edge, in a dried-up tributary of the Khan.

Henri Mouhot

Although he was the first European to reach the isolated royal city of Louang Phabang, French explorer **Henri Mouhot** was far better known for his nineteenth-century journey to Cambodia, a trip that gained him renown as the "discoverer" of **Angkor Wat**, the famed Khmer temple complex built by Suryavarman II. Mouhot was hardly the first Westerner to stumble upon Angkor, but the eloquence of his journals, published posthumously in English and French, captured the majesty of the ruins and piqued his European readers' imagination. His writings circulated widely, and their influence is immediately apparent in such works as *The English Governess at the Siamese Court*, written in 1870 by Anna Leonowens, the governess of *The King and I* fame, and in which certain passages bear remarkable similarity to Mouhot's work.

Mouhot, who turned to England for sponsorship of his journeys after finding a lack of interest in his native France, spent much of his three years in **Southeast Asia** travelling through the difficult terrain of northeastern Thailand, Cambodia and Laos. His travels in Laos were the final episode in a life of insatiable exploring that took him far from his Jersey home, and his writings on the country bear the same descriptive flair that brought Angkor to life for his European audience. Mouhot set off from Bangkok for Laos in December 1860, aware that no Westerner in recent memory had travelled to the heart of Siam's isolated vassal state and lived. Putting aside premonitions that it was his destiny to die in Laos, he travelled through the Forest of the King of Fire, the present-day Thai provinces of Korat and Loei, and on to Louang Phabang through Paklai, all the while dazzling the Lao with his long red beard and filling his journals with his customarily frank insights on those he encountered, including the children who brought the naturalist insects for his collection in exchange for a bit of brass wire or a "cigarette, for it is a common thing for them to leave their mother's breast to smoke". It took him seven months to reach **Louang Phabang**, a "delightful little town", the setting of which he likened to Geneva's. In Louang Phabang, Mouhot was received by King Tiantha, an encounter he described in detail: "After waiting for ten days I have at length been presented to the king with great pomp. The reception room was a shed such as they build in our villages on fête-days, but larger and hung with every possible colour. His Majesty was enthroned at one end of the hall, lazily reclining on a divan, having on his right hand four guards squatting down, and each holding a sabre; behind were the princes all prostrated, and farther off the senators, with their backs to the public and their faces in the dust."

Using Louang Phabang as a base, Mouhot made several exploratory trips in the surrounding countryside, but contracted a fever and, three months after his arrival in the royal city, died at the age of 35, his famously descriptive diary trailing off with the words "Have pity on me, oh my God...!" Mouhot was buried in the shadow of Phou Souwung Mountain, on the banks of the Nam Khan River, his explorations a harbinger of the colonies of France in Laos and Cambodia.

The Pak Ou Buddha Caves

Without a doubt Louang Phabang's most popular day-trip, a river excursion to the **Pak Ou Buddha Caves** (daily 8am–sunset; $1), 25km north of Louang Phabang at the confluence of the Mekong and Nam Ou rivers, is one of the best quick trips you can make out of the city. Numerous caves punctuate the limestone cliffs on both sides of the Mekong in this vicinity, but the two "Buddha Caves" of **Tham Ting** and **Tham Phoum** are the best known. These caves have been used for centuries as a repository for old Buddha images that can no longer be venerated on an altar, either because they are damaged to the point of disfigurement – termite holes, burn marks and broken limbs being afflictions common to wooden Buddhas – or simply because newer images have crowded them out. In former times, before the caves became a tourist attraction, the inhabitants of Louang Phabang didn't give much thought to the caves or their contents except during **Lao New Year**, when boatloads of townsfolk would make the pilgrimage upriver and ritually bathe the semi-abandoned Buddhas to gain merit. The practice survives to this day and is worth seeing if you happen to be around. If not, the caves still deserve an hour or so, if only to gaze at the eerie scene of hundreds upon hundreds of serenely smiling images covered in dust and cobwebs. Tham Ting, the lower cave, just above the water's surface, is more of a large grotto and is light enough to explore without an artificial light source. The upper cave is unlit, so bring a torch (flashlight).

Boats to Pak Ou are easily arranged at the South Pier landing in Louang Phabang and cost $15–20 per boat, depending on the size, to charter for the trip there and back. The ride upriver takes less than an hour. If you want to see the **Whisky Village** (see below) on the opposite side of the Mekong from the Pak Ou Caves, tell the boatman before you leave or you may end up paying more later. A tuk-tuk to the caves is around $10 return from Louang Phabang, plus $2 to cross the Mekong.

Whisky Village

Opposite the Buddha Caves on the far side of the Mekong is the "mouth" of the "Ou" River – "Pak Ou" in Lao. The scenery here at the entrance of the Nam Ou is dramatic, with a huge limestone peak rising up over the junction of the two rivers. South of Pak Ou, on the banks of the Mekong, is a village that produced stoneware jars for thousands of years, but has now forsaken that activity, having found that distilling liquor is more lucrative. The inhabitants of **BAN XANG HAI**, referred to by local boatmen as the "**Whisky Village**", are quite used to thirsty visitors stopping by for a pull on the bamboo straw. The liquor is *lào-láo*, made from fermented sticky rice, and pots filled with the hooch are lined up on the beach awaiting transport up or down the river.

As it's logical to see the Pak Ou Caves and the Whisky Village on the same trip, most boatmen hired in Louang Phabang are happy to treat it as a package, assuming that after you've seen a cave-full of Buddhas you'll be ready for a good, stiff drink. **Boats** to either or both destinations are easily arranged in Louang Phabang.

Tad Se

The wide **Tad Se** waterfall wanders down a gradual slope, serenely cascading through trees and easing through a dozen clear-blue pools, like some elaborate Zen meditation retreat, until it finally flows into the Nam Khan River. The pools here aren't good for swimming like those at Kouang Si, but are fine for a bit of splashing around. The excursion to the falls follows Route 13 south along the beginning of its most dramatically pretty stretch, winding around mountains and past hillside teak plantations, and culminates with a short trip by pirogue downstream to the waterfall. If you've come by your own transport, turn left off Route 13 17km south of town, and head for **Ban En** (marked Ban Aine on a blue roadside sign), 2km away. Here you'll need to hire a boat ($1) for the short journey to the falls, which are downstream on the opposite bank. The boat cruises downriver for five minutes past tobacco fields and drop-door bamboo fishing traps. You can also get to Ban En very easily by tuk-tuk (around $8 return). If you're on a motorbike, be wary of buses and trucks careering through the final turns of the journey up from Vientiane.

Kouang Si

One of the best day-trips from Louang Phabang is **Kouang Si** waterfall (daily 8am to sunset; $2), a picturesque, multi-level affair that tumbles 60m before spilling through a series of crystal-blue pools. The spray from the falls keeps the surrounding grounds cool even at midday. It's a great spot for a picnic and a refreshing swim – there are picnic tables and changing rooms at the site. The **upper pool** has a nice view of the falls, though swimming is only allowed at the **lower pool**, which lacks a direct view. If you didn't pack lunch, pay a visit to the vendors nearby selling *tam màk hung*, fruit and drinks.

If you're up for some exercise, the steep path on the opposite side of the falls leads to the top and a grassy **meadow** filled with brilliantly coloured butterflies. Tread carefully though, as the path can get quite slippery; more than a few barefoot trampers have slipped and broken a leg here.

There are several options for **getting to the waterfall**, which is situated 35km southwest of Louang Phabang. The easiest is to charter a tuk-tuk ($6) or rent a motorcycle in Louang Phabang, but the most scenic approach is by boat down the Mekong River; the same boatmen who run the trips to the Pak Ou Caves will take you to the falls ($10–12 per boat). The boat option, a pleasant cruise down the Mekong River, entails taking a tuk-tuk for the last portion of the journey, something that needs to be established when negotiating the boat fare. The whole trip takes half a day if you don't linger too long at the falls.

The road to Kouang Si follows the Mekong through pretty scenery and villages populated by a variety of different **ethnic groups**, including Hmong. The first village southwest of Louang Phabang is **Ban Lak 8**, settled in the 1960s by Lao Theung fleeing fighting along the Vietnamese border to the north. Three newer villages – the Hmong village of Ban Na Ouane, the Lao Theung village of Ban Nun Sa-at and Ban Thin Keo, a lowland Lao settlement – were resettled here from the mountain near the waterfall by the government, which was fretting that their slash-and-burn methods of farming were affecting the falls.

Accommodation near the waterfall is available at a charming guesthouse, *Vanvisa 2* (❸), in Ban Tha Pene. It's run by the owners of the *Vanvisa* in Louang Phabang and offers six basic rooms with en-suite bathrooms. To find it, turn right before the hill leading out of the village, cross the footbridge over the stream and you'll see it on the left.

Mount Phaban

Phou Phaban is the highest peak in the immediate vicinity of Louang Phabang and, so far, remains well off the beaten tourist track. The Nam Khan River flows right around the flanks of this 2212-metre peak, around 30km upriver from the city. You can get close to the peak by chartering a passenger boat to take you up from **Xiang Ngeun**, 24km south of Louang Phabang. On the way to the turbulent rapids at the base of the mountain, where boats have to turn around, you can stop at a **cave** and a natural **hot spring** with cold and hot pools. Upriver, beyond the rapids, the Nam Khan flows through over 100km of unchartered jungle all the way to the Nam Et NBCA.

Travel details

Buses

Louang Phabang to: Muang Nan (5 daily; 3hr); Nam Bak (2 daily; 2hr 10min); Nong Khiaw (2 daily; 2–3hr); Oudomxai (3 daily; 5–6hr); Pakkhon (5 daily; 3hr); Pakmong (5 daily; 2hr); Vang Viang (6 daily; 6–7hr); Viang Kham (1 daily; 4hr 40min); Vientiane (7 daily; 10–12hr).

Slow boats

Louang Phabang to: Nong Khiaw (infrequent; 7–8hr); Pakbeng (1 daily; 10hr); Thadua (daily; 6–8hr); Vientiane (infrequent; 3 days).

Domestic flights

Louang Phabang to: Pakxe (2 weekly; 1hr 30min); Phongsali (4 weekly; 35min); Phonsavan (2 weekly; 35min); Vientiane (up to 4 daily; 40min).

The northeast

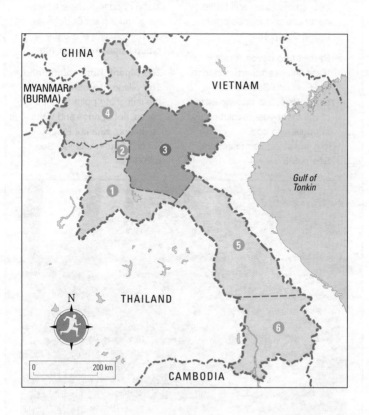

CHAPTER 3 # Highlights

* **Route 1** From Nong Khiaw to Nam Neun junction, ride across the rooftop of Indochina to one of the least-visited parts of the country. See p.175

* **Suan Hin** These ancient circles of upright slabs of rock in a remote forest still baffle historians and archeologists today. See p.183

* **Pathet Lao caves** A major Viet Minh headquarters during the First and Second Indochina Wars, this historic base of the thirty-year revolutionary struggle also boasts incredible limestone karst scenery. See p.185

* **Plain of Jars** Fields of ancient giant stone urns scattered across the Xiang Khouang Plateau stand as witnesses to a vanished civilization. See p.194

* **Muang Khoun** Travel back in time to the ancient kingdom of Xiang Khouang where temple ruins and a giant Buddha are all that remains of a once proud kingdom. See p.198

* **The Muang Kham hinterland** The village of Muang Kham is the launching point for trips to caves, hot springs and visits to Hmong, Khamu, Black Tai and Phuan villages. See p.200

△ Suan Hin

The northeast

D ifficult to reach and short on typical tourist sights, the remote **north-east** is, not surprisingly, one of the least-visited parts of Laos. However, a frontier friendliness among the inhabitants, who come from more than two dozen ethnic groups, and the challenge of tough travel in remote reaches lend the region a certain allure for those who enjoy blazing their own trail.

Topographically diverse, the northeast region extends from the towering peaks that border the Vientiane Plain, across the Xiang Khouang Plateau, over the jagged backbone of the Annamite Mountains, and into the watershed of the Nam Xam River, which flows into Vietnam. The area encompasses **Houa Phan** and **Xiang Khouang provinces**, the **Xaisomboun Special Zone** and part of **northern Louang Phabang province**. Historically, this swath of Laos was the domain of two independent principalities – the Tai federation of Sipsong Chao Tai in Houa Phan and the Phuan Kingdom of Xiang Khouang. Sandwiched between expansive empires to the west and east, both entities struggled to maintain their sovereignty until the late nineteenth century, when the French finally folded most of their territory into unified Laos.

The kings of the defunct royal house of **Xiang Khouang** came from the same family tree as those of Louang Phabang, both kingdoms claiming descent from Khoun Borom, the celebrated first ancestor of numerous Tai–Lao legends. Yet, unlike in Louang Phabang, few physical traces of Xiang Khouang's splendour survive. In the place of the distinctive Xiang Khouang-style temples are bomb craters doubling as fishing holes and houses erected on piles crafted from bomb casings – reminders that this was one of the most heavily bombed pieces of real estate in the world, and a testimony to the rugged perseverance of the Phuan, Black Tai, Hmong and Khamu peoples who inhabit the province. Much of the bombing was directed at the strategic **Plain of Jars**, which takes its name from the fields of ancient, giant funerary urns that are the northeast's main tourist draw. Indeed, until fairly recently, for most visitors a trip to the region meant a flying visit to Xiang Khouang's provincial capital **Phonsavan** to see the Jar sites, and a quick side trip to nearby **Muang Khoun**, the former royal seat of Xiang Khouang, where a handful of ruins whisper of the kingdom's vanished glory.

Even fewer travellers make the journey to **Houa Phan**, an impenetrable sea of rugged green mountaintops lost in mist and shallow valleys, far from the Mekong River and the traditional centres of lowland Lao life. The only provincial centre in Laos east of the Annamites is Houa Phan's capital **Xam Nua**, a chilly frontier town closer to Hanoi than Vientiane, a proximity that lends it a distinctly Vietnamese flavour. This lightly populated region is home to more

than twenty ethnic groups, most of them Tai, including the Black, Red and White Tai, all of whom share a distinctly Houa Phan character – a fortitude shaped by the remote mountainous terrain and by years spent living in the heart of the **Pathet Lao's liberated zone**. After the Pathet Lao rose to power in 1975, the communists further exploited Houa Phan's isolation by transforming their liberated zone into a massive prison camp. Thousands of former Royal Lao soldiers were interred in the province's notorious re-education camps. Houa Phan's wartime history has been etched into the land at **Viang Xai**, a short ride from Xam Nua. Dozens of **caves** hidden in the sawtoothed limestone karsts of Viang Xai served as the headquarters for the Pathet Lao during their Thirty Year Struggle.

Travel practicalities

Poor roads and unreliable **transport** conspire with rugged mountains to keep the northeast remote, though two border crossings allow tourists to travel here from Vietnam. As a result, travelling in this part of Laos is still something of an adventure, so leave on the earliest possible vehicles, bring some food and bottled water, and be prepared for breakdowns while on the road.

At present, the only way to get to the region from elsewhere in Laos is to bus in along one of the difficult overland routes (Route 1 and Route 7) from Louang Phabang province, or to fly into Xam Nua or Phonsavan and begin exploring the region from there.

Unless you plan on exiting to Vietnam, the most logical route for travellers is the **circle route** through Nong Khiaw, Xam Nua, Phonsavan and Phou Khoun or vice versa. Owing to a lack of direct transport and long waits in between transfers along Route 1, you should allow two days to get from Nong Khiaw to Xam Nua by public transport (though Louang Phabang–Xam Nua via Nong Khiaw can be done in a day with your own vehicle), and then another day to swing back out to Phou Khoun on Route 13. Route 1 is paved from Nong Khiaw to Viang Thong, but beyond the town of Sop Xuang it becomes progressively worse until finally hitting tarmac again at the **Nam Neun** junction, where paved Route 6 links Xam Nua to Phonsavan and the Plain of Jars. There are direct sawngthaews connecting Viang Thong with Xam Nua, Nam Neun and Phonsavan. The 140-kilometre stretch of **Route 7** from Phonsavan to Phou Khoun is mostly paved, but can still take as long as six hours to travel during the wet season. To get from Phonsavan to Vientiane takes a full day by bus.

At some points, you may find sawngthaew drivers unwilling to depart because there aren't enough travellers; passengers are at times asked for more money, or to wait, sometimes for hours. You can save hours of endless waiting by **chartering** a sawngthaew, though note that drivers will still want to pick up passengers en route and collect the extra fares.

Nong Khiaw to Nam Neun

The journey from **Nong Khiaw** to **Nam Neun** along Route 1 is one of northern Laos's great road journeys, crossing numerous mountain ranges and valleys. It's a tough trip but the scenery more than makes up for the discomfort. If you're travelling by sawngthaew you'll probably have to change vehicles at **Viang Kham**, and again at **Viang Thong** (sometimes known as Muang Hiam), the first major town of Houa Phan province. Travellers may have to overnight in Viang Thong or Viang Kham depending on the weather and road conditions. Both towns have basic guesthouses.

Viang Kham

Roughly 50km from Nong Khiaw, the town of **VIANG KHAM** snakes along Route 1 for several kilometres. Buses and sawngthaews stop at the **bus stop** on a hill high above the river, 3km out on the northeast edge of town. If you're staying overnight you'll have to hike into town or flag down a passing motorcycle. Both of the town's basic **guesthouses** are located close to the river, one on each side of the bridge. The guesthouse on the eastern side of the river – a two-storey concrete house about eight houses before the bridge – is the better of the two (❶).

There's little to see in the town, which amounts to two rows of wooden houses flanking Route 1, but many of these have traditional looms for weaving. The river that cleaves the town is the **Nam Xuang**, which eventually winds its way to Louang Phabang. Although highway upgrades have made river transport somewhat redundant, it may be possible to find a boatman willing to make the journey south. Green Discovery Adventures (Ⓦwww.greendiscoverylaos.com), which has offices in Vientiane, Louang Phabang, Louang Namtha and Vang Viang, can organize river trips on request.

Southeast through Phou Loei NBCA

Continuing east, Route 1 labours up forested hills and through ethnic minority villages, with their rough huts precariously perched along the ridges above a sea of mountains. The **scenery** is simply spectacular, with row upon row of mountain ranges extending into the distance.

Route 1 passes through **Phou Loei NBCA**, covering an area of 1465 square kilometres. In the high, mountainous divide separating Louang Phabang, Houa Phan and Xiang Khouang provinces, the park consists of north–south ranges, with its highest peak, **Phou Soy** at 2257m, at the northern end. None of the ridge-top Hmong villages along Route 1 has any formal accommodation, and any trekking has to be self-arranged with a licensed guide.

A chorus line of tall palms on either side of the highway announces **Sop Xuang**, 50km east of Viang Kham. There's nowhere to stay here, but it does have several *főe* shops and a solitary *hân kin deum* (an "eat–drink shop"), which can be counted on for noodles and warm beer, though passenger vehicles don't tend to linger here. From here there's one last mountain range to cross before Viang Thong.

Viang Thong

VIANG THONG, more popularly known by its old name **Muang Hiam**, lies in the upper valley of the Nam Khan River, which sweeps across the wide swath of rice fields on the town's western flank. The town itself winds along the bottom of the narrow river valley and its main street begs for a high-noon shoot-out. A pleasant diversion if you find yourself having to hang around for a bus is the thirty-minute walk to the nearby **hot springs**. To get there, cross the bridge, turn right at the *Phu Kae* guesthouse and walk 1km, past the hill on the left and rice fields on the right. Rising steam and a narrow path on your left mark the way to the swampy clearing where scalding water bubbles up from the ground. While the pools are large enough for a good soak, they're far too hot; a tiny pool near the main road is cooler and a popular spot for villagers to bring their infants for a warm bath.

After the long overland loop to reach Viang Thong, it's strange to think that the swift-flowing river through town ends its journey in distant Louang Phabang. Starting from the Nam Et NBCA north of Viang Thong, the Nam Khan River heads southwest between two ranges of high mountains, over difficult rapids and through dense jungles. The entire area is a big blank on most maps and no passenger boats travel this length of the river. Locals say it's not possible, though it wouldn't take much arm-twisting to get kayaking expedition organizers in Louang Phabang to give it a shot. Green Discovery (see p.165) is your best bet.

Practicalities

For an extended stay, the most pleasant of Viang Thong's three **accommodation** options is the *Phu Kae* (●), a white house containing a handful of rooms with shared bathroom, though the location, on a hill just west of the river, is less convenient. If you're coming in from the west you'll see it to the left before crossing the river bridge. For those passing through quickly, the other two options, near the bus lot, make a better choice. Just west of the new market, the friendly *Santisouk* (●) is an extremely basic, rickety two-storey building that stuffs truck-drivers and itinerant Chinese merchants into its tiny, thin-walled rooms. The communal bathing facilities at the back, however, are not ideal, with everyone competing for showers just before daybreak, hurrying to get back on the road. There is a very humble restaurant just opposite. The *Souksakhone* (●), on the same side of the road just to the east of the market, is virtually indistinguishable from the *Santisouk*, with plain, rudimentary rooms and concrete communal facilities.

Don't expect culinary satisfaction in Viang Thong. There's little to choose from among the handful of **restaurants** clustered at the heart of town. *Fŏe* is, as usual, easy to come by, and, if you're lucky, you may get a simple soup and a plate of boiled chicken to go with some sticky rice. In the mornings though, even a fried egg can be too much to ask for. The **dry goods store** west of the new market does *fŏe* and three-minute noodles, and directly opposite is a Lao **coffee shack**.

To **move on**, it's imperative that you track down a vehicle early, as vehicles for Viang Kham, Xam Nua, Nam Neun and, less frequently, Phonsavan depart from the bus stand next to the market between 6am and 7.30am each morning. If there are no direct buses to Xam Nua or Phonsavan, catch a sawngthaew to Nam Neun – a gruelling two to three hours to the east over a huge mountain range along a rocky, potholed road – from where onward connections can be made. For Xam Nua, there's also a converted Soviet truck which leaves daily. If you arrive in Nam Neun too late in the morning you may well wind up stuck there overnight, as vehicles travelling Route 6 leave early.

Nam Neun

From Viang Thong, Route 1 crosses the mountains down to the tiny settlement of Houa Phou (the actual junction of Route 1 and Route 6) before winding a further 6km down into a deep river valley to the village of **NAM NEUN**. Everyone travelling through the northeast by road eventually winds up in Nam Neun, which is the launching point for buses heading north to Xam Nua or south to Phonsavan. Although it's just fifty tin-roofed shacks around a dirt lot in the middle of nowhere, there is a rugged friendliness about the place. The steep valley walls and churning river make Nam Neun a diamond in the rough, and for many it's a very welcome spot to break the journey from Nong Khiaw.

The town is set in a steep valley perched above the swift-flowing **Nam Neun River** – spanned here by a sturdy Russian-built bridge – which flows out of the Nam Et NBCA and eventually empties into the Gulf of Tonkin at Vinh. Of the two **guesthouses**, the extremely basic *Nam Neun* (❶), at the bus lot, is the cheaper. Much better, though, is the eight-room *Phouchomkub* (❶), a small compound of whitewashed, blue-roofed buildings, which has a terrific location right on the river and next door to the town's only wat. The beautiful two-storey house further along the road was part of a Japanese development project. **Food** is available in Nam Neun, but it's fairly elementary. A small selection of grilled meats on bamboo skewers and bags of sticky rice can be bought in the pint-sized market, and two or three restaurants cater to travellers in transit with bowls of instant noodles and warm drinks.

Houa Phan province

Sometimes known as Xam Nua after the name of its capital city, sparsely populated **Houa Phan province** is a sea of misty mountains, dotted with isolated bowl-like valleys. The country's northeasternmost province, it's also one of the most spectacularly beautiful provinces in all of Laos, with some of the north's highest mountains, a large number of diverse ethnic groups, extensive forest cover and one of Laos's largest NBCAs. There are also enough caves, waterfalls and limestone karst scenery to give Vang Viang hoteliers sleepless nights: you only need to drive the road in from Nam Neun to realize what amazing tourist potential Houa Phan has. The problem of course is infrastructure – there are at present very few roads, though Chinese, Vietnamese and Lao crews have upgraded many of the road links to China and Vietnam.

The difficult terrain and the province's proximity to Vietnam made Houa Phan the perfect headquarters for the Pathet Lao, who operated out of the caves that honeycomb the karst formations in Viang Xai for the better part of their Thirty Year Struggle. Along with Phongsali, Houa Phan was set aside as a regroupment area for the communist forces under the Geneva Agreements of 1954. While the province formed the backbone of the Pathet Lao's liberated zone, not all of Houa Phan was under communist control: for years, the 1786-metre **Phou Pha Thi** was crowned by a "blind bombing" device to guide air raids on Hanoi (see box on p.183).

The real muscle behind the Pathet Lao during the war, **Vietnam**, retains much political and economic control over Houa Phan, and a steady flow of Vietnamese goods, electricity, merchants and construction workers arrives in the Lao province via three border points – one of which is open to foreign travellers. Travelling beyond Xam Nua town is a more attractive option than it used to be now that the **Na Meo border crossing** gives overland access to Thanh Hoa province in Vietnam. It's not usually hard to find transport up to the border at least, but you'll need to have a Vietnamese visa in advance to use the crossing.

Houa Phan is predominantly populated by various Tai groups – Red, Black, Neua and White – and, in the towns, migrants from Vietnam and China. With more than twenty **ethnic groups** in the mix, it's perhaps not surprising that even residents from neighbouring Xiang Khouang complain about the difficulty of understanding Houa Phan dialect. During the centuries before French rule, the area was part of a Black Tai principality, known as the Sipsong Chao Tai, which spanned the present-day Lao–Vietnamese border. The principality fell under the sway of the lowland Lao kingdoms of Louang Phabang, Xiang Khouang and Vientiane and under the control of the greater powers that in turn controlled them – Siam and Vietnam. Stone pillars (known as Suan Hin), located several kilometres off Route 6 near Houa Muang, suggest that the area was a hub of some forgotten culture long before Tai–Lao and Vietnamese rulers squabbled over this region.

Xam Nua

You could be forgiven for thinking that you'd crossed into Vietnam on descending into **XAM NUA**, the provincial capital and the only sizeable Lao town east of the Annamite Mountains. Unlike the rest of Laos, which drains west into the Mekong, all of Houa Phan province's rivers flow southeast to the Gulf of Tonkin – Xam Nua itself sits in the narrow Nam Xam River valley. If you want to feel like you're in the middle of nowhere, Xam Nua fits the bill, feeling very much like a hill station, sitting in a bowl surrounded by low, pleasant hills with the narrow river rushing through its centre. Vietnamese logging has contributed to a small construction boom, which has brought about new multistorey buildings – an unsightly mixture of modern Thai and Chinese styles – springing up everywhere and climbing the flanks of the surrounding hills.

Although there's little to see in the town itself, it serves as a comfortable base for the Viang Xai Caves, or a stopover on the push to northern Vietnam.

Arrival and information

Transport from Nam Nuen and Vieng Thong offloads at the **bus station** on Phathy Road, the town's main street. Across the big bridge over the Nam Xam, Route 6 continues to the airport 3km away. If you've arrived at the **airport**,

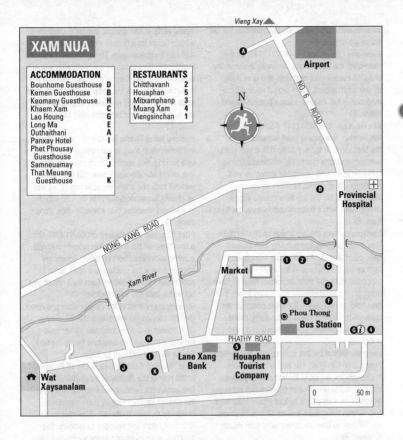

XAM NUA

ACCOMMODATION

Bounhome Guesthouse	D
Kemen Guesthouse	B
Keomany Guesthouse	H
Khaem Xam	C
Lao Houng	G
Long Ma	E
Outhaithani	A
Panxay Hotel	I
Phet Phousay Guesthouse	F
Samneuamay	J
That Meuang Guesthouse	K

RESTAURANTS

Chitthavanh	2
Houaphan	5
Mitxamphanp	3
Muang Xam	4
Viengsinchan	1

taxis (15,000K) will be on hand to shuttle you to a hotel. There's a **tourist office** (Mon–Fri 8am–noon & 1–4pm), located in the small building at the front of the *Lao Houng Hotel*, where transportation and guides can be arranged for a trip to Suan Hin. **Exchange services** are available at the bank on the Phathy Road towards Wat Xaysanalam. There is 24-hour electricity in Xan Nua, but no Internet services at the time of writing.

Accommodation

Despite the lack of tourists in Xam Nua, there's certainly no shortage of **accommodation** available around the bus station, along Phathy Road and out by the airport. While most group tours tend to stay out by the airport, the hotels close to the market or on Phathy Road are much more convenient for independent travellers, being within short walking distance of all the town's best restaurants.

Bounhome Guesthouse ☎064/312223. Housed in a modern building in which everything works. All rooms are smallish but clean. The more expensive rooms, with en-suite bathrooms, are on the ground floor, while guests on the top floor use a shared bathroom and toilet downstairs. ②

Kemen Guesthouse ☎064/312726. On the opposite side of the river from most of the other places to stay, Kemen feels more like a homestay – especially if you get one of the rooms in the old wooden house. Rooms in the newer concrete building are adequate though lacking charm, but they do have

179

en-suite bathrooms, while the bathrooms in the old house are shared. ❷

Keomany Guesthouse ☎064/312142. On the main drag, the three-storey *Keomany* is something of a Chinese trucker's rest stop, and is as noisy as you might expect, but is okay if other accommodation is full. All rooms share bathrooms and toilets. ❶

Khaem Xam ☎064/312111. Facing the river, this newish, four-storey hotel is hands down the best value in town. Family-run, it has eighteen immaculately clean, big-windowed rooms, many en suite with piping hot water, as well as rooms using shared facilities which are also spotless. On the top floor there's a nice sitting room with a balcony overlooking the Nam Xam. ❷

Lao Houng Near the big bridge ☎064/312028. This dreadful sprawling building with several open courtyards and a television lounge was built by the Vietnamese in the 1970s and is supposed to be the most important hotel in town. Although it's dark, gloomy and falling apart, it may hold an odd charm for those nostalgic for state-built hotels in China in the early 1980s. The rooms, however, are run-down and overpriced. ❷

Long Ma Behind the bus station, next to the *Phou Thong* ☎064/312230. The best of the Chinese trucker places, the *Long Ma* has perfectly good, big, tiled rooms with shared facilities and hot water. Travellers on a very tight budget should head here first. Rooms 5 and 6, as well as 12 and 13 above, are the best as they are corner units with double windows. ❷

Outhaithani Directly opposite the airport entrance ☎064/312121, ☎312415. Primarily

aimed at fly-in tour groups, this hotel consists of a huge house on a hillside with three log cabins and four bungalow units. Though smaller than the bungalows, the log cabins are preferable and are actually much nicer inside than they look. All the accommodation has hot water and the restaurant is about the only one in town to attempt a Western breakfast. A possible alternative to being in town. ❹

Panxay Hotel Phathy Rd. One of the few French-era buildings in town to survive the war, this very odd-looking, two-storey French mansion looks like an old schoolhouse inside and has rooms without bath and a few en-suite rooms, as well as shared accommodation. The concrete *that* in the front indicates that a temple once stood there. ❷

Phet Phousay Guesthouse ☎064/312943. On a small lane off No. 6 Rd is this modern concrete building with three floors of rooms. Rooms are clean and large but spartan, and noise tends to echo around in the building. Each floor has shared hot water, bath and toilet facilities. ❷

Samneuamay West of the *Panxay Hotel* and down the first alley on the left ☎064/312407. A new hotel housed in a substantial two-storey building with a flat roof and balconies facing the lane. Rooms are tiled and well kept. ❷

That Meuang Guesthouse South off Phathy Rd to the rear of the *Panxay Hotel* ☎064/312141. Two connected buildings of a similar quality to the *Khaem Xam* but slightly more expensive. There are thirteen spotlessly clean rooms, all with tiled floors and en-suite bathrooms. The big draw is the outdoor terrace where you can sit with a beer and take in the view of the surrounding hills. ❷

The Town

There's little to occupy the traveller in Xam Nua, save absorbing the rugged frontier atmosphere of this most un-Lao outpost. Most of the town is on the southern side of the river, although it's starting to sprawl out towards the airport. However, with the hills pressing in on all sides, there's precious little room for the town to grow. The main street is the two-kilometre-long, four-lane **Phathy Road** – a huge central boulevard lined with institutional-looking government buildings and bearing the unmistakeable mark of the Vietnamese, who rebuilt the town after the war.

There are almost no cultural sites, but you can walk up Phathy Road to the **victory monument**, an easy climb that affords a good view of the valley, and a bit further on, near the main street's end, to **Wat Phoxai** (officially Wat Xaysanalam). Construction of the wat began in 1958 and took nearly a decade to complete, whereupon it was almost immediately destroyed by the bombing. The modest structure that now stands here was completed in the 1980s. It was until very recently the only wat in town and there are only

Xam Nua textiles

Experts on **Lao textiles** all seem to agree that the most sophisticated pieces, in terms of both design and colour scheme, are produced in the region around **Xam Nua**. A fashion revolution followed the political revolution in 1975, when the victorious communists abandoned their headquarters near Xam Nua and moved into Vientiane. The wives of the new leaders enthusiastically sported the Tai Daeng styles of Xam Nua, and it wasn't long before the look caught on. Today the bold, spidery patterns of Xam Nua textiles are a favourite all over Laos.

Among Lao textiles, the work of the Tai Daeng and Tai Nua stand out. Classified by ethnologists as "tribal Tai", these ethnic groups are related culturally and linguistically to the lowland Lao. However, unlike the lowland Lao, they are animists for the most part, though Mahayana Buddhist influence can be seen in their textile motifs. These groups believe that death is the most important rite of passage in a person's life, and the funeral ceremony is correspondingly elaborate. To prepare for it, a woman will weave a special skirt to wear to the grave. A geometric design woven into the waistband of the skirt will serve to ward off spirits that might attempt to block her passage into the "Garden of Golden Mangoes". Another significant textile used by the Xam Nua cultures is a "shaman's shawl", worn by spirit mediums while performing healing ceremonies. Symbols on these shawls are remarkably similar to those found on bronze frog-drums of the sixth-century-BC Dong-son culture which was centred in northern Vietnam. Other motifs found on Xam Nua textiles include the swastika, a Hindu symbol that was adopted by Mahayana Buddhism, and the stylized "third eye". Perhaps the most striking and the most "Lao" of the Xam Nua motifs are realistic *naga* imprinted in the textiles by tie-dyeing.

a handful of resident monks. As journalist Christopher Kremmer wrote in *Stalking the Elephant Kings*: "if you're tired of seeing monks in Laos, come to Xam Nua." The town's three other prewar wats, including the 200-year-old Xiang Khouang-style Wat Inpeng, were never rebuilt. The sad little spires along Phathy Road leading up to the wat indicate where these holy sites once were.

Much more cheerful is the vibrant **market**, on the street running in front of the river, which is a good place to get a feel for the province's character. Vietnamese goods, many of which are bought by merchants at weekend border markets in Xiang Khoun and Na Maew, flood the stalls in a display of vegetables, meats and the occasional severed water-buffalo head. The market buzzes throughout the day, its vendors bundled against the cold with their heads wrapped in colourful scarves, a sartorial twist that most likely lent the province its name – "Houa Phan" means "wrapped head". Sadly, most of the vendor ladies have traded in their traditional turbans for cheap Chinese hand towels.

Behind the wet market is a large, block-long shed housing the **indoor dry market**. Here you'll find all manner of individual wooden stalls selling various goods, including a smattering of Lao **textiles**, although much of the best stuff gets sent directly to Louang Phabang or Vientiane. Although a lot of cloth is produced in Houa Phan, it's all made in people's homes, not factories. If you're looking for loom-woven cloth rather than cotton prints it's better to come to the market in the afternoon. The alley behind the dry market houses all kinds of electrical shops bulging with refrigerators, televisions, rice-cookers, bicycles and home karaoke systems.

Eating and drinking

Xam Nua has several tourist-class **restaurants**. The *Chitthavanh* (℡064/312265), facing the river a few doors down from the *Khaem Xam*, is widely considered the best restaurant in town, with a range of reasonably priced dishes and an English-language menu – all the NGO and foreign engineers eat here. A couple of doors over, the signless *Viengsinchan* is similar and does a decent beef noodle soup, good Lao coffees and even sells Lao textiles. In the alley running directly behind the *Viengsinchan*, the *Mitxamphanp* is above-average noodle shack. The *Samneuamay* restaurant, just past the bridge on the road to Nam Neun, is also one of the town's government-recommended tourist restaurants. For Western food, the *Houaphan Restaurant*, 211 Phathy Road (℡064/312190) is good, serving up dishes like chicken Kiev and fish with white sauce. In fact, the menu here is one of the most sophisticated you'll see anywhere in Laos, featuring pâté, spare ribs, roast duck and many other delicacies (including Lao food) all thanks to Chef Sengmanee, who cooked in Bangkok for two years before returning home to Xam Nua. In terms of decor, service and quality, the *Houaphan* could certainly hold its own even in Louang Phabang. The town's other Western restaurant is the Lao-French restaurant at the *Outhaithani Hotel* (℡064/312121), which knows how to fry a buffalo steak with *pomme frites*. There's also a selection of French wines. As for **drinking**, the two best places in town for a sundowner with a view of the mountains are the terrace at the *That Meuang Guest house* and the patio at the *Outhaithani*.

Around Xam Nua

To conveniently visit the nearby hot springs, mountains, caves, waterfalls and Hmong villages you need to charter transportation. Unfortunately there's no motorcycle rental in Xam Nua but vans can be hired through the town's tourist office.

West of Xam Nua is the **Nam Et NBCA**, linked with neighbouring Phou Loei NBCA (see p.176) in Louang Phabang province. The two parks together total 3400 square kilometres, making them the second-largest conservation area in the country after the Khammouane NBCAs. The terrain here is extremely rugged and mountainous, and from the ridge tops it seems as if the mountains recede into infinity. The park is very remote and currently has no access roads, but can be reached by following the Nam Et River from Muang Et.

Phou Pha Thi

Some 35km northwest of Xam Nua, **Phou Pha Thi**, a 1786-metre-high limestone mountain, is the tallest peak in northern Houa Phan and the most distinctive mountain in the province: a broad-based massif, with a near-vertical summit. The Nam Xam River, which flows through the centre of Xam Nua and all the way to the Gulf of Tonkin, runs directly down from the peak's southern flanks.

Phou Pha Thi is famous for being an important Lima Site during the **Second Indochina War** when the CIA and Special Forces set up a navigation radar tower on the summit. As this secret mountain base, run by the CIA and guarded by 300 Thai mercenaries, was in the very heart of Pathet Lao territory, the story of its eventual capture and destruction is the stuff of local legend (see box opposite). Visits to the summit of Phou Pha Thi are not allowed, but a van can be hired in Xam Nua for the ride to the foot of the mountain.

The fall of Phou Pha Thi

In a decision that would prove to be the turning point of the war in Laos, US President Lyndon Johnson ordered the installation of a navigational beacon to guide air strikes against the North Vietnamese atop **Phou Pha Thi**. Here, US air force cargo helicopters dropped off the components of the device, code-named Commando Club, which was assembled a few hundred metres from fields growing some of the best opium in Laos. Hmong soliders, not known for their ability to defend fixed positions, were assigned to protect the latest in military wizardry.

A few weeks before Commando Club became operational in late 1967, a couple of monks were caught on the summit of Phou Pha Thi carrying cameras and sketch books; they were Vietnamese spies, and soon after Commando Club began directing its all-weather, high-altitude air strikes on the Hanoi valley, two Soviet-built biplanes, dark-green museum pieces with cloth-covered wings and wooden propellers jury-rigged to fire mortar shells, buzzed the site – the only time during the war that the North Vietnamese attacked a target with biplanes. The planes were shot down, but the Vietnamese, provoked by this high-profile site that threatened their security, moved more troops into Laos. By the time North Vietnamese commandos scaled the summit with grappling hooks and ropes to take the position on March 10, 1968, the nineteen Americans operating Commando Club knew the end was near. The **fall of Phou Pha Thi** was typical of the lack of unified command that plagued the United States' war in Laos. As historian Roger Warner wrote in *Shooting at the Moon*: "The radar installation belonged to the air force, but the CIA was supposed to defend it. The CIA couldn't defend it as it chose, because the ambassador didn't want "unauthorized" weapons on the mountaintop. Kept from direct accountability for its own men, the air force lost interest, even though it had proposed the installation in the first place, and, on the mountain itself, nothing held the villagers from wandering where they pleased, including to the little opium patch near the summit, which they harvested just as they always had."

Phou Pha Thi also signalled a shift in the demands the US placed on its Hmong allies: they were no longer being armed to defend their own mountaintops, but were now pawns of the war in Vietnam. Eight Americans were pulled off Phou Pha Thi, leaving eleven dead or missing – the beginning of prolonged confusion, as Warner indicates, over the fate of Americans missing in action in Laos, and for whom the search continues today.

Suan Hin

Located just off Route 6, 50–60km southwest of the town of Houa Muang, the **Suan Hin** or "Stone Garden" is a standard stop on any organized day-trip out of Xam Nua. Surrounded by forest, the megalithic stone gardens consist of large slabs of rock that have been stood upright and arranged in circles. The age and origin of the sites as well as the culture that created them remain a mystery, though the pillars have been linked by archeologists to the stone funerary urns of the Plain of Jars.

Nam Nua waterfall and the road to Viang Xai

The road heading east out of Xam Nua passes through the Striped Hmong village of **Ban Houa Khang** before descending into a valley of rice fields surrounded by shaggy karsts – the first glimpse of the heart of Pathet Lao territory. Passing through the lowland Lao town of **Ban Muang Liat** and the Hmong village of **Houai Na**, you'll arrive at a fork, 21km from Xam Nua. Bearing left leads to Sop Hao and Xiang Khoun on the old French road to Hanoi, right to **Viang Xai**, 8km away, and eventually the Vietnamese border town of Na Maew. Three kilometres down the Viang Xai road you'll come to a bridge over a swift-flowing stream, and from here a track leads off left to the top of a seventy-metre waterfall, **Tad Nam Nua**. Cutting away from the path, it's possible to scramble along the rocks and riverbank to a viewpoint at the crest of the falls. The classic frontal view is harder to attain: back at the junction, take the Sop Hao road for roughly 2km where you'll find a track leading for over 1km through paddies and eventually across a stream and a sticky thicket of bamboo. A local guide, encouraged with the offer of a few thousand kip, is probably in order here.

Viang Xai

Arriving in **VIANG XAI** ("City of Victory"), you wouldn't know the Pathet Lao and their communist allies in Vietnam had won the Second Indochina War. Sprawled across a valley surrounded by the cave-riddled karst formations used by the Pathet Lao as their wartime headquarters, Viang Xai was cobbled together by comrades from Russia, North Korea and Vietnam as well as labourers from Houa Phan's notorious re-education camps (see box on pp.186–187). In 1973, at the end of the war, there were plans to make Viang Xai the heart of the newly socialist nation, but in the end Laos's socialist friends could not be convinced to foot the bill to turn a backwater into a gleaming new capital, and so the Pathet Lao leadership decamped to Vientiane. With time, Viang Xai couldn't even compete with nearby Xam Nua as a provincial hub. People moved out and many buildings fell into a state of crumbling decay. Today, a victory arch made of oil drums is the gateway to this wax museum of empty kerbed streets, lined with broken street lamps, and ugly empty, utilitarian structures. A stupa, crowned with a communist star and lost among the weeds, completes the setting. The only sign here that still trumpets the Pathet Lao's triumph with authority is the socialist victory statue that greets visitors as they make their way down the wide main street towards the market. The statue depicts a peasant, a soldier and a worker, one foot atop a bomb inscribed "USA".

Practicalities

Very few travellers stay in Viang Xai, most preferring to do the caves (see pp.193–196) as a **day-trip** from Xam Nua, which has much better food and accommodation. However, for those who can afford the time, the scenery, countryside and ambience around Viang Xai deserve further exploration, evoking that of Guilin in China. In fact, if you want to know what Vang Viang was like before it was overrun with trippy backpackers, Viang Xai is the place for you.

Sawngthaews from Xam Nua to Viang Xai (10,000K; 30min) leave every hour until mid-afternoon and stop in front of the market. Alternatively, you could charter a sawngthaew for $5 from Xam Nua, which will allow you to stop off at the Nam Nua falls en route. You must **register and pay** a 10,000K entrance and guide fee at the Viang Xai **tourist office** (daily 8am–noon & 1–4pm) before you can tour the caves. From the market, bear left at the big stupa, and the tourist office is in the middle of the second block on the right. With the caves, market and hotel all spread out across the valley and few tuk-tuks for hire, you could end up doing a fair bit of walking in Viang Xai. Be sure not to miss the last sawngthaew back to Xam Nua at about 3pm or you'll have to hitch-hike back.

There is only one **hotel** in Viang Xai – the wood and bamboo bungalow *Naxay* (①) – located near the market. Outside of town, the former *Vieng Xay Hotel*, surrounded by pine trees and karst scenery, has been closed for renovations for years now. The hotel was originally constructed to put up visiting dignitaries. According to Christopher Kremmer's book, *Stalking the Elephant Kings*, this was where the Lao royal family, sent into internal exile in Houa Phan in 1977, lived before they disappeared. Indeed, the hotel seems to have been used as a sort of transit centre for high-ranking officials of the fallen royalist government on their way to the "re-education" camps set up by Vietnamese and Russian "foreign experts".

Aside from the bowls of *fŏe* rustled up in the daytime by the **noodle stalls** in the bare-bones market, satisfying meals can be hard to come by in Viang Xai. If you're planning to stay for more than one night you may want to bring supplies from Xam Nua's market.

The Pathet Lao caves

When American air force Chief of Staff General Curtis LeMay jested that the United States would bomb the enemy "back to the Stone Age", what he hadn't realized was that living like cavemen would prove to be the key to the survival of the North Vietnamese Army and Pathet Lao during the heaviest aerial bombardment in history. Like Vang Viang in central Laos and Mahaxai in the south, the limestone karst formations in the valleys east of Xam Nua are pockmarked with **caves** and crevices – a perfect hideout for the Pathet Lao's parallel government. **Viet Minh** army units began using the caves and enlarging them in the early 1950s while fighting the French in the days before Dien Bien Phu. Soon, the Lao leftists had joined the Vietnamese underground, and by the middle of the 1960s, Viang Xai and the surrounding area had become a troglodyte city of thousands living in the more than one hundred caves. The caves – some at the foot of hills, others high up, hidden by surrounding escarpments and accessible only by scaling steps cut into sheer rock faces – were an impregnable fortress, but even poking your head outside could prove deadly as craters near the caves attest. Jacques Decornoy, a French journalist and one of the rare Westerners permitted to visit the caves during the war, wrote that his room in a "hotel" grotto was "a dangerous place if one puts one's nose out of the mountain: sometimes one cannot finish shaving because of the jets raiding from Thailand". When Decornoy visited the caves and the grassy fields surrounding them in 1968 he found "a terrain turned over hundreds of times by explosions and no longer resembling anything at all – a chaos of red earth, broken rocks, devastated trees".

The inhabitants of the caves followed a routine of sleeping by day and working at night in the fields outside or in the caves themselves: caverns held weaving mills, printing presses and workshops where American bombs and worn-out trucks were upgraded into farming tools and appliances. On Saturdays, adults would take a break and attend **classes** consisting of professional, cultural and political courses as well as lessons in algebra, geometry and geography. As the liberated zone's director of education explained to Decornoy, "a teacher must be a propagandist of the people. He must know how to run a meeting, how to explain the central political line, he must be a shooting instructor and link manual work with theoretical teaching."

The conclusion of the war didn't bring the hardships experienced in the caves to an end: what changed were the inhabitants. After 1975, the caves became a "**re-education camp**" for functionaries of the Royal Lao government – from the lowliest foot soldier to the former king (see box on pp.186–187). For years, the Vientiane government and Houa Phan officials, who regard Viang Xai as a national treasure and a symbol of revolutionary resolve along the lines of Mao's Long March, treated the caves as if they were a military secret, but they are now more welcoming to foreigners interested in visiting the site. The caves have

Re-education camps

The first group of prisoners to be transported to **re-education camps** – the Pathet Lao's means of neutralizing its wartime enemies – arrived by invitation in full military dress months before the communist takeover in December 1975. After receiving letters signed by Prince Souvannaphouma, seventy high-ranking Royal Lao Army officers and provincial governors came to what they thought would be an important meeting and were whisked off to the Plain of Jars, where they were fêted with a banquet and a movie. Any hope of a uniquely Lao solution to the Second Indochina War ended there, as these officials were shortly thereafter flown off to Houa Phan, where they were stripped of their rank and separated into small work parties. In the following months, thousands of civil servants and army officers voluntarily entered the re-education centres in Houa Phan, Attapu and Phongsali after being assured the "seminars" would last only a few weeks. With their opponents safely out of the way in the most remote corners of the country, or having opted already to flee to Thailand, the Pathet Lao moved ahead with the final stage of their bloodless takeover virtually unopposed.

Joined later by thousands more who arrived somewhat less willingly, the internees were turned loose in the fenceless camps, which were heavily guarded and hemmed in by the extreme geographical features of the Lao wilderness, and left to forage for food and build their own shelters out of bamboo. Each morning, a bell was rung at 5am and the prisoners were assigned a job for the day – cutting wood in the jungles, building roads, working in the fields. In the evenings, self-criticism and political indoctrination sessions were held. Although there was no physical torture, mindless rules were established in order to control the captives, who were never allowed to settle into one place. The cumulative effect of the "re-education", according to a former Royal Lao Army officer, who spent thirteen years in a Houa Phan camp, was a sort of "brainwashing". Life in the camps was hard – the officer is certain that he only survived because of a Green Beret survival course he attended in the United States – and many ran off or died of malaria. While women were not arrested, wives and families could opt to join their husbands in the camps. Some did, but many more, having lost their principal wage earner, fled to Thailand.

Drug addicts, prostitutes and other "anti-social" elements, although considered the least threatening to the new regime, were also rounded up and shuttled off to **Ang**

---

been **restored**: furniture has been replaced, electric lights have been plugged in and the gardens around the cave entrances have been tended.

Only five caves are open to the public, and the guided tour takes about two hours. Each of these caves, named after the Pathet Lao leaders who lived there, had multiple exits, an office and sleeping quarters, as well as an emergency chamber for use in case of chemical-weapons attacks (these chambers were kitted out with a Soviet oxygen machine and a metal door of the sort you'd find on an old submarine). After the Paris peace accords were signed in 1973, a few of the leaders built a house outside their cave, where they lived until moving to the former American compound on the outskirts of Vientiane in 1975 in order to take up government office. Don't expect any information from your guide should you inquire about the fate of the Lao royal family – all questions about the doomed royals will be met with feigned incomprehension.

Tham Than Kaysone

Tours usually begin with the cave of **Kaysone Phomvihane** (see p.258), who became leader of the Lao communist movement at its formation in 1955, and remained unchallenged in his post as head of the Lao People's Democratic

Nam Ngum near Vang Viang (see p.111), where an estimated three thousand people were placed on "Boy Island" and "Girl Island". In 1977, the **royal family** too was arrested and banished to Camp 01 at Sop Hao, in Houa Phan, where the king and crown prince reportedly died of starvation two weeks apart in May 1978. The queen is said to have died in 1981, and, like her husband and son before her, was buried in an unmarked grave outside the camp. The only government acknowledgement of their deaths came a decade later, when Party Secretary General Kaysone mentioned in an aside during a visit to Paris that the king had died of old age.

There are **no official figures** for the number of people who were interned in the camps, but estimates based on reports by former inmates and their families suggest that at the height of the camps, in 1978–79, the number of internees may have been as high as fifty thousand. Whatever willingness supporters of the Royalist regime had to work with the new government quickly evaporated when it became clear that those interned in the camps weren't coming home anytime soon. Confronted with the prospect of being sent off for re-education, more than three hundred thousand people, nearly a tenth of Laos's population, fled the country. According to political scientist Martin Stuart-Fox, this **mass exodus** cost the fledgling government much of its educated class, setting the new Laos back a generation.

The first group of prisoners, low-ranking members of the former regime, was **released** in 1980, and despite finally being deemed fit to live in socialist Laos, many took the first chance they got to cross the Mekong. As the 1980s wore on, more and more prisoners were gradually released under pressure from Western nations and the human rights organization Amnesty International, which reported that in 1985 seven thousand people remained in the camps, a number which had dwindled to 33 by March 1991. The camps may now be empty, but the current number of political prisoners in Laos is not known, and Amnesty International has described Laos as "a country which has a zero-tolerance policy towards dissent in any form". Amnesty International believes that two out of five Lao students arrested in 1999 for trying to hold a peaceful demonstration in Vientiane are still imprisoned, serving ten-year sentences. Lao authorities have admitted that one of the five students died in detention, but the whereabouts of the remaining two detainees are disputed.

Republic from its inception in 1975 until his death in 1992. Born in Savannakhet of a Lao mother and a Vietnamese father, Kaysone spent far more time in Viang Xai than the Pathet Lao's face man, Prince Souphanouvong. While the Red Prince was off playing Vientiane's game of cat-and-mouse politics, Kaysone stayed in Houa Phan, attending frequent meetings in Hanoi – a risky two-day journey from Viang Xai – with North Vietnamese leaders Ho Chi Minh and General Vo Nguyen Giap, the legendary military strategist behind the French defeat at Dien Bien Phu.

Around the corner from the tourist office and to the left, Kaysone's cave has a large brown house and a meeting hall in front of it, as well as stairs leading to the cave's main entrance – during the war, the cave was accessed by rope. It's one of the larger caves and has an outdoor terrace, which was used for cooking.

Tham Than Nouhak

In the escarpment across the street from Tham Than Kaysone, **Nouhak Phoumsavanh's cave** is tiny compared with those of the other leaders, kitted out with only a bedroom and an emergency room. A peasant's son with only a primary school education, Nouhak was born in Savannakhet in 1916 and was

3

recruited by the Viet Minh while operating a bus line connecting Thakhek, Savannakhet and Vinh in the early 1940s. Nouhak proved himself to be a valuable courier to the Viet Minh and he quickly rose to prominence in the Lao communist movement. Nouhak was Kaysone's right-hand man during the war and the second-ranking member of the party's political bureau for years, eventually becoming chairman of the state assembly and, after Kaysone's death, state president.

Tham Than Souphanouvong

A stand of pomelo trees lines the path to **Prince Souphanouvong's cave**, tucked into a narrow indentation in an escarpment northwest of the tourist office. Fit for a prince, the cave has a garage grotto for his car and an outdoor kitchen on a natural patio. Yet reminders of the struggle linger around Souphanouvong's Viang Xai hideaway: a reddish discolouration high up on the cliff face marks the spot where a bomb crashed into the karst. Off to the right, a red stupa bears the ashes of one of the prince's sons who was killed during the war. Considered for years by the West to be the Pathet Lao's most important leader, the Red Prince was one of three remarkable sons of Prince Boun Khong, the viceroy of Louang Phabang. His brothers, Phetsarath and Souvannaphouma, were both former prime ministers, and all three played a major role in shaping twentieth-century Lao history. Souphanouvong lived here with his wife and ten children from 1963 to 1973. In 1975, Souphanouvong became president of the new government, although real power remained with Kaysone.

Tham Than Phoumi

Just west of Souphanouvong's cave is that of **Phoumi Vongvichit**, a cave artificially improved with the aid of dynamite to enlarge the living space and make room for a garage. Phoumi was born the son of a governor of Vientiane province in 1909 and went on to join the Indochinese civil service where he served as secretary to the French resident of Xiang Khouang. As an official in Houa Phan during the Japanese occupation, Phoumi aided Free French guerrillas, but when France reoccupied Laos he joined forces with Souphanouvong in northern Vietnam. Quiet, clerkish Phoumi, who had a knack for communist jargon, became minister of information and culture and, after Souphanouvong became ill, acting president of the Lao PDR before retiring from government in 1991.

Tham Than Khamtay

Beyond the decrepit grandstand and weedy athletic field on the north side of town, you'll come to the cave of **Khamtay Siphandone**. A postman in the former colonial government, Khamtay was born in 1924 into a peasant family in Champasak. As the returning French troops marched on Savannakhet in 1946, Khamtay, then with the Lao Issara, the early Lao independence movement, took with him the entire finances of the province – 150,000K – and ran off to join resistance forces on the Bolaven Plateau. In the grounds are Viang Xai's one mark of modernity – street lamps of the kind you might see in any suburban cul-de-sac, some evidence of the guide's insistence that the current president still pays annual visits to his old haunt. Behind Khamtay's house stands an imposingly thick man-made wall, built to protect the artificially dug cave's entrance from bombing raids. Inside, one doorway once opened onto an added feature of Khamtay's cave, a kilometre-long secret tunnel – now shoulder-deep in water – that leads to a cavernous chamber, formerly used as a meeting hall and, bizarrely, for the odd circus performance.

Located to the south of Route 6A, the **Nam Xam NBCA** is the smallest individual NBCA in Laos at just 580 square kilometres. The conservation area basically encompasses a broad bend in the **Nam Xam River** where it makes a lengthy detour around two large mountains within the NBCA, before extending over to the Vietnamese border to the east that comprises the park's eastern boundary. The tallest peak is located in the centre of the park and is 1741m. The eastern area of the park is said to provide a habitat for elephants, bears, tigers, and gibbons. The park can only be reached by four-wheel-drive vehicle; ask about trips at the tourist office in Xam Nua.

Xiang Khouang and the Plain of Jars

When the buffalo fight the grass gets flattened

Lao proverb

Xiang Khouang province lies at the crossroads of important trade routes leading north to China, south to Thailand and east to Vietnam, and has been coveted throughout the centuries by rival Southeast Asian empires. Ironically, for all its strategic importance, Xiang Khouang, hemmed in by a ring of dramatic mountains, including the country's tallest peak, Phu Bia, is still rather difficult to reach by road. Faced with the prospect of a long road trip via Route 7 or Routes 1 and 6, many visitors opt for a flight into **Phonsavan**, which also gives an unforgettable view of the treeless flatlands and crater-ridden landscape of the **Plain of Jars**, for which the province is best known. A plateau of grassy meadows and low rolling hills situated at the centre of the province, the Plain takes its name from the clusters of chest-high funerary urns found there. For people with a very deep interest in archeology and Southeast Asian history the jars are worth the journey to Xiang Khouang, but for some tourists they are something of an anticlimax, not worth the expense of the **compulsory tours** to them. It has been remarked upon that if it weren't for their holes, the jars would simply be boulders. At the end of the day they're best appreciated for what they are: traces of an ancient, vanished civilization that prospered on the Xiang Khouang Plateau.

As the flattest area in northern Laos, the Plain of Jars is also a natural gathering point for **armies** – a fact not lost on military commanders of the early kingdoms of Lane Xang, Vietnam and Siam and later the Soviet Union, France and America, the Viet Minh, the Pathet Lao and the Lao Royalists. Fought

Safety in Xiang Khouang

Occasional attacks by mountain **bandits or insurgents** have given Xiang Khouang province an uncertain reputation. Vehicles have been attacked, and on one occasion in the mid-1990s a bus was bombed in downtown Phonsavan. Such incidents have been sporadic, the last occurring in 1999. The official word is that such attacks are the work of bandits rather than insurgents. At any rate, hundreds of tourists visit the area each month without incident. Of more immediate danger are the **mines**, **bomblets** and **bombs** littering the province. The three main Jar sites have been cleared of Unexploded Ordnance (UXO), but it's advisable to stick to the paths, and not to pick up or kick any object if you don't know what it is. See Basics, p.64, for more details.

over dearly in the Second Indochina War, the region was bombed extensively between 1964 and 1973, transforming the Plain into a wasteland, which leaves a lasting impression on those who fly over it into Phonsavan.

With much of the literature of the province's historical Phuan kingdom (see below) destroyed and many of the customs lost, **Hmong culture** and festivals have come to play an important role in Xiang Khouang life. Boun Phao Hmong, or the Festival of the Hmong, celebrated throughout the province in November, draws overseas Hmong back each year for an event featuring water buffalo and bull fights. In December, Hmong New Year, a time for young Hmong to find a husband or wife, is celebrated, as is the lowland Lao festival of Boun Haw Khao, a two-day holiday in which food is offered to the dead. It has a distinctly Xiang Khouang flavour, however, with the addition of horse races, horses being especially prized by villagers who work Xiang Khouang's far-flung fields.

Some history

Even the **legends** surrounding the jars reveal how thoroughly life in Xiang Khouang has been overshadowed by **war**, with local lore telling of how the jars were created to hold rice wine by an army of giants to celebrate a military victory. Although the identity of the civilization that built the jars remains a mystery, local folktales telling of the arrival of the Phuan people (see p.349), the lowland Lao group that still dominates the ethnic make-up of the area today, date back as far as the seventh century, when the divine Tai–Lao first ancestor Khoun Borom (see p.135) sent his seventh and youngest son, Chet Chuong, to rule over the Tai peoples of Xiang Khouang. Although the time frame for this version of events may be a bit premature, Xiang Khouang was nonetheless one of the earlier areas settled by Tai peoples in Laos, and by the fourteenth century, an independent **Phuan principality**, known as Xiang Khouang and centred on modern-day **Muang Khoun**, had already begun to flourish here. While the **Kingdom of Xiang Khouang** had the wealth to build exquisite pagodas, it never amassed the might necessary to become a regional power. Sandwiched between the great empires lying to its east and west, Phuan kings maintained a semblance of independence over the years by offering tribute to Vietnam and Lane Xang and eventually Siam. Whatever price the royal house paid, however, it was not enough to keep Xiang Khouang from being repeatedly annexed, overrun and forcibly depopulated, beginning with the invading armies of the **Vietnamese** on their way back from sacking Louang Phabang in the late 1470s through to the Second Indochina War, when nearly every village in the province was obliterated.

It was a Phuan revolt against Vietnam's attempt to annexe Xiang Khouang, a satellite of the Lane Xang empire, referred to by the Vietnamese as Tran Ninh, that helped provoke Vietnam's invasion of Lane Xang in 1478. Nearly four hundred years later, Vietnam was drawn into another major conflict over Xiang Khouang, but this time it was with Louang Phabang's suzerain, **Siam**. As the nineteenth century progressed, the Kingdom of Xiang Khouang was battered towards extinction. In 1869, warrior horsemen from southern **China** raced across the plain, slaughtering villagers or carrying them off into captivity. These Black Flag bandits pillaged the riches of the kingdom and plundered the contents of the jars. Those that fled didn't get far: Lao and Thai soldiers on their way to Xiang Khouang to quell the invasion rounded up the refugees and frogmarched them through the jungle to the Chao Phraya River Valley in Siam, where they became slaves to Thai lords. The tortuous march lasted over a month, with many dying along the way, lost to sickness and starvation. In two generations, Siamese armies and Chinese bandits reduced the population by three-quarters through death and forced migration. The Phuan state never recovered.

Xiang Khouang enjoyed better protection from its neighbours with the arrival of the **French**, who considered the province's temperate climate – which can be downright cold by any measure for several months of the year – suitable for European settlement and plantation agriculture. The primary cash crop, however, was **opium**, a trade the French quickly moved to control (see box, pp.220–221). Muang Khoun was chosen as the French provincial capital and the devastated former royal seat of the defunct kingdom was transformed into an architectural gem of French Indochinese villas and shophouses, which might have rivalled the charm of Louang Phabang and Savannakhet had Xiang Khouang not returned to its familiar role as battleground a few decades later.

One hundred years after the carnage of the Chinese bandits, American planes wreaked destruction that was equally indiscriminate, levelling towns and forcing villagers to take to the forest, as the two sides in the **Second Indochina War** waged a bitter battle for control of the Plain of Jars, which represented a back door to northern Vietnam. Throughout much of the 1960s, Xiang Khouang was the site of a seesaw war, with the royalist side led by Hmong General Vang Pao gaining the upper hand in the rainy season and the communist side launching offensives in the dry months. Yet again, Xiang Khouang was caught between superior powers, and once more the refugees flowed south.

Today, villages have been rebuilt and fields replanted. Many of the valley-dwelling, wet-rice farmers, as well as a majority of the townsfolk in Phonsavan, are descendants of the Phuan kingdom. In addition to the Lao, the Phuan are joined by a third lowland group, the Black Tai, and also the Khamu – a Lao Theung group who ruled the lowlands until they were forced into the hills with the arrival of the Tai groups over a thousand years ago – and a significant population of Hmong, who arrived in Laos from China in the nineteenth century and now make up roughly a third of the provincial population.

Phonsavan

The capital of Xiang Khouang province, **PHONSAVAN** has gradually emerged as the most important town on the Plain of Jars since the total devastation of the region in the Second Indochina War. The bomb-casing collections in many guesthouse lobbies are grim galleries reflecting the area's tragic past when possession of the strategic plain was seen as the key to control of Laos. It was the new communist government that designated Phonsavan the new provincial capital, and parked Laos's fledgling collection of Soviet MiGs nearby, a smug reminder of who won the battle for this bitterly contested area. Hastily rebuilt in the aftermath of decades of fighting, Phonsavan has only now, 30 years after the end of conflict, begun to recover economically, thanks in a large part to international interest in the world-famous Jar sites scattered around the perimeter of the plain. Tourism has given the town new life: bombs at the Jar sites have been cleared away and Khoun Cheuam's jar – the largest of the scores of jars in the area – stares down from tourism posters across the country. Although most visitors come only to see the Jar sites, the Xiang Khouang Plateau is a place of great natural beauty and its backroads are well worth exploring.

Arrival, transport and information
Landing at the **airport**, you'll need a tuk-tuk (50,000K) for the four-kilometre ride into town. Alternatively you can get a free lift with one of the hotel reps.

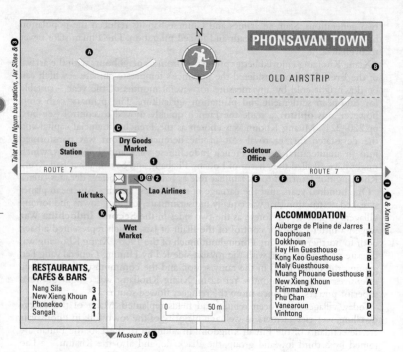

PHONSAVAN TOWN

N

OLD AIRSTRIP

Ⓐ

Ⓑ

Ⓒ

Bus
Station

Dry Goods
Market

❶

Sodetour
Office

ROUTE 7

ROUTE 7

Ⓔ   Ⓕ   Ⓖ

Ⓗ

Ⓘ Ⓙ & Xam Nua

Ⓓ @ ❷

Lao Airlines

Tuk tuks

Ⓚ

Wet
Market

ACCOMMODATION

Auberge de Plaine de Jarres	I
Daophouan	K
Dokkhoun	F
Hay Hin Guesthouse	E
Kong Keo Guesthouse	B
Maly Guesthouse	L
Muang Phouane Guesthouse	H
New Xieng Khoun	A
Phimmahaxay	C
Phu Chan	J
Vanearoun	D
Vinhtong	G

**RESTAURANTS,
CAFÉS & BARS**

Nang Sila	3
New Xieng Khoun	A
Phonekeo	2
Sangah	1

0   50 m

▼ Museum & Ⓛ

Arriving by bus, you'll be dropped at the **bus lot** opposite the dry goods market and the post office, from where most guesthouses are an easy walk. Vehicles travelling towards Vientiane and Xam Nua all leave from here; those heading for Muang Khoun and other points south leave from the Talat Nam Ngum bus station, 3km to the southwest of town on the road to the Jar sites. The main **tuk-tuk stand** is on the main road just opposite the *Daophouan Guesthouse*. For journeys further afield than the town or the jar sites, four-wheel-drives can be hired through most hotels and travel agencies.

Lao Airlines, next to the post office, has flights to Louang Phabang and Vientiane. The Lane Xang Bank (Mon–Fri 8am–noon & 1–4pm) is on the main road, at the south end of town across from the *Phudoi Hotel*, and can **exchange** US dollar traveller's cheques. There is also an exchange kiosk at the airport. Next to Lao Airlines is an **Internet shop**; phone calls can be made next to the post office.

Accommodation

Phonsavan has many **guesthouses and hotels**, most of which line Route 7, east of the dry goods market. Before Route 7 opened to tourists, Phonsavan previously catered mostly to fly-in package tour groups. Consequently, the town was not well set up for independent travellers; there were few good restaurants and many guesthouses are very overpriced. However, with Route 7 now open and increasing numbers of backpackers making the trip to Phonsavan this situation has corrected itself. If you've got money to spend, two **luxury resorts** sit on the hills to the south overlooking town, both of which offer great views and spacious, charming bungalows with fireplaces, though you will feel cut off from town (and cheaper restaurants) if you've arrived without your own transport. For these two hotels you'll need to reserve beforehand, especially in the high season, as both tend to be booked well in advance by tour groups.

Auberge de Plaine de Jarres ☎ 061/312044. Overlooking the town from a hill to the southeast, this very classy lodge is set in landscaped grounds surrounded by pine trees and bougainvillea. There are deluxe two-room cabins with fireplaces and private bathrooms, and there's also a French restaurant with spectacular views. **⑦**

Daophouan ☎ 061/312171. The eleven rooms in this three-storey building are a notch above others in the same price bracket, and all are en suite with hot water. Definitely one of the top choices in town, but a bit pricey even with breakfast included. **④**

Dokkhoun Route 7 east of centre ☎ 061/312189. Three separate buildings with a lobby full of UXO as a decorative feature. The ten rooms in the newest wing have en-suite bathrooms with hot water, much better value though pricier than the older ones in the back buildings. **③**

Hay Hin Guesthouse Route 7, east of centre ☎ 061/312252. Super-basic, with plywood walls and poor construction, the *Hay Hin* has two-bed rooms, with or without cold-water bathroom. **②**

Kong Keo Guesthouse ☎ 061/211354. Situated 200m off Route 7 next to the old airstrip. Whether you're looking for an inexpensive, clean room with spotless, shared hot-water facilities or a deluxe bungalow with hot-water en-suite bathroom in a quiet garden, *Kong's* is simply the best value in town. Kong himself is a real character and his nightly bonfires are legendary. A very good deal – just watch out for that *lào-láo*. **②**

Maly Guesthouse West of the museum ☎ 061/312156, ℱ 312003. This has pleasant rooms, hot-water showers and an excellent restaurant, and if you need Western-style comfort, the VIP rooms upstairs in the new building are amongst the nicest in town, with wall-to-wall carpeting, TV and huge picture windows.

Popular with group tours, but it's a bit isolated and far from the centre. **⑤**

Muang Phouane Guesthouse Route 7 ☎ 061/312046. Located in a large compound, the *Muang Phouane* is a single-storey house that has been adapted to take boarders. All rooms are clean and have en-suite bathrooms with hot water. **②**

New Xieng Khouang On the road leading up behind the bus station ☎ 061/312049. Recently renovated, this used to be Phonsavan's short-stay motel, next to its most popular disco. Some rooms are spacious and come with a sitting area, while smaller rooms have just enough space for a bed; all have en-suite facilities. The cavernous restaurant on the premises serves food which is better than the lack of patrons would suggest. **③**

Phimmahaxay ☎ 061/312208. On the first corner north of the bus lot, this newish, six-room hotel in a modern three-storey building has big rooms with good-quality mattresses, but only shared hot-water facilities. **②**

Phu Chan ☎ 061/312264. Sitting on the hillside roughly 2km southeast of town, this friendly resort has twelve wooden cabins, each with two large rooms, a roomy common area, a cosy fireplace and striking views of the surrounding landscape. **⑥**

Vanearoun Next to the *Phonekeo Restaurant* on Route 7 ☎ 061/312070. Older and starting to show some real wear, this place has more of a local clientele. The more expensive rooms have en-suite hot-water bathrooms; cheaper rooms share facilities. Best kept as a fallback. **②**

Vinhtong Route 7 ☎ 061/212622. Basic but clean, with tiled floors, rattan walls and en-suite bathrooms with hot water. There are also some bigger units out back for slightly more money. The lobby has a big UXO collection and tourist information on the surrounding sites. **②**

The Town

The original settlement of Phonsavan was, like every other town on the plain, obliterated during the war. The town you see today is a modern **reconstruction** that has largely gone up over the last ten years. There is really nothing of note to see, although the town grid is nicely laid out on a rather grand scale. Indeed, if the length and width of Phonsavan's empty boulevards are anything to go by, local officials have very big plans for this little place. In keeping with this, there are a lot of large new government buildings around town including the **Xiang Khouang Museum**, resembling a step pyramid, at the big intersection by the Lane Xang Bank. After being under construction for ages, the museum looks to be completed but was still shut at the time of writing, for reasons unknown.

Aside from the museum, the only real sights in town are the two main **markets** located on Route 7 at the town's main junction, where most of the hotels and restaurants are found. The **wet market** behind the post office is well worth a wander, the amount and variety of the fresh produce on sale giving a good indication of just how much people's lives here have improved since the government quietly swept communist economics under the rug. Opposite the post office on the northern side of the main road is a **dry market** where all manner of consumer durables are sold. On the eastern side of the market you can sometimes find – in addition to a huge assortment of knick-knacks and everyday items – colourful pieces of Xiang Khouang's heritage for sale: small squares of **Hmong textiles**, intricately handwoven in electric greens, oranges and yellows, known as *paj ntaub* (pronounced "pang dao"), and other articles of Hmong traditional clothing. *Paj ntaub* can sell for $100, hats for $300, a reflection of the intense workmanship that goes into producing the textiles, but also indicative of the buying power of Hmong relatives overseas, who send money from southern California, Minnesota and beyond to keep themselves in the colours of the old country and the family left behind in greenbacks. Another worthwhile souvenir to seek out is the "*khan nyu*" umbrella – beautifully constructed, mulberry-paper umbrellas are an old Xiang Khouang art and require dozens of steps, from crafting the bamboo struts to oiling the hand-made paper. Oil from the fruit of the *màk nyao* tree produces yellow umbrellas, while oil from *màk bao* roots produces red umbrellas. If you can't find the umbrellas in the market, ask at *Sangah* restaurant or the *New Xieng Khouang*.

Eating, drinking and nightlife

Phonsavan is not the best town in Laos for **places to eat**. Most travellers gravitate to the *Sangah*, just east of the main bus station, which serves passable steak and chips and Lao dishes. Once the staff get to know your face they're quite friendly and this is the best place in town to meet other travellers. The *Phonekeo*, across the street, is always empty because the food is even less inspiring than that at the *Sangah*. If you're a true fan of *föe*, make the effort to seek out the locally well-regarded *Nang Sila*, 600m west of the dry goods market, on the left, in a two-storey grey house. Nearby, directly outside the post office, there are no fewer than three carts selling hot *cha-shao bao*, steamed Cantonese buns filled with sweet red pork. The food at *Kong Keo Guesthouse* is worth trying – they've been getting cooking lessons from all the falangs passing through, and have added things like mashed potatoes, fresh fruit salad and home-made peanut butter to their menu. For a splurge, the views from the French restaurant up at the *Auberge de Plaine de Jarres* are outstanding. Given the setting and views, it's really quite inexpensive, with Lao entrees for $2 and French entrees for $5. You'll need to call (☎061/312044) and place your order a few hours in advance with the Lao manager, who speaks both English and French. The restaurant of the *New Xieng Khouang* does decent Western fare as well as quasi-Thai dishes.

Phonsavan has a handful of karaoke establishments with the usual cat-like hostesses and caterwauling patrons. However, most travellers opt for drinking a late-night Beer Lao at the *Kong Keo*.

The Plain of Jars

Many visitors mistake the Jar sites for the **PLAIN OF JARS** and vice versa. The latter is a broad rolling plain covering an area roughly 15km across at the

△ The Plain of Jars

centre of the Xiang Khouang Plateau, which sits high above the Mekong and the Vientiane Plain. The ancient **Jar sites** scattered around the perimeter of the plain led the French to name the region the Plain de Jars – the PDJ to the American pilots who flew over it. Topographically, the plain is something like the hole in a doughnut with concentric rings of increasingly high mountain peaks around it. Although the jars are the main tourist attraction of Xiang Khouang Province, there's much more to see here. The Plain itself offers beautiful scenery, which most visitors, obsessed with seeing the jars, completely overlook. With its bare rolling red, brown and purple hills, pine trees and eucalyptus, the plain is a would-be paradise for horseback-riding. Away from the main highway there are countless backroads to explore as well as friendly **Phuan and Hmong villages**, where it may seem that you're the first foreigner the children have seen. Note that for the time being, the jars and other outlying areas can only be visited if you're accompanied by a licensed guide.

The presence of the jars attests to the fact that Xiang Khouang, with its access to key regional trade routes, its wide, flat spaces and temperate climate, has been considered prime real estate in mainland Southeast Asia for centuries, but the story of the plain as a **transit route** for ancient man has yet to be told. As a natural corridor between the coasts of southern China and the vast plains of Korat beyond the Mekong, the Plain of Jars has certainly seen the passage of many tribes and races, perhaps even groups of *Homo erectus*, who ranged from northern China to Java between one million and 250,000 years ago.

The Jar sites

The **Jar sites** are among the most important prehistoric archeological sites in Southeast Asia. Clusters of stone jars thought to be 2000 years old, along with seemingly older stone pillars, are scattered across the Plain and also in other

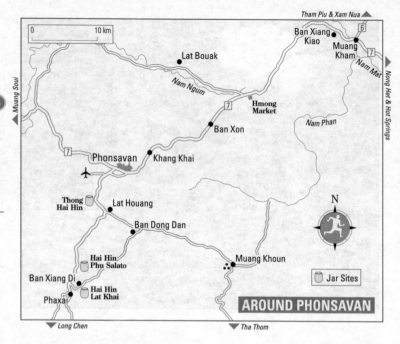

parts of Xiang Khouang and Houa Phan province. The largest urns measure 2m in height and weigh as much as ten tonnes. Little is known about the **Iron Age megalithic civilization** that created these artefacts; war and revolution kept archeologists from working on the sites for decades. By the time French archeologist Madeleine Colani began excavating at the Jar sites in the 1930s, most of the urns had been looted, although she did find bronze and iron tools as well as coloured glass beads, bronze bracelets and cowrie shells. Colani theorized that the jars were **funerary urns**, originally holding cremated remains. More recent discoveries have revealed underground burial chambers, further supporting Colani's theory. Because of the great age of the jars and the unsolvable mystery of their origin, they have perhaps become famous beyond their aesthetic merits.

Of the dozens of Jar sites, **three main sites** close to Phonsavan have been officially opened for tourists, largely because they are accessible and have a greater concentration of jars. The closest one, known as Site 1, just 2km southwest of town, has over two hundred jars. Sites 2 and 3 are much more scenic and are located about 10km southwest of the market village of **Lat Houang**, which is 10km south of Phonsavan, on the road to Muang Khoun.

Site 1

Site 1 or **Thong Hai Hin** ("Stone Jar Plain") is the most visited of the sites, but unfortunately its proximity to the nearby air base, which houses the Lao PDR's squadron of ageing MiGs, somewhat mars the landscape. There's a pavilion built for a visit by the Thai crown prince, a member of Laos's surrogate royalty – where you can also buy drinks. Following the path from the pavilions to the jars, you'll quickly come to **Hai Cheaum** ("Cheaum Jar"), a massive jar 2m high that was named after the Tai–Lao hero of lore, who is celebrated in one version of the jar myth as the liberator of the people of the Plain of Jars from a cruel overlord named Chao Angka. Legend has it that the jars were made to ferment rice wine to celebrate the victory; as the jars bear a passing resemblance to *lào hái* jars used today, the liquor-loving locals didn't have to stretch their imaginations too far to come up with this theory. Walk downhill a little way and you'll find yourself amid another group of jars, one of which has a crude human shape carved onto it. In the hill off to the left is a large **cave** that the Pathet Lao used during the war, and which, according to local legend, was used as a kiln to cast the jars. Erosion has carved two holes in the roof of the cave – natural chimneys that make the cavern a worthy kiln of sorts. Colani suggests that the cave was used as a crematorium: in and around the cave she found the remains of what she believed to be commoners not lucky enough to be interred in the stone funeral urns, which were reserved, she argued, for the ashes of the nobility.

Sites 2 and 3

Back on the Phonsavan–Muang Khoun road, the turn-off for **sites 2 and 3** is 3km further on at Lat Houang. Zipping across the flats surrounding Lat Sen, the town that played host to the old French airstrip, towards Phaxai and the Jar sites, you'll pass narrow dirt runways on the grassy meadows and hillsides. These clearings are used by hunters to trap swallows in nets that they trigger from camouflaged huts at one end of the strip; smoky fires bring bugs to the surface of the clearing, attracting the swallows. The most skilful hunters can catch several hundred birds on a good day, netting a tidy sum. The birds are sold at Phonsavan's market.

Ten kilometres on from the turn-off, you turn left along a dirt track – a road in slightly worse condition than the Phaxai road – and follow it for 2km through a village just large enough to support a tiny monastery, until you wind up at two adjacent hills, one on either side of the road. Nearly a hundred jars are scattered across the twin hills here, lending the site the name **Hai Hin Phou Salato** ("Salato Hill Stone Jar Site").

The gateway to Site 3, the most atmospheric of the three, lies in the village of Ban Xiang Di, 4km up the Phaxai road on the left. Large Lao Phuan houses line the way to Wat Xiang Di, a simple wooden monastery 1km from the turn-off, where you'll find the path leading to **Hai Hin Lat Khai**, also known as Hai Hin Xiang Di. There's a depressing, bomb-damaged Buddha here that the guides like to point out. Pick up the path at the back corner of the monastery compound, which hops a stream and cuts uphill through several fields before arriving at a clearing with more than a hundred jars and sweeping views of the surrounding countryside.

Practicalities

Visitors to the jar sites must be accompanied by a licensed **guide**; tuk-tuks aren't allowed to go and private taxis and vehicles must be registered for "safety" and have a "special permit" to serve the Jar sites – a system introduced by the big tourist hotels and travel agencies keen to keep this lucrative line of business for themselves.

All three sites, together with old Xiang Khouang (see p.198), can be seen in a day, with hotels and tour companies generally pitching the four spots as a package. Lane Xang Travel, Sodetour and Inter-Lao (see p.43) all operate such **day-tours** but, at $50–100 for a van with driver and English-speaking guide, it's the most expensive way of seeing the sites. A much cheaper option is to book a vehicle and guide ($30 for six persons) through one of the Phonsavan guesthouses or restaurants. Mr Manopet, at the *Sangah* restaurant, or Mr Boualin Phommasin, at the *Phonekeo* restaurant, both arrange inexpensive, non-agency tours. Mr Kong at *Kong Keo Guesthouse* also regularly rounds up foreigners for cut-rate trips out to the Jar sites. Bear in mind when organizing a non-agency tour that the price is determined by the type of vehicle used. Tours include the price of entry to the sites.

Muang Khoun (Old Xiang Khouang)

A ghost of its former self, **MUANG KHOUN**, old Xiang Khouang, 35km southeast of Phonsavan, was once the royal seat of the minor kingdom Xiang Khouang, renowned in the sixteenth century for its 62 opulent stupas, whose sides were said to be covered in treasure. Years of bloody invasions by Thai and Vietnamese soldiers, pillaging by Chinese bandits in the nineteenth century and a monsoon of bombs that lasted nearly a decade during the Second Indochina War taxed this town so heavily that, by the time the air raids stopped, next to nothing was left of the kingdom's exquisite temples. The town was all but abandoned, and centuries of history were drawn to a close. All that remains of the kingdom's former glory is an elegant Buddha image towering over ruined columns of brick at Wat Phia Wat, and That Dam, both of which bear the scars of the events that ended Xiang Khouang's centuries of rich history. Although the town has been rebuilt and renamed, it has taken a back seat to Phonsavan, and, with little in the way of amenities for travellers – there are a few *fŏe* shops around the market, but the lone hotel has closed – it's most convenient to visit Muang Khoun as a day-trip.

A long row of low-slung wooden shophouses, centred on the market, springs up along the road from Phonsavan in the shadow of towering **That Dam**, signalling your arrival in Muang Khoun. A path alongside the market leads up to the blackened hilltop stupa, the base of which has been tunnelled straight through to the other side by treasure seekers hoping to find more than a simple bone of the Enlightened One inside. A British surveyor who travelled through the area in the service of the Siamese king in 1884 – shortly after the invasions by Chinese Haw – surmised that the bandits pillaged the stupa, making off with 7000 rupees' weight of gold. Continuing on the main road beyond the market, you'll pass the ruins of a villa, the only reminder that this town was once a temperate French outpost of ochre colonial villas and shophouses, and arrive at the ruins of sixteenth-century **Wat Phia Wat**. Brick columns reach skywards around a seated Buddha of impressive size, a mere hint at the temple architecture for which the city was renowned. The only remaining example of Xiang Khouang-style architecture is Wat Khili in Louang Phabang (see p.152), but Wat Khili has been modified so many times that you wouldn't know its link to Xiang Khouang's monasteries unless you viewed it from the back. The recently completed temple at **Wat Siphoum**, the uninspiring structure nearest the market, bears little trace of the old designs for which the city's monasteries were known and serves notice of how much of Xiang Khouang's culture has been lost.

Phonsavan to Muang Kham

Many of the ethnic groups that populate Xiang Khouang are well represented in the area between Phonsavan and Muang Kham to the northeast, and a trip out to the village of **Muang Kham** and its nearby hot springs by rental car or sawngthaew makes an interesting excursion. Route 7, being upgraded by Vietnamese road crews at the time of writing, winds through valleys hemmed by hills bursting with *dok bua khom* – yellow flowers that are crushed into a natural fertilizer for vegetable gardens – passing dusty Khamu, Black Tai, Phuan and Hmong villages, with their wooden huts.

Leaving Phonsavan, you first pass through **Khang Khai**, the town that became the seat of Prince Souvannaphouma's neutralist government after the Battle of Vientiane in December 1960, before arriving in **Ban Xon Tai**, 12km north of Phonsavan, where two village women etched the name of their hometown into Pathet Lao lore when they shot down an American plane during the war. Apparently armed with little more than rifles, the heroines inspired the addition of the adjectives "patriotic" and "brave" to generations-old songs praising the beauty of Xiang Khouang women. Eleven kilometres further along on Route 7, a **Hmong market** sets up weekly on early Sunday mornings, attracting Hmong from numerous villages in the area.

In the hills to the west of the market are the beginnings of the **Nam Ngum River**, one of the Mekong's most important tributaries. Theoretically, it's possible to kayak or raft the Nam Ngum all the way down from the Xiang Khouang Plateau to the Ang Nam Ngum Reservoir. In the not-so-distant past foreigners who tried this were arrested by overzealous Lao army soldiers unable to figure out why anyone would want to attempt such a thing unless they were a spy. Nowadays it is sometimes possible to go **white-water rafting** on the river through the adventure tour operator Green Discovery in Vang Viang (☏023/511230, ⓦwww.greendiscoverylaos.com).

Three kilometres beyond the market you'll pass through the Hmong village of Tha Cho before arriving in **Daen Thong**, 12km further on, a village peopled by Khamu, a midland tribe that makes up around seven percent of Xiang Khouang's population. Widely considered to be among the original inhabitants of Laos, the ancestors of the Khamu are thought by some to have built the funerary urns scattered across the Plain of Jars. The next village, **Ban Lao**, was settled by Black Tai (Tai Dam), who fled to Laos several decades ago from Dien Bien Phu, the Vietnamese valley where the final battle of the First Indochina War was fought. After a further 7km, a dirt track forks off to the east leading to another Black Tai village, **Ban Xiang Kiao**, while the main road continues over a bridge spanning the Nam Mat stream and winds its way into Muang Kham, a large village formerly known as Chomthong.

Muang Kham

Situated in a long flat valley at the northeastern edge of the Plain of Jars, 51km from Phonsavan, **MUANG KHAM** lies at the convergence of the roads to Louang Phabang, Houa Phan and Vietnam and is a pit stop for trucks ferrying goods between Laos and its eastern neighbour. Other than the drivers of the hulking lorries in the market compound, few travellers stay the night here, preferring to base themselves at Phonsavan, and visit the sights around Muang Kham as a day-trip. Indeed, the town is basically just a T-junction with a small market and the usual Kaysone monument. There are two no-frills **guesthouses**, the better being *My Xay Guesthouse* (❶), which occupies a two-storey building directly opposite the market and is usually full of Chinese traders. On the main road (Route 7) that runs in front of the market and the square stand a few **noodle shops**, some of which also serve a selection of *khao keng* dishes (stir fries and curries) to cater to hungry truckers – look for the selection of pots and trays holding lukewarm food set up on tables outside the restaurant. **Buses and sawngthaews**, heading north to Nam Neun and Xam Nua, east to Nong Het and south to Phonsavan, stop in the market compound.

Around Muang Kham

There are several sights around Muang Kham on the itineraries of day-tours out of Phonsavan. None is worth a special journey all the way from Phonsavan in its own right, but collectively they're a good excuse to see more of rural Xiang Khouang province, especially if you're on a flying visit to the Plain of Jars. A sombre pilgrimage to **Tham Piu**, a cave in which hundreds seeking refuge from the wartime bombing were killed when a fighter plane fired a rocket into the grotto, has begun to draw an increasing number of visitors. The turn-off for the cave lies on the left-hand side of Route 6, 4km north of Muang Kham. Follow the road 1500m to the foot of the hill and you'll find a steep set of stairs climbing up to the wide mouth of the cave. No memorial has been erected and only blackened rock testifies to the tragic incident.

From Muang Kham, Route 7 east towards the Vietnamese border leads you to two **hot springs**, Baw Nam Hon Lek and Baw Nam Hon Nyai – "Little Hot Spring" and "Big Hot Spring". The smaller of the two lies a little over 3km from town, on an unsignposted road leading off Route 7 to the right, but is usually passed over in favour of the larger spring, which has been converted into a resort of sorts, further east along Route 7. After passing through the tiny Na Ba market and crossing a bridge, turn right at Ban Nam Dien – 16km from Muang Kham – and head for the cliffs to find the spring. The road ends at the resort's gate, 3.5km away from Route 7, where you'll need to pay an entrance fee (5000K). The hot spring fills a swampy green pond of no remarkable beauty, but blooming flowers in the rainy season attract Phonsavan couples, who make the trip out on weekends to picnic and canoodle. A crude piping system draws the spring's steamy water to the site's main attraction: the **hot baths**, which are situated in a long shed among a small cluster of rustic bungalows. A warm bath (5000K) – there are two large tubs per private room – is certainly worth the trip during Xiang Khouang's chilly winters. The **bungalows** were constructed for the use of visiting dignitaries (if none is in residence, it's usually possible to get accommodation; ❹) by Kaysone's wife, known for her appreciation of herbal cures, and are managed by the proprietors of the small restaurant in the compound. A variety of Lao food is on the menu, but you'll most likely end up eating whatever the cook managed to find in the market that day.

The best way to visit these sites is to hire a car and driver for the day in Phonsavan ($40), which allows you to stop at the various villages along the way and linger in the hot baths. A cheaper but more difficult alternative is to catch either a sawngthaew to Muang Kham from Phonsavan or a bus going to Nam Neun or Ban Nong Het, both of which will pass through Muang Kham. Once in Muang Kham, you can hire a tuk-tuk at the market to take you to Tham Piu, the hot springs, or both.

Beyond Ban Nong Het is the **Nong Het border crossing** to Nghe An province in Vietnam, as yet little used by travellers due to a lack of long-distance public transport. You must have obtained a visa in advance in order to enter Vietnam here.

Muang Soui

From Phonsavan, Route 7 winds west towards the mountainous edge of the Plain of Jars and then begins working its way through the mountains to the outpost of Muang Phoukhoun on Route 13. This section of the French-built highway – a favourite target of Hmong insurgents as recently as the 1990s – grinds through pine-topped hills and steep-banked stream beds for 48km to **MUANG SOUI**. Roughly at the halfway mark, the road fords the Nam Ngum

Xaisomboun Special Zone

Carved out of parts of Vientiane, Xiang Khouang and Bolikhamxai provinces in 1994, the **Xaisomboun Special Zone**, extending over more than 7000 square kilometres, was created in an effort to quell anti-Vientiane insurgent activities, and has been administered by the Lao military ever since. Much of the southern sector is empty wilderness, but the district is home to **Phou Bia**, Laos's tallest mountain at 2819m. Located approximately halfway between Phonsavan and Ang Nam Ngum Reservoir, Phou Bia is closed to tourists as it still has an insurgency problem; at the moment, the closest you can get to seeing it is out of the window on the Phonsavan–Vientiane flight.

The zone is accessible via Route 13B, which runs off Route 13 just north of Ang Nam Ngum and then branches off at Pha Volo into separate roads north to Phonsavan. Due to improvements in the security situation, the military have recently returned two districts to Vientiane province, but Xaisomboun is still not considered totally safe for travel, and anyone determined to visit may well be turned away by the authorities. As long as remnants of the disbanded Hmong army continue to stage hit-and-run attacks on civilian and military targets, the new name the communists have chosen for the former Hmong stronghold, Xaisomboun, or "Bountiful Victory", will remain a rather premature one at best, given the government's inability to bring the isolated zone under its control.

as the river builds up steam en route to the Nam Ngum Dam, and then passes a pair of villages populated by Hmong, who were forcibly resettled here in the late 1990s.

Once a significant village known for its temples, Muang Soui was yet another casualty of the intense fighting in Xiang Khouang province. Now rebuilt alongside **Nong Tang**, a pretty lake hemmed in by stubby limestone karsts and praised for its serenity in local folk songs, it's a sleepy town of wooden shophouses and a small market. Nearby is **Tham Pha**, a forest cave that shelters a Buddha image and a *that*. One kilometre from town, an old 1500-metre-long landing strip, in a state of disuse, cuts across Route 7 as it begins its ninety-kilometre journey towards Muang Phoukhoun.

Travel details

Buses and sawngthaews

Nam Neun to: Phonsavan (1–2 daily; 6hr); Viang Thong (1 daily; 3hr); Xam Nua (2 daily; 2hr 30min).
Nong Khiaw to: Nam Bak (hourly; 30min); Viang Kham (2–3 daily; 2hr).
Phonsavan to: Muang Kham (4–5 daily; 1hr 30min); Muang Khoun (2–3 daily; 1hr); Muang Soui (1–2 daily; 2hr); Nam Neun (1–2 daily; 6hr); Nong Het (daily; 4hr); Phaxai (daily; 40min); Xam Nua (daily; 6hr).
Viang Kham to: Louang Phabang (daily; 4hr 40min); Nong Khiaw (2–3 daily; 2hr); Viang Thong (2 daily; 4hr).

Viang Thong to: Nam Neun (1 daily; 3hr); Viang Kham (2 daily; 4hr); Xam Nua (1 daily; 6–7hr).
Xam Nua to: Muang Et (1 daily; 5hr); Nam Neun (2 daily; 2hr 30min); Viang Thong (1 daily; 6–7hr); Viang Xai (10 daily; 30min); Vientiane (daily; 30hr).

Flights

Phonsavan to: Louang Phabang (2 weekly; 35min); Vientiane (4 weekly; 40min).
Xam Nua to: Vientiane (3 weekly; 1hr 10min).

The far north

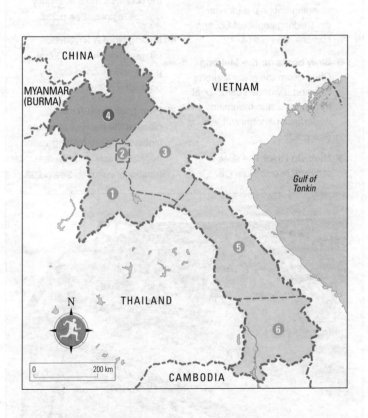

CHINA

MYANMAR
(BURMA)

VIETNAM

Gulf of
Tonkin

THAILAND

N

0   200 km

CAMBODIA

CHAPTER 4

Highlights

✳ **Hill-tribe trekking** With dozens of tribal ethnic groups still relatively unaffected by the modern world, northern Laos is a big trekking destination. See opposite

✳ **Nam Ha NBCA** Hike, kayak or raft, but don't miss this stunning national park near the trekking centre of Louang Namtha. See p.214

✳ **Slow boats on the Mekong** Chug down the great Mekong River on a wooden cargo boat through the vast mountain wilderness of northern Laos. See p.225

✳ **Nam Ou River** The spectacularly scenic Nam Ou, flanked by jagged karst and rustic riverside villages, can be explored using local river boats. See p.231

✳ **The Phongsali Loop** Take the week-long loop from Louang Phabang through some of the country's most ethnically diverse regions. See p.232

✳ **Muang Ngoi** A tiny idyllic village, surrounded by karst peaks and reached only by boat. See p.235

✳ **Phongsali town** A restful place at the heart of a remote highland region, offering vast tropical forests and diverse traditional cultures. See p.238

△ Getting around by pick-up

The far north

While history has seen the rise and fall of a Lao dynasty enthroned at Louang Phabang, little has changed on the elevated **northern fringes** of the former kingdom. Decades of war and neglect have done their part to keep this isolated region of Southeast Asia from developing and have unwittingly preserved a way of life that has virtually vanished in neighbouring countries. While the fertile valleys of the Upper Mekong and its tributaries have for centuries been the domain of the **Buddhist lowland Lao**, the hills and mountains to the north have been the preserve of a scattering of animist tribal peoples, including the **Hmong**, **Mien** and **Akha**. Anthropologists, gleaning evidence largely from oral tradition, speculate that some of these tribal peoples, such as the **Khamu**, were actually here before the lowland Lao migrated onto the scene; others, such as the Akha, are relative newcomers. The highlanders make their living by painstakingly clearing and cultivating the steep slopes while bartering with the lowland Lao for anything that they themselves cannot harvest, hunt or fashion with their own hands. It is largely the chance to experience first-hand these near-pristine cultures that draws visitors to the region today.

In the past, visitors only had a few set options for travelling around the far north, considered by many to be the highlight of any trip to Laos. The most popular route was from Louang Phabang up through Muang Sing to Xiang Kok and then back down the Mekong, either exiting at Houayxai or returning back down the Mekong to Louang Phabang. Today working out a travel itinerary for a journey through the far north is not so simple, since there are now many different routes and transport options. While the traditional route described above is still very popular, a number of variations on this theme are also possible, with many travellers using **Routes** 2 and 3 to swing up to **Route 1**. Aside from river travel along the Mekong between Louang Phabang and Houayxai (see box, p.225, for more), in season it is also possible to travel upcountry by boat along the **Nam Tha** and **Nam Ou rivers**.

Whichever way you choose to go, the two most popular northern towns are the tourist centre of **Louang Namtha**, with its excellent trekking and river trips, and **Muang Sing**, a laid-back Tai Leu town that lies within the borders of the **Golden Triangle**, formerly the world's most notorious opium-producing zone. Both towns have become popular bases for trekking, owing to their comfortable accommodation and easy access to nearby Akha, Mien and Tai Dam villages. Along the Mekong River there are a number of river-port towns with boat traffic, accommodation and roadheads leading up into the interior. These include **Xiang Kok**, just a short journey from Muang Sing; **Houayxai**, an official border crossing with Thailand, **Pakbeng**, an important stop for

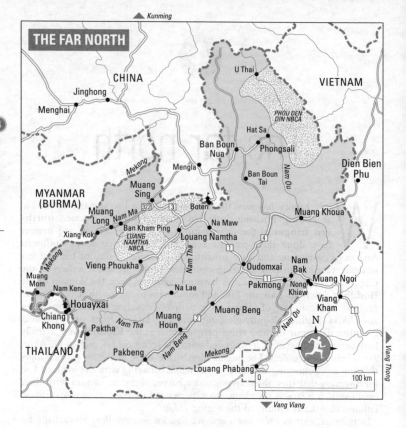

THE FAR NORTH

CHINA

Kunming

VIETNAM

Jinghong

Menghai

U Thai

PHOU DEN
DIN NBCA

Hat Sa

Ban Boun
Nua

Phongsali

Mengla

Dien Bien
Phu

Ban Boun
Tai

MYANMAR
(BURMA)

Muang
Sing

Boten

Muang Khoua

Muang
Long

Nam Ma

322

3

Xiang Kok

Ban Kham Ping

Na Maw

LUANG
NAMTHA
NBCA

Louang Namtha

4

Vieng Phoukha

Nam Tha

Oudomxai

Nam
Bak

Muang
Mom

Nam Keng

Na Lae

Pakmong

Nong
Khiaw

Muang Ngoi

Houayxai

Viang
Kham

Chiang
Khong

Paktha

Nam Tha

Muang
Houn

Muang Beng

Nam Ou

13

N

THAILAND

Pakbeng

Nam Beng

Mekong

Viang
Thong

Louang Phabang

0   100 km

Vang Viang

slow boats on the Louang Phabang to Houayxai route; and of course, Louang
Phabang itself.

Another route is the **Phongsali Loop**, which can combine both river and
road travel and takes nearly a week to complete, passing through the most
spectacular scenery in northern Laos. Although the loop can be done in either
direction, most travellers opt to begin in Louang Phabang, ascending the **Nam
Ou River** by passenger boat. Leaving the river at the town of **Hat Sa**, you
travel by sawngthaew over the mountains to **Phongsali**, a provincial capital
situated on a plateau blessed with a year-round temperate climate. Inhabited
mainly by the easy-going Phu Noi people, this tidy town is reminiscent of
highland towns in southern China's Yunnan province. From Phongsali, you
travel by sawngthaew down to the city of **Oudomxai**, the most important road
junction in the far north. It can be used as a jumping-off point for either of the
two main tourist loops described above, or for journeys into China through the
border crossing at Boten.

For those who are less interested in covering ground and are simply looking
for a picturesque place to chill while spending as few kip as possible, a relatively
short sawngthaew ride up Route 13 from Louang Phabang, followed by an
even shorter boat trip, will put you in **Muang Ngoi**. This blessedly isolated
village, ringed by jagged karst mountains, is only reachable by ferry. There's not

The art of sawngthaew travel

Until very recently, transport in northern Laos was limited to its network of rivers, with travellers at the mercy of the water level. Today, with the introduction of four-wheel-drive Toyota **pick-up trucks**, mobility in the mountainous north has greatly improved. Enterprising drivers have converted their pick-ups into buses of sorts, adding two rows of benches bolted to the pick-up's bed and covering the whole affair with a tarpaulin stretched over a steel frame, giving shelter from sun and rain. Unfortunately, long-distance travel on these vehicles can be excruciatingly uncomfortable, especially on potholed roads.

While there is nothing a passenger can do about the sad state of Lao roads, knowing where to sit in the pick-up can make the trip a bit more tolerable. The **front seat**, next to the driver, is obviously the best. Everyone knows this and drivers usually charge extra for this choice spot. Being able to speak a bit of Lao may help you secure this seat as drivers enjoy conversing on long hauls and a Lao-speaking foreigner is considered an entertaining diversion. Often though, the driver will bring along a friend or family member and this seat will be reserved. This leaves passengers riding in the bed with a dilemma: relative comfort or a view.

The **innermost seats**, those nearest the cab, are a smoother ride but afford almost no view of the passing scenery. For this reason, non-Lao passengers often try to stake a claim on the seats nearest the tail-gate. Unfortunately, passengers in these seats have to put up with clouds of dust and choking exhaust fumes, as well as amplified jolts and knocks. If the pick-up has a **back bumper** that is wide enough to stand on, adventurous passengers may opt to perch on that while clinging precariously to the tarp-frame. This affords unobstructed views and gusts of fresh air, but watch out for those car-sick Lao passengers who poke their heads out of the sides and hurl into the wind.

much to do but enjoy the scenery, and a bunch of dirt-cheap guesthouses has cropped up; this is the northern Lao version of the laid-back traveller's scene in the south's Don Det.

Among the great pleasures of travelling through northern Laos are chance encounters with the region's distinctively dressed hill-tribe peoples. **Guided treks**, long a popular tourist diversion in neighbouring Thailand, are now established in Laos, with Louang Namtha and Muang Sing the two main centres for organized trekking. In fact, self-organized treks are actually discouraged in these two towns where the government, understandably, is trying to regulate the industry. In other northern towns, however, it is still possible for travellers to trek independently by simply using a town with accommodation as a base, getting directions and then hiking to a nearby tribal village. Muang Long is currently the most popular base for self-organized trekking, but there are also excellent untapped opportunities to be explored in Phongsali province, particularly in the vicinity of Ban Boun Tai, Muang Khoua and the provincial capital. For advice on behaviour when trekking, see the box on p.215.

Oudomxai

OUDOMXAI sits at the junction of Routes 1, 2 and 4, in a small basin surrounded by mountains. From this high point rivers flow to the north, south, east and west, making it an important trading town. The town also straddles a major trade route to China, and even today it is the most Chinese city in northern

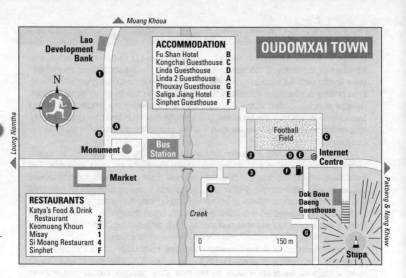

▲ Muang Khoua

OUDOMXAI TOWN

Lao Development Bank

N

ACCOMMODATION
Fu Shan Hotel	B
Kongchai Guesthouse	C
Linda Guesthouse	D
Linda 2 Guesthouse	A
Phouxay Guesthouse	G
Saliga Jiang Hotel	E
Sinphet Guesthouse	F

Football Field

Internet Centre

Monument

Bus Station

Market

RESTAURANTS
Katya's Food & Drink Restaurant	2
Keomuang Khoun	3
Misay	1
Si Moang Restaurant	4
Sinphet	F

Creek

Dok Boua Daeng Guesthouse

0   150 m

Stupa

Laos. Trucks to and from China pass this way daily and most of the town's hotels, nightclubs and brothels are run by mainland Chinese. There are so many Chinese traders and tourists here that the Chinese yuan is as readily accepted as the US dollar. The town was once known as Muang Xai, but after the civil war it was renamed Oudomxai, which means "Abundant Victory".

There is little to actually see in Oudomxai – in fact it is the least appealing town in all of northern Laos. Although the valley itself is quite pretty, the town has grown up along the two main roads without any planning and is a sprawl of ugly concrete buildings. Even its varied population, including Lao, Chinese and Khamu, is not as colourful as elsewhere in northern Laos. The locals prefer to wear Chinese-made "Western-style" clothing and, except for the occasional Hmong villagers in town for a day of trading, there is no way to tell the ethnic groups apart. However, if you travel around the north long enough there's a very good chance you'll end up having to stop over here at some point, like it or not. To this end, the town makes a pretty good rest stop – there is 24-hour electricity, email, a laundry service, hot water and even herbal sauna and massage to be had here.

The only real sight is **Phou Xay Hill**, which is located just east of the bridge. A long flight of stairs on the northern side of the hill, just beside the *Dok Boua Daeng* guesthouse, leads to the summit, crowned by a white stupa with a golden spire which provides good views over the entire valley and is an excellent place to watch the sunset. Near the stupa is a traditional wooden building with a red roof used by monks. The town's main temple, **Wat Santiphap**, is on a rise just north of town. At sunset you'll often find monks from the wat up at the Phou Xay stupa practising their English with passing visitors.

Practicalities

The **airport** lies 3km east of town; shared tuk-tuks wait there for the town's three weekly arrivals from Vientiane. Buses and sawngthaews from all four points on the compass arrive at the town's only **bus station**, a big dirt lot between the river and the Kaysone monument, which stares out from an odd

The hill tribes

The Lao Soung (literally, the "high Lao") are comparative newcomers to Laos, having migrated from China at the beginning of the nineteenth century and settled on the only land available to them, at elevations over 1000m above sea level. Among the Lao Soung are the country's most colourfully dressed ethnic groups, such as the Hmong, Mien, Lahu and Akha. You may well encounter these peoples trading at lowland markets or sometimes walking along the roadside in single file, but seeing a Lao Soung village at first hand is often one of the highlights of a trip to Laos, providing a chance to reflect on an age-old existence that, for some travellers, seems to compare favourably with their own.

The Hmong

▲ Hmong woman

Most numerous among the Lao Soung are the **Hmong**, with a population of approximately 200,000. Their apparel is among the most colourful to be found in Laos, and the Hmong are divided into several sub-groups including the White Hmong, Red Hmong, Blue Hmong and Striped Hmong named for the predominant colour of their costumes. Collectors prize Hmong silver jewellery; Hmong babies receive their first silver necklace at the age of one month, and by the time they are adults they will have several kilogrammes of silver jewellery, most of which is cached until special occasions such as Hmong New Year. Their written language uses Roman letters and was devised by Western missionaries.

As many Hmong fought on the side of the Royal Lao Government during the war, the tribe has been persecuted since the Revolution; pogroms caused many to flee for refugee camps in Thailand, from where some were subsequently able to make their way to the USA and France. Within Laos, Hmong use of slash-and-burn agriculture has given the government an excuse to resettle them at lower elevations. Tight controls on the media, including the occasional arrest of foreign reporters, continues to keep reports of unrest among the Hmong and Lao military drives against them, out of the press.

Hill-tribe treks

Slow to assimilate to the relatively modern ways of the lowland Lao, the hill-tribe communities offer a glimpse of traditional Southeast Asian lifestyles. Until recently, travellers wishing to visit their villages in the northern provinces had to arrange things independently, but the resulting encounters led to problems such as the smoking of opium (it was invariably offered to trekkers, many of whom were keen to have a pipe or two). These days, treks to the villages are organized by tour agencies or guesthouses – you'll find an abundance of both in trekking centres such as Louang Namtha (see p.210) and Muang Sing (see p.215). Despite the advent of organized trekking, Laos doesn't seem to be headed in the same direction as neighbouring Thailand, which is home to many of the same tribes and has been offering trekking packages to tourists for nearly two decades. By the late 1990s, many tribal villages in northern Thailand had pickup trucks and satellite dishes; in the absence of a tourism boom in Laos, the trekking experience here is still very pristine.

▲ Upland village, northern Laos

The Lahu

The **Lahu** inhabit areas of northwestern Laos, as well as Thailand and Burma. A branch of the Lahu tribe known as the Lahu Na, or Black Lahu, are known first and foremost for their hunting skills. Formerly they used crossbows but now manufacture their own muzzle-loading rifles which they use to hunt birds and rodents. Old American M1 carbines and Chinese-made Kalashnikov rifles are used to bring down larger game, and Lahu hunters are sometimes seen at the side of the road displaying a freshly bagged deer or boar for sale.

The Mien

The **Mien** are linguistically related to the Hmong and also immigrated into Laos from China, but their culture is much more Sinicized; the Mien use Chinese characters to write their documents and worship Taoist deities. Like the Hmong, they cultivate opium, which they trade for salt and other necessities that are not easily obtained at high elevations, and are known to be astute traders. It's estimated that nearly half the country's Mien population fled after the communist victory, eventually settling in the USA and France; today Xainyabouli province, northwest of Vientiane, has the largest population of Mien in Laos.

The costume of Mien women is perhaps Laos's most exotic, involving intricately embroidered pantaloons worn with a coat and turban of indigo blue. The most striking feature is a woolly red boa, attached to the collar and running down the front of their coat.

▼ Mien women wearing traditional red boas

The Akha

The Akha are another of the highlands' stunning dressers. They believe that art is more appropriately displayed on one's body, as opposed to hanging it on walls. Catching a first glimpse of the Akha women's distinctive headgear – covered with rows of silver baubles and coins – is surely one of the highlights of many a Lao visit.

Speakers of a Tibeto–Burman language, the Akha began migrating south from China's Yunnan province to escape the mayhem of the mid-nineteenth century Muslim Rebellion. This was followed by another exodus after the Chinese communist victory in 1949 and again during the Cultural Revolution. They now inhabit parts of Vietnam, Burma (Myanmar) and Thailand as well as Laos, where they are found mainly in Phongsali and Louang Namtha provinces.

▲ Akha weavers at work

▼ Spirit gate at the entrance to an Akha village

Akha villages are easily distinguished by the elaborate "spirit gate" leading into the village. This gate is hung with woven bamboo "stars" that block spirits, plus talismanic carvings of helicopters, aeroplanes and even grenades, as well as crude male and female effigies with exaggerated genitalia. The Akha are animists and, like the Hmong, rely on a village shaman and his rituals to help solve problems of health and fertility or provide protection against malevolent spirits. Chickens and pigs are sometimes sacrificed and chicken bones are utilized to divine the future. As with the Hmong and Mien, the Akha use opium to soothe the day's aches and pains, and some Akha also use massage to the same effect. The Akha raise dogs as pets as well as for food, but do not eat their own pets; dogs that will be slaughtered for their meat are bought or traded from another village.

The Akha are fond of singing and often do so while on long walks to the fields or while working. Some songs are specially sung for fieldwork but love ballads are also popular. There is even a sort of "Akha blues": songs about poor Akha villagers struggling through life while surrounded by rich neighbours.

little park on a hill in the centre of town. From here buses leave early in the morning for Louang Namtha, the Chinese border at Boten, Pakbeng, Muang Khua, Phongsali, Vientiane and Louang Phabang. Heading east towards Nong Khiaw, you may need to change vehicles in Pakmong, the last sawngthaew for which leaves mid-afternoon.

Lao Development **bank** is housed in an impressive two-storey house on a hilltop 500m north of the market. There's also a BCEL bank west of the bus station, opposite the Konica Express lab. Both banks exchange foreign currency and traveller's cheques, and accept Visa. Oudomxai's **Internet café**, which does Internet phone calls, is located by the hideous *Saliga Jiang Hotel* on the main street. For the road-weary, there's a Lao Red Cross **sauna** (daily 4–7pm; ℡081/312391) with traditional massage (20,000K per hour) and a herbal sauna (10,000K; bring a towel and sarong) located behind the stalag-like *Phouxay Hotel*.

Accommodation

There are many **hotels** in Oudomxai, but most are dirty and run-down, particularly those on the western side of the bus lot. Most of the newer guesthouses are found on the east side of the river on or just off the main road, but likewise most of them are badly built and poorly maintained. Furthermore, Oudomxai is a dirty-weekend town for mainland Chinese tourists, so many of the hotels here are involved in the sex trade. Since travellers from four directions all start converging on Oudomxai at about 3pm as their buses come in, it is desirable to secure a room at one of the better guesthouses immediately. If you can't get a room at the *Sinphet*, *Linda*, *Linda 2* or *Kongchai*, you'll find that all of the ten other places to stay between the bridge and Phou Xay Hill are in pretty much the same sad shape, with tatty, run-down rooms all going for about $4.

Fu Shan Hotel Just west of the Kaysone monument. Built with mainland Chinese money, the *Fu Shan* is a typical communist government-built hotel – a huge three-storey rectangle covered in bathroom tiles. Although it's the biggest hotel in town and boasts a lobby, a Chinese restaurant and a tacky nightclub, its main claim to being the top hotel in town is the presence of TVs in the rooms. Otherwise, the rooms are ordinary, run-down and very poor value. ❸

Kongchai Guesthouse At the east end of the football field, 20m north up the first alley east of the *Linda* ℡081/211141. The friendly *Kongchai* has simple, reasonably priced rooms with en-suite bathrooms and hot water. The rooms at the front of the building overlook the field and have views of the mountains. ❷

Linda Guesthouse East of the bridge ℡081/312147. Despite its ugly facade, the *Linda* has seventeen rooms which are on a par with the *Sinphet* in terms of decor and cleanliness (though slightly more expensive), as well as a few VIP rooms at the front which feature a/c and windows facing the street. ❷

Linda 2 Guesthouse North of Kaysone monument. Because it's relatively far from the eating places east of the river, this newer branch of the popular *Linda Guesthouse* is much more likely to have a

vacant room. The place itself is another ugly, block-shaped building, but inside the rooms are cleaner than usual for Oudomxai. ❷

Phouxay Hotel At the end of the lane along the west side of Phou Xay. This spooky government-run establishment must rate as one of Laos's most bizarre hotels. Set in a huge compound surrounded by a brick wall topped with barbed wire, the four brick barracks facing a courtyard would make a perfect location for a film about the cultural revolution. The ancient-looking rooms are mostly used by transiting civil servants and bureaucrats. ❶

Saliga Jiang Hotel Main street near the *Linda* ℡081/312468. This four-storey Chinese hotel covered in brown bathroom tiles is probably the best of a bad lot if you arrive too late and the *Lindas* are full. There's a Chinese restaurant downstairs, karaoke entertainment – and lots of Chinese working girls in and out of the lobby. ❸

Sinphet Guesthouse East of the bridge, before Phou Xay Hill ℡081/312324. Formerly the *Pholay* (and indeed the old sign is still up), this place is the pick of the bunch, a family-run concern in the old-fashioned Southeast Asian style with inexpensive rooms above and a good traveller's café below. Rooms have fan, en-suite bathroom and hot water. The catch is that there are only six rooms and they fill up very quickly. ❷

Eating

Oudomxai has plenty of **restaurants**, particularly Chinese-run places. The restaurant at the *Sinphet Guesthouse* is the best option, serving up good stir-fry dishes – try the pork fried in ginger and the pork fried with basil leaves – and passable European fare. It's also renowned for frozen yoghurt and great fruit smoothies. Three buildings west of the *Sinphet* is another traveller's café, *Keomoung Khoun*, which isn't as good as the *Sinphet* but does passable fried rice or noodles. Directly opposite just inside the alley is *Katya's Food & Drink Restaurant*, which is clean and worth trying. For dinner, the *Si Moang Restaurant* is one of the town's better-organized establishments, a big place with proper tables and seating in a large dining room. To find it, take the first alley on the right, east of the bridge, cutting through the barracks, then turn right at the T-junction and it's on the first corner. The *Misay*, about 400m north past the *Fu Shan Hotel*, is one of Oudomxai's longest-running eating places and worth the short hike. They serve Lao food only, in a comfortable dining room with good seating and an English menu.

Louang Namtha and around

Straddling Route 3, four hours' drive northwest of Oudomxai, **LOUANG NAMTHA** was heavily contested during Laos's civil war, which is to say that it was razed to the ground. Once the fighting stopped, the surrounding hills were stripped of their trees and the mammoth logs were trucked away to China. Today, the once devastated and depopulated valley is making a comeback as a booming tourist area with rafting, kayaking and trekking. Although the town itself supplies a host of good restaurants, hotels and tourist services, the real reason to come to Louang Namtha is to visit the **Nam Ha NBCA**, walk or cycle to nearby Hmong and Leten villages, take a trek in the hills, or go kayaking or rafting on the Nam Tha and Nam Ha rivers. Louang Namtha is also a launch base for passenger-boat trips down the Nam Tha River to Houayxai.

Arrival, transport and information

The **airport** and **boat jetty** are both located 7km south of the main town, down Route 3, while the **bus station** sits three streets west of the main street. Situated in a long valley sandwiched between mountain ranges, the town is

---

Trekking and boat trips

A trekking permit for the Nam Ha NBCA is supposed to be bought through the **Louang Namtha Guide Services Office** (GSO). Likewise, guides who have been approved by the GSO are also supposed to be used for treks in the province. In practice however, most visitors go through either the travel agency Green Discovery or the *Boat Landing Guesthouse* (listed on p.212), both of which are licensed by the GSO. The GSO itself (daily 8am–noon & 1–5pm; ☏086/211534) is located east of the dry market and post office.

For **kayaking** and **rafting** trips, visit the Green Discovery office (☏086/211484, ⓦwww.greendiscoverylaos.com) on the main street next door to Pla-Net Computer. Green Discovery offers a number of river packages on the Nam Tha and the Nam Ha rivers, ranging from one to three days and staying in tribal villages en route. Prices vary and are significantly cheaper when there are more people joining the tour, but you're generally looking at about $30 a day per person for two people.

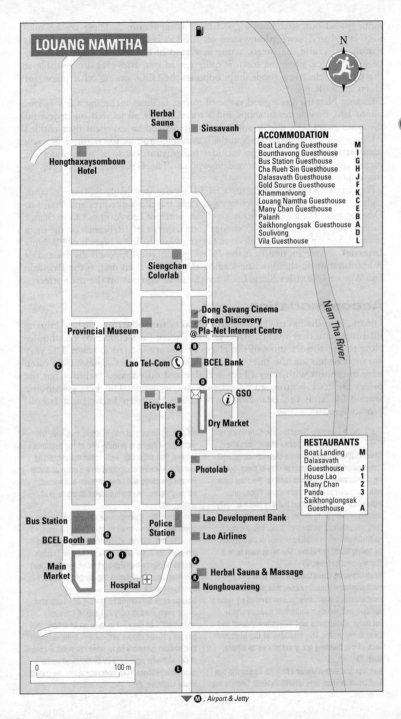

LOUANG NAMTHA

N

Herbal Sauna ■ ■ Sinsavanh ①

Hongthaxaysomboun Hotel

Siengchan Colorlab

Provincial Museum

Nam Tha River

■ Dong Savang Cinema
■ Green Discovery
@ Pla-Net Internet Centre

Ⓐ Ⓑ
Lao Tel-Com (☎) ■ BCEL Bank

Ⓒ Ⓓ

Bicycles ✉ (i) GSO
■ **Dry Market**

Ⓔ
②

Ⓕ ■ **Photolab**

③

Bus Station
BCEL Booth Ⓖ

Ⓗ Ⓘ

Main Market

Police Station

Hospital ✚

■ Lao Development Bank

■ Lao Airlines

Ⓙ
Ⓚ ■ Herbal Sauna & Massage
■ Nongbouavieng

Ⓛ

ACCOMMODATION	
Boat Landing Guesthouse	M
Bounthavong Guesthouse	I
Bus Station Guesthouse	G
Cha Rueh Sin Guesthouse	H
Dalasavath Guesthouse	J
Gold Source Guesthouse	F
Khammanivong	K
Louang Namtha Guesthouse	C
Many Chan Guesthouse	E
Palanh	B
Saikhonglongsak Guesthouse	A
Soulivong	D
Vila Guesthouse	L

RESTAURANTS	
Boat Landing	M
Dalasavath Guesthouse	J
House Lao	1
Many Chan	2
Panda	3
Saikhonglongsak Guesthouse	A

0   100 m

▼ Ⓜ , Airport & Jetty

quite spread out, stretching a good 6km along Route 3. There are no tuk-tuks, but shared **sawngthaews** are on hand at both the airport and the bus station and cruise the streets, acting as a kind of bus system; using them can be a good idea, since the town is quite spread out. **Bicycles** are available at the Chinese electrical goods shops opposite the GPO, among other places, for about 20,000K per day.

Louang Namtha has a good range of tourist facilities including a few colour photo labs, bicycle rental shops and a travel agency, all located on or just off the main street. The tourist authority has produced an excellent flyer entitled "Things to do in Louang Namtha", available around town or at ⓦwww .theboatlanding.com. The list includes information on local wats, waterfalls, picnic sites, handicraft coops and viewpoints. The GSO (see box, p.210) has free copies.

For currency **exchange** there's a BCEL service unit (daily 8.30am–3.30pm) right at the bus station, which accepts cash, traveller's cheques and Visa. Lao Development Bank on the main street just north of Lao Airlines can exchange foreign currency and traveller's cheques, and there's a BCEL branch on the main street almost opposite Lao Telecom. Louang Namtha has a branch of Pla-Net's **Internet** service located near the *Palanh* guesthouse. Opposite the Bureau of Administration in the dirt lane leading east off the main drag is the Paseutsin Lao Women's **Textiles** Shop. Look for the small sign out on the main street.

Accommodation

Louang Namtha has the best selection of **accommodation** north of Louang Phabang, with over twenty places to stay. Except for a couple of guesthouses close to the airport, most of the places to stay are located in town. The very cheapest hotels are the ones run by Chinese for other Chinese; they often have big rooms with several beds available and only shared facilities, but the prices are rock-bottom and foreigners are welcome. The best guesthouse around by far is the *Boat Landing*, which is northern Laos's most famous eco-style resort.

Boat Landing Guesthouse 6km south of the centre on the banks of the Nam Tha River ☎086/312398, ⓦwww.theboatlanding.com. Hands down the best place to stay in town, boasting comfortable bungalows right on the river bank, with hot-water en-suite bathrooms. Prices are higher than the competition but this place actually delivers – everything works and it's good value. They run officially sanctioned treks into the Nam Ha NBCA and are a reliable source of information for taking boats to Paktha. The restaurant here is also the best in town. ❻

Bounthavong Guesthouse Just east of the main market ☎086/312256, this is a well-run establishment with clean rooms divided by woven bamboo and wooden walls that deaden ambient noise. Bathrooms and toilets are shared and there is hot water. The verandas at the front and back of the building are good places to sit and read. ❷

Bus Station Guesthouse Entrance facing the bus field on its eastern side ☎086/211090. Despite the off-putting name and odd location, this new, ten-room guest house is actually one of the best deals in town. The attractive, well-constructed building is inside a walled compound so it's quite peaceful. Rooms are clean and have en-suite bathrooms, although there was no hot water at the time of writing. ❶

Cha Rueh Sin Guesthouse On the corner opposite the main market, this Chinese-run cheapie is a last resort; rooms are grubby and the staff are surly and speak no Lao or English. Rooms all share bathing and toilet facilities, and you may be able to halve the posted price of $2 by haggling. ❷

Dalasavath Guesthouse On the southern end of the main road ☎086/211299. A Chinese restaurant that decided to take on boarders, this has very rustic rooms with woven bamboo walls that should probably have been changed a couple of dry seasons ago; slightly better (and more expensive) rooms have concrete walls. All rooms share facilities. ❷

Gold Source Guesthouse One street west of the main road ☎086/211253. This quiet little establishment looks like a modern house; inside rooms are clean if smallish, some with en-suite bath and hot water. One room is a "suite", with a larger bed and bathroom. ❷

Khammanivong On the main road 50m south of Lao Airlines. Ten simple rooms with shared bathrooms in an attractive, new wooden house. All the rooms have wood floors, large windows and Lao textile quilts. There are hot showers and the rear balcony has mountain views. ❷

Louang Namtha Guesthouse Straight north up the road running along the west side of the bus field ☎086/312087. A work in progress, with a huge mansion, two nicely built thatched bungalows overlooking the pond out back and another concrete building under construction. Good value. ❷

Many Chan Guesthouse Main street, opposite the dry market ☎086/312209. Eight simple rooms on the second floor of a wooden house with toilets and hot shower below. The rooms are spartan but very clean. Run by the friendly and helpful Miss Manychan and her family, this is the favourite backpacker place in town, so it fills up very quickly. ❷

Palanh Main street directly opposite *Saikhonglongsak* ☎086/312439. The rooms here, some with shared bath, are about standard quality but slightly more expensive than average. ❷

Saikhonglongsak On the main street ☎086/212257. One of Louang Namtha's first restaurants, subsequently converted into a guesthouse. Rooms in this three-storey modern building have en-suite baths with hot water. Try to get a room at the back of the building if you are bothered by street noise. ❷

Soulivong On the corner one block east of the GPO ☎086/312253. This large, newish, three-storey house with a peaked blue roof has rooms with tile floors and en-suite bathrooms, and hot water in the evenings. The rooms on the second and third floors are the best. ❷

Vila Guesthouse On the main road 1km south of town at Km 2 ☎086/312425. If you're looking for something clean and modern in town and don't mind paying a bit more then this huge two-storey mansion is your best bet. There are nine rooms, seven with en-suite bathrooms, and an upstairs balcony with mountain views. Behind the main house is a smaller wooden house which has a charming restaurant (breakfast included). ❹

The Town and around

In the town itself, the only formal attraction is the **Louang Namtha Provincial Museum** (Mon–Fri 8.30am–noon & 1–3.30pm; 5000K), housed in a green-roofed building behind the Kaysone monument, where you'll find displays of traditional hill-tribe costumes and artefacts, a model depicting battles that took place in the area during the civil war and a rusty collection of weaponry.

The town boasts two traditional **Lao saunas**, one being the Luang Namtha Herbal Sauna, located just west of *House Lao* restaurant. The other is the Herbal Sauna & Massage, a fascinating affair in a traditional grass-roofed building on stilts. On the main road between the *Dalasavath* and *Khammanivong*, it's reached by a thirty-metre-long bamboo bridge. Both saunas are open daily from 4.30pm to 7.30pm, and charge around $1 for a sauna, $2 per hour for a massage.

The most straightforward **day-trip** consists of renting a bicycle and heading out for the surrounding villages. One good self-organized trip is to charter a tuk-tuk to take you up the road towards Na Toei, get off with your bicycle where the pavement ends 15km from town, and then coast all the way back down the mountain, a downhill run of about 8km back to the valley floor.

Eating

Louang Namtha's food scene has improved greatly since a few years ago, when it was all fried rice and noodle soups; these days there are travellers' cafés and even upmarket **restaurants**. Small food stalls with low tables and chairs sell pre-prepared satay, eggs, cold noodles and spring rolls outside the old Dong Savang cinema opposite the museum near the Pla-Net. Plenty of fŏe places are dotted around the bus lot and in the Morning Market.

Moving on from Louang Namtha

Sawngthaews for **Muang Sing** and **Oudomxai** leave from Louang Namtha's bus station. Travellers with a valid visa for **China** can take a Chinese-operated bus in the morning from here to the border crossing at Boten and on to Jinghong. Sawngthaews only go as far as the border. The trip down Route 3 to Houayxai is one of those dusty Lao journeys that are fast disappearing with the ongoing road-paving programme, but the road is still quite bad in parts. The route is plied by sawngthaews, taking between eight and ten hours ($8). During the dry season, passengers eat a lot of dust and during the monsoon season they get wet and the mire is sometimes barely passable. If the ride gets too much, there is basic lodging in the village of Vieng Phou Kha, 66km south of Louang Namtha. Once the upgrading of the road has been completed the journey should take under six hours.

The Nam Tha is navigable from about July until January, during which time travellers heading for **Houayxai** have the option of going by passenger boat. Unless you have unlimited time to wait around, it's most convenient to charter a boat outright ($140 pays for a boat that holds up to ten people). If the water levels are high it's a one-day trip, but if the water is low it takes one and a half days, with an overnight stop in Na Lae. Boatmen usually only go as far as Paktha, where the Nam Tha meets the Mekong. From there you get a speedboat for the last 36-kilometre stretch along the Mekong to Houayxai (1hr; 300 baht per person). It's very important to strike a clear deal with your boatman, as boatmen have been known to renegotiate the fare en route if they run into adverse conditions. Important questions to ask include whether the boat will be able to make the trip to Paktha or if a change of boat at Na Lae is necessary. The Guide Services Office in town has a very useful free flyer explaining the different possible routes and programmes you could negotiate, with approximate prices.

Boat Landing Restaurant *Boat Landing Guesthouse*. A great place to sample quality Lao food, with a wide choice of northern specialities such as *sa*, *aw lahm*, *moke* and a range of other dishes such as green pumpkin soup, tofu stuffed with green peppers and "rock algae chips" (*khai paen*, patties made with river moss). If you've made it all the way to Louang Namtha, don't miss this wonderful restaurant.

Dalasavath South of Lao Airlines. Belonging to the guesthouse of the same name, this restaurant is in a nice open *sala* surrounded by greenery, which gives it a bit of local atmosphere. There's good Asian and Western food and their beer garden is a great spot for drinks.

House Lao On the main street at the north end of town, opposite the *Sinsavanh Guesthouse*. This marvellous Lao-style restaurant is the flashest in town. Completely built of wood, it has a covered deck and there's a bar and a balustrade around the top. The location along the main drag is poor, but the atmosphere and the Lao specialities make it a top choice.

Many Chan Main street. The town's most popular travellers' café, with inexpensive tasty food including Western and Asian dishes and good coffee.

Panda Restaurant Just north of the bus station. Very cheap Western dishes and stir-fries out of a tiny shack, with plastic chairs and a sandwich board outside. Despite the odd location, the place gets rave reviews and does a roaring business most evenings. Most dishes under $1.

Saikhonglongsak On the main street. Like the *Many Chan*, this guesthouse has a very popular travellers' café at street level serving Western and Asian food. The coffee is the best in town and the owner is quite a humorous fellow.

Nam Ha NBCA

Established in 1993, the **Nam Ha NBCA** is one of Laos's most convenient and easily accessible conservation areas. Covering 1,470 square kilometres contiguous with the Xiang Yong Protected Area in Yunnan, China, the park straddles two high mountain chains and boasts two peaks in excess of 2000m. The

Trekking etiquette

While it is possible to organize trekking entirely on your own, if you arrange to be accompanied on your trek by a local who will act as a **guide** and **interpreter**, your experience will be greatly enhanced. Do-it-yourself trekkers often find that their visit to a hill-tribe village degenerates into an exercise of mutual gawking. A good guide will be able to explain customs and activities that you might otherwise find incomprehensible and can help you to interact with the hill folk, who may be unaccustomed to or apprehensive of outsiders. If you do decide to do a trek independently, using a bit of common sense and following a few rules should make for a smooth, memorable visit.

(1) Never trek alone. While Laos is a relatively safe country in terms of violent crime, there have been **robberies** of Western tourists in remote areas. Owing to the government's total control of the Lao media, word of these incidents is suppressed, making it impossible to ascertain just how much risk is involved in solo trekking. Encountering armed men while hiking through the woods does not necessarily mean you are going to be robbed, but it is best to treat all such encounters with caution. If you are approached by armed men and robbery is clearly their intent, do NOT resist.

(2) Most hill-tribe peoples are animists. **Offerings** to the spirits, often bits of food, left in what may seem like an odd place, should never be touched or tampered with.

(3) The Akha are known for the elaborate **gates** which they construct at the entrances to their villages. Far from being merely decorative, the gates are designed to demarcate the boundaries between the human and spirit worlds. It goes without saying that climbing onto such a gate to pose for a photograph is poor form.

(4) Many hill folk are willing to be **photographed**, but, just like everyone else, do not appreciate snap-and-run tactics. Old women, particularly of the Hmong and Mien tribes, are not always keen on having their picture taken. It's best to make it clear to a potential subject that you wish to photograph them and to gauge their response before taking a photo.

(5) Passing out sweets to village kids is a sure way to generate mobs of young beggars with rotten teeth. Likewise, the indiscriminate handing out of **medicine**, particularly antibiotics, does more harm than good. Unless you are a trained doctor, you should never attempt to administer medical care to hill people.

NBCA is an important biological habitat for many forest creatures, including 37 species of large mammals and 288 species of birds. The best-known of the park's rivers are the **Nam Ha** and the **Nam Tha**, both of which are developed for **kayaking** and **rafting** trips.

The park is accessible by car, with Route 3 crossing the NBCA in two separate places. Within the NBCA itself are some 25 **hill-tribe villages**, the most populous ethnic groups being Akha, Hmong, Khmu and Lantaen, and multi-day trekking tours between these settlements are also possible. More **information**, as well as bookings for organized tours within the NBCA, can be obtained through the Louang Namtha Guide Services Office, Green Discovery or the *Boat Landing Guesthouse* (see p.212).

Muang Sing and around

In a short space of time, **MUANG SING**, located some 60km northwest of Louang Namtha, has progressed from a quaint, middle-of-nowhere Tai Leu village to a talked-about-on-three-continents backpacker haven. Ten years ago,

△ Trekking in the Louang Namtha area

barely a trickle of travellers made it to Muang Sing, but since then its residents have opened dozens of guesthouses and restaurants to cater to tourists and trekkers in search of exotic **hill tribes** in traditional garb. The town is smaller and more compact than Louang Namtha and the people are friendlier. The valley is also prettier, and though the **trekking** industry is not yet as well organized, Muang Sing has over the last few years slowly emerged as the premier hill-tribe trekking destination in northern Laos.

Lying within the boundaries of the region known as the Golden Triangle, Muang Sing has a long connection with **opium**. During the late French colonial era, Muang Sing became an important collection point and way-station for the French colonial government's opium monopoly. In the post-colonial period and before the communist takeover, quantities of local opium found their way to RLA-controlled refineries near Houayxai. After the country reopened for tourism in the 1990s there was a big tourist rush into Muang Sing to "see it before it's spoiled". Some of these tourists came to seek out and experiment with opium smoking and for a brief period opium dens even reappeared, although these have been closed down by the authorities.

Today, while it's true that Muang Sing has a growing trekking industry and attracts increasing numbers of tourists, it is still an agreeable and friendly place, where great, sway-backed sows drag their teats down the main road and young novice monks play *kataw* and ride bicycles around the monastery grounds.

The Town and around

Muang Sing is pretty much a one-street town, although the dirt lanes running west of the main road have some quaint neighbourhoods. Tucked behind *Muangsing Guesthouse* is the town's principal **temple**, the ancient-looking Wat

Sing Jai, which has a wonderfully rustic *sim* painted in festive hues. The monastery is run by a young abbot and adherence to Buddhist precepts is surprisingly relaxed. If you come in the morning there's usually a lot of activity, mostly the village ladies coming to pray and make offerings.

On the corner of the main road, a few metres from the monastery's main entrance, stands a simple but elegant wooden structure, the former residence of a local lord, which has been converted into a **museum**. Unfortunately, museum hours vary and it is sometimes closed for days on end. If you are lucky enough to catch the museum while it's open (admission 5000K) you'll see local textiles, tribal costumes, folk utensils and some Buddha images.

Muang Sing's morning **market** is famous for its colourfully dressed vendors and shoppers, though nowadays camera-toting tourists almost outnumber the locals who are more likely to be wearing tracksuits and Nike knock-offs. If you want to take a photo of a vendor, it's only polite to buy something first and try to have a little conversation. The market convenes very early, just after sunrise, and the tribal vendors tend to have left by about 8am, though goods are on sale all day long. Most of the vendors with fixed stalls are Chinese traders from Yunnan who bring goods such as cooking oil, trainers, Western-style clothing and electrical and household goods from factories in China. Local ethnic peoples generally set up a small table and sell vegetables, fruits, herbs and spices. This connection, of Chinese lowlanders trading with the mountain peoples of the

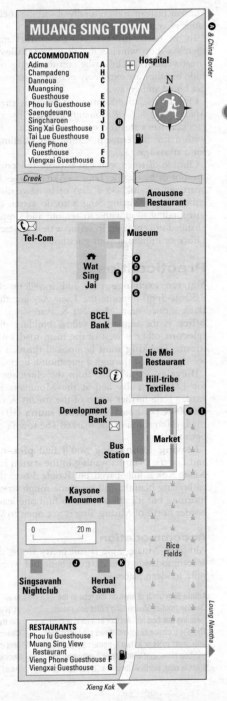

MUANG SING TOWN

A & China Border

N

ACCOMMODATION

Adima	A
Champadeng	H
Danneua	C
Muangsing Guesthouse	E
Phou Iu Guesthouse	K
Saengdeuang	B
Singcharoen	J
Sing Xai Guesthouse	I
Tai Lue Guesthouse	D
Vieng Phone Guesthouse	F
Viengxai Guesthouse	G

Hospital

Creek

Anousone Restaurant

Tel-Com

Museum

Wat Sing Jai

BCEL Bank

Jie Mei Restaurant

GSO

Hill-tribe Textiles

Lao Development Bank

Market

Bus Station

Kaysone Monument

0   20 m

Rice Fields

Singsavanh Nightclub

Herbal Sauna

Loung Namtha

RESTAURANTS

Phou Iu Guesthouse	K
Muang Sing View Restaurant	1
Vieng Phone Guesthouse	F
Viengxai Guesthouse	G

Xieng Kok

Yunnan Plateau and culturally absorbing them in the process, goes back thousands of years to the Han Dynasty.

To the north, just between the market and the *Jie Mei* Chinese restaurant, there's a shop which sells hill-tribe **textiles** and handbags. Many wandering street **vendors** in hill-tribe costume hang around the guesthouses; they aren't rude but they are extremely persistent, so practise your Lao with them till they get bored and go away.

One of the nicest things in town is the **herbal sauna** attached to the *Muang Sing View Restaurant*. Entered by a rickety bamboo bridge over a creek, it has a steam room connected to a big drum full of water and herbs with a fire underneath. Come out smelling like lemongrass soup, then go for a **massage** ($2).

Outside of town, you can explore the **countryside** and traditional villages on foot or by bicycle. Trips to Akha villages further afield can also be done by chartered tuk-tuk ($5 a day) or by sawngthaew. But the best way to see hill tribes around Muang Sing is to do a trek of one to three days through the surrounding mountains, to remote and unspoilt villages where life has barely changed in centuries. To set up a trek, contact the Muang Sing Guide Services Office or inquire at your guesthouse.

Practicalities

You can **exchange** cash and traveller's cheques at the BCEL (Mon–Sat 8.30am–3pm) opposite the *Vieng Xay* guesthouse, or at the Lao Development Bank service unit (Mon–Sat 8.30am–4pm) on the market square. The **post office** is the unmarked yellow building directly opposite the market. The **telecom** office is west of the main road, on the street running parallel to the stream. **Trekking** must be booked through the Guide Services Office (GSO; see opposite) or through a guesthouse licensed by them.

Bicycles are available from the *Anousone* restaurant opposite the museum for 12,000K a day and at the Mountain Tour postcard shop on the main road, a little further north of the stream. A very good traditional Lao massage (20,000K per hour) and **herbal sauna** (10,000K) can be found on the main road, 100m south of the market. The town's electricity is usually available from 6pm to 10pm.

Leaving Muang Sing, you'll find **pick-ups** to Muang Long, Xiang Kok and Louang Namtha waiting in the station in front of the market. The road to Xiang Kok is fully paved, but Route 3 over the mountains through the NBCA to Louang Namtha still has some rough stretches. Most vehicles depart in the morning but it's still possible to find one leaving at around 2pm. The Chinese border north of Muang Sing is not open to Westerners.

Accommodation

Although Muang Sing is still pretty rustic, the town now has a fair range of accommodation options, from basic old wooden buildings to comfortable en-suite modern places.

Adima 8km north of town on the road to the Chinese frontier. Muang Sing's first eco-resort, featuring bamboo architecture in a rural setting. There is a choice of rooms in two big bungalows with grass roofs or in two A-frame cabins. The bamboo restaurant with a deck overlooking the fields is nice, worth visiting even if you stay in town. You can get a free lift out to the resort daily at 10am from the *Vieng Xay Guesthouse*, which is run by the same family. ❷

Charmpadeng Northeast corner of the market. The best of the four budget hotels facing the market. Rooms 1, 2 and 3 on the second floor have terrific views over the rice fields towards the mountains. ❷

Danneua Main road just north of the *Muangsing Guesthouse*. It's in a very big, ugly concrete building, but the eight upstairs rooms are clean and modern and have en-suite bathrooms. There's a nice wide balcony overlooking the main drag. ❷

Muangsing Guesthouse Main street. This very friendly place, run by the Kumda family, is the backpacker favourite. In the newer, modern building behind the original guesthouse there are one- and two-bed rooms with shared bath. In winter they'll supply you with a thermos of hot water for bathing. The sitting area on the roof is also good for sunsets and there's a nice little coffee shop downstairs. The mother is a marvellous woman from Louang Phabang who speaks English, Thai and Mandarin. ❷

Phou Iu Main road south of market. The best-built hotel in town with spotlessly clean rooms with high ceilings, tile floors and modern bathrooms. Open less than a year, it's a steal at just over $5 and there's a clean, spacious restaurant downstairs. If you want something clean and modern this is the best option. ❷

Saengdeuang Main road 100m north of the museum. This well-constructed, two-storey building has eight rooms and a clean restaurant downstairs. But the real draw here are the two traditional thatched bungalows with wood-tile roofs out back. The bungalow rooms have wooden floors, big windows and en-suite bathrooms. ❷

Singcharoen West off the main road. Muang Sing's biggest tourist hotel, with 22 rooms aimed at package tour groups from France. Institutional and devoid of atmosphere, but if you need something clean and modern with an en-suite bathroom, this fits the bill. ❹

Sing Xai Guesthouse East of the market near the *Champadeng Guesthouse*, this rather plain establishment seems to attract the spillover from its more popular neighbour. The rooms here are spacious but empty, and noise tends to echo around. The shared bath and toilet facilities are just barely adequate. ❷

Tai Lue Guesthouse Main road, close to the *Muangsing Guesthouse*. This rather picturesque wooden building built in the Tai Leu style was the town's first and only hotel until the mid-1990s. The original rooms have been refurbished and are pleasingly rustic. There is a veranda along the second storey and the rooms that front it all share bath and toilet facilities. Newer concrete rooms at the back have en-suite facilities. Downstairs is a rather laid-back restaurant featuring the usual mixture of Chinese, Lao and travellers' fare. ❷

Vieng Phone Main road, close to the *Muangsing Guesthouse*. One of a handful of popular restaurants that decided there was money to be made by renting out rooms. As might be expected, the rooms are a bit of an afterthought, smallish and with shared toilet facilities. ❷

Vieng Xay Guesthouse Main road, close to the *Muangsing Guesthouse*. Yet another restaurant with a couple of rooms for rent upstairs. Rooms are small but clean, and toilet and bathing facilities are shared with the family who run the restaurant. ❷

Eating

Food is rather pricey in Muang Sing – your food expenses will easily exceed your room bill. The *Vieng Xay* and *Vieng Phone*, right next to each other on the main street, are the most popular travellers' cafés in town. The *Phou Iu Guesthouse* has the nicest sit-down restaurant and serves fresh fish brought in from fish farms in nearby China. The *Muang Sing View Restaurant* has a a big open *sala* made of bamboo, rattan, grass and wood with potted plants all around, and a superb view over the rice fields. There is one noisy **nightclub**, the karaoke-infested *Singsavanh*, near *Singcharoen Hotel*.

Villages and treks around Muang Sing

Muang Sing is located in the centre of a flat, triangular plain surrounded on all sides by high mountains. The Nam Youan River flows down to the plain from China, and numerous other streams water the valley. Scores of **hill-tribe settlements** are located both in the valley basin and all through the surrounding mountains; ethnic groups in the region include Tai Leu, Tai Dam, Akha, Mien, Hmong and others.

Until fairly recently, trekking around Muang Sing was a do-it-yourself venture using local youths as guides and hoping for the best. In 2002, however, the LNTA opened a **Guide Services Office** (GSO) in Muang Sing to establish some control over trekking in the area. This is by no means necessarily a negative development as the local townspeople had made very little progress towards developing a trekking industry on their own, and self-proclaimed "guides" were demanding as much as $40 a day without offering any kind of programme or even being able to speak English. Near the Lao Development Bank, the GSO gives out information about trekking as well as licensing official guides. It's a good idea to visit the office before attempting to go on a trek, just to suss out the current official policies.

The Akha Road (Route 322)

The road which links **Muang Sing** and **Xiang Kok** passes through one of Laos's most remote regions. While the peaceful scenery of forest-covered hills belies it, the history of this region is tied to the production of illicit drugs: opium, heroin and, more recently, methamphetamine. It is believed that most meth is produced in labs in neighbouring Myanmar, but smugglers use routes through Laos on their way south to Bangkok, a principal market and distribution point for the drug, which finds its way to discos and dance clubs all over Southeast Asia. Travellers are unlikely to see any indication of this activity from the road, though.

A brief history of opium

"Opium" – the word alone conjures up romantic images of the old Orient. Westerners' glamorization of the drug is based largely upon a thread of memory passed down from the age of European imperialism, when the empires of the British, French, Dutch and Portuguese were built partly upon encouraging and sustaining the opium habits of millions of Asians. In 1773, Britain's East India Company opened a Pandora's box of addiction by targeting China as a market for Indian opium, and by 1900 there were 13.5 million addicts in that country alone. By then, the Chinese were cultivating their own opium crop, and their appetite for the drug had spread to expatriate Chinese settlements throughout Southeast Asia as well as North America. The governments of Europe's colonies in Asia set up monopolies to regulate and tax opium consumption, which in turn enriched and strengthened Europe's grasp on the region.

Opium was introduced to Laos from two directions. Opium cultivation and use was known among **tribal peoples** such as the Hmong and Mien, who brought the poppy's seeds with them as they migrated south into Laos during the nineteenth century. Because the best parcels of arable land in Laos were already occupied by the lowland Lao and Tai Leu, the tribal immigrants were forced to live at high elevations. But the newly arrived tribals soon made an important discovery: opium poppies used up less of the soil's nutrients than other crops, reducing the frequency with which farmers had to perform the labour-intensive slash-and-burn technique. Growing opium and trading it for rice made their lives easier. By the early twentieth century, the **government of French Indochina** began encouraging the migration of Vietnamese and Chinese to Vientiane and the cities of southern Laos, primarily to stimulate trade, and opium addicts among these immigrants created a demand for the drug. Despite these subsequent developments, it is doubtful that the small amounts of opium grown in the hills of northern Laos ever reached the opium dens of the south. Indeed, the French opium monopoly, Opium Régie, suppressed cultivation of the poppy among the tribals in northern Laos in order to tax and control the supply of opium to the licensed dens of Indochina.

By the beginning of World War II, **taxes** on the sale of opium throughout French Indochina made up fifteen percent of the colonial government's revenues. When

While the Lao government has mundanely designated this 75-kilometre stretch of road **Route 322**, a more apt designation might be the **Akha Road**, given the high density of Akha villages through which it passes. The Akha of this isolated region have had little contact with the lowland Lao, and this is reflected in their dress. Indeed, the area is one of the few in Laos where you will see Akha men still wearing their traditional headgear: disc-shaped red turbans or tall hats festooned with seed-beads. The road is paved all the way and sawngthaews run in both directions early morning. The main stop between Muang Sing and Xiang Kok is **Muang Long**, long known as an excellent base for self-organized **trekking**.

Muang Long

MUANG LONG (also called Long) is an up-and-coming Tai Leu town surrounded by Akha and Hmong villages. If you're looking for good trekking in unspoilt areas and don't mind very basic food and facilities, then Muang Long is the place for you.

In town itself there are a few "sights". At dawn a parade of tribal peoples comes down from the hills to trade at the makeshift **market**. Besides the usual basketloads of peppers, tubers and gourds, villagers bring pieces of rare eaglewood which they gather from the dense forest. This resinous wood, used

global war disrupted the traditional maritime route of opium into Indochina, Opium Régie turned to the **Hmong** farmers. Past French attempts to deal with the Hmong on the issue of opium had been disastrous, leading to Hmong uprisings in the provinces of Houa Phan and Xiang Khouang. Their fear of provoking the obstinate Hmong led the French to select tribal leaders to act as brokers. The result was an 800 percent increase in Hmong opium production within four years. By the close of World War II, a weakened France had lost control of much of Laos to the Viet Minh and their protégés, the fledgling Pathet Lao. A rivalry formed between two powerful Hmong opium brokers and they took opposing sides, one supporting the colonialist French, the other the communists. The defeat of the French at Dien Bien Phu in 1954 put them out of the picture for good, but the Americans were soon to fill the vacuum.

America's efforts at combating the spread of communism in Southeast Asia created what has been termed a "Cold War opium boom". US involvement in the civil war in Vietnam escalated during the 1950s, leading to all-out intervention and the commitment of American troops in the 1960s. In Laos, a similar situation was occurring, but with a crucial difference. Instead of sending troops into "neutral" Laos, the US sought by unconventional means to preserve the illusion of non-intervention; CIA operatives trained the Hmong guerrillas who had previously sided with the French, using their cash crop to fund their operations. A Byzantine alliance between the Royal Lao Government, opium warlords and the CIA was formed. Utilizing its own fleet of "Air America" aircraft, the CIA coordinated the collection of opium, which was transported to refineries in the **Golden Triangle**, the resulting heroin eventually finding its way to markets all over the globe. By the war's end, the production of opium in the Golden Triangle, which overlaps into Myanmar and Thailand, had reached epic proportions.

Opium **eradication programmes** in Thailand have had much success in curtailing cultivation of the opium poppy there, and although Myanmar and Laos continue to grow opium, most experts agree that the once lucrative poppy crop has been largely replaced by the production of methamphetamine, which is in high demand in Bangkok and other urban centres in the region.

in Middle Eastern countries in the manufacture of perfumes and incense, is warehoused here before being shipped off to Bangkok, where it fetches astonishingly high prices at shops in the small Arab quarter off Bangkok's Sukhumvit Road. There's also a diminutive Tai Leu **stupa** resembling those found in China's Xishuangbanna region, which stands a few metres off Muang Long's main road. If you look closely at concrete tablets built into the stupa, you'll see examples of the Tai Leu script, which differs greatly from written Lao.

Pick-up trucks going in both directions stop on the main road in the morning before noon. Muang Long has a couple of basic **guesthouses**, the *Muang Long* (❷) and the two-storey, wooden *Sysengphet* (❷), both on the main road; a small "restaurant" downstairs from the *Sysengphet* does Lao food and sticky rice.

Around Muang Long

Muang Long lies in a flat narrow valley bottom, with the Nam Ma River flowing right down the valley to enter the Mekong at Xiang Kok. Two tributaries intersect the Nam Ma right at the junction of Muang Long: the Nam Dok Long flows down from the north while the larger Nam Louang River enters from deep in the mountains to the south. Together, the two **river valleys**, heavily populated with ethnic tribes, form corridors into the mountains north and south of Muang Long.

There are several easy areas to explore around Long, which can be done as **day-trips**. To the south of town, there's a new road under construction up the Nam Louang river valley, which will eventually cross the mountains to connect with Route 3 at Vieng Phoukha. If you follow this road up into the mountains there's a scenic waterfall and tribal villages. To the north of town is another road leading to Ban Jamai, which will eventually go all the way to Ban Chak Keun. Another option is to take Route 322 south towards Xiang Kok to the village of Somphammai where you then take a dirt road south into the mountains which leads to a number of **Akha villages**.

Another good location near Long is up Route 322 to the village of **Ban Cha Kham Ping** near Kilometre 35. This is the narrowest section of the Ma River valley and the steep mountains come right to the edge of the road. At Ban Cha Kham Ping there's some amazing pristine subtropical **rainforest** which, with a guide, would be well worth the effort of reaching. There's no guesthouse here, but a homestay should be possible if you can't get back to Long before dark. Regardless of what routes you take, if you do go for a do-it-yourself trek in this region, keep in mind that wandering around on remote trails in these mountains without a **guide** is foolhardy.

Xiang Kok and around

A rowdy frontier town on a remote stretch of the Mekong, **XIANG KOK** is the last river-town stop before China. The Upper Mekong scenery here is fantastic, the river narrow, fast and studded with islets of craggy stone, and the region's remoteness gives it a real wilderness feel. The local economy seems to be based on trade between Thailand and China and smuggling. Xiang Kok itself is ramshackle. There's a customs post, half a dozen guesthouses, a few shops and a brothel. Chinese cargo trucks transfer loads at the boat landing before heading back to China.

From Xiang Kok you can currently only travel **downriver**, but note that the boatmen, who know well that many travellers need to get down to Houayxai

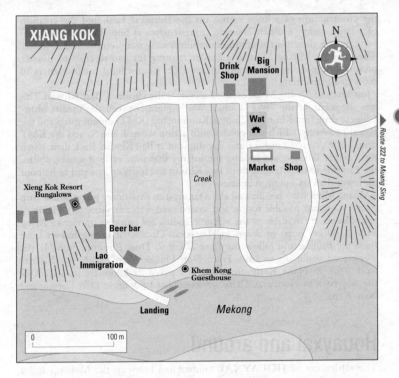

and exit into Thailand before their visas expire, have a reputation for extorting money from tourists. If you're unlucky and there are no other passengers, you may have to pay more than $100 to hire a boat outright. Note also that it's a good idea not to take a speedboat from Xiang Kok to Houayxai; these speedboats frequently crash and fatalities are all too common.

Most budget travellers **stay** at the *Khem Kong Guesthouse & Restaurant* (❷), near the customs office above the boat landing. The six double rooms here are passable and the toilet and (cold) shower facilities are shared. The best place in town is the *Xieng Kok Resort* (❷), on the embankment overlooking the river and landing. Built by a Thai investor, the resort has twelve comfortable, self-contained bungalows with en-suite bathrooms and charming balconies overlooking the Mekong. There are also a couple of dirty and dismal Chinese trucker hostels in town. Food can be ordered at all the guesthouses. Electricity in Xiang Kok is from private generators and generally available from dusk until 9pm.

Muang Mom

At the time of writing, **MUANG MOM** was the only Lao village on the Mekong between Xiang Kok and Houayxai with tourist accommodation. Located on a flat stretch on the river banks about an hour's trip north of Houayxai by speedboat, it is also the last town connected by road to Houayxai. There is really no reason to visit here unless you want to experience village life on the Mekong. A tiny place, Muang Mom slept through the aborted tourist boom which occurred during the late 1990s and saw the construction of a huge casino on the Burmese bank and the creation of a large, tacky "Golden Triangle" tourist town at Sop Ruak on the Thai bank, where dozens of shopping complexes now stand empty and deserted. Theoretically, Muang Mom is a border crossing for Lao to cross to Burma, presumably to go to the casino; in any case, it's not legal for foreigners to cross to Burma here.

Just south of Muang Mom on the Lao side is the village of **Ban Khwan**. This was the scene of the 1967 "Opium War" fought between the upstart Shan-Chinese drug lord Khun Sa, Chinese Kuomintang (KMT) opium gangs and the Royal Lao Army, which was goaded into action when Khun Sa and the KMT drug barons started a major three-day slug-out at Ban Khwan. Back then, when the Golden Triangle was gaining the infamy that now earns it tourist dollars, the Lao side of the Mekong from Ban Khwan to Houayxai was said to harbour no fewer than six opium refineries.

Muang Mom has a noodle stall and a family-run two-storey **guesthouse** with twelve basic but passable rooms and shared cold-water facilities (②). Plenty of **speedboats** are available at the village's landing for journeys upriver to Xiang Kok ($100 per boat) or down to Houayxai. Occasional **sawngthaews** leave from the landing and follow the river 20km to **Don Pheung**, probably the worst road you'll see in Laos. From Don Pheung there's fairly good gravel road 30km to **Nam Keng**, from where a paved 27-kilometre road leads all the way back to Houayxai. There are speedboat landings in Don Pheung and Nam Keng.

Houayxai and around

The settlement of **HOUAYXAI**, sandwiched between the Mekong and a range of hills, is a popular border crossing with Thailand and has long been an important crossroads for traders. Driving caravans of pack-ponies laden with tea, silk and opium, travelling Chinese merchants from Yunnan, known locally as "Jin Haw", would pass through Houayxai on their way south to Chiang Mai, and again on the return north with their loads of gold, silver and ivory. The old Jin Haw mule caravans became scarce after World War II, however, and had all but disappeared by the 1960s. Today, Chinese goods are still much in evidence, but exotic cargoes of silks and opium have been replaced by dirt-cheap hand tools and brittle plastic wares that are floated down the Mekong by the barge-load.

Most tourists hurry through Houayxai, either rushing through to Thailand at the end of their visas or entering from Chiang Khong but immediately heading downriver by slow boat. If time permits though, Houayxai is worth a day or two and makes a good base for day-trips to the nearby Bokeo **gem mines**.

The Town

Houayxai boasts only two proper "sights", one of which is best viewed from Chiang Khong across the river: the high, black walls of hilltop **Fort Carnot** (not open to visitors), once home to troops of the French Foreign Legion and now a barracks for the Lao army. Decidedly more friendly is **Wat Chom Khao Manilat**, also situated atop a hill. The gaudy modern *sim* is barely worth doing a lap around, but the adjacent, tall, Shan-style building, which was originally a *sim* but is now being used as a classroom for novice

Slow boats on the Mekong

Originally, the Mekong's **slow boats** (*heua sa*) were primarily for cargo and the occasional Lao passengers who relied on them for trade and transport in a part of Laos where roads are sometimes impassable. Since the Lao government eased travel restrictions allowing foreigners to ride these antiquated diesel-powered boats, thousands of tourists have made the two-day journey between Houayxai and **Louang Phabang**, stopping overnight at the village of **Pakbeng**. The boats run in both directions (downriver is the journey most tourists do) and there are many other private vessels leased by tour companies that do the same trip but won't pick up individual travellers. You'd be foolish to risk your life travelling the river in one of the **speedboats** (*heua wai*) which also make the journey from Houayxai to Pakbeng and Louang Phabang (6hr); crash helmets and life-vests are supposed to be provided, but don't forget to bring earplugs.

Despite the popularity of the trip with tourists and the huge amount of money being generated, almost no concessions were originally made towards their comfort, save for ticket booths at each end of the journey. But these days, as a result of overcrowding on the boats and other problems, special tourist boats have been launched with proper seating, a toilet and other comforts. If this isn't your cup of tea, it is still possible to take one of the old cargo boats, though your chances of securing passage will be greatly enhanced if you can speak Lao.

Most travellers agree that the journey is one of those once-in-a-lifetime experiences. The riverbanks along the Mekong are sparsely populated, though the forest is not as pristine as one might imagine. Logging and decades of slash-and-burn agriculture have left their mark, and, on the more accessible slopes and summits, trees have been supplanted by rows of corn stalks and banana trees. Of as much interest are the glimpses into local **village life**. Fisher-folk utilizing bamboo fish-traps and prospectors panning for gold can be seen among the sandbars and jagged rocks that make this stretch of the Mekong a treacherous obstacle course. Along the way, boats often call briefly at tiny villages situated at confluences, and the villagers take the opportunity to hawk fish, game and other local products to passengers and crew. If you want to help these rural people, buy something from them – even if it's only a bunch of bananas.

The slow-boat **fare** from Houayxai is $9 to Pakbeng or $18 to Louang Phabang, payable in Thai baht, dollars or kip; speedboats charge $15 and $30 respectively. Bring along food and bottled water, as none is available on board. It's important to arrive at the landings as early as possible in order to secure a boat. If there are no other passengers, it may be necessary to hire the boat outright.

monks, is made of picturesquely weathered teak. Behind the modern *sim* is a collection of *heuan pha*, literally "cloth houses", built to store belongings of the dead. Originally, these homes for the spirits were fashioned from cloth or mulberry paper, but nowadays many are constructed from plywood – a practice unique to parts of northern Laos and northern Thailand. The top of the stairway leading up to the monastery from Houayxai's main road is a perfect place to watch the sun set. Other wats in town include Wat Keo Phonsavan Thanarom and Wat Khon Keo.

A handful of shops in town by the ferry crossing offer cut **gemstones** with wide and simple facets. Unlike in Thailand, where most Lao gems are eventually marketed, the gem merchants of Houayxai have so far not succumbed to hard-sell tactics. Prospective buyers can spend time fingering stones and chatting with the merchants and then walk away without making a purchase, and this is probably what you should do unless you are an expert and can

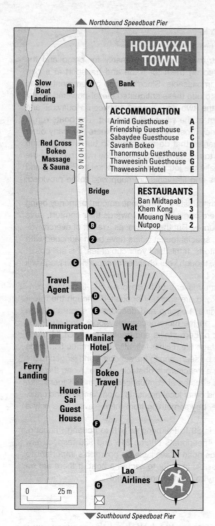

▲ Northbound Speedboat Pier

HOUAYXAI TOWN

Slow Boat Landing

🅐 Bank

ACCOMMODATION
Arimid Guesthouse	A
Friendship Guesthouse	F
Sabaydee Guesthouse	C
Savanh Bokeo	D
Thanormsub Guesthouse	B
Thaweesinh Guesthouse	G
Thaweesinh Hotel	E

Red Cross Bokeo Massage & Sauna

KHAMKHONG

Bridge

RESTAURANTS
Ban Midtapab	1
Khem Kong	3
Mouang Neua	4
Nutpop	2

Travel Agent

Immigration

Wat

Manilat Hotel

Ferry Landing

Bokeo Travel

Houei Sai Guest House

Lao Airlines

N

0   25 m

▼ Southbound Speedboat Pier

discern quality stones from inferior ones.

Houayxai has a traditional Lao **herbal sauna** (daily 5–9pm; sauna 10,000K for 3hr, massage 25,000K per hr) run by the Red Cross in Bokeo. It's located opposite the Agriculture Forest Office, just past the wooden bridge as you go north up the main road.

Practicalities

For travellers crossing over from Thailand's north, Houayxai is their first taste of Laos, an experience that usually begins in **Chiang Khong**, just across the river in Thailand, where you can absorb the sights and sounds of Houayxai from over the sluggish brown river. Houayxai's immigration station and **ferry pier** are directly opposite Chiang Khong's pier, which also has an immigration post. Arriving in Houayxai from Thailand, make absolutely sure that you go through Lao immigration formalities and have your passport **stamped**. A number of travellers have reported that the Lao authorities are purposely not stamping the passports of incoming visitors, who don't realize it until they arrive in Louang Phabang, where the authorities give them a choice of going back to Houayxai to get their passports stamped, or paying a hefty fine – usually $100. Aside from boat traffic up and down the Mekong, **sawngthaews** and **buses** arrive daily from Louang Namtha. Houayxai's only **Internet** shop is next door to the *Savanh Bokeo*.

Accommodation

In the not-too-distant past Houayxai underwent an **accommodation** boom and there are now a dozen places to stay, all on or just off the main road (Khamkhong Road). Unfortunately there aren't any really quaint family-run guesthouses here, most places to stay being modern Thai-style establishments.

Arimid Guesthouse On its own small lane running between the main road and bank, north of the slow-boat landing and opposite the petrol station. A collection of a dozen thatched cottages, quite pleasant if a bit squeezed together, with en-suite bathrooms and hot water. The restaurant is one of the nicest in town. If you're looking for something a bit more Lao flavour, or are planning on staying in Houayxai a few days, this is a good spot to be. ❷

Moving on from Houayxai

Travellers arriving in Houayxai can strike up or down the Mekong by boat, or bus overland up Route 3 to **Louang Namtha**. Those exiting Laos here can obtain a thirty-day visa on arrival from Thai immigration (daily 8am–5.30pm) in Chiang Khong on the Thai side. From Chiang Khong, there are direct buses to Chiang Rai or Chiang Mai. Boats shuttle you across the river in a minute for 20 baht.

Houayxai has three different boat piers, two for speedboats and one for slow boats, approximately 500m north of the ferry pier. **Slow boats** leave every morning about 9am for Louang Phabang. The southbound speedboat pier is located at Ban Tin That, 2km downriver; speedboats going upriver to Xiang Kok leave from the northbound speedboat pier at Nam Keng, a ridiculous 27km north of town by a paved road (the sawngthaew fare there is 15,000K) which continues through Don Pheung (57km from Houayxai) and Muang Mom (77km), both of which also have speedboat landings. Note that there is no regular service for Xiang Kok ($12 per person), so you just have to take your chances or hire your own boat. Nam Keng has clothing shops and noodle stands but no accommodation.

It's possible to take a daily **truck** up Route 3 all the way to Louang Namtha (8hr), but this is a tough trip as stretches of the road are unpaved and very dusty (or muddy). This journey can be broken at Vieng Phoukha, 66km short of Louang Namtha, where there is one basic guesthouse, the *Phongsavath* (❷).

Friendship Guesthouse 50m south of the ferry landing ☎084/211219. A multistorey modern place almost identical to the *Thaweesinh* in price, standard and appearance. They have a huge roof from where you can enjoy the sunset over the Mekong. Good value. ❸

Sabaydee Guesthouse North of the ferry landing. This modern, new hotel boasts spotlessly clean rooms featuring tiled en-suite bathrooms. The four back corner units offer terrific views of the Mekong. The best deal in town. ❷

Savanh Bokeo North of the ferry landing. About the cheapest deal in town, with large two-, three- and four-bed rooms and shared facilities in a nice old wooden house. ❷

Thanormsub Guesthouse North of the ferry landing ☎084/211095. This blue-roofed house is a newish establishment whose central passage leads to fourteen very clean, tiled rooms with en-suite bathrooms and hot water. There are no views here but five corner rooms have windows on two sides. Three rooms are also available with a/c. Very good value. ❸

Thaweesinh Hotel Main road north of the ferry ☎021/211502. This four-storey, concrete building may not have much Lao ambience but it's clean and modern, with a nice rooftop patio, and is popular with group tours coming across from Thailand. There's a wide selection of rooms, ranging from windowless singles ($2) to a/c doubles with TV ($8). All rooms have tiled floors and en-suite bathrooms. *Thaweesinh* also has a cheaper guesthouse of the same name next to the post office. ❸

Eating

The *Mouang Neua* **restaurant** opposite the *Thaweesinh Hotel* specializes in tourist fare and has an English-language menu; the vegetable omelette is a must. Rustic *Nutpop*, near *Thanormsub Guesthouse*, does stir-fry dishes, cold beer and fruit smoothies in an outdoor setting, while nearby, *Ban Midtapab* offers excellent fish and views across the Mekong. The restaurant at the *Arimid Guesthouse*, opposite the bank at the north end of town, is quite good and is a comfortable place to sit and relax. There are also riverside restaurants overlooking both the ferry landing and the slowboat landing, the best of which is the one just down the path to the former. Just down the path to the ferry landing is the *Khem Kong Mekong Riverside*, which has a nice view of the river and specializes in – what else – Mekong river fish.

Around Houayxai: the Bokeo gem mines

While not as well known as Mogok in Burma or Pailin in Cambodia, the **gem mines** of Bokeo province are said by some to be just as rich. Indeed, the name of the province – "baw kaew" – actually means "gem mine", and locals claim that when it rains hard, the sapphires wash right out of the hills.

Deposits of corundum (the crystalline form of aluminium oxide, the substance which rubies and sapphires are made of) are plentiful around Houayxai and, when not working their rice fields, farmers take to the gem fields, digging shallow pits into the red earth until the yearly monsoon fills their excavations with rainwater. In 1996, a Danish firm won a contract from the Lao government to mine a 72-square-kilometre tract of land near Houayxai for twenty years. Once the operation was up and running a few years later, the Lao government took over the mine and deported or jailed the foreigners. The mine is fenced off and closed to casual visitors, but watching the antics of part-time prospectors, who have turned the land surrounding the mine into a cratered moonscape, is an interesting half-day diversion.

You can make the half-hour ride to the gem fields by tuk-tuk for a few dollars per person. Bokeo Travel, across from the *Houei Sai Hotel*, can arrange a trip there by Land Rover for about $20 for half a day. The trip is sometimes combined with a visit to one of the primitive **gem–cutting factories** on the outskirts of town. These small-scale operations depend on part-time prospectors for their supply of rough gemstones, and all but shut down during the rainy season.

Pakbeng and around

The bustling, frontier river port of **PAKBENG** is the halfway point between Houayxai and Louang Phabang, and the only sizeable town or roadhead along the 300-kilometre stretch of river between them. As slow boats don't travel the

THE FAR NORTH | Pakbeng and around

△ Slow boats at Pakbeng

228

Mekong after dark, a night here is unavoidable if you're travelling this way – a taste of backcountry Laos complete with hill tribes and rustic accommodation. As you stumble off the slow boat at the end of a long day, the ramshackle settlement of wood-scrap, corrugated tin and hand-painted signs that constitutes the port area can be a bit of a culture shock. Since Pakbeng is many travellers' first night in Laos, the expression on a lot of faces is one of "What have I got myself into?". Don't worry: Pakbeng is typical of the northern backwoods only, and provided you don't miss your morning boat you'll be sipping lattes in Louang Phabang in no time.

The Town

Although first impressions of the town are generally unfavourable, Pakbeng is actually a very interesting place. Once extremely poor, it is now growing rapidly, with even a few big mansions going up. The town's change of fortune is due to its role as an important **trading post**; goods from Thailand come down the river from Houayxai and then make their way up into the interior from here. Tourism has also been a big boon for the town, with the slow boats alone disgorging up to a hundred hungry backpackers a day.

Since most tourists to Pakbeng come by slow boat, arriving late and leaving early, many people think the port area around the landing is Pakbeng. In fact, the real town lies past the top of the hill and stretches for a good kilometre along the main road that follows the Mekong before turning north to Muang Beng and Oudomxai. The town is well worth a wander and has a couple of pleasant **wats** overlooking the Mekong. There's no accommodation or restaurants in the old town, although you will find a few noodle ladies and some stalls selling sausages and sticky rice. Along the only street are a shop selling hand-beaten silver jewellery and the "UN Harmony Income Generation Project" – a shack selling handicrafts and nicely made local clothes and purses under the slogan "Be Lao, Buy Lao".

The small **market** is located right at the top of the landing road past the *Donevilasak* where the road turns sharply right towards the town proper. There's not a lot happening here but it's worth visiting and there are some *fŏe* stalls. The market convenes every morning and goes most of the day, and is frequented by Hmong women and children, although it appears that traditional dress has gone out of fashion among the Hmong in this vicinity. Heading out of town in either direction will quickly take you to very poor,

PAKBENG PORT

Market

N

RESTAURANTS
Bounmy   3
Dokkhoune   1
Pinekham   2
Souksakkhong   4

ACCOMMODATION
Bounmy Guesthouse D
Donevilasak   A
Luang Say   C
Sarika   B

Ticket Booth

Floating Speedboat Shed

0   25 m

traditional villages where you'll soon be the centre of attention. The road towards the resort takes you to just such a village in no time.

Pakbeng does not yet have any trekking or organized outdoor-adventure tours but this doesn't mean there's nothing to do in the area. The owner of the *Bounmy* guesthouse can organize various activities on request, including fishing trips on the Mekong, boat trips to villages and guides for walks to the surrounding tribal villages and forests.

Practicalities

Slow boats stop at the landing at the bottom of the port road. **Speedboats** pull up to the floating speedboat shed which, for some reason, is well away from the concrete steps up the embankment, forcing arrivals to climb the muddy hillside. **Sawngthaews** from Oudomxai stop first in Pakbeng town and then down at the port area.

The town has a lot of small **shops** selling imported foods and household products, since it's an important distribution centre for the interior. There are also several pharmacies. Electricity in Pakbeng is by generator from 6pm until 10pm.

Accommodation

Once the boat pulls in, don't waste any time securing a **room**. From the landing, the majority of guesthouses are just up the hill well before the town itself. They're all pretty much the same: a very basic wooden room with a bed, mosquito net and a fan, and with shared cold-water bathrooms out back.

Bounmy Guesthouse Turn left from the boat landing and walk about 200m. The only guesthouse not on the main road, this comprises three big houses right next to the Mekong. At the time of writing, the owner was replacing the original buildings with better two-storey concrete and wood houses. The newly rebuilt unit has eleven tiled rooms with en-suite bathrooms. There are still cheaper basic rooms with shared facilities in the original buildings and a nice open restaurant with a two-tier deck over the Mekong. ❸

Donevilasak The last place at the top of the hill, this has the benefit of being a real house rather than just something that was thrown up in a hurry during the tourist boom. Rooms are small but clean; facilities are shared. ❷

Luang Say About 800m down the road running west from the landing. The most luxurious place in these parts, with eighteen luxury Lao-style bungalows, featuring all mod-cons including hot water. On stilts, the bungalows are connected by a beautifully built covered walkway which leads

Moving on from Pakbeng

If you're continuing to **Louang Phabang** or **Houayxai** by **slow boat** (see p.225), be down at the landing before 8am to avoid being left behind. Going downriver, some captains stop briefly at the caves at **Pak Ou** (see p.168) before Louang Phabang, charging each passenger who disembarks a couple of thousand kip extra. If you're up for it, this does work out cheaper than chartering a boat from Louang Phabang, but leaves little time for exploring.

Speedboats leave to go up and down the river throughout the morning. There's a government-run ticket booth above the boat landing that controls all the traffic, so it's impossible to bargain your own deal with the boat drivers, as much as they'd be willing. The foreigners' speedboat fare is $12 to either Louang Phabang or Houayxai.

Sawngthaews up Route 2 to Muang Houn, Muang Beng and Oudomxai leave from outside the *Sarika* between 7am and 9am, depending on how many passengers they have.

to the reception. The resort even has its own boat pier and fancy restaurant with uniformed staff. And you thought this was the middle of nowhere. ⑧

Sarika A big three-storey concrete building right above the landing. This is the largest

guesthouse in town, with fifteen rooms, all with cold-water en-suite bathrooms. It's aimed at package groups and rather overpriced; you can't bargain a discount, even when they are empty. ④

Eating

Because of the fierce competition, many of Pakbeng's **restaurants** now boast tablecloths and even candles, although the most you can expect in these parts is just a decent stir-fry. The best places are on the eastern side of the street and have Mekong views. *Dokkhoune*, *Pinekham* and *Souksakkhong* are all pleasant, and the *Bounmy* across the street has a bit of candle-lit atmosphere. The restaurant at the *Sarika* is the most formal and has a big balcony overlooking the river. The best option is out at the *Luang Say*, which features an outdoor patio bar with a view of the Mekong, a great place for a sundowner. In the morning, makers of takeaway submarine sandwiches line the road down to the boat landing (the *Pinekham* restaurant also does good takeaway sandwiches).

Route 2: Pakbeng to Oudomxai

Trucks up and down the Nam Beng river valley between Pakbeng and Oudomxai run daily between 8am and 9am, leaving from the foot of the hill. The journey along the 150-kilometre-long wreck of a road, which passes through Hmong and Tai Leu villages, takes about eight hours. There are two very basic guesthouses in **MUANG HOUN**, a small town 52km north of Pakbeng known for its textiles. The inhabitants, perhaps descendants of Tai Yuan who migrated here from what is now northern Thailand, continue to weave in a style that looks remarkably like that of old Chiang Mai. During the Seventies, Muang Houn was the site of a military base that trained and indoctrinated disenfranchised Thai students who would later return to Thailand and take part in the communist insurgency in "red zone" frontier provinces such as Loei and Nan. Muang Houn may only have very basic accommodation and food, but it can serve as an off-the-beaten-track basecamp for self-organized trekking.

The Nam Ou River Valley

After a few days of lounging in Louang Phabang's French bistros, sipping imported wine and munching on watercress salad, it's easy to forget that there are places relatively near which offer very little in the way of creature comforts, no matter how many kip you are willing to spend. The **Nam Ou River**, which starts on the China border, drains all of Phongsali province and flows down through western Louang Phabang province to meet the Mekong above Louang Phabang, is just such a place. Much of the Phongsali province watershed is devoid of roads and still well covered with old-growth forests, and the river and its many tributaries remain in many ways as they were when nineteenth-century French explorers passed through.

An important Mekong tributary, the Nam Ou holds a cherished place in Lao lore as the original route followed by Louang Phabang's founding father, Khun Lo, and later by Fa Ngum, the warrior-king, as he headed towards Louang Phabang to claim the throne and found the Kingdom of a Million Elephants. The river begins its journey in the southern flanks of the mountains separating Laos and Yunnan in China. This northernmost part of Laos, Phongsali province,

Slow boats on the Nam Ou

Every rainy season, transport slows to a crawl in the northern province of Phongsali, which is why its rivers are still widely plied by small boats. Take one of the boats on the **Nam Ou** and the descriptions of nineteenth-century French explorers spring to life from the pages of their journals. For many people, the inconvenience and unpredictability of the journey are more than made up for by the pristine beauty of the land and the hospitality of the people who inhabit it.

The southern leg of the journey is the six-hour ride between Louang Phabang and **Nong Khiaw** which is wildly scenic, especially the karst forests around Nong Khiaw and Muang Ngoi. Closer to Louang Phabang, where the river follows Route 13, extensive logging and slash-and-burn agriculture have stripped the surrounding mountains: only where the slopes are too rocky or too steep for cultivation have stands of forest been left intact. In an effort at reforestation, however, rows of young teak trees, recognizable by their enormous leaves, have been planted. After the road leaves the river, the scenery takes a turn for the spectacular, with vertical limestone peaks and pristine little white-sand beaches.

Upriver from Nong Khiaw the scenery continues to impress, possibly even surpassing that of the stretch below Nong Khiaw, the river snaking through impenetrable jungle. Because many of the surrounding mountains are simply too steep for slash-and-burn agriculture, the forests have been left virtually untouched. When the river is not too high and fast, this leg is also blessed with shelves of squeaky-clean beach, perfect for taking a lazy swim and admiring the dramatic scenery. However, this primeval landscape lasts only a third of the distance to **Muang Khoua** and is then replaced by arable hills with a beaten, domesticated air about them. The journey between Nong Khiaw and Muang Khoua takes approximately five hours.

Beyond Muang Khoua, it's another 100km to **Hat Sa**, the last town of any size on the Nam Ou until U Thai, far to the northeast. The mountainous scenery on the Muang Khoua–Hat Sa leg doesn't rival the stretch of river on either side of Nong Khiaw, the slopes having long ago been cleared, cultivated and left fallow. Though gracefully drooping thickets of bamboo have replaced the old-growth forest, here and there a solitary behemoth survives, conveying some idea of the majestic heights that the now-vanished canopy must once have reached.

Passenger boats continuing up the Nam Ou River beyond Hat Sa are few and far between, but it is possible to charter a boat to explore Laos's northernmost corner. The going price for an all-day boat trip shouldn't be more than $50. North of Hat Sa there's no formal accommodation but it should be possible to find lodging in villages.

is hemmed in by high mountains on three sides, and the Nam Ou is joined by no less than eight major tributaries before entering Louang Phabang province and beginning its final run down to the Mekong. Two of these tributaries, the Nam Khang and the Nam Houn, pass within the huge **Phou Den Din NBCA**, along the border with Vietnam. The main city of the upper Nam Ou is **Phongsali**, the provincial capital. To the east, **Hat Sa** effectively acts as Phongsali's river port on the Nam Ou. The other two important towns on the Nam Ou are Muang Khoua and Nong Khiaw: **Muang Khoua** sits astride the river where **Route 4** continues from Oudomxai to Dien Bien Phu, Vietnam, while **Nong Khiaw** is located where **Route 1** crosses the river on its way from Oudomxai to Phan province in the extreme northeast. All of these towns have tourist accommodation and can be reached by road or by boat along the Nam Ou.

The **Phongsali Loop** is a popular travellers' route starting and ending at either Louang Phabang or Oudomxai, and involving a combination of river travel on the Nam Ou and tough road travel between Phongsali and Oudomxai. Many travellers do the first part of the loop as far as Phongsali by boat up the Nam Ou from Louang Phabang, taking in Nong Khiaw, Muang Khoua, Muang Ngoi and Hat Sa en route, and then do the return portion by road (the account below follows this sequence). You can shorten the loop by exiting at either Nong Khiaw or Muang Khoua, both of which have daily sawngthaews to Oudomxai. More than a few people never even finish the loop, deciding that the boat journey up the Nam Ou to Hat Sa is so beautiful that they want to return the same way.

Pakmong and Nam Bak

The road route from Louang Phabang to Nong Khiaw takes about two and a half hours. Well-maintained Route 13 takes you north out of Louang Phabang, hugging the Nam Ou for much of the way. Over halfway along, the road veers away from the river and into a wide valley, passing through **Hmong villages** whose inhabitants have been resettled here from the highlands by the Lao government in an ongoing programme to control and assimilate them. The majority of villages along this stretch are located far from the road, but periodic glimpses of the people who inhabit them reveal something about the labour-intensive lives they lead. When not engaged in cultivating their teetering hilltop gardens, the highlanders spend daylight hours hunting and gathering in the forest. Women carry firewood using ingeniously designed back-pack baskets fitted with a wooden yoke and head-strap to distribute the weight, and almost every male above the age of 15 can be seen shouldering a firearm of some sort, long-barrelled muzzle-loading rifles and the occasional M1 carbine.

Straddling the junction of Route 1 and Route 13, **PAKMONG** roughly separates the northeast from the northwest. There's no reason to stay in Pakmong, but it's a key spot for bus and sawngthaew transfers – whether you're headed northwest to Oudomxai, east to Viang Thong or south to Louang Phabang.

Like Pakmong, the quiet settlement of **NAM BAK**, situated in the Nam Bak river valley just a fifteen-minute drive east from the Pakmong junction, loses out to the much more dramatic scenery of its neighbour, Nong Khiaw, further downriver. Despite the fact most travellers head straight for Nong Khiaw or Muang Ngoi, three guesthouses line the road – all basic, two-storey buildings. Handiest for the market and onward transport is the *Vanmisay* (❷), with a handful of cramped but clean rooms up a creaky flight of steps where you see a small balcony overlooking the road; the bathroom and basic bathing facilities are around the back. A noodle and coffee shop sits across from the dusty market, where you'll also find the queue for Nong Khiaw-bound sawngthaews. From here it's a quick, thirty-minute ride to Nong Khiaw, via pretty villages with shaggy thatch-roofed houses surrounded by all manner of fruit trees.

Nong Khiaw

Resting at the foot of a striking red-faced cliff, amid towering blue-green limestone escarpments, the dusty town of **NONG KHIAW** on the banks of the Nam Ou River lies smack in the middle of some of the most dramatic scenery in Indochina. Unfortunately local entrepreneurs were slow to realize that there was money to be made from the backpackers who use the town as a hub, and in the meantime Muang Ngoi, which is even more scenic, was "discovered". Now few people stay here except for those pressing up the Nam Ou.

Though there's very little to see in the town itself, Nong Khiaw makes a good base for **day-trips** in the scenic surrounding countryside. Aside from day-trips to Muang Ngoi, there's a cave just 1km to the east along Route 1 which has a big staircase leading up to the entrance (1000K). There are also hill-tribe villages in the area, including Khamu settlements, but to reach these you need a local guide.

Practicalities

Although the old town stretches a kilometre along a dirt road parallel to Route 1, all of Nong Khiaw's tourist facilities are located by the big bridge over the Nam Ou. Here, at the western end of the bridge, you'll find the boat mooring, the bus lot and most of the guesthouses and restaurants. At the eastern end of the bridge on the opposite bank is **Ban Lao**, a village of about two dozen homes that also has a couple of guesthouses and a very popular tourist restaurant. From the western side of the bridge, walking south down the main street takes you west through the old town, its dirt street lined with dusty old wooden buildings, until you emerge back on Route 1 about 2km west of the bridge.

The most scenic route to Nong Khiaw is the six-hour boat trip up the Nam Ou from Louang Phabang, but since most locals now prefer to travel to Nong Khiaw by road (on Route 13), catching a passenger **boat** on the Nam Ou isn't as easy (or cheap) as it used to be. The best method is get a group of fellow travellers together and hire a passenger boat ($80 for ten people). Passenger boats going up river to Muang Ngoi (1hr) and Muang Khoua (5hr) also leave from the landing. As for road transport, there are frequent departures to **Pakmong**, but sawngthaews headed for **Viang Thong** are very scarce. There's a daily bus that comes through about 10pm from Louang Phabang en route to **Phonsavan**, but if you want to make the trip in daylight you have to do it in stages by sawngthaew.

Nong Khiaw boasts eight simple **guesthouses** and several **tourist restaurants**. The *Sunset* is the town's best tourist restaurant with a great sundeck and lovely views as well as some very good food. A couple of travellers' cafés can be found just west of the *Philasouk*, both of which do passable stir-fries and coffee. The big no-name restaurant right over the water next to the western end of the bridge is a very pleasant spot to sit, with a big open deck and good views of the mountains and river.

Accommodation

Manypoon At junction of the main street and Route 1 near the bridge. This rather endearing guesthouse has seven simple rooms in a lovely house with a small garden, and is arguably the best value in town. The upstairs rooms are the nicest and there's a small balcony with a fine view east and another little balcony looking north. ❷

Phayboun Route 1, a short walk to the west of the bridge. Built for group tours, *Phayboun* was originally just a wooden building but a new concrete wing has been added, giving it a total of twenty rooms. The rooms are all a cut above the rest, especially those in the new wing, which feature en-suite bathrooms. ❷

Philasouk Next to the bridge opposite the bus stop. A good choice, with a dozen rooms in a big old wooden house. The rooms are basic but comfortable and the shared facilities are clean. Aside from a good location, the house has genuine atmosphere. ❶

Sai Nam Ou Right over the river by the boat landing. Favoured by some budget backpackers as it's right next to the river, *Sai Nam Ou* is basically a big shack thrown together out of nipa palm and bamboo. The deck, at least, has a million-dollar view of the river and karsts. ❶

Somnyot At the corner leading down to the landing. This building with a tin roof and seven rooms is a good choice if you don't like wooden guesthouses: the *Somnyot* has concrete walls. Rooms have big windows and are on a par with those at the *Manypoon*. 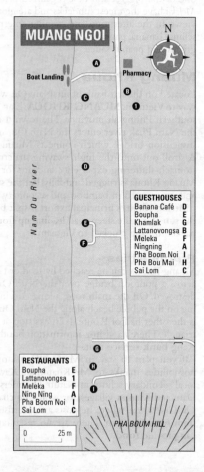 ❶

Sunset Across the river, the *Sunset* is the "in" place with backpackers, largely because of its excellent restaurant and lovely two-level sundeck overlooking the river. It's also clean and very well run. ❶

Muang Ngoi

Tiny **MUANG NGOI** on the right bank of the Nam Ou has already surpassed larger Nong Khiaw and Muang Khoua in popularity and is attracting lots of travellers, many of whom are lulled into staying a week or more. Located an hour's boat ride north of Nong Khiaw, Muang Ngoi is a totally idyllic and friendly village set among spectacular scenery. The fact that it can only be reached by river gives it an edge-of-the-world feel. Although it's easy enough to just hang out in the village sipping coffee and swinging in a hammock, there are a lot of **activities** to pursue here, including trekking with the local guide to hill-tribe villages, canoeing on the river, organized fishing trips, making outings to the caves and waterfall and just generally exploring on the islands and beaches on either side of the river. The scenery is superb, easily rivalling Vang Viang's.

Day-trips out of Muang Ngoi are easy to organize; just ask at your guesthouse. Fishing- and boat-trips to the waterfall and caves cost about $1 per person. For more serious trekking, the local school teacher, Mr Kongkeo, acts as a guide for interested foreigners and charges about $10 a day per person for multi-day treks, which get rave reviews.

Accommodation and eating

Muang Ngoi is a one-street village, along the dirt lane running from the landing to the foot of Pha Boum Hill. Behind the village is a football field and beyond that rice paddies. All of the bungalow places are along the river bank facing west over the Nam Ou. Many of these **places to stay** have a grand total of only three rooms and none has en-suite bathrooms or hot water. The best are those with large bamboo decks affording a view of the river: five-room *Pha Boom Noi* (❶) at the extreme end of the village has the best views of the valley. If their rooms are all full, *Pha Bou Mai* (❶) right next door will do. Friendly three-room

MUANG NGOI

N

Boat Landing

Pharmacy

Nam Ou River

GUESTHOUSES
Banana Café	D
Boupha	E
Khamlak	G
Lattanovongsa	B
Meleka	F
Ningning	A
Pha Boom Noi	I
Pha Bou Mai	H
Sai Lom	C

RESTAURANTS
Boupha	E
Lattanovongsa	1
Meleka	F
Ning Ning	A
Pha Boom Noi	I
Sai Lom	C

0   25 m

PHA BOUM HILL

Khamlak (●) is also good, with a nice deck and three more units currently under construction, while *Meleka* (●) has the nicest sundeck in town and three units for rent. *Boupha* (●) right next door has five rooms and a pleasant deck, as well as the town's only free-standing bungalow. If staying in a flimsy nipa structure isn't your style, try *Sai Lom* (●), which features five small rooms in a proper house, as well as an excellent sundeck with superb views. *Lattanovongsa* guesthouse (●) is also in a two-storey wooden house on the main street just above the landing. A few metres south and also on the river is the excellent *Banana Cafe & Guesthouse* (●), which offers rustic but very clean wooden and bamboo rooms and bungalows in a grove of banana trees on the river bank.

Virtually all of the town's bungalow operations serve **food** – indeed it's their chief money earner. However, since most of them are trying to prepare ten different orders at once in a primitive hut with no electric lights and only an open fire to cook over, the service can be pretty slow. If you're in a hurry you'll get faster service at any of the village's proper **restaurants**, in wooden houses lining the main drag. One of the best is *Lattanovongsa*, which has a large dining room partially made out of old bombs. The *Ning Ning* right by the landing is one of the biggest and best-organized places. For alfresco dining, *Sai Lom* and *Meleka* have the nicest sundecks and are glorious places just to sit and take in the views. In the afternoon and evening enterprising locals set up little food **stalls** selling banana pancakes and Lao snacks such as green crepes with chopped greens and peanut sauce.

Muang Khoua

Located on the left bank of the Nam Ou where Route 4 crosses the river on its way to Vietnam, **MUANG KHOUA** is an important crossroads and outpost in southern Phongsali province. The town itself is built on a steep hillside where the Nam Phak river enters the Nam Ou, and is named for an ancient rust-clad suspension bridge which connects Muang Khoua with the village of Natun. A stroll out onto the high, swaying structure is worth it for the view, but is a stomach-fluttering experience and not for the vertigo-prone. The area around Muang Khoua is rugged and hilly, but the surrounding hills have been clear-cut and are covered in bamboo and secondary growth.

Muang Khoua's principal export is split bamboo shoots, which are laid out in the sun along the steep road leading up from the river. Once dry, the shoots are packed up and trucked to Vietnam.

Practicalities

Muang Khoua can be reached by road or river. At one time Route 4 continued across a pontoon bridge over the Nam Ou at Muang Khoua, but it has been destroyed. Off the main road, a long curving road leads down to the boat landing on the pebble beach along the Nam Ou. The dirt road on the opposite bank is the other half of Route 4. Trucks stop at the town square, which is actually a triangle. There's a visitor-information booth here, and across the street is a Lane Xang **bank** service unit.

If you plan to stay in Muang Khoua over a weekend, there are **trekking** possibilities thanks to Mr Khamman Xayavong, who teaches English at the local secondary school in Natun. He offers guided treks to Phu Noi, Akha, Tai Dam and Khamu villages, for which he charges $10 per person: ask at the *Nam Ou Guesthouse*, where he posts an advertisement. Muang Khoua has electricity from 6pm to 10pm. There are no restaurants in town, but all the guesthouses can provide **food**.

Moving on from Muang Khoua

Passenger **boats** bound for Hat Sa upriver and Nong Khiaw downriver leave most days. The fixed passenger rate is around $5 per person for either direction. A slow boat (seating twelve) or a speedboat (seating eight) can be hired for $20–25, depending on your bargaining skills. The journey takes five hours by slow boat, less than two hours by fast. While the river is navigable year round by passenger boat, fast boats don't make the journey when the water is low.

Trucks to Oudomxai ($1.50) leave from in front of the police station early in the morning, the dusty trip taking approximately three hours. At Km 62, the T-junction leading to Oudomxai and Phongsali, is the very busy village of **Sin Sai** where you'll find a decent little guesthouse over the river which can be used as a base for trekking in this ethnically diverse area. To the east, the Vietnam border has a crossing that leads to Dien Bien Phu, but so far it has not been officially opened to third-country nationals. During the **monsoon** season, if the road to Phongsali is washed away, taking a boat up the Nam Ou is the only way to continue north from Muang Khoua.

Accommodation

Muang Khoua has some half a dozen **guesthouses**. At the town square opposite the bank is the two-storey *Sing Savanh* (①) which is basic but clean and has newly refitted bathrooms. To the right, down the path to the suspension bridge over the Nam Phak, is *Ketsana* (☎088/412065; ①), comprising two houses, one old, one new, which have been joined together. It has the best and cleanest rooms among the budget guesthouses, and the location next to the Nam Phak is nice. The most popular backpacker option is the *Guesthouse Nam Ou* (①). Like the *Sing Savanh*, it has simple but tidy rooms, and you can't beat this funky old guesthouse's terrific location, balanced right on the hillside looking down on the river and landing. The owner, who speaks both English and French, has built a long wooden staircase down the hillside to the landing road, so you no longer need to find your way up the hill. If you've arrived by truck just follow the yellow signs from the square.

If *Nam Ou* is full and you want to be on the river, *Sengali* (①) just up the landing road has passable if somewhat grungy rooms in a rickety two-storey with a nice new covered veranda. Room no. 3 has its own balcony with a terrific view of the river. At the very top of the road on the main street is the fanciest place in town, the new *Muang Khoua Hotel* (④), built by a Chinese-Lao investor. This palatial red-roofed building features a grand spiral staircase outside, huge windows and a terrific rooftop patio with great views of the river. Directly opposite, the far more humble *Manichan* (①) has very basic but clean rooms with shared facilities.

Hat Sa

The village of **HAT SA** consists of barely sixty homes, most of which are constructed from the ubiquitous bamboo and palm thatch, although concrete construction has reached even this remote outpost. Most travellers bypass Hat Sa since they're either in a hurry to start downriver or they've come up from Nong Khiaw and have already had their fill of rustic riverside accommodation. But for those looking to experience the trials, hardships and romance that greeted wayfarers of yesteryear, Hat Sa and the villages further up the Nam Ou are about as far off the beaten track as you can get and are worth exploring, especially if you find Nong Khiaw and Muang Ngoi too touristy.

Phou Den Din NBCA

Phou Den Din is Laos's northernmost NBCA and runs along the Vietnam border for over 100km. The scenery here is rugged and mountainous, rising up to the peaks in the Phou Den Din range which reach heights of over 1800m and form the border with Vietnam. The 1310-square-kilometre park is said to contain Asian elephants and Asiatic black bears as well as leopards and tigers. This is one of Laos's most inaccessible NBCAs and at present the only way to get in here is by organizing an expedition by pirogue as far up the Nam Ou as possible and then continuing in by foot.

Hat Sa is reached in five hours by passenger boat from Muang Khoua ($5): the same trip downriver only takes about four hours. By speedboat (as risky as the Mekong speedboats), it's less than two hours from Muang Khoua, but if you've come to Laos to see and appreciate the country you should really stick to the "slow" passenger boats. Depending on water levels, Hat Sa is about the northernmost Nam Ou town served by speedboats, but it's possible to continue upriver by passenger boat.

Visitors are put up in a basic **hut** run by the woman who lives next door, and who can provide **meals** of fried sticky rice, with noodles at one of the huts near the river. Hat Sa has no electricity yet: the shops near the river sell cheap Chinese torches and batteries.

Sawngthaews to Phongsali ($2) leave before noon from the landing. Although it's only a twenty-kilometre trip, it takes an hour to reach Phongsali, which is on the other side of the mountains.

Phongsali

After either the three-day river trip from Louang Phabang or the tortuous road from Oudomxai, visitors usually opt to spend a couple of nights in **PHONG-SALI** to rest up. Happily, it's an engaging place with an invigorating climate and comparatively comfortable accommodation, the perfect antidote for those suffering from travel fatigue. The town, perched just below the peak of Phou Fa ("Sky Mountain"), looks and feels every bit the capital of Laos's northernmost province. The altitude gained becomes apparent once the sun drops below the horizon and the chill sets in. On clear nights, as soon as the lights go out, the view of the heavens is unparalleled. The crisp air seems to amplify the stellar glow and the Milky Way is splashed across the sky like a giant, luminescent cloud.

A wide slice of terrain wedged between China's Yunnan and Vietnam's Lai Chau provinces, Phongsali province would surely be a part of China today were it not for the covetous nineteenth-century French. During the Second Indochina War, Phongsali came under heavy Chinese influence, a fact evident in the fortress-like former Chinese consulate, now the *Phou Fa Hotel*. It was during this time also that much of the province was stripped of its hardwood forests, compensation for China's support for the Pathet Lao. The town's inhabitants are made up of the Theravada Buddhist, Tibeto-Burman speaking Phu Noi people and the Chinese Haw, descendants of Yunnanese traders who annually drove caravans of pack-ponies south into old Siam.

The Town

On a slope directly behind the *Phongsali Hotel* is the town's **old quarter**. A wander through these friendly but medieval-looking lanes is like stepping back in time. Phu Noi grannies, wearing their traditional white leggings, sun themselves with one eye shut and the other on the lookout for free-range fowl, lest they pilfer the rice, soybeans and peppers left drying on mats by the roadside. Haw men wearing flappy Chinese trousers lead horses down the broken cobblestone lanes. Interspersed among the squat houses of mud bricks and rough-hewn planks are a few architectural standouts, including one distinctly Chinese building with a beautifully carved wooden facade that looks like it belongs on the backstreets of old Kunming. The quarter's three main streets run parallel for a stretch and then converge at a basketball court-cum-market from which leads Phongsali's main commercial thoroughfare, a tidy street of low shophouses, some with roofs constructed of oil drums hammered flat and laid out like shingles. Situated on the opposite bank of the town's green bathing pond is **Wat Kaew**, the local monastery.

Anyone interested in seeing what Phongsali's ethnic groups dressed like before the influx of cheap "Western-style" clothing from China can pay a visit to Phongsali's **museum**, located across from the *Phongsali Hotel*. Here the traditional costumes of some of Laos's more obscure groups – the Lolo, the Pala and the Loma among them – are displayed on whimsical wooden mannequins with painted gourds for heads.

Outside of town, it's possible to do a short hike to two **ethnic villages**. Heading west on the track just below the *Phou Fa Hotel* will bring you to two Phu Noi villages of bamboo and thatch huts: Khoun Souk Noi, located about 5km outside Phongsali, and, some 4km further, Khoun Souk Louang. Both villages are known locally for their rice-liquor production, and, depending on how you present yourself, you may be invited to partake of a shot or two.

Practicalities

Card-operated long-distance **telephones** are located in front of the post **office**. The **bank** opposite the post office will exchange US dollars, Thai baht, Chinese yuan and traveller's cheques into kip. There is electricity from 6pm to 10pm.

Passenger vehicles leave at around 7am from the bus lot in front of the museum for the nine-hour journey south to Oudomxai ($4). Pick-ups and sawngthaews to Hat Sa ($2) leave in the morning and cover the twenty-kilometre distance in an hour. There are northbound vehicles but the border crossing to China is not open to third-country nationals. If there's no direct vehicle to go north to U Thai, Ban Pakha or Bosao, it's better to take a vehicle to Ban Boun Nua, 30km southwest of Phongsali, and then get a connection from there.

Opposite the bus station is the *Phongsali* **hotel** (❷), a four-storey block that can be noisy early in the morning. The rather tatty rooms come with three or four beds and shared bath. Located 500m west of the post office, this newish *Phongsali Guesthouse* (❷) is somewhat isolated and much quieter than the competition. Accommodation here consists of two- and three-bed rooms with shared bath. The *Phou Fa Hotel*, near the immigration office, is a renovated former Chinese consulate (❹). With high brick walls and an underground bunker, it has some atmosphere but is a bit overpriced, its en-suite singles and doubles small and dank. A "beer garden" on the premises has a view all the way to Oudomxai. The downstairs **restaurant** at the *Phongsali Hotel* is worth checking out for its good Chinese food, especially the house speciality *phat mi kawp*, crispy fried noodles.

Phongsali to Oudomxai

Regardless of which direction you travel this route, it's a long, hard journey requiring a total of nine gruelling hours in a sawngthaew or truck ($4). This is unfortunate, as the view from inside the covered bed of a sawngthaew is almost zilch, especially when the vehicle is crowded. If you are lucky enough to get a seat with a clear view, however, you are in for some unforgettable sights. This road passes through some prime **Akha territory**, and the tribal women use the thoroughfare to hike between villages and conduct trade. It's very common in fact to see groups of Akha women parading their wonderful apparel along the roadsides. A few of the villages actually straddle the road and afford fleeting snapshots of Akha life: women displaying glittering headdresses and betel-stained smiles, men shouldering long-barrelled muskets, and gaggles of gaping kids clad only in a layer of ochre-coloured dust. If for the entire ride you are stuffed into the tarp-covered bed of a pick-up, then a tranquillizer is suggested.

Another option is to break the journey at **BAN BOUN TAI**, 80km (three hours' drive) south of Phongsali. Ban Boun Tai is a large village, populated by lowland Lao and often frequented by the inhabitants of nearby Akha villages. The village itself is pretty unremarkable but, if you spend a whole day here, it is possible to **trek** into an Akha village on the main road some 15km south. Treks out here can be arranged with the owner of the village's only restaurant. Sawngthaews from Phongsali to Oudomxai arrive at Ban Boun Tai late in the morning and stop at a small store where the proprietor can point you to the no-name **guesthouse** (❶) that has doubles with mosquito net and shared toilet and bath. A short walk from the store stands the town's only **restaurant**, which serves the usual noodles but can sometimes do fried fish dishes on request. Departing from Ban Boun Tai, it's best to park yourself outside the small store (late morning if you're going south, afternoon if going north) and wait. Make sure you flag down the sawngthaew, or it won't stop. Hitching a ride on a passing truck is also possible, but drivers will expect to be paid for the favour. There is no electricity in Ban Boun Tai.

Travel details

Buses and sawngthaews

Hat Sa to: Phongsali (2hr).
Louang Namtha to: Boten (4 daily; 2hr); Houayxai (8hr); Jinghong, China, via Boten (daily; 11hr); Muang Sing (4 daily; 2hr 30min); Oudomxai (4 daily; 4hr); Xiang Kok (daily; 4hr).
Louang Phabang to: Nam Bak (2 daily; 2hr 10min); Nong Khiaw (2 daily; 2–3hr); Oudomxai (daily; 7hr); Pakmong (5 daily; 2hr).
Muang Sing to: Louang Namtha (4 daily; 2hr 30min); Xiang Kok (2 daily; 2hr 30min).
Nam Bak to: Nong Khiaw (hourly; 30min); Pakmong (hourly; 10min).
Nong Khiaw to: Viang Kham (2–3 daily; 2hr), Louang Phabang (2 daily; 2–3hr).
Oudomxai to: Boten (4hr); Jinghong, China, via Boten (12hr); Louang Namtha (4hr); Louang Phabang (3 daily; 5hr); Muang Khoua (5hr); Muang Sing (6hr); Pakbeng (8hr); Phongsali (11hr), Vientiane (daily; 19hr).
Pakmong to: Louang Phabang (5 daily; 2hr); Nam Bak (hourly; 10min); Oudomxai (3 daily; 3hr).
Phongsali to: Hat Sa (2hr); Oudomxai (11hr).

Boats

Houayxai to: Louang Namtha (passenger boat 1–2 days); Louang Phabang (slow boat 2 days; speedboat 6hr); Pakbeng (slow boat 1 day; speedboat 3hr); Xiang Kok (speedboat; 4hr).
Louang Namtha to: Houayxai (passenger boat 1–2 days); Paktha (passenger boat 1–2 days).
Louang Phabang to: Houayxai (slow boat 2–3 days; speedboat 6hr); Nong Khiaw (passenger boat daily; 8hr); Pakbeng (slow boat 1 day; speedboat 3hr); Vientiane (slow boat variable; 3 days).
Muang Khoua to: Hat Sa (slow boat 6hr; speedboat: 2hr).
Nong Khiaw to: Muang Khoua (4hr).

Domestic flights

Houayxai to: Vientiane (3 weekly; 50min).
Louang Namtha to: Vientiane (3 weekly; 1hr).
Oudomxai to: Vientiane (3 weekly; 50min).
Phongsaly to: Vientiane (2 weekly; 1hr 30min).

South central Laos

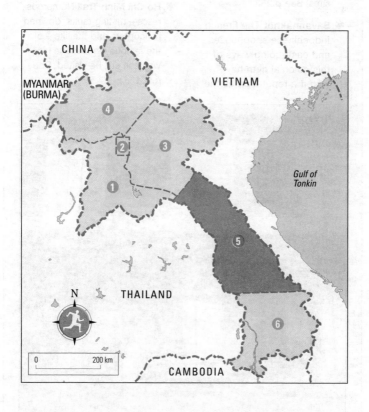

CHINA

MYANMAR
(BURMA)

VIETNAM

④

②　③

①

Gulf of
Tonkin

⑤

N

THAILAND

⓪　　　200 km

⑥

CAMBODIA

CHAPTER 5 **Highlights**

✳ **Mahaxai Caves** Excellent hiking, cycling and cave-exploring near Thakhek. See p.251

✳ **Tham Lot Kong Lo Cave** This seven-kilometre stretch of underground river is one of Asia's most unusual kayaking sites. See p.253

✳ **Savannakhet** The French-Indochinese shophouses and easy-going ways of this colonial gem have won it a reputation as the south's Louang Phabang. See p.254

✳ **That Ing Hang** This revered sixteenth-century Buddhist stupa next to the Mekong provides a great excuse for a bicycle ride out of Savannakhet. See p.260

✳ **Ho Chi Minh Trail** Numerous relics – rusting tanks, downed helicopters and the like – of the famous clandestine highway can still be visited. See p.261

△ Shophouse fun-and-games, Savannakhet

South central Laos

M
any travellers see very little of **south central Laos**, spending just a night or two in the principal towns of **Thakhek** or **Savanna-khet** before pressing on to the far south or crossing the border into Vietnam. However, those willing to take time out from the more popular north and south of the country will find that there is much more to the region than the main Mekong towns, not least the otherworldly beauty of the Mahaxai stone formations at the edge of the **Khammouane Limestone NBCA** near Thakhek, and the largest of all Laos's conservation areas, the massive **Nakai-Nam Theun NBCA** to the northeast.

The three narrow provinces that dominate this part of Laos, namely **Bolikhamxai**, **Khammouane** and **Savannakhet**, are squeezed between main-land Southeast Asia's two most formidable geographical barriers: the Mekong River and the Annamite Mountains. The mighty **Mekong** has long served as a lifeline for the inhabitants of this stretch of the interior, providing food and a thoroughfare for trade and transport. In the late nineteenth century, European colonialism turned the life-giving "Mother of Waters" into a political boundary, and the Lao on its west bank were incorporated into Siam. During the 1970s and 1980s, the river became a further political and economic divide, when short-lived but draconian post-revolutionary policies forced large numbers of the inhabitants of the towns along this stretch of the Mekong, primarily ethnic Vietnamese and Chinese, to flee across the river into Thailand.

East of the river, the elevation gradually increases, culminating in the rugged **Annamite Mountains**, which, throughout much of recorded history, have divided Indochina culturally into two camps, Indian influence prevailing west of the chain and that of China dominating the east. Until very recently these mountains made up one of the region's least inhabited areas and were teeming with wildlife, including some of Asia's rarest and most endangered species, such as the tiger, Javan rhinoceros and Indian elephant. In recent years, however, this area has been the target of heavy logging, and some observers claim that the damage done to the forest since the start of the new millennium is irreversible.

As might be expected, the three principal settlements and provincial capi-tals of south central Laos – Pakxan, Thakhek and Savannakhet – are all on the Mekong. **Pakxan**, the smallest of these, lies at the mouth of the Xan River, which flows down from the 2620-metre Phou Xaxum on the Xieng Khouang Plateau. **Thakhek** now sees few foreign visitors, though it was once a casino town that drew gamblers from Thailand. East of Thakhek is a dramatic landscape of imposing and impossibly vertical mountains of the kind often depicted in old Chinese scroll paintings, which forms the

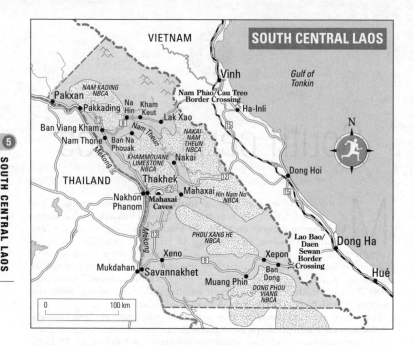

southern boundary of the **Khammouane Limestone NBCA**. Easily visited on a day-trip from Thakhek, these awesome limestone formations are riddled with labyrinthine tunnels and caverns. **Savannakhet** has been described as southern Laos's equivalent of Louang Phabang, its inhabitants living comfortably among architectural heirlooms handed down by the French. Situated at the junction of two ancient trade routes, the town also displays evidence of other cultures – Vietnamese, Thai and Chinese – that have left their mark while passing through.

Aside from the main north–south artery of **Route 13**, central Laos has three important highways – Routes 8, 12 and 9 – which cross the region from west to east, connecting the Mekong River Valley with the provincial interior, and extending beyond into Vietnam. The northernmost highway, **Route 8** – paved and served by daily buses from Vientiane – snakes up through mountains, rainforests and the Phu Pha Maan "stone forest" before winding down to the city of Vinh on the Gulf of Tonkin. The middle route, **Route 12**, begins at Thakhek and crosses the Annamites, connecting with Vietnam's Highway 15. This route is not served by public transport and, in any case, the border crossing is the only one on the three routes that is not open to foreigners. Southernmost of the three is **Route 9**, served by daily buses connecting Savannakhet to Dong Ha on the coast of Vietnam.

Near **Xepon**, Route 9 bisects another route of more recent vintage: the **Ho Chi Minh Trail**. Actually a network of parallel roads and paths, the trail was used by the North Vietnamese Army to infiltrate and finally subdue its southern neighbour. The area is still littered with lots of war junk, some of it dangerous. The best way to view these rusting relics is to use Xepon as a base, making trips to nearby Muang Phin and Ban Dong.

Pakxan and Pakkading

Route 13 passes through **PAKXAN**, capital of Bolikhamxai province and the northernmost major settlement on the narrow neck of Laos, but few travellers actually stop over in this small and sleepy Mekong town, and the ferry crossing here to and from **Beung Kan** in Thailand is little used. For years there have been plans to upgrade Route 4 from Phonsavan to Pakxan, which would make it possible for northbound travellers from Savannakhet to head straight to the Plain of Jars without having to make a detour to Vientiane. When and if this happens, the increased through traffic and ensuing facilities will make spending a night in Pakxan a more tempting option than it is at present.

The town is slowly growing, however, and a number of guesthouses and restaurants have opened. Pakxan officials have tried to boost tourism by altering the timing of its annual **boat racing festival**, which usually takes place some time in October, so as not to conflict with the much larger races in the capital.

Practicalities

The town's **bus station** is on Route 13 next to the Lane Xang **bank**, which changes money. **Accommodation** is decidedly downmarket here. The long-running *BK Guesthouse*, on the road leading down to the river (☎054/212638; ❶), is a reasonable standby, and north up the same road you'll find *Hongxakham Guesthouse* (☎054/212362; ❶). Just beyond it is the *Villaysak Hotel* (☎054/212311; ❶), with fan and air-conditioned rooms, some with TV.

A handful of **restaurants** with river views can be found where Route 13 crosses the Xan. Of these, the *Tavendeng Saysane* is the most geared towards non-Lao, with a smattering of English-speaking staff. Located just beyond it, the *Paknamxan Restaurant* is more of a local favourite; just across the bridge, the *Saynamxan Restaurant* is the oldest in town and does good fish dishes.

Pakkading

Forty kilometres southeast of Pakxan, **Nam Kading NBCA** is Bolikhamxai province's largest conservation area and a place of dramatic scenic beauty. Running parallel to the Mekong and encompassing 1740 square kilometres, the park has a chain of mountains down its length, the highest peak being the 1588-metre **Mount Pha Pet**, which can clearly be viewed as you travel Route 13. Unfortunately, this is likely to be as intimate a glimpse of the reserve as you'll get, as there are no facilities for visitors whatsoever.

Behind the ridge on the eastern boundary of the NBCA, the **Nam Mouan** and **Nam Theun** rivers converge to form the **Nam Kading**, so named because the waterfalls where the Nam Theun spills off the plateau are said to make a "kading" sound – the sound of a water buffalo's bell. The Nam Kading flows out through a gap in the mountains to join the Mekong at the village of **PAKKADING**. There are a number of good fish **restaurants** along the highway here, making it a favourite lunch spot for truckers and travellers plying Route 13.

To the east of Pakkading, the highway crosses a Russian-built bridge and heads south out of town. Drivers often pause to light a cigarette before crossing the bridge, and then respectfully toss the lit cigarette into the swift waters below, an offering to appease the feisty water serpent believed to live at the river's mouth. Every year a buffalo is sacrificed to the water serpent, though the offerings weren't enough to spare the lives of a Russian engineer and several Lao workers who died during construction of the bridge.

Route 8 via Lak Xao

At the tiny junction town of **Ban Viang Kham**, 47km south of Pakkading, **Route 8** begins its journey over the Annamite Mountains to Vietnam. These days the majority of travellers pass through here on direct, air-conditioned buses running the Vientiane–Vinh route, but it's worth pausing at the frontier town of **Lak Xao**, a base for trips to both the **Ho Chi Minh Trail** and the **Nakai-Nam Theun NBCA**.

Tracing a centuries-old trading route to Vietnam, Route 8 zigzags through hilly countryside, dotted with woods and tiny stream valleys, the southern horizon punctuated by black-topped limestone pillars draped in lush vegetation. An hour's drive along this route takes you to the village of **NA HIN**, which sprang up during the construction of the **Theun-Hin Boun Dam**, completed in 1998. The hydroelectric potential of the area is vigorously demonstrated during the monsoon season, when the rains recharge a medley of waterfalls on the surrounding hillsides. The densely forested hill guarding the valley's southeastern side alone supports as many as six sizeable falls, all visible from the highway.

Today Na Hin has found a new lease of life as a gateway into the Phou Hin Poun NBCA, more popularly known as the **Khammouane Limestone NBCA** (see p.252). The village boasts a **guesthouse**, and from the bus station there are direct daily connections to both Vientiane and Thakhek.

Continuing east on Route 8, you pass **Ban Phonhong** and cross a toll bridge spanning the Nam Theun, the river that powers the Theun-Hin Boun Dam. The road then reaches **KAM KEUT**, a quaint, shady village of traditional homes, set in an expansive valley of rice fields hemmed in by a low wall of hills. It was once the principal settlement in the area, but has seen its population diminish in recent years, as Lak Xao has emerged as the regional hub.

Lak Xao

If you've made the stunning journey east to the sprawling boom town of **LAK XAO**, the town itself comes as something of a disappointing sight, but is spared from being a complete blot on the landscape by the impressive limestone escarpment which stands sentinel on the outskirts of town. Few travellers pass through Lak Xao, and for most it's little more than a launch pad for trips into Vietnam, 35km to the east.

Carved out of the hills by the logging company, Phudoi, in the 1980s, Lak Xao facilitates border trade with Vietnam, as well as providing a base for loggers. The town's **logging industry** continues to thrive, as the continual buzz of chainsaws and roar of trucks testify. Helicopters haul the logs out of the forests, some of the priciest wood, namely that of the coniferous Mai Long Len trees, being prized by both the Chinese and Japanese, who use the lumber to construct beds and coffins. It's thought that this fragrant wood possesses the ability to heal respiratory ailments as well as preserve corpses. The wealth tapped from the surrounding forests is reflected in the town **temple**, located next to the hotel. Lavish by a country town's standards, the wat has been embellished by merit-making donations from Phudoi company officials.

Once known for selling exotic wildlife, Lak Xao's **market** has largely cleaned up its act since recent scientific discoveries heaped international attention on the nearby conservation zone. With representatives of international environmental organizations regularly passing through, mouse deer and other goodies are no longer as obviously available. The market does however have some interesting stalls, selling **silver jewellery** from minority tribes and old silver bars etched with Chinese characters. You might also see villagers of the Hmong tribe, some of whom are dressed in their finest traditional clothes.

Another market is held monthly about 35km to the east, just inside the Lao border. **Vietnamese traders** come here to hawk everyday goods such as spanners, mouse traps, Hanoi beers and pharmaceuticals. The market may not be of great interest in itself, beyond offering an insight into cross-border trade, but the journey out is scenic, passing through wide valleys and vibrant green fields. Shared tuk-tuks leave for the market from Lak Xao's own market.

Practicalities

Buses to Lak Xao stop in the lot outside the market. To the west of the market is the *Phouthavong Guesthouse* (T 054/341071; ●), a well-run place with clean rooms. More established, and a bit more worn, is the *Souriya Guesthouse* just opposite (T 054/341111; ●), which has en-suite bathrooms with bathtubs. Near the market, the *Thiphavongsay* **restaurant** has a range of traditional Lao dishes; next door is a **bank** which can exchange dollars and Vietnamese dong.

The Nam Phao/Cau Treo border crossing

If you want to reach the **Nam Phao/Cau Treo** border crossing into Vietnam from Lak Xao, your best option is to charter a tuk-tuk (50,000K) from the town's market. Shared tuk-tuks (10,000K) can be found, but are often overcrowded and leave infrequently – except when the monthly border market's on. For those crossing into Laos from Vietnam, there's usually a tuk-tuk on hand, but you may well have to charter it outright (expect to pay 100,000K to Lak Xao).

Crossing the border (daily 7.30am–5pm) can be a hassle, so it's best to start your journey early to ensure you don't end up stuck at the border. On the Vietnamese side there's usually a small army of touts ready to pull you into a van headed for Vinh. Neither immigration post is near a town of any size; the settlement on the Vietnamese side of the border is **Cau Treo**, 105km west of Vinh on Highway 8. A small exchange kiosk sits in the Lao terminal, but don't expect to get a decent rate.

Thakhek and around

Less visited than Savannakhet to the south, **THAKHEK**, capital of Khammouane province, is gradually gaining popularity as the best base to explore the nearby **Mahaxai Caves** and karst formations, and the massive **Khammouane Limestone NBCA**. It is also an entry point into Laos from Nakhon Phanom in Thailand, as well as being a good place to break the long journey down Route 13 to Savannakhet.

Thakhek's roots date back to the Chenla and Funan empires. The name Thakhek, which means "Visitor's Landing", is relatively new, but is a reference to the town's importance as far back as the eighth century. As Sikhotabong, and later Lakhon, Thakhek was a principality spanning both banks of the Mekong, and a hub for trade routes connecting civilizations in Vietnam, Thailand and Cambodia. Its former spiritual centre, the shrine of That Phanom, is now in present-day Thailand and is still the holiest site in ethnically Lao northeastern Thailand. When the kingdom of Lane Xang was formed under the leadership of Fa Ngum in the fourteenth century, Sikhotabong's governor oversaw the

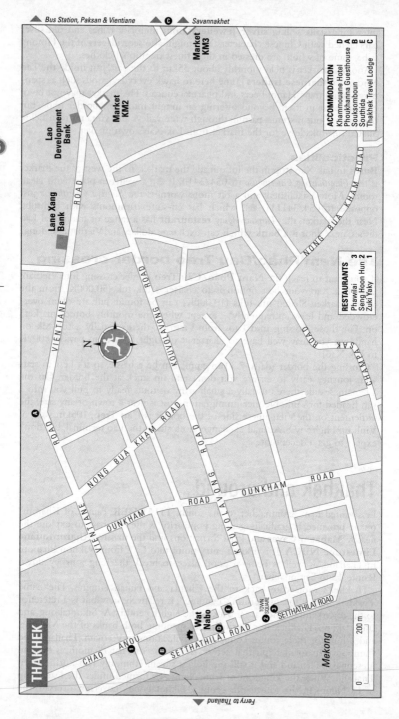

THAKHEK

▲ Bus Station, Paksan & Vientiane ▲ C ▲ Savannakhet

Market KM3

Market KM2

Lao Development Bank

Lane Xang Bank

ROAD

VIENTIANE

NONG BUA KHAM ROAD

KOUVOLAVONG

CHAMPASAK ROAD

ROAD

NONG BUA KHAM ROAD

VIENTIANE

OUNKHAM ROAD

OUNKHAM ROAD

KOUVOLAVONG ROAD

ROAD

N

CHAO ANOU

Wat Nabo

TOWN SQUARE

SETTHATHILAT ROAD

SETTHATHILAT ROAD

Mekong

▼ Ferry to Thailand

0   200 m

ACCOMMODATION
Khammouane Hotel   D
Phoukhanna Guesthouse   A
Souksomboun   E
Southida   B
Thakhek Travel Lodge   C

RESTAURANTS
Phawilai   3
Seng Hoon Hun   2
Zuki Yaky   1

southern extent of the Lao empire. Under the French, the town became an administrative outpost with a bustling Vietnamese community: the colonial administration thought that an influx of Vietnamese workers was the key to finally turning a profit on their sparsely populated Lao territory. By the 1940s, the town was 85 percent Vietnamese. After the revolution, large numbers of these Vietnamese families fled across the Mekong to Nakhon Phanom on the opposite bank, with the result that Thakhek has slipped into being the sleepy Lao town it is today.

Arrival, information and transport

Bus passengers disembark either at the Kilometre 2 Market (2km from the riverbank), or at the main **bus station**, located near Souksomboun Market about half a kilometre northwest of the centre. There are plenty of **tuk-tuks** on hand at both markets, which you'll probably want to use, as the town is very sprawling. The town **tourist office** (Mon–Fri 8–11am & 2–4pm) is on the edge of the river near the tiny town square, but the best place for local information is the *Thakhek Travel Lodge* (see p.250).

To change **traveller's cheques**, head for BCEL on Vientiane Road, or the Lao Development Bank opposite the Kilometre 2 Market. There's also a kiosk run by the same bank at the ferry pier, but they only exchange cash. For **Internet access**, look on Kouvolavong Road and around the town square. Also on the town square there are two IDD telephone booths and a Kodak Express film shop.

Motorbikes for exploring the Mahaxai caves and karst formations can be rented at most guesthouses for about $8 a day; the *Travel Lodge* and *Southida* (see below) also have vans for rent. **Bicycles** are available from various guesthouses ($2 a day) for getting around town.

The **ferry** to **Nakhon Phanom** in Thailand leaves daily during daylight hours from the ramp near the Immigration Office, making crossings every half hour or so (50 baht). From Nakhon Phanom bus terminal, buses leave for Ubon Ratchathani, Mukdahan, Khon Kaen and Nong Khai. There is also a direct Thakhek–Hanoi bus which departs from Talat Souksomboun every Saturday at 9pm.

Accommodation

There are several good **accommodation** choices in Thakhek. If you want to stay by the Mekong, just head straight for the old town square and then walk north up riverside Setthathilat Road, where you'll find a choice of four hotels.

Khammouane Hotel Setthathilat Rd ☎051/212216. If you want to be right by the Mekong, the best bet is the huge *Khammouane*, recently renovated, with large rooms and great sunset views from the balcony. There's also a huge roof patio with terrific views of both the Mekong and the mountains. The rooms are all pretty similar but have a range of different prices depending on whether you want a/c, TV or hot water. Good value. ❷

Phoukhanna Guesthouse Vientiane Rd, about 1km from the river ☎051/212092. A choice between a/c rooms in a 1960s-era building and larger fan rooms in a newer annexe behind it. The cheaper rooms have the advantage of receiving less ambient noise from noisy Vientiane Rd. ❸

Souksomboun Setthathilat Rd ☎051/212225. Formerly the *Sikhot*, this old French colonial police station right on the riverfront features surreal, retro 1970s interior decor with smoked mirrors and yards of vinyl that is more Las Vegas than Lao. In the motel annexe off to the side, there are equally spacious, cheaper fan rooms, but without any atmosphere. Behind the hotel is an on-again, off-again disco that can attract hordes of young Thakhek youths on motorbikes. ❸

Southida Chao Anou Rd ☎051/212568. Decent hotel, in a new three-storey building just around the corner from the *Khammouare*, with tiled-floored, a/c rooms and en-suite bathrooms with hot water. There's a good restaurant downstairs, and they rent mini-vans, 50cc motorcycles and bicycles. ❸

Thakhek Travel Lodge ☎020/515137, ℮travel @laotel.com. Located up a side road halfway between the Kilometre 2 and 3 markets, this three-storey guesthouse is the most popular budget option in town. It features dormitories and fan rooms with shared facilities, as well as a/c en-suite rooms, all reasonably priced. They also rent bicycles, motorbikes, and vans. Dorm beds $2, ❶–❸

The Town

A wander round the streets leading out from Thakhek's tiny **town square** reveals French villas and shophouses, crumbling into overgrown gardens, and too-wide dirt streets contribute to the almost haunted atmosphere. Aside from French-era architecture, there is little to see around the square except the potholed dirt road running south along the Mekong to a big concrete *sala*. In houses just a block from the main square, locals cook their suppers over open fires in their backyards and cows graze on the verge. This tranquil air of neglect is all the more evocative when set against the town's colourful history. During the Second Indochina War, Thakhek was a sort of Havana on the Mekong, with visiting Thais flocking to its riverbank casino; these days, it's Nakhon Phanom on the opposite bank that's the big metropolis. Separated only by the Mekong River, the two Lao peoples living on each bank couldn't have a more different way of life.

For most visitors this lost-in-time atmosphere is the main draw. There are a few nice colonial-era buildings around the town square, and on **Chao Anou Road**, north of the square, is a fine row of 1920s shophouses featuring interlocking swastika designs of moulded stucco (although this Hindu motif appears in Lao weaving, it is rare in Lao architecture). Between Chao Anou and Setthathilat is a large temple, Wat Nabo.

Thakhek's main attraction is 6km to the south and easily reached by tuk-tuk. Known locally as Muang Kao, **Wat Pha That Sikhotabong** is one of the country's holiest pilgrimage sites and a great scenic spot, especially at sunset. The golden Lao-style stupa occupies spacious grounds on the banks of the Mekong, a prominent position that makes it visible from the opposite bank. Restored three times in the past fifty years, the stupa was built in the nineteenth century under the orders of Chao Anou, the revered Lao king, who tried in vain to throw off the yoke of Thai control and reunify the once-powerful kingdom of Lane Xang. A pair of whitewashed sandstone nagas, pilfered from some Khmer temple, are arranged symmetrically near a small altar, where pilgrims leave offerings of candles and incense. Ruins in the immediate vicinity of the stupa are said to be all that remains of a shrine erected as long ago as the reign of King Nanthasen in the tenth century.

The third lunar month, which usually falls in July, is the best time to visit, when the temple celebrates its annual *bun* and a carnival-like atmosphere prevails. Walking out of the south gate, you'll find an excellent open-air **restaurant** – more of a large shelter with a corrugated tin roof, really – where you can order up Lao mainstays such as roast chicken, *tam màk hung* and sticky rice.

Eating and drinking

Though there are plenty of places to eat on or close to the town square, many of Thakhek's best local **restaurants** are far out on the outskirts of town. The most popular place with local expats is the humble *Seng Hoon Hun* (no English sign) under the huge tree at the west side of the town square. Aside from decent stir-fries, they have an ice-cream freezer with imported Magnum bars. Nearby, at the southwest corner of the square, is *Phawilai*, which serves up noodles, grilled chicken, and *mu yáw*, a bland local sausage, which you can wash down with cold beer. For a proper sit-down meal, the restaurant at the *Southida* is the best bet in the **old quarter**. Five doors up on Vientiane Road is *Zuki Yaky*, a Korean barbecue place. *Thakek Travel Lodge* is a bit of a trek if you're staying near the Mekong, but it's got the best Western breakfasts in town.

Mahaxai Caves

East of Thakhek, potholed Route 12 is swallowed up by a surreal landscape of karst formations. Hidden among the sea of jagged limestone hills are the **Mahaxai Caves**, many of which lie within the Khammouane Limestone NBCA. A number of the more easily accessible caves are popular both with Lao families on a weekend picnic and with foreign tourists. These more visited caves line the Thakhek–Mahaxai road, the furthest one only about 20km from Thakhek. Not all of these caves are worth visiting, but those that are make a day-trip through the strange beauty of this area a must if you're passing through Thakhek.

The easiest way to reach the caves is by renting a motorbike ($8 per day) or chartering a tuk-tuk from Thakhek, but some visitors prefer to cycle out or catch a Mahaxai-bound bus to the caves and then explore on foot. Public transport can be tricky, however: pick-ups and buses travel the road frequently enough in the morning but aren't so reliable late in the afternoon. To get back, you'll have to flag down one of the buses or pick-ups coming from Mahaxai – of which there are several a day – although again, you can't count on catching one late in the afternoon. If you want to do a **walking tour** of the caves, a good point to start is **Tham Ban Tham**, on the road to Mahaxai 7km from Thakhek; from here you can walk to **Tham En**, taking in other caves en route, a twelve-kilometre walk in all.

The caves

To find the first cave, turn south down the dirt road that turns off Route 12 towards **Ban Tham**, a small village nestling at the base of the first limestone escarpment. The gaping mouth of the tautologically named **Tham Ban Tham** ("tham" meaning "cave") should be visible from the highway. Cut through the village to find the concrete stairs leading up to the cave, which contains a shrine, centred around a sizeable Buddha image. Perched partway up the side of the hill, Tham Ban Tham offers a commanding view of the surroundings, and is particularly pretty at sunset. If you've come with a local, ask to see the shrine to Ganesh, an elephantine rock hidden in a tunnel within the main cavern. From Ban Tham, follow the road cutting north to get back on the main road.

Just before the second wooden bridge along this road, roughly 17km from Thakhek, a dirt path on the right leads to **Tham Xiang Liap**. After 300m the trail reaches a stream, which flows into the entrance of the cave on the opposite bank (during the monsoon, the water level may be too high to enter the cave). While not the most inspiring cave, Tham Xiang Liap is a pleasant stop chiefly for its seclusion and the novelty of scrambling across a stream full of rocks into the half-submerged cave mouth. Nearby is the disappointing **Tha Falang**, reputedly a favourite spot during colonial times with Thakhek's French residents, who would come here to picnic by a stream among the hills. To get here, continue east along the main road, crossing the second wooden bridge. A sign reading "Limestone NBCA" in English accompanied by a crudely drawn district map marks a sandy turn-off on the northern side of the road, a few hundred metres from the bridge. Bearing right, you'll reach a small clearing 1km away on the left, and here on the bank is the *tha*, or landing. It's a pretty unexceptional spot though, and it's not clear what drew Laos's former colonial masters: the area only musters some charm during the rainy season, when the water-sculpted rocks are submerged and the hills a vibrant green. During the dry season, the brackish water stagnates against the rocks.

Drink vendors set up shop in the recesses of two cliffs 100m beyond the turn-off for Tha Falang, signposting the path leading to **Tham Sa Pha In**, which is without question the best of the caves. A small sign on the left points towards the path leading to the cave, a short walk from the main road. Look for the bamboo gate to find the cave entrance. The cave was renamed for the Hindu god Indra after the Second Indochina War, when villagers claimed to see the Hindu deity's image reflected in the pool. Illuminated by an inaccessible opening in the ceiling of the cave, the pool glows emerald green, the colour of Indra's skin. You can pause to light a candle by the shrine in the back of the cave before clambering down to sit by the pool, where swifts dive-bombing the surface and the drone of insects conspire to give the deep cavern an other-worldly atmosphere. A sign at the mouth of the cave asks visitors not to touch the water, which is considered sacred.

The most visited of Mahaxai's caves, **Tham En**, named for the large number of sparrows that are said to inhabit the cave and popular for what the Lao call its natural air conditioning, lies another 4km up the road; it's easily located by the gate, where an official collects 2000K per visitor, plus a vehicle fee. A concrete stairway takes you deep into the tunnel mouth, but there is still plenty of room to clamber around on the rocks and climb up to one of the several cave mouths that offer commanding views of the forest outside. On weekends, the cave is packed with day-tripping locals snacking on roast chicken, playing cards and picnicking. Pint-sized bungalows, designed to provide tourist accommodation, were started here but never finished.

Mahaxai

Fifty kilometres east of the Mahaxai Caves lies the beautifully situated town of **MAHAXAI**, engulfed in limestone karst formations, on the banks of the Xe Bang Fai River. A bumpy fifty-kilometre drive from Thakhek, this lively little town lacks sights of its own but is nevertheless a charming place offering visitors enchanted by the strange beauty of Khammouane's karst formations a chance to soak up the surroundings at a more measured pace.

Buses and pick-ups grind to a halt at the central market, next to an old tin-roofed temple. You'll find just one **hotel**, with huge rooms (❷), as well as several noodle shops and *tam màk hung* vendors, all just steps away. Hiring a boat to cruise the river, which stretches from the mountainous Vietnamese border to the Mekong, can be a bit of a chore – ask by the river or around town – but if you can swing it, a two-hour round-trip by motorized pirogue is scenic in either direction, with the upstream route taking in stunning cliffs and the downstream option skimming through gentle rapids, past submerged water buffalo and villagers catching fish. Most cave touring originates in Thakhek, but the area surrounding Mahaxai is also honeycombed with caves – ask the villagers.

Khammouane Limestone NBCA

The most accessible of Khammouane province's three NBCAs is the Phou Hin Poun NBCA, more popularly known as the **Khammouane Limestone**

△ Kayaking through Tham Lot Kong Lo Cave

NBCA. Unlike the neighbouring Nakai-Nam Theun and Hin Nam No NBCAs to the east, the Khammouane Limestone NBCA can be accessed by road or river from a number of approaches, making it the most practical and affordable of the three to visit.

The best way to experience the park is on one of the organized tours that a number of tour companies operate, and that generally include kayaking, hiking and **village stays**. The tours are best booked out of Vientiane, from where they depart, although it is still possible to link up with tours from Thakhek provided you make arrangements with the tour operator by phone or fax. Although it will not allow you to penetrate the interior of the park to the degree a professionally organized expedition can, a do-it-yourself tour from Thakhek is also easily arranged and affordable.

The chief highlight of many of the tours is the journey by kayak through the wonderfully dramatic **Tham Lot Kong Lo Cave**, a natural seven-kilometre river tunnel through a limestone karst mountain into a hidden valley. Bring a torch (flashlight) and some rubber flip-flops as it can be necessary to wade through the more shallow stretches of the river. Green Discovery (☎021/251564, ⓦwww.greendiscoverylaos.com) also offers a Kong Lo Cave cycling/kayaking tour out of the capital.

There's an **eco-resort** within the park, the *L'Auberge Sala Hine Boun* (☎051/214315, ⓦwww.salalao.com; ⑤), on the banks of the Nam Hin Poun River; it's reached by taking a tuk-tuk from **Na Hin** (on Route 8) to Ban Na Phouak on the northern boundary of the NBCA, and then a boat up the Nam Hin Poun ($15; 2hr). The resort features comfortable bungalows and is within easy day-hiking distance of a number of hill-tribe villages, Tham Thieng cave and Tham Lot Kong Lo. A kayak excursion through the underground river can be arranged here for around $30 per person, though note that boatmen do the paddling rather than you. Given the remoteness of the area, advance booking is advised.

Savannakhet and around

SAVANNAKHET (known locally as "Sawan") is Laos's third-largest city after Vientiane and Louang Phabang, and the surrounding area that makes up Savannakhet province, stretching from the Mekong River to the Annamite Mountains, is Laos's most populous region; for centuries the inhabitants fought off designs on their territory from both Vietnam and Thailand. The city is also southern Laos's most visited provincial capital, its popularity with travellers due in part to its central location on the overland route between Vientiane and Pakxe and between Thailand and Vietnam, the two countries linked to each other by a 240-kilometre-long road carved by the French. Aside from being an important junction, Savannakhet also possesses very impressive **architecture**, including shophouses of ochre-coloured stucco that are reminiscent of parts of Hanoi, that can make for a worthwhile couple of days' stay.

Savannakhet's inhabitants, as travellers who have recently arrived from Vietnam are quick to note, are much mellower than their neighbours east of the Annamite Mountains, despite the fact that a large percentage of the town's population is ethnic Vietnamese, descendants of entrepreneurs who migrated to Laos during French rule. Most have been living here for generations and consider themselves to be more Lao than Vietnamese in habit and temperament.

Arrival, information and city transport

Most **buses** offload at the station on the north side of the town, with **tuk-tuks** on hand to make the two-kilometre run into the city centre (10,000K). The passenger **ferry** between Savannakhet and Mukdahan in Thailand uses the landing at the Immigration Office in the town centre. The **airport** is on the southeastern side of the town, off Makaweha Road a few blocks from the centre, but most of the flights here operate on a private charter basis, and tickets aren't on sale to the general public.

As Savannakhet is incredibly spread out, you may find **tuk-tuks** easier than trying to walk the long blocks outside the old quarter, especially in summer. Tuk-tuks can be flagged down around town and cost 5000K for short distances within the centre. Bicycles are another excellent way of seeing the town and can be rented at *Santiphab Hotel* near the square and at some guesthouses. Savanbanhao Tourism on Senna Road (℡041/212944), three blocks north of the church, has vans with drivers for hire. The **Tourism Administration office** (℡041/212755) seems to move frequently; at the time of writing, it was located on Latsaphanit Road, just south of the square.

Moving on to Vietnam and Thailand

A daily bus to **Vietnam** leaves Savannakhet at 10pm. Different cities are served, including Dong Ha, Hué and Da Nang ($8–11), depending on the day of the week you travel. All the Vietnam buses stop in Dong Ha, where Route 9 meets Vietnam's Highway 1, so you can transfer there for other Vietnamese cities, including Hanoi.

A bridge spanning the Mekong and linking **Mukdahan** in Thailand and Savannakhet may well be open by the time you read this. Otherwise, crossing over to Thailand usually entails using the passenger **ferry** to Mukdahan (50 baht), departing roughly twice an hour during peak times, hourly during the heat of the day. You'll find an exchange kiosk in the ferry terminal on the Lao side. On the Thai side, frequent buses leave for That Phanom and Ubon Ratchathani.

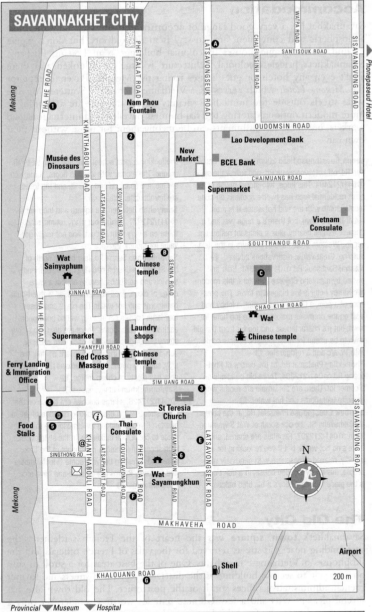

SAVANNAKHET CITY

Mekong

THA HE ROAD

PHETSALAT ROAD

Nam Phou Fountain

KHANTHABOULI ROAD

Musée des Dinosaurs

LATSAVONGSEUK ROAD

CHALEUNSINH ROAD

WATPA ROAD

SISAVANGVONG ROAD

SANTISOUK ROAD

OUDOMSIN ROAD

Lao Development Bank

New Market

BCEL Bank

CHAIMUANG ROAD

Supermarket

LATSAPHANIT ROAD

KOUVOLAVONG ROAD

Wat Sainyaphum

Chinese temple

SENNA ROAD

Vietnam Consulate

SOUTTHANOU ROAD

KINNALI ROAD

CHAO KIM ROAD

Wat

Chinese temple

THA HE ROAD

Supermarket

PHANYPUI ROAD

Laundry shops

Red Cross Massage

Chinese temple

SIM UANG ROAD

Ferry Landing & Immigration Office

St Teresia Church

SAYAMUNGKHUN ROAD

LATSAVONGSEUK ROAD

SISAVANGVONG ROAD

Food Stalls

Thai Consulate

Mekong

SINGTHONG RD

KHANTHABOULI ROAD

LATSAPHANIT ROAD

KOUVOLAVONG ROAD

PHETSALAT ROAD

Wat Sayamungkhun

MAKHAVEHA ROAD

N

Airport

KHALOUANG ROAD

Shell

0   200 m

ACCOMMODATION		RESTAURANTS	
Leena Guesthouse **C**	Santyphab **D**	Baw Bun Shop **5**	Rendezvous **3**
Nanhai **A**	Savanbanhao **B**	Hoongthip Garden Restaurant **2**	Sakura Korean BBQ **6**
Phonevilay **G**	Sayamungkhun **E**	Lao-Paris 4 Seasons Café **4**	
Saisouk Guesthouse **F**		Mekong Riverside **1**	

Accommodation

Savannakhet has a very good range of **accommodation**. Generally, the most atmospheric and convenient area to stay is in the old city, but don't expect to find charming guesthouses in colonial buildings as in Louang Phabang. Savannakhet's priceless colonial architecture is largely overlooked and there aren't even any hotels or guesthouses facing the Mekong River (except for the *Mekong Hotel*, which serves as a Vietnamese brothel). Scattered on the wide streets outside the immediate vicinity of the old city are a handful of more modern options, catering to Thai business travellers and international aid workers, but these establishments can be inconvenient for those without their own car.

Leena Guesthouse Head 200m east along Chao Kim Rd, off Latsavongseuk Rd, and follow the signs ☏ 041/212404. This huge, two-storey house in a quiet residential area has twelve spotless en-suite rooms, some with a/c and hot water. It is a bit out of the old town, but there's a huge wat and a Chinese temple nearby, plus a pleasant restaurant serving Western breakfasts downstairs in the next building. Great value; reservations advised. ❷

Nanhai Santisouk Rd ☏ 041/212371. Built and owned by mainland Chinese investors, this modern five-storey hotel is the biggest in town. The presence of a pool, a Chinese restaurant, a lobby and a lift on the premises makes this the top hotel in town, but it's characterless and too far from the old town to be useful for most tourists. Rooms come with TV, a/c and a refrigerator. ❺

Phonevilay Phetsalat Rd, at the corner of Khalouang Rd ☏ 041/212284. Three big buildings on a corner lot. There are six simple a/c rooms with en-suite bathrooms and hot water. ❸

Saisouk Guesthouse Phetsalat Rd, at the corner of Makhaveha St, a block south of Wat Sayamungkhun ☏ 041/212207. Facilities are shared, and there's no hot water, but if you're looking for a friendly, relaxed atmosphere with genuinely nice people, this lovely wooden house, in a quiet area, is the place for you. There's a big tiled balcony

overlooking a local school yard and palm trees all around. The rooms, with wooden floors, some with a/c too, are spacious and well lit, and the toilets are immaculately clean. ❶

Santyphab Between the square and the river ☏ 041/212277. Central but dingy rooms, strictly for those on a very tight budget, and not really good value for money. ❶

Savanbanhao Senna Rd, four blocks north of the St Teresia Church ☏ 041/212202. Unfriendly service and no atmosphere at all, but a wide range of clean, good-value rooms, all with en-suite bathrooms and hot water. The place comprises four large houses set in a big walled compound, each with six a/c rooms. There are also two single-storey buildings around the back with cheaper, non-a/c rooms. In the unlikely event it's full, the ugly, similarly priced *Savanphathana* right next door has plenty of cheap rooms. ❷

Sayamungkhun Latsavongseuk Rd ☏ 041/212426. A large colonial-era house on the main street, within easy walking distance of the old quarter: if you're looking for atmosphere this is the place to come. The building is in the style popular with successful Chinese merchants of the time, essentially Western but with some Oriental motifs and features. Rooms are en suite and have a/c. Excellent value. ❷

The Old City

Savannakhet's **town square** was the heart of the French settlement, the surrounding neat grid streets reserved for the villas of French officials and the shophouses of Vietnamese merchants. One of the best areas for a stroll or spin on a bicycle to see old buildings is the district of tree-lined streets and former French administrative offices south of the post office. The old town also has several pleasant wats and a few Chinese temples worth a wander. Yet only a kilometre or two away from this bastion of French civilization, the paved roads became dirt paths meandering through traditional Lao villages that were largely unaffected by French rule and remain culturally pristine to this day.

The **Old French Quarter** boasts some fine examples of European-inspired architecture, though most of this looks much more ancient than it really is – it's

△ St Teresia Catholic Church

doubtful that any of these crumbling structures predate the early twentieth century. The main square is dominated by the octagonal spire of **St Teresia Catholic Church**, built in 1930, its thick masonry walls keeping the interior blessedly cool even on the hottest of days. Objects of interest include an old teakwood confessional and, high up on the walls, a set of hardwood plaques, with Vietnamese mother-of-pearl inlay, depicting the fourteen stations of the cross. Not surprisingly, the biblical characters have distinctly Asian faces: Christ resembles a Confucian sage, while the Roman soldiers look more like turban-wearing Mongols. On Saturday and Sunday mornings, Mass is said in Lao to an overwhelmingly ethnic-Vietnamese congregation. Just south of here, the **Thai Consulate**, housed in a 1926 mansion on Kouvolavong Road, is a fine example of how beautiful French-era buildings can be when properly restored.

Vietnamese and Chinese joss houses and schools in the area attest to the wealth and influence of Savannakhet's merchant class. Gravitating towards urban areas and searching for business opportunities, the Chinese found their way to Savannakhet in small numbers before the arrival of the French. But the Vietnamese came for the most part at the encouragement of the French, who doubted the business acumen of ethnic Lao. After the revolution, most of Savannakhet's ethnic Vietnamese and Chinese fled across the Mekong into Thailand, taking their capital and entrepreneurial skills with them. Even today, thirty years after the revolution, much of Savannakhet is empty of people, its shops shuttered, and packs of stray dogs roaming the streets. Only recently have the Chinese and Vietnamese started coming back in any numbers to invest, gradually reclaiming many of the old French-era shophouses and opening up a few businesses.

Wat Sainyaphum
Just north of the ferry landing, on the road running along the Mekong, sits **Wat Sainyaphum**, Savannakhet's largest Buddhist monastery. Nearly all the

structures at the wat, save for the school building in the northwest corner of the compound, have been recently restored in garish, circus-like hues. It is worth a visit, however, especially if you are looking for a serene, shady spot to catch up on your postcard-writing.

Musee des Dinosaurs

Set up with some help from French paleontologists, the **Musee des Dinosaurs** on Khanthabouli Road (daily 9am–noon & 1–4pm; free), north of Wat Sain-yaphum, showcases finds from the five digs going on in the countryside around Savannakhet. However, there's nothing much of interest aside from a few old bones and photos of the digs, and the opportunity to chat with the friendly curators, who appreciate foreign visitors and a chance to converse in English.

Provincial Museum

Housed in a peeling colonial-era mansion, 1km south of the ferry landing, the unkempt **Provincial Museum** (daily 8am–noon & 2–4pm; 5000K) is mostly

Kaysone: the man behind the bamboo curtain

When the leaders of Laos set about honouring their prime minister and communist party leader **Kaysone Phomvihane** on his death in 1992, they turned to North Korea. Experts at producing bronze work in the heroes-of-socialism style, North Korean sculptors executed 150 bronze busts of Kaysone, which have since been erected in pavilions throughout Laos. Whether these bronzes are a faithful portrayal of Kaysone is a matter of irrelevance to most Lao, since from 1958 until 1975, the man who led the Lao People's Revolutionary Party from its inception in 1955 was rarely seen in public. Only now that the state has begun remaking itself in his image is the cloud of secrecy surrounding the man dissipating, but the lack of biographical details about his life makes it difficult to discern the private Kaysone from the state-cultivated one.

What is known is that Kaysone was born in Savannakhet in 1920, the only son of a Vietnamese civil servant father and a Lao mother. As a teenager he left for Hanoi, where he studied at a law school under the name of Nguyen Tri Quoc before dropping out to devote himself to the life of a revolutionary. By 1945, he had attracted the attention of the great North Vietnamese leader Ho Chi Minh, who sent Kaysone back to his hometown, instructing him to infiltrate a Lao nationalist movement supported by the American Office of Strategic Services, a forerunner of the Central Intelligence Agency. Kaysone would later match his wits against the CIA as commander of the communist forces during the Second Indochina War.

When **Souphanouvong** arrived on the scene in Savannakhet later on in 1945, Kaysone and his followers deferred to the leadership of the prince, whom Kaysone followed to Bangkok after the French returned to power in 1946. Soon after, Kaysone became a member of the newly formed Committee for Resistance in the East, chaired by Nouhak Phoumsavanh, coordinating anti-French guerrilla raids along the Lao–Vietnamese border and responsible for liaisons with the Viet Minh, a tie that was to earn him the trust of the North Vietnamese, who eventually recruited him into the Indochinese Communist Party (ICP). After training at the Viet Minh's military academy, Kaysone became commander of the Latsavong brigade, the guerrilla unit in southeastern Laos that marked the beginnings of the Lao People's Liberation Army. Although unknown in national circles (it would take years for the international press to recognize him), Kaysone was already a force to be reckoned with, and, in 1950, when Souphanouvong formed the national resistance government that came to be known as the Pathet Lao, Kaysone was named defence minister. In this capacity, Kaysone spent the next four years recruiting and training members for given over to old photographs of Kaysone, Savannakhet's most revered native son (see box, below), and the events leading up to the communist takeover in 1975. There's a giant bust of the great leader, and pictures of him bear-hugging a variety of dictators including Ho Chi Minh, Fidel Castro, Hun Sen and Jiang Zemin. In a sign of the times, the collection of captured RLA light artillery pieces formerly lined up in the weedy yard in front of the museum and pointed at Thailand has been discreetly removed.

Around Savannakhet

A **bicycle ride** out in any direction from the centre of town gives you an opportunity to view the difference in lifestyles between the ethnic Vietnamese of the town and the ethnic Lao in the countryside. As you head out, brick and stucco give way to teak and bamboo, while rows of shade trees come to an abrupt halt and fruit trees – mango, guava and papaya – begin to appear in every yard. Children walking to and from school carry small cylindrical

the Pathet Lao's fighting force, of which he formally became commander in 1954. On the formation of the Lao People's Party the following year, Kaysone became secretary general – a post he would hold for the next 37 years. His control of the revolutionary movement was further solidified in 1959 when Souphanouvong and other Pathet Lao leaders were jailed in Vientiane. Though Kaysone relinquished his post as commander of the army to Khamtay Siphandone in 1962, he continued to direct military strategy until the end of the Thirty Year Struggle in 1975. He also led several delegations over these years to the Soviet Union, where he was received with all the honours accorded a communist party leader.

It was only fitting that Kaysone – a man who disdained the perquisites of military rank, indeed who was never even referred to by rank, and adopted the atypical surname of Phomvihane, the Lao word for the Sanskrit *brahmavihara*, or "Four Principles of Great Leadership" (kindness, mercy, sympathy and impartiality) – should emerge as the first prime minister of the Lao People's Democratic Republic in December 1975. For the next seventeen years, Kaysone firmly held the reins of power in Laos and, among diplomats, earned a reputation as a clever man, eager to learn and willing to acknowledge his mistakes. He has also been called the most pragmatic of Southeast Asia's socialist leaders, praise he earned after he ditched the botched socialist economic policies of the late 1970s and initiated reforms – long before change took root in the Soviet Union and Vietnam, Laos's socialist backers. Indeed, Kaysone's Laos hardly fitted the mould of a typical socialist country at all by the time of his **death** at the age of 72 in 1992, when Buddhist monks from wats around the capital chanted funeral incantations and received alms during a seven-day period of mourning in his honour. Until Kaysone's death the country's leadership rarely presented itself to the public as anything but a group, but the former prime minister's greying hair and full face has since become the image employed by a party reaching out for symbols of nationalism, his name invoked in speeches and the source of inspiration for a museum erected at his former Vientiane home (see p.109). But what is perhaps more striking than the party's decision to transform Kaysone into a "man of the people", who relished simple food and knew all the country songs by heart, are the pedestals upon which his bust has been placed. Shaded by red and gold pavilions topped by tiered parasols, Kaysone's monuments exude something of the regal splendour once reserved for the Theravada Buddhist monarchs who ruled over the kingdom of Lane Xang.

baskets, indicating a preference for sticky rice over steamed rice, and older Lao men favour a sarong in traditional shades of purple, orange and black over the shorts or trousers worn in urban areas. Depending on the season, **rice fields** are either being ploughed, planted, weeded or harvested by hand. The farmers are busiest in the hours just after dawn and before dusk, wisely spending the hottest time of the day snoozing in hammocks suspended in the shade.

That Ing Hang

A much revered Buddhist stupa dating from the sixteenth century, **That Ing Hang** is located just outside Savannakhet and can be reached by bicycle or motorcycle: follow Route 13 north for 13km until you see a sign on the right and follow this road for a further 3km. The stucco work that covers the stupa is crude yet appealing, especially the whimsical rosettes that dot the uppermost spire. Off to one side of the stupa stands an amusing sandstone sculpture of a lion, grinning like a Cheshire cat, which could only have been hauled here from one of the Khmer ruins downriver.

The stupa is best visited during its annual festival in February when thousands make the pilgrimage, camping in the walled courtyard that surrounds the stupa. During the celebrations, the door to a small chamber at the base of the stupa is opened, and male devotees queue up to make offerings to the Buddha images inside. By custom, women are prohibited from entering this inner sanctum.

Eating

The food and service at Savannakhet's **travellers' cafés** are passable, but the town does have some good local **restaurants**. One famous local noodle dish worth seeking out is *baw bun* (Vietnamese rice noodles served with chopped-up spring rolls and beef). Vietnamese spring rolls are also quite good here. Other local delights include bamboo shoots and watermelon and *sin Savannakhet* – sweet, dried, roasted beef.

There are a few local Lao restaurants such as *Xokxay* and *Savanhlath* on and around the town square. In the evenings, shops selling soft drinks – the fruit shakes are in a class of their own – and a few *tam màk hung* vendors crop up on the riverbank in front of Wat Sainyaphum, a pleasant spot to catch the sunset over Thailand and mingle with locals.

Baw Bun Shop Fourth shophouse from the river in the alley behind *Santyphab Hotel*. Not only is this place hard to find (there's no English sign) but it's only open until noon or so. Still, if it's *baw bun* you're after, this is the place.

Hoongthip Garden Restaurant 79 Phetsalat Rd ☏041/212262. The nicest restaurant in town, housed in a big wood building with open sala-style seating under a green roof in Thai-Lao style. If you're after a good meal in pleasant surrounds with some atmosphere, look no further.

Lao-Paris 4 Seasons Café 30 Chaleunmoung Rd, near the river. Many travellers seem to end up at this Vietnamese shophouse near the river. The food may not be the greatest, but it's a pleasant enough place for a beer or an iced coffee.

Mekong Riverside North end of Tha He Rd. For some unfathomable reason, this is the only restaurant in town to take advantage of the view across the Mekong, and the tables on a wooden terrace outside a large house supply an excellent sunset vista. Not to be confused with the badly botched *Mekong Hotel* just down the street.

Rendezvous 179 Latsavongseuk Rd, at the corner of Simuang Rd. A travellers' café with an English menu and a few Western dishes like pancakes, though it does a much better job with Chinese fare.

Sakura Korean BBQ Sayamungkhun Rd. Very good Korean barbecue with a choice of beef or fish and lots of fresh veggies and glass noodles. Cheap, delicious and highly recommended.

Directory

Airlines Lao Airlines, at the airport, southeast of the city centre ☏041/212140.

Banks and exchange The Lao Development Bank and the BCEL are near the intersection of Latsavongseuk and Oudomsin roads, the former facing Oudomsin Road and the latter facing Latsavongseuk Road.

Consulates Thailand, Kouvolavong Road, one block south of the square (Mon–Fri 8.30am–noon & 2–3.30pm; ☏041/212373); tourist visas require two photos and, provided you apply before noon, the visa is ready the same afternoon. Vietnam: on Sisavang Vong Road (Mon–Fri 7.30–11am & 1.30–4.30pm; ☏041/212418); visas cost $55, require two photos and take three working days.

Hospitals and clinics The biggest hospital is located on Khanthabouli Road, near the provincial museum; a 24hr clinic operates on Phetsalat Road, a block south of the *Hoongthip Hotel*.

Internet access A handful of Internet places can be found in town, charging somewhere in the neighbourhood of 15,000K per hr.

Laundry Fast and cheap at the laundry shops along Kouvolavong Road, north of the town square.

Markets Talat Nyai (main market), at the north end of town towards the bus station, has four levels of goods. A market was recently constructed on Latsavongseuk at the corner of Chaimuang Road. Stalls selling fresh fruit daily can be found on Latsavongseuk at the corner of Soutthanou Road.

Massage The Red Cross clinic offers traditional massage on Kouvolavong Rd across from the Chinese temple.

Newspapers A few copies of the *Bangkok Post* arrive at the minimart, next to the *Santyphab Hotel*, daily around 5pm, and there's a free reading copy at the *Lao-Paris* café (see opposite).

Pharmacy The biggest pharmacy is on the corner of Oudomsin and Senna roads.

Post and telephone The GPO is on Khanthabouli Road, a few blocks south of the town square (Mon–Fri 8am–noon & 1–5pm, Sat & Sun 8–11am). The Telcom building, with overseas phone and fax services, (daily 8am–10pm) is just behind it.

Swimming The *Phonepaseud Hotel*, on Santisouk Rd northeast of the centre, has a 25m pool which is open to non-guests for a small fee.

East to Xepon and the Vietnam border

From Savannakhet, the newly paved **Route 9** heads east through a series of drab and dusty towns, passing Muang Phin and then Xepon, where it begins its climb up into the Annamite Mountains. The road ends its Lao journey at the **Lao Bao pass**, before crossing into Vietnam and continuing down to **Dong Ha**, where it joins Highway 1. The French completed the road in 1930, as part of an Indochinese road network intended to link Mekong towns with the Vietnamese coast, bringing in Vietnamese migrants and trucking out Lao produce. Today, the Thais, too, have an interest in Route 9 as a trade corridor, linking their relatively poor northeastern provinces with the port of Danang in Vietnam. For the time being, Route 9 is an easy ride, but unless the road is maintained there is a very real possibility that it will revert to the bumpy, dusty track it once was in the not so distant past.

While most travellers barrel through to and from Vietnam on the direct buses, the frontier is not without sites of interest. As you approach **Muang Phin**, Route 9 begins to cross the north–south arteries of the **Ho Chi Minh Trail**, a network of dirt paths and roads that spread throughout southeastern Laos, running from the Mu Gia Pass in Bolikhamxai province south through Attapu and into Cambodia. While much of the debris from the war lies off the beaten track, some of these war relics are easily accessible. Another place worth stopping in to explore the surrounding area is the recently rebuilt market town of **Xepon** which, along with neighbouring towns, is populated predominantly by Phu Tai people, a lowland Lao group. To the west, the valleys have long been inhabited by Lao, drawn south centuries ago by the prospect of river valleys ripe for wet-rice cultivation. They also benefited from their proximity to the trading route from Hué, the ancient Vietnamese royal seat, to Savannakhet and on to Siam.

Xeno and Muang Phin

Route 9 heads past teak plantations until, 35km from Savannakhet, it reaches **XENO**, where it intersects the country's north–south axis, Route 13. Once a French military outpost and later a Royal Lao airfield, Xeno these days is known mostly for its gypsum quarries. There's no reason to stop here, but should you find yourself stuck for the night, you can take advantage of the air-conditioned rooms at the town's sole hotel, the multistorey *Pounlaodi* (●), across from the market.

You'll know you've reached **MUANG PHIN**, roughly 100km east of Xeno, when your bus halts right in front of the massive Vietnamese-Lao friendship monument, a testament to communist cooperation during the Second Indochina War, and exuding far more revolutionary zeal than anything found in Vientiane. The golden rendering of a Pathet Lao and North Vietnamese soldier dwarfs the town, whose run-down appearance attests to Muang Phin's unfortunate position on one of the fronts during the war. There's little to recommend Muang Phin as a stopover, but if you're here you may opt for a quick trip to check out what's left of a downed American helicopter, one of the more easily accessible **war relics** on the Ho Chi Minh Trail. Follow the road that strikes south from the friendship monument for 30m and you'll find it on your left.

If and when **Route 23** is reconnected to Toumlan, Muang Phin will become a convenient hub for travellers wanting to cut down directly to Salavan, as well as a base for visiting the huge Dong Phou Viang NBCA just south of town. But these days, the town is little more than a through point on the road to the border. There are two new private **guesthouses** here; *Sikham* (●) just west of the bus station, and a little further down the street there's also the *Sysamphone* (●).

Vietnamese influence

Ties between Muang Phin and **Vietnam** go back a long way. During much of the eighteenth and nineteenth centuries, the area's Phu Tai inhabitants paid tribute to the court in Hué. In the middle of the nineteenth century, the Vietnamese rulers, having just wrapped up a war with Siam, were content to exact a light tribute of wax and elephant tusks from the Phu Tai, preferring to leave the Tai minority's territory as a loose buffer zone between regional powers. By this point, Vietnamese merchants, following the traditional trading route across the Lao Bao pass, were already arriving in Muang Phin with cooking pans, iron, salt and fish sauce, and returning east with cows and water buffaloes in tow. A story told by an early French visitor to the town attests to the business acumen of one of these merchants. Upon arriving in town, the merchant found prices too high, but was reluctant to return home without making a good profit. With a quick conversion to Buddhism the merchant's problem was solved: he shaved his head and shacked up in the local temple where he could defray his expenses until prices dropped, at which point the merchant donned a wig, bought up a few buffalo and hightailed it back to Hué. Today, a planned link to the Vietnamese power grid reflects the continuing influence exerted by Vietnam in this area.

Xepon

A picturesque village in the foothills of the Annamite Mountains, 40km from the Vietnamese border, **XEPON** is a pleasant rural stopover for those in transit on the route to Vietnam or Savannakhet. Cows and water buffalo meander along red dirt roads, pausing to graze in the fields that separate the village's wooden homes, and flame trees add a splash of fire to the misty green hills surrounding the settlement. To look at the crumbling, custard-coloured school building, perched on a hill overlooking the market, you'd think Xepon was much older than it is. In fact, the original town of Xepon was destroyed during the war – along with every house of the district's two hundred villages – and was later rebuilt here 6km west of its original location, on the opposite bank of the Xe Banghiang River. The old city (written as "Tchepone" on some old maps) had been captured by communist forces in 1960 and became an important outpost on the Ho Chi Minh Trail. As such, it was the target of a joint South Vietnamese and American invasion in 1971 (see p.264), aimed at disrupting the flow of troops and supplies headed for communist forces in South Vietnam.

Practicalities

Xepon is such a small town that even the **market**, where the bus drops passengers, fails to generate much of a buzz, despite being the hub of everyday life. From the market, it's a short walk uphill to the government **guesthouse** (❶), a long wooden structure with blue trim, which offers dormitory-style accommodation and an outdoor pump for a shower. The caretaker drops by once or twice a day to check for new arrivals and clean up the rooms. The forestry department runs a somewhat nicer guesthouse (❶) at the edge of town, 1500m from the market, also featuring dormitory-style rooms. There's no water, so be prepared to bathe in the nearby stream. To get here, take a left at the second road west of the market and follow the road to the foot of the hill.

There's an excellent **noodle shop** on the western side of the market complex, popular with locals. Run by a family from Vientiane, the shop makes a hearty bowl of *fŏe*, loaded with chunks of roasted chicken and garlic. A second eating option is the small **restaurant** (across from the market and marked by an English sign) run by a chatty Phu Tai woman. Noodles, omelettes and stir-fried vegetables can be selected from an English-language menu scrawled on a chalk board, although the innards mingled into the *làp sin* may not appeal to all.

There are no official exchange services in Xepon, but cash can always be exchanged at the market. From Xepon, sawngthaews run up to Ban Dong as well as the border town of Daen Sawan, where you can continue by motorcycle taxi to the Lao Bao border post.

The Ho Chi Minh Trail at Ban Dong

Heading east out of Xepon, you'll cross a Russian bridge, built to replace the destroyed French one, the shrapnel-riddled remains of which lie in the river below. The highway gradually climbs through the foothills of the Annamite chain, passing bomb craters – often obscured by brush – and unexploded ordnance, dragged to the roadside by villagers clearing their land. Women squat by the road with their intricately woven baskets, selling bamboo shoots – a local speciality. The area's abundant bamboo crop is in fact partially a by-product of the spraying of defoliants by American forces who hoped to expose the arteries of the Ho Chi Minh Trail: hardy bamboo is quick to take root in areas of deforestation.

Operation Lam Son 719

On the outskirts of the village of Ban Dong on Route 9 sit two rusting American tanks, all that remains of a massive invasion and series of battles that have become a mere footnote in the history of the decade-long American military debacle in Indochina. In 1971 US President Nixon, anticipating a massive campaign by North Vietnamese troops against South Vietnam the following year (which happened to be an election year in the US), ordered an attack on the Ho Chi Minh Trail to cut off supplies to communist forces. Although a congressional amendment had been passed the previous year prohibiting US ground troops from crossing the border from Vietnam into Laos and Cambodia, the US command saw it as an opportunity to test the strengths of Vietnamization, the policy of turning the ground war over to the South Vietnamese. For the operation, code-named **Lam Son 719**, it was decided that ARVN (Army of the Republic of Vietnam) troops were to invade Laos and block the trail with the backing of US air support. The objective was Xepon, a town straddled by the Trail, which was some 30–40km wide at this point. Nixon's national security adviser, Henry Kissinger, was later to lament that "the operation, conceived in doubt and assailed by scepticism, proceeded in confusion". In early February 1971, ARVN troops and tanks pushed across the border at Lao Bao and followed Route 9 into Laos. Like a caterpillar trying to ford a column of red ants, the South Vietnamese troops were soon engulfed by North Vietnamese (NVA) regulars, who were superior in number. Ordered by President Thieu of South Vietnam to halt if there were more than 3000 casualties, ARVN officers stopped halfway to Xepon and engaged the NVA in a series of battles that lasted over a month. US air support proved ineffectual, and by mid-March scenes of frightened ARVN troops drastically retreating were being broadcast around the world. In an official Lao account of the battle, a list of "units of Saigon puppet troops wiped out on Highway 9" included four regiments of armoured cavalry destroyed between the Vietnam border and Ban Dong.

Rows of bamboo-and-thatch drink shops, competing to quench the thirst of Vietnamese truckers, signal your arrival in **BAN DONG**, and are the only feature that distinguish this seemingly unremarkable village from the handful of other villages on this stretch of Route 9. However, Ban Dong is a popular stop on any tour of the **Ho Chi Minh Trail**, and villagers are slowly growing accustomed to tourists poking around for a glimpse of the Republic of Vietnam's American-made tanks left over from one of America's most ignominious defeats during the war, at the battle known as **Lam Son 719**.

The tank that's easiest to find lies five minutes' walk off the road that cuts south out of town towards Taoy, which was once a crucial artery of the Ho Chi Minh Trail. Shaded by a grove of jackfruit trees, it rests atop a small hill east of the road, and has been partially dismantled for its valuable steel. Someone has scrawled a message in red paint on the iron carcass, warning locals that they should leave the rest of the tank intact as a monument to Pathet Lao military triumph. In truth, the tanks speak of the might of the North Vietnamese Army, which routed South Vietnamese troops in their attempted invasion of Laos (see box above). UXO-Lao, the Lao National Unexploded Ordnance Programme, cleared Ban Dong of unexploded war debris in 1998, but it's still a good idea to ask a villager to show you the way, as you should always take extra care when leaving a well-worn path, and vegetation in the rainy season can obscure the tank's location. If you're travelling by public transport, the best time to visit Ban Dong is in the morning, as there are no late-afternoon buses plying this stretch of highway, and Ban Dong has no accommodation. For getting back in the afternoon, check to see if another bus will swing through town to pick you up; otherwise you'll have to rely on flagging down a ride.

Daen Sawan and the border

The quality of the road takes a dive as it makes its final push towards the mountain pass of Lao Bao, leading to Vietnam. After passing through many small ethnic minority villages, you come to **DAEN SAWAN**, the last town on the Lao side of the pass.

For a remote border town, Daen Sawan is quite tourist-friendly. There is a Lao May Bank in town, as well as at the Lao Immigration Office on the border. The rates are not good, so if you're arriving from Vietnam, only change what you need; $20 is more than enough to get you to Savannakhet. There's **accommodation** at the *Friendly* guesthouse (❶), which has basic rooms with shared bathrooms and a helpful owner who speaks fairly good English. Attached to the guesthouse is the *Loung Aloune* **restaurant**, which can muster up a tasty plate of fried rice, along with the usual smattering of Lao dishes. Baguettes are on offer at another shop nearby.

There are two buses a day from here to Savannakhet, leaving in the morning, the last at 10am; and there's also an early-afternoon bus to Xepon.

The Daen Sawan/Lao Bao border crossing

A short distance from the Lao immigration post is the **Daen Sawan/Lao Bao** border crossing into Vietnam. Motorcycle taxis can be hired in Daen Sawan for the final one-kilometre ride to the Lao immigration post. Even if you're on a direct bus into Vietnam, you may find yourself waiting a couple of hours in Daen Sawan.

Travellers **to Vietnam** must have a valid visa and the crossing is not always hassle-free: Vietnamese officials may send you back if your visa is not stamped for "Lao Bao", and motorcyclists have also reported problems, with officials sometimes unwilling to allow larger bikes to enter. On the Vietnamese side, there are motorcycle taxis to take you down the hill to **LAO BAO** town where buses leave every thirty minutes for the twenty-kilometre journey to Khe Sanh; some buses go straight through to Dong Ha on Route 1, where bus or train connections can be made to Hanoi and Hué. If you've entered Laos **from Vietnam** and are not on a through bus, you'll have to get a motorbike 1km down to **Daen Sawan**.

Travel details

Buses

Daen Sawan/Lao Bao to: Muang Phin (3 daily; 2hr); Savannakhet (2 daily; 5hr); Xepon (4 daily; 1hr).

Lak Xao to: Thakhek (1 daily; 5hr); Vientiane (3 daily; 8hr).

Muang Phin to: Daen Sawan/Lao Bao (3 daily; 2hr); Savannakhet (3 daily; 3hr); Xepon (3 daily; 1hr).

Savannakhet to: Daen Sawan/Lao Bao (2 daily; 5hr); Danang (4 weekly; 10hr); Hué (3 weekly; 8hr); Muang Phin (3 daily; 3hr); Pakxe (3 daily; 6hr);

Thakhek (9 daily; 2hr); Vientiane (6 daily; 12hr); Xepon (2 daily; 4hr).

Thakhek to: Hanoi (weekly; 24hr); Lak Xao (3 daily; 4hr); Mahaxai (5 daily; 2hr 30min); Pakxe (3 daily; 9hr); Savannakhet (9 daily; 4hr); Vientiane (10 daily; 8hr).

Xepon to: Daen Sawan/Lao Bao (4 daily; 1hr); Muang Phin (3 daily; 1hr); Savannakhet (2 daily; 4hr).

Ferries

Thakhek to: Nakhon Phanom (every 30min during daylight; 10min).

6

The far south

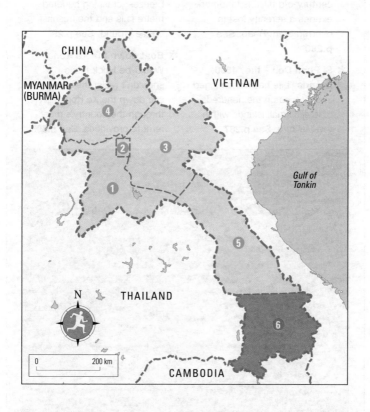

CHAPTER 6   # Highlights

* **Champasak** Kick back for a day or three in this laid-back backpacker town, among temples, sacred mountains and Khmer ruins. See p.278

* **Wat Phou** The most harmonious Khmer ruin outside of Cambodia, this fifteen-century-old hillside landmark exudes a serenity lost in overrun Siem Reap. See p.280

* **Si Phan Don – the "4000 Islands"** Life has not changed in centuries on the hundreds of idyllic small islands within the Mekong. See p.287

* **Dolphin-watching at Khon Island** See the rare and endangered Irrawaddy freshwater dolphins in one of their last surviving habitats. See p.295

* **Explore the Bolaven** Ascend the Bolaven Plateau for cool breezes, crashing hundred-metre falls and the freshest coffee around. See p.297

* **Boat down the Xe Kong** Would-be Huck Finns shouldn't resist the chance to slip down the Xe Kong River through the country's most remote provinces. See p.305

△ Carvings at Wat Phou

The far south

The tail end of Laos is anchored by the provinces of **Champasak**, **Xekong**, **Attapu** and **Salavan**, a region that lay at the crossroads of the great empires that ruled Southeast Asia centuries ago – Champa, Chenla and Angkor. Bordered by Thailand, Cambodia and Vietnam, the **far south** conveniently divides into two sections, dictated primarily by topography, with **Pakxe**, the region's most important market town, as the hub. In the west, the **Mekong River** cuts Champasak province roughly in half, while further east, the fertile highlands of the **Bolaven Plateau** separate the Mekong corridor from the rugged Annamite Mountains that form Laos's border with Vietnam.

The dozens of ancient Khmer temples scattered throughout the lush tropical forests and jade rice paddies on either bank of the Mekong hold mysteries yet to be unravelled by today's archeologists. Pilgrims from the lowland Lao communities that dominate the Mekong River Valley of the far south gather relics from these sites, ignorant of the gods that inspired them, and place them upon their gaudy, modern Theravada Buddhist temples. In the last years of the monarchy, even members of the royal family had the audacity to plunder statues of deities to decorate their modern villas, as if proclaiming a rightful link to the *devaraja*, the god-kings who ruled over Angkorian Cambodia. The most famous of these temples, **Wat Phou**, is the spiritual centre of the region and the main tourist attraction in southern Laos. An imposing reminder of the Angkorian empire that once dominated much of Southeast Asia, Wat Phou is one of the most impressive Khmer ruins outside Cambodia, and lies a few kilometres from the town of **Champasak**, the former royal seat of the defunct Lao kingdom of the same name.

From here it makes sense to go with the flow of the river south to **Si Phan Don**, where the Mekong's 1993-kilometre journey through Laos rushes to a thundering conclusion in the series of picturesque **waterfalls**. The region's name means "Four Thousand Islands", a reference to the vast number of land masses dotted with long-established ethnic Lao villages and rice paddies, which the Mekong wraps around before spilling over the Khone Falls into Cambodia. These waters support some of the most important freshwater fisheries in Southeast Asia.

Much of the area east of the Mekong lies off the beaten track and is likely to appeal most to the intrepid and those who relish a dose of "real travelling". Typically, travel in this region involves journeying on hard wooden seats along bumpy roads to remote towns or out-of-the-way spots of raw natural beauty. Just east of Pakxe, the **Bolaven Plateau**, with its rich agricultural bounty and crashing waterfalls, straddles the borders of three remote provinces, an area

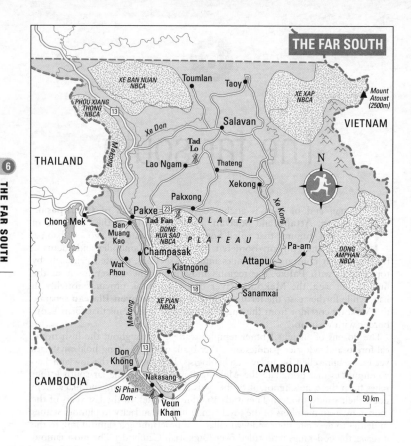

THE FAR SOUTH

with a long history of settlement by midland Mon-Khmer groups, whose names – Laven, Taoy, Alak, Katang, Ngae – are seldom heard outside Laos. The isolation of the thickly forested hills in this region has made it an ideal place for insurgents throughout the ages to hide out – from anti-French rebels to the North Vietnamese in the Second Indochina War. The latter transformed trails and roads along Laos's eastern edge into the Ho Chi Minh Trail, a thoroughfare along which supplies and troops made their way into Cambodia and South Vietnam. American forces and their allies, the Royalist Lao and the Thai, subjected the area to some of the most intensive bombing in history, a campaign that included the use of chemical defoliants such as the notorious Agent Orange. By braving the primitive transport linking the far-flung villages of Salavan, Xekong and Attapu, you'll witness the resilience of the land, still home to a diverse variety of wildlife, and travel among peoples as cut off from the rest of Laos as they have ever been.

Pakxe, the region's commercial and transport hub, provides the most convenient **gateway** to the far south, with travellers arriving either from Savannakhet or from Thailand via the Chong Mek border crossing. It's also possible to arrive from Stung Treng in Cambodia, via the Mekong (see p.25). Getting around in the deep south can be exhausting, as transport is limited to slow, crowded buses navigating poorly paved roads, some of which are impassable in the rainy season. Another drawback to the network stitching together the southern provinces is that it can be difficult to avoid backtracking, but, on the bright side, several significant towns can be reached by river, providing a more comfortable, if time-consuming, mode of travel. The most pleasant **time of year** to visit the region is during the cool season (Nov–Feb), when the rivers and waterfalls are in full spate and the scenery is greenest.

Some history

The **early history** of the far south remains a hot topic of debate among archeologists. Although the ruins of an ancient city buried near Champasak (and not far from Wat Phou) indicate that the area was the centre of a thriving civilization as early as the fifth century, no one seems sure if the town was part of **Champa**, a Hinduized kingdom that ruled parts of central Vietnam for more than fourteen centuries, or the **Chenla** kingdom, which is thought to have been located near the Mekong River in present-day northern Cambodia, extending through what is now southern Laos. The **Khmer** were the first people to leave a clear imprint on the area, and the temple ruins that survive throughout the far south along the Mekong River suggest the region was an important part of the Khmer empire from the eighth to the twelfth century, when the Angkor empire was at its height. It is also thought that the better part of southern Laos was dominated by ethnic Khmer, in particular the **Mon-Khmer ethnic groups** that still inhabit the Bolaven Plateau region and the Annamite Mountains.

The **ethnic Lao** are relative newcomers to the region, having made their way slowly south along the Mekong from the Lao heartland of the Upper Mekong, as Angkor's power, and its hold over present-day southern Laos, waned. By the early sixteenth century, the centre of the ethnic Lao world was shifting steadily south, and King Phothisalat spent much of his time in Vientiane. Eventually, his son and successor Setthathilat officially transferred the capital of Lane Xang from Louang Phabang to Vientiane in 1563. While the origins of the first ethnic Lao principality in the Champasak region are unclear, legends trace the roots of the **Lao kingdom of Champasak** back to Nang Pao, a queen said to have ruled during the mid-seventeenth century. The story goes that **Nang Pao** was seduced by a prince from a nearby kingdom and gave birth out of wedlock, initiating a sex scandal for which she has been remembered ever since. The queen is said to have acknowledged her mistake by decreeing that every unwed mother must pay for her sin by sacrificing a buffalo to appease the spirits, a tradition continued into the late 1980s by unwed mothers, known as "Nang Pao's daughters", from some of the ethnic groups in the area. Legend has it that Nang Pao's actual daughter, Nang Peng, ceded rule over the kingdom to a holy man, who in turn sought out **Soi Sisamouth**, a descendant of Souligna Vongsa, the last great king of Lane Xang, and made him king in 1713.

Soi Sisamouth ascended the throne of an independent southern kingdom in the wake of the dissolution of Lane Xang at the turn of the eighteenth century. With his royal seat centred on present-day Champasak, near Wat Phou, Soi Sisamouth extended the new kingdom's influence to include part of present-day Thailand, as well as Salavan and Attapu. But the king, and his successor Sainyakuman, only managed to maintain a tenuous independence and, after its capital was captured by Siamese forces in 1778, Champasak was reduced to being a **vassal of Siam**, and so it remained until the French arrived more than one hundred years later. King Yo made a gambit to regain independence for Champasak when he joined forces in 1827 with his father Anou, Vientiane's legendary last king, in an ill-fated fight to throw off the yoke of Siamese domination. The botched rebellion had disastrous consequences for both kingdoms – the kingdom of Vientiane was left to ruin while Champasak was drastically reduced in size.

Siam gobbled up so much of Champasak's territory that there was little left for the **French** when they arrived late in the nineteenth century and claimed all territory east of the Mekong River. Caught between French ambition and a still-powerful Siam, Champasak was split in half, and its king, Kam Souk, was forced to rule from the left bank, severed from a large number of his subjects. Champasak's meagre territory was reunited by the Franco-Siamese treaty of 1904, but Kam Souk had to travel to Pakxe to swear his allegiance to France and was treated as little more than a civil servant, stripped of the royal privileges that the kings of Louang Phabang and Cambodia were permitted to keep.

Although Kam Souk's son, **Prince Boun Oum na Champasak**, successfully parlayed his birthright into a prime spot in the national limelight, it seems Nang Pao's kiss of death was reserved especially for him. In exchange for the title of Inspector General for life, Prince Boun Oum renounced his claim to the throne of a sovereign Champasak in 1946 and recognized the king of Louang Phabang as the royal head of a unified Laos, effectively ending the Champasak royal line. Although Boun Oum continued to perform the ritual duties that lent legitimacy to his princely title until the mid-1970s, when the right-leaning prince fled the country after the communist takeover, he spoke of the kingdom as being doomed from the start on account of Nang Pao's misdemeanour: "With an unmarried mother as queen, everything started so badly that the game was lost before it began."

Pakxe

Capitalizing on its location at the confluence of the Xe Don and the Mekong rivers, roughly halfway between the Thai border and the fertile Bolaven Plateau, **PAKXE** is the far south's biggest city. For travellers, the place is mostly a convenient stopover en route to Si Phan Don and Wat Phou, though it's also a more comfortable base than Pakxong for exploration of the Bolaven Plateau and nearby NBCAs, and the border crossing to Thailand just west at Chong Mek makes Pakxe a logical entry or exit point for travellers doing a north–south tour of Laos.

Unlike other major Mekong towns, Pakxe is not an old city. Rather it has risen in prominence, from relatively recent beginnings a hundred years ago as a French administrative centre, to being the region's most important market town, attracting traders from Salavan, Attapu, Xekong and Si Phan Don, as well as from Thailand. The diverse population of Vietnamese, Lao and Chinese today numbers some 60,000.

Arrival and city transport

Pakxe is served by an airport, three bus stations, a sawngthaew station, and a passenger boat landing. **Buses** to and from the north use either a lot next to the **Champasak Plaza**, centrally located, or the **Northern Bus Station**, 7km north of the city on Route 13. Buses to and from points south and east use the **Southern Bus Station**, 8km southeast of town on Route 13 at the big T-junction. Tuk-tuks from either bus station into town cost around 10,000K.

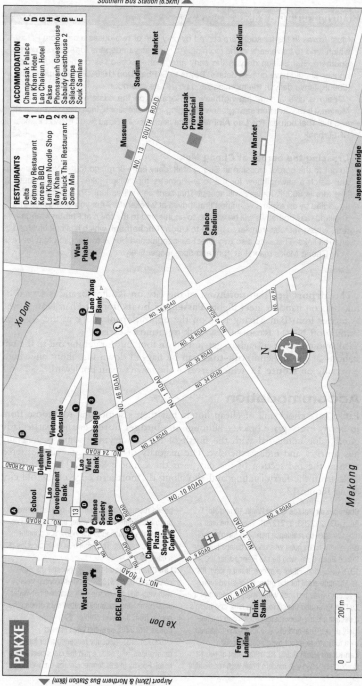

PAKXE

Southern Bus Station (6.5km) ▲

RESTAURANTS	
Delta	
Ketmany Restaurant	
Korean BBQ	
Lan Kham Noodle Shop	
May Kham	
Seneluck Thai Restaurant	
Some Mai	

ACCOMMODATION	
Champasak Palace	C
Lan Kham Hotel	D
Lao Chaleun Hotel	G
Pakse	H
Phonsavanh Guesthouse	A
Sabaidy Guesthouse 2	B
Salachampa	F
Souk Samlane	E

Market

Stadium

Museum

Stadium

Champasak Provincial Museum

NO. 13 SOUTH ROAD

New Market

Japanese Bridge

Wat Phabat

Palace Stadium

Xe Don

Lane Xang Bank

NO. 38 ROAD

NO. 36 ROAD

NO. 35 ROAD

NO. 34 ROAD

NO. 1 ROAD

NO. 40 RD

NO. 42 ROAD

N

Vietnam Consulate

Massage

NO. 46 ROAD

NO. 24 ROAD

Mekong

Diethelm Travel

Lao Viet Bank

School

Lao Development Bank

13

Chinese Society House

NO. 23 ROAD

NO. 12 ROAD

NO. 5 ROAD

NO. 6 ROAD

Champasak Plaza Shopping Centre

NO. 10 ROAD

NO. 1 ROAD

NO. 8 ROAD

NO. 9 ROAD

Wat Louang

BCEL Bank

Xe Don

NO. 11 ROAD

NO. 8 ROAD

Drink Stalls

Ferry Landing

Airport (2km) & Northern Bus Station (8km) ▲

0   200 m

Moving on from Pakxe

Most towns in the far south are served by only one or two buses a day from Pakxe, which tend to leave early in the morning. An express van departs for Attapu from the Southern Bus Station daily in the early afternoon – schedules change, but guesthouses should have current details. **Boats** to Si Phan Don (16,000K) via Champasak (5000K) leave daily in the mornings and arrive late afternoon.

There is also a huge **sawngthaew lot** located on the eastern side of the New Market. Here you'll find sawngthaews heading in all directions, including Champasak and the Thai border. The **Lao Airlines** office is on No. 11 Road (☎031/212252), near BCEL bank.

Crossing the border at Chong Mek

To get to the border crossing at Chong Mek (daily 8am–8pm), go to the New Market and catch a sawngthaew for the forty-kilometre trip, which takes around an hour. The fare is 8000K (drivers will accept Thai baht as well as kip). The border itself is straddled by an expansive market that thrives at weekends. After you've crossed into Thailand, sawngthaews will be waiting to shuttle you to the town of **Phibun Mangsahan**, where you can transfer to buses to **Ubon Ratchathani**, which has plentiful road and rail links. There are also two direct air-conditioned buses to Bangkok that leave from Chong Mek's market at 4pm and 5pm respectively.

The **airport** lies 2km northwest of the city on Route 13, and is served by tuk-tuks on hand to greet flights. **Passenger boats** from Si Phan Don as well as ferries from Ban Muang Kao, on the opposite bank, dock at the Xe Don landing off No. 11 Road, an easy walk from most hotels.

Pakxe is compact enough to get around on foot, but for getting out to the bus stations or the museum, **tuk-tuks** can be flagged down just about anywhere, especially on **Route 13**, which serves as the town's main boulevard.

Accommodation

Pakxe isn't chock-full of cheap hotels, but there's something to choose from in nearly every price bracket, although the **budget hotels** are not particularly good value compared with the north of the country; the south is generally less touristy and more expensive. The majority of places to stay are scattered around the old section of the city, near the Chinese Society House, a short walk from the ferry landing, and also along the northern edge of the old city, along Route 13.

Champasak Palace Cnr of Route 13 and No. 1 Rd ☎031/212263, ☎212781. Though he didn't actually take up residence here, the town's fanciest, ninety-room hotel was once a palace built for Prince Boun Oum, who fled to France after the 1975 revolution. Fit for a prince, if not a king, it's an absolute steal for the price: royal-sized rooms lead onto wide terraces with sweeping views of the Xe Don River and the surrounding hills, and there's a decent ground-floor restaurant serving moderately priced Thai and Chinese food, accompanied by a fully stocked (but overpriced) bar. ⑥
Lan Kham Hotel Route 13, 150m east of No. 12 Rd ☎031/213314. A modern hotel with reasonably

priced rooms, ranging from two-bed fan rooms up to a/c rooms with hot water en-suite and TVs. Downstairs, attached to the lobby, is a popular noodle restaurant. The hotel also rents bicycles ($2 a day). ②
Lao Chaleun Hotel Directly opposite the Salachampa ☎031/251333. Another modern hotel, with very tidy a/c rooms with attached hot-water bathrooms, and centrally located right around the corner from the West Market. ③
Pakse No. 5 Rd, near the West Market ☎031/212131. Recently reopened after lengthy renovations, and once again the city's best-value hotel. Rooms in this former cinema are well kept,

and everything works. The more expensive rooms have views of the river, as well as satellite TV and fridge. Downstairs is a popular restaurant. ⑤

Phonesavanh Guesthouse No. 12 Rd, a block north of Route 13. The long-running but uninviting *Phonesavanh Hotel* has a newish annexe which has seven newer rooms at the same low prices. All rooms have en-suite bathrooms but no hot water; some also have a/c. ②

Sabaidy Guesthouse 2 No. 24 Rd ☏ 031/212992. All budget travellers seem to head straight to this guesthouse, sited in an old residential area and hence quieter than the middle of town just across Route 13. Rooms are clean if spartan, and the dorm is the best in town. ①

Salachampa No. 10 Rd, near Champasak Plaza ☏ 031/212273. An elegant restored French villa, with teak floors, breezy verandas and a sitting room, filled with antique furniture, that's an atmospheric place to write postcards or read. All rooms have bathrooms and a/c, but spurn the cheaper modern cottages on offer; rooms in the old building are spacious, with high ceilings. Breakfast – Lao coffee with French bread – is included in the rate. ③

Souk Samlane No. 10 Rd, behind the Chinese Society Building ☏ 031/212002. A range of uninspiring but sanitary rooms, some with attached bathrooms and balconies. The cheaper en-suite rooms have no hot water. ①

The Town

Nestling between the Mekong and a bend of the Xe Don, Pakxe's centre, where you'll find the market and most of the hotels and restaurants, is surrounded by water on three sides. For some reason the streets in the centre of the city have all been laid out diagonally, but it's such a small place that finding your way around isn't a problem.

Along No. 11 Road, the street that follows the Xe Don, are a few remaining examples of crumbling Franco-Chinese **shophouses** and the town's main temple, **Wat Louang**. Turning away from the river here, you'll soon find yourself by the big new **Champasak Plaza Shopping Centre**, built on the site of the old market that was razed by fire in 1998. In the interim, the market vendors all moved out to a new venue located east along No. 38 Road, known in English as the **New Market**, and there seem to be few takers willing to occupy the overpriced spaces in Champasak Plaza.

For one of the few surviving examples of colonial architecture in the far south, be sure to check out the **Chinese Society House**, on No. 5 Road near the *Hotel Salachampa*, yet another French-era building. With many of the town's French-influenced buildings in disrepair or already replaced by modern shophouses, the Society House, beautifully renovated in 1998, is an elegant example of a style on the way out in rapidly modernizing Pakxe.

Along Route 13

On a low hill just west of Wat Pha Baht stands the **Champasak Palace Hotel**, a majestic eyesore resembling a giant cement wedding cake, and one of the few prominent reminders of the late Prince Boun Oum na Champasak, a colourful character who was the heir to the Champasak kingdom and one of the most influential southerners of the last century. Legend has it that Boun Oum needed a palace this size so that he could accommodate his many concubines. The palace, left incomplete after the one-time prime minister wound up on the wrong side of history and left for France in the 1970s, was converted into a hotel by Thai investors, who retained its original wooden fittings, tiled pillars and high ceilings. The stucco motifs on the gables depicting the country's post-revolutionary zeal were not in the prince's original plans. **Wat Pha Baht**, just east of the bridge that crosses north over the Xe Don, features a stylized Buddha's footprint, but like the rest of Pakxe's monasteries, the architecture doesn't reflect much divine inspiration.

The **Champasak Provincial Museum** (Mon–Fri 8–11.30am & 2–4pm; 3000K), 1500m east of the town centre on Route 13, houses some fine examples of ornately carved pre-Angkorian sandstone **lintels** taken from sites around the province, situated in the rear gallery. The upper gallery contains a dusty selection of costumes and jewellery from tribal peoples, and a small display of antique ethnic clothing. The rest of the museum is given over to the obligatory display of photographs and artefacts of the long Lao struggle to establish a workers' paradise on earth.

The New Market

The **New Market** (Talat Dao Heuang) on No. 38 Road is well worth a visit, and is certainly big enough to remind you of Vientiane's Morning Market. Along with the usual array of mounds of tobacco, plastic ware and live chickens, specialities available at the market include tea, coffee and a variety of fruit and vegetables, much of this from the bountiful Bolaven Plateau, as well as fish from the islands of Si Phan Don, including gigantic golden carp featherbacks, and the fermented fish paste known as *pa dàek*, sold out of ceramic jars.

Eating and drinking

Pakxe has the best range of **restaurants** south of Savannakhet, not just because of its size but because of the number of foreigners working here and its mix of ethnic Vietnamese, Chinese and Lao communities. Most of the town's better restaurants are found either on Route 13 between No. 12 and No. 24 roads, or on No. 46 Road just east of No. 24 Road.

Aside from restaurants, there are also a handful of **karaoke lounges** in the town proper, though more peaceful spots for a cold beer are the cheap drink stalls under the shady trees directly above the ferry landing, where you can look out over the Mekong and Xe Don rivers.

Delta Restaurant Route 13, near the Lao Viet Bank. This is the best place in town for a Western meal, especially breakfast. There's also Thai food, as well as a few vegetarian dishes.

Ketmany Restaurant Route 13. Aside from Thai and Lao food, this simple place offers ice cream, cakes and coffee.

Korean BBQ No. 46 Rd, just east of No. 24 Rd. Serving very tasty, inexpensive, BBQ meat steamboats – absolutely great with cold beer.

Lan Kham Noodle Shop Route 13, below the hotel of the same name. This very clean noodle shop is only open at lunchtime, when it's packed.

May Kham On the corner of Route 13 and No. 12 Rd. This place is always empty, and with only a few tables, doesn't really look like a restaurant, but offers an extensive array of Chinese dishes, including outstanding stewed duck with black mushrooms.

Seneluck Thai Restaurant Route 13. Run by a marvellous bunch of Laos who have lived and worked in Thailand, and a good evening hangout, with decent food to boot.

Some Mai No. 46 Rd, just east of No. 24 Rd. Almost across the street from the Korean BBQ, the *Some Mai* is also a steamboat place, where you pay just $1 per meat platter and get all the veggies, noodles and broth included.

Listings

Banks and exchange BCEL, No. 11 Rd; Lao Development Bank, Route 13 opposite the *Lan Kham Hotel*; Lao Viet Bank, Route 13, opposite the *Champasak Palace Hotel*.

Consulates Vietnam, on No. 24 Rd (Mon–Fri 8–11am & 2–4.30pm; ☎031/212058); visas cost $50, require two photos and take five working days.

Hospital South of the market on No. 9 Rd.

Internet access These come and go; your best bet is to look around the Champasak Plaza Shopping Centre.

Post office At the corner of No. 8 and No. 1 roads (daily 7.30am–9pm).

Telephones International calls and faxes at Telecom, on the corner of No. 1 and No. 38 roads (daily 8am–9pm).

Tour agencies Diethelm Travel, No. 21 Rd, north of Route 13 ☎031/212596; Inter-Lao Tourisme, in the lobby of the *Champasak Palace Hotel* ☎031/212778.

Around Pakxe

As more and more tourists make their way south to Pakxe, the number of **day-trip options** has begun to grow. **Ban Saphai**, a silk-weaving village north of the city, offers the chance to see villagers weaving *sin* according to age-old practices, and experience life in a traditional town on the island of **Don Kho** in the middle of the Mekong. In the hills south of the city, the villagers of **Kiatngong** raise elephants, which can be hired for trekking, while nearby **Ban Phapho** presents the opportunity to observe elephants being trained for work in the forest.

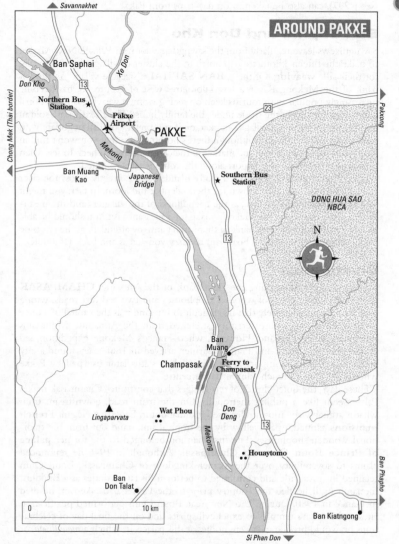

From Pakxe, daily passenger boats ply the forty-kilometre stretch of the Mekong south to the charming riverside town of **Champasak**, past misty green mountains and riverbanks loaded with palm trees. An up-and-coming backpacker resort, Champasak also serves as the gateway to **Wat Phou** and other **Khmer ruins**. Although it is easily possible to visit Wat Phou as a day-trip from Pakxe, there is plenty of cheap accommodation available in Champasak, and basing yourself here allows you to take in the sights at a leisurely pace. With its old wooden houses, three temples, Khmer ruins, mountains and river-boat trips, plus guesthouses and good food, it's easy to imagine Champasak becoming another Muang Ngoi in no time.

Other sights, such as the coffee plantations and waterfalls of **Bolaven Plateau** (see p.297), can also be taken in on day-trips from Pakxe.

Ban Saphai and Don Kho

Sawngthaews leave regularly from the sawngthaew lot near Pakxe's New Market to make the fifteen-kilometre trip north to the cluster of villages known locally for their **silk weaving**. Of these, **BAN SAPHAI**, a sizeable village on the left bank of the Mekong River, a few kilometres west of Route 13, has become increasingly popular with tourists keen on seeing women weaving on traditional hand looms, set up in the shade under the family house. Their textiles are sold in one or two shops in the village's market, or, if you prefer, you can negotiate with one of the weavers directly, although there's nothing here that you won't find in Pakxe. Sawngthaews stop at the market in the centre of town; check to see when they return to Pakxe, as transport along the route is rather limited.

The villagers of **DON KHO**, a shady island located directly across the river from Ban Saphai, are also known for their talent at the loom. In fact, you might well opt to head straight here, as the friendliness of the villagers and the meandering dirt paths along the Mekong make for a pleasant visit. You should be able to hire a boat from the riverbank (if there aren't any, the attendant at the riverside petrol station can scare up a boatman) to ferry you across and back (10,000K).

Champasak

Meandering for 4km along the right bank of the Mekong, **CHAMPASAK** is an unassuming town of wooden shophouses and two red dirt roads, with a pace so decidedly leisurely that it's difficult to imagine it as the capital of a once bustling kingdom, whose territory stretched from the Annamite Mountains into present-day Thailand. However, when France's Mekong expedition, led by Doudart de Lagrée and Francis Garnier, arrived in 1866, they found a city which was the most important in the south, a status later usurped by Pakxe when it became a French administrative centre.

These days, the quiet cluster of ten villages that constitutes Champasak makes Pakxe seem like a pulsing metropolis. On the main road, downstream from what is arguably the most under-used roundabout in Laos, two elegant **French mansions**, tanned a pale yellow by the tropical sun, stand out from the traditional wooden shophouses. The first mansion belonged to the former **palace of Prince Boun Oum na Champasak**. Although in 1946 he renounced claims to sovereignty over the former kingdom of Champasak, Boun Oum retained his royal title and continued to perform his ritual duties as a Buddhist monarch until he fled the country prior to the Pathet Lao takeover; he died in France in 1980. During Lao New Year, Boun Oum performed purification rites at the town's temples to expel evil spirits, and on the final day of celebrations he would preside over ceremonies at this palace, in which a *maw thiam*, or

△ Colonial-era buildings, Champasak

medium, called the spirits of Champasak's past rulers, and a *basi* ceremony was held. Since the advent of the new government, however, the pageantry has been abandoned and New Year ceremonies in this former royal seat have become a strictly family affair.

As is the case with the nagas in front of Boun Oum's house, which were taken from Wat Phou, the area's most exquisite **pre-Angkorian relics** wound up in the late prince's private collection. One local villager working with a team of archeologists in the ancient city is old enough to remember Boun Oum looting one site. Pieces from the collection are now on display in the small museum at the entrance to Wat Phou.

Practicalities

Buses and **sawngthaews** (10,000K from Pakxe) will let you off at Champasak's tiny roundabout, where you'll find almost everything you need, including a **post office** (open until 9pm weekdays for phone calls), and a tiny wooden bank, which can exchange cash and traveller's cheques. The **boat and ferry dock** is about 2km north of the roundabout; **tuk-tuks** are available at the dock.

There aren't any proper hotels in town, but there are several **guesthouses**, the most popular of which is the *Vongpasit* (❷), 2km south of the roundabout, which has en-suite bungalows and a restaurant with a nice deck overlooking the Mekong. Just south of the roundabout, *Kham Phou* (❶) has roomy doubles and triples and wooden en-suite bungalows in the garden. Fifty metres south, the *Souchittra Guesthouse* (❶) has above-average rooms in another old wooden house with a shared bath, plus self-contained bungalows on the lawn overlooking the Mekong. There's also a spacious veranda from which you can gaze upon the rather haunted-looking colonial-era mansion across the street. The town's oldest guesthouse is the *Saythong* (❶), just south of the roundabout and above a restaurant overlooking the Mekong; it has basic rooms with shared facilities in an old wooden house, but, frankly, has been surpassed by all the places listed above. *Dok Champa GH & Restaurant*, on the roundabout, offers the best selection of **Lao dishes** in town and also rents bicycles, as do most of the guesthouses.

When it comes to **moving on**, three buses pass through Champasak each morning en route to Pakxe (1hr 30min) and can be hailed from the town's main road. It's also possible to cross the river to Ban Muang and then get a shared sawngthaew. For **bus connections** to Si Phan Don, cross the river (ferries leave when full) to Ban Muang and wait for a bus heading south on Route 13, or alternatively take the daily **boat** from Pakxe, which calls at Champasak at around 9am. Boats to Houaytomo (around $8) can be arranged through your guesthouse or directly with the boatmen who hang out at the boat landing.

Wat Phou

One of the most evocative Khmer ruins outside Cambodia's borders, **Wat Phou** (daily 8.30am–4.30pm; 15,000K), 8km southwest of Champasak, should be at the top of your southern Laos must-see list, occupying a setting of unparalleled beauty. It's not hard to see why the lush river valley here, dominated by an imposing 1500-metre-tall mountain, **Lingaparvata**, at the foot of which Wat Phou resides, has been considered prime real estate for nearly two thousand years by a variety of peoples, in particular the Khmer. The surrounding forests are rich with wildlife, including the rare Asiatic black bear. The pristine state of the environment – it is without question one of the most scenic landscapes chosen by the Khmer for any of their temples – was a major factor in UNESCO's decision to propose the area as a World Heritage site. A few kilometres up the road, an ancient buried city, with ruins dating back to the fifth

The legacy of the Angkorian empire

In the mid-nineteenth century, French explorers began stumbling across the **monumental ruins** of a centuries-dead empire that had once blanketed mainland Southeast Asia. Soon word of these "lost cities" reached Europe and an intrigued populace groped for theories to explain such grandeur amid the sparsely inhabited jungles of an "uncivilized" corner of Asia. Surely, they mused, these monuments were the work of expatriate Romans or perhaps some far-wandering tribe of Israelites. Further exploration and the subsequent colonization of much of Indochina by France brought these mysterious monuments to the attention of French scholars and archeologists, some of whom were to dedicate their entire careers to unravelling the secrets of these tantalizing remnants of an empire.

In time, the **Khmer**, the inhabitants of modern-day **Cambodia**, were rightfully acknowledged to be the descendants of the founders of a highly sophisticated culture, whose influence stretched north to Vientiane in Laos and as far west as the present-day border of Thailand and Burma. From its capital, located at Angkor in what is now northwestern Cambodia, a long line of kings reigned with absolute authority, each striving to build a monument to his own greatness which would outdo all previous monarchs. With cultural trappings inherited from earlier Khmer kingdoms, which in turn had borrowed heavily from Indian merchants that once dominated trade throughout Southeast Asia, the Khmer rulers at Angkor venerated deities from the **Hindu** and **Buddhist** pantheons. Eventually, a new and uniquely Khmer cult was born, the *devaraja* or god-king, which propagated the belief that a Khmer king was actually an incarnation of a certain Hindu deity on earth. Most of the Khmer kings of Angkor identified with the god Shiva, although Suryavarman II, builder of **Angkor Wat**, the most magnificent of all Khmer monuments, fancied himself an earthly incarnation of Vishnu. An intriguing account of life at Angkor was penned by Chou Ta-Kuan, a Chinese traveller who visited the capital in the thirteenth century. In it he tells of imposing stone temples stunningly sheathed in gold and a king loyally guarded by an army of spear-wielding amazons.

century, is currently the object of intense archeological interest. Experts are unable to agree on who the inhabitants of this city were, with some calling it a western outpost of the Champa kingdom and others celebrating it as the cradle of Khmer civilization.

Wat Phou, which in Lao means "Mountain Monastery", is actually a series of ruined temples and shrines dating from the sixth to the twelfth centuries. Although the site is now associated with Theravada Buddhism, sandstone reliefs indicate that the ruins were once a **Hindu place of worship**. When viewed from the Mekong, it's clear why the site was chosen. A phallic stone outcropping, easily seen among the range's line of forested peaks, would have made the site especially auspicious to worshippers of Shiva, a Hindu god that is often symbolized by a phallus.

Archeologists tend to disagree on who the original founders of the site were and when it was first consecrated. The oldest parts of the ruins are thought to date back to the sixth century and were most likely built by the **ancient Khmer**, although some experts claim to see a connection to Champa. Whatever the case, the site is still considered highly sacred to the ethnic Lao who inhabit the region today, and is the focus of a **festival** in February, attracting thousands of Lao and Thai pilgrims annually.

Tuk-tuks can be hired in Champasak for the eight-kilometre journey to Wat Phou. The drivers charge 10,000K per passenger, and wait for you while you visit the ruins.

In 1177, armies from the rival kingdom of Champa, taking advantage of a period of political instability, were able to sack Angkor, leaving the empire in disarray. After some years of chaos, **Jayavarman VII** took control of the leaderless Khmer people. Convinced that the old state religion had somehow failed to protect the kingdom from misfortune, Jayavarman VII embraced Mahayana Buddhism and went on to expand his empire to include much of present-day Thailand, Vietnam and Laos. But the days of Khmer glory were numbered. Soon after the death of Jayavarman VII the empire began to decline and by 1432 was so weak that the **Siamese**, who had previously served as mercenaries for the Khmer in their campaigns against Champa, were also able to give Angkor a thorough sacking. The Siamese pillaged the great stone temples of the Angkorian god-kings and force-marched members of the royal Khmer court, including the king's personal retinue of classical dancers, musicians, artisans and astrologers, back to Ayuthaya, then the capital of Siam. To this day, much of what Thais perceive as Thai culture, from the sinuous moves of classical dancers to the flowery language of the royal Thai court, was actually acquired from the Khmer. After the collapse of the Angkorian empire, Siam moved in to fill the power vacuum and much of the Khmer culture absorbed by the Siamese was passed on to the Lao.

Following the **revolution in 1975**, the communist leaders of Laos, who identified with the newly reunified Vietnam and saw Thailand and its culture as decadent and Americanized, made a vigorous attempt to cleanse the new Laos of "reactionary" culture and iconography. Casualties of these purges include former royal Lao icons such as the image of the Hindu deity Airavata, and the **three-headed elephant**, formerly found on the Lao flag and on all Lao currency. Despite revolutionist efforts to revise the past, you don't have to look very hard to find major evidence of the legacy of the ancient Khmer in modern-day Laos. **Written Lao**, with its gracefully curving lines, was adapted from a script developed by the Siamese, who had borrowed heavily from an alphabet devised by the ancient Khmer.

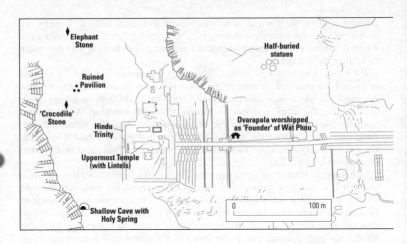

Elephant Stone

Ruined Pavilion

'Crocodile' Stone

Hindu Trinity

Uppermost Temple (with Lintels)

Shallow Cave with Holy Spring

Half-buried statues

Dvarapala worshipped as 'Founder' of Wat Phou

0   100 m

The site

At the entrance to the site, a small **museum** houses pieces of sculpture found among the ruins as well as some said to have belonged to Prince Boun Oum. The **stone causeway** leading up to the first set of ruins was once lined with low stone pillars, the tips of which were formed into a stylized lotus bud. Stone pedestals along the way indicate that a few statues may have lined this path as well. On either side of the causeway there would have been reservoirs known in Khmer as *baray*. As ancient Khmer architecture is rich in symbols, it is surmised that these pools represented the oceans that surrounded the mythical Mount Meru, home of the gods of the Hindu pantheon.

Just beyond the causeway, on either side of the path, two megalithic structures of sandstone and laterite mirror each other. According to local lore, they are segregated **palaces**, one for men and the other for women. Archeologists are sceptical though, pointing out that stone was reserved for constructing places of worship, and, even if this hadn't been the case, the vast interiors of both buildings were roofless and would have afforded little shelter. The structure on the right as you approach is the best preserved. Its carved relief of Shiva and his consort Uma riding the sacred bull Nandi is the best to be found on either building. As with much of the architecture of the pharaohs of ancient Egypt, that of the Khmer kings of Angkor was monumental and symmetrical. Even in their ruined state, you can imagine the awe these stacked and carved stones must have inspired, especially with the spectacle of a majestic royal procession passing through their midst.

As the path begins to climb, you come upon jagged stairways of sandstone blocks. Plumeria (frangipani) trees line the way, giving welcome shade and littering the worn stones with delicate blooms known in Lao as *dawk jampa*, the national flower of Laos. At the foot of the second stairway is a shrine to the legendary founder of Wat Phou. The statue is much venerated and, during the annual pilgrimage, is bedecked with offerings of flowers, incense and candles. When and why this one statue has come to be venerated in such a fashion is unknown, and once again, local folklore and archeological record diverge – according to archeologists, the statue is actually that of a *dvarapala*, or temple guardian. In the field behind this statue, half buried in the ground, lie the headless torsos of two similar statues.

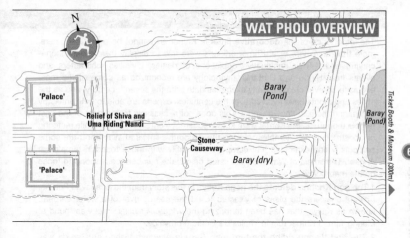

Continuing up the stairs, you come upon the final set of ruins, surrounded by mammoth mango trees. This uppermost temple contains the finest examples of **decorative stone lintels** (see box, pp.284–285) in Laos. Although much has been damaged or is missing, sketches done by Georges Traipont, a French surveyor who visited the temple complex in the waning years of the nineteenth century, show the temple to have changed little since then. On the exterior walls flanking the east entrance are the images of *dvarapalas* and *devatas*, or female divinities, in high relief. On the altar, inside the sanctuary, stand **four Buddha images**, looking like a congress of benevolent space aliens. Originally, this altar would have supported a Shivalinga, a phallic stone representing Shiva. Today, it's crowded with a collection of ancient odds and ends gathered from the surrounding area. Doorways on each side of the altar lead to an empty room with walls of brick; it is thought that these walls constitute the oldest structure on the site, dating back to the sixth century.

To the right of the temple is a Lao Buddha of comparatively modern vintage, and just behind the temple is a relief carved into a half-buried slab of stone, depicting the Hindu trinity – a multi-armed, multi-headed Shiva (standing) is flanked by Brahma (left) and Vishnu (right). Continuing up the hill behind the temple, you'll come to a **shallow cave**, the floor of which is muddy from the constant drip of water that collects on its ceiling. This water is considered highly sacred, as it has trickled down from the peak of Lingaparvata. In former times, a system of stone pipes directed the run-off to the temple, where it bathed the enshrined Shivalinga. By tradition, this water was utilized in ceremonies for the coronation of Khmer kings and later the kings of Siam. Even today, Lao pilgrims will dip their fingers into a cistern located in the cave and ritually anoint themselves. Foreign visitors should resist the temptation to use this water to scrub off some trail-dust – indeed, doing so would be extremely poor form, not so different from going into a church and washing your face in the baptismal font.

If you follow the base of the cliff in a northerly direction, a bit of sleuthing will lead you to the enigmatic **crocodile stone**, which may have been used as an altar for pre-Angkor period human sacrifices, though there is no hard evidence that ritual sacrifice was a part of the ceremonies that took place here. Nearby is a pile of sandstone rubble that once formed a pavilion and is thought by archeologists to be one of the oldest structures on the site. A few metres away

Decorative lintels at Wat Phou

The importance of the **decorative lintel** in Khmer art cannot be overstated. Here, more than anywhere else, Khmer artisans were free to display their superb stone-carving skills. Their imaginative depictions of deities, divinities, characters and events from Hindu and Buddhist mythology are recognized as some of the most exquisite art ever created. Early examples date from the seventh century, and as the styles and motifs have evolved over the centuries, experts are able to date lintels by comparing them to known works. This does not necessarily fix the date of the host temple though, as the Khmer were known to remove or replace lintels while restoring or constructing new temples. Among the decorative lintels at **Wat Phou** are some particularly fine examples that compare favourably with those found in temples at Angkor. The lintels at Wat Phou are listed below; the numbers correspond to those on the map below.

1 The god Krishna defeats the naga Kaliya In this story from the Bhagavad Purana, Krishna answers the pleas of villagers to rid the nearby river of a water serpent, known as Kaliya, that has been terrorizing the village. A similar lintel was found at Muang Tam, a Khmer ruin in Thailand's Buriram province.

2 The god Vishnu riding the bird-man Garuda Although Vishnu on Garuda was a common theme in Khmer art, images of the two were rarely depicted on lintels. After conquering the Khmer in 1432, the Siamese adopted the Garuda to symbolize their own monarchy – hence an image of Garuda is found on all Thai banknotes and official documents.

3 The god Indra riding the three-headed elephant Airavata Despite being a Hindu god, Indra holds a significant place in Theravada Buddhist mythology. Until the Lao revolution, Airavata was the official symbol of the Lao monarchy. The image of the three-headed elephant was formerly found on the Lao flag and Lao currency and can still be seen on the facade of the former royal palace in Louang Phabang.

4 Indra on Airavata A larger and more detailed depiction of #3.

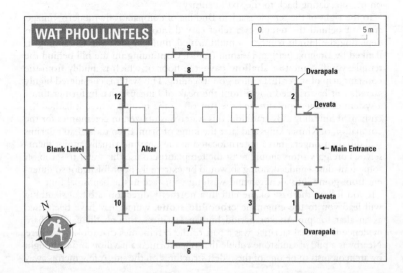

5 Deity atop Kala Although this deity is very commonly depicted on lintels, it is uncertain just who it is supposed to be. As the deity is holding a mace and sitting in the "royal ease" pose, perhaps it depicts a generic king or ruler. Kala, a temple guardian also commonly found on Khmer lintels, is sometimes confused with Rahu, who is believed to devour the sun and moon during eclipses. Kala is usually depicted with two stylized garlands spewing from the corners of his mouth.

6 Deity atop Kala (see #5) On the portico above the lintel is what is left of a scene from the Churning of the Sea of Milk myth, a contest between gods and demons for possession of the elixir of immortality. This scene is depicted most spectacularly on the bas-reliefs at Angkor Wat in Cambodia.

7 Krishna killing Kamsa From the Bhagavad Purana, this lintel is a gruesome depiction of Krishna tearing his uncle in half. According to this myth, it was foretold that King Kamsa's death would come at the hands of one of his own family members. This prophecy launched the king on an orgy of killing which was only halted when his nephew put him to death.

8 Deity atop Kala (see #5)

9 Deity atop Kala (see #5) On the ruined portico above this lintel are the remains of a depiction of the god Vishnu in his incarnation as Narayana, reclining in cosmic slumber as he floats atop a naga on the waters of a vast primordial ocean.

10 Shiva as a rishi atop Kala A unique lintel depicting Shiva as a rishi, or wandering ascetic, perched above Kala. The image of the Hindu sage, usually dressed in a tiger skin and sitting in an attitude of meditation, has been adopted by Buddhism in Laos and Thailand, and is the object of veneration at numerous small monastery shrines in both countries.

11 Deity atop Kala (see #5) Sadly, this lintel has been badly damaged, possibly by looters trying to remove part of the sculpture for the thriving stolen-antiquities trade in Thailand.

12 Deity atop Kala (see #5)

to the north is the **elephant stone**, a huge, moss-covered boulder carved with the face of an elephant. This carving is relatively recent, probably dating from the nineteenth century.

If you were to hike straight up the mountain to the **summit of Lingaparvata**, it would take two days of rigorous climbing over vertical cliff-faces and dense forest. In 1997, an Italian team of archeologists did just that. On the very tip of the natural phallic outcropping that is the peak of the mountain, they discovered a small Shivalinga of carved stone. Sadly, the archeologists found it necessary to remove this artefact that had crowned the sacred mountain for untold centuries, catching raindrops that would eventually filter down to the cave of lustral waters at the foot of the mountain. The trophy now rests in the small museum at the entrance to Wat Phou.

Hong Nang Sida Temple

Situated about 1km south of Wat Phou, **Hong Nang Sida** is a small twelfth-century Khmer temple, built on an ancient thoroughfare that once stretched from Wat Phou to Angkor Wat. The trail leading south to the temple from Wat Phou through the rice paddies is easy to locate during the dry season, but you may have to ask the guards at the entrance to Wat Phou for directions once the rains have started and the trail becomes obscured by weeds. This little-visited ruin can be taken in in just a few minutes: the dimensions of Hong Nang Sida are modest compared to those of Wat Phou, and very few of the sandstone blocks from which it was constructed are adorned with carvings. Still, as with Wat Phou, the warm light on the venerable stone walls is particularly magical during sunrise and sunset.

Houaytomo Temple

If your thirst for Khmer temples has yet to be quenched, a visit to **Houaytomo**, a tenth-century temple, is an option. Best visited as a day-trip from Champasak, the ruin is set in the midst of a lush forest on the banks of a stream, for which it is named. Also known by various other names, including Oum Muang, the temple is thought to have been dedicated to the consort of Shiva in her form as Rudani, and was "discovered" by Frenchman Etienne Edmond Lunet de Lajonquière early in the twentieth century.

Although much of the structure has collapsed and some of the lintels have been removed, a couple of interesting pieces of sculpture remain *in situ*, most notably an unusual stone pillar located inside the laterite sanctuary. The pillar is crudely carved with the moustached faces of a mysterious deity, perhaps Shiva. Archeologists working for UNESCO speculate that it is a *mukhalinga*, literally "phallus with face", and that it dates from the seventh century. Lined up outside the walls of the temple is a collection of lintels, obscured by a thick layer of moss. As the whole area is shaded by the forest's thick canopy, it's cool and pleasant even at high noon.

The best way to reach Houaytomo is to hire a **pirogue** in Champasak (2hr; around $8) to zip you south along the river, skimming the surface, past Lao children at their favourite swimming holes. When the river is high enough, the boat will be able to navigate the Houaytomo Stream and dock at the ruins. During the dry season, when the river level lowers and the water turns a sparkling blue-green, you'll have to disembark on the banks of the Mekong and walk a couple of kilometres. When the river is low, a trip to Houaytomo can be combined with a stop at the beaches of **Don Deng**, the river island opposite Champasak, for a lazy stroll in the sand; the sandy bank here provides an excellent place for a swim.

Kiatngong, Phou Asa and Ban Phapho

Located approximately 50km southeast of Pakxe, **KIATNGONG** is one of several villages in the area whose inhabitants keep **elephants**. Recently, it's become possible for tourists to hire out elephants for treks up nearby **Phou Asa**, a jungle-clad hill with some mysterious ruins atop its summit. Phou Asa is thought to date back to the nineteenth century, and the site's layout suggests it was possibly used as a fort, though archeologists admit that the crudely stacked stone walls and pillars are an enigma. Local villagers, believing the ruins to be the remains of an ancient Buddhist monastery, periodically make pilgrimages to the site to leave offerings at a "Buddha's footprint" carved into a low cliff below the ruins. From the summit, commanding views of the surrounding dense jungle, rice fields and villages lend credence to the fort hypothesis.

Elephants have been traditionally used by the people of Kiatngong to haul timber and rice. Villages located far in the interior used to hire Kiatngong's elephants and mahouts to carry their rice harvest to main roads, where it could be transferred to trucks. Recently, though, new roads have made this mode of transport obsolete and mahouts have begun selling off their elephants. The last time villagers organized a hunt to round up wild elephants was in 1988, and many are turning to water buffalo as a more practical beast of burden. A steady stream of potential elephant trekkers, however, will ensure that at least for the time being, villagers here will continue to keep elephants as their ancestors did for centuries.

The **best way to get here** is by your own transport: Diethelm in Pakxe (see p.276) rents out vans – or pick-ups in the rainy season – to the village, charging $50 for the round trip, but it's much cheaper to hire a sawngthaew from the New Market to Kiatngong. Once in Kiatngong, you'll find elephant hire costs about $10 for a trek that takes in Phou Asa and the ruins on its summit. The best time to come is at dusk, when spectacular sunsets can be enjoyed from the top of the hill. It's also possible to get here by bus from Pakxe in less than two hours, but you may have to flag down a passing bus or sawngthaew to return to Pakxe at the end of the day. Some wooden cottages have been built for tour groups that sometimes overnight in the village, and it is usually possible to stay here – just contact the village headman.

Another elephant village, **Ban Phapho**, is involved in the training of elephants for the timber trade. As in Kiatngong, elephant trekking can be arranged at the village, located some 20km from Kiatngong, although Ban Phapho lacks the picturesque ruins and views that make Kiatngong the more popular destination, though it does have a very basic **guesthouse** here with shared facilities. Both villages can be visited in one day if you charter a vehicle from Pakxe.

Xe Pian NBCA

Just southeast of Houaytomo and running the entire length of Route 13 all the way to Si Phan Don is the **Xe Pian NBCA**, roughly triangular in shape and bounded by Route 18 to the north. Although many tourists travel right alongside it for almost 150km on route to Don Khong, few are aware they are right next to Laos's southernmost NBCA and one of the country's largest (2665 square kilometres) nature reserves. The terrain here is mostly plains, although there are mixed deciduous forests and several peaks between 300m and 800m. In the east, the **Xe Kong** flows into Cambodia through the park, and tigers, elephants, leopards and **rhinoceros** may survive here. The best way to visit the NBCA is from Pakxe, where tour companies can organize four-wheel-drive trips through the north of the park.

Si Phan Don

In Laos's deepest south, just above the border with Cambodia, the muddy stream of the Mekong is shattered into a fourteen-kilometre-wide web of rivulets, creating a landlocked archipelago. Known as **Si Phan Don**, or Four Thousand Islands, this labyrinth of islets, rocks and sandbars has acted as a kind of bell jar, preserving traditional southern lowland Lao culture from outside influences. Island villages were largely unaffected by the French or American wars, and the islanders' customs and folk ways have been passed down uninterrupted since ancient times. As might be expected, the Mekong River plays a vital role in the lives of local inhabitants, with 95 percent of island families fishing for a living. Ecological awareness among locals is high, with nearly half of the villages in the district participating in voluntary fisheries conservation programmes.

The archipelago is also home to rare wetland flora and fauna, including an endangered species of freshwater **dolphin**, which it's sometimes possible to glimpse during the dry season. Southeast Asia's largest – and what many

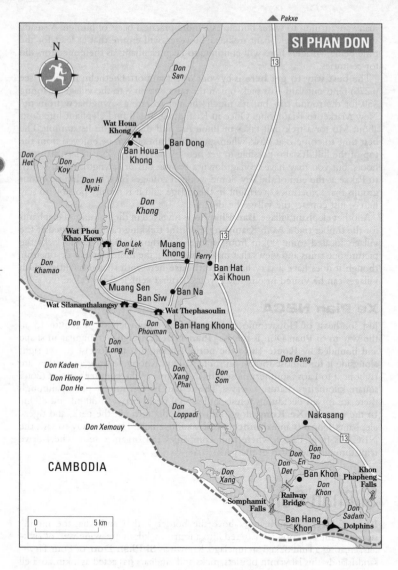

SI PHAN DON

N

Don San

Wat Houa Khong

Ban Dong

Ban Houa Khong

Don Het

Don Koy

Don Hi Nyai

Don Khong

Wat Phou Khao Kaew

Don Lek Fai

Muang Khong

Ferry

Ban Hat Xai Khoun

Don Khamao

Muang Sen

Ban Siw

Ban Na

Wat Silananthalangsy

Wat Thephasoulin

Don Tan

Don Phouman

Ban Hang Khong

Don Long

Don Beng

Don Kaden

Don Hinoy

Don He

Don Xang Phai

Don Som

Don Loppadi

Nakasang

Don Xemouy

CAMBODIA

Don Xang

Don Det

Don En

Don Tao

Ban Khon

Khon Phapheng Falls

Somphamit Falls

Railway Bridge

Don Khon

Don Sadam

Ban Hang Khon

Dolphins

0   5 km

consider to be most spectacular – waterfalls are also located here. The area's biggest sightseeing attractions, the **Khon Phapheng** and **Somphamit** waterfalls, dashed nineteenth-century French hopes of using the Mekong as a trade artery into China. The remnants of a French-built railroad, constructed to carry passengers and cargo past these roaring obstacles, can still be seen on the islands of **Don Khon** and **Don Det**, along with a rusting locomotive and other ghosts of the French presence. The most developed place to base yourself is the popular island of **Don Khong**, with its collection of quaint villages and ancient temples, but there's also plenty of accommodation on Don Khon and Don Det.

Don Khong

The largest of the Four Thousand Islands group, **DON KHONG** draws a steady stream of visitors, most of whom use it as a base to explore other attractions in Si Phan Don. Don Khong is surprisingly wide for a river island, though, and is known locally for its venerable collection of **Buddhist temples**, some with visible signs of a history stretching back to the sixth or seventh century. These, together with the island's good-value accommodation and interesting cuisine, based on fresh fish from the Mekong, make Don Khong the perfect place for indulging both adventurous and lazy moods. The islanders, an amiable lot, seem to be taking the mini-onslaught of foreign travellers in their stride.

Don Khong has only three settlements of any size, the port town of **Muang Sen** on the island's west coast, the east-coast town of **MUANG KHONG**, where most of the accommodation and cafés are situated (see the map on p.291), and the smaller town of **Ban Houa Khong**, where slow boats from Pakxe moor. Like all Si Phan Don settlements, both Muang Sen's and Muang Khong's homes and shops cling to the bank of the Mekong for kilometres, but barely penetrate the interior, which is reserved for rice fields.

The best way to explore Don Khong and experience the traditional sights and sounds of riverside living is to rent a **bicycle** from one of the guesthouses and set off along the road that circles the island. Don Khong's flat terrain and almost complete absence of motor vehicles make for ideal cycling conditions. For touring, the island can be neatly divided into **two loops**, southern and northern, each beginning at Muang Khong, or done all in one big loop that takes about three hours without stops.

Southern loop

The chain of picturesque villages that line the south coast makes the **southern loop**, roughly 20km long, the more popular of the two itineraries. Following the river road south from Muang Khong, you soon cross a rotting wooden bridge, with an inscription indicating that it was constructed in 1963 by USAID (United States Agency for International Development), which was sometimes used as a front for shadowy CIA activities during the Second Indochina War. Take care to stick to the narrow path along the river, and not the road that parallels it slightly inland. A couple of kilometres south of Muang Khong lies the village of **Ban Na**, where the real scenery begins. Navigating the trail as it snakes between thickets of bamboo, you come upon traditional southern Lao wooden houses trimmed with painted highlights of white and royal blue. They're all surrounded by plots of barren, hard-packed earth, kept tidy by frequent sweeping with a stiff coconut-frond broom and enclosed by low fences of split bamboo.

Near the tail of the island the path forks. A veer to the left will lead you to the tiny village of **Ban Hang Khong** and a dead end; keeping to the right will put you at the gates of **Wat Thephasoulin**, parts of which were constructed in 1883. The *sala* and monks' quarters, composed of teak-plank walls and terracotta tile roofs, are particularly pleasing to the eye, making this a good place for a breather and a swig on the water bottle. From here the path soon skirts the edge of a high riverbank, at intervals opening up views of the muddy Mekong flowing sluggishly southwards. The dense canopy of foliage overhead provides welcome shade as you pass through **Ban Siw**, whose quaint gingerbread houses, decorated with wood filigree, look invitingly cosy. The bamboo-and-thatch drink shops that line this section of the path are a good place to linger while enjoying a rejuvenating sip of coconut juice. Worth a look is the village monastery, **Wat Silananthalangsy**; the recently restored *sim* lacks charm, but a school building at the back of the compound has been left in a wonderfully decrepit state. This is often the case in Laos, as Buddhist laymen believe that much more merit is acquired by donating money towards the restoration of a structure that shelters Buddha images than by rebuilding a mere school for novice monks.

As you continue on from here, the path widens at the approach to Muang Sen, Don Khong's sleepy port. While there is nothing to see, it's a recommended stop for rest and refreshment before heading east via the shade-stingy eight-kilometre stretch of road that leads back to Muang Khong.

Northern loop

The long, sometimes shadeless, route of the **northern loop** rewards handsomely with access to what is certainly one of southern Laos's most idyllic spots. The total distance of approximately 35km is probably best covered by **motorbike**; in the hot season, industrial-strength sun block and a wide-brimmed hat are a must.

Starting from Muang Khong, you begin by heading due west on the road that bisects the island. During the hot season the plain of fallow rice paddies that makes up much of the island's interior looks and feels like a stretch of the Kalahari. After the rains break and rice paddies are planted, the scenery is actually quite beautiful.

Just before **Muang Sen**, turn right at the crossroads and head north; follow this road up and over a low gradient and after about 4km you'll cross a bridge. Keep going another 1500m and you'll notice large black boulders beginning to appear off to the left. Keeping your eyes left, you'll see a narrow trail that leads up to a ridge of the same black stone. Park your bike at the foot of the ridge, and, following the trail up another 200m to the right, you'll spot a cluster of monks' quarters constructed of weathered teak. These structures belong to **Wat Phou Khao Kaew**, an evocative little forest monastery situated atop a river-sculpted stone bluff overlooking the Mekong. Until a recently built *sala* of modern materials added a bit of the late twentieth century to the landscape, you could wander the grounds of this wat and almost believe that the clock had been turned back a hundred or so years. The centrepiece is a crumbling **brick stupa** crowned with a clump of grass; a fractured pre-Angkorian stone lintel sits at the base of the stupa and, assuming it was once fixed to it, would date the structure to the middle of the seventh century.

Nearby sits a charming miniature *sim*, flanked by plumeria trees. A curious collection of carved wooden deities, which somehow found their way downriver from Burma, decorates the ledges running around the building. In 1998, a life-sized **bronze Buddha** image was stolen from the altar, only to turn up hidden under a hastily made tent of branches in an isolated stretch of forest on the mainland. The antique image's *ushnisha* (flame-like finial on the crown of the head) was missing, but the Buddha was otherwise intact. Undoubtedly it had been destined for Thailand's black market in plundered antiquities. At present, the image is stored at the police station in Muang Khong. If you want to have a look at the inside of the *sim*, ask one of the resident monks to unlock the door for you, or you can peer through the windows on either side of the main entrance, which faces the river.

If, after a look round Wat Phou Khao Kaew, you're still feeling energetic, continue another 6km north to **Ban Houa Khong**, on the outskirts of which stands the modest **residence of Khamtay Siphandone**, former revolutionary and ex-prime minister. Not far away is a **monastery** that has been restored to reflect the status of the village's most important part-time inhabitant. The wat is not all that remarkable, except perhaps for the collection of artefacts in the main temple. Sharing the altar with rows of Buddha images is a gargoyle-like object, actually a *somasutra* from an ancient Khmer temple, used to channel lustral water onto an enshrined Shivalinga. Next to the altar is a display case filled with small Buddha images and other dusty relics.

Pushing on from Ban Houa Khong, you follow the road east to Ban Dong and then south to Muang Khong, a journey totalling 13km. On arriving at the northern outskirts of Muang Khong, just before reaching the high school, you pass a trail bordered with white stones, which leads to **Tham Phou Khiaw**, or Green Mountain Cave. Although it has gained quite a reputation among travellers, based no doubt on the obscurity of its location, the cave is no Lost City of Gold: in reality, it's a shallow grotto sheltering one termite-riddled Buddha and a number of clay pots containing crude votive tablets, each with an image of the Buddha pressed into it. Unless you're here during the Lao New Year celebrations, when islanders visit the site to make offerings and ritually bathe the images, or the Bun Bang Fai festival, a month later, when bamboo skyrockets are launched in a rainmaking ritual, it's not really worth the effort; the trail leading up to the cave is overgrown at other times of the year and you'll have to hire a local guide.

Practicalities

A total of seven **buses to Don Khong** leave from Pakxe's bus station daily. Two of these go directly to Muang Khong, crossing the Mekong by ferry from

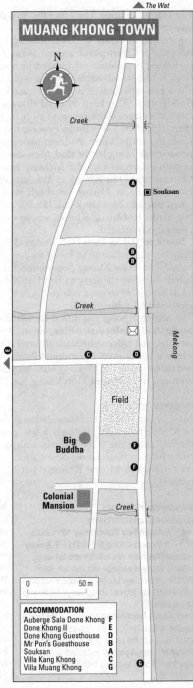

▲ The Wat

MUANG KHONG TOWN

N

Creek

■ Souksan

Creek

Mekong

Field

Big Buddha

Colonial Mansion

Creek

0   50 m

ACCOMMODATION
Auberge Sala Done Khong	F
Done Khong II	E
Done Khong Guesthouse	D
Mr Pon's Guesthouse	B
Souksan	A
Villa Kang Khong	C
Villa Muang Khong	G

Ban Hat Xai Khoun. The other five pass through Ban Hat Xai Khoun on their way to Nakasang.

A couple of **boats to Don Khong** leave daily from **Pakxe** around 8am, stopping at **Champasak** around 10am. The trip downriver takes eight hours or longer, depending on how many stops are made en route, and costs $3 from Pakxe. It's advisable to bring water and food along; otherwise your only chance of refreshment is from the snack vendors who converge on the boat during stops. Also keep in mind that these boats have no toilet, and during stops at villages there is a mad rush by passengers to disembark and relieve themselves. The Lao woman's sarong allows the wearer to simply squat on the bank and retain some modesty; passengers who wander too far in search of privacy risk being left behind. Men should bear in mind a local taboo against urinating directly into the Mekong while standing on the roof of the boat. On reaching Don Khong in the late afternoon, boats **dock** at either Ban Houa Khong or Muang Sen, both on Don Khong's west coast. From here you'll need to hire a tuk-tuk ($1.50) or motorcycle for the eight-kilometre trip across to Muang Khong, where the best selection of food and accommodation is located.

Boats to Pakxe from Don Khong ($5) usually leave from Ban Houa Khong daily, but the only way to know for sure is to ask at your guesthouse. A Pakxe-bound bus leaves Muang Sen around 8am and passes through Muang Khong before boarding the ferry to Ban Hat Xai Khoun and heading north up Route 13. It is possible to get a ride to Pakxe by private vehicle every 7am at *Mr Pon's Restaurant* (2hr 30min; $1).

In Muang Khong you'll find the island's only **post office**, just south of the bridge, and a **telecom office**, about 200m west of the ferry landing, where international calls can be made (Mon–Fri 8am–noon & 1–4pm; Sat 8am–noon). There is also a small Agricultural Promotion Bank. Several of the guesthouses and shops facing the Mekong offer **bicycles** for rent; the *Villa Kang Khong* also rents out **motorbikes**. Don Khong has 24-hour electricity.

Accommodation

Most of the island's accommodation is concentrated in Muang Khong. Over in Muang Sen there are only a few guesthouses, including *Say Khong* (❷), directly above the ferry landing, with spacious doubles and triples with fans and a balcony; and *Muong Sene Guest House* (❶), situated a little further east, on the road to Muang Khong – but Muang Khong has much better eating options.

Muang Khong accommodation

Auberge Sala Done Khong 100m south of the ferry landing ☎031/212077. A nicely restored French-era villa with a/c and hot water, catering largely to package-tour clientele. When there are no package tourists the place is wonderfully serene, and you can almost imagine it belongs to you alone. ❺

Done Khong Guesthouse Adjacent to the ferry landing ☎031/214010. This long-established place has basic but rather grubby rooms with shared facilities, a popular restaurant and very friendly staff speaking both English and French. ❷

Done Khong II 300m from the ferry landing on the road to Muang Sen. Set in an airy teak house with verandas offering commanding views of the countryside. Accommodation ranges from dorm beds to comfortable en-suite doubles. ❷

Mr Pon's Guesthouse 150m north of the ferry landing. A great place to stay, offering tidy rooms in a wooden house with private or shared facilities, hot water, and a very popular restaurant downstairs. Mr Pon has also built an annexe next door with more rooms. ❶

Souksan 300m north of the ferry landing ☎031/212071. Lao Chinese-owned establishment with a restaurant and accommodation ranging from dormitory beds to fairly luxurious bungalows, priced according to whether or not you switch on the a/c. ❺

🏃 **Villa Kang Khong** 100m west of the ferry landing ☎031/213539. Helpful, French-speaking owner, Mr Thongleuam, offers slick service at budget prices, making the spacious, comfortable rooms in this French-colonial-era teak house excellent value. Highly recommended. ❷

Villa Muang Khong 300m south of the ferry landing ☎031/213011. Smallish, modern, bungalows with fan and attached toilet. There's a restaurant on the premises, but meals need to be ordered a day in advance. ❺

Eating

All of Don Khong's guesthouses serve food, and, as you might expect, **fish** is the island's staple. The islanders have dozens of recipes, all worthy of a place on your plate – from the traditional **làp pa** (a Lao-style salad of minced fish mixed with garlic, chillies, shallots and fish sauce) to fish steamed in coconut milk – but whatever you do, be sure to try the island speciality, **mók pa**. Steamed in banana leaves, this sublime fish dish has the consistency of custard and takes an hour to prepare.

For this and just about anything else, *Mr Pon's Guesthouse* stands out as having the best **restaurant** in Muang Khong. If it's Chinese food and a perfect river view you're after, head for the restaurant at the *Souksan*, which stands on stilts above the Mekong. *Done Khong Guesthouse*, once the only place to eat in town, remains popular and its banana crepes are divine. If you're staying at the *Villa Kang Khong*, don't miss out on the immaculately served **breakfast** – eggs, sliced and toasted baguettes and Lao coffee.

The people of Si Phan Don are very proud of their *lào-láo*, which has gained a reputation nationally as one of the best **rice whiskies** in Laos. For those who haven't taken a liking to Lao white lightning, you're in luck: Muang Khong has devised a gentler blend known as the "Lao cocktail", a mix of wild honey and *lào-láo* served over ice with a dash of lime.

Don Khon and Don Det

Tropical islands in the classic sense, **DON KHON** and **DON DET** are fringed with swaying coconut palms and inhabited by easy-going, sarong-clad villagers. Located south of Don Khong, the islands are especially stunning during the rainy season when rice paddies in the interior have been ploughed and planted in soothing hues of jade and emerald. Besides being a picturesque little haven to while away a few days, the islands, linked by a bridge and traversed by a trail, provide opportunities for some leisurely trekking. In fact, there are as yet only a handful of motor vehicles on the islands, making them one of the precious few places in Southeast Asia not harried by the growl and whine of motorbikes. There is, however, a fee of 5000K for a day pass or 10,500K for seven days to be on the islands.

A delightfully sleepy place with a timeless feel about it, **BAN KHON**, located on Don Khon at the eastern end of the bridge, is the largest settlement on either island and has the most upmarket accommodation (see p.296). A handful of quaintly decrepit French-era buildings with terracotta tile roofs adds some colonial colour to the village's collection of rustic homes of wood, bamboo and thatch. A short walk west of the old railroad bridge, past the ticket booth, stands the village monastery, **Wat Khon Tai**. Just behind the newly built *sim* is the laterite foundation of what was once a Khmer temple dedicated to the god Shiva. As with several Buddhist temples in southern Laos, this one was built upon the ruins of an ancient Hindu holy site, suggesting that the otherwise humble Ban Khon is around 1000 years

6

△ Remains of the old French train

old. On a pedestal nearby stands a Shivalinga, which was probably enshrined in the original Khmer temple. Because Khmer Shivalinga are usually simple and lack the intricate carving for which Khmer art is famous, they are rarely the target of art thieves and so stand a better chance of remaining on or near their original place of enshrinement.

Taking the southwestern path behind the wat, you'll soon be aware of a low, almost inaudible purr that gradually becomes a roar the further you proceed. After following the path for 1500m, you'll come to a low cliff overlooking **Somphamit Falls**, a series of high rapids that crashes through a jagged gorge. Fishermen can sometimes be seen carefully negotiating rickety bamboo catwalks suspended above the violently churning waters.

To see the remnants of Laos's **old French railroad**, follow the trail south from the old railroad bridge. A short distance back from the bridge lies the rusting locomotive that once hauled French goods and passengers between piers on Don Khon and Don Det, bypassing the falls and rapids that block this stretch of the river. Nearby, behind thick brush bordering rice fields, is an overgrown **Christian cemetery** that includes the neglected tomb of a long-forgotten French family that died on the same day in 1922 – some say murdered by their Vietnamese domestics. It is actually possible to follow the former railroad all the way across both islands; however, with the exception of two alarmingly precarious bridges constructed from railroad scrap and lengths of rail recycled as fences, there are few signs that a railway ever existed.

A similar but shorter walk is from Don Khon to Don Det across the bridge and along the three-kilometre elevated trail to the small village at the northern end of the island. Here several **guesthouses** have opened just a stone's throw from an incongruous industrial structure once used for hoisting cargo from the train onto awaiting boats; it's all that remains of the railroad's northern terminus.

Dolphin-spotting

Don Khon's most popular attraction is the **dolphins** which can be spotted off the southern side of the island. To get there, take the railroad trail for 4km through rice paddies and thick forest to the village of **Ban Hang Khon**, the jumping-off point for dolphin-spotting excursions. The April–May dry season,

The Irrawaddy dolphin

Communities that live beside waters inhabited by dolphins often spin legendary tales of the bond that links man and beast. The distant stretches of southern Laos, where the rare **Irrawaddy dolphin** cruises the Mekong and its tributaries, are no exception. Indeed, this freshwater dolphin holds a unique place among the Lao: it's the one creature exempted from a Lao diet famous for consuming everything that hops, flies, swims or crawls. The bluish-grey dolphin (*orcaella brevirostris*), known as *pa kha* in Lao, grows to a length of 2.5m and is distinguished from its dolphin relatives by a blunted beak. It lives in coastal waters stretching from the Bay of Bengal to the northern Australian coast, and inhabits the Irrawaddy River in Burma, the Mahakam in Kalimantan, Indonesia and the Ganges in India. The dolphins are rare in Lao waters, as most are unable to swim beyond the Khone Falls near the Lao–Cambodian border. Those that do make it this far upstream favour a fifty-metre-deep pool off the southern tip of Don Khon, but have also been seen in the Xe Kong, Xe Kaman and Xe Pian Mekong tributaries in the southeastern province of Attapu.

Villagers from Si Phan Don tell of dolphins saving people from drowning and pulling them from the jaws of crocodiles. They are thought to be reincarnated humans, to possess a human spirit, and are even said by some to have breasts like a woman. That the dolphins are a "human fish" is etched into local lore in the *Lam Si Phan Don*, a traditional folk song from the area. In one version of the *lam*, the raft of Nang Sida – the wife of Rama whose kidnapping sets the *Pha Lam Pha Lak* (the Lao version of the Ramayana) in motion – plunges over the Khone Falls, killing her and her loyal boatman. She is reborn as a river tern (*nok sida* in Lao), he as a dolphin; theirs is a relationship played out daily in the river, with the dolphin leading the tern to its meals.

But the dolphins may soon be no more than legend. Over the past one hundred years their **population** in the Mekong has dwindled from thousands to little more than one hundred today. Gill-net fishing and, across the border, the use of poison, electricity and explosives have cut into their numbers. In the past, fishermen were reluctant to cut costly nets to free entangled dolphins, causing them to drown, but this no longer happens, as Lao villagers are now compensated for their nets – part of an initiative begun by the **Lao Community Fisheries and Dolphin Protection Project**. The use of explosives, however, remains common across the border. Khmer soldiers began the practice of tossing hand grenades into the river and scooping up the fish which floated to the surface. Some shot the dolphins for sport, and the Khmer Rouge, during its 1970s reign of terror, reputedly killed them by the hundreds in the Tonle Sap, extracting oil from their skins.

Fortunately, the grassroots fisheries conservation effort, of which the dolphin is the most visible symbol, is meeting with success, and villagers from nearly half of Khong District's villages voluntarily participate in the **Si Phan Don Wetlands Project**, which encourages communities to set aside conservation zones and establish laws to regulate how and when fish are caught, a step towards protecting one of the world's most ecologically diverse river systems. Participating fishermen say the changes have already registered improvements, with catches larger outside the zones than they were in those areas in previous years. A few villagers have even claimed that *ngeuak* – mythological water serpents – have returned to Lao waters.

when the Mekong is at its lowest, is the best time of year to catch a glimpse of this highly endangered species. The dolphins tend to congregate in a deep-water pool, and boats can be chartered from the village to see them ($8). During the rest of the year, chances of seeing the dolphins decrease, as deeper water allows them more range.

Sadly, however, if current trends continue, dolphin-spotting off Don Khon may soon be a thing of the past. The present dolphin population here is less than ten, down from thirty in 1993.

Khon Phapheng Falls

Despite technically being the largest waterfall in Southeast Asia, **Khon Phapheng**, to the east of Don Khon, is not all that spectacular. Indeed, it's best described as a low but wide rock shelf that just happens to have a huge volume of water running over it. The drop is highest during the March–May dry season and becomes much less spectacular when the river level rises during the rainy season. Still, the sight of all that water crashing down on its way to Cambodia is quite mesmerizing, and a well-built tourist pavilion above the falls provides an ideal place to sit and enjoy the view. There's also no shortage of food shacks serving snacks. Most tourists do the falls as a package from Don Khong (see below) but it is also possible to get there by sawngthaew from Ban Hat Xai Khoun (opposite Muang Khong) or Nakasang (5000K). There is a 10,000K admission fee for foreigners and 1000K extra for a motorcycle.

Practicalities

It is possible to do both Don Khon and Don Det plus the waterfall at Khon Phapheng as a **day-trip** from Don Khong, although Don Khon on its own is worth a few days' visit. Muang Khong's guesthouses and restaurants offer boat trips (10,000K per person) on which you can see the waterfalls and the defunct railroad. The boat can't go directly to Khon Phapheng Falls, so the boatman will take you to the right bank and wait there while a sawngthaew (another 10,000K per person) collects you and takes you on the thirty-kilometre round-trip to the falls (admission not included).

The cheapest option for **getting to the islands** independently from Muang Khong is to take the ferry (5000K) across the river to Ban Hat Xai Khoun and then get a bus to **Nakasang**, where you can get a boat to Don Khon or Don Det ($1–2). The boats depart from the landing, a short walk from the market. It's possible to join a Don Khon day-trip and negotiate a one-way, discounted price.

From the southern end of Don Khon, it's possible to charter a boat down the river to **Veun Kham** ($5 for up to three passengers), where there is a Lao immigration office and a **border crossing** into Cambodia.

Accommodation and eating

Although Don Khon was the first island to take off with travellers, Don Det has already surpassed its larger neighbour in popularity. There's not a huge difference in the two islands, and **where you stay** is largely a matter of shopping around for a bungalow or room to suit your taste and budget.

On **Don Khon**, most of the bungalows are located near Ban Khon on the north end of the island. The fanciest place here is the *Sala Don Khone* (T031/251461; ❷), east of the railway bridge near the Don Khon landing. The rooms in this converted French-era bungalow, which was once a hospital, feature air conditioning and hot-water showers. It also offers Lao-style wooden bungalows and a nice riverside restaurant. Next door is *Mr Bounh's* (❶), offering simple bungalows with shared facilities in a quiet compound close to the river. In Ban Khon is *Pon's River Resort* (❶), a collection of stilted bamboo huts with shared facilities and a decent restaurant.

Bungalow places are scattered all the way around **Don Det**, but the largest concentration is on the north side of the island. Some of the more long-running are *Santiphab* (❶), next to the railroad bridge and popular with backpackers, and, about 2km further up the trail from the bridge, *Mr Tho's Bungalows* (❶), basic bamboo-and-thatch huts and hammocks from which you can idly watch river life passing by. If they're full, try *Souksan Bungalow* (❶), on the northern tip of the island.

Food, not accommodation, is the real money-earner here, and every bungalow place has **restaurants** serving Lao food and the usual traveller's fare, so you may want to take some of your meals at the bungalow you're staying at.

The Bolaven Plateau

As gradual as Route 23's eastwardly climb out of Pakxe is, there's no mistaking when you've reached the **Bolaven Plateau**, roughly 30km from Pakxe. The suffocating heat of the Mekong Valley yields to a refreshingly cool breeze, and coffee and tea plantations, exulting in the rich soil, begin cropping up along either side of the highway. Hilly, roughly circular in shape, and with an average altitude of 600m, the high plateau has rivers running off in all directions and then plunging out of lush forests along the Bolaven's edges in a series of spectacular waterfalls, some more than 100m high, before eventually finding their way to the Mekong. Four provincial capitals – Pakxe, Salavan, Xekong and Attapu – surround the Bolaven, while the main settlement on the plateau itself is the town of **Pakxong**.

△ Coffee beans being dried, Bolaven Plateau

The French, recognizing the fertility of the terrain, cleared wide swathes of forests and planted strawberries, coffee, tea and cardamom. Although it was cardamom that provided the south's chief export during colonial times, coffee is the crop that dominates the plateau these days, earning the well-paved highway that links Pakxe with Pakxong the moniker the **Coffee Road**. Introduced to the area by the French in the 1920s, coffee plants are now crammed into every spare centimetre of land; the villagers hope to earn extra kip by hawking their private crop to brokers, who sell the roasted beans upcountry and around the world.

Long before the French planted their first coffee crop, midland **hill tribes** were practising swidden agriculture on the plateau. Today, twelve ethnic groups, including lowland Lao, Laven, Alak, Suay and Taoy, live in the area. Given that ethnic minorities are in the majority here, it's only fitting that the plateau takes its name from one of these groups, the **Laven**.

Historically, the Bolaven has yielded more than just rich agricultural pickings. For the French, controlling the area was a headache during the early years of their rule. An Alak holy man, believed to possess supernatural powers, sparked a rebellion against the land's new colonial masters, a revolt which, fuelled by anger at the disruption of established political and economic relationships in the area, spilled into the Mekong basin and neighbouring Thailand. This rebel spirit was later co-opted by the Pathet Lao in their attempt to create a nationalist history of rebellion against foreign powers. During the Second Indochina War, the plateau's elevated terrain provided a strategic military position as well as access to the far-flung outposts of Salavan and Attapu. The legacy of decades of battle still haunts the people of the plateau, with farmers tending to their crops amid fields laden with unexploded bombs.

One of the easiest waterfalls to access here is **Tad Lo** on the forested northern edge of the plateau, a popular spot with travellers looking for somewhere pleasant to relax for a few days and enjoy the plateau's cool climate. You can lounge in the pools of the Xe Set River below the waterfall and do some elephant trekking to nearby tribal villages. South of Route 23 between Pakxe and Pakxong is the **Dong Hua Sao NBCA**, containing the **Tad Fan Waterfall**. **Pakxong** was levelled in bombing raids during the war and has not been able to rekindle the charm it once possessed.

Lak Sao-et, the tiny village 21km from Pakxe along Route 23, is an important junction for **bus transfers** – there are connections here for Tad Lo and Salavan in the northeast, and for Pakxong and beyond. Makeshift thatch lean-tos at the junction are great for **fruit**, including sun-yellowed bunches of bananas, suspended from bamboo poles, and pineapples and durians – the last of these are fresh off the plateau and are known for their exceptional creaminess.

Dong Hua Sao NBCA

Located in the southwest quarter of the Bolaven Plateau, **Dong Hua Sao** is, at the time of writing, the only NBCA up on the plateau itself, though another two areas of the plateau are under consideration for NBCA status; assuming the proposals go through, the three protected areas would merge into a single conservation area totalling 2465 square kilometres and covering the greater part of the outer Bolaven Plateau, and featuring a 1300-metre peak in the west.

Falling water enthusiasts will get a kick out of **Tad Fan**, a cascade some 100m high, set amid primeval jungle that stretches as far as the eye can see. Of several waterfalls in the area, this one is the easiest to locate. Travelling east on Route 23 from Pakxe to Pakxong, turn right at the Kilometre 38 marker onto a dirt road that leads through a coffee plantation and then forks; take the branch to the left and you will end up at the edge of a cliff overlooking the falls. A trail leads down to a better vantage point, but it's not advisable to attempt this slippery path during the rainy season, as it's a long drop down into the abyss. If you're travelling by **bus**, ask to be let off at Tad Fan, and you'll be able to walk the dirt road in.

At the falls, you'll also find the *Tad Fane Resort* (T021/350160, W www .tadfane.com; ❸) which has a restaurant and ten nicely built Lao-style bungalows near the falls.

Pakxong

Laos's famed coffee capital, **PAKXONG**, some 60km east of Pakxe, was rebuilt after the war and is just now beginning to find a market for its traditional cash crop. Those searching for some epicentre of coffee culture will be disappointed, but arriving on the plateau from the baking lowlands, especially during the torrid March–May hot season, will make you wonder how a bit of altitude can turn the cruel midday sun into a shoulder-warming friend.

The vast majority of Pakxong's inhabitants are **Laven**, an ethnic group that has almost completely assimilated with the ethnic Lao. About the only trait that differentiates the Laven from the lowland Lao, besides language, is their hospitality which, believe it or not, actually exceeds that of the lowlanders. This is especially apparent during Lao New Year, when foreign guests are sure to be welcomed with prodigious amounts of potent rice liquor.

Lao Java

In the early twentieth century, the French were looking for ways to make their newest chunk of Indochina profitable. Laos had become a disappointment when the grand scheme of using the Mekong as a trade link to China turned out to be impractical, but the French soon had other plans. Would **coffee**, which had been successfully introduced to Vietnam, also thrive in Laos? It seemed worth a try. Saplings were brought from the orchards around Buon Me Thuot in Vietnam and planted at varying degrees of elevation. From the banks of the Mekong on up to the Bolaven Plateau, rows of arabica and robusta were carefully nursed. After four years, the first harvest saw mixed results: coffee at lower elevations failed to fruit, but planters on the Bolaven were rewarded for their patience.

By the 1940s, **coffee plantations** covered the plateau and the future looked bright until a bout of the blight caused the arabica trees to wither and die. Next, war and revolution intervened, and by the 1980s, the once painstakingly tended trees had gone wild. However, interest in Lao coffee has been rekindled over the last decade and the old plantations have benefited from a certain amount of foreign investment. A blight-resistant strain of arabica was recently introduced from Costa Rica, and the "Association des Exportateurs du Café Lao" is hoping to increase annual coffee production and make Lao coffee known to aficionados around the globe. Planters are also optimistic, citing tales of recent harvests so bountiful that branches snapped under the weight of the clusters of beans.

Although coffee made its way to Laos via Vietnam, the **coffee-drinking etiquette** and accoutrements of Laos have a flavour all their own. The tin-drip, used in Vietnam to filter coffee into a glass, is rare in Laos; the Lao favour pouring hot water through a sock-like bag filled with ground coffee. For more on Lao coffee, see p.51.

The temperate weather and amiable locals notwithstanding, Pakxong's sights are almost nil. The **town** itself is a small collection of mould-blackened concrete shophouses lining wide, dust-scoured streets, which wouldn't look out of place on the set of a spaghetti Western. A gatepost at the entrance of the market is possibly the only structure in town to have survived the war. Beyond it is a depressing block of ramshackle shops and noodle stands. Despite the bleakness of the town, the surrounding countryside and **coffee plantations** provide some diverting scenery, especially during March and April when the coffee trees are covered with intoxicatingly fragrant white blossoms.

Perhaps noting the lack of ambience, some of Pakxong's residents have begun exploring the decorative possibilities of **unexploded ordnance**. At the Shell service station on Route 23 just west of town, a 110-kilo bomb and other sundry bits of ordnance, all of it presumably still live, have been painted and sit neatly arranged in a garden near the petrol pumps.

Practicalities

If only Pakxong boasted a cosy guesthouse surrounded by gardens where you could enjoy the invigorating climate. Sadly, it does not. The town's only **accommodation**, *Pakxong* (②), 500m beyond the market, is dingy and uncomfortable. Supposedly this building was prefabricated in Germany by some NGO and used as their quarters before being left to the Lao – who have no way of replacing fixtures when anything breaks. **Moving on**, buses headed for Xekong and Attapu pass the town, and sawngthaews leave from the market for Pakxe.

Tad Lo

The ten-metre-high **Tad Lo**, a waterfall on the banks of the Xe Set 90km northeast of Pakxe and about 30km southwest of Salavan, draws a steady stream of foreign visitors, providing the perfect setting for a few days' relaxation and the opportunity to ride an elephant along the breezy western flank of the plateau. In the hot season, the pools surrounding **Tad Hang**, the lower falls, are a refreshing escape from the heat; large boulders in the river shade a few surprisingly deep swimming holes and are perfect spots for lounging in the sun. Just be sure to clear the water before darkness, however, when the floodgates of a dam upstream sometimes unleash a torrent of water without warning.

Elephant treks ($5 for 2hr) through the forested hills around Tad Lo are easy to arrange through any of the guesthouses here. Sitting high up in the howdah, you get some sense of the grace of these regal beasts, which for centuries were cherished by Lao and French travellers alike for their ability to glide through tricky terrain. A ride typically involves a round-trip from the *Tad Lo Resort*, and involves a short stop at Tad Lo, 500m upstream, before pulling through a nearby village inhabited by midlanders of Alak ethnicity, who have a long history of settlement on the plateau.

Practicalities

The road between Pakxe and Salavan is mostly dirt but is flat and in good condition. The turn-off for Tad Lo is 88km northeast of Pakxe, just beyond the village of **Lao Ngam**. Buses will drop you at the turn-off where a congregation of restaurants and general stores crowds the mouth of the 1500-metre dirt road that leads to Tad Hang, the lower falls, which can be reached by tuk-tuk (5000K per person). When leaving, find a tuk-tuk to take you back to the highway, where you can pick up a morning bus to Salavan or Pakxe.

A chanting mob, two thousand-strong, descended on Savannakhet in April 1902, convinced by a holy man that any bullets fired at them would be miraculously transformed into frangipani flowers. Three times they attacked, and each time they were mown down by troops from France's "Garde Indigène". The rout, which left 150 dead, marked the climax of the so-called **Holy Man's Revolt**, which had its origins with the arrival of the French in 1893 and simmered on for many years afterwards in the highlands of the south.

The French brought with them administrative changes, increased taxation and reshuffled the traditional relationships that had guided life in Laos for generations. At first, resistance was textbook Lao. Villagers avoided direct confrontation, preferring to make their displeasure about the new order known through passive means: villages undercounted their populations, adapted a generally uncooperative attitude, or simply left. The first serious opposition didn't arise until eight years after the French employed gunboat diplomacy to wrest control of Lao territory from Siam.

When **Ong Kaew**, an Alak tribesman believed to possess supernatural powers, prophesied that "the end of the world as we know it" was nigh, he found willing listeners among midland tribes living along the plateau, chafing under increased taxes and *corvée* labour demands instituted by the French commissioner of Salavan. Sensing that Ong Kaew was gaining too much influence, the commissioner ordered the burning of a pagoda erected in the holy man's honour. This only served to increase support for Ong Kaew, and in April 1901, he and a band of rebels attacked the commissioner and his guard. Soon after, nearly all of the Bolaven region was in revolt.

By 1902, the revolt had spilled across the Mekong and briefly gained the support of older lowland Lao families, who felt threatened by the collapse of the social and economic order to which they were accustomed. After the disastrous march on Savannakhet, Ong Kaew and another Lao Theung leader, **Ong Kommadam**, whose son would later continue to resist the French and ultimately become a Pathet Lao leader, retreated across the Xe Kong as villages were burned and less fortunate leaders rounded up and executed. But the defeat at Savannakhet and renewed attempts by France to pacify the Bolaven region did little to dispel the holy man's popularity, and it took a new commissioner at Salavan, **Jean Dauplay**, to force Ong Kaew to surrender in 1907. Three years later, with the holy man's influence over the Bolaven inhabitants as strong as ever, Dauplay arrested Ong Kaew, who died "during a jail break" the next day. The revolt was effectively over.

Not all was lost during the insurrection. French authorities were careful to place more of the burden on lowland Lao when they raised taxes in 1914, and Ong Kaew had unwittingly sown the seeds for what the Pathet Lao would later claim to be the stirrings of Lao nationalism.

High on a hill overlooking Tad Hang, but reachable on foot, perches the *Tad Lo Resort* (☎031/214184; ❸), with thirteen rooms in an assortment of **bungalows**, ranging from the very basic to well-appointed structures at the river's edge. Across the river bridge, *Saise* **guesthouse** has a couple of rooms with shared facilities in a raised house, plus some very pleasant en-suite ones in the "Green House", a few hundred metres upstream (both types ❷). It's the best deal to be found in the area, especially the VIP rooms, which have balconies overlooking the river.

Choices for **eating** are limited, but the *Tad Lo Resort* has a relaxed open-air restaurant, with rattan furniture and commanding views of the Xe Set, where you can choose from a range of moderately priced French and Lao dishes. Be sure to try their *mók pa*, fish with chillies steamed in banana leaves.

The remote provinces

Salavan, **Xekong** and **Attapu**, cut off from the Mekong River Valley by the Bolaven Plateau and made remote by the rugged jigsaw of the Annamite Mountains, are some of the least-visited provinces in Laos. Until recently, poor infrastructure and the scars of war conspired to keep the region isolated. With the Ho Chi Minh Trail streaming across their borders, these provinces were victims of some of the heaviest bombing during the Second Indochina War. Villages were decimated, roads destroyed and in some places the dangerous litter of battle still lies about. Yet these factors kept the densely forested mountains of Attapu and Xekong pristine until the beginning of this century. Today, intense **logging** along the Vietnamese border is turning parts of this once rich ecosystem into a moonscape. For the time being, however, the provinces are still home to a variety of wildlife and numerous ethnic minority villages.

Arcing around the **Bolaven Plateau**, these provinces can be seen in a convenient clockwise loop from Pakxe. From Lak Sao-et (see p.312), 21km east of Pakxe, head northeast for roughly 100km along well-maintained Route 20 towards Salavan, where bus connections are available for the bumpy ninety-kilometre trip to **Xekong** via **Thateng**, the dusty northern gateway to the Bolaven Plateau. Just east of the plateau, uninspiring Xekong provides a jumping-off point for the pretty five-hour boat trip along the babbling Xe Kong to **Attapu**, capital of Laos's southeasternmost province.

From Attapu, it can be a rough haul back to Pakxe up the eastern flank of the Bolaven and through the coffee plantations surrounding Pakxong, as the steep, poorly engineered Attapu–Pakxong road, a seasonal route cut by a South Korean hydroelectric company working in the area, becomes nearly impassable in the rainy season. At the moment, no public buses and very few private vehicles travel Route 18, the shortcut to Si Phan Don, which shadows the southern edge of the Bolaven, although the Asian Development Bank once had plans to upgrade the road as far as Vietnam.

Salavan

Located on a flank of the former Ho Chi Minh Trail north of the Bolaven Plateau, Salavan province was held by the Royal Lao government until 1970, when an NVA push to consolidate control over the Trail drove the Royalists out. The provincial capital, also called **SALAVAN**, was, thanks to its proximity to the Trail, all but obliterated during the war by B-52 strikes. It wasn't until the late 1980s that rebuilding began; in the interim, the province was used as a re-education camp in which high-ranking RLA officers were given plots of land to till, many dying of malaria.

Scrap collectors have all but dismantled what few war relics were left here. About the only prewar building in evidence is **Wat Phon Kaew**, comprising a shrapnel-pocked gateway and a ruined stupa in the grounds of the provincial hospital.

Today, Salavan town is a peaceful backwater, scorched in the hot season by desert-like winds. Many new buildings of permanent materials have replaced the rickety wooden structures that were the norm up until the 1990s, and nowadays you'd need a guide with knowledge of what the old Salavan looked like in order to glimpse any evidence of Salavan's tumultuous history. Unless you are simply looking for a very out-of-the-way place to hang out, there isn't much reason to gravitate here, though the town can be used as a base to explore Mon-Khmer villages in the area.

Practicalities

The daily buses that pull into Salavan's **bus station** connect the town with Pakxe, Xekong and Pakxong, with smaller buses and pick-up trucks heading off from here to the province's interior. Overly optimistic maps suggest the possibility of travelling north to Savannakhet province (through Toumlan to Muang Phin and through Taoy on to Ban Dong), but these roads, effectively taken out during the war, are now overgrown and lacking key bridges.

If you're interested in travelling to the outer districts of the province, seek out the helpful **provincial tourism officer**, Mr Bounthone, whose office is located at the *Saise Guesthouse*. He can point you in the direction of any interesting festivals taking place in nearby ethnic minority villages, and update you on the progress of repairs to roads and bridges you might need to traverse.

Salavan has a number of **guesthouses**, including *Sinsamai* (❷), just north of *Nong Vilaivane Restaurant*, which offers rooms with a fan or air conditioning; other choices in town include the *Thipphaphone* (❷) and the *Chindavone* (❷).

Aside from the adjoining Lao restaurant, the **market** offers a group of stalls selling pre-made Lao food and sticky rice. Also in the vicinity, the *Nong Vilaivane*, a tidy little **restaurant** with bamboo interior, has a dusty rack of foreign liquor and an English-language menu with a short list of inexpensive Lao, Chinese and Vietnamese dishes.

In the immediate vicinity of the market you'll find the **post office** as well as a branch of Phak Tai **bank**, where you can exchange US dollars and Thai baht in cash only.

The Xe Kong River Valley

The **Xe Kong** is one of Laos's great rivers, starting high in the Annamite Mountains from the eastern flanks of the 2500-metre-high Mount Atouat and flowing southwestward around the southern edge of the Bolaven Plateau. It enters Cambodia via the Xe Pian NBCA, eventually joining the Mekong River in that country, north of Stung Treng.

The main towns along the Xe Kong in Laos are **Xekong** and **Attapu**, which are linked by a paved road. Roads into the vast forest interior are still extremely poor, but various tributaries link the Xe Kong to no less than four of Laos's most pristine NBCAs, and **boat trips** down the Xe Kong are a possibility.

If you're heading this way from Salavan, the first part of the journey involves a laborious climb through rich jungle and midland tribal villages up the steep curves of the Bolaven Plateau to **Thateng**, 40km away. A dusty, ramshackle congregation of threadbare markets and crooked wooden houses with thatch roofs, Thateng was where the French commissioner to Salavan, Jean Dauplay, "the father of Lao coffee", chose to settle in the 1920s. Sadly, Thateng's strategic location as the gateway to the plateau, a grip on which was considered key to controlling the bulk of the far south, made it a prime target for American bombs. The town was basically wiped out, and although villagers returned after the war, the place is nowadays little more than an unappealing transit point.

Xekong

In 1984, a wide expanse of jungle was cleared of trees and graded flat in order to found the town of **XEKONG**. Created partly because the nearby town of Ban Phon was deemed no longer habitable owing to unexploded ordnance, Xekong, some 50km east of Thateng, is now the capital of a new province, created when Attapu was divided in half. Xekong has some of a frontier feel but not much of interest, though intrepid travellers may be attracted by the prospect of a scenic journey downriver from here to Attapu.

Three major branches of the **Ho Chi Minh Trail** snaked through the jungle surrounding Xekong, and consequently this area was one of the most heavily bombed in Laos. Animist tribal peoples living in the adjacent hills, under constant threat of attack from the sky, erected talismans above their huts to ward off falling bombs. Some of these strange war relics are still in place: rusting tail-fins from dud bombs have been arranged to form a protective X over thatched roofs, and, in at least one village, carved wooden miniatures of helicopters, looking like militaristic weather vanes, are mounted above the tribal meeting house. Some of these tribes produce **hand-woven textiles** that are highly sought-after by collectors. Decorative patterns feature traditional motifs such as animals and plants, alongside stylized fighter planes and bombs of obvious inspiration.

Despite the dropping of bombs and defoliants, the area is host to a surprisingly large and varied **wildlife** population. Herds of wild elephants regularly raid village rice barns, and tigers have been seen lapping at the pools below Tad Xe Noi, a waterfall 25km south of Xekong. Other rare species known to inhabit the wilds of Xekong include the Siamese crocodile and pygmy slow loris. There is even thought to be a small population of Sumatran rhinos deep in the jungled hills.

If you're ready to devote half your visa time to Xekong, prepare yourself for this cruel hitch: the astonishing amount of **UXO** that blankets this province makes exploration extremely dicey. UXO disposal teams assigned to the province conclude that, like parts of Europe that were heavily fought over during both world wars, Xekong will be losing victims to UXO for decades to come. Despite all this, the average traveller to Laos has little to worry about if a few simple rules are followed. Although it may seem obvious, the number-one rule is not to be a trailblazer. When in rural areas, always stay on well-worn paths, even when passing through a village. For more advice on UXO, see p.64.

As if the danger of UXO weren't enough, there is a disturbing beasty lurking in Xekong's waterways: the *pa pao*, an innocuous-looking blowfish with a piranha-like appetite and, according to locals, a particular fondness for lopping off the tip of the male member. The risk of losing a plug of flesh to a ravenous blowfish notwithstanding, the journey by **pirogue** down the stretch of river between Xekong and Attapu (see opposite) is undoubtedly the best way to view this most inaccessible corner of southern Laos.

Practicalities

Buses to and from Pakxe operate from the lot outside the morning market, about 1km from the main market. A handful of **tuk-tuks** await arriving buses and will ferry you into the centre for 5000K. Heading into town, you'll pass a branch of the Lao Phattana bank where you can **exchange cash** and traveller's cheques, and the **post office** and telecom building where international calls can be made. A daily bus plies the paved route that follows the Xe Kong south to Attapu; it leaves the morning market at 7am, arriving in Attapu about two hours later, and departs for the trip back to Xekong at noon. Daily buses also go to Salavan on a paved road.

Sekong Souksamlane (☎038/212022; ❷), 500m downriver from the market, has decent if somewhat overpriced **rooms**. A cluster of cheap places to eat surrounds the hotel, and the hotel's **restaurant** cooks rather good Thai food at reasonable rates. The array of handicrafts that lines its walls is for sale, though there's a better selection in the small shop in an adjacent building. However, it's not always open and it's difficult to find someone with the key, so if you're here for some serious shopping, head over to the market where the prices are better.

Xekong to Attapu by river

If you've made it as far as Xekong, the scenic **Xe Kong**, which meanders through little-visited countryside, provides a strong incentive to charter a motorized pirogue for the journey south to **Attapu** – not cheap at $30–50, but well worth the expense. To find a boat in Xekong, follow the road that passes in front of the *Sekong Souksamlane* hotel south for 1km until you reach a boat landing on the riverbank, where you'll have to negotiate a price with the boatmen.

The pirogues make the journey to Attapu through gentle rapids and past lushly forested riverbanks, where people living in the surrounding hills come to catch fish and bathe. The journey usually takes four hours, but late in the dry season it can take seven, and at this time the shallow waters require passengers to walk short stretches of the journey along the bank. Although the fare doesn't rise at this time of year, captains limit the number of passengers to two, thereby increasing the price per person. Keep in mind that this river can be hazardous during high waters, and if you're not a strong swimmer you should probably give it a pass; more than one tourist has drowned on this journey.

During the Second Indochina War, US aircraft struck at the threads of the Ho Chi Minh Trail running parallel to the river, hoping to disrupt the endless tide of men and supplies streaming southwards. Bombs invariably wound up in the river and the resulting explosions sent scores of fish floating belly-up to the surface, unintentional war reparations quickly collected by villagers living amid a battlefield. Today's depleted fish catches are still blamed on the war, but more modern fishing equipment has surely had an impact, as has the use of explosives for catching fish, a technique that was utilized by Vietnamese soldiers during the war and remains part of the Cambodian fisherman's arsenal along some stretches of the river. One victim of such high-impact methods, the **Irrawaddy dolphin** (see p.295), until the 1980s a frequent visitor to Attapu's maze of rivers in the rainy season, now rarely visits these waters.

Attapu

A leafy settlement of almost twenty thousand people, most of whom are Vietnamese, Chinese or lowland Lao, remote **ATTAPU** occupies a bend in the Xe Kong just south of where it is joined by the **Xe Kaman**. Access to the town relies on the poorly engineered roads from Pakxong and Xekong, and hence Attapu can be difficult to reach, especially if the road from Xekong is washed out, but it's a pleasant destination compared to the hot and dusty towns of Xekong and Salavan.

It was near this distant outpost, capital of Laos's southeasternmost province, that the Ho Chi Minh Trail diverged, with one artery running south towards Cambodia and the other into South Vietnam. But despite its role as the final staging point in Laos for North Vietnamese supplies, Attapu somehow eluded the grave effects of war that wiped other southern cities off the map. That the town remains an oasis among rugged mountains perhaps reflects what some American military advisors mocked as the reluctance of the Royal Lao Army, who controlled Attapu in the late 1960s, to engage their opponents in battle – a trait that prompted the Americans to nickname the Royalist troops "the Fastest Army Running", a moniker derived from the army's old French acronym FAR. When the Pathet Lao announced that they intended to take the city in April 1970, Royal Lao troops lived up to their reputation and fled. Five years later, the Pathet Lao made the entire province a **re-education camp** (see p.186), resettling political enemies and forbidding them to leave the province for years. The Pathet Lao perhaps thought it only fitting to punish opponents with a dose of what they had had to endure, living in the country's remotest areas during their Thirty Year Struggle; what better place than one which, even by nineteenth-century Lao standards, was known for its "extreme unhealthiness", as reported by French explorer François Jules Harmand, who visited Attapu in 1877. This reputation festers to this day, with Attapu registering the country's highest rate of malaria.

Such tumultuous history lends new currency to the old legend surrounding Attapu's name. When the first lowland Lao immigrants to the region asked the indigenous people what the name of their town was, the latter thought the Lao were pointing to a pile of water buffalo dung, or *itkapu* in their language, and responded accordingly. With a slight change in pronunciation to accommodate the Lao accent, the town of "buffalo shit" was born.

The Town

Attapu has no warehouse of tourist attractions: the way to enjoy this town is by leisurely wandering in its rambling red-dirt lanes, absorbing the easy-going pace and chatting with the genial residents. In the evening, head to the southern end of town, where the Xe Kong pauses to flow east to west, and the high riverbank invites you to catch a sunset over the river. If it's sights you crave, walk over to the town's main **wat**, which occupies a massive block in the heart of town. On the northern side of the compound, standing out among the gaudy modern temple architecture, you'll find a handsome French-style monastery school building.

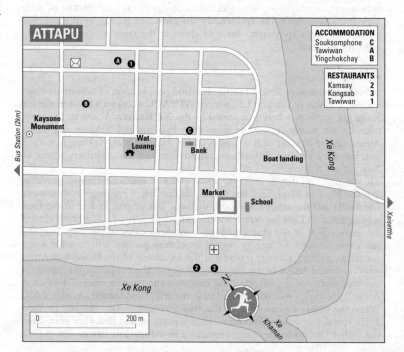

ATTAPU

ACCOMMODATION
Souksomphone C
Tawiwan A
Yingchokchay B

RESTAURANTS
Kamsay 2
Kongsab 3
Tawiwan 1

Bus Station (2km)

Kaysone Monument

Wat Louang

Bank

Boat landing

Xe Kong

Market

School

Xe Kong

Xaisettha

Xe Kong

Xe Khaman

0   200 m

If you're arriving by bus, note the recently built monument at the bus station, commemorating Lao-Vietnamese cooperation during the war. The monument, depicting Pathet Lao and NVA soldiers waving flags and Kalashnikov rifles aloft, is a near copy of the one in Muang Phin, Savannakhet province. Not surprisingly it is Vietnamese-built, and is supposed to welcome visitors from that country arriving on the extension of Route 18 to the Vietnamese border – if and when that road is ever finished.

Practicalities

In the rainy season, getting to and from Attapu by road can be something of a challenge, and you may well find yourself getting out to push a bus axle-deep in mud. Arriving by **bus**, you'll find yourself next to a market (**Talat Noi**) on the northwestern outskirts of the city, 3km from the centre. If you're on the **express bus** from Pakxe, don't get off here, as the bus may continue into town. Boats from Xekong dock at the **ferry landing**, just upriver from the new bridge. A good point of orientation is Attapu's only **bank**, a branch of Lao Development Bank, which is about in the centre of the town, and can be reached from the ferry landing by following the road into town.

Attapu has one **hotel** and a handful of **guesthouses**. The block-like *Yingchokchay Hotel*, in a huge compound (☏036/211031; ❷), has air-conditioned rooms with fridge and satellite TV, plus some very cheap, good-value fan rooms. The oldest of the guesthouses is the well-run but sometimes surly *Souksomphone* (❶), which has seven rooms, most with double beds and private bathrooms; look for the modern building opposite the bank. Near the post office, *Tawiwan* (❶), formerly the official government guesthouse, has rooms with creaky wooden floors and shared bathrooms in a cluster of two-storey houses set back from the road. Come here only if you want to get a taste of what accommodation was like in all of provincial Laos during the 1980s and early 1990s.

At the eastern end of the *Tawiwan* compound is its **restaurant**, Attapu's longest running; here you'll find good, moderately priced noodle and rice dishes. Most visitors opt to do a sunset dinner at one of two riverside places, *Kamsay* and *Pa Kongsab*, but at neither establishment is the food all that good – beer and karaoke are the staples here. The restaurant at the *Yingchokchay Hotel* is the only place in town with Western breakfasts.

Moving on from Attapu, the bus to Xekong leaves at noon and arrives at Xekong's morning market at around 2pm. The **express bus** leaves Attapu for Pakxe at 6am, making the nonstop trip in a lightning-quick four hours. Otherwise you're stuck with the gruelling regular bus, which can take twice as long. **Boats** to Xekong can be arranged through the owner of the *Souksomphone*; for more on this route, see p.305.

Across the river from Attapu

When François Jules Harmand asked about **crossing to the left bank** of the Xe Kong River during his visit in the late 1870s, the village chief answered each question about the possibility of such a trip with *baw dai* ("No can do") – a refrain the French explorer heard so often he was pressed to consider whether the Lao language possessed any other words than these. Visitors today will have less trouble, at least in getting as far as **Pa-am**, an Alak village some 40km east of Attapu, reached via the Route 18 extension that will eventually link Attapu with Vietnam. Pick-ups doing the trip leave from the Talat Noi bus station when full. The scenery on the journey isn't exactly lush – this area was deforested in the past decade, and in fact the newly upgraded road is more about giving Vietnamese logging companies access to Lao timber than it is about linking Attapu and Pleiku in Vietnam. The only thing worth seeing in Pa-am is a rusting surface-to-air missile parked under a mango tree. The missile, stencilled in both Russian and Vietnamese, is one of a very few surviving pieces of wartime hardware that have not been carted away by scrap collectors.

Around a dozen **ethnic minorities** live in these hills and, with many of the same groups living on the Vietnamese side of the mountains, these peoples reflect the porous nature of many of the borders in Southeast Asia. As the indigenous people of this area, these groups are considered by lowland Lao to be close to the spirits of the land, a belief that inspires some superstitious ethnic Lao to fill their pockets with Parrot Brand soap – the garlic of toiletries, believed to ward off black magic – before entering tribal villages.

In the late nineteenth century, when the region was in Bangkok's sphere of influence, some of these midland villages paid tribute to Siam – usually in the form of **gold dust** stored in the quill of a large bird's feather – in order to hedge their bets against being captured in a slave hunt, a practice abolished by the French. The sight of these flecks of gold convinced French explorers that hidden riches might lie in the mountains, and they dug mines, but the colonial administration saw little profit from these ventures. Indeed, a brief visit to the villages outside Attapu is evidence enough that the area is no gold mine.

Attapu once shared neighbouring Xekong's rich variety of **wildlife**. Lured by this abundance, Suay villagers arrived here several centuries ago to capture wild elephants. Although the Suay migrated west in the eighteenth century, poachers in these hills still hunt exotic animals, which they sell off to buyers from Vietnam. The fact that such work has become quite lucrative gives villagers added incentive to continue this practice, and those that do are not keen on individuals seen to be poking around.

Travel details

Buses

Attapu to: Pakse (3 daily; 4–7hr) via Pakxong (2 daily; 5hr); Xekong (1 daily; 2hr).
Champasak to: Pakse (3 daily; 2hr 30min).
Pakse to: Attapu (2 daily; 4–7hr); Ban Phapho (3 daily; 3hr); Ban Saphai (hourly; 30min); Champasak (3 daily; 1hr); Chong Mek (every 30min; 45min); Muang Khong (2 daily; 5hr); Kiatngong (3 daily; 2hr 30min); Muang Sen (2 daily; 5hr 30min); Nakasang (5 daily; 3hr); Pakxong (hourly; 2hr); Salavan (5 daily; 3hr); Savannakhet (3 daily; 6hr); Thakhek (3 daily; 8–10hr); Vientiane (3 daily; 12–15hr); Xekong (2 daily; 4–5hr).

Pakxong to: Attapu (2 daily; 5hr); Pakxe (hourly; 2hr).
Salavan to: Pakse (5 daily; 3hr); Taoy (1 daily; 5hr); Toumlan (1 daily; 2hr); Xekong (2 daily; 4hr).
Xekong to: Pakse (2 daily; 4–5hr); Salavan (2 daily; 4hr).

Boats

Pakxe to: Champasak (1–2 daily; 1hr 30min); Don Khong (1–2 daily; 8–10hr).

Flights

Pakxe to: Vientiane (1 daily; 1hr 20min).

Contexts

Contexts

History

Laos as a unified state within its present geographical boundaries has only existed for little more than one hundred years. Its national history stretches back six centuries to the legendary kingdom of Lane Xang, a rival to the empires of mainland Southeast Asia until it splintered into a cluster of weak principalities dominated by their more powerful neighbours.

The beginnings

As long as forty thousand years ago, Laos was inhabited by **hunter–gatherers** who lived in relatively permanent sites and used tools made of stone, wood and bamboo, not terribly different from many of those still in use in rural Lao villages today. By 8000 BC, these peoples had become **farmers**, growing beans, peas and rice and domesticating animals. Excavations at a site in present-day northeastern Thailand reveal that copper and bronze work in the region dates back four thousand years – as early as anywhere in the world. **Ironworking** was the next step forward, and by 500 BC the inhabitants of the Khorat Plateau in northeastern Thailand were using ploughs with iron tips, pulled by water buffalo, to cultivate wet rice. The sophistication of the metallurgy of the region is perhaps best indicated by the bronze drums crafted by the Lac Viet people of northern Vietnam in the first millennium BC, ritualistic artefacts discovered in 1920 near Dong Son in Vietnam and later at several sites in Laos.

The **earliest indigenous culture** in Laos to have been investigated by archeologists was that of an iron-age megalithic people that lived in what is now Xiang Khouang province on the Plain of Jars. These people built stone pillars which were positioned next to underground burial chambers, and large stone funerary urns to hold the ashes of their dead. The civilization is thought to have progressed from crafting the three-metre tall stone slabs to the massive jars after the development of iron tools. Bronze objects as well as beads foreign to the region suggest that the civilization was a wealthy one and lay at the centre of trade routes to China, Vietnam and points south. However, very little else is known about this people and what became of them.

By this time, broad linguistic and cultural groups were beginning to emerge in Southeast Asia. Small villages were developing and between them there was regular communication and trade in such items as pottery, salt and metal tools. The early inhabitants of Laos and the surrounding parts of central and southern Indochina spoke Austroasiatic languages such as Mon and Khmer, while the ancestors of the lowland Lao spoke proto-Tai languages, and were still living in the river valleys of southeastern China. What is known about this group of **Tai** people comes mostly from documents written by their neighbours. Tai peoples described in early Chinese documents were valley- and lowland-dwelling subsistence farmers who typically cultivated wet rice and vegetables and, unlike the Chinese and Vietnamese, lived in houses built on piles. They reared water buffalo less for use as beasts of burden than as symbols of wealth and status or for use in ritual.

The **Tai villages** of the first millennium AD were probably much like the villages of rural Laos today, and would have consisted of a small cluster of households sharing labour during harvests. A need for mutual protection against outside forces most likely drove such villages together into larger units known as *muang* – a term which refers to both a group of villages and the central town in a network of villages.

With the lowlands to the east and northeast densely settled by Vietnamese and Chinese populations, the Tai peoples slowly **migrated** west and south-west into northern Laos and southern Yunnan, and eventually as far as Assam in northeastern India, displacing the sparse indigenous population of Austro-nesian and Austroasiatic groups and forcing them into the less desirable upland areas – where their descendants still live today. This migration is reflected in the Lao legend of Khoun Borom (see box on p.135). By the ninth century, the Tai were spread across upland Southeast Asia and surrounded by **Nanchao**, a well-organized military state located in southwestern China; a Vietnamese state on the verge of independence from China; Champa, an Indianized king-dom on the coast of Vietnam; Angkorian Cambodia; and the Mon and Pyu kingdoms of Burma.

Indianized influences

The cultural roots of the present-day Lao lie in **Indian civilization**. From the first century AD, Indian traders made their way east through Southeast Asia by land and by sea en route to China. Hinduized enclaves sprang up along the routes they travelled. The first of these to emerge were along the coast of Indochina, and included the **Funan** empire, a Mekong Delta state with trading links as far as Persia, and **Champa**, which was centred near Danang in Vietnam. Later, inland civilizations developed in Burma, Cambodia and Thailand. It was these classical Indianized civilizations along with individual Indian traders and travelling monks, rather than Chinese culture, that would shape the identity of the Lao, an influence evident today in the sharp difference between the Tai groups who underwent Indianization, became Buddhist and incorporated Pali and Sanskrit words into their languages, and those that did not.

The foundation of Buddhist civilization in Thailand and Laos was laid by a unique Theravada Buddhist cultural complex identified with the Mon people and known as **Dvaravati**. This civilization grew up around the overland trade route stretching from the Indian Ocean to the Gulf of Thailand, and dominated the Central Plain of Thailand for several centuries, although more as a cul-tural influence than an empire. Monastery boundary stones, clay votive tablets, Indian-influenced Buddhist statuary and objects foreign to Southeast Asia (such as coins and lamps found at sites across Thailand and parts of Laos) suggest that Dvaravati was a prosperous, expansive civilization that flourished between the sixth and ninth centuries. Dvaravati sites appear to have been most densely clustered around the lower Chao Phraya River Valley of Thailand, along what were regular routes of communication and trade. These lines of contact were significant for the Tai *muang* that were to emerge in Laos, as they contributed to the spread of Buddhism in the area. This is evidenced by the discovery of eleventh- and twelfth-century relics in Louang Phabang and near Phonhong on the Vientiane Plain, the earliest Buddhist statuary yet discovered in these parts of Laos.

The Khmer

As the ninth century drew to a close, Dvaravati's influence over central Southeast Asia was rapidly being eclipsed by the **Khmer Empire** of Angkor. The Khmer empire was ruled by kings who were usually identified with the Hindu gods Shiva or Vishnu, although Mahayana Buddhism later came into vogue at the Khmer court. At its height, the empire extended from its core of Cambodia and the southern half of northeastern Thailand into Vietnam, central Thailand and Laos, where the Khmer built dozens of Angkor-style temple complexes. As a result of this expansion, the Khmer gained control over important trade routes between India and China from which they derived their wealth and strength. The empire was held together by an extensive network of communications and institutions, as well as a system of highways linking key centres of the empire, traces of which are visible between Wat Phou and Angkor.

As the empire grew, Khmer governors, who were sometimes princes with ties to the royal house at Angkor, were placed in control of newly acquired areas, bringing with them tax collectors, judges, scribes and monks and ordering the construction of enormous religious monuments. The people then living in what is now southern Laos were probably predominantly Khmer as far north as Savannakhet, although by the eleventh and twelfth centuries, ethnic Tai made up a significant portion of the population on the fringes of the Angkor empire.

Early Tai principalities

The first record of contact between the Khmer empire and a Tai state occurred sometime after the seventh century near Chiang Saen in far northern Thailand, where a Tai state known as **Yonok** emerged along the Mekong River in the vicinity of Bokeo province. By the late tenth century, Buddhism was blossoming in Yonok, transforming the localized Buddhism into an institutionalized religious tradition with ties to the civilizations of the Mon and Ceylon. It was around this time that the Tai were beginning to move onto the lowland plains, suitable for extensive cultivation of rice, and develop into organized states, although none was yet large enough to dominate their non-Tai neighbours.

Though the origin of the first Lao principalities is ill defined to say the least, it appears that the first significant Tai centres in what is now Laos took root in the north, at Louang Phabang and Xiang Khouang, both of which are identified in legends as areas ruled by the sons of Khoun Borom.

By the thirteenth century, Louang Phabang, along with Chiang Saen, Jinghong (the Tai Leu capital located in Yunnan) and a Black Tai centre near the Da River in Vietnam, had emerged as one of the chief Tai centres of the Upper Mekong, an area settled by people who called themselves **Lao** and lived under the threat of invasion from Nanchao and Vietnam. A century later, Louang Phabang, then known as Xiang Dong Xiang Thong, had become but one of many small Lao principalities that existed on the fringes of two larger Tai states that had emerged: **Lan Na**, centred on Chiang Mai, and **Sukhothai**, the principality which is viewed as the cornerstone in Thailand's development. These states had capitalized on the collapse of the region's classical Indianized empires, Angkor and Pagan, their growth fuelled by large bases of rice land and manpower. Inscriptions from the Siamese *muang* of Sukhothai indicate that Lao rulers from Xiang Dong Xiang Thong were paying tribute to the Sukhothai by the late thirteenth century.

Yet even as the sun began to set on Angkor in the thirteenth century, the Khmer empire's most lasting impact on its still nebulous northern neighbour was to come in the form of a helping hand to the young exile who was to transform the petty Lao principalities scattered across Laos and portions of Thailand into a power in mainland Southeast Asia.

The rise of Lane Xang

Lao legends tell of a young prince belonging to the ruling family of Xiang Dong Xiang Thong who was cast out of the fledgling Lao principality, only to wind up in the Khmer court at Angkor where he was taken in, educated and married to a Khmer princess (see p.136). The generosity of Angkor, by that point on the verge of collapse and perhaps desperate for an ally, didn't stop there. Provided with an army by the Khmer king, this prince, **Fa Ngum**, fought his way up the Mekong valley atop a war elephant in 1351 – subduing first the principalities of the lower Mekong valley, Sikhotabong (present-day Thakhek) and Kham Keut (near Lak Xao), before proceeding to the Plain of Jars where, with the aid of an exiled Phuan prince, he captured Muang Phuan, the capital of the principality of Xiang Khouang.

Descending the Nam Ou River, Fa Ngum finally reached Xiang Dong Xiang Thong, where he ascended the throne in 1353 and began the reign that is popularly considered the cornerstone in Laos's development. Fa Ngum called his new kingdom **Lane Xang Hom Khao**, the Kingdom of a Million Elephants and the White Parasol, a name signifying military might and royal prestige. In the ensuing two decades of his reign, Fa Ngum expanded Lane Xang south through the Vientiane Plain into northeastern Thailand, northeast to the Black Tai area west of the Black River and north into Sipsong Pan Na (present-day Xishuangbanna in China).

Lane Xang was a decentralized state. Its three principal hubs, Xiang Khouang, Sikhotabong and Vientiane, were virtually autonomous. Their main contribution to Xiang Dong Xiang Thong was a share of their revenue and manpower – the greatest asset in a sparsely populated land – in deference to the greater reserves of men and prestige of that city's ruling line. These three *muang* in turn claimed a share of the income and manpower of smaller towns surrounding them. Given the ever-shifting balance of power in the region over the course of the next few centuries and because these and other smaller *muang* remained virtually autonomous, Lane Xang's frontiers were fluid, with *muang* often shifting allegiances or even paying tribute to two empires at once.

With Fa Ngum and his Khmer queen, Kaew Keng Nya, came Cambodian monks and artisans, a new civil administrative system and a code of laws. Although Fa Ngum and his Khmer retinue are also credited with introducing Buddhism to Lane Xang, it seems more likely that the religion was already a presence in the area, as suggested by the discovery of Buddhist statuary dating from the eleventh and twelfth centuries. But it is fairly certain that Buddhism flourished during the reign of Fa Ngum and probably grew further with the arrival of his second queen, Kaew Lot Fa, from the Siamese Kingdom of **Ayuthaya**, another neighbouring state with a strong Buddhist tradition and elaborate court rituals.

Though Fa Ngum was a strong leader, there was a fair amount of internal strife, and after twenty years on the throne, Fa Ngum was ousted by his ministers. He was succeeded by his only son, **Oun Heuan**, who ascended to the throne in 1373 and ruled for 43 years, ushering in an era of peace during which the city flourished. This period of stability was due in part to his marriage into the ruling houses of both Ayuthaya and Lan Na, his more powerful neighbours to the south and west. Oun Heuan is remembered as Samsenthai or king of Three Hundred Thousand Tai, a name signifying the number of Lao men available to Lane Xang for labour and military service. After Oun Heuan's death, a period of bitter political infighting began – with eight kings in 22 years – which left the kingdom severely weakened.

The leading ministers of the town restored stability to Lane Xang by offering the throne to the ruler of Vientiane, Vangburi (1438–79), the only surviving son of Oun Heuan. Whereas Fa Ngum had merely tipped his hat to Theravada Buddhism, Vangburi was a devout Buddhist, taking the name **Sainyachakkaphat Phaen Phaew** (a name derived from the Pali term for "Universal Buddhist Monarch") upon his coronation and promptly appointing new abbots in key monasteries. Theravada Buddhism, slower to take hold east of the Mekong at first, now served to legitimize the rule of the kings of Lane Xang. In return for the king's patronage the monks taught that the king ruled because he possessed superior moral merit.

Sainyachakkaphat took pains to heal the rifts wrought by two decades of struggle over the throne and tried to return Lane Xang to its former glory. However, his rule was not to last. **Vietnam**, angered by Lane Xang's betrayal of the Vietnamese struggle against the occupying forces of China's Ming Dynasty and further provoked by a Phuan revolt against Vietnamese control over Muang Phuan, invaded Lane Xang in 1479. Lao chronicles record the causes behind the attack somewhat differently, however, noting that Emperor Le Thanh Tong had been offended, not by the massacre of his mandarins and soldiers, but by the fact that the Lao's response to his request for hair from a recently captured white elephant, an animal revered by the Lao, was to send him a box full of dung. Whatever the cause, five columns of Vietnamese troops swept through Xiang Dong Xiang Thong a year after the revolt in Muang Phuan, and Sainyachakkaphat, humiliated, abdicated and fled. The Lao king's younger brother, Souvanna Banlang, regrouped the Lao troops and eventually chased off the Vietnamese troops, whose final retort was the sacking of Muang Phuan on their way home.

Yet Xiang Dong Xiang Thong's destruction proved to be a catalyst for Lane Xang's first golden age, a century when the civil administration was fine tuned, striking temples were built and epic poems composed.

The kingdom of the Pha Bang

Souvanna Banlang's three successors – La Saen Thai (1486–96), Somphou (1496–1500) and Visoun (1500–20) – ruled over a peaceful and prosperous Lane Xang, their reigns marked by strengthened ties and an upswing in trade with Ayuthaya. The wealth generated by trade went into the adornment of Xiang Dong Xiang Thong. These rulers also reorganized the government, appointing ministers to oversee specific departments, establishing an extensive hierarchy among government officials and dividing the capital into districts and sub-districts, all of which served to make the kingdom more stable than it had ever been before.

Buddhism flourished, under **Visoun** in particular, as monks took up residence in the city and the monasteries became centres of literary culture, where sacred Pali texts were studied. It was during also his reign that the Lao Buddhist world view came together. Visoun ordered the composition of the *Nithan Khoun Borom,* which brought together legends concerning the origin of the Lao, Khoun Borom and the founding of Xiang Dong Xiang Thong – complete with grand stories of Fa Ngum's deeds – and placed these tales within the framework of Theravada Buddhism. Arguably, Visoun's most important act was bringing the **Pha Bang** to Xiang Dong Xiang Thong from Vientiane in 1512, a defining event in the development of Lao identity. The golden Buddha image, installed at Wat Visoun, became the palladium of the ruling dynasty and the symbol of unity and power of the kingdom itself.

Whereas Visoun and his immediate predecessors had ruled over a peaceful state concerned primarily with domestic affairs, Visoun's son Phothisalat and grandson Setthathilat had major ambitions for Lane Xang, which they saw as being the equal of Ayuthaya. **Phothisalat** (1520–47) was a man driven by profound piety. He gave generously to the monastic order and left his mark on the spiritual life of Xiang Dong Xiang Thong when, in 1527, he broke with local traditions and banned the practice of animism, ordering the destruction of associated religious buildings. In pursuit of his expansionist aspirations, Phothisalat established a wide network of regional relations, which included taking a Lan Na princess as his queen. He chose to reside at Vientiane, which had the advantage of being closer to the trade routes linking Lane Xang with Vietnam, Ayuthaya and Cambodia. Vientiane was also closer to the population centre of the expanding Lao world: with the downfall of Angkor in the previous century, the Lao had begun to shift into the middle Mekong Valley and onto the Khorat Plateau where the land was flatter and more fertile.

Phothisalat's aggressiveness contributed to the souring of relations with Ayuthaya. Tensions between the neighbours flared up over the now weakened state of Lan Na; Lane Xang prevailed, and Phothisalat's son **Setthathilat** (1548–71) assumed the throne at Chiang Mai in 1546. He quickly hurried home, however, after the death of his father, who was crushed beneath his elephant during a display of his riding skills. In his hasty departure, Setthathilat nonetheless managed to pilfer Lan Na's talismanic Emerald Buddha, the sacred **Pha Kaew** that today is the palladium of the ruling line in Bangkok.

The Burmese invasions

Setthathilat was only 14 when, in 1548, he assumed the throne of Lane Xang. But the young king's hold over Lan Na gradually slipped away, as internal disputes in Chiang Mai and the rise of a powerful Burmese kingdom in the west dashed hopes of a greater Lao state, one that would unify Lane Xang and Lan Na. Wary of the growing **Burmese threat**, Setthathilat reacted defensively. In 1563, he officially moved his capital to Vientiane and quickly set about building brick ramparts around the city. In deference to Xiang Dong Xiang Thong, the Pha Bang was left behind and the city was renamed after the revered image, while the Emerald Buddha was placed in the newly constructed Haw Pha Kaew in Vientiane.

Lane Xang managed to forge an alliance with Ayuthaya, but the Tai states proved no match for the armies of the Burmese warrior-kings who reduced Lan Na, Ayuthaya and Lane Xang to vassalage in a matter of a decade, and sacked Vientiane in 1565. The invaders were eventually repelled by a guerrilla campaign led by the king. After reclaiming Vientiane, Setthathilat renovated That Phanom in Sikhotabong and built That Louang in the capital, in an effort to lift the morale of his vassals in the central Mekong; they had misgivings about being ruled by a royal line whose roots were in Louang Phabang, especially one that was taxing their resources by waging a costly war.

By the end of 1569, Lane Xang was the only Tai power remaining. Burma once again set its sights on Vientiane, which fell for the second time, and once again Setthathilat regained his capital – but this time the heavy demands on the *muang* of the central Mekong brought resentment to boiling point. Setthathilat was lured into a campaign against the mountain peoples of the south by the powerful ruler of Sikhotabong, and was never seen again. The king's downfall revealed a major weakness in Lane Xang: the monarchy still depended on the loyalty of its vassals, but the latter no longer felt any strong allegiance to the king or to Lane Xang. With the death of Setthathilat, Lane Xang plunged into turmoil as the Burmese retook Vientiane and extended their rule to the Vietnamese frontier. By the early 1580s the kingdom was in such disarray that no king sat on the throne for nearly a decade. It would take half a century for Lane Xang to recover.

Sourinyavongsa and the Golden Age

The decisive character who returned stability to Lane Xang and eventually ushered in its **Golden Age** was Sourinyavongsa (1637–94). Although rarely seen in public, he was a popular king, known for his firm administration of justice, and ruled over a peaceful and prosperous kingdom. The **first Europeans** to reach Lane Xang, a mission from the Dutch East India Company led by Gerritt van Wuysthoff and a party of Jesuits, arrived during Sourinyavongsa's reign to find a flourishing Buddhist kingdom whose wealth was poured into the construction of religious monuments and the monastic order. Monks – more numerous than the soldiers of Germany, as one visitor observed – came from as far as Cambodia and Burma to Vientiane, which had emerged as a regional centre of Buddhist studies.

Sourinyavongsa ensured his reign was peaceful by aligning Lane Xang with neighbouring powers through marriage, although he did not hesitate to resort to force when necessary – after all it was a violent struggle among relatives that won him the throne in the first place. When the ruler of Xiang Khouang refused to offer his daughter in marriage to Sourinyavongsa, Lane Xang invaded Xiang Khouang, seizing the woman in question and taking several thousand captives, who were resettled near the capital. Thereafter Xiang Khouang paid regular tribute to Vientiane and was forced to break off its relationship with Vietnam. Sourinyavongsa took the daughter of the Vietnamese emperor as a concubine and established the boundaries between the two states in a treaty with Vietnam which identified all people living in houses on piles as Lao subjects and all living in homes that rested on the ground as Vietnamese. The frontier with Ayuthaya remained unchanged, with both countries respecting the watershed line between the Mekong and the Chao Phraya rivers, a border established by Setthathilat. Lane Xang was left holding sway over the northern and eastern portions of the Khorat Plateau.

Closer to home, Sourinyavongsa avoided the bitter rivalries that contributed to the downfall of Setthathilat, by striking a balance between the regional interests of the kingdom. He appeased the powerful families of the central Mekong by dividing the powers of state among three chief ministers – the minister of the palace conducted foreign relations and ran the royal secretariat; a second commanded the army and oversaw Vientiane; and a third, the viceroy, the powerful ruler of Sikhotabong, ruled the south.

While the new balance of power provided the stability Lane Xang needed to flourish, no provisions were made to maintain that stability after the king's death. In the end, the kingdom paid the price for Sourinyavongsa's stern brand of justice: the king had executed his only son for adultery, leaving no obvious heir to the throne when he died in 1694. Once again royal succession turned into a political crisis; this time around, however, the country's three regions went their separate ways.

The division of Lane Xang

Vientiane was taken over by a Lane Xang prince who returned from exile in Vietnam to establish a new kingdom there, although Vietnam exacted a heavy price in silver bars, elephants and rhinoceros horns for their assistance in the endeavour. Very soon, however, **Setthathilat II** (1698–1735), as this king chose to call himself, had trouble on his northern flank. Sourinyavongsa's grandsons – Kingkitsalat and Inthasom – had fled Vientiane to Chiang Hung (present-day Jinghong in Yunnan) some years before and sought assistance from their mother's relatives in Sipsong Pa Na. With the aid of a cousin, the princes raised an army, captured Louang Phabang in 1706 and soon after marched on Vientiane. Setthathilat appealed for help from Ayuthaya. The king of Ayuthaya negotiated a division of the territory at the bend in the Mekong, south of Paklai, making Kingkitsalat the first ruler of an independent Louang Phabang kingdom, and leaving Setthathilat II to rule over Vientiane.

Meanwhile, in the south, a new ruling house had emerged at **Champasak**. Little is known of the origins of this *muang*, although legends trace its roots to a holy man who, ruling the kingdom as a regent for an unmarried queen, sought out a young prince to take the throne. The prince, sometimes said to be a long lost son of Sourinyavongsa, assumed the throne as King Soi Sisamouth in 1713. Thus the new ruling lines of each of the three major principalities, Louang Phabang, Vientiane and Champasak, could claim, however tenuously, some link to Fa Ngum and, by extension, to Khoun Borom. Family ties notwithstanding, it didn't take long for these isolated principalities of inland Southeast Asia to be at each other's throats, making these weak states easy prey for their larger neighbours. The rivalry between Louang Phabang and Vientiane was particularly bitter, deteriorating further when a second wave of Burmese invasions swept across the Tai world in the 1760s and forces from Vientiane aligned with the invaders and helped sack Louang Phabang.

Ayuthaya, which had flourished since the last wave of Burmese invasions, was next. The Burmese breached the walls of Ayuthaya and took the city in 1767, razing everything to the ground and hauling off tens of thousands of prisoners. The city was abandoned, but with remarkable speed the Siamese built a new kingdom, one that was to succeed at the expense of the Lao states.

The rise of Siam

Under the charismatic leadership of King Taksin, a military genius, the **Siamese** quickly rebuilt their kingdom downriver from Ayuthaya near Bangkok, and within a decade had retaken its territory, conquered Lan Na, and were prepared to expand to the east to secure its perimeter. Taking advantage of a peaceful Burma and a distracted Vietnam, twenty thousand Siamese soldiers set out towards Vientiane in 1778.

A second army of ten thousand swept east through Cambodia and, after conquering first Champasak and then Sikhotabong, turned north and marched on Vientiane. Here, the two Siamese forces met before the ramparts of Vientiane and were joined by a battalion from Louang Phabang bent on revenge. The city fell, and hundreds of prisoners, including the royal family, were dragged back to Siam and forcibly resettled on the plains north of the Siamese capital. The two Buddha image palladia of Lane Xang, the Pha Bang – which had been relocated to Vientiane by Setthathilat II in 1705 – and the Pha Kaew, were hauled off as well and enshrined in Thonburi (that part of Bangkok west of the Chao Phraya River). By reducing Champasak and Vientiane to vassal states and bringing Louang Phabang into an unequal alliance, Siam had extended its empire to the Annamite Mountains and forced the Lao world to adjust to a predominantly Bangkok-centred existence for the next century.

Anou's rebellion

The captured Lao princes returned to Vientiane as vassal kings, beginning with Nanthasen (1782–92). He brought with him the Pha Bang, which the Siamese king had decided was bad luck for his kingdom. Nanthasen didn't waste time in rekindling the old conflict with Louang Phabang, which his forces conquered in 1792. But Siam was wary of allowing any of the Lao vassal states to improve their position at the expense of another, and so recalled Nanthasen. He was replaced by Inthavong (1792–1804), the elder brother of the accomplished general Anou, who served as viceroy and led Lao armies to fight in the name of Siam in battles with Burma. By the time of Inthavong's death at the turn of the century, Vientiane had begun to pay tribute to Vietnam and, when **Anou** (1804–28) was chosen to ascend to the throne, he immediately notified the Vietnamese.

Siam became increasingly alarmed by Vietnam's growing influence, and, worried that Vietnam had its eye on Champasak, decided to run the risk of turning Anou into a powerful, and potentially dangerous, vassal by appointing Yo (1819–27), Anou's son, to the Champasak throne. Anou, who envisioned restoring Lane Xang to its former glory, made good on Bangkok's fears. On the pretence of coming to Siam's aid in the event of an attack by the British, who had by this time established a presence in Burma, Anou's and Yo's troops advanced across the Khorat Plateau early in 1827, and by late February had come within a few days' march of Bangkok. However, Anou misjudged the strength of the Siamese, who struck back fiercely, capturing Yo and sacking Vientiane. Anou fled to Vietnam. When he returned to Vientiane with a small force several months later, fighting broke out which resulted in Anou's capture. Siamese forces destroyed every building in the capital, save for Wat Sisaket, and dragged the entire population back to Thailand, where they were resettled. Vientiane was abandoned to the jungle; it was still in ruins when French explorers arrived four decades later. The Lao king was placed in an iron cage and exposed to the sweltering heat of Bangkok, where he died, an example to Siam's vassals of the price of rebellion. Anou was the last Lao ruler to attempt to liberate the former territories of Lane Xang.

Although the primary source of tension between Siam and Vietnam lay in Cambodia, both jockeyed for control over the fragmented Lao *muang* during the decades that followed Anou's defeat. Siam undertook a massive programme of resettlement of the Lao to the thinly populated Khorat Plateau, whose cities and villages remain predominantly Lao today. By force and diplomacy, Siam depopulated the area east of the Mekong, particularly in south central Laos, leaving a wasteland of burned villages and rice fields. Only Louang Phabang managed to stay intact. Vietnam countered by formally incorporating Lane Xang's eastern territory back into the organization of its state.

Xiang Khouang represented the greatest source of conflict in the struggle. Situated on the Plain of Jars, the Phuan principality occupied an area that was effectively a back door for a military invasion of Vietnam. In the aftermath of Anou's defeat, the Vietnamese emperor executed Noi, the Phuan ruler, allegedly for his treachery against Anou, and the area was made a province known to the Vietnamese as Tran Ninh. Siam, with the assistance of Louang Phabang, quickly moved to retake the principality and, when it did, much of the Phuan population was forcibly resettled to the south.

By the middle of the nineteenth century, the Lao territories had become a buffer zone between the two powers. Siam was dominant in the Mekong valley; the Vietnamese held sway in the east; joint control was exercised over what was left of Muang Phuan. This balancing act was soon upset, however, by **marauding Chinese**, remnants of Chinese rebellions, who swept through the northern Lao territories on horseback in the 1870s and 1880s. Siam, its position in Laos endangered by the incursions, launched a series of military expeditions. The last of these campaigns backfired when the Siamese commander angered a White Tai chief, leading to the sacking of Louang Phabang and eventually to Siam's loss of Laos to the French.

French conquest

As the nineteenth century wore on, French governments became increasingly imperialistic. In the Far East, with Britain threatening to dominate trade with China, France saw Vietnam, and by extension Laos, as a potential route into the resource-rich Yunnan region of China. France acquired her Indochina colonies in a rather haphazard fashion, often through the exploits of individual adventurers or the unilateral action of French officials. By the time the Mekong Exploration Commission of 1867–68 set off from Saigon for Laos and Yunnan, **Cochinchina** (present-day southern Vietnam) was already a French possession. Interest in Laos, however, quickly waned after the explorers, led by Doudart de Lagrée and the charismatic Francis Garnier, found that significant stretches of the river were unnavigable.

Interest in Laos was rekindled by French explorer **Auguste Pavie**, who conducted a "conquest of hearts" in the name of France in the 1880s and 1890s while trekking across Laos in search of political alliances and trade routes. As vice-consul in Louang Phabang, Pavie was the chief advocate of France's extension of the Indochina empire to the banks of the Mekong. He won an important ally for France by rescuing the northern kingdom's ageing king Oun Kham almost singlehandedly when the city, left virtually undefended by the Siamese, was torched in 1887 by a White Tai leader from Sipsong Chao Tai, out for revenge against Siam. Pavie's effort led the king to state: "[Louang Phabang] is not a conquest of Siam. Louang Phabang, wanting protection against all attacks, voluntarily offered its tribute. Now through Siam's interference, our ruin is complete… we will offer tribute to France…"

The relentless efforts of Pavie, coupled with gunboat diplomacy in Bangkok, eventually forced Siam to relinquish its claim to all territory east of the Mekong in 1893, although not before nearly sparking a war between Siam, Britain and France. Britain and France eventually settled on the Mekong River as the boundary between British Burma and French Laos and agreed to guarantee Siamese independence in the Chao Phraya River Valley in order to ensure a buffer zone between the two Western powers.

French rule

For half a century, Laos was ruled as a **French colony**, but for all Pavie's determination, it was regarded as the least important of the five components of French Indochina, the other four being Annam (central Vietnam), Tonkin (the north), Cochinchina (the south) and Cambodia. The boundaries with Burma, China, and Vietnam that were adopted by France – essentially the limits of the Mekong watershed – were carved with indifference to the complex existing political structures and ethnic groupings. In short, the borders meant nothing to the peoples of Laos. In the south, the kingdom of Champasak was split in two (a situation remedied by subsequent Franco–Siamese treaties, which added land west of the Mekong in the south and in Xainyabouli, and roughly established the border Laos shares with Thailand today). In the north, two Tai Leu *muang* were severed from Sipsong Pa Na, an act which served to foster political instability in that region. After initially dividing the Lao territories into three regions which were administered from Vietnam, the French eventually settled on **Vientiane** as their administrative capital and split the country up into eleven provinces, with the kingdom of Louang Phabang as a nominal protectorate.

After France realized that the Mekong was a poor transport route and that explorers' claims of an Eldorado were but a pipe dream, Laos became the neglected backwater of its Southeast Asian acquisitions. Accordingly, the French presence in Laos was minimal. Whereas forty thousand French competed for civil service jobs in Saigon and the Mekong Delta, only a hundred such jobs were available in Laos. The French found the Lao work ethic suspect and regarded the hill peoples with disdain, and so brought in Vietnamese to fill most of the upper and middle ranks of the civil service (Lao occupied positions such as junior clerks and translators) and the bulk of the spots in the Garde Indigène, the paramilitary police force.

The French made do with limited administrative manpower by simply floating their administration on top of existing feudal court structures. The royal houses of Xiang Khouang, Champasak and Louang Phabang – Vientiane's ruling line had been eliminated after Anou's defeat – were preserved, although France reduced the status of the rulers of Xiang Khouang and Champasak to that of governors and reserved the right to approve the successors to all three houses. Outside the cities, the French established an administrative system that pitted various ethnic groups against one another, effectively cutting costs at the same time as they deflected resentment away from themselves.

In order to cover the cost of administration, France imposed heavy **taxes** on opium, alcohol and salt, levied a head tax on males between 18 and 60, and required all adult males to perform unpaid *corvée* labour. Often required to walk days to work sites far from their villages, while supplying their own food, villagers sometimes responded by simply clearing out of an area altogether, returning once the project was completed. Such measures provoked several **revolts**, some led by messianic religious figures, in the late nineteenth and early twentieth centuries, with the first large uprising beginning on the Bolaven Plateau in 1901 (see box, p.301). It seems these disturbances were more in response to central government intrusion into rural life and the disruption of old orders than they were specifically anti-French. However, the fact that such uprisings occurred largely among upland peoples, upon whom the French made harsher demands and for whose customs they showed less respect, suggests that the methods employed by the colonial administration didn't lie too far away from the cause. Later, these revolts were construed as forerunners of the nationalist Lao Issara and Pathet Lao movements.

While explorers' reports that Laos was teeming with **natural resources** proved overly optimistic, the French did manage to exploit, among other things, tin deposits near Thakhek and teak trees, which were cut and floated down the Mekong, and introduced coffee. France's chief agricultural exports were cardamom from the Bolaven Plateau area and, from the highlands of Xiang Khouang, **opium**, a product that was later allegedly used by the CIA and the Pathet Lao to finance their respective war efforts. For its part, the French Indochina Government established a monopoly over opium, which accounted for one-seventh of its total budgetary receipts and brought the Hmong of Xiang Khouang into the money economy faster than most other groups in Laos.

Trade was in the hands of Chinese merchants, as it had been for centuries. Goods followed traditional routes from Laos and the west bank of the Mekong across the Khorat Plateau towards Bangkok and away from French Vietnam. The same Chinese merchants who exported cardamom, sticklac and benzoin, skins and ivory to the trading houses of the Siamese capital were already importing cheap British and German products by the time the French established themselves in Laos.

With trade flowing towards Bangkok, minimal exports and a depleted population providing an insufficient tax base, the colony remained dependent on **federal subsidies**. The French hoped to remedy these problems by building roads and, eventually, a railway from the Vietnamese coast – a project derailed first by the Great Depression and then by World War II – and by encouraging mass Vietnamese migration, in order to tackle the age-old problem of too much land and too few people. Although relatively few Vietnamese wound up settling west of the Annamites, Vientiane and southern Mekong towns such as Thakhek and Savannakhet had substantial Vietnamese populations. Had it not been for World War II, the French may well have succeeded in making the Lao a minority in their own land, in which case Laos might not exist today.

For all its talk of the "civilizing mission" of their particular brand of imperialism, France appeared to have no mission in Laos, other than to deny territory to the British. Elsewhere in Indochina, the French built schools, universities, a railway network and an extensive highway system. Although the French did construct a skeletal highway system linking Laos with Vietnam and rebuilt monuments destroyed by the Siamese in the early 1800s, few improvements were made to Laos's educational or health-care systems.

World War II

The fall of France to Germany in 1940 changed everything for Laos. The initial fallout from events in Europe was the **Japanese occupation** of Laos. Vichy France was left responsible for the administration of Indochina and gave the Japanese the right to move and station troops throughout the region. Sensing an opportunity to avenge its defeat of 1893, Siam, renamed **Thailand** in 1939, seized the west-bank territories of Xainyabouli and Champasak, leaving the Lao angry with both the Thai for encroaching on their territory and the French for failing to defend the country.

To counter the appeal of Thai nationalist propaganda, the French encouraged a weak **nationalism** among the Lao elite. This movement was spearheaded by Charles Rochet, a colonial official whose affection for the people of Laos had left him embittered at France's neglect of the colony. Rochet met with movement leaders weekly, devising ways to generate Lao pride through a renaissance of literature, theatre, music and dance, patriotic rallies and the creation of a national development programme. Schools were built, the health-care system improved and the first Lao newspaper was published. And, in a sign that Lao nationalism was coming of age, a suggestion to romanize the Lao language was stymied by the viceroy of the royal house of Louang Phabang, Prince Phetsarath. Rochet's efforts met with the criticism of colonial officials who felt that he was arousing dangerous sentiments. They were to be proved right, although it would be left to the Japanese to shatter the illusion of French power and provide the spark for Lao independence.

In March 1945, the Japanese staged a pre-emptive strike to neutralize French forces in Indochina, imprisoning French soldiers and civil servants. In a major blow to French prestige, Japan proclaimed an end to France's colonial regimes. Japanese forces reached Louang Phabang by the following month and forced Sisavang Vong, the pro-French king, to declare independence, forcing his hand by hauling off the crown prince to Saigon. Somewhat less reluctantly, **Phetsarath**, who could trace his family line back to Anou, the last king of Vientiane, became prime minister. The eldest of three remarkable brothers who would have a profound impact on Lao history, Phetsarath was now the second most powerful political figure after King Sisavang Vong.

Free Laos

Nationalists across Indochina moved to take advantage of the power vacuum created by the end of World War II and **Japan's surrender**. In Laos, an independent-minded Lao elite formed a government which became known as the Lao Issara, literally "**Free Laos**", while next door the Viet Minh seized power and Ho Chi Minh proclaimed the establishment of the Democratic Republic of Vietnam.

The rapid awakening of the Lao elite after years of French rule left them factionalized, with support split between opposition to the Japanese and opposition to the French. A power struggle ensued as King Sisavang Vong welcomed the return of the French and Phetsarath reaffirmed the independence of Laos and declared the union of the Kingdom of Louang Phabang and the territory of Champasak in a single, independent Kingdom of Laos.

The king repudiated Phetsarath by dismissing him as prime minister and viceroy on October 10.

In response, the newly constituted **Lao Issara government** deposed the king two days later. This new government, which based itself in Vientiane, contained some of the key figures who would dominate politics in Laos over the course of the next few decades, including Phetsarath's younger brothers Souvannaphouma and Souphanouvong, both educated in Paris. Before joining the new government in Vientiane as Minister of Foreign Affairs and Chief of the Liberation Army, **Souphanouvong** was flown to Hanoi by an American general to meet Ho Chi Minh. After winning the North Vietnamese leader's support he returned to Laos on foot with a contingent of Viet Minh soldiers – the first instance of Vietnamese armed support for a Lao nationalist movement. As the group crossed the Annamite Mountains, Souphanouvong took a solemn oath to continue the struggle until an independent Laos had been won.

The **Potsdam Agreement** marking the end of World War II failed to recognize the Lao Issara government. Under the terms of the agreement, the Japanese surrender was accepted by the Chinese Nationalists north of the Sixteenth Parallel and by the British to the south, where French reoccupation forces were gathering steam, their return facilitated by the British. In March 1946 French forces, along with their Lao allies, made their way slowly up the Mekong Valley. Lao Issara volunteers, led by Souphanouvong and assisted by the Viet Minh, resisted the French near Thakhek, but the French successfully reoccupied Vientiane in April 1946 and Louang Phabang three weeks later. Thousands of Lao Issara supporters and Vietnamese fled to Thailand, where Prince Phetsarath established a government-in-exile in Bangkok. Although the Western community readily donated blood to help heal Prince Souphanouvong from the wounds he suffered at Thakhek, the United States and Britain did not respond to Lao Issara appeals for support, even as Souphanouvong repeated US President Franklin Roosevelt's statement that the French should not be allowed to return to Indochina.

The Kingdom of Laos

In 1947, the newly constituted **Kingdom of Laos** began to take shape. Prince Boun Oum of Champasak, who had helped the French in the south, renounced his claim to a separate southern kingdom, strengthening the French position in Vientiane and paving the way for Laos to be unified under the royal house of Louang Phabang. The territories west of the Mekong were restored, elections for a Constituent Assembly were held and a new constitution proclaimed. The members of the new government, which was a decidedly pro-French body, were drawn from the elite that had benefited from the French presence all along. The government lacked cohesion, however, with loyalties to leading families and regional factions counting for more than national unity. Furthermore, the king opted to remain in Louang Phabang rather than move to Vientiane.

The French by now were increasingly bogged down in their struggle with the **Viet Minh** which had erupted in December 1946 and would become known as the First Indochina War. What had begun as a police action had rapidly become a costly "war without borders" that was to last eight years and cost the lives of 93,000 on the French side and an estimated 200,000 Viet Minh supporters. The Viet Minh did not confine their efforts to Vietnam, with the Vietnamese nationalists coordinating and participating in Lao Issara guerrilla raids, led by Souphanouvong, on French convoys and garrisons. The Viet Minh's influence over Souphanouvong took its toll on the unity of the Lao Issara. By May 1949 the rift had become irreparable and Souphanouvong was removed from his post. In July, France appealed to the more moderate elements of the Lao Issara by conceding greater authority to the Vientiane government. The Lao Issara announced its dissolution. As Souvannaphouma, along with two dozen moderate Lao Issara leaders, returned to Vientiane on board a French transport plane, Souphanouvong set out from Bangkok on foot for Viet Minh headquarters. Meanwhile, the leader of the movement, Phetsarath, remained behind, refusing to return to Laos until 1957, when his title of viceroy was finally restored by the king.

The Pathet Lao

When Souphanouvong arrived at Viet Minh headquarters in Tonkin in late 1949, he was warmly welcomed by Ho Chi Minh, who had ambitious plans for him. Souphanouvong, who sought only arms and money, also received some advice from Vo Nguyen Giap, the legendary Vietnamese general who in a matter of a few years would defeat the French at Dien Bien Phu. In the course of the meeting, Giap told the Lao prince to keep away from towns, saying "Remember, those who rule the countryside rule the country."

While the moderate members of the dissolved Lao Issara joined the new **Royal Lao Government** (RLG) in 1950, Souphanouvong founded his own government, which saw itself as the successor to the Lao Issara. In August 1950, in a far corner of northern Laos, Souphanouvong presided over the **First Resistance Congress**, which was supervised by the Viet Minh. The Congress adopted a twelve-point manifesto, at the bottom of which appeared the notation "**Pathet Lao**", literally "the Land of the Lao". This became the name by which his resistance group was to be known. The manifesto called for a truly independent and unified Laos to be governed by a coalition government with the RLG, and the Pathet Lao pledged cooperation with the Vietnamese and Khmer in the common struggle against the French.

In the years immediately following the congress, the Pathet Lao focused on recruiting members in northern and eastern Laos. Pathet Lao cadres moved into remote villages, promoting literacy, building schools and organizing village militias. Like the Viet Minh before them, the Pathet Lao expanded their influence village by village. Kaysone Phomvihane directed the Committee for the Organization of the Party, which recruited new cadres, until the **Lao People's Party** was formally established in 1955.

Given that the RLG already controlled the major population centres, and that the Pathet Lao alliance with the Viet Minh carried with it, in the minds of some ethnic Lao, the threat of Vietnamese domination, the Pathet Lao had more success appealing to highland minorities than to the lowland Lao. Minority cadres were offered a chance to play a part in the national struggle, as displayed by the inclusion of two tribal resistance leaders, Faydang Lobliayao, a Hmong from the important Lo clan of Nong Het, and Sithone Kommadam, the son of the great Laven leader of the Bolaven Revolt.

The First Indochina War

By the early 1950s, the **First Indochina War** had engulfed the region. Chinese military aid flowed to the Viet Minh, while the United States, smarting from the fall of China to the communists, supported France. After the routing of the nationalists in China and the outbreak of the Korean War, the French could portray, with greater success, their struggle against the Viet Minh not as a colonial war but as a fight in defence of the "Free World".

For the Viet Minh, Laos was an extension of their battle against the French. Twice in 1953 they staged major invasions of Laos. In their first attack, the Viet Minh nearly reached Louang Phabang, causing panic to sweep through Vientiane and people to flee across the Mekong. In Louang Phabang all was calm, however, as a blind monk had prophesied that the invaders would not take the city and battle preparations had given way to celebrations long before the Viet Minh ran out of supplies, leaving the French baffled. The Viet Minh seized large areas of the country during the offensives and turned them over to the Pathet Lao.

By this point, Souphanouvong had formally established the headquarters of the resistance government in **Xam Nua**, which lay at the heart of an extensive "liberated zone"; meanwhile in Paris, Souvannaphouma was pressing the French for complete independence. By the time full independence was granted in October 1953, however, Laos was a divided country, with large areas controlled by the Pathet Lao and the rest of the country under the RLG.

Taunted by the Viet Minh invasions of Laos, which France was obliged by treaty to defend, General Henri Navarre, the French Commander-in-Chief in Indochina, ordered the French Expeditionary Force's parachute battalion to establish a massive base in **Dien Bien Phu** in November 1953. Navarre reasoned that by creating a camp in this isolated valley along the traditional invasion route of Laos, he could force the Viet Minh into an open battle – while at the same time protecting Laos – and end the war in eighteen months. The war did end, but not quite as he expected. The Viet Minh encircled the valley and began a bloody assault that lasted 59 days and cost the lives of twenty thousand Viet Minh soldiers. The French were forced to surrender on May 7, 1954. Their efforts to restore the pre-World War II status quo in Indochina had collapsed.

The Geneva Conference

On May 8, the nine delegations attending the **Geneva Conference** called to discuss the situation in Korea shifted their focus to Indochina. The government in Vientiane was represented by Phoui Sananikone, the scion of Vientiane's leading family and a leader of the anti-Japanese resistance in northern Laos during World War II. The Viet Minh arrived with a young Lao by the name of Nouhak Phoumsavanh, who proposed that the Pathet Lao resistance government of which he was a member be represented as well. Phoui defended the sovereignty of the Vientiane government and the proposal was rejected. The conference's final declaration included Phoui's proclamation that the RLG would not pursue a policy of aggression nor would it allow a foreign power to use its soil for hostile purposes. The **Agreement on the Cessation of Hostilities** was signed on July 20 – by the Viet Minh and France – which in addition to a ceasefire also called for a regrouping of opposing forces, leading to elections in two years.

Although Laos was reaffirmed as a unitary, independent state with a single government, the Pathet Lao did manage to win de facto recognition as an insurgency group and were allotted the provinces of Phongsali and Houa Phan in which to regroup. Meanwhile, Vietnam was divided at the Seventeenth Parallel and the stage was set for a widening of the conflict into an ideological battle between the superpowers.

America intervenes

The **United States** had since 1950 been funding an estimated seventy percent of the French war effort in Indochina. In 1951, the US signed an economic aid agreement with the government of Phoui Sananikone which aimed to speed up the development of a free and independent Laos. After the 1954 Geneva Accords, which the US did not sign, considering them a sell-out to international communism, strengthening the anti-communist governments of Indochina became a priority for President Dwight Eisenhower's administration. The withdrawal of the French military left a power vacuum on the edge of a historically expansionist state, a worrisome state of affairs in the eyes of the United States.

As of 1955, the US was financing most of the Lao government budget and completely bankrolling the Royal Lao Army, countering the Viet Minh, which was shouldering the entire cost of the Pathet Lao's army. Feeling that the French were not taking their responsibility of training the Lao army seriously enough, the US skirted the terms of the Geneva agreement by training select officers in Thailand and by equipping and expanding the police force. Other funds went into churning out propaganda, building roads and communications networks, and propping up the kip. The Americans bought truckloads of the local currency above the black market rate, burned the notes and gave the government US dollars in exchange. Merchants exploited the programme by trading in bags of kip for dollars. They then bought luxury goods which they subsequently sold to Thailand for a profit.

For the next eight years, the US spent more on foreign aid to Laos per capita than it did on any other Southeast Asian country, though the overwhelming majority of the aid was military. As US dollars poured into the country, the army grew increasingly powerful and existing rivalries between leading families were reinforced, with the clans more concerned with improving their social standing than exercising responsible power. Fretting over recent communist takeovers around the world, US policies were motivated by the fear of the so-called **Domino Effect**. As President Eisenhower prepared to turn over the helm to John F. Kennedy, he told his successor: "If Laos is lost to the free world, in the long run we will lose all of Southeast Asia."

The quest for unity and neutrality

After Geneva, the priority of the RLG was to regain control of the two Pathet Lao provinces so that elections could be held in accordance with the peace settlement. But when elections finally went ahead in December 1955, it was without the Pathet Lao, disgruntled at being refused its demands for changes to the electoral law and freedom for its front organization, the Lao Patriotic Front (behind which stood the Lao People's Party), to operate as a political party. The elections resulted in the formation of a government led by **Prince Souvanna-phouma**, who entered into negotiations with his half-brother Souphanouvong in the belief that national unity and neutrality were the key to the preservation of the state. The two sides cut a deal in November 1957 to include two Pathet Lao members in a coalition government in exchange for the reintegration of Houa Phan and Phongsali into the rest of Laos.

Left alone, it seemed, the people of Laos could work out their problems on their own, or so Souvannaphouma thought. However, when elections the following May gave leftist candidates 21 seats in the National Assembly, the US embassy and the CIA actively promoted the creation of the right-wing Committee for the Defence of National Interests, known as the CDNI, and withheld aid from Souvannaphouma's government, forcing its collapse in July. Power in Vientiane had shifted from the National Assembly to the American Embassy.

With the collapse of the government, any hope for a neutral, united Laos was rapidly disintegrating. After a right-wing government – led by **Phoui Sananikone** – took charge in August, the truce put in place by the Geneva Accords began to unravel. Civil war seemed inevitable. In January, claiming that a North Vietnamese invasion was imminent, Phoui demanded and received emergency powers for a year, effectively shutting the Pathet Lao out of Vientiane's political arena and opening the door for the Royal Lao Army to gain control of the Ministry of Defence. A ruthless and powerful military figure, **General Phoumi Nosavan**, assumed the post of vice minister of defence. The story goes that in 1949 he drew matchsticks to decide between staying on with Prince Souphanouvong in his alliance with the Viet Minh or travelling to Vientiane to cooperate with French forces. A decade later, no such indecision hampered Phoumi as he eagerly auditioned for the role of strong-man. Immediately stepping up harassment of the Pathet Lao's political front, he did not disappoint the Americans.

After negotiations to integrate two Pathet Lao battalions into the Royal Lao Army stalled, one battalion slipped back to Houa Phan, where the communist forces were preparing to resume their insurgency. The government considered the leftist troops to be in rebellion and responded by arresting Pathet Lao leaders in Vientiane, including Souphanouvong. As skirmishes signalled a return to the battlefield, the lost opportunity for peace was underscored by the passing of the country's most powerful political figures, Prince Phetsarath and King Sisavang Vong, who died within two weeks of each other in October.

Phoumi's coup and the growth of the Pathet Lao

Phoui's failure to rein in the increasingly powerful military had sown the seeds for his ousting. With a helping hand from the vehemently anti-communist CDNI, General Phoumi, by now in charge of the ministry of defence, staged a **coup** in December. His troops took to the streets of Vientiane under the pretext, yet again, of a Pathet Lao attack. Although Phoumi failed in his bid to lead the newly formed government, it was nonetheless controlled by the military and staunchly aligned with the USA and Thailand. Rigged elections held in April left the leftists without a seat, much to the satisfaction of the USA.

The **corruption** of the generals and politicians in Vientiane and the purge of communist cadres in the countryside gave the Pathet Lao propaganda machine ample material with which to win hearts and minds. With Souphanouvong biding his time in jail reading Greek classics, Kaysone Phomvihane, as head of Pathet Lao military operations, expanded his control over the organization's leadership. Communist forces were active throughout most of the country, and by 1960, roughly twenty percent of the population was no longer under government control.

Although the Royal Lao Army generals were far too concerned with vying for influence to worry about the communists' successes in indoctrinating the rural population, the men guarding Souphanouvong and his comrades certainly took note. As the new government – one which was set on a show trial for the Red Prince – was taking shape, all fifteen Pathet Lao prisoners, along with their guards, slipped off in the night. Souphanouvong began his now legendary five-hundred-kilometre march to Pathet Lao headquarters in Houa Phan.

The Laotian crisis

The Pathet Lao weren't the only ones fed up with the self-serving politicians and generals in Vientiane. In August 1960, a disgruntled 26-year-old army captain named **Kong Le** seized control of Vientiane, much to the surprise of the United States and the Cabinet, whose ministers were away in Louang Phabang. Proclaiming himself a neutralist, Kong Le called for an end to "Lao killing Lao" and an end to foreign interference in the affairs of the country. He then invited Souvannaphouma to lead a new government.

Laos began to split apart. As the Pathet Lao took advantage of the confusion and seized more territory, Phoumi regrouped what troops he could in Savan-nakhet, where he gained the backing of the CIA. Planes belonging to Air America, a civilian contract airline operating in Asia which was later revealed to be a front for the CIA, began flying into the Mekong River town with arms and bundles of money.

In November, Phoumi's men, coordinated by American advisors and assisted by a group of crack Thai troops, began a march on Vientiane, as Moscow and Washington – both of whom saw Laos as an excellent place from which to control Southeast Asia – looked on. The Soviet Union began airlifting supplies to Kong Le's neutralist forces in the capital. Laos was now at the heart of a Cold War showdown.

By the time Phoumi's troops reached Vientiane in December, the neutralists had allied themselves with the Pathet Lao and the Viet Minh. With both sides reluctant to spill Lao blood, a sloppy battle ensued which was won by the right-ists. The neutralists retreated north and eventually joined Pathet Lao forces on the Plain of Jars. Souvannaphouma, who fled for Phnom Penh before the battle, was formally ousted as prime minister by King Sisavang Vatthana and replaced by Prince Boun Oum of Champasak.

But by March 1961, as a neutralist–Pathet Lao offensive got under way, President Kennedy announced American support for a **political settlement** involving the neutralization of Laos. This was an acknowledgement that America saw military victory as unlikely given the incompetence and reluctance to fight on the part of the Royal Lao Army, something that Kennedy sensed when

Soon after Soviet aircraft began dropping weapons and supplies by parachute to Pathet Lao and neutralist forces stationed on the Plain of Jars in December 1960, a Central Intelligence Agency operative by the name of Bill Lair boarded an H-34 helicopter in Vientiane and flew off into the mountains of Xiang Khouang in search of **Vang Pao**, a little-known Royal Lao Army lieutenant-colonel. With Laos in the midst of a crisis that held the rapt attention of the world's superpowers, the 30-year-old Hmong officer was holding out against the communist forces who had taken over the Plain of Jars and the surrounding hillsides, an area heavily populated by Hmong. Lair and Vang Pao had been preparing for this meeting, albeit unknowingly, for a decade. The Texan had spent the better part of the 1950s training members of Thailand's national police in guerrilla warfare, a measure taken against the perceived threat of an invasion by communist China. Vang Pao, meanwhile, had been earning his reputation as a ruthless and clever soldier by leading raids against North Vietnamese forces stationed in Laos, first as a police officer and later as a member of a group of French-trained hill-tribe irregulars.

As retold in Second Indochina War correspondent Jane Hamilton-Merritt's *Tragic Mountains,* Vang Pao made clear in his meeting with Lair that the Hmong and the United States shared a common enemy: "For me, I can't live with communism. I must either leave or fight. I prefer to fight." In the cool of a hillside thatch hut, the seeds of the CIA's so-called **secret army** were sown. To Lair and Vang Pao, American and Hmong needs were a perfect fit. The United States provided weapons and training for the indigenous population, who were led by one of their own in a fight for their own cause.

The **Hmong** were naturals as guerrilla soldiers. Determined to defend their homeland, they knew the terrain and could run circles around the Pathet Lao and the North Vietnamese. After a three-day crash course in the weapons of modern warfare, Vang Pao's initial force of several hundred soldiers won their first battle, ambushing a curious band of Pathet Lao who had tracked the supplies descending from Air America planes by parachute. Operation Momentum, as the project was known, was a success. The clandestine army developed into an effective **guerrilla fighting force**, their numbers swelling to twenty thousand over the course of the decade. Hmong soldiers rescued downed American pilots, learned to fly fighter planes and bravely marched into battle, often trailed by their wives and children. Most importantly, Vang Pao's slapdash band of irregulars were all that stood between the Mekong and the North Vietnamese.

At first, US costs were low and Americans few and far between, a far cry from the battle next door in Vietnam where the United States threw increasing amounts of money and troops at the problem with little to show for it. But a low-cost, home-grown war run out of the hip pocket of a lone CIA agent wasn't what the United States military had in mind for Laos. As the 1960s progressed, the war in Laos escalated, advisors flooded the American ranks, and the role of air power grew to criminal proportions, and with it the role of the Hmong. Although they were best at guerrilla warfare, the Hmong were often called upon to fight conventional battles and defend high-profile sites. Casualties soared as the troops were increasingly involved in set-piece battles with a seemingly more and more determined North Vietnamese force; an estimated 25 percent of the Hmong who enlisted to fight were killed in battle.

By 1968, Vang Pao's forces were no longer fighting for their homeland, they were fighting for the United States, pawns of the **war in Vietnam**. The institutionalization of the Laos war had reduced Operation Momentum to a bloated recruitment programme churning out war-weary Hmong mercenaries. Half a world away in Washington DC, former ambassador to Vientiane William Sullivan, questioned in Senate hearings as to whether the US had any responsibility for the well-being of Vang Pao and his people, made it painfully clear where the Hmong stood: "No formal obligation upon the United States; no."

he first met the diminutive Phoumi and commented, "if that's our strongman, we're in trouble". With Cuba, Berlin and numerous other hotspots on the radar, Washington worried about spreading itself too thinly. The president, pronouncing the country's name as "Lay-oss" – figuring that it might prove difficult to rally support for action in a country called "Louse", concluded his March 23rd speech on the "Laotian Crisis" saying: "All we want in Laos is peace, not war; a truly neutral government, not a Cold War pawn; a settlement concluded at the conference table and not on the battlefield."

The United States had already begun to hedge its bets, however. Lao army troops were training in Thailand, US army advisers had arrived with new weapons and a handful of planes, and the CIA launched Operation Momentum (see opposite), which established a **clandestine army** recruited from the Hmong and under the command of Vang Pao, a Hmong lieutenant-colonel, whose military brilliance would earn him the rank of general in the Royal Lao Army by the end of the Second Indochina War.

Two months after Kennedy's speech, a **second conference** was convened at **Geneva**, but despite the determination of the Soviet Union and the US to neutralize tensions over Laos, it took a year and a decisive defeat for the royalist army at Louang Namtha before the feuding Lao factions reached an agreement on the formation of a **second coalition government**. The second coalition, however, was a failure, dissolving after the April 1963 assassination of a neutralist cabinet member. Fearing arrest or assassination, Pathet Lao ministers fled the capital.

The tacit agreement

Following the second round in Geneva, Washington's priority was South Vietnam, where, by 1962, it already had ten thousand military advisers and support troops. By October 1962 American and Soviet military personnel had withdrawn from Laos, but only forty North Vietnamese had cleared the checkpoints, leaving an estimated five thousand troops in Laos.

Laos was being drawn increasingly into the **Second Indochina War**, as North Vietnam and the United States undermined the country's neutrality in the pursuit of their agendas in Vietnam. Lao territory was a crucial part of the North Vietnamese war effort. They could not risk allowing the United States to use northern Laos, in particular the Plain of Jars, to threaten North Vietnam and they needed to control the mountainous eastern corridor of southern Laos in order to move soldiers and supplies to South Vietnam along the Ho Chi Minh Trail (see p.261). The US saw no option but to challenge North Vietnam's strategy. Eventually, all sides with a stake in Laos came to the same conclusion about the Geneva Accords: while they would have loved to point an accusing finger at the opposition's violations of the agreement, they had much more to gain by quietly pursuing their own agendas. So the right-wing Lao, the Americans and the Thais on the one side and the Pathet Lao, the North Vietnamese and their Chinese and Soviet backers on the other all tacitly agreed to pretend to abide by the accords, guaranteeing Laos's neutrality while keeping the country at war.

Even after the collapse of the second coalition government in 1963, patriotic Souvannaphouma was determined to keep the vision of a neutral Laos alive. He first flew to Beijing and Hanoi to seek support for extricating Laos from the war in Vietnam. Next he travelled to the Plain of Jars for a three-way meeting with his half-brother Souphanouvong, who he refused to believe was really a committed communist, and Defence Minister Phoumi, who had already asked Saigon to send troops into Laos in pursuit of communist soldiers there. After the negotiations proved futile, an exhausted Souvannaphouma returned to Vientiane and, on April 18, 1964, with tears rolling down his cheeks, he announced his plans to resign, prompting Phoumi's rightist rivals to launch a surprise coup the next day. Under house arrest, Souvannaphouma appeared on his balcony, as US Ambassador Leonard Unger shouted encouragement to the embattled prime minister from the garden next door – an event which the French ambassador, present at the time, dubbed "la diplomatie à la Roméo et Juliette". Within a matter of days, the prince was back in power and the generals were out. The US had decided that they liked the neutralist prince after all.

Excluded from the new government, the Pathet Lao went on the offensive, chasing Kong Le's remaining neutralists off the Plain of Jars and into an alliance with Vang Pao and his Hmong army. The communist offensive fitted neatly into what would become the standard seesaw pattern of fighting in northern Laos, in which each side went on the offensive when the season best suited them. As the rains drew to a close in October and the roads dried up, the communists would begin their attacks, concluding their operations by the monsoons, during which time they would try to hold their newly won territory, while the rightists – with US air support and better supply lines favouring them during the rains – would go on the offensive. Pushing out from the Mekong Valley, the royalist and Hmong forces would usually retake what was lost, with the end result that neither side wound up controlling more than they had at the beginning.

But as the communists pressed on in the spring of 1964, they came up against a whole new enemy: **airpower**. Single-prop T-28 aircraft hammered at communist positions, scaring off their soldiers who had never faced aeroplanes before. Within a matter of weeks, T-28 bombing runs were joined by US jets, which were sent over Laos as they happened to be in the neighbourhood. Once the bombing began, Washington apparently decided it wasn't such a bad idea. News reports produced by the few journalists in Laos could be controlled, the US reasoned. They were right: although the bombing campaign would be reported for years by Pathet Lao and North Vietnamese radio, it would take five years before the United States public heard anything about it.

Escalation

Souvannaphouma initially gave his permission for US flights over Laos, but after two American jets were downed over northern Laos the prime minister had second thoughts and once again threatened to resign unless the bombing raids ceased. However, Souvannaphouma was in no position to argue. The US had restored him to power and paid his government's budget. And it would be only thanks to US backing that Souvannaphouma, trying to preserve a minimum of freedom of action, would remain in power for the next decade in the face of successive coups.

In 1964, a new phase of the war in Laos began. With the US pushing hard for an **escalation of the bombing** in the summer, Souvannaphouma, prodded by the US embassy, declared that the North Vietnamese were using the eastern flank of Laos to send combatants and supplies to South Vietnam along what would become known as the **Ho Chi Minh Trail**. He then gave the go-ahead for what were euphemistically known as "armed reconnaissance" flights over

Laos, permission that essentially became a blank cheque for the US to bomb wherever it pleased.

The war was intensifying next door in **Vietnam**, too. Whatever misgivings US President Lyndon B. Johnson had about the Southeast Asia problem he had inherited from his predecessors, he was determined not to go down as the president who lost to the communists. Although Johnson, facing an election in November 1964, initially decided to keep his plans for the escalation of the war in Vietnam secret from voters and from Capitol Hill, he was able to make his stand against communism more public in August when the *USS Maddox* came under attack off the coast of North Vietnam. In response to the incident, US senators passed the **Gulf of Tonkin Resolution**, which became Johnson's justification for the Vietnam War. No such resolution was passed regarding Laos; after all, the country was "neutral".

When Ambassador William Sullivan assumed his post in Vientiane near the end of 1964, his assignment was to wage war while maintaining the fiction of the Geneva Accords, which he had personally helped to negotiate. He came to the Lao capital aware of US plans for Operation Rolling Thunder – a sustained carpet-bombing campaign against North Vietnam designed to go "after the manure pile" rather than simply swatting flies, as the Commander of the US Air Force, General Curtis Le May, eloquently put it. Even before the Vietnam operation began, Sullivan established his own programmes for Laos, called **Operation Barrel Roll** in the north and **Operation Steel Tiger** in the south.

Sullivan set the tone for the US campaign in Laos – ground troops were kept out (apart from reconnaissance missions and raids on the Ho Chi Minh Trail area) and military planes had to take off outside the country. The war took place in total secrecy. As British journalist Christopher Robbins wrote in *The Ravens*, based on interviews with pilots who fought in "the Other Theatre", "There was another war even nastier than the one in Vietnam, and so secret that the location of the country in which it was being fought was classified... The men who chose to fight in it were handpicked volunteers, and anyone accepted for a tour seemed to disappear as if from the face of the earth."

From 1964 until the ceasefire of February 1973, United States planes flew 580,944 sorties – or 177 a day – over Laos and dropped 2,093,100 tonnes of bombs – equivalent to one planeload of bombs every eight minutes around the clock for nine years – making Laos the most heavily bombed country per capita in the history of warfare.

The turning point: 1968

On March 10, 1968, communist forces overran a strategic limestone massif in Houa Phan which the US had crowned with a high-tech bombing guidance device that directed attacks on Hanoi and was guarded by Hmong troops. The **fall of Phou Pha Thi** (see box, p.183) underscored the lack of unified command that plagued the various US factions – the embassy, the CIA and the air force – responsible for fighting the Laos War.

According to Roger Warner in his book *Shooting at the Moon*, while some involved in directing the US war effort thought the US had erred by provoking the North Vietnamese with the installation of this direct threat to Hanoi's security, others argued that the North Vietnamese escalation in Laos was simply a part of the same intensive effort that produced the January 31 **Tet Offensive**, in which a combined force of 70,000 communists violated a truce to launch attacks on more than a hundred cities across South Vietnam. In a Washington reeling from Tet, which brought with it the popular perception that the communists were winning the war in Vietnam, President Johnson vetoed requests for a massive troop expansion, and on March 31 he suspended bombing north of the Twentieth Parallel to jump-start the peace talks in Paris that would grind on for five years. By the year's end the bombing had completely ended.

The suspension of bombing in Vietnam was terrible news for Laos, as the US Air Force's reaction was to send more planes over Laos than ever before. Swarms of planes circled the country, zeroing in on their targets with the help of a new breed of forward air controllers known as Ravens, introduced in the wake of the Phou Pha Thi disaster. These pilots, "sheep-dipped" in civilian clothes, flew single-engine Cessna propeller planes, with a hill-tribe translator in the backseat to communicate with ground forces, guiding up to three hundred American sorties per day. The early days of Operation Momentum, when the CIA quietly waged a grassroots guerrilla war, were a distant memory.

Nixon's presidency

In order to facilitate pulling out of Southeast Asia while saving face for the United States, President **Nixon** initiated a policy of "**Vietnamization**". This involved a gradual withdrawal of US forces coupled with an intensification of the air war and more materiel support, as well as pursuing communist sanctuaries with greater intensity in the hope that South Vietnam could hold its own against the North.

The first major test of this strategy was the United States' **invasion of Cambodia**, which lay at the end of the Ho Chi Minh Trail. Until 1970, Cambodia, under the leadership of Prince Norodom Sihanouk, had stayed neutral in the war. Neutrality for Sihanouk, however, meant allowing the North Vietnamese to operate on Cambodian soil and the United States to bomb the North Vietnamese with B-52s. On March 18, 1970, a right-wing pro-US general named Lon Nol replaced Sihanouk in a coup and, two weeks later, US and South Vietnamese troops invaded the regions of the country nearest South Vietnam.

The operation set off a political uproar in the US. Massive **anti-war demonstrations** spread across America after four National Guardsmen opened fire on demonstrators at Kent State University in Ohio, killing four. Politically, the Cambodian "incursion", as it was termed, and subsequent protests prompted the US Congress to pass a measure forbidding the use of American ground troops in Cambodia and Laos. Had they not, US ground troops might have taken part in **Lam Son 719** (see p.264) – one of the most disastrous operations undertaken by the United States in the whole of the war. In February 1971, nearly 20,000 South Vietnamese troops, backed by American air power, drove across the Annamite Mountains, in the hope of cutting North Vietnamese supply lines in the vicinity of Xepon, 40km west of the border. After years of strategically bombing the veins of the Ho Chi Minh Trail, Washington appeared to recognize that aeroplanes couldn't stop people. The move proved catastrophic. Five thousand South Vietnamese were killed or wounded, 176 Americans died and more than one hundred US army helicopters were shot down, with an estimated six hundred more damaged. Images of South Vietnamese troops clinging to the skids of American helicopters in a desperate bid to flee the massacre carried the message that even with massive US support the South Vietnamese didn't stand a chance, pushing US policymakers closer to the realization that the war was a lost cause.

Washington had begun to realize that Southeast Asia was merely a small part in the Cold War, and that as long as the US continued to fight in Indochina, it would continue to give the Soviet Union and China – the two communist giants, whose border forces had clashed in March 1969 – a reason to cooperate. By the time Nixon announced that his national security advisor, Henry Kissinger, had secretly visited China in July 1971 and that he would soon visit China himself, the president seemed ready to sacrifice South Vietnam – and by extension Laos and Cambodia – in order to create an opening with China.

With **peace talks** deadlocked in Paris, Nixon sent Kissinger, with former Laos ambassador Sullivan at his side, to take charge. On January 27, 1973, the United States, North Vietnam, South Vietnam and the Viet Cong at last signed the **Paris Accords**, under the terms of which a ceasefire was established and all remaining American troops were to be repatriated by April. In reality the accords would accomplish little more than smoothing the US withdrawal from Indochina.

The Pathet Lao takeover

While the US saw an agreement on Laos as an afterthought that would be quickly resolved, Souvannaphouma held out against a settlement, wanting assurances from the Americans that the North Vietnamese would pull their troops out of Laos. But the Vietnamese had never acknowledged having troops in Laos in the first place and, with the US already committed to a withdrawal, there was little Washington could do for Vientiane. The North Vietnamese knew this and took the position that they would only withdraw from Laos and Cambodia after a new government had been put in place. Late in February, the Vientiane government and the Pathet Lao signed an Agreement of the Restoration of Peace and Reconciliation, which neither the US nor the North Vietnamese signed – as if they had never been in Laos in the first place.

Continued negotiations resulted in the formation of a **third coalition government** in April 1974, with leftists taking half the ministerial portfolios and the remainder going to the right. Souvannaphouma once again presided as prime minister and Souphanouvong headed the policy-making National Political Consultative Council, which met in Louang Phabang.

When Phnom Penh and then Saigon fell to communist forces in April 1975, a complete communist takeover in Laos appeared a foregone conclusion. "Liberating" towns as they went, Pathet Lao forces gradually closed in on Vientiane, where demonstrations were held in the capital against the continuing US presence and right-wing political and military figures. A Pathet Lao force of fifty women soldiers symbolically "liberated" Vientiane on August 23. Power was slowly but surely shifting to the Pathet Lao.

Relieved of his RLA command by Souvannaphouma after refusing to stop fighting, Vang Pao was finally persuaded to leave Laos in May by the US, whose representatives were pulling out as well. A mass exodus of Hmong towards Thailand followed. An estimated thirty thousand Hmong – nearly a tenth of the tribe's entire population within the borders of Laos – had died during the war. As thousands fled, their suffering continued, as many were robbed and shot while trying to flee to Thailand.

Lowland Lao generals of the royalist side were more willing to try to cooperate with the new government. Although large numbers fled the country, many more chose to stay and serve the new government. Thousands of civil servants and military officers went willingly to re-education camps (see pp.186–187) in the remote northeast and southeast of the country after being told these "seminars" would only last a few weeks.

The absence of right-wing figures opened the door to further Pathet Lao advances which culminated in a **National Congress of People's Representatives** on December 2, 1975, when the congress proclaimed the Lao People's Democratic Republic and accepted the abdication of King Sisavang Vatthana.

The Lao People's Democratic Republic

The **Thirty Year Struggle**, with its roots in the short-lived Lao Issara government, was over. The man in charge was the little-known party secretary-general **Kaysone**, who was named prime minister. When Kaysone appeared at a reception on December 5 it was the first time he had been seen in public in seventeen years. The man who had been the face of the Pathet Lao all along, Souphanouvong, assumed the role of president. The prince essentially became a figurehead – after all, it wouldn't do to have a communist country run by a French-educated prince.

Unlike their comrades in Vietnam and Cambodia, the Pathet Lao took power in a **bloodless coup**. After overthrowing the government of Souvannaphouma and abolishing royalty, the Pathet Lao named the prince and the king as advisors to the new government and demonstrated further flexibility by inviting the United States to maintain its embassy in Vientiane.

The Pathet Lao's flexibility ended there, however, as they continued to round up civil servants and military personnel with ties to the royalists until as many as fifty thousand people were in **re-education camps**, which turned out to be malaria-ridden labour camps, heavy on self-criticism sessions. Whatever willingness to cooperate with the new regime there was left among the lowland Lao quickly evaporated as the government refused to allow the return of people in camps. Many, on their release, left the country. By the mid-1980s Laos had lost ten percent of its population – including an overwhelming majority of its educated class.

Considerable problems faced the new government, which took over a country stripped of money and resources. The **economy** was now a shambles, crippled by the termination of US aid, runaway inflation and the closure of the border with Thailand – the country's primary source of imports, which resulted in severe shortages of basic foods. Thirty-five thousand ethnic Vietnamese and Chinese – the traditional merchants of the country – boarded up their shops in Vientiane and crossed the Mekong. Intent on ushering in a socialist state, the Pathet Lao followed **Eastern bloc models**: they collectivized farms, centralized control of prices and nationalized what little industry there was. The revolution was extended to the personal sphere as well. The government required long-haired teenagers to get haircuts and women to wear traditional skirts in an effort to develop Lao socialist men and women. Prostitutes and petty thieves were shipped off to re-education camps of their own on islands in the middle of Ang Nam Ngum.

As living standards declined within Laos and the number of refugees in camps in Thailand swelled, **opponents of the regime** found ready recruits. The Thailand-based Lao National Revolutionary Front produced anti-government propaganda and sent sabotage teams into Laos, while remnants of the Hmong secret army went on the offensive in northern Laos, capturing a town on the outskirts of Louang Phabang in March 1977. Fearing that opponents might rally around the figure of the king, the government arrested the royal family and banished them to Houa Phan, where the king, queen and crown prince died, something officially acknowledged only in 1990.

Vietnamese forces helped quell the Hmong revolt, and in July, Vientiane and Hanoi signed a 25-year **Treaty of Friendship and Cooperation** which formalized Vietnamese political, economic and military assistance, including the stationing of more than 30,000 Vietnamese troops in Laos over the next decade. Relations were also close with the Soviet Union, which sent hundreds of technicians and advisers to Laos, drawing it firmly within the Soviet sphere of influence.

The new thinking

By 1979, external and internal difficulties facing the new government forced it to re-evaluate its policies; as a result, its agricultural cooperative programme was suspended and a less rigid form of socialism was adopted. Despite the changes, little had been accomplished by the time the Pathet Lao celebrated its tenth anniversary in power and the completion of its first five-year plan in December 1985. Heavily dependent on foreign aid, Laos remained one of the world's poorest countries. The time had come, in the eyes of Kaysone, for a change.

After overcoming opponents of reform, Kaysone was able to implement the **New Economic Mechanism**, approved by the Fourth Party Congress in November 1986, which essentially introduced a market economy. Without an upheaval among the party's leaders – many of whom had worked together since their days in the Indochinese Communist Party in the 1940s – the ageing hard-liners of the Pathet Lao embarked on a series of reforms, generally known as *jintannakan mai* or the New Thinking, which was as thorough as anything to be found in Eastern Europe at the time. By the late 1980s, the centralized social-ist economy had been largely dismantled. Farmers could own their own land and sell their crops at free-market prices, state-owned businesses had to make a profit or close their doors and wholly owned foreign investment projects, protected against nationalization, were authorized.

Political changes did not accompany the economic reforms, however. Local elections held in 1988 – the first since 1975 – and subsequent national elections in 1989 did provide some popular legitimacy for the government, but candidates were approved by the party prior to polls. And although the re-education camps wound down, the government showed in 1990 that it would deal strictly with **dissent** when it arrested three critics whom it accused of "activities aimed at overthrowing the regime". The three, former government officials who called for democracy and the creation of a multiparty system, were sent off to Houa Phan where, according to Amnesty International, one has since died in prison and two are still being held.

For many, less government intrusion in people's lives and an abundance of material goods flooding the markets, brought on by the opening up of the economy, went a long way towards smoothing over discontent. Of course, the discontented could also vote with their feet – crossing the Mekong and blending in with the ethnic Lao population of northeastern Thailand. But by the late 1980s, the Mekong had once again become a two-way street, as Lao refugees were invited to return, and Western tourists began to visit the country.

In 1991, the Fifth Party Congress endorsed the long-awaited **Constitution**, which guaranteed basic freedoms and the right to private ownership of property. The congress served to indicate that the party was no longer above the law when one member of the politburo was demoted for corruption. Economic reform also received an endorsement, with the party replacing the communist red star in the national crest with the That Louang stupa and eliminating the word "socialism" from the national motto.

The 1992 **death of Kaysone**, who had led the communist movement since the inception of the Lao People's Party in 1955, presented a serious challenge to the regime, but a smooth transition, resulting in the appointment of **Nouhak Phoumsavanh** as state president and **Khamtay Siphandone**, the prime minister, as president of the party, ensured the government's political stability.

Regional integration

As communism began to collapse in Eastern Europe and Vietnam began to withdraw its forces from Laos, the government improved ties with Thailand and with other capitalist countries, notably Japan, Australia and Sweden. Cooperation with the United States in the search for missing US servicemen on Lao soil and control of the opium trade improved ties with the United States, culminating in the re-establishment of full ambassadorial relations in 1992. With the collapse of the Soviet Union in 1991, Laos also began to smooth over difficulties with China which had arisen as a result of Vientiane's alliance with the USSR and Vietnam. China has in fact emerged as Laos's most important foreign military ally, as well as a powerful economic force on Laos's northern border. Thus, by the early 1990s, Laos enjoyed relatively good relations with all its border countries, allowing it to slip back into its familiar role of a crossroads between contending regional powers.

The Australian-financed **Friendship Bridge** to Thailand – opened in 1994 outside Vientiane – as well as membership in the **Association of Southeast Asian Nations** in July 1997 were two important signs that Laos had finally begun to shake off decades of isolation. But for the **Sixth Party Congress**, the Friendship Bridge to Thailand symbolized the way in which the New Thinking was being corrupted, as economic reforms brought a host of new problems, including corruption, gambling dens, brothels and increased crime. The conservative policies introduced by the congress indicated the party intended to slow the pace of reforms and would attempt to contain the fallout from "socially evil outside influences", in part by appealing to traditional Lao values. (While Lao newspapers routinely pummelled the sleazy side of the Thai economic miracle – as well as the Thai inclination to "look down on Lao people" – the *Far Eastern Economic Review* indicated that the government didn't allow such frictions to interfere with the generous helpings of Thai aid, trade and investment upon which it has relied in recent years.)

Laos today

Economic reforms, with the accompanying social problems, increased official corruption and growing income disparity, represent a great challenge to internal order in the eyes of the party, more so than the continuing insurgency in Hmong-dominated areas in the north. The party clings to this view despite the fact that in the mid-1990s and again in the first few years of the new millennium, there was a slight upswing in insurgent activities, reportedly by the group known as the Chao Fa, perhaps owing to anger at government attempts to **resettle** highland groups. The official reason for resettlement was to put an end to opium cultivation and slash-and-burn agriculture, and bring far-flung villagers closer to hospitals and schools. The consequences in some cases have proved fatal for the highlanders, who have contracted valley-related diseases such as malaria.

In June 2006, former Minister of Defence **Choummali Saignason** took the reigns of power from Khamtay Siphandone. Choummali is the first post-revolution leader of Laos that is not a member of the ageing old guard, but little else is known about him. However, it is safe to say that his appointment is not a sign of changing times in Laos – Choummali is expected to maintain the status quo. With absolutely no possibility of a homegrown opposition leader coming to the forefront, the government is under little pressure to initiate political reforms.

Despite the prospect of Laos reaping rewards from the sale of power – from grand new hydroelectric projects – to its neighbours, the country continues to rank among the world's poorest and least developed. Indeed, the World Bank has said that Laos's social indicators are more akin to those of sub-Saharan Africa than they are to the rest of Southeast Asia. Roughly half the adult population is illiterate, some forty percent lack access to safe drinking water and the country continues to be mired at the bottom of World Health Organization rankings. In the meantime, Laos continues to shrewdly manipulate international governments as well as non-governmental organizations in order to keep aid flowing in. Not that this is too difficult: Laos's recent history as a pawn in the cold war, and its peoples' sufferings as a result of that era, makes the country a perfect candidate for international assistance, while human-rights abuses continue to be overlooked.

Religion and belief systems

The multiplicity of belief systems in Laos mirrors the complexity of its mulligan stew of ethnicities. Theravada Buddhism is the majority religion, practised by approximately two-thirds of the population, followed by animism and ancestor worship. The remainder practise Mahayana Buddhism and Taoism, and a small percentage of the population follow Christianity or Islam.

Buddhism

Lao legend has it that Buddhism came to Laos in the fourteenth century, but archeological evidence suggests that Buddhism existed in parts of what is now Laos as early as the eighth century. **Theravada Buddhism**, sometimes referred to as the "southern school" of Buddhism owing to its geographic spread, is prevalent in Sri Lanka, Myanmar (Burma), Thailand and Cambodia as well as Laos. The vast majority of lowland-dwelling ethnic Lao, whose numbers make up over half of the population of Laos, are adherents of Theravada Buddhism, as are other ethnic groups such as the Tai Leu, Phuan and Phu Noi, plus a fraction of the tribal Tai groups, such as the Phu Tai, Tai Daeng and Tai Dam. Lao-style Theravada Buddhism is a fascinating blend of indigenous and borrowed beliefs and rituals. During Laos's many years of vassaldom to the various kingdoms made up of lands that now lie within Thai borders, many outside religious beliefs and customs found their way into the Lao royal courts of Louang Phabang, Vientiane and Champasak and, from there, into the valleys of the interior via the tributaries of the Mekong River. The Hindu customs and beliefs that were adopted by the Thai after their sack of Angkor, in what is now Cambodia, were also passed on, in diluted form, to Laos.

Later, Chinese and Vietnamese immigrants brought with them **Mahayana Buddhism**, the so-called "northern school" of Buddhism. As the immigrants prospered and assimilated, the images of their gods found their way into urban monasteries. Go into one of these monasteries today and, alongside images of the Buddha, you may well see a representation of a Hindu god such as Ganesh or a Mahayana Buddhist deity such as Kuan Yin.

The ideological rift between the two Buddhist schools is as vast as the one that divides Catholicism and Protestantism. Theravada Buddhism is the more austere of the two and has been described as having an "every man for himself" philosophy, that is to say, each individual adherent is believed to be responsible for his or her own accumulation of merit or sin. Mahayana Buddhism is more of a "group effort", with adherents praying for divine assistance from *bodhisattva*, near-Buddhas who have postponed their enlightenment in order to serve as the compassionate protectors of all mankind.

For most Lao Buddhists, religion in everyday life revolves around the all-important practice of **making merit**, or *het bun*. This accumulation of merit is paramount to a Theravada Buddhist's spiritual strategy, a way to dilute the destructive effects of any sin that may have been accrued by bad deeds, while at

Most ethnic Lao men become novice monks at some time in their lives, usually before marriage. Monks take **vows** to uphold no less than 227 precepts. These range from abstinence from sexual relations, alcohol and the wearing of any sort of ornamentation to more arcane rules such as a prohibition on urinating while standing upright (so as not to soil robes). Laos's history of social upheaval and a generally relaxed attitude towards rules, however, have meant that, especially in rural monasteries, not all of the precepts are strictly adhered to. For most Lao males, the time spent wearing a robe is short, usually no more than three months or so during the rainy season. Interestingly, a man who has yet to do time in a monastery is referred to as *dip* or "unripe", alluding to the fact that many Lao don't consider a man complete without some time spent in the monastery; before the advent of public schools, lessons in reading and writing at the monastery were about all the education the average Lao could hope for.

As the state religion, Buddhism enjoyed royal patronage up until the time of the **revolution**. In the years leading up to the revolution, the communists cleverly used Buddhist monks, many of whom were unhappy with widespread government corruption, as instruments for diffusing propaganda. Once the cause had been won, however, the communists moved to gain total control, banning the practice of alms-giving. This effectively made it impossible to remain a monk, as it is against Buddhist precepts for monks to cultivate plants or raise animals for food. The move backfired, however, as lay people were shocked at the new regime's heavy-handed treatment of the monkhood and resented being deprived of any opportunity to make merit. Popular outcry forced the government to rescind the draconian measures, but only after large numbers of monks fled to Thailand or abandoned their robes and became laymen. Today, the study of Marxist–Leninist theory is still mandatory for all monks, but Lao Buddhism has made a strong comeback and economic reforms and liberalization have helped to increase the numbers of men in the monkhood to pre-revolution levels.

the same time ensuring that the next incarnation will be better than the present one. Many of the holidays in the Lao calendar are associated with Buddhist festivals and give the visitor a chance to observe the practice of merit-making, whether it be ritually bathing Buddha images or donating new robes to monks. Making merit is accomplished most readily by giving **alms** to Buddhist monks and novices. This enchanting practice can be witnessed just after dawn, when barefoot monks solemnly walk through the neighbourhood or village surrounding their monasteries in order to collect offerings of food from laypeople. Merit thus acquired is believed to bring the giver good fortune in this life and the next, and also to dilute the destructive effects of sin that may have been accumulated. Male adherents may also make merit for themselves and their families by taking vows and becoming a novice monk for a limited period of time. Even more merit may be acquired by becoming an ordained disciple of the Buddha.

Animism and ancestor worship

Predating Buddhism in Laos, **animism** is the belief that natural objects – such as hills, trees, large rocks or plots of land – are inhabited by spiritual entities or possess supernatural powers. While the Buddhist Lao still harbour vestiges of these beliefs, some midland and highland tribal peoples are exclusively animist.

△ A spirit house

Building structures and cultivating land are believed to displace the spirits and so an alternative home must be provided. An easily recognized example of animism among Buddhists is the practice of erecting a **spirit house** on plots of land. Ordinarily found in a corner of a piece of property, a spirit house is the customary abode of the *jao bawn*, or spirit of the site, and resembles a miniature house or sometimes a model of Mount Meru, the Hindu Mount Olympus, atop a pedestal. The idea is to make the spirit house a more habitable place than the dwellings for humans located on the same plot of land; naturally, if the *jao bawn* is comfortable in its digs, it is less likely to cause trouble for people living in the vicinity. Offerings to keep the spirit of the site propitiated may include flowers, incense, candles or sweets. A much simpler offering to *jao bawn* that visitors may note is the practice of pressing spirit offerings of sticky rice against trees or rocks. Another manifestation of animism that can be readily seen is the **talaew**, a six-pointed star made from strips of bamboo and placed over doors and gates or in rice fields. The device is thought to bar evil spirits from entering and doing harm.

After the revolution, the communists discouraged many animist practices, such as the annual sacrifice of water buffalo in tribal villages in the south, believing that such worship wasted resources and held back the progress of the nation. As with Buddhism, animism quickly revived once official suppression was relaxed.

Ancestor worship in different forms is also practised by many of the highland tribes that migrated to Laos from China, including the Akha, Hmong and Mien. Practices vary, but all believe that the spirits of deceased ancestors have the ability to affect the lives of their descendants. The ancestors are thought to be rather helpless and dependent on the living for earthly comforts; the ancestors reward descendants who remember them with offerings, but can become harmful if neglected.

Other beliefs

The Mien also worship **Taoist** deities, and are known for the crude but charming painted images of these deities which are traditionally displayed on the Mien altar.

Hinduism, or Braminism, was first introduced to what is now southern and central Laos by the Khmer, who adopted many Hindu traditions and beliefs from Indian traders who began arriving in the ports of Southeast Asia in the first century AD. Some elements of the annual ceremonies at Wat Phou, the ancient Khmer site in Champasak province, reflect Hindu rituals handed down to the Lao from the days when the Khmer kings at Angkor ruled much of Southeast Asia. While the Laos' recognition of Hindu divinities is minimal compared with that of their Thai cousins, two such deities, namely the multi-armed, four-faced **Brahma** and the green-skinned **Indra**, have become icons in the Theravada Buddhist pantheon and so are commonly depicted in Lao monasteries. Images of **Ganesh**, the so-called elephant god, can be found on the premises of some Buddhist monasteries and shrines, particularly in the south. The *shivalinga*, or stone phallus symbolizing the god **Shiva**, was commonly enshrined at ancient Khmer temples and, because many Lao Buddhist monasteries were built on top of ancient Khmer sites, the *shivalinga* and other bits of Khmer statuary are often found on Buddhist altars, particularly in the south.

Christianity arrived in Laos in 1642 in the form of an Italian Jesuit missionary but, according to his journal, he was far from successful. Not until the French colonial period did Christian missionaries scramble to make converts throughout Laos. While they had little success with the Buddhist Lao, a number of the animist highlanders were converted. A significant number of Laos's ethnic Vietnamese population is Catholic and the largest concentration of Catholics is found in southern Laos, particularly Savannakhet, which boasts the country's most elaborate Catholic church. Lao Christians also fared badly after the revolution. Because the communists saw Christianity as a "Western", and therefore potentially subversive, religion, missionaries were expelled and churches throughout the country were closed. An example of one such church is located near Kilometre Five on Tha Dua road outside Vientiane. The former Methodist church here is now a garage for fire engines.

Followers of **Islam** are found mainly in Vientiane, where a small community of Cham Muslims, refugees from the Khmer Rouge reign of terror in Cambodia, reside in the vicinity of a mosque located near the Nam Phou (fountain). In northern Laos, small pockets of Chinese Muslims (known locally as *jin haw*), descendants of mule-caravan traders from Yunnan, can be found in Phongsali and other highland towns.

Art and temple architecture

The vast majority of works of art created in Laos – sculpture, painting, architecture, even decorative motifs on jewellery – are inspired by Buddhism, with the important exception of Lao textiles. The motivation behind much Theravada Buddhist art relies heavily on the concept of making merit. Wealthy patrons looking to acquire religious merit and dilute an accumulation of sins can do so by commissioning the crafting of an image of the Buddha or by financing the building or restoration of any of the structures found in monastery grounds.

Owing to Laos's distance from lucrative trade routes and its tumultuous history, the patronage of the religious arts never reached the heights that were attained in neighbouring Cambodia, Thailand and Burma (Myanmar). Nevertheless, a style did develop that is distinctively Lao and, although the number of works which exhibit a high degree of refinement is rather small, Lao art makes up for it with a vigour and whimsy that rarely fails to charm.

Sculpture

The historic Buddha was a prince who gave up his wealth and birthright in order to pursue the "middle path" – a philosophy of moderation – towards enlightenment. Just before his death, the Buddha was said to have discouraged his followers from making images of him, saying that it was his teachings that should be worshipped, not a likeness of him. For a time after the Buddha's passing, Buddhists used **symbolic imagery** to recall the enlightened one. An empty throne or a royal parasol was sometimes depicted commemorating the Buddha's decision to abandon his life of luxury and seek the path to enlightenment.

However, human nature being what it is, adherents needed something more concrete. The **first images of the Buddha** were probably made several centuries after the Buddha's death. By that time, no living artist had actually seen the Buddha, but a list of physical traits said to be unique to the Buddha had been passed down. The result of this list of fairly rigid attributes is that Buddha images from all over Asia share much the same characteristics. Lao images are no different and many of their seemingly bizarre features, toes of equal length for instance, are due to the strictness with which the aesthetic canon has been followed. In much the same vein, the attitude of the Buddha's arms and hands, or *mudra*, are rich with **symbolism** and must be depicted accurately if they are to be understood. Most of these gestures correspond to Buddhist theory or to events that occurred during the Buddha's lifetime. Besides the standard gestures and poses, the Lao have invented a couple of their own. One is a standing Buddha with arms to its sides and fingers pointing downwards, known as the "Beckoning Rain" pose. Buddhas with this *mudra* are found only in Laos and parts of northern Thailand. A similar standing Buddha with arms crossed at the wrists is also a Lao-invented *mudra*, known as "Contemplating the Tree of Enlightenment". The most sacred Buddha image in the country, the Pha Bang (see p.148), is also a standing Buddha, this time with arms held out in a blocking gesture, known as the "Dispelling Fear" pose.

Observant visitors will notice that one *mudra* in particular is especially popular with the Lao. This is found on Buddhas sitting in a half-lotus position, with the left hand resting palm-upward on the image's lap and the right hand extended down and touching the earth with the fingertips. Known as "Victory Over Mara", this pose commemorates the historic Buddha's triumph over Mara the Tempter, a Satan-like figure that tried unsuccessfully to distract the Buddha from his path to enlightenment.

The best place to see sculpted images of the Buddha is on an altar in a Buddhist **monastery**. Typically, a massive central image, usually constructed of brick and stucco, is flanked by numerous smaller images cast from bronze or carved from hardwood. In Louang Phabang, the Pha Bang undeniably gets the most attention, but the superb reclining Buddha enshrined in a small "chapel" at Wat Xiang Thong is perhaps the best example of Lao sculpture to be found in the country. The Haw Pha Kaew, a museum in Vientiane with a small but outstanding collection, is a must-see for those interested in more sophisticated examples of Lao sculpture. **Caves** are a less obvious venue for admiring Lao Buddhas, and by the time an image is deposited in a cavern, it is usually damaged. The caves at Pak Ou near Louang Phabang surely house the largest concentration of Lao Buddhas on earth.

Temple architecture

Of all Lao architectural elements, the *that*, or **stupa**, is probably easiest for the visitor to appreciate. This is due mainly to the fact that it is at once readily recognizable and varied in design. The concept of the stupa – a monument atop a reliquary containing sacred relics of the Buddha – originated in India and spread throughout Asia. In each country where Buddhism took root, the local architects and artisans put their own ideas to work when designing a stupa, and thus the bell-shaped stupas of Sri Lanka have little in common stylistically with the multi-storied "pagoda" stupas found in China and Japan. Vientiane's That Louang stupa, the national symbol of Laos, is a fusion of aggressive angles and graceful curves that make it quite different from designs predominant in neighbouring countries (although stupas in this style can also be found in the northeast of Thailand where ethnic Lao predominate). This design of stupa is probably the greatest single Lao contribution to Buddhist architecture.

Within a typical Lao wat there are a number of buildings serving different functions, but it is the **sim**, the structure in which the monastery's principal Buddha image is enshrined, that gets the most attention from Lao architects and artisans. Lao *sim* have two main styles: the **Vientiane style** owes much to the Bangkok school of architecture, while the **Louang Phabang style** shares characteristics with that of Chiang Mai in northern Thailand. From a distance, the difference between the two styles is easily discerned. The roof of a Vientiane-style *sim* is high and steep, while a Louang Phabang-style roof gently slopes nearly to the ground.

Variations on *sim* design were produced by the Phuan and Tai Leu ethnic groups. The rare **Xiang Khouang style**, once found in the province of the same name, is low and squat, designed to withstand the weather of the windswept Plain of Jars. The handiwork of the Phuan people, this style did not survive Laos's violent history. Examples of architecture produced by the Tai Leu are very similar to that found in the Xishuangbanna region of China's Yunnan province. The *sim* at Muang Sing's Wat Sing Jai is a picturesque example of the Tai Leu style.

Decorative features on the *sim* and other structures found at a Lao wat are in a variety of mediums. Carved wood, moulded stucco and, to a lesser extent, mirrored-glass mosaics typically ornament the exterior while, inside, detailed murals cover entire walls. Doors and windows of the *sim* are often made from teakwood, ornately carved with the figures of celestial beings or demons upon a background of stylized flames or floral forms known as *lai lao* – "Lao pattern". The structure's wooden pediments – triangular segments of the upper facade that support the roof – are another place to look for pleasing examples of *lai lao*, along with carved depictions of Hindu deities such as Kala and Indra atop Aira-vata. Many of these motifs have origins in ancient Khmer ornamentation, such as that found at Wat Phou in Champasak province. Lao stuccowork is sometimes gilt-covered and almost always looks better from a distance. The use of stucco for ornamentation was introduced to Laos by the Khmer or possibly the Mon, but the methods and designs of Lao stuccowork owe more to the Tai Yuan of what is now northern Thailand. Likewise, the use of mirrored glass also came to Laos via Thailand. The mosaics at Wat Xiang Thong are Laos's most famous example of ornamentation using this medium but the works are modern, having been created in the late 1950s. Lao murals are meant to be read like a story and those found on the walls of the *sim* usually depict one of the tales from the Jataka tales, the Lao version of the Ramayana (see box, p.361), or scenes of local life.

The Lao belief that religious merit can be made by **restoring** old monastery buildings ensures that nearly all Lao *sim* are restored every fifty years or so. The artisans who restore these buildings are under little pressure to be true to an earlier design. Indeed, it is believed that the more lavish the new design, the more merit is likely to be made by the patron who commissioned the restoration. The result is that much of the decoration on Buddhist buildings in Laos is nowhere near as old as the structure it adorns.

Textiles

An art historian once described Lao art as a provincial version of the art of Thailand. He was obviously quite ignorant of the existence of **Lao textiles**. Indeed, in discussions about art, Lao textiles are often overlooked or relegated to the level of "handicraft". Recently, though, Lao textiles have begun enjoying the recognition that they deserve.

The matrilineal society of the lowland Lao and tribal Tai meant that when a man married, he immediately set up house on the property of his new bride's parents. Sometimes this entailed leaving his home village and subsequently, when this couple's son came of age, he would do the same. With such a custom, men's roots in a village were never deep and this was reflected by their simple dress: it told almost nothing of a man's background. Women, on the other hand, were the heirs to a weaving tradition that reflected their ethnic and geographical origins. Techniques improved with each new generation and were passed on.

Each **ethnic group** had its own particular patterns and colours, which varied from village to village but were still recognizable as belonging to that group. Sometimes, as with the Tai Daeng, these variations were great – indeed, one could fill a hefty book with the myriad designs found in Tai Daeng weaving. According to experts, the "grammar" of a textile can be read to reveal not only the ethnicity of the wearer, but also her marital and financial status. Because all women in a village wove and wore similar patterns and a woman normally wore only what she herself had made, it was apparent at a glance who had mastered the art of weaving – a highly desirable skill in the eyes of young men looking for a prospective bride. Not surprisingly, a woman's most striking apparel was saved for festival days when all the young men from the village and beyond would be in attendance.

The many years of war in Laos had a predictable effect on textile weaving. Quality weaving requires peace and stability. Refugees fleeing a war are unlikely to take their looms along with them, especially the heavy bed-sized looms of the lowland Lao. Looms can be rebuilt once conditions improve but, by sad coincidence, peace in Laos was accompanied by the introduction of inexpensive, mass-produced textiles. The importance that Lao mothers once placed on teaching their daughters the secrets of the loom rapidly faded. As a result, however, antique pieces have become highly sought-after collectables, and museums as far afield as Australia have hired textile experts to scour Lao villages for examples of nineteenth- and early twentieth-century Lao weaving.

Laos's ethnic mosaic

While many of Southeast Asia's nations are ethnically diverse, Laos is one of the few that is still visibly so. That is to say, it is one of the last countries whose minorities have not been totally assimilated into the culture of the majority. This is partially because the majority is only in the majority by a thin margin and partially due to the relatively short period of time that the majority has had to reshape the country in its own image.

In an effort at categorization, the Lao government officially divides the population into three groups. Which group an ethnicity fits into is determined by the **elevation** at which that ethnicity dwells; thus many unrelated ethnic groups may be grouped together if they reside at one elevation. This method of categorization may be seen as a tenuous majority's subtle means of proclaiming cultural superiority over its sizeable population of minorities while at the same time trying to bring them into the fold. In this section we discuss two of these three groups, namely the **lowland Lao** and the **Mon–Khmer groups** who live at somewhat higher elevations; the third group is covered by the separate colour section on the **hill tribes**.

The lowland Lao

The so-called **Lao Loum** (or lowland Lao) live at the lowest elevations and on the land best suited for cultivation. For the most part, they are the **ethnic Lao**, a people related to the Thai of Thailand and the Shan of Burma. The lowland Lao make up between fifty and sixty percent of the population, and are the

△ The *basi* ceremony

group for which the country is named. They, like their Thai and Shan cousins, prefer to inhabit river valleys, live in dwellings that are raised above the ground, and are adherents of Theravada Buddhism. Laos is by no means the only place where ethnic Lao dwell. Most of Thailand's northeastern region is populated with ethnic Lao and, owing to internal migration patterns caused by economic factors, Bangkok has the largest concentration of ethnic Lao anywhere. This fact is not lost on the Lao of Laos who feel that history has deprived them of much of their original territory.

Of all the ethnicities found in Laos, the culture of the lowland Lao is dominant, mainly because it is they who hold political power. Their language is the official language, their religion is the state religion and their holy days are the official holidays. As access to a reliable water source is key to survival and water is abundant in the river valleys, the ethnic Lao have prospered. They have been able to devote their free time – that time not spent securing food – to the arts and entertainment, and their culture has become richer for it. Among the cultural traits by which the Lao define themselves are the cultivation and consumption of sticky rice as a staple, the taking part in the animist ceremony known as *basi* (see p.66), and the playing of the reed instrument called the *khaen*.

Akin to the ethnic Lao are the Tai Leu, Phuan and Phu Tai, found in the northwest, the northeast and mid-south respectively. The **Tai Leu** of Laos are originally from China's Xishuangbanna region in southern Yunnan, where nowadays they are known as the "Dai minority". In Laos, their settlements stretch from the Chinese border with Louang Namtha province, through Oudomxai and into Xainyabouli; among foreign visitors, the best known Tai Leu settlement is Muang Sing. The Tai Leu are Theravada Buddhists and, like the Lao, they placate animist spirits. They are known to perform a ceremony similar to the *basi* ceremony which is supposed to reunite the wayward souls of their water buffalo. They are also skilled weavers whose work is in demand from other groups that do not weave, such as the Khamu.

The **Phuan** are in the same historical predicament as such Southeast Asian peoples as the Mon and Cham: they were once a recognized kingdom, but are now largely forgotten. The kingdom's territory, formerly located in the province of Xiang Khouang (the capital of which was formerly known as Muang Phuan), was at once coveted by the Siamese and Vietnamese. Aggression from both sides as well as from Chinese Haw bandits left the kingdom in ruins and the populace scattered. A British surveyor in the employ of a Siamese king reached Muang Phuan in the 1880s and remarked that the Phuan "exhibited refinement in all they did, but their elegant taste was of no avail against the rude barbarian". To this day, there are villages of Phuan as far afield as central Thailand, inhabited by the descendants of Phuan villagers who were taken captive by the Siamese during military campaigns over a hundred years ago.

The Phuan are Theravada Buddhists, but once observed an impromptu holy day known as *kam fa*. When the first thunder of the season was heard, all labours ceased and villagers avoided any activity that might cause even the slightest noise. The village's fortune was then divined based on the direction from which the thunder was heard.

The **Phu Tai** of Savannakhet and Khammouane provinces are also found in the northeast of Thailand. They are Theravada Buddhists and have assimilated into Lao culture to a high degree, although it is still possible to recognize them by their dress on festival days. The predominant colours of the Phu Tai shawls and skirts are an electric purple and orange with yellow and lime-green highlights.

The "tribal Tai"

Other Tai peoples related to the Lao are the so-called "**tribal Tai**", who live in river valleys at slightly higher elevations and are mostly animists. These include the rather mysteriously named Tai Daeng (Red Tai), Tai Khao (White Tai) and Tai Dam (Black Tai). Theories about nomenclature vary. It is commonly surmised that the names were derived from the predominant colour of the womenfolk's dress, but others have suggested that the groups were named after the river valleys in northern Vietnam where they were thought to have originated. These Tai groups were once loosely united in a political alliance called the **Sipsong Chao Tai** or the Twelve Tai Principalities, spread over an area that covers parts of northwestern Vietnam and northeastern Laos. The traditional centre was present-day **Dien Bien Phu**, known to the Tai as Muang Theng. When the French returned to Indochina after World War II, they attempted to establish a "Tai Federation" encompassing the area of the old Principalities. The plan was short-circuited by Ho Chi Minh who, after defeating the French, was able to manipulate divisions between the Tai groups in order to gain total control.

The **Tai Dam** are found in large numbers in Houa Phan and Xiang Khouang provinces, but also inhabit northern Laos as far west as Louang Namtha. This ethnic group are principally animists and have a system of Vietnamese-influenced surnames that indicate political and social status. The women are easily recognized by their distinctive dress: long-sleeved, tight-fitting blouses in bright, solid colours with a row of butterfly-shaped silver buttons down the front and a long, indigo-coloured skirt. The outfit is completed with a bonnet-like headcloth of indigo with red trim.

Mon–Khmer groups

The ethnic Lao believe themselves and their ethnic kin to have inhabited an area that is present-day Dien Bien Phu in Vietnam before migrating into what is now Laos. Interestingly, there is historical evidence to support their legends. As the Lao moved southwards they displaced the original inhabitants of the region. Known officially as the **Lao Theung** (*theung* is Lao for "above"), but colloquially known as the *kha* ("slaves"), these peoples were forced to resettle at higher elevations where water was more scarce and life decidedly more difficult.

The **Khamu** of northern Laos are thought to number around 350,000, making them one of the largest minority groups in Laos. Speakers of a Mon–Khmer language, they have assimilated to a high degree and are practically indistinguishable from the ethnic Lao to outsiders. Their origins are obscure. Some theorize that the Khamu originally inhabited China's Xishuangbanna region in southern Yunnan and migrated south into northern Laos long before the arrival of the Lao. The Khamu themselves tell legends of their being northern Laos's first inhabitants and of having founded Louang Phabang. Interestingly, royal ceremonies once performed annually by the Lao king at Louang Phabang symbolically acknowledged the Khamu's original ownership of the land. The Khamu are known for their honesty and diligence, though in the past they were easily duped by the lowland Lao into performing menial labour for little compensation. Their lack of sophistication in business matters and seeming complacency with their lot in life probably led to their being referred to as "slaves" by the lowland Lao. Unlike other groups in Laos, the Khamu are not known for their weaving skills and so customarily traded labour for cloth. The traditional Khamu village has four cemeteries: one for adults who died normal deaths, one for those who died violent or unnatural deaths, one for children and one for mutes.

A large spirit house located outside the village gates attests to the Khamu belief in **animism**. Spirits are thought to inhabit animals, rice and even money. Visitors to the village must call from outside the village gate, enquiring whether or not a temporary village taboo is in place. If so, then a visitor may not enter, and water, food and a mat to rest on will be brought out by the villagers. If there is no taboo in effect, male visitors may lodge in the village common-house if an overnight stay is planned, but may not sleep in the house of another family unless a blood sacrifice is made to the ancestors. There is no ban on women visitors staying the night in a Khamu household as it is thought to be the property of the women residents.

The village common-house also serves as a home for adolescent boys, and it is there that they learn how to weave baskets and make animal traps as well as become familiar with the village folklore and taboos. The boys may learn that the sound of the barking deer is an ill omen when a man is gathering materials with which to build a house, or that it is wrong to bring meat into the village from an animal that has been killed by tiger or has died on its own. Young Khamu men seem to be prone to wanderlust, often leaving their villages to seek work in the lowlands. Their high rate of intermarriage with other groups during their forays for employment has contributed to their assimilation.

Another Mon–Khmer-speaking group which inhabits the north, particularly Xainyabouli province, are the **Htin**. They excel at fashioning household implements, particularly baskets and fish traps, from bamboo (owing to a partial cultural ban on the use of any kind of metal), and are known for their vast knowledge of the different species of bamboo and their respective uses.

Linguistically related to the Khamu and Htin are the **Mabri**, Laos's least numerous and least developed minority. Thought to number less than one hundred, the Mabri have a taboo on tilling the soil which has kept them semi-nomadic and impoverished. Half a century ago they were nomadic hunter-gatherers who customarily moved camp as soon as the leaves on the branches that comprised their temporary shelters began to turn yellow. Known to the Lao as *kha tawng leuang* ("slaves of the yellow banana leaves") or simply *khon pa* ("jungle people"), the Mabri were thought by some to be naked savages or even ghosts, and wild tales were circulated about their fantastic hunting skills and ability to vanish into the forest without a trace. The Mabri were said to worship their long spears, making offerings and performing dances for their weapons to bring luck with the hunt. Within the last few decades, however, they have given up their nomadic lifestyle and now work for other groups, performing menial tasks in exchange for food or clothing.

The Bolaven Plateau in southern Laos is named for the **Laven** people, yet another Mon–Khmer-speaking group whose presence predates that of the Lao. The Laven were very quick to assimilate the ways of the southern Lao, so much so that a French expansionist and amateur ethnologist who explored the plateau in the 1870s found it difficult to tell the two apart. Besides the Laven, other Mon–Khmer-speaking minorities are found in the south, particularly in Savannakhet, Salavan and Xekong provinces. Among these are the **Bru**, who have raised the level of building animal traps and snares to a fine art. The Bru have devised traps to catch, and sometimes kill, everything from mice to elephants, including a booby-trap that thrusts a spear into the victim.

The **Gie-Trieng** of Xekong are one of the most isolated of all the tribal peoples, having been pushed deep into the bush by the rival Sedang tribe. The Gie-Trieng are expert basket weavers and their tightly woven quivers, smoked a deep mahogany colour, are highly prized by collectors. The **Nge**, also of Xekong, produce textiles bearing a legacy of the Ho Chi Minh Trail that snaked through their territory and of American efforts to bomb it out of existence. Designs on woven shoulder bags feature stylized bombs and fighter planes, and men's loincloths are decorated with rows of tiny lead beads, fashioned from the munitions junk that litters the region.

The **Alak** and **Katu** have of late been brought to the attention of outsiders by Lao tour agencies who are eager to cash in on the tribal custom of sacrificing water buffalo, in a ceremony reminiscent of the final scene in the film *Apocalypse Now*. The Katu are said to be a very warlike people and, as recently as the 1950s, carried out human sacrifices to placate spirits and ensure a good harvest. The ethnic Lao firmly believe that these southern Mon–Khmer groups are adept at black magic, and advise visitors to keep a cake of fragrant soap on their person to foil the sorcery of tribal witchdoctors.

The environment

A landlocked state in the heart of tropical Southeast Asia, Laos covers a land area of nearly 237,000 square kilometres, a size comparable to that of England. Laos is dominated by rugged highlands cut by narrow river valleys and shares in two of Southeast Asia's most prominent geographical features: the **Annamite Mountains** and the **Mekong River**, with the Mekong picking up more than half of its water flow during its nearly two thousand-kilometre journey through Laos.

With a heat and humidity typical of a tropical region, Laos's climate nourishes a natural wealth of wildlife that includes rare or endangered species. Early French explorers marvelled at the sheer beauty of Laos's landscape, as they dodged tigers and collected samples of strange and wonderful insects. Indeed, the country's former name, the Kingdom of a Million Elephants, boasts of these tropical riches. In the recent past, Laos has surprised the scientific world with a new species of plant or animal life discovered or redis-covered in the country's forests and rivers. Sadly, Laos's natural wonders have been greatly diminished since the late nineteenth century – there are at most a few thousand elephants roaming the country's frontiers today, and the forest continues to shrink each year. Despite the efforts of a handful of concerned international groups, the Lao government's efforts at **conservation** have been half-hearted and ineffectual. Lucrative **logging** and **mining** contracts have been awarded to Chinese and Vietnamese firms, bringing riches to government and military officials but leaving the environment much poorer as a result. Likewise, the **damming** of Lao rivers to generate hydroelectricity that can be sold to neighbouring countries is seen as a way for Laos to generate capital, but the ill effects that dams and the reservoirs behind them have on the environment are often ignored.

Climate and geography

Laos has a **tropical monsoon climate**, with a rainy season extending from May to October, a cool dry season from November to February and an at times excruciatingly hot dry season in March and April. Although the rainy season occurs at roughly the same time throughout the country, rainfall varies significantly from place to place, with the highest amounts – 3700mm annually – soaking the Bolaven Plateau in the far south, and considerably less falling in Mekong River cities such as Savannakhet (1440mm), Vientiane (1700mm) and Louang Phabang (1360mm). Such high average rainfall fail to reveal the fact that in some years droughts severely affect rice yields.

Agriculture plays a significant role in Laos's economy as the vast majority of people in Laos live off the land. Rice, as the cornerstone of the Lao diet, accounts for eighty percent of agricultural land. For the most part, farmers employ one of two cultivation systems when growing rice. In the lowlands, farmers generally practise the wet-field paddy system, while swidden cultivation (also known as shifting or slash-and-burn agriculture) is primarily employed in the highlands. Large level areas along the Vientiane Plain, in Savannakhet and in Champasak are perhaps the areas best suited for extensive paddy rice cultivation in the country, and these places have not surprisingly emerged as the country's population centres. Other crops include cardamom, coffee, corn, cotton, fruit, peanuts, soybeans, mung beans, sugarcane, sweet potatoes, tobacco and various vegetables.

Swidden cultivation techniques practised by the Lao Theung and Lao Soung date back thousands of years and vary from group to group, with some peoples living in permanent villages around which they rotate cultivation within a large swath of forest, and others shifting their settlements from hillside to hillside. Nearly all midland and upland groups rely on swidden rice cultivation. A debate over the practice rages among environmentalists, with some charging that the technique is highly destructive to the forest and others arguing that, when practised correctly in a sparsely populated environment, such as is found throughout many parts of Laos, swidden cultivation is sustainable and keeps the soil fertile and the forests in balance.

The Lao government has used shifting agriculture among tribal peoples, especially the Hmong, as a reason to forcibly **resettle** thousand of highland families. The stated policy is to protect forest habitats and to bring hill peoples closer to community resources such as hospitals and schools. While this may have been beneficial for forests, the effects on resettled peoples are often no less than disastrous.

The Mekong

With such a limited land base for agriculture, it's no surprise that **freshwater ecosystems** are of massive importance to Laos. The heart and soul of Laos's freshwater ecosystems is the **Mekong River**, the longest river in Southeast Asia, and, in terms of volume, the tenth largest in the world, carrying 475,000 million cubic metres to the sea each year. With the beginnings of its 4180-kilometre journey in a frozen stream high up in the Plateau of Tibet, the Mekong travels the entire length of Laos before slipping through Cambodia and fanning out into the "Nine Dragons" that constitute the river's delta in Vietnam. The Mekong is joined by fourteen major tributaries during the course of its 1993-kilometre journey through Laos. Nearly all the rivers and mountain streams in the country eventually find their way into the Mekong, as ninety percent of Laos drains into the river.

Rural life revolves around the Mekong River System, which encompasses everything from the myriad mountain streams to the flooded rice paddies to the river itself. It generates power, waters crops, provides a place to bathe and is an all-important source of fish. In most of lowland Laos, as well as in many parts of the highlands, fish and other aquatic animals provide more than seventy percent of the animal protein in people's diet. Nowhere in Laos is this more evident than in the country's southernmost tip, where every family fishes and every meal includes something from the Mother of Waters. It is in this region that the Mekong expands to attain its greatest width – 14km at the height of the rainy season – and journeys through the country's best known **wetlands**: Si Phan Don and the Khone Falls. These wetlands are of regional importance, as a nesting ground for birds and a spawning ground for fish, and are home to the rare Irrawaddy dolphin, whose numbers are in a drastic state of decline (see p.395).

Forests

To know the Mekong, as *Mekong Currency* author Liesbeth Sluiter says, one must meet the forests, which possess an intimate relationship with the river and its tributaries; forests soak up the rains of the monsoon, slowly releasing the water into streams and back into the air. The country is dominated by mixed **deciduous forests**, in which trees survive lengthy periods of minimal rainfall by shedding their leaves in order to conserve water. Tall, pale-barked **dipterocarps**, a group of tropical hardwoods prized for their timber, tower over these monsoon forests, ranging in height from ten to forty metres. Natural stands of teak, rosewood and mahogany were once common features of Laos's deciduous forests, though these much sought-after hardwoods, considered ideal material for building everything from furniture to the decks of yachts, have been substantially reduced in number.

Bamboo, hardly in short supply, thrives in Laos's monsoon climate and appears in more varieties in Laos than in any other country with the exception of two of Laos's neighbours, China and Thailand. Growing at astonishing rates during the rainy season, bamboo rules the understorey of the deciduous forests, surviving in soils too poor for many other types of vegetation and dominating secondary forests – those areas where a new generation of plants has grown up after forest has been stripped bare by swidden agriculture, rampant logging or the harsh excesses of chemical defoliants. Flexible bamboo is used by the Lao for making everything from houses to Laos's national musical instrument, the *khaen*, while bamboo shoots find their way into a variety of Lao dishes. Other, less common forest types in Laos include dry dipterocarp forests, noteworthy for their more open canopies and found along the arid plateaus of southern Laos; and rare old growth pine forests and semi-evergreen and hill evergreen forests, the latter soaked by frequent rainfall and possessing moss-covered forest floors and dense undergrowth.

Conservation zones and wetlands

In the early 1990s, the government of Laos established a system of **National Biodiversity Conservation Areas** throughout the country, which put under protection more than twelve percent of the country's total land area, one of the highest ratios in the world. However, that has not stopped the Lao government from leasing logging and mining concessions within NBCAs. Forests have been particularly damaged in the south along the Vietnamese border – where until recently never before seen species were turning up – and in the northeast.

Ironically, many of the roads that run through these areas were cut due to the need to get logging vehicles in and the valuable timber out. In time perhaps these roads will be paved and plied by regular transport. As yet only a few parts of the conservation areas are accessible and open for tourism – such as the caves of the Khammouane Limestone NBCA near Thakhek; most are well off the beaten track. A survey of some of the more interesting areas follows.

Southern Laos

Flush against the Vietnam border in Khammouane and Bolikhamxai provinces and to the south of Lak Xao, the **Nakai–Nam Theun** is without question one of the world's more important biodiversity areas. Indeed, three of the last five large mammals to be discovered or rediscovered worldwide inhabit this area. A lost world of evergreen forests, savanna and jagged, mist-shrouded peaks, the Nakai–Nam Theun is one of the richest wildlife and forest areas remaining in Southeast Asia. It is best known for the recent discovery of the saola, a large mammal resembling a shaggy brown and white deer with spindly horns; and the giant-antlered muntjak and the black muntjack, as well as the rediscovery of the Indochinese warty pig, which had been described a century ago – by a Jesuit priest in Shanghai who purchased a few skulls of the creature from southern Vietnam in 1892 – before being lost to science.

Once a royal hunting reserve, this area is now the largest single "protected" area in Laos, extending over 3700 square kilometres, with an elevation ranging from 500m on the Nakai Plateau to mountain peaks of well over 2000m, and is home to at least eleven globally threatened large mammal species. Its forests provide habitat for most of the mainland Southeast Asia fauna, including such rare animals as tiger, lesser slow loris, clouded leopard – a small tree-dwelling cat which hunts birds and monkeys by night – Asiatic black bear and elephant. More than four hundred bird species, among them the endangered white-winged duck, crested argus, beautiful nuthatch and greater spotted eagle, have been recorded here, the highest diversity of any site surveyed in Laos. The area is also noteworthy for its forests, composed of stands of wet and dry evergreen, cypress forest, old growth pine, found only in parts of Southeast Asia, and riverside forest – all of which are regionally threatened habitats. Nakai–Nam Theun is also treasured for its four river systems. However, their hydroelectric potential now figures large in national development plans, which involve the construction of the **Theun–Hin Boun Dam**, west of the NBCA, and the massive **Nam Theun 2**, which when completed will flood 450 square kilometres of forest, put nearly 400 elephants at risk, and require the resettlement of at least 1000 families.

Further south, spectacular waterfalls plunge from soaring escarpments cloaked with pristine evergreen forests in **Dong Hua Sao**, a 910-square-kilometre zone to the east of Pakxe and the south of Pakxong, which encompasses a flat, upland area along the Bolaven – of immense floral and faunal interest – and the lowlands along the Plateau's southern flank. With its habitat further diversified by the presence of sandstone flats and wetlands, Dong Hua Sao is home to nearly 250 species of birds, including the rare Siamese fireback, green peafowl and red-collared woodpecker as well as primates, including the endangered douc langur and gibbons, sun bear and the world's largest species of wild cattle, the gaur, once a prized trophy among big game hunters during colonial times.

Shadowing the Laos–Cambodia border and spanning the southern stretches of Attapu and Champasak provinces, the **Xe Pian** is for the most part covered by semi-evergreen forest, interspersed with tracts of dry dipterocarp forest. Wetlands and riverine systems are also an important feature of the Xe Pian, which takes its name from the snaking Xe Pian River that bisects the reserve's eastern and southern flatlands. As home to eight threatened bird species, the protected area is of global significance for wildlife conservation and supports numerous lowland bird species as well as a wealth of migrants. Woolly-necked storks and nesting sarus cranes are both thought to inhabit the wetlands of the Xe Pian. Gibbons also fill the central forests of the Xe Pian with their unmistakable hooting, and villagers have reported seeing kouprey, the elusive grey forest ox whose global population is thought to number no more than three hundred, hog deer and Eld's deer, as well as wild water buffalo and rhinoceros. Rhino horns are prized by the Lao, who believe them to possess magical properties, and the Chinese, who consider them a useful ingredient in aphrodisiacs. Black bears, sun bears, peacocks, leopards and otters, hunted for their skins which are sold to Cambodians, have also been spotted in the area, as have two rare river creatures: the Irrawaddy dolphin, which is said to still pay seasonal visits to the Xe Pian, and the Siamese crocodile, already extinct in most Southeast Asian rivers.

Just west of the Xe Pian lie two **wetlands** of regional significance, Si Phan Don and the Khone Falls. Here, the Mekong concludes its journey through Laos, swirling past the countless outcroppings of soil and rocks that constitute the "Four Thousand Islands" of the region's name. Considered the richest fishing grounds in Laos, Si Phan Don possesses large tracts of seasonally flooded forest, along the banks of the Mekong and on the dots of land in between, which constitute a crucial spawning ground for the unknown number of fish species inhabiting this portion of the river. At the southern tip of Si Phan Don – and the entire country for that matter – lie the Khone Falls, an eight-kilometre wide series of channels composed of waterfalls and rapids flowing between rocky islands. The falls, which begin 5km north of the Cambodian border, are a vital passageway for the Mekong's many species of migratory fish.

The seasonally flooded islands here are also an important sanctuary for **birds** and represent one of the last nesting areas of the river tern, greater thick-knees and river lapwing, all of which appear as the water level begins to recede in January. The trees of the wetlands' flooded forests also provide perches for thick-billed pigeons, pied hornbills and green imperial pigeons and offer a welcome spot for blue-tailed bee-eaters to rest after one of their aerial insect chases. The area is also one of the rare places in Southeast Asia visited by red-headed and white-rumped vultures, whose numbers are on the decline owing to hunting and a shortage of food, caused partly by the fact that Laos now has fewer tigers, whose leftovers make a favourite vulture snack. Other rare or endangered birds making the rounds in the area are the grey-headed fish eagle, the woolly-necked stork and the giant ibis.

Beneath the surface, Laos's lower Mekong area possesses a stunning array of **fish species**, including giant golden carp, featherbacks, eels and freshwater rays that grow well over a metre in length, fish that climb the Khone Falls by sucking their way up the rocks with their lips and the mysterious *ba leum*, a fish weighing 200kg that fishermen attempt to snare with the entrails of dogs attached to a hook at the end of a thirty-metre length of rope. But the jewel of the Mekong is without a doubt the blunt-nosed Irrawaddy dolphin, a handful of which still frolic in the waters between Laos and Cambodia.

Central and northern Laos

East of Ang Nam Ngum and less than two hours' drive from Vientiane, centrally located **Phou Khao Khouay** is perhaps the most accessible of the conservation zones and as such must balance its role as a recreational site for Vientiane residents intent on picnicking near its waterfalls and as a preserve for endangered species such as tiger, Asiatic black bear and green peafowl. In this often steep upland area large tracts of evergreen forests dominate the valleys and hillsides, while coniferous and scrub forests flourish in the thin soils masking sandstone bedrock formations at higher elevation.

In the far northern corner of northeastern Houa Phan province, elephants roam the bamboo forests of **Nam Et** protected area, more than half of which lies 1000m above sea level. Nam Et has been severely affected by shifting cultivation which has left the area with relatively little dense forest. As such it may find itself reduced in size in the near future, but nonetheless remains an important refuge for bears, endangered cats, such as the clouded leopard and tiger, wild cattle, and dhole, the rare, reddish wild dogs that hunt in packs. To the southwest of Nam Et, **Phou Loei**, occupying more than 1400 square kilometres in Louang Phabang and Houa Phan provinces, is one of the most important wildlife and evergreen forest conservation areas in northern Laos. Composed of rugged highlands, most of which are well over 1000m, and cut by the Nam Khan and Nam Xuang rivers, Phou Loei has a significant amount of bamboo forests and grasslands resulting from swidden cultivation – still the primary form of agriculture among villagers living in the area. Hunting and fishing with poison present further challenges to managing this NBCA, whose wildlife includes silver pheasants, banteng, hog deer, bears and cats, as do the creation of new settlements in farflung areas noted for their pristine forests.

Environmental issues

In its rush to develop by capitalizing on key natural resources, primarily its wetlands and forests, Laos must come to terms with a number of critical, often interrelated, **environmental issues**. Perhaps the greatest source of concern for conservationists is Laos's many **hydroelectric dam** projects. It is no secret that dams have the potential to cause a serious negative impact on the environment, yet for Laos, the Mekong and its tributaries, with an estimated hydroelectric potential of more than 18,000 megawatts – more than half the river's total estimated potential – represent an alluring means for generating much-needed foreign exchange. Dams, in the view of the International Union for the Conservation of Nature, are not necessarily incompatible with conservation goals; instead, they represent a critical challenge to the integration of conservation and development objectives. No project better illustrates this than the $1.2 billion, 600-megawatt Nam Theun 2 dam which will directly affect the Nakai–Nam Theun conservation zone.

Laos's potential for hydropower development is inextricably linked to its forests, which protect the catchments that provide the water that ultimately generate the energy. **Deforestation** is a major problem, with the country's primary forest cover having steadily declined over the past five decades from an estimated seventy percent at the time of the French withdrawal from Indochina to roughly ten percent today. Laos's forests are threatened by the clearing of lowland forest for permanent agriculture, the use of chemical defoliants during the Second Indochina War, infrastructure development, shifting agriculture, new settlements and logging; large companies from Asian countries continue to win logging concessions from the government.

Developing and enforcing a set of regulations governing logging is a difficult task given the government's limited resources and the vast tracts of forest spread through the country; simply designating biodiversity conservation zones isn't enough to preserve the country's natural wealth. One positive development occurred in 1995, when the governor of Attapu and six other officials from the southeastern province were convicted of timber smuggling. Nonetheless, the case also demonstrated that some of the very people who should be protecting this natural resource are abusing their power by exploiting the forests for their personal gain.

Deforestation places increasing pressure on Laos's rural population, who rely on the forest for food, firewood, construction materials, herbs, medicine and a host of other things. The declining forests also threaten Laos's wildlife, which is already struggling to survive other intense pressures, including **hunting** and the **wildlife trade**. Despite the country's relatively low population density, the level of hunting has increased in recent decades, the result of the increased availability of guns and explosives, improved access to previously remote areas via newly cut logging roads and the exorbitant prices that rare and endangered species fetch on international markets. The gathering of forest products is also on the rise. While much of the wildlife trade is for local food consumption and use in traditional medicine, large quantities of wildlife and wildlife products are sold to Thailand, Vietnam and China. Thus, while posters and pamphlets warning villagers against hunting vulnerable species are visible in government offices and noodle shops throughout the country, elephant ivory, bear paws, pangolin scales, turtle shells, rare types of orchids, tiger parts and bird bills – all highly valued items in this cross-border trade – continue to find their way onto restaurant tables in Hanoi and into traditional medicines in Bangkok and Hong Kong.

Literature and myths

Classical Lao literature has its roots in the **Jataka** tales, a collection of 547 stories about the Buddha's previous lives. The tales recount the events and experiences which led to his incarnation as Siddhartha Gautama, the prince who sought the meaning of life and attained enlightenment. Penned in India and Sri Lanka, they spread with Buddhism to Southeast Asia.

Of more direct impact on Lao literature were an additional fifty tales that employed the same basic theme as the Jataka. Known as the **Panyasa Jataka**, these were perhaps composed by the Mon and abridged by the Tai Yuan of Lan Na, a kingdom centred around Chiang Mai in what is now northern Thailand. Contacts between Chiang Mai and Louang Phabang resulted in the Panyasa Jataka arriving in Laos where the stories were modified and expanded upon. Eventually the Lao versions came to differ significantly from the Tai Yuan versions, in that the former deviated from strict religious themes and became more entertaining, even to the point of having some sexual content.

Two types of story emerged: prose and poetic. Prose stories contained much Pali, the language of the Theravada Buddhist scriptures, and were written in a script called *phasa tham*, or Dharma language. These would have been comprehensible only to monks who had studied the language. Much more popular with lay people were the poetic stories, written using the Lao script and containing mostly Lao vocabulary. As Lao is a tonal language, these poems did not rhyme as poetry composed in English sometimes does. Instead, tones and alliteration were used to produce a rhythm. Both types of stories were recorded by writing on the fronds of a certain kind of palm with a stylus, and some of the longer versions made use of hundreds of palm leaves. These surprisingly durable palm-leaf manuscripts were kept in a special library in the monastery grounds or sometimes in private homes. Occasionally, the stories were copied anew, but there was no pressure on the scrivener, usually a monk, to remain true to the original. The result was literally hundreds of versions and variations of these stories that not only taught values but also contained a wealth of information about traditional Lao society. During certain festivals, villagers would gather at the local monastery or in a private home to hear the stories read aloud and in this way some favourites eventually emerged. The *Sang Sin Sai* in particular is felt by many Lao to be the pinnacle of Lao literature. As with all of these stories, the plot takes a back seat to the poetry itself and the author is obscure. Attributed to "Pangkham", the story is almost certainly the product of many authors and editors.

Today, with the rapid spread of electrical power to all parts of Laos, the novelty of television has meant that the reading of the old stories is not quite the event that it once was. Still, the fact that most ethnic Lao men spend some time in the monastery as a monk or novice ensures that the stories are in no immediate danger of being forgotten.

A tradition of oral folk tales known as **Xiang Miang**, after the name of the central character, were eventually transcribed as both poetry and prose. The stories seem to be almost the opposite of the Jataka-style morality tales: Xiang Miang is a lazy but clever trickster who enjoys outwitting authority figures, especially the king. In a typical exploit he covets the king's prized cat and so decides to kidnap it. Once he has the cat safely home, Xiang Miang teaches it to shun the fresh fish it is accustomed to by beating the cat every time it nears a fish placed on the floor. The cat soon learns to eat rice and when the king

The Ramayana

Of the Indian literature to become established in Southeast Asia, the Hindu **Ramayana** is by far the best known. This epic poem, with its host of vivid characters possessing comic-book hero attributes, arrived in Southeast Asia during its "Indianization" at the hands of Hindu traders. In the original, Hanuman, the King of the Monkeys, assists the god Rama in rescuing his wife Sita from the many-headed, multi-armed demon Ravana.

Once the Ramayana became established in Southeast Asia, however, it didn't take long for local variations to emerge. The inhabitants of Java, Bali, Burma, Cambodia and Thailand all composed their own distinct versions and eventually the story spread from coastal areas into the Indochinese hinterland. Although a version of the poem was well known to the Khmer who once inhabited what is now southern Laos, the Ramayana's introduction to the ethnic Lao came much later via Siam.

French colonization brought scholars who, perhaps because they were already familiar with the Khmer version of the poem, tended to overemphasize the Ramayana's significance to Lao literature, proclaiming it Laos's most important work. Later, Indian scholars, eager to aggrandize the influence of Indian culture in a country they considered an outpost of "Greater India", echoed French opinions. In fact, the Lao version of the Ramayana, known as **Pha Lak Pha Lam**, was never popular at the village level. Suitably modified to suit Lao tastes, it did, however, become a favourite of the Lao court. This popularity is reflected in depictions of the Ramayana in murals and reliefs found at Buddhist monasteries, especially those that were patronized by the monarchy.

arrives to claim his cat, Xiang Miang "proves" it doesn't belong to the king by letting the cat choose between a plate of rice and plate of fish. Knowing that going near the fish will bring on a beating, the cat chooses the rice and the king goes home empty handed.

The present climate for Lao writers living in Laos has been described as "tricky". Laos is still rather **restrictive** in what it will allow to be published, but a few Lao writers manage to make social commentary without the government's approval by publishing in Thailand in the Thai language.

Books and maps

A s Laos is one of the least-known countries in Southeast Asia, it should
be no surprise to find that books about it are hard to come by, to say
nothing of quality works on the country. You're likely to have more luck
searching for many of the titles listed below at an online bookstore such
as ❽www.amazon.com, ❽www.powells.com or Thailand's ❽www.asiabooks
.com than you would wandering the aisles of your local bookshop. While
some books will need to be specially ordered, others, such as those published
by White Lotus in Bangkok, will be easier (and sometimes cheaper) to find at
bookshops in Bangkok or Vientiane.

A number of **maps** of Laos are available internationally, as well as in bookshops in major Thai cities and in Vientiane. Rough Guides' own map of Laos
(along with Vietnam and Cambodia), published in 2006, is printed on tearproof
plastic at a scale of 1:1,200,000. Also worth checking out is the 2005 Laos map
produced by Golden Triangle Rider in Thailand.

In the book reviews below, the abbreviation o/p means "out of print"; titles
marked 🏃 are particularly recommended.

Culture, society and environment

Sucheng Chan (ed) *Hmong Means
Free* (Temple University Press). Fascinating personal narratives by three
generations of Hmong refugees from
five different families, which describe
their lives as farmers on the hilltops
of Laos, as refugees in the camps of
Thailand and as immigrants in the
United States.

Patricia Cheesman *Lao-Tai Textiles:
The Textiles of Xan Neua and Muang
Phuan* (Studio Naenna). Highlighting
two of Laos' most interesting regions
with regards to textiles, and featuring
lots of photos of the eye-catching
patterns and colours that have caught
the attention of textile collectors all
over the world.

Brett Dakin *Another Quiet American* (Asia Books). A very personal
account of contemporary Laos by
an American who lived in Vientiane
during the 1990s.

Natacha Du Pont De Bie *Ant Egg
Soup: the Adventures of a Food Tourist*
(Hodder/Sceptre) A foodie goes to
Laos in search of culinary adventure
– and finds that the Lao have learned
to eat just about anything.

🏃 **Grant Evans** *The Politics of Ritual and Remembrance: Laos Since
1975* (University of Hawaii Press). A
provocative collection of anthropo-
logical essays focusing on the rituals
and social structures of Laos yesterday
and today, and the attempts by the
post-1975 government to reinvent
"Laos".

🏃 **Anne Fadiman** *The Spirit
Catches You and You Fall Down:
A Hmong Child, Her American Doctors, and the Collision of Two Cultures*
(Noonday Press). An excellent exploration of the sad, absorbing tale of
Lia Lee, a severely epileptic child,
born to a family of Hmong refugees
living in California, who clash with
their daughter's Western doctors over
how to treat the child's condition.

Betty Gosling *Old Luang Prabang*
(Oxford University Press). A descrip-
tion of the history, geography and
culture of the former royal capital,
exploring the relationship between
royalty, mythology, religion and ritual.

Stephen Mansfield *Culture Shock!
Laos* (Times Books International). A
cultural starter kit detailing how to

avoid such faux pas as touching your spouse in public, pointing your foot at someone and eating your sticky rice with chopsticks. A helpful introduction if you're off to work in Laos and interesting even if you're only planning an extended visit.

Mayoury Ngaosyvathn *Lao Women: Yesterday and Today* (Lao State Publishing Enterprise). A pioneering study about women in Laos that examines the status of women with regard to family, religion and society. While dissecting Lao women's portrayal in myths, legends and court chronicles, this insightful case also assesses the obstacles preventing women from becoming equal partners in socialist Laos.

Henri Parmentier *L'Art du Laos* (o/p). An excellent source, if it can be tracked down, of rare photographs of Lao temple architecture and art

published by the Ecole Française d'Extrême-Orient in the early 1950s. The text, in French, should be taken with a grain of salt, however, given the overly condescending tone of the author.

Phia Sing et al. *Traditional Recipes of Laos* (Prospect Books). Not only is this one of the rare books explaining how to prepare Lao cuisine, it's the only book containing the recipes of the former royal chef and master of ceremonies of Louang Phabang.

Liesbeth Sluiter *The Mekong Currency* (International Books). An earthy account of green issues along the Mekong corridor, in Laos, Cambodia and Thailand, Sluiter's book does an excellent job of presenting environmental concerns from the perspective of the fishermen and farmers whose livelihoods are sustained by the Mekong and its tributaries.

Travellers' accounts

Marthe Bassenne *In Laos and Siam* (White Lotus). The evocative account of a French expatriate woman's 1909 journey up the Mekong River to Louang Phabang.

Louis Delaporte *A Pictorial Journey on the Old Mekong* (White Lotus). Volume three of the Mekong Exploration Commission's report is devoted to the exquisite illustrations of the artist who accompanied French explorers Francis Garnier and Doudart de Lagrée during their 1866–68 expedition.

Francis Garnier *Travels in Cambodia and Part of Laos* (White Lotus). The English translation of the first volume of the report by France's Mekong Exploration Commission, which set out from Saigon to find a backdoor route to China via the Mekong, details the group's travels from Cambodia to Louang Phabang.

Francis Garnier *Further Travels in Laos and in Yunnan* (White Lotus). Volume two of the Mekong Exploration Commission's report focuses on the weary explorers' travels in Upper Laos and Yunnan, with entries on a Muslim uprising in China and Garnier's explorations of alternative trade routes.

F.J. Harmand *Laos and the Hill Tribes of Indochina* (White Lotus). A cultural barbarian by today's standards, the French explorer nevertheless produced a valuable report on his late-nineteenth-century journey through southern Laos, researching the region's natural history and searching for an overland route from Champasak to Hué. The account, which records funerary and religious customs of the highland tribal minorities of the Bolaven Plateau, also focuses on his encounters with the Phu Tai people of the Savannakhet region, and is liberally sprinkled with amusing and insightful anecdotes.

Harry Hervey *King Cobra: An Autobiography of Travel in French Indo-China* (o/p). An American writer's account of his journey from Saigon to Vientiane, where he mingles with French expatriates and Lao royalty. Although his historical facts are often quite askew, Hervey, who sought to unlock the mysteries of the Angkorian empire, is a rare traveller for the early twentieth century, offering open-minded observations recorded in lush, detailed prose.

Henri Mouhot *Travels in Siam, Cambodia, and Laos* (White Lotus, Bangkok). The account of the final journey of the legendary "discoverer of Angkor Wat", filled with his characteristically blunt observations of the people of Laos, from the tobacco-hungry infants to the uncouth court officials that he encountered on his journey to Upper Laos which resulted in his death outside Louang Phabang.

History

Laos: A Country Study (Federal Research Division). One in a continuing series of books prepared by the Federal Research Division of the United States Library of Congress, this comprehensive (though somewhat outdated) study provides background and analysis of Laos's economic, social and political institutions, as well as the cultural and historical factors shaping them. Also available at ⊛countrystudies.us/laos.

Nina S. Adams and Alfred W. McCoy (eds) *Laos: War and Revolution* (o/p). A gem of a book, albeit somewhat dated, collecting political speeches, historical essays on subjects from Air America to the ancient Thai–Vietnamese struggle over the country, interviews with Lao politicians and refugees, and essays by French journalists and Vietnamese soldiers. With an academic leftist slant, the book arose out of the desire of the Committee of Concerned Asian Scholars to remedy the lack of information regarding Laos available during the United States' "bitter war against the people of Laos".

Kennon Breazeale and Snit Smuckarn *A Culture in Search of Survival: The Phuan of Thailand and Laos* (Yale University Press). An impressive history tracing the migrations and forced resettlements during the nineteenth century of the Phuan people of Xiang Khouang.

🏃 **Jane Hamilton-Merritt** *Tragic Mountains: the Hmong, the Americans, and the Secret Wars for Laos, 1942–1992* (Indiana University Press). This impressive account of the Hmong, written by a Pulitzer Prize-nominated correspondent during the Second Indochina War, ranges from the personal to the political as it follows the Hmong from the battlefields to life after the war.

Victor T. King *Explorers of Southeast Asia: Six Lives* (Oxford University Press). Six different authors examine the journeys of various nineteenth-century European explorers, including Frenchmen Henri Mouhot and Francis Garnier.

Christopher Kremmer *Bamboo Palace: Discovering the Lost Dynasty of Laos* (HarperCollins). A continuation of the author's earlier *Stalking the Elephant Kings*, which tracked his journey into remote Laos in search of the monarch who disappeared shortly after the communists took over in 1975. By interviewing a former inmate of Laos' re-education camps, Kremmer is able to piece together the last days of the royal family, some of whom perished due to harsh living conditions in the caves of Houa Phan province.

Alfred W. McCoy *The Politics of Heroin: CIA Complicity in the Global Drug Trade* (Lawrence Hill Books). Laos, not surprisingly, figures prominently in this exhaustively researched, revised and expanded version of McCoy's landmark *The Politics of Heroin in Southeast Asia*.

Mayoury Ngaosyvathn and Pheuiphanh Ngaosyvathn *Paths of Conflagration: Fifty Years of Diplomacy and Warfare (1778–1828)* (Ithaca). A re-examination of the relationship between Laos and Thailand which draws on a wealth of new source material in examining Chao Anou, the Lao king who rebelled against Siamese suzerainty during the early nineteenth century.

Christopher Robbins *The Ravens: Pilots of the Secret War of Laos* (o/p). Although difficult to find, this book on America's secret war is well worth reading. Many of the details of America's secretive Laos operations during the Second Indochina War didn't come out until this gripping work by Robbins, a British journalist, was published in 1987. Based on interviews with American pilots who fought in Laos, this hard-to-find book is well worth tracking down.

Stan Sesser *The Lands of Charm and Cruelty: Travels in Southeast Asia* (Picador/Vintage Departures). Among the five insightful essays in this superb book is a 53-page segment on Laos during the late 1980s and early 1990s. In presenting a well-observed account of the country as it struggles to rebuild itself after the war, Sesser mixes reflections on Laos's recent history with insights into the country's political leadership, culture and economic reforms. The book builds on articles Stesser originally wrote for *The New Yorker*.

Martin Stuart-Fox *A History of Laos* (Cambridge University Press). Written by an Australian scholar who covered the Second Indochina War as a foreign correspondent, this work represents the best available overview of Laos's history, although it's extremely light on the country's early history.

Martin Stuart-Fox *Buddhist Kingdom Marxist State* (White Lotus, Bangkok). Fox outlines the history and politics of modern Laos from French rule to the present, with particular emphasis on the Lao PDR during the Pathet Lao's first two decades in power.

Martin Stuart-Fox and Mary Kooyman *Historical Dictionary of Laos* (Scarecrow Press). A encyclopedia of key people and events in the history of Laos which, though expensive and difficult to find, is worthwhile for the many insightful nuggets of information tracked down by the authors, and the extensive bibliography.

John Tenhula *Voices from Southeast Asia: The Refugee Experience in the United States* (Holmes & Meier). A moving collection of oral histories, told through narrative, dialogue and poetry, of Indochinese refugees, many of whom have relocated to the United States.

Roger Warner *Shooting at the Moon: The Story of America's Clandestine War in Laos* (Steerforth Press). Winner of the Overseas Press Club's award for the best book on foreign affairs, Warner's thoroughly researched and crisply written account of American involvement reads like an adventure novel. Letting tragic events speak for themselves, Warner brings to life the key players and significant events as he follows the secret war from its origins at the end of World War II to the American withdrawal from Indochina.

Language

Language

Language

L ao belongs to the Tai family of languages, which includes Thai; Shan (Tai Yai), spoken in Myanmar (Burma); Phuan, spoken in Laos and parts of Thailand; and Tai Leu, spoken by the Dai minority of southern China's Yunnan province. Besides Lao and its "cousin" languages, such as Tai Leu and Phuan, sundry other languages are spoken within the borders of Laos. These include tongues belonging to the Mon–Khmer and Tibeto–Burman families of languages which are spoken by upland tribal peoples, as well as Vietnamese and Chinese spoken by immigrants from Laos's neighbouring countries.

French was once the second language of the educated and elite classes, and fluent French-speakers may be found among the over-50s, usually an indication that they were once functionaries of the old royal regime. But despite subsidies from the French government to open a French-language school in Vientiane and convince the Lao government to display French-language signage at government offices, French has fallen out of favour. Since economic liberalization came into effect, **English** has become the preferred foreign tongue among the younger generation, who are convinced that learning English is the key to obtaining a high-paying job in the tourism sector. During the 1980s, Lao students were sent to study abroad in fellow Soviet-bloc countries such as Poland, East Germany and Cuba, and hence it is sometimes possible to find a Polish-, German- or Spanish-speaking Lao, though they will be the first to admit that their language ability has become rusty with years of disuse.

Travellers will find that getting around in urban areas can be done using basic English. Once out in the countryside, however, the situation changes, and visitors will have to make an effort to learn some Lao phrases to get by. Travellers shouldn't feel too put out if they consider that urban Lao sometimes experience similar problems when travelling in rural areas.

One of the greatest obstacles to building a nation that successive Lao governments have had to deal with is language. While Lao as it is spoken in Vientiane has official language status, there are pockets of Laos where no dialect of Lao, much less the Vientiane version, will be heard. With little money or resources to post qualified teachers to isolated villages, **Vientiane Lao** is simply not being learned in these areas. The Lao government has experimented with the somewhat drastic step of relocating tribal children to lowland towns where they live in huts in the school grounds and where, theoretically, they are exposed to language and lifestyles that will help them assimilate and become more "Lao". In the meantime, many of the non-Lao-speaking ethnic groups in rural areas will continue to live as they always have done, speaking their own tongue among themselves while maintaining a handful of Lao phrases to conduct trade or other dealings with the lowland Lao.

To fully understand the contemporary state of the Lao language in urban areas, it is necessary to look at how it relates to Thai. The spoken Thai of Bangkok and the spoken Lao of Vientiane are similar, as akin as Spanish is to Portuguese. As vassals of the Thai, the Lao absorbed a fair amount of Thai vocabulary, mainly through the Buddhist monkhood and channels between the royal courts. This shared vocabulary was, for the most part, taken from **Pali**, in which the scriptures of Theravada Buddhism were written. During the Lao civil war, Thailand sided with the Lao royalists. The communist victory and death of the Lao monarchy saw the end of flowery court language, but although the communist government temporarily suppressed Lao Buddhism, no direct attacks on Pali-derived vocabulary were mounted. Some aspects of everyday spoken and written Lao were targeted, however. In an effort to erase class divisions, the communist government discouraged the use of personal pronouns that flaunted status or begged servitude. A typical banned pronoun was "*doi kha noi*", which translates into English as "I" but which literally means "I, small slave". Such a personal pronoun would have been used in the old days by a commoner speaking to a superior of noble rank.

After the revolution the Lao government also made official changes to the **Lao alphabet** in order to simplify it, as well as purge it of aspects that the communists felt were too similar to Thai. The Lao government's policies had, for a time anyway, the desired effect of levelling class divisions, and the simplified alphabet has no doubt made teaching the illiterate to read an easier task. However, the changes and simplifications have had an unforeseen effect on the Lao language. What the government didn't anticipate was the growing sophistication of the **Thai media** and subsequent boom in popularity of Thai films, television and popular music in Laos. Every day, tens of thousands of Lao tune in to receive a dose of Thai, with its stratified personal pronouns and honorifics. Even broadcasts of the Thai royal language, almost identical to the extinct Lao royal language, can be heard daily on the Thai television news. These factors have conspired to give the Lao something of an inferiority complex about their own language, and they often compare it unfavourably to Thai by saying that Thai sounds more "beautiful" and "polite" than Lao.

Transliteration

Visitors who travel between Laos and Thailand may notice the similarity in the scripts of the two countries. This is because the Lao script was actually based on an early version of written Thai. During colonial times, the French considered replacing the **Lao script** with an alphabet similar to *quoc ngu*, the Romanized script now used to write Vietnamese. The project was never implemented, as French influence was waning at the time, but devising the system presented quite a challenge. The Lao language contains sounds that don't exist in French, or any other Western European language for that matter, making transliteration an inexact exercise at best.

Imperfect as it was, the fledgling **French transliteration system** has had some staying power. The Lao seem comfortable with the French system, and many educated Lao prefer to have their names transliterated in the French manner, which serves to differentiate them from the Thai, who use a different system. Official maps of Laos produced by the Lao government use a modified form of the old French system. This can create problems for English speakers who assume that the system was created for them. But if you keep in mind, for example, that the Lao "ou" rhymes with the French "vous", not the English "noun", reading Lao place names shouldn't be a problem. The transliteration of place names in this book follows the modified French system used by the Lao National Geographic Service. For the transliteration of Lao words in the following section, a simplified version of the same system is used. This is not to say that travellers will find exactly the system in use throughout Laos: the Lao are quite cavalier when it comes to **consistency** in transliteration. In Vientiane, for instance, it is possible to see the Arch of Victory monument transliterated as "Patouxai", "Patousai", "Patuxai" and "Patusai".

Consonants

b as in big

d as in dog

f as in fun

h as in hello

j (or ch) as in jar

k as in skin (unaspirated)

kh as kiss

l as in luck

m as in more

n as in now

ng as in singer (this combination sometimes appears at the beginning of a word)

ny as in the Russian nyet

p as in speak (unaspirated)

ph as in pill

s (or x) as in same

t as in stop (unaspirated)

th as in tin

w (or v) as in wish

y as in yes

Vowels

a as in autobahn

ae as in cat

ai as in Thai

aw as in jaw

ao as in Lao

e as in pen

eu as in French fleur

i as in mimi

ia as in India

o as in flow

oe as in Goethe

u (or ou) as in you

ua (or oua) as the UA in truant

Tones and markers

Lao is a **tonal language**, which means that the tone a speaker gives to a word will determine its meaning. While the tone system may make some visitors despair of ever learning any Lao, mastering a handful of simple phrases will greatly enhance your travels in Laos. The Lao are always delighted by foreigners who make the effort to converse with them in their own language and will reciprocate with more than the usual graciousness.

The dialect of Lao spoken in Vientiane has **six tones**. This is not quite as impossibly complicated as it sounds. In English, tones are used to express emotion or differentiate between a question, statement or exclamation; "Really?" sounds quite different from "Really!" Lao uses these same tones to differentiate between meaning. The Lao word *sang* spoken like a question ("sang?") means "granary" but if spoken as an exclamation ("sang!") it means "elephant". Depending on its tone, *sang* can also mean either "craftsman", "laryngitis", a species of bamboo, or "to build".

Originally, all Lao words were monosyllabic, as with most tonal languages, but with the introduction of Buddhism to Laos, the language began to absorb polysyllabic words from the Indian languages Pali and Sanskrit. Speakers of non-tonal languages generally find these polysyllabic loan words easier to understand and say than the monosyllabic words that rely mostly on tone to be understood.

Since it is impossible to learn the six tones properly without actually hearing them, try getting a speaker of Vientiane Lao to recite **numbers one to nine** in **Lao** to you, since all six tones feature in these numbers (shown on p.374). Number one is a mid tone (unmarked) and since the mid and low tones are so similar, the beginner may pronounce these two tones identically. Number two is a rising tone (~), number five is a low-falling tone (`), number six is a high tone (´), and number nine is a high-falling tone (^).

Lao words and phrases

As a stranger you should remember to utter a greeting first when you meet someone. Questions the Lao commonly ask in conversation may seem personal to Westerners ("Are you married?") but this is simply an indication of the importance of the family in Lao culture. Questions in Lao are not normally answered with a yes or no. Instead the verb used in the question is repeated for the answer; for example: "Do you have a room?" would be answered "Have" in the affirmative or "No have" in the negative.

Greetings and small talk

sabai di	Hello (said with a smile)	jâo mí âi nâwng ják khón	How many brothers and sisters do you have?
sabai di baw	How are you?		
sabai di	I'm fine	jâo taeng ngan léu baw	Are you married yet?
jâo wâo phasã angkit dâi baw	Can you speak English?	taeng ngan lâew	Yes, I'm married
wâo baw dâi	No I can't	yáng baw taeng ngan	No, I'm not married
khói wâo phasã láo dâi nói neung	I only speak a little Lao	jâo mí lûk ják khón	How many kids do you have?
jâo khào jai baw	Do you understand?	mí lûk sãwng khón	I've got two kids
khói baw khào jai	I don't understand	yáng baw mí lûk	I don't have any kids
jâo má tae sãi	Where are you from?	thiàw méuang láo muan baw	Are you enjoying Laos?
khói má tae angkit/ amelika/awsteli/ nyu silaen	I'm from England/ America/Australia/ New Zealand	muan lãi	I'm enjoying it very much
jâo seu nyãng	What's your name?		
khói seu	My name is....	lá kawn	Goodbye
jâo anyu ják pi	How old are you?	sok di	Goodbye (in reply)

Places and directions

pai sãi	Where are you going? (often used as a familiar greeting)	phù la phán kip	One thousand kip per person
		...yu sãi	Where is the...?
pai talat	To the market	bân phak yu sãi	Where is the guesthouse?
pai bân phak	To the guesthouse		
pai hong haem ...	To the ... *Hotel*	thà heuá yu sãi	Where is the boat launch/pier?
pai thà heuá	To the boat launch/pier		
pai khiw lot	To the bus station	hân kãi ya	Drugstore
pai baw	Will you go?	paisani	Post office
pai thao dai	How much will you go for?	sathani tamluat	Police station
		phiphithaphan	Museum

sathanthut thai	Thai embassy	kai	It's far
sathanthut jin	Chinese embassy	baw kai	It's not far
sathanthut wiatnam	Vietnamese embassy	pai sêu sêu	Go straight
... yu kai baw	Is the ... far away?	lîaw khwã	Turn right
doen bin yu kai baw	Is the airport far away?	lîaw sãi	Turn left

Accommodation

mí hàwng wàng baw	Do you have a room?	hàwng suam yu sãi	Where is the toilet?
mí hàwng sãwng tiang baw	Do you have a double room?	si phak ják khéun	How many nights will you stay?
hàwng mí phat lóm baw	Does the room have a fan?	si phak sãwng khéun	I will stay two nights
mûng	Mosquito net	lút lakha baw dâi	Sorry, no discounts
hàwng nâm	Bathroom	het anamai hàwng dâi baw	Can you clean the room?
suam	Toilet	khãw kajae dae	Can I have the room key?
ae yen	Air conditioning		
phà hom	Blankets	yâi hàwng dâi baw	Can I move to another room?
nâm hâwn	Hot water		
khãw beung hàwng kawn dâi baw	Can I see the room?	hàwng nî mí nyung lãi	This room is full of mosquitoes
khéun la thao dai	How much per night?	hàwng nî siãng dang	This room is too noisy
khéun la jét phán kip	Seven thousand kip per night	mí bawlikan sak phà baw	Do you have a laundry service?
lút lakha dâi baw	Can you discount the price?	mí lot thip hâi sao baw	Do you have bicycles for rent?

Shopping

an nî khãi baw	Is this for sale?	jîa hàwng nâm	Toilet paper
thao dai	How much?	thian	Candles
an nî thao dai	How much is this?	ya kan nyung baep jút	Mosquito coils
khói yak sêu...	I'd like to buy ...	koep tae	Flip-flops
ya sùp	Cigarettes	an nî thao dai	How much is this?
ya	Medicine	ngóen dawn khit thao dai	How much is it in dollars?
khãwng kao	Antiques		
khãwng thilaleuk	Souvenirs	khói mí tae ngóen kip	I only have kip
seuà phà	Clothes		
phà mãi	Silk cloth	phaeng lãi	It's very expensive
mí ... baw	Do you have ...?	lút lakha dâi thao dai	How much of a discount can you give?
mí sabu baw	Do you have soap?		
yã si khâew	Toothpaste		
sabu fun	Washing powder		

On the road

lot nî pai ... baw	Does this vehicle go to...?
pai ... thao dai	How much is it to go to...?
sai wela ják sua móng	How many hours will it take?
lot si awk ják móng	What time will the bus depart?
si hâwt ják móng	What time will we arrive?
bawn nang nî wàng baw	Is this seat vacant?
wàng	It's vacant
baw wàng	It's taken
mão lot/heuá dâi baw	Can I hire the vehicle/ boat outright?
mão lot/héua thao dai	How much to hire the vehicle/boat outright?
baw tâwng hap phù doi sãn khon eun	Don't pick up any other passengers
tók lóng lakha baw	Do you agree to the price?
tók lóng	I agree
baw tók lóng	I don't agree
jàwt nî dae	Please stop here
jàwt thai bao dae	Please stop so I can urinate
lot pen nyãng	What's wrong with the vehicle?
jàwt yu nî don baw	Will we be parked here for long?

Emergencies and health

suay dae	Help!
jâo suay khói dâi baw	Can you help me?
mí ubatihet	There's been an accident
khói tâwng kan hã mãw	I need a doctor
khói baw sabai	I'm not well
khói pen khai	I have a fever
thâwng khói baw di	I have diarrhoea
khói jép nák	I'm in a lot of pain
song khói pai hong mãw dae	Please take me to the hospital
khói theuk mã/ngu kát	I've been bitten by a dog/snake
hàwng suam yu sãi	Where is the toilet?
pâm doen thang khãwng khói siã hãi	I lost my passport
kheuang khãwng khói siã hãi	My pack is missing

Common answers to questions

baw hû	I don't know
baw mí	There isn't/aren't any
baw dâi	It cannot be done
baw nàe	It's uncertain

Numbers

0	sun	10	síp
1	neung	11	síp ét
2	sãwng	12	síp sãwng
3	sãm	13	síp sãm
4	si	14	síp si
5	hà	15	síp hà
6	hók	16	síp hók
7	jét	17	síp jét
8	pàet	18	síp pàet
9	kâo	19	síp kâo

20	sao	90	kâo síp	
21	sao ét	100	hôi	
22	sao săwng	200	săwng hôi	
30	săm síp	1000	phán	
31	săm síp ét	2000	săwng phán	
32	săm síp săwng	10,000	síp phán	
40	si síp	50,000	hà síp phán	
50	hà sip	100,000	săen	
60	hók síp	200,000	săwng săen	
70	jét síp	1,000,000	lân	
80	pàet síp	2,000,000	săwng lân	

Days of the week and time

wán thít	Sunday	tawn láeng	Early evening
wán jan	Monday	tawn khám	Late evening
wán angkhán	Tuesday	thiang khéun	Midnight
wán phut	Wednesday	athit nà	Next week
wan phahát	Thursday	athit thi lâew	Last week
wán súk	Friday	deuan nà	Next month
wán săo	Saturday	deuan thi lâew	Last month
mêu ní	Today	pi nà	Next year
mêu wan ní	Yesterday	pi thi lâew	Last year
mêu eun	Tomorrow	tawn ní	Now
tawn sâo	Morning	theua nà	Later
thiang wán	Noon	ta kî	Just now
tawn bai	Afternoon		

A food and drink glossary

Useful phrases

êu ... dâi bawn nãi	Where can I buy...?
sêu ahãn dâi bawn nãi	Where can I buy food?
hàwng ahãn yu sãi	Where is a restaurant?
khãw laikan ahãn dae?	Do you have a menu?
mi...baw?	Do you have...?
baw phét	Not spicy
khói kin te phák	I am vegetarian
khói ao...	I would like...
khãw sék dae?	Can I have the bill?
khói baw dâi sang náew ní	I didn't order this
ní nyãng?	What's this?
sai/baw sai	With/without

baw sai nâm pa	Without fish sauce
khãw baep nân ján neung	I'd like a plate of that
khói kin sîn baw dâi	I can't eat meat
baw sai nâm tan	No sugar
baw sai nâm kâwn	No ice
soen sàep	Bon appétit
kâew	Bottle
mâi thu	Chopsticks
jawk	Cup/glass
sàep	Delicious
sawm	Fork
hãn kãi fõe	Noodle shop
buang	Spoon
hân ahãn	Restaurant

375

Staples

bai hóhlapha	basil
boe	butter
hét	mushroom
hua phák bua	onion
hua phák thiam	garlic
jaew	sauce
jeun khai	omelette
kai	chicken
kha	galingale
khai dao	egg, fried
khào jâo	rice, steamed
khào ji	bread
khào niaw	rice, sticky
khing	ginger
kûng	shrimp
màk kheua	aubergine
màk len	tomato
màk phét	chilli
mu	pork
nâm kat	coconut milk
nâm pa	fish sauce
nâm tan	sugar
naw mâi	bamboo shoots
nok	bird
nóm sòm	yoghurt
pa	fish
pa dàek	fish paste
pét	duck
phák	vegetables
phák nâm	watercress
phák salat	lettuce
phông sú lot	MSG
pu	crab
sìn ngúa	beef
tâo hû	bean curd
tôm khai	egg, boiled

Noodles

fõe	rice noodle soup
fõe hàeng	rice noodle soup without broth
fõe khùa	fried rice noodles
khào piak sèn	rice noodle soup, served in chicken broth
khào pûn	flour noodles with sauce
mi hàeng	yellow wheat noodles without broth
mi nâm	yellow wheat noodles

Everyday dishes and "drinking food"

kaeng jèut	mild soup with pork and vegetables
khào ji pateh	bread with Lao-style paté and vegetables
khào ji sai boe	bread with butter
khào khùa or khào phát	fried rice
khào khùa sai kai	fried rice with chicken
khùa khing kai	chicken with ginger
khùa phák baw sai sìn	stir-fried vegetables without meat
làp mu	minced pork
man falang jeun	chips
mũ phát bai hólhapa	pork with basil over rice
pîng kai	grilled chicken
pîng pa or jeun pa	grilled fish
tam màk hung	spicy papaya salad
tôm yam pa	spicy fish soup with lemongrass
yam sìn ngúa	spicy beef salad
yáw díp	spring rolls, fresh
yáw jeun	spring rolls, fried

Fruit

lamut	sapodilla
màk hung	papaya
màk kîang	orange
màk kiang	rose apple
màk kûay	banana
màk lînji	lychee
màk mángkhut	mangosteen
màk mî	jackfruit
màk mo	watermelon
màk muang	mango
màk náo	lime/lemon
màk nat	pineapple
màk ngaw	rambutan
màk nyám nyái	longan
màk phom	apple

màk sida	guava	khào niaw màk muang	sticky rice with mango
thulian	durian	nâm wăn	sweets in coconut milk
		nâm wăn màk kûay	banana in coconut milk

Sweets

kalaem	ice cream
khào lăm	sticky rice in coconut milk cooked in bamboo

Drinks

bia	beer	nâm deum	water
bia sót	beer, draught	nâm hâwn	water, hot
kafeh	coffee	nâm kâwn	ice
kafeh dam	black coffee	nâm màk phâo	coconut juice
kafeh net	instant coffee	nâm sá	tea
kafeh hawn	hot coffee	nâm soda	soda water
kafeh (nóm) hawn	hot Lao coffee (with sweetened condensed milk)	nâm tào hû	soy milk
		nâm yén	water, cold
		nóm	milk, usually sweetened condensed
kafeh (nóm) yén	iced coffee (with sweetened condensed milk)	owantin	Ovaltine (a chocolate drink)
lào-láo	rice whisky	sá jin	tea, Chinese
màk kuay pan	banana shake	sá yén	tea, iced
màk mai pan	fruit shake		

Glossary

Akha highland ethnic group

ARVN Army of Republic of Vietnam, the defunct South Vietnamese Army

baht Thai currency, also a unit for measuring gold

ban house or village

basi animist Lao ceremony

bia sot draught beer

bombi type of anti-personnel bomb which explodes when touched

Brahma Hindu god

bun (or boun) festival

dawk jampa plumeria (frangipani) blossom, the national flower of Laos

devaraja god-king a Khmer concept of divine kingship

devata female divinity

don (or dawn) island

dvarapala guardian divinities at doors and gateways of Khmer ruins

falang white person, person of European descent

fõe Vietnamese noodle dish ("pho" in Vietnamese) found throughout Laos

hân kin deum casual eating and drinking spot

HCMT Ho Chi Minh Trail, series of trails used by the NVA to infiltrate South Vietnam

heua sa slow boat

heua wai speed boat

Hmong highland ethnic group

Indra Hindu god

jataka mythological tales of the Buddha's previous lives

jumbo three-wheeled motorized taxi

kataw a game similar to volleyball, but played without the use of the arms; also played in Thailand and Malaysia, where it's called *takraw*

kha slave; formerly used as a pejorative for hilltribes

Khamu an upland ethnic group

khào rice

khào ji French bread

khào niaw sticky rice

khiw lot bus stand

Khmer Cambodian

khwaeng province

kip Lao currency

lak kilometre, often used in place names

lam wong traditional dance

Lane Xang ancient Lao kingdom

Lao Loum lowland Lao, mostly ethnic Lao.

Lao Soum highland Lao; hill tribes.

Lao Theung speakers of Mon–Khmer languages who live at higher altitudes than the Lao Loum.

lào hái rice wine sipped from straws out of a large stoneware jar

lào-láo strong alcoholic drink made from sticky rice

làp minced meat dish

lintel horizontal beam or stone over a door or window

LNTA Lao National Tourism Administration

lustral water holy water used to bathe a Buddha image

makara mythical water monster

maw thiam spirit medium

Mien a highland ethnic group

muan fun, enjoyable

muang (or meuang) city or town

mudra hand and arm positions depicted in Buddhist and Hindu imagery

mukhalinga phallic-shaped stone symbolic of Shiva with an image of the god's face carved into it

naga benevolent mythical water serpent (pronounced "nak" in Lao)

nam river

nam phu (or **nam phou**) fountain

NBCA National Biodiversity Conservation Area

ngeuak malevolent mythical water serpent

NTAL National Tourism Authority of Laos

NVA North Vietnamese Army

pa dàek fermented fish paste, used as seasoning

pa kha Irrawaddy dolphin

pa pao blowfish with a vicious bite found in southern Laos

pak mouth of a river

Pathet Lao communist guerrilla movement which gained control of Laos in 1975

Patouxai monument in Vientiane

Pha Bang a Buddha image belived by many to be the talismanic protector of the Lao nation

Pha In Hindu god Indra

Pha Lak Pha Lam Lao version of the Ramayana

Pha Phut the Buddha

Pha Phutthahup Buddha image

phi spirit or ghost

phu (or **phou**) hill or mountain

Phuan lowland ethnic group

pirogue narrow dug-out canoe

Ramayana epic poem of Indian origin (Pha Lak Pha Lam in Lao)

rishi hermitic ascetic

Royal Lao Army (RLA) army of the defunct Kingdom of Laos

sala pavilion with a raised floor and roof but no walls

samana re-education camp, derived from the word "seminar"

sawngthaew pick-up truck used for public transport

Shiva Hindu god

Shivalinga phallic-shaped stone symbolic of Shiva

shophouse Southeast Asian property, usually built in terraces and comprising a shop at ground level with residential areas above

sim building in a monastery housing the main Buddha image

sin women's wrap-around skirt

Sipsong Chao Tai the Twelve Tai Principalities, a loose federation that once included parts of northwest Vietnam and northeast Laos

soi lane or alley

somasutra stone pipe for channelling lustral water

stupa Buddhist structure built to contain holy relics ("that" in Lao)

tad (or **tat**) waterfall

Tai ethnic Thai

Tai Dam lowland Lao ethnic group, found in Houa Phan and Xiang Khouang provinces

Tai Leu lowland Lao ethnic group, found in northwest Laos

Tai Yuan northern Thai

talat market

Talat Sao Vientiane's morning market

thanon road or street

that Lao word for Buddhist stupa

tuk-tuk three-wheeled motorized taxi

ushnisha finial symbolizing enlightenment found on the crown of the head of Buddha images

UXO unexploded ordnance

Vishnu a Hindu god

wat Buddhist monastery

wiang (or **viang**) town surrounded by wooden palisades

xe river (southern Laos only)

xiang town surrounded by brick or earthen ramparts

Travel store

Available from all good bookstores

ROUGH GUIDES

NOTES

Small print and Index

A Rough Guide to Rough Guides

Published in 1982, the first Rough Guide – to Greece – was a student scheme that became a publishing phenomenon. Mark Ellingham, a recent graduate in English from Bristol University, had been travelling in Greece the previous summer and couldn't find the right guidebook. With a small group of friends he wrote his own guide, combining a highly contemporary, journalistic style with a thoroughly practical approach to travellers' needs.

The immediate success of the book spawned a series that rapidly covered dozens of destinations. And, in addition to impecunious backpackers, Rough Guides soon acquired a much broader and older readership that relished the guides' wit and inquisitiveness as much as their enthusiastic, critical approach and value-for-money ethos.

These days, Rough Guides include recommendations from shoestring to luxury and cover more than 200 destinations around the globe, including almost every country in the Americas and Europe, more than half of Africa and most of Asia and Australasia. Our ever-growing team of authors and photographers is spread all over the world, particularly in Europe, the USA and Australia.

In the early 1990s, Rough Guides branched out of travel, with the publication of Rough Guides to World Music, Classical Music and the Internet. All three have become benchmark titles in their fields, spearheading the publication of a wide range of books under the Rough Guide name.

Including the travel series, Rough Guides now number more than 350 titles, covering: phrasebooks, waterproof maps, music guides from Opera to Heavy Metal, reference works as diverse as Conspiracy Theories and Shakespeare, and popular culture books from iPods to Poker. Rough Guides also produce a series of more than 120 World Music CDs in partnership with World Music Network.

Visit www.roughguides.com to see our latest publications.

Rough Guide travel images are available for commercial licensing at www.roughguidespictures.com

Rough Guide credits

Text editor: Richard Lim
Layout: Pradeep Thapliyal
Cartography: Karobi Gogoi, Maxine Repath
Picture editor: Nicole Newman
Production: Katherine Owers
Proofreader: Janet McCann and Susannah Wight
Cover design: Chloë Roberts
Photographer: Tim Draper
Editorial: **London** Kate Berens, Claire Saunders, Geoff Howard, Ruth Blackmore, Polly Thomas, Alison Murchie, Karoline Densley, Andy Turner, Keith Drew, Edward Aves, Nikki Birrell, Helen Marsden, Alice Park, Sarah Eno, Joe Staines, Duncan Clark, Peter Buckley, Matthew Milton, Tracy Hopkins, David Paul, Lucy White, Ruth Tidball; **New York** Andrew Rosenberg, Steven Horak, April Isaacs, AnneLise Sorensen, Amy Hegarty, Sean Mahoney, Ella Steim
Design & Pictures: **London** Simon Bracken, Dan May, Diana Jarvis, Mark Thomas, Jj Luck, Harriet Mills; **Delhi** Madhulita Mohapatra, Umesh Aggarwal, Ajay Verma, Jessica Subramanian, Ankur Guha, Sachin Tanwar, Anita Singh

Production: Sophie Hewat, Aimee Hampson
Cartography: **London** Ed Wright, Katie Lloyd-Jones; **Delhi** Rajesh Chhibber, Jai Prakash Mishra, Ashutosh Bharti, Rajesh Mishra, Animesh Pathak, Jasbir Sandhu, Amod Singh, Alakananda Bhattacharya
Online: **New York** Jennifer Gold, Kristin Mingrone; **Delhi** Manik Chauhan, Narender Kumar, Shekhar Jha, Rakesh Kumar, Amit Verma, Amit Kumar, Rahul Kumar
Marketing & Publicity: **London** Richard Trillo, Niki Hanmer, Louise Maher, Jess Carter; **New York** Geoff Colquitt, Megan Kennedy, Katy Ball; **Delhi** Reem Khokhar
Custom publishing and foreign rights: Philippa Hopkins
Manager India: Punita Singh
Series editor: Mark Ellingham
Reference Director: Andrew Lockett
PA to Managing and Publishing Directors: Megan McIntyre
Publishing Director: Martin Dunford

Publishing information

This third edition published February 2007 by
Rough Guides Ltd,
80 Strand, London WC2R 0RL
345 Hudson St, 4th Floor,
New York, NY 10014, USA
14 Local Shopping Centre, Panchsheel Park,
New Delhi 110017, India
Distributed by the Penguin Group
Penguin Books Ltd,
80 Strand, London WC2R 0RL
Penguin Putnam, Inc.
375 Hudson Street, NY 10014, USA
Penguin Group (Australia)
250 Camberwell Road, Camberwell,
Victoria 3124, Australia
Penguin Books Canada Ltd,
10 Alcorn Avenue, Toronto, Ontario,
Canada M4V 1E4
Penguin Group (NZ)
67 Apollo Drive, Mairangi Bay, Auckland 1310,
New Zealand
Cover concept by Peter Dyer.

Typeset in Bembo and Helvetica to an original design by Henry Iles.

Printed and bound in China

© Jeff Cranmer and Steven Martin 2007

No part of this book may be reproduced in any form without permission from the publisher except for the quotation of brief passages in reviews.

400pp includes index

A catalogue record for this book is available from the British Library

ISBN 9-78184-353-506-5

3 5 7 9 8 6 4 2

Help us update

We've gone to a lot of effort to ensure that the third edition of **The Rough Guide to Laos** is accurate and up to date. However, things change – places get "discovered", opening hours are notoriously fickle, restaurants and rooms raise prices or lower standards. If you feel we've got it wrong or left something out, we'd like to know, and if you can remember the address, the price, the time, the phone number, so much the better. We'll credit all contributions, and send a copy of the next edition (or any other Rough Guide if you prefer) for the best letters. Everyone who writes to us and isn't already a subscriber will receive a copy of our full-colour thrice-yearly newsletter. Please mark letters: "**Rough Guide Laos Update**" and send to: Rough Guides, 80 Strand, London WC2R 0RL, or Rough Guides, 4th Floor, 345 Hudson St, New York, NY 10014. Or send an email to **mail@roughguides.com**
Have your questions answered and tell others about your trip at
www.roughguides.atinfopop.com

Acknowledgements

Steven Martin thanks Linda McIntosh, Settasak Akanimart, and Benjamin Sirirat for assistance during the updating of this edition.

SMALL PRINT

Readers' letters

Thanks to all the readers who have taken the time to write in with comments and suggestions (and apologies if we've inadvertently omitted anyone's name):

Jonathan Blair, Russell Briggs, Roger Burrows, Paolo Cortini, Vibeke Dank, Hilary Dennison, Antoinette Figliola and William Kaderli, Jamison Firestone, Quentin and Ann Hunter, Sarah Jhirad, Dave Key, Daniel Knights, H. Kolia, Audrey Letouze, Kate Lloyd-Williams, Gordon Macniven, Katie May, Chris Mitchell, John Moran, Robert Neumark Jones, Yan Plihal, Sarah Riches, Paul Taylor, Nathan van der Veer & Esther Gernette, Graham Wade, Jake Wetherall, Brett Wyatt.

Photo credits

Index

Map entries are in colour. For a list of map symbols used in this book, see p.399. Lao personages are indexed according to first name – thus Khamtay Siphandone is under K. Certain physical features are indexed under the Lao terms for those features – *tham* for caves, *tad* for waterfalls, *phou* for mountains.

Map symbols

maps are listed in the full index using coloured text

----	International boundary
---	Chapter division boundary
===	Major road
──	Minor road
⫶⫶⫶⫶	Steps (town maps)
──●──	Rail line
── ──	Ferry route
────	River
▪▪▪▪▪	Wall
♦	Point of interest
♦	Border crossing
⌃⌃	Mountain range
▲	Mountain peak
⑊⑊⑊	Hill
🌢	Waterfall
∴	Ruin
⌒	Cave
♠	Temple/monastery
⌃	Stupa/that

🏯	Chinese temple
⊙	Statue/monument
✈	Airport
★	Bus/taxi stand
🏮	Petrol station
◉	Accommodation
▣	Restaurant
☏	Telephone office
@	Internet access
ⓘ	Tourist information
⊠	Post office
⊞	Hospital
▭	Market
◯	Stadium
▮	Building
╪	Church/cathedral
▨	Park/National Biodiversity Conservation Area (NBCA)
▨	Forest